"THE NATIONS OF THE WEST" (popularly called "The Pioneers"), designed by A. Stirling Calder and modeled by Mr. Calder, F. G. R. Roth, and Leo Lentelli, topped the Arch of the Setting Sun at the Panama-Pacific Exposition held at San Francisco in 1915. Facing the Court of the Universe moves a group of men and women typical of those who have made our civilization. From left to right appear the French-Canadian, the Alaskan, the Latin-American, the German, the Italian, the Anglo-American, and the American Indian, squaw and warrior In the place of honor in the center of the group, standing between the oxen on the tongue of the prairie schooner, is a figure, beautiful and almost girl-ish, but strong, dignified, and womanly, the Mother of To-morrow. Above the group rides the Spirit of Enterprise, flanked right and left by the Hopes of the Future in the person of two boys. The group as a whole is beautifully symbolic of the westward march of American civilization.

"THE NATIONS OF THE WEST"

HISTORY
OF THE
UNITED STATES

A STUDY IN AMERICAN CIVILIZATION

BY

CHARLES A. BEARD

AND

MARY R. BEARD

REVISED EDITION

New York

THE MACMILLAN COMPANY

1944

Set up and electrotyped. Published October, 1934.
Reprinted January, 1935; August, 1935;
November, 1935; October, 1936; April, June,
September, 1938; November, 1939; December, 1940;
June, 1941; February, July, 1942; August, 1944.

Λ

First edition copyrighted and published March, 1921.
Revised editions copyrighted and published in 1929, 1932.

PREFACE

This is no superficial revision of our *History of the United States* originally issued in 1921. On the contrary the original text has been entirely rewritten and thoroughly simplified to meet the new demands on high schools which have been created by the unprecedented increase in enrollment during the past few years. And what is still more important, new chapters have been added to bring the work into harmony with the present trend in American thinking.

The first edition contained several departures from traditional narrative history, especially of politics. Besides making extensive use of the topical, or "unit," method, it laid emphasis on the social and economic aspects of our history and on the place of our country among the world powers. Owing to the recent changes in the spirit and substance of historical writing and the rapid advance of social studies in the schools, it is no longer necessary to repeat the argument for this type of textbook. The former opposition to it has almost completely disappeared.

It only seems necessary to indicate here the nature of the new lines of progress marked out in this revision. While retaining all the significant features of the older edition, it widens the scope to include American culture in the broadest sense: thought as well as commerce, science as well as politics, and art as well as industry, as illustrated in Chapters IV, IX, XVI, and XXX. In making this extension we have tried to coördinate the text with the growing interest of the American people in civilization in the large — to introduce high-school pupils to intellectual issues which are being discussed by educated people everywhere and to explain the background of those issues.

Mankind lives not by politics alone nor by bread alone but also by things of the spirit which form ideals, inspire love of beauty, and ennoble action.   To reinforce this new treatment of American history, fresh illustrations and more illustrations have been chosen, particularly from American works of art, and fitted into the text by appropriate references.

C. A. B.
M. R. B.

New York City.

CONTENTS

PART I: THE COLONIAL PERIOD

PART II: CONFLICT AND INDEPENDENCE

Contents

FULL–PAGE INSERTS

MAPS

A SMALL LIBRARY IN AMERICAN HISTORY

SINGLE VOLUMES:

BASSETT, J. S.   *A Short History of the United States*
ELSON, H. W.   *History of the United States of America*

SERIES:

"Epochs of American History," edited by A. B. Hart

HART, A. B.   *Formation of the Union*
THWAITES, R. G.   *The Colonies*
WILSON, WOODROW.   *Division and Reunion*

"Riverside Series," edited by W. E. Dodd

BECKER, C. L.   *Beginnings of the American People*
DODD, W. E.   *Expansion and Conflict*
JOHNSON, A.   *Union and Democracy*
PAXSON, F. L.   *The New Nation*

PART I. THE COLONIAL PERIOD

CHAPTER I

AMERICA DISCOVERED BY EUROPE

Europe Once Frightfully Ignorant of Geography. Six hundred years ago, students of geography in western Europe knew little about the surface of the earth. They were familiar with the general location of the British Isles, the coast of Europe bordering on the Atlantic, and the outline of the Mediterranean Sea. They also had vague ideas about northern Africa and the form of southern Asia from the Red Sea to the lower part of China. Of Russia and the vast regions stretching eastward into China, they knew almost nothing. Some of them thought that the world was flat and none suspected that two huge continents, now called North America and South America, lay far across the Atlantic. Concerning Australia and innumerable islands of the ocean, they had no knowledge at all.

Preparing for a Great Adventure

Early Oriental Travel and Trade. But long before Columbus made the fateful voyage of 1492 that discovered America, European missionaries, merchants, and sea captains had begun to add new bits of land and water to the maps which had come down from ancient times. Far back in the days of Julius Cæsar, before the birth of Christ, the Romans had carried on a great trade with India and China. After the Roman Empire fell and Europe broke up into many independent states, that trade declined, but it never stopped entirely. During the middle ages, it flowered again and steadily increased until it became an important part of European commerce.

In 1245, almost two hundred and fifty years before Columbus set sail on his first voyage, a missionary was sent by the Pope beyond the Black Sea into "the land of the Great Khan." On his return this traveler told wonderful stories about Cathay, as he

3

called China, and declared that the country was rich in gold, silver, grain, silk, and "everything that tends to support mankind." About thirty years later, the son of a Venetian merchant, Marco Polo, went overland to China with his father and uncle, and stayed a long time in the Orient. When he came back to Italy in 1295, Marco thrilled all the people who listened to his tales or read his accounts of the glories of the East.

From Sherwood and Mantz: "The Road to Cathay"

MARCO POLO RETURNING TO VENICE FROM THE ORIENT

While the travelers were spreading a knowledge of Asia among the people of Europe, merchants were quietly building up trade between the two continents. From the East were imported into Europe tea, silks, spices, perfumes, tapestries, and other luxuries. By land and by sea, these goods were brought to ports on the eastern shore of the Mediterranean. Thence they were carried, mainly by Italian business men, to Venice, Florence, Genoa, and other near-by cities. Goods not sold in Italy were forwarded to trading towns in France, Holland, England, Germany, and other countries of western Europe.

In managing the western branch of their business, Italian merchants at first worked principally through the port of Marseilles in southern France, from which they sent their boxes and bales of Oriental merchandise northward to various market cities. Later however they found it cheaper to fit out vessels and ship their goods through the Strait of Gibraltar, by water, to ports on the Atlantic.

The Search for New Routes to the East. Naturally, the cost of freight from China to Paris or London by these routes was very high. Goods had to be packed and repacked many times. At every important commercial town through which they passed, local merchants took their toll of profits. Robbers beset caravans by land and pirates stole cargoes at sea. To make things worse for European merchants, Constantinople, a great freight center which had long been under their control, fell into the hands of the Turks in 1453, and this event was followed by frequent wars between the Christians and the Mohammedans, which were harmful to trading enterprises.

Even if Constantinople had not been captured by the Turks, intelligent merchants in Italy would have tried harder and harder to lower the cost of bringing goods from the East to their markets in Europe. As a matter of fact, they had cut the freight charges, as we have seen, by dispatching cargoes in ships along the Atlantic coast to various ports instead of taking them overland by wagon or on horseback. And as early as 1292 they tried to discover an all-water route to the Orient by sending an expedition down the west coast of Africa in the hope that it might get around the southern end and reach India or China.

This attempt failed, but the dream did not vanish. Throughout the fourteenth and fifteenth centuries, efforts were made to realize it, for the business men of those far-off times were eager to solve the problem of the water way to the Orient. If this way could be found to the East, freight rates would be reduced, the journey made easier, and trade increased. While the merchants expected to profit from it, the people knew that they would benefit from lower prices and more goods. Then as now trade was a strong motive for courageous undertakings. Furthermore there

was continual excitement over the adventure of discovering new
sea routes, just as there is to-day over efforts to make air routes
commercially successful.

Development in the Art of Navigation. But the merchants of
Europe were dependent upon other classes of people for success in
solving their water-route problem, in the same way that business
men of our own times interested in aviation are dependent on inventors, weather forecasters, map makers, and daring pilots.
Fortunately for the traders engaged in Oriental business, aid was
at hand. Here and there throughout Europe were "cartographers,"
as they were styled, busy in monasteries and libraries with the
study of the earth's surface. To the old maps handed down by
the Greeks and the Romans, these men added new patches of land
and water as they pieced together the stories told by returning
missionaries, sailors, and merchants. One of these geographers,
who lived in Venice, made a map in 1459 showing Africa ending
in a point, with a water route around it to India and China.
About the same time, an astronomer in Florence, named Toscanelli,
came to the conclusion that India could be reached by sailing due
west across the Atlantic. He drew a map showing the course and
wrote a letter stating the reasons for his belief.

In addition to making maps, some cartographers worked out the
theory that the world was round, not flat as most of the common
people believed. It is true that this was an old idea inherited
from the wise men of ancient Greece, but few sailors in the early
middle ages had ever heard of it.

While knowledge of the earth was increasing, some inventor
made a tiny instrument, known as the compass, which enabled
sailors to tell directions on the pathless sea. Hitherto they had
steered by the sun and stars; now they could keep on their course
when the sky was cloudy and neither sun nor stars could be seen.
The name of the inventor is unknown and so is the date of the
invention, but before Columbus was born every ocean-going
ship had its compass, and navigators felt safer in experimenting
in strange waters. As the years passed, other instruments were
devised; for example, the astrolabe was improved so that the
sailor could find his distance from the equator by taking the height

of the sun. In the meantime shipwrights learned how to build bigger and better ships, stronger and faster, safer and more attractive to adventurous minds, just as in the twentieth century engineers are designing more reliable airplanes.

Yet maps, theories about the shape of the earth, and sturdy vessels would have been worthless without hardy navigators willing

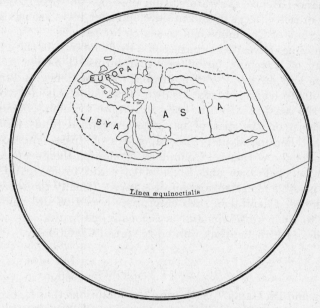

AN ANCIENT ROMAN MAP OF THE WORLD
Little more than this was known at the beginning of the period of exploration.

to take every risk. Courage for distant sea voyages was early found however among the sailors who had got experience in the Mediterranean or along the Atlantic coast of Europe. It was they who grew more bold as they were inspired by inventions and rewards offered by merchants and princely patrons. They were pioneers, in the true sense of that word, prepared to brave the dangers of sailing unknown seas and visiting strange places. Many lives were lost among these pilots of the sea, as lives are lost to-day among pilots of the air, but the quest for ways to master nature and to serve mankind went on unabated.

Money for Adventure. Still another thing was necessary to promote commerce by the sea in those days. It cost a great deal of money to buy ships, pay sailors, and launch expeditions, and small merchants did not have vast sums at their command. Hence, as aviators in our time have to appeal to governments or rich citizens for aid in developing air travel, so navigators in the time of Columbus had to search for patrons.

Sometimes a wealthy prince took a lively interest in the exciting venture of searching far-off seas and furnished money to geographers and navigators. For instance, Prince Henry of Portugal (1394–1460) equipped from his own purse many ships for voyages down the coast of Africa in quest of a route to India. Sometimes sovereigns, on the plea of navigators, supplied funds for expeditions. Ferdinand and Isabella, rulers of Spain, appropriated money for the voyages of Columbus. Following their example, the monarchs of France and England gave aid to navigators and made possible many voyages of discovery. Usually the sovereigns who invested capital in such enterprises hoped to add new territories to their kingdoms and occasionally, as in the case of Ferdinand and Isabella, they wanted to spread Christianity.

The Great Explorers

Diaz and Da Gama. Such were the conditions that favored the extension of searches on the high seas and finally brought about the discovery and exploration of the New World. Among the sailors who led in this work, several won immortal fame. If we take them up in the order of their adventures, we must put Bartholomew Diaz at the top of the list. Commanding ships sent out by the king of Portugal in 1486, Diaz rounded the Cape of Good Hope, showing that there probably was a water route all the way to India. This was made certain when Vasco da Gama, also flying the Portuguese flag, sailed around the Cape in 1498, visited India, and returned home the next year to report wonderful opportunities for trade with that country.

Columbus. Greater and more courageous than these navigators was Christopher Columbus, an Italian, born in or near Genoa. After starting out early in life as a sailor, Columbus drifted to Portugal and then to Spain, spending his time either on sea voyages or in the study of geography. He was familiar with the theory that the world was round and with Toscanelli's idea that India could be reached by sailing west. In fact he came to the same conclusion himself and wanted to test his beliefs.

Having no wealth of his own, Columbus appealed to many people for money to make the experiment, without success for a

From the painting by M. I. Danforth

THE LANDING OF COLUMBUS

long time. Finally he persuaded Ferdinand and Isabella to help him and in 1492 he was able to sail away on his daring adventure which brought him, after weeks of anxious watching and waiting, within sight of land — one of the Bahama Islands — on October 12. For many days he cruised about in the neighboring waters and then went back to Spain, thinking that he had reached Asia and that the fabled wealth of China and Japan was within easy reach of the land he had seen. On his arrival in Spain, he was honored by the king and queen and cheered by the crowds in the streets. Money was raised for new voyages and Columbus made three more trips across the Atlantic. He visited numerous islands and even touched the coast of South America but he found no magnificent cities prepared to exchange their wares for Spanish goods, no stores of gold and silver to be won by trade or the sword. Bitterly disappointed himself and bitterly disappointing others, Columbus spent his later years in poverty and died without knowing that he had discovered a new world which was to be richer in the end than the Europe he had known.

Cabot and Vespucci. After Columbus had broken the way, and the terrors of the deep had been proved imaginary, there was no lack of mariners willing and even eager to sail hither and yon exploring. In 1497 John Cabot, an Italian sea captain, made a voyage to the west for Henry VII, the king of England, and skirted along the shores of North America, probably off Labrador, giving England a claim in the New World. A few years later Amerigo Vespucci, also an Italian, who worked first for the king of Spain and then for the king of Portugal, made, according to his story, four voyages across the Atlantic. On one of these he sailed along the upper shores of what is now South America and declared that he had discovered in fact a continent. In honor of his exploits, map makers gave the name America to this strange land.

Magellan and the Trip around the World. Bolder than either Cabot or Vespucci, a Portuguese sailor, Magellan, set out in 1519, under Spanish auspices, on what proved to be the most amazing voyage in the annals of the sea. He passed along the eastern shore of South America, pushed through the straits at the southern end which bear his name, and sailed on day after day over the wide Pacific until he reached the islands now known as the Philippines. There Magellan was killed in a quarrel with the natives but his men completed the journey, reaching Spain in the autumn of 1522. At last the world had been circumnavigated and the position of South America was fairly determined.

Two years after Magellan's men returned, the king of France also decided to take part in the great work of exploration. He laughed at the claims of Portugal and Spain to all that had been found by the navigators and asked, in a jovial mood, to see Adam's will bestowing upon them their monopoly of the earth. Then he sent an Italian seaman, Verazzano, on an expedition across the

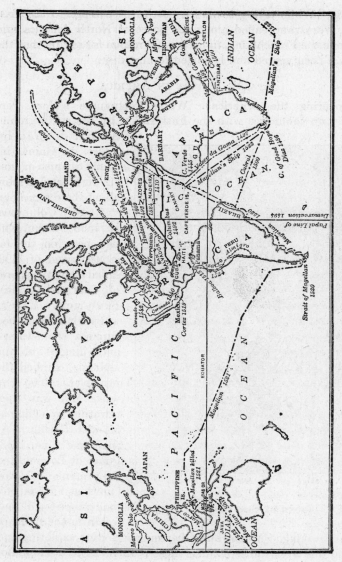

Voyage of Discovery and Exploration

Atlantic. While trying to find a northwest passage to the East Indies, Verazzano sailed along the coast of North America and thus gave the French king, in his turn, a reason for saying that the land had been visited and belonged to him.

SPAIN'S EMPIRE IN AMERICA

Uncovering the Americas. While Portuguese sailors were building up commerce with the East Indies by the route around

Courtesy of The Metropolitan Museum of Art

PANEL TAPESTRY TYPICAL OF THE CIVILIZATION FOUND BY SPANIARDS

Africa opened by Vasco da Gama, intrepid Spanish explorers were learning more about the regions first visited by Columbus. In 1508 Pinzon, who had been on the famous voyage of 1492, sailed along the shores of Central America. Five years afterward Balboa pushed through the swamps and jungles of the Isthmus, climbed the mountains to the west, and was then rewarded by a glimpse of the Pacific. At the same time, 1513, Ponce de Leon visited the mainland, now known as Florida, and took possession of that region in the name of the Spanish king. Meanwhile other mariners were exploring and charting the West Indies, adding those islands to the dominion of the Spanish monarch.

The Conquest of Mexico by Cortes. In their restless quest for land and treasure, the Spaniards soon came upon the grand empire of Mexico, stretching northward from the Isthmus which Balboa had discovered. Under a mighty ruler, Montezuma, the natives were tilling the fields and raising bountiful crops: they had built fine highways and splendid cities; they had temples for the worship of their gods; they worked in metals and stone; they had palaces and treasuries overflowing with gold, silver, and jewels.

Booty such as this the Spanish explorers had long been seeking. So a band under Hernando Cortes, in 1521, attacked the Mexicans, seized their capital, overthrew their government, annexed their country to Spain, and carried off a large part of their wealth. In the wake of the soldiers followed Catholic missionaries who converted the natives to Christianity and with their labor built monasteries and churches on Spanish models in all parts of Mexico. A large number of Spaniards moved to the new country and settled down as soldiers, landlords, priests, and government officials. They forced the conquered people to till the fields, build and adorn churches, and serve them in their households. In this way, Mexico, now styled New Spain, was changed into a province of subject peoples ruled from Madrid.

The Conquest of Peru by Pizarro. While the Spaniards were subduing Mexico, they heard rumors of another rich empire far to the south, in Peru. Thereupon, one of their leaders, Pizarro, gathered a group about him, numbering fewer than two hundred men, and set out on an unknown path to find the distant realm. After a slow and perilous journey he and his companions came upon a country superior in many ways to Mexico and especially rich in the kind of booty they were hunting. They immediately attacked and overcame the natives and stripped the temples, palaces, and tombs of their treasure. Besides wringing vast wealth from Peru, they annexed that region to the Spanish empire.

Explorations in North America. Stories of the fabulous riches won by the conquerors of Mexico and Peru led other Spanish captains to undertake long journeys into North America. They too searched for cities and fertile fields to seize and exploit not by the labor of their own hands, but by the toil of natives enslaved by war. Not discouraged by the fruitless expedition of Ponce de Leon, another soldier, Hernando de Soto, who had fought with Pizarro, decided to try his luck on the mainland. At the head of a small army, he landed on the coast of Florida, looking for new kingdoms to conquer. But instead of wonderful cities, he found only miserable Indian villages; instead of wide-reaching acres cultivated by prosperous farmers, he encountered jungles, forests, and swamps. Yet, with grim determination, De Soto's company pressed inland, every hour hoping that the next would reveal fortune and fame. At last, in 1541, the stern captain reached the broad waters of the Mississippi. But there he died, and his unhappy followers dropped his body in the darkness of the night down to the bottom of the river he had discovered. Then they made their way back to Spanish settlements as best they could.

While De Soto was on this luckless journey, another Spanish adventurer, Coronado, explored the southwestern part of what is now the United States, all the way from Mexico to the Kansas region. He too found no glorious cities and precious booty, but he opened the path for missionaries and gave the king of Spain a claim to the territory. In due time, the Spanish flag was hoisted on the coast of California and missions for the conversion of the Indians were scattered from the Gulf of Mexico to the Pacific.

Extent of the Spanish Rule in America. Thus, by the middle of the sixteenth century, the king of Spain boasted ownership over Cuba, Porto Rico, and all the other islands of the West Indies. On the mainland, he ruled Mexico and Peru and, in fact, laid claim to the whole of North and South America except Brazil which had been conquered by the intrepid Portuguese. Over vast regions, Spanish missionaries preached to the Indians and used them as laborers in the fields and artisans about the missions. Spanish learning was introduced by the founding of schools and universities. From American dominions Spanish officials annually shipped home huge cargoes of gold, silver, and precious stones. Having won their holdings by the sword, the Spaniards forbade French, English, and all other European merchants to enter their ports in the New World.

FRANCE AND ENGLAND ENTER THE RACE

The Search for the Northwest Passage. Naturally the king of France grew envious as he heard repeated accounts of the harvest gathered from conquest and trade by his brother monarchs in Spain and Portugal. Not dismayed by the failure of Verazzano to find anything but uninhabited sea coasts during his voyage of 1524, the French king clung to the hope of better luck next time. Under his royal patronage Jacques Cartier sailed, in 1534, for the coast of North America to hunt for the shortest water route to China. Cartier explored the gulf at the mouth of the St. Lawrence River and came to the conclusion that possibly he had actually found the long-sought passage. The next year he was at the gulf again and pushed far up the river where, however, he found mere Indian villages instead of Chinese cities or the gateway to the Orient. Still hopeful, Cartier returned a third time and established a colony in the St. Lawrence Valley. This colony failed to prosper and he never reached Asia, but he gave his sovereign a claim to a very fertile country.

The Work of Champlain. From time to time, other French explorers followed Cartier, but none did anything very extraordinary until Samuel de Champlain came on the scene in 1603. He traveled far and wide in Canada and, in what was later called New England, established a post at Quebec in 1607, discovered the lake which has received his name, and wrote numerous books on the Indians and his various explorations. When he died at Quebec in 1635, the grasp of France on the territory to the north of the St. Lawrence was firmly fixed. As the American historian, Parkman, says, "Champlain has been fitly called the Father of New France."

Francis Drake. For a long period after the voyage of John Cabot in 1497, the English paid little attention to the work of exploration that had been pressed with such zeal by their neighbors. But in the reign of Queen Elizabeth there grew up in England a number of hardy sea captains, such as Drake, Raleigh, Hawkins, Frobisher, and Gilbert, who were determined to challenge Spain's right to rule so much of the earth and monopolize so much trade.

Under the leadership of these men, the English navy was increased until it became big enough to break the power of Spain on the sea.

The most famous of these captains, Francis Drake, gave the Spanish a taste of what was to come by sailing around the world, in 1577–1580, and robbing Spanish vessels and ports as he passed.

From an old print

QUEEN ELIZABETH

Though his queen was at peace with the king of Spain, Drake looted and burned trading posts down the eastern coast of South America and up the western coast, capturing ships and filling his vessels with treasure. After skirting along the western shores of North America, he refitted his ships and sailed across the Pacific. At the end of three years spent in freebooting, Drake rode safely home into English waters. Overjoyed with gifts from his cargoes, Elizabeth knighted Drake for his achievements.

Angry over such piratical conduct, the Spaniards, eight years later, sent a proud fleet — the *Armada* — into the English Channel to test the might of their rival then and there. Between the prowess of the English sailors and the havoc of a terrible storm, the *Armada* was utterly routed. Thus the way was cleared for the English to try their hand at building an empire in North America.

Sir Walter Raleigh's Attempts at Colonization. Among the friends of the English sea-rovers was a soldier-courtier, Sir Walter Raleigh, who decided that the next great task before his country was to create "an English nation" in the New World. With the aid of his queen, Raleigh tried to start this second England in 1585 by planting a colony on the coast of what is now North Carolina. His first effort failed; three more experiments proved equally fruitless; and in the end Raleigh had to confess defeat. The new nation of which he dreamed and for which he worked was to be built by other Englishmen and in other ways. But as a forerunner, a pioneer in colonization, Raleigh helped to break the path for the men and women who succeeded in establishing the thirteen English colonies in America.

References

John Fiske, *Discovery of America*.
E. J. Payne, *History of the New World Called America*.
Sherwood and Mantz, *The Road to Cathay*.
Edward Channing, *History of the United States*, Vol. I.

Questions

1. What did the people of Europe know about geography six hundred years ago?

2. Why did Europeans try to find out about other continents?

3. Explain how travelers, missionaries, and traders help to spread knowledge of geography.

4. Give some of the causes of the search for the water route to China.

5. Describe the services rendered to exploration by map makers, inventors, navigators, and rich patrons.

6. Tell about the work of Diaz, Da Gama, Columbus, Cabot, and Magellan.

7. Trace the steps in the growth of the Spanish Empire in North and South America.

8. Who were the leaders in Spanish adventure on the mainland?

9. Outline early French explorations.

10. For what was Francis Drake famous? Sir Walter Raleigh?

Research Topics

Biographies. Turn to any good encyclopedia, look up the names of the persons mentioned in this chapter, and report on their lives.

Geography. Consult the *Encyclopædia Britannica* under the titles "Geography" and "Map" for the history of the way in which European knowledge of geography grew from crude beginnings to great exactness.

Navigation. Consult an encyclopedia and report on the compass, astrolabe, navigation, and shipbuilding.

CHAPTER II

THE GREAT MIGRATION TO AMERICA

Among all the peoples of Europe that explored, searched, and discovered in the New World, the English alone founded settlements which grew into a new nation primarily European in population. Italians, Spaniards, Portuguese, French, Dutch, and Swedes were never able to do anything just like this. The Spaniards, it is true, conquered and ruled great regions, such as Mexico and Peru, and the French established a colony in Canada peopled from their own country. But the Spanish provinces were inhabited mainly by Indian races and the French colony finally passed under British dominion. So one naturally asks: "How did it happen that the work of the English was so unusual?"

Why England Led in Colonization

The Sea Power. Since American colonization had to be carried on across the ocean, a successful colonizing nation had to possess a navy strong enough to defend its merchant ships and its settlements. Repeated wars among the countries of Europe over trade and territory proved this many times. Toward the close of the sixteenth century, English statesmen saw clearly that only by "ruling the waves" could they protect overseas possessions against their rivals and people them with colonists. So they built a navy and strengthened it from decade to decade. Thus they were able to strike down the Spanish in 1588, the Dutch in a series of conflicts, and the French in two hundred years of struggle. By commanding the sea, Great Britain made it possible for her colonists to go forth to distant regions, plant settlements in peace, trade in security, and hold fast to the regions they occupied.

Growth of Business Enterprise. But a great navy could not found colonies. That was a task for civilians, not for warriors alone. It called for organizing talent, for capital, to pay the first

18

expenses, and for business men to direct the shipping of settlers and supplies across the ocean. Now, owing to their fortunate position on an island, the English had long enjoyed peace at home and had promoted industry and commerce in safety. They had learned how to form business companies and push their trade in various parts of Europe. They had money to invest in enterprises that promised to pay a profit and they were looking about for opportunities for investment when their leaders turned their interest to the New World.

People to Till the Soil. When colonization in America was proposed, it was viewed as an experiment in agriculture as well as trade. It was therefore necessary to find farmers who were willing to leave their birthplace to work on the soil in distant lands. At the opening of the seventeenth century, England had two types of farmers who could be counted on to do this. The first were the yeomen — owners of small farms — who were noted for their steady habits and their pride in their crops and their freedom. The second were farm laborers — men and women who worked for the landowners for wages. Generally speaking, these laborers were the descendants of serfs, or people once bound to the land and compelled to labor for their masters a certain number of days in the year. That is, they belonged to a class which had tilled the soil for centuries. But by 1600 the English serfs had been released from their ancient bondage and were "free" to leave their home country for the colonies. In fact, many of them were very glad to go because they were landless and miserably poor. The colonies seemed to offer agricultural laborers a chance to earn wages and perhaps acquire farms of their own.

Women Colonists. Labor in the fields and forests was necessary to successful colonization but so were homes. And homes could not be established without the coöperation of women. As it happened, England had many types of women who could join the men in distant lands. Some had business experience of their own, others were skilled in industrial arts, such as spinning and weaving, and others knew all the branches of farming. They were to be the mothers of young colonists, besides being workers themselves in agriculture and manufacturing, and often managers of estates and industries. Recognizing the importance of women in colonization, the English companies and proprietors that planted settlements in the New World offered especially large grants of land to married men and sold land to maidens as well as bachelors. The work of colonization was hard and hazardous but many women in England were willing to take the risks.

Religious Disputes. Among the various motives which drove British people to cross the sea to America, the desire for freedom to worship God in their own way was one of the most impelling. Once, of course, all the nations of western Europe belonged to a single church, the Catholic Church, with the Pope of Rome at its head, and no person was allowed to choose his own religion. But at the opening of the sixteenth century, a great religious movement, known as the Protestant Revolt, changed this state of affairs.

In England, this movement ended in a break with the Pope and the establishment of the Church of England by law. To this church, known as the Anglican Church, every subject of the king was forced to belong. But all his subjects did not like this new order. The Catholics, who had never approved the Protestant Revolt, naturally wanted to restore their religion and with it the headship of the Pope. On the other hand, many Protestants were dissatisfied with the Anglican Church because it had retained a large part of the Catholic faith and ceremony. Some of these dissenters wanted to modify the established religion and others wanted freedom to form their own churches.

Among the moderate reformers were the Puritans, who wished merely to "purify" the Church of England by removing some of its Catholic features. The more radical Protestants, calling themselves Independents or Separatists, proposed to set up churches for themselves — little self-governing congregations or democracies. Before the Protestant Revolt had advanced very far, there were Baptists, Quakers, Presbyterians, and other dissenting sects, each proclaiming its particular form of salvation.

Since the law of England forbade all religions except the one established by the government, Dissenters and Catholics alike were liable to punishment for disbelief — heresy — and in fact were sometimes cruelly punished in England. Hence it is not sur-

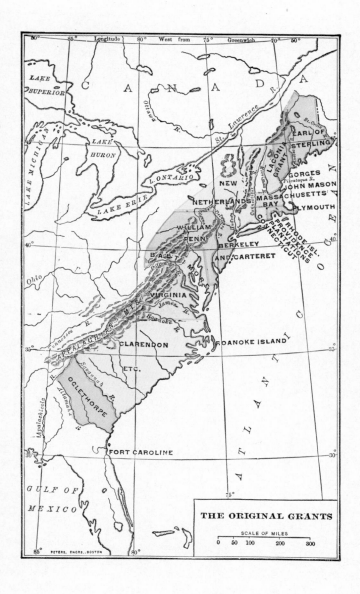

THE ORIGINAL GRANTS

SCALE OF MILES

0   50   100   200   300

prising that a great many people in the British Isles were anxious to flee to the New World where they believed they could worship God according to their faith.

Political Disputes. While the religious controversy was raging in England, a political quarrel arose between the king and the Parliament, especially the lower branch, or House of Commons, which was composed of members elected by merchants and the smaller landowners. This quarrel started when the king insisted on forcing everybody to conform to the Anglican Church and on ruling and taxing the country in his own way. Under James I (1603–1625), the dispute became very bitter and under his son and successor, Charles I, it broke out in a civil war.

In the course of this struggle, Charles was put to death and an attempt was made to change the monarchy into a republic. After years of turmoil however the monarchy was restored in 1660. Yet the ferment was not over; in 1688 James II was driven into exile, another monarch was chosen in his place, and Parliament was given the sole right to lay taxes on the people. Since many of those who resisted the king on account of taxation were Puritans in religion, the whole conflict with Charles I was known as the "Puritan Revolution." Naturally England was not a merry country to live in during this series of wars and revolutions, and colonists were readily recruited among persons eager to escape to America to find political peace and religious freedom.

How the Colonies Were Founded in America

Problems of the Early Migration. Yet in the early part of the seventeenth century it was no light matter to cross the wide Atlantic Ocean and found homes in the American wilderness. No ships, strong and comfortable, sailed regularly from the Old World to the New. There were no industries running and farms cleared to give immediate employment to the immigrants. The land to which the colonists came was claimed by the king of England and could not be occupied without his consent. Moreover, wild Indians claimed a large part of it, too, and sometimes fought hard to keep their fields and forests from invaders. Even after they were safely settled on this side of the water, immigrants had to work many months before they could harvest a crop of grain for their bread.

For these reasons early migration had to be carefully planned. At first individuals could not go to America alone; it was always necessary for people to go in bands. Every expedition cost a large sum of money — to pay for the ship, for tools and implements, for seeds, and for supplies of food and clothing to keep the settlers alive until they could get started for themselves. Every expedition had to be organized with leaders to manage it, soldiers to defend it, artisans such as carpenters and stonemasons to do work calling for special skill, and farmers to raise crops. Arrangements had to be made for the safe transportation of women and children. Finally the English king's permission to settle on land in his dominions beyond the seas had to be obtained.

The Trading Company. Evidently a colonial enterprise called for more money than the ordinary citizen in England could furnish. So the first successful colonies in America were managed by groups of people united in trading companies or corporations. A company is simply a society of citizens who put their money together in a common enterprise, choose directors and a manager, and share the profits, if there are any. Companies had long been engaged in European commerce when the English migration to America began.

The early colonial trading company was composed of men and women from different social ranks — noblemen, merchants, and commoners — each of whom invested a sum of money in the undertaking. When the society was formed, it got a charter from the king. After naming the members of the corporation, this charter usually gave them the right to elect certain officers and to manage their business affairs at regular and special meetings. It also gave them a grant of land in America and authorized them to sell this land in lots to individuals and to carry on trade.

In fact a company was a little government set up by the king for New World enterprise. Sometimes its members remained in England, as in the case of the Virginia Company, and sent out agents to direct its colony. When the members of the company came over the sea themselves, as in the case of the Massachusetts Company, they formed the direct government of the region they occupied. In that instance the stockholders became the voters while the elected head of the company served as governor of the colony. Four of the thirteen American colonies — Virginia, Massachusetts Bay, New Netherland, and Georgia — were founded by trading corporations.

The Religious Congregation. A second agency which helped men and women to get to America during the first days of colonization was the religious congregation composed of people bound

From the painting by Benjamin West
WILLIAM PENN TREATING WITH THE INDIANS

by a common religious faith. "And the multitude of them that believed were of one heart and one soul," we are told in a passage of the New Testament describing the early Christian Church at Jerusalem. In the same spirit, almost sixteen hundred years later, a leader among the Pilgrims who founded the settlement at Plymouth, in 1620, wrote concerning that colony: "We are knit together as a body in a most sacred covenant of the Lord . . . by virtue of which we hold ourselves strictly tied to all care of each other's good and of the whole." These Pilgrims bought the land on which they settled from a trading company; but they governed themselves as a kind of religious brotherhood.

The Proprietor.   A third and very important agency in promoting migration to America was the proprietor or proprietary. As the name, associated with the word "property," implies, the proprietor was a person to whom the king granted land in America. This land the proprietor could hold, use, and manage for his own benefit and profit or sell to other persons. He could keep a part and dispose of the rest on terms satisfactory to himself. The proprietor always was a rich and influential person who could furnish or borrow the money, collect the ships, supply the stores, and assemble the people for a plantation beyond the sea. He could grant to his settlers such rights of self-government as he pleased, subject, of course, to the rules laid down in his own charter from the king. Sometimes a single proprietor was given a vast tract. Sometimes two or more were associated as partners. Six colonies — Maryland, Pennsylvania, Delaware, New Jersey, and the two Carolinas — owe their main origins to this system.

Virginia Leads the Way

The Founding of Jamestown.   Late in 1606 three ships with one hundred and forty-three emigrants on board dropped down the Thames River on their way to distant America. They were being sent over by the London Company just chartered by James I. In the following spring these pioneers reached a spot on a broad river in Virginia which seemed attractive and there they built a fort and log cabin, naming the place Jamestown in honor of their king. Thus the first permanent English colony was begun.

Early Difficulties.   Yet for a time the colony did not prosper. Among the settlers were too many "gentlemen" hoping to get rich quickly by the discovery of gold; there were too few mechanics and farmers and no women at all. "Nothing," wrote Captain John Smith, one of the little band, "is to be expected thence but by labor." In spite of this warning, the Company was slow to meet the demand for industrious workers. It was easier to enlist adventurers and gold seekers as emigrants than to collect people willing to toil in the fields and forests. So wrangling broke out in the colony; idlers refused to plant and reap; and the community almost perished with hunger in the "starving time" of 1609. To make matters worse disease attacked them and reduced their numbers until it seemed that the entire colony would vanish.

Growth of the Colony. In fact at first the whole business was a mere experiment. Members of the London Company kept demanding gold from the colonists, but finally most of them saw that the best hope for profits lay in tobacco growing. So land was sold in large lots to encourage this enterprise. If the chief industry was to be tilling the soil, then labor, order, and home life were necessary to prosperity. After beginnings had been made, a few women came over with their husbands and finally in 1619 the Company sent out ninety maidens whose passage was paid by the planters they married on their arrival. When it found that this plan worked well, the Company shipped other groups of women from time to time, thus helping to make Virginia a colony of homes. An adequate supply of labor for the fields, however, was not quickly provided; when in 1619 a Dutch sea captain brought a shipload of negroes to Virginia, the planters hastily bought them as "servants" and thus started the slave system which was to be so fateful in American history.

Local Government Established. As the population increased, it became more difficult for the Company to control the colony by governors sent out from London one after another to act as its agents. Virginia was far away. It took weeks for complaints to reach London and more weeks for orders in reply to arrive. Some governors were unduly harsh and others angered the colonists by trying to make too much money out of their office. Governor Argall, for instance, seems to have been a sea captain with the manners of a pirate and his methods almost caused a rebellion.

With a view to making the colonists more contented, the London Company decided in 1619 to invite the planters to share in the government of Virginia. It asked them to elect two citizens from each settlement and borough to meet with the governor and his council for the purpose of making decisions about local affairs. This Assembly, or "House of Burgesses," as it was called, was the first "people's legislature" on the American continent.

Virginia Becomes a Royal Province. Yet the creation of a local legislature did not end the Company's troubles over Virginia. On the contrary, the king of England was now grumbling because he thought it was giving the settlers too much liberty. When in 1623 more than three hundred colonists were killed in an Indian war, the king decided to abolish the Company. The next year he took away its charter, broke up the corporation, and made Virginia a "royal" province. This meant that henceforward the king was to rule Virginia through a governor and council appointed by himself, and aided by the House of Burgesses. But harmony did not come automatically.

Bacon's Rebellion. Many and lively were the contests that arose between the king's governors and the people of Virginia. The severest conflict that occurred between 1624 and 1776 was known as "Bacon's Rebellion" — a popular uprising which sprang from two sources. In the first place, the governor and wealthy citizens tried to deprive poor men of the right to vote in elections. In the second place, they neglected to defend the frontier against the Indians.

Taking things in his own hands, a young planter by the name of Nathaniel Bacon raised a small army, defeated the Indians, marched on the Jamestown government in 1676, and drove the governor from his capital. Just at the moment of triumph, however, Bacon died and his followers were dispersed by the governor with great loss of life. But some reforms were made and there were no more serious outbreaks until the beginning of the Revolution a century later when the thirteen colonies united in a common rebellion against English rule.

Congregations and Corporations in New England

The Plymouth Colony. Shortly before the London Company was dissolved, it granted a small part of its territory to the "Pilgrims" whose religious congregation we have already mentioned. Now, as Separatists in religion, the Pilgrims had come into conflict with the king and the Church of England. Persecuted in the land of their birth, some of them had fled to Holland in search of liberty of worship.

Although they were well received by the Dutch, the Separatists were English in tongue and in customs and they never felt quite at home. Moreover the conditions of their labor in Holland were very severe. Therefore after much praying and examination of hearts, a party of Separatists decided to go to America to try their fortunes. In the summer of 1620 they sailed for Southampton where they were joined by another party of their own sect. They

From a "Thistle" print — *Copyright Detroit Publishing Company*

THE "MAYFLOWER" IN PLYMOUTH HARBOR

A painting by W. F. Halsall.

were out on the sea when one of the vessels, the *Speedwell*, began to leak so badly that they had to return to port. But at last in September a little company of Pilgrims, picked from both groups, sailed on the *Mayflower* for the New World.

Having permission to settle in Virginia, the Separatists tried to reach that colony but were driven by storms to Cape Cod where they had no rights at all. After exploring the shore line for four or five weeks, they landed at a point which they named Plymouth, stepping, it is said, from their row boats to the ledge now celebrated as Plymouth Rock.

Growth of the Plymouth Colony.　Before the *Mayflower* passengers went ashore, the men met in the cabin of the ship and drew up a "compact" for the government of the colony.　By this bond they agreed to stand together and to obey rules made by themselves for the common good.　Thus they looked not to a king or a royal charter for their law but to a pledge made and signed by their own hands.　Having bound themselves to a peaceable and orderly mode of life by the Mayflower Compact, the Pilgrims started to build their houses on the shore overlooking the harbor.

Soon the bitter, gray winter closed down upon them, and when summer came again, about one-half were dead, including their governor, John Carver.　Still they refused to despair.　Electing a new governor, William Bradford, they went on with their work. When the planting season arrived, the survivors put out several acres of corn under the direction of friendly Indians who had visited them and taught them the arts of field, forest, and stream. Trade in furs and lumber was gradually developed along the coast and new bands of immigrants joined the forerunners.　But the number of Separatists in England, upon whom the Pilgrims could draw for labor, was limited and there was no simple staple, like tobacco, to make them rich.　So at the end of seventy years when in 1691 Plymouth was merged with Massachusetts, the colony had only about seven thousand inhabitants in all.

The Puritan Colony of Massachusetts Bay.　The tiny religious brotherhood at Plymouth was just about ten years old when settlements began to appear in the region to the north under the direction of a strong corporation, chartered by Charles I in 1629 as the Massachusetts Bay Company.　In several striking respects the new concern differed from the London Company which planted Virginia.　The founders of Jamestown were as a whole loyal members of the Church of England, not religious reformers. The Massachusetts Bay Company, on the other hand, was composed principally of Puritans, who, after failing to change the English Church to suit their views, decided to migrate to America and establish the kind of religious worship they preferred.　Unlike members of the Virginia Company, who remained in England and tried to govern Virginia through agents sent across the sea. members of the Massachusetts Bay Corporation, accompanied by other Puritans, came in person to their colony. In 1630 the great experiment began, when more than a thousand men, women, and children arrived in New England under the leadership of their governor, John Winthrop.

Growth of Massachusetts. The Puritan colonization opened with settlements at Boston and other points near the Bay. As the number of immigrants increased and the population multiplied, new towns were built in the inland regions. A lucrative business in furs, shipping, and fishing was soon developed, and within a very short time Massachusetts was a thriving colony.

Separated from England by so great a distance, the Puritans lost touch with the Anglican Church and instead of fretting about purifying it they formed new "Congregational" churches of their own. With a view to keeping control over local affairs, they refused to allow any man to vote who was not a member of one of these churches. As they settled in communities they governed themselves according to decisions made at town meetings attended by the voters.

With the spread of settlements into the interior, the members of the Company found it harder to meet in one place to make laws for their government and so they provided for a general assembly to which the towns were to send delegates. Before their first governor, John Winthrop, died in 1649, Massachusetts had grown into a populous and powerful colony, almost independent of England, except in name.

The Founding of Rhode Island. Very early in the development of Massachusetts, two citizens, Roger Williams and Anne Hutchinson, began to criticize its management. Williams believed that every person had the right to worship God as he pleased and that neither the government of England nor of Massachusetts should interfere with this right on any pretext. Mrs. Hutchinson, besides holding similar views, also objected to certain religious doctrines of the Puritans. Alarmed by the teachings of these agitators, the rulers of Massachusetts banished them both.

With a few loyal companions, Roger Williams went down to the head of Narragansett Bay where, in 1636, he founded the town of Providence. Near by, on Rhode Island, Anne Hutchinson, accompanied by her faithful followers, planted another settlement two years later. From these roots sprang the colony of Rhode Island — a union of many towns which was granted a royal charter by King Charles II in 1663.

Connecticut and New Hampshire. During the lively dispute raised by Roger Williams and Anne Hutchinson in Boston, other

From Brown Brothers, New York

ANNE HUTCHINSON

A statue by Cyrus E. Dallin, State House, Boston.

groups of discontented people, under the leadership of an able preacher, Thomas Hooker, set out for the Connecticut River Valley. In this movement, some were seeking a larger religious liberty and others were looking for lands more fertile than the stony soil of Massachusetts. Copying the example of the mother colony, the pioneers of the new country settled in towns, instead of scattering over the country on isolated farms. In this way the beginnings of Hartford, Windsor, and Wethersfield were made. Learning the need of union in a terrible war with the neighboring Pequod Indians, the men of the wilderness towns held a meeting in 1639, drew up a plan of government — "The Fundamental Orders of Connecticut" — and pledged loyalty to its terms.

While the Connecticut River country was being opened by these Puritans, others under the leadership of a rich London merchant,

Theophilus Eaton, and a famous preacher, John Davenport, established settlements at New Haven and several points along the Sound. Like their neighbors to the north, these little towns were federated, in their turn — under an agreement, styled "The Fundamental Articles of New Haven," which declared that the Scriptures hold a perfect rule for the government of all men in church and state and family. In 1662 the two colonies, with one capital at Hartford and the other at New Haven, were fused, and granted a royal charter by Charles II.

Other offshoots from Massachusetts to the north beyond the Merrimac River grew into thriving communities and early displayed signs of independence. Their position and their importance were recognized by the king in 1679, when they were made a separate colony — the royal province of New Hampshire.

The New England Confederation. Although the New England colonies pursued separate ways, they were very much alike in laws, manners, and religion. For this reason Plymouth, Massachusetts, Connecticut, and New Haven were able, in 1643, to form a union for defense against the Indians, known as the New England Confederation. Again in 1686 when the king placed New England, New York, and New Jersey under one governor, Edmund Andros, the Puritans resisted almost as a unit the attempt to oust their governors in favor of a royal agent. After three years of opposition to Andros, they had the pleasure of seeing him driven off, when his sovereign, James II, was dethroned. Then each colony settled back in its own habits.

FIVE PROPRIETARY COLONIES

Maryland. Among the men of affairs in England, who watched the experiments in New England and Virginia, was a Catholic gentleman, Sir George Calvert, later Lord Baltimore, high in the favor of King Charles I. In 1632 Baltimore obtained from his monarch a charter making him the proprietor of a large tract of land northeast of Virginia. But he died before the paper was signed and the charter was issued to his son and heir, Cecilius Calvert, who founded the new colony, naming it Maryland in honor of the queen.

It was natural for the second Lord Baltimore to favor people of his own religious faith when he selected colonists. And as Catholics had suffered from persecution in England no less than the Puritans, many of them were ready to move to America. However, Baltimore was more interested in selling his land and building a prosperous colony than in maintaining a particular sect; therefore he also invited Protestants of every denomination to come to his settlement.

In the course of time, the Protestants outnumbered the Catholics and made plans to control the colony themselves. But out of this strife came the celebrated Toleration Act of 1649 which declared that all who vowed their faith in Jesus Christ should be permitted to worship according to their consciences. Catholics and Protestants were thus recognized. Under the mild rule of the descendants of Lord Baltimore (except for a short period), Maryland continued to live until the eve of the American Revolution.

From an old print

CHARLESTON HARBOR IN COLONIAL TIMES

The Carolina Proprietors. The success of the Baltimores inspired other royal courtiers with the desire to make money out of colonies in the New World. Accordingly eight noblemen secured from Charles II in 1663 a tract of land south of Virginia which they called Carolina. To start exploiting it, they sent out an expedition and established a settlement named Charleston, which was removed to the site of the present city in 1680. With the expansion of plantations inland, this town became a thriving seaport. In the meantime the northern part of Carolina was being settled by Quakers and other immigrants from Virginia.

Desirous of selling their land to the best advantage, the proprietors granted religious toleration to various Protestant sects, and this action attracted to their colony Puritans from New England, Dutch from New York, Huguenots from France, Presbyterians from Scotland and Ireland, Germans and Swiss from the Continent. As the colony grew, the difficulties of supervision multiplied especially owing to the fierce objections of the settlers to taxes and other dues on land. To make the business of government simpler, the proprietors divided their grant into North and South Carolina but, to their surprise, that did not improve affairs. Weary at last of the contest with unruly colonists, which brought neither profit nor glory, the owners of the Carolinas sold out to the king in 1729, and each of these colonies then became a royal province with a royal governor of its own.

Pennsylvania and Delaware. While the Carolina proprietors were trying to put their experiment on a firm basis, another proprietor, William Penn, was founding a new colony west of the Delaware River. Early in life, Penn had adopted the faith of the Friends, a Protestant sect popularly known as Quakers, and as he grew into manhood he became deeply interested in finding a haven in the New World for people of his particular religious belief. Fortunately for his plans, he inherited from his father a claim against the king, Charles II, for a large sum of money. After much haggling Penn managed in 1681 to obtain payment in a grant of land in America — Pennsylvania, as the king named it.

Finding that his territory had no coast line, Penn induced the king's brother, the Duke of York, to turn over to him the Delaware region to the southeast, which had been wrested from the Swedes by the Dutch and from the Dutch by the English. Although these lower counties were assigned to Penn on the same terms as his larger grant, they were formed into the separate colony of Delaware in 1702, and remained in that status under the Penn family throughout the colonial era.

As soon as Penn got his grants straightened out, he set to work in a practical manner to secure more settlers for his territory —

which was already inhabited by a few thousand Swedes and Dutch on the Delaware and by Quakers who had preceded him in the search for religious liberty. To push the work along Penn came himself at the head of an expedition in 1682. When he planned his first town, Philadelphia, "city of brotherly love," he made the streets unusually wide in order to avoid the overcrowding that existed in European cities; for Penn was an idealist as well as a shrewd business man. Treaties of peace were made with the Indian natives and they were paid for their land, showing that Penn

From an old print

A GLIMPSE OF OLD GERMANTOWN

was a "Friend" in practice as well as religion. By promising general toleration, Penn induced many Scotch-Irish Presbyterians and German Protestants to join pioneers of his own sect in developing Pennsylvania. Before long the colony became populous and prosperous. Trade flourished and farms were laid out westward into the interior. After William Penn died, both Pennsylvania and Delaware remained in the control of his family until American independence was established.

NEW YORK, NEW JERSEY, AND GEORGIA

New York, First Known as New Netherland. One of the most strategic colonies in America was founded by the Dutch.

These hardy people had early been trading rivals of the Spaniards and the English in all quarters of the world. They, too, had taken part in the search for a water route to the Far East; under their direction in 1609 Henry Hudson, an Englishman in command of Dutch vessels, sailed up the great river that now bears his name, looking for the long-desired passage through the New World. A few years later the Dutch West India Company bought the island of Manhattan from the Indians and planted a trading settlement,

From an old print

OLD DUTCH FORT AND ENGLISH CHURCH NEAR ALBANY

called New Amsterdam, at the lower end. For the purpose of occupying the Hudson River Valley, the Dutch Company granted big estates to rich men, known as "patroons" or patrons, who agreed to transport settlers. These patroons advanced the money to pay the passage of emigrants and to buy seeds and tools. The emigrants, on their part, bound themselves to work for the patroons.

The English Seize New Netherland. For about forty years the Dutch continued to hold and develop their colony of New Netherland but from the outset its fate was uncertain. England claimed the very ground on which they settled and on their eastern frontier they were menaced by the advance of Connecticut pioneers. Even on the high seas they were challenged by the English navy; so protection for the colony was always a serious question.

Finally in 1664 the blow fell. Charles II granted the whole region between the Hudson and Delaware rivers to his brother, the Duke of York, and without warning an English fleet rode into the harbor of New Amsterdam with a command to surrender. The Dutch governor, Peter Stuyvesant, protested violently but, being helpless, yielded to the conqueror. New Netherland was henceforward known as New York.

Englishmen now came in large numbers to settle beside the Dutch who remained in the colony as English subjects. And when Louis XIV, the king of France, prohibited all except Catholic worship in his country in 1685, many of his Protestant subjects, known as Huguenots, fled to New York, a party of them founding New Rochelle, named for their French home. As long as the Duke of York owned the colony, it was regarded as a proprietary province. On his coronation as James II, king of England, in 1685, New York became a royal province.

New Jersey. When the English wrested New Netherland from the Dutch, they also seized the land to the west of the Hudson River where a few settlements had been made. Shortly afterward that region was granted to Lord Berkeley and Sir George Carteret who, as proprietors, began to colonize it. The name New Jersey was given to it because Carteret had once been governor of the Isle of Jersey in the English Channel.

In this colony rich land was offered for sale at low prices and religious toleration was promised to all Protestants, thus attracting to it Puritans, Quakers, and Scotch-Irish Presbyterians. Like people in other colonies, the settlers in New Jersey often quarreled with the owners of their territory and in time both Berkeley and Carteret were glad to get rid of their property. In 1702 New Jersey became a royal province. At first it was attached to New York but later, in 1728, it was given a separate royal governor.

Georgia. The thirteenth and last of the English colonies was founded far to the south, below South Carolina. The leader in this enterprise was a man of humane spirit, James Oglethorpe, who wanted to help the poor debtors and other prisoners crowded in English jails. After worrying a long time about their miserable lot, he determined to try to improve it by giving them an opportunity in the New World to make an honest living. He proceeded to form a company, or board of trustees, to aid him in this venture and in 1732 obtained from George I a grant of land to the south of the Savannah River. Charitable citizens of England were persuaded to make contributions for the scheme on the ground that they would be aiding the poor, while business men were invited to invest with the object of making profits. In the interest of good order, slavery and the sale of rum were forbidden in Georgia. Substantial settlers were also induced to come, and the colony was started in high hopes with the founding of Savannah.

The prisoners taken to Georgia however did not prove to be very diligent or competent workmen. Therefore the trustees began to send colonists of a different kind from England, Scotland, and Europe. With the growth of the colony, a demand arose for a repeal of the laws against slavery and rum and finally the government yielded on both points. Negroes were then imported to till the plantations laid out in the lowlands. Now assured of an abundant labor supply, more men of wealth came to the colony to acquire land and increase their fortunes. Thus, Georgia, though started as a kind of social experiment, became very much like her neighbor, South Carolina. Indeed, in 1752, the trustees, defeated in their original plan, turned their colony over to the king, who governed it as a royal province.

How the People Got over the Sea

Immigrants Who Paid Their Way. No matter how a colony was started or managed, the passage of immigrants to America had to be paid. Many of the immigrants, of course, were eager to come and had the money with which to defray the cost of the voyage. What proportion could pay their way is not known, though undoubtedly a large number belonged to this class. An American historian, Henry Cabot Lodge, claims that "the settlers of New England were drawn from the country gentlemen, small farmers, and yeomanry of the mother country. . . . Many of the emigrants were men of wealth, as the old lists show, and all of them, with few exceptions, were men of property and good standing. They did not belong to the classes from which emigration is usually supplied, for they all had a stake in the country they left behind." But certainly not all the immigrants in New England were free and well-to-do and in some of the other colonies a very large number were far from that fortunate state.

Indentured Servants. In fact tens of thousands of emigrants were too poor to pay for their passage; this we know from the shipping records. To meet the cost of the sea voyage, shipowners and other persons of means often supplied the passage money to emigrants in return for their promise, or bond, to work for a term of years to repay the sum advanced. This system was called bond, or indentured, servitude.

It is probable that the number of bond servants brought to America exceeded the original Puritans, the yeomen, the Virginia gentlemen, and the Huguenots combined. All the way down the coast from Massachusetts to Georgia these servants — men, women, and children — were to be found in the fields, kitchens, and workshops, serving out terms of labor generally ranging from five to seven years. In the proprietary colonies the proportion of bond servants was very high. The proprietors diligently sought workers of every nationality to till their fields, for land without labor was worth no more than land in the moon. Hence the gates of the proprietary colonies were flung wide open. In Pennsylvania, it was not uncommon to find a master with fifty bond servants on his estate. It has been estimated that two-thirds of all the immigrants into Pennsylvania between the opening of the eighteenth century and the outbreak of the Revolution came in bondage. In the other Middle colonies the number was doubtless not so large; but it formed a considerable part of the population.

The story of this traffic in white servants is one of the most arresting chapters in the history of American labor. Bondmen differed from the serfs of the feudal age in that they were not bound to the soil but to changing masters who bought them at their convenience. They likewise differed from the negro slaves in that their servitude had a time limit. Still they were subject to many special hardships. It was, for instance, a common practice to punish them more severely than freemen for the same offense. A free citizen of Pennsylvania who indulged in horse racing and gambling was let off with a fine; a white servant guilty of the same unlawful conduct was whipped at the post and fined as well.

The life and work of bond servants were regulated by strict rules. They could not marry without their master's consent; nor engage in trade; nor refuse to do the work assigned to them. For an attempt to escape or indeed for any violation of the law, the term of service was extended. The condition of white bondmen in Virginia, according to Lodge, "was little better than that of slaves. Loose indentures and harsh laws put them at the mercy of their masters." It would not be unfair to add that such was their lot in all the other colonies.

Cruel as was the system in many ways, it gave thousands of people in the Old World a chance to reach the New in the hope of freedom and the winning of a home. When their weary years of servitude were over, if they survived, they might obtain land of their own or settle as free working people in the towns. For many of them the gamble proved to be a losing venture because they found themselves unable to rise out of the state of poverty and dependence into which servitude carried them. For thousands, on the other hand, bondage proved to be a real avenue to liberty and prosperity.

The Transported — Involuntary Servitude. In their hurry to secure settlers, the companies and proprietors also resorted to, or connived at, the practice of kidnaping men, women, and children in the streets of English cities. In a single year, 1680, it is officially estimated, "ten thousand persons were spirited away" to America. Many of the victims of such violence were young children, for the traffic in youth was highly profitable. Orphans and dependents were sometimes shipped off to America by relatives unwilling to support them. In 1627 about fifteen hundred helpless children were thus transported to Virginia.

In this gruesome business occurred many tragedies and very few romances. Parents were often separated forever from their children and husbands from their wives. Hundreds of skilled artisans — carpenters, smiths, and weavers — disappeared from England as if swallowed up by death. A few dragged off to the New World to be sold into servitude for a term of five or seven years later became well-to-do. In one case a young man who was forcibly carried over the sea lived to make his way back to England and to prove that he was a nobleman. But many victims of the kidnapers sank down into poverty.

Akin to the kidnaped, at least in economic position, were convicts deported to the colonies in lieu of fines and imprisonment. Against this practice, other colonists cried out long and heartily, but in vain. Indeed, they often made too much of its evils, for many of the "criminals" were only mild offenders against unduly cruel laws. A peasant caught shooting a rabbit on a lord's estate or a luckless servant girl who stole a pocket handkerchief was treated like a hardened thief or highwayman. Some offenders were intelligent "political criminals"; that is, persons who criticized or opposed the harshness of the English government. This class included at one time Irish who revolted against British rule in Ireland; at another, Cavaliers who were loyal to the king against the Puritan revolutionists; Puritans, in turn, sent over after the monarchy was restored; and Scotch and English subjects in general who joined in political uprisings against the king.

The African Slaves. Rivaling in numbers, in the course of years, the white people carried to America against their will were the African negroes brought to the colonies and sold as slaves. When this form of bondage was introduced into Virginia in 1619, it was looked upon as a temporary custom that would pass as the white population grew in size. Moreover it does not appear that those planters who first bought negroes at the auction block intended to set up a system of bondage for life. Only by a slow process did chattel slavery take deep root and become the leading source of the Southern labor supply. In 1650, thirty years after the introduction of slavery, there were only three hundred Africans in Virginia.

The great increase in later times was due in no small measure to the zeal for profits that seized slave traders both in Old and New England. By fair means or foul they seized negroes in Africa and crowded Southern ports with vessels freighted by human cargoes. The English Royal African Company sent to America annually between 1713 and 1743 from five to ten thousand slaves. Nor were shipowners of New England far behind their English brethren in pushing this terrible traffic.

As the number of the negroes steadily rose, and as whole sections were overrun with slaves and slave traders, white settlers in the Southern colonies grew alarmed. In 1710 Virginia sought to cut down the trade by placing a duty of £5 on every slave imported. This effort was futile, for the royal governor vetoed it. From time to time similar bills were passed by colonial legislatures only to meet with royal disapproval. South Carolina in 1760 strictly forbade importation; but the measure was vetoed by the British king. As late as 1772 Virginia in a petition to George III declared: "The importation of slaves into the colonies from the coast of Africa hath long been considered as a trade of great inhumanity and under its present encouragement, we have too much reason to fear, will endanger the very existence of Your Majesty's American dominions."

All such protests were without avail. The negro population rose swiftly, until at the time of this petition it amounted to more than half a million. In five colonies — Maryland, Virginia, the two Carolinas, and Georgia — the slaves nearly equaled or actually exceeded the whites in number. In South Carolina they formed almost two-thirds of the population. Even in the Middle colonies of Delaware and Pennsylvania about one-fifth of the inhabitants were from Africa. To the North, the proportion of slaves steadily fell although chattel servitude was on the same legal footing as in the South. In New York about one in six and in New England one in fifty was a negro, including a few freedmen.

Nationality of the European Immigrants

The English. In leadership and origin the thirteen colonies, except New York and Delaware, were English. During the early days in all, save these two, the main, if not the sole, current of immigration was from England. The colonists came from every walk of life. Most of them were yeomen, or small landowners, farm laborers, and artisans. With these were associated merchants and "gentlemen," as the wealthier landlords were called, who brought stocks of goods or fortunes of their own to the New World. Scholars came from the universities of Oxford and Cambridge to preach the gospel or to teach. Now and then the son of an English nobleman left his baronial hall behind and cast his lot with America. These people represented every Christian faith — members of the Established Church of England; Puritans who had labored to reform that church; Separatists, Baptists, and Friends, who had left it; and Catholics, who clung to the religion of their fathers.

New England was almost purely English. During the years between 1629 and 1640, the period of harsh Stuart government, about twenty thousand Puritans emigrated to America, settling in the colonies of the far North. Although other settlers came from time to time, the greater portion of the New England people sprang from this original stock. Virginia, too, for a long time drew nearly all her colonists from England alone. Not until well into the eighteenth century did the Scotch-Irish and German immigrants rival the English in numbers.

The population of the later English colonies — the Carolinas, New York, Pennsylvania, and Georgia — was enlarged by a stream of immigrants directly from Great Britain and by wanderers from the older settlements. New York was invaded by Puritans from New England in such numbers as to cause an Anglican clergyman there to lament that "free thinking spreads almost as fast as the Church." North Carolina was first settled toward the northern border by immigrants from Virginia, who were joined by the Quakers from New England.

The Scotch-Irish. Next to the English in numbers and influence were the Scotch-Irish, Presbyterians in belief, English in tongue. Both religious and economic reasons sent them across the sea. Their Scotch ancestors had settled in the north of Ireland whence the native Irish had been driven by English armies about the middle of the seventeenth century. There the Scotch flourished for many years, enjoying in peace their own religion and making money by the manufacture of fine linen and woolen cloth.

Then suddenly they got an awful shock. Toward the end of the century their religious worship and the export of their cloth were both forbidden by the English Parliament in London. As a result, within a few years, twenty thousand Scotch-Irish left Ulster alone for America; and throughout the eighteenth century the migration continued to be heavy. Although no exact record was kept, it is reckoned that the Scotch-Irish and the Scotch who came directly from Scotland composed one-sixth of the entire American population on the eve of independence.

These newcomers made their homes chiefly in New Jersey, Pennsylvania, Maryland, Virginia, and the Carolinas. Coming late upon the scene, they found much of the land along the seaboard already taken up. For this reason they became mainly a frontier people, settling the interior and mountain regions. There they cleared the land, laid out small farms, and worked as "sturdy yeomen on the soil," hardy, industrious, and independent in spirit, sharing neither the luxuries of the rich planters nor the leisure of the merchants in the towns. To their agriculture they added woolen and linen manufacture, which, flourishing under the supple fingers of their tireless women, made heavy inroads upon the trade of the English merchants in the colonies. Of their labors a poet has sung:

> O, willing hands to toil;
> Strong natures tuned to the harvest-song and bound
>   to the kindly soil;
> Bold pioneers for the wilderness, defenders in the field.

The Germans. Third among the colonists in order of numerical importance were the Germans. From the very beginning, they appeared in colonial records. Some of the artisans and carpenters in the first Jamestown colony were of that nationality. Peter Minuit, the famous governor of New Netherland, was from Wesel on the Rhine, and Jacob Leisler, leader of a popular uprising against the royal government in New York, was from Frankfort-on-Main. The wholesale migration of Germans began with the founding of Pennsylvania. William Penn, who was very active in searching for thrifty farmers to cultivate his lands, made a special effort to attract competent peasants from the Rhine country. A great association, known as the Frankfort Company, bought more than twenty thousand acres from him and in 1684 established a center at Germantown for the distribution of immigrants. In New York, Rhinebeck-on-the-Hudson became a similar center.

From Maine to Georgia special favors were offered to the German farmers and in nearly every colony, in time, their settlements were to be found. In fact the migration became so large that German princes were frightened at the loss of so many good subjects and England was also disturbed by the rush of foreigners into her overseas dominions. Yet nothing stopped the movement. By the end of the colonial period, the number of Germans had risen to more than two hundred thousand.

SETTLEMENTS OF GERMAN AND SCOTCH-IRISH IMMIGRANTS

The majority were Protestants from the Rhine region and South Germany, driven out by wars, religious controversies, oppression, and poverty. Though they were chiefly farmers, there were among them skilled artisans who aided in the rapid upbuilding of industries in Pennsylvania. Their iron, glass, paper, and woolen mills, dotted here and there among the thickly settled regions, added to the wealth and independence of the colony.

Unlike the Scotch-Irish, the Germans did not speak the language of the original colonists or mingle freely with them. They kept to themselves, built their own schools, founded their own newspapers, and published their own books. Their clannish habits often irritated their neighbors and led to occasional agitations against "foreigners." However, no serious clashes seem to have occurred; and in the days of the Revolution, German soldiers from Pennsylvania fought in the patriot armies side by side with soldiers from the English and Scotch-Irish sections.

Other Nationalities. Though the English, Scotch-Irish, and Germans made up the bulk of the colonial population, there were other racial strains. From France, after 1685, came the Huguenots fleeing from a decree of the king which inflicted frightful penalties upon Protestants. From "Old Ireland" came many native Irish, Celtic in race and Catholic in religion. Like their Scotch-Irish neighbors to the north, they were unhappy under the government and the Church of England imposed upon them by the sword. How many came we do not know, but shipping records of the colonial period show that boatload after boatload left the southern and eastern shores of Ireland for the New World. Undoubtedly many of these passengers were Irish of the native stock, for Irish names appear constantly in the lists.

Likewise engaged in a battle for religious toleration, Jews found in the American colonies more freedom than they had enjoyed in England, France, Spain, or Portugal. The English law did not actually give them the right to live in any of the dominions, but owing to the easy-going habits of the Americans they were allowed to filter into the seaboard towns. The treatment they received there varied. On one occasion the mayor and council of New York forbade them to sell by retail and on another prohibited the exercise of their religious worship. Newport, Philadelphia, and Charleston were more hospitable, and had large Jewish groups, consisting principally of merchants and their families.

Though the small Swedish colony in Delaware was quickly submerged beneath the tide of English migration, the Dutch in New York maintained their customs for more than a hundred years after the English conquest in 1664. At the end of the colonial period over one-half of the 170,000 inhabitants of the province were descendants of the original Dutch — still distinct enough in their customs to give a decided cast to the life and manners of New York. Many clung as loyally to their mother tongue as they did to their big farmhouses or their Dutch ovens; but they were slowly losing their identity as the English pressed in beside them to farm and trade.

The melting pot had begun its historic mission.

References

E. Channing, *History of the United States,* Vols. I and II.

J. A. Doyle, *The English Colonies in America* (5 vols.).

J. Fiske, *Old Virginia and Her Neighbors* (2 vols.).

A. B. Faust, *The German Element in the United States* (2 vols.).

H. J. Ford, *The Scotch-Irish in America.*

L. Tyler, *England in America* (American Nation Series).

R. Usher, *The Pilgrims and Their History.*

T. J. Wertenbaker, *The First Americans.*

Questions

1. Explain how England led in colonization.

2. America has been called a nation of immigrants. Why?

3. Why were individuals unable to go to America alone at first? What agencies made colonization possible? Discuss each of them.

4. Make a table of the colonies, showing what agencies aided in their establishment and growth.

5. Give three important events and dates in connection with the founding of Virginia; five in connection with New England; four in connection with Maryland, Pennsylvania, and Delaware; and five in connection with New York, New Jersey, and Georgia.

6. Who were John Smith, John Carver, William Bradford, John Winthrop, Roger Williams, Anne Hutchinson, Thomas Hooker, Theophilus Eaton, John Davenport, Lord Baltimore, William Penn, Peter Stuyvesant, Lord Berkeley, and James Oglethorpe?

7. Compare the way immigrants come to-day with the way they came in colonial times.

8. Contrast indentured servitude with slavery and serfdom.

9. Account for the eagerness of companies and proprietors to secure colonists.

10. Why did the slave system grow?

11. In what way did the North derive advantages from slavery?

12. What nationalities were represented among the early colonists? What is meant by the "melting pot"?

Research Topics

The Chartered Company. Compare the first and third charters of Virginia in Macdonald, *Documentary Source Book of American History,*

1606–1898, pp. 1–14.   Analyze the first and second Massachusetts charters in Macdonald, pp. 22–84.   Special reference: W. A. S. Hewins, *English Trading Companies*.

Congregations and Compacts for Self-government.   A study of the Mayflower Compact, the Fundamental Orders of Connecticut, and the Fundamental Articles of New Haven in Macdonald, pp. 19, 36, 39.   Reference: Charles Borgeaud, *Rise of Modern Democracy*, and C. S. Lobingier, *The People's Law*, Chaps. I–VII.

The Proprietary System.   Analysis of Penn's charter of 1681, in Macdonald, p. 80.   Reference: Lodge, *Short History of the English Colonies in America*, p. 211.

Studies of Individual Colonies.   Review of outstanding events in the history of each colony, using Elson, *History of the United States*, pp. 45–135, as the basis.

Biographical Studies.   John Smith, John Winthrop, William Penn, Lord Baltimore, William Bradford, Roger Williams, Anne Hutchinson, Thomas Hooker, and Peter Stuyvesant, using any good encyclopedia.

Indentured Servitude.   In Virginia, Lodge, *Short History*, pp. 69–72; in Pennsylvania, pp. 242–244.   Contemporary account in Callender, *Economic History of the United States*, pp. 44–51.   Special reference: Karl Geiser, *Redemptioners and Indentured Servants* (Yale Review, X, No. 2 Supplement).

Slavery.   In Virginia, Lodge, *Short History*, pp. 67–69; in the Northern colonies, pp. 241, 275, 322, 408, 442.

The People of the Colonies.   Lodge, *Short History*, Virginia, pp. 67–73; New England, pp. 406–409, 441–450; Pennsylvania, pp. 227–229, 240–250; New York, pp. 312–313, 322–335.

Questions for Debate

1. The motives of immigration in the seventeenth century were essentially different from the motives of immigration in the twentieth century.

2. The desire for greater political and religious liberty had more to do with the settlement of America (the thirteen colonies) in the seventeenth century than economic reasons.

Historical Fiction

Washington Irving, *A History of New York by Diedrich Knickerbocker*.
Mary Johnston, *To Have and to Hold*.
Emma Rayner, *In Castle and Colony*.

CHAPTER III

INDUSTRY ON LAND AND SEA

THE LAND AND THE WESTWARD MOVEMENT

The Meaning of Land Tenure for Humanity. The way in which the land of a country is held, acquired, bought, sold, and divided among the heirs of deceased persons helps to shape the life and character of a people. If land is owned in large lots or estates by a few persons only, we have one type of agriculture and society; if it is owned in small farms by many people, we have another type. Beyond any doubt a man who possesses a farm outright is more independent than one who rents the land he tills or who works for a landlord.

During the age of colonial America, a large part of the land in Europe was held in great estates, each owned by a proprietor for whom the tillers of the soil worked as tenants or serfs. On the death of the landlord the entire estate usually passed to his eldest son, who kept it together in one piece as his father had done. The law favored this form of inheritance, which was known as primogeniture, meaning right of the first-born. Naturally the system prevented the division of estates into small parcels of land which farmers and laborers could buy and thus become free home owners. It was very difficult indeed for the mass of the people of Europe to purchase any land for themselves and thus escape dependence on the owners of large tracts, who gave them employment. In such circumstances proprietors of estates had enormous power over their renters and laborers, who made up the bulk of the population.

Experiments in Common Tillage. In the New World with a vast territory awaiting the plow, it was impossible to introduce everywhere the system of lords and tenants that existed in crowded Europe. So it happened that almost every kind of tenure was tried.

48

In the early days of the Jamestown colony, the land, though owned by the London Company, was tilled in common by the settlers. No man had a separate plot for himself. The motto of the community was: "Labor and share alike." All men were supposed to work in the fields and receive a share of the crops. At Plymouth,

From *The Holliday Historic Photograph Co.*

A MASSACHUSETTS MANSION BUILT IN 1718

the Pilgrims tried a similar plan: the joint produce of their labor was divided with rough equality among the workers.

But in both colonies communistic experiments were failures. Angry at the lazy men in Jamestown who idled their time away and yet expected regular meals, Captain John Smith issued a manifesto: "Everyone that gathereth not every day as much as I do, the next day shall be set beyond the river and forever banished from the fort and live there or starve." Even this terrible threat did not bring a change for the better. Not until each man was given a plot of his own to till did the settlers work hard and the colony prosper. In Plymouth, where the communal scheme lasted for five years, the results were similar to those in Virginia, and in a short time the system was given up for one of separate fields in which every person could "set corn for his own particular." Some other New England towns, refusing to profit by the experience of their Plymouth neighbor, also tried common ownership and labor, only to abandon the idea sooner or later and change to individual ownership of the land. "By degrees it was seen that even the Lord's people could not carry the complicated communist legislation into perfect and wholesome practice."

Feudal Elements in the Colonies — Quitrents, Manors, and Plantations.   Radically different from common ownership of land was the semi-feudal tenure found in the proprietary colonies, in the seaboard regions of the South, and to some extent in New York. The proprietor was a feudal lord in that he held his land by a direct grant from the king. He could keep any part of it for his personal use or dispose of it all in large or small lots. While he generally kept for himself a huge block of land, it was impossible for him to manage directly very much of his grant. Consequently he sold most of it in parcels for lump sums in cash and usually on condition that the purchasers make to him an annual payment in money, known as "quitrent." In Maryland, the proprietor sometimes received as much as £9000 (equal to about $50,000 to-day) in a single year from this source.

In the royal provinces, the king of England claimed all revenues collected in this form from the land, a sum amounting to £19,000 a year at the time of the Revolution. Wherever it was laid however, by king, proprietor, or company, the people grumbled about it and called it a feudal tax on freeholders; and it became an item among the grievances listed against the mother country.

Besides selling small plots of land subject to this perpetual quitrent, the king, companies, and proprietors also granted huge estates or manors to individuals, with or without quitrent liabilities. In the colony of Maryland alone there were sixty manors of three thousand acres each, owned by wealthy men and tilled by tenants. In New York also there were many manors of wide extent, some of them dating back to the days of the Dutch West India Company when favorable terms were made with patroons to induce them to bring over settlers. The Van Rensselaer, Van Cortlandt, and Livingston manors were so large and populous that each was entitled to send a representative to the provincial legislature. The tenants on these New York manors were in somewhat the same position as serfs on old European estates. They were bound to pay the owner a rent in money and kind; they ground their grain at his mill; and they were subject to his judicial power because he held court and meted out justice, in some instances even the death sentence.

The extensive manors of New York however were of slight consequence as compared with the plantations of the Southern seaboard — huge estates, far wider in expanse than many a European barony and tilled by laborers more servile than any feudal tenants, namely, by slaves. It must not be forgotten that this system became the chief feature of a large section and gave a decided bent to its economic and political life.

The Small Freehold.   Yet in the upland regions of the South and throughout most of the North, the drift was against all forms of servitude and tenantry and in the direction of the freehold, that is, the small farm owned outright and tilled by the possessor and his family. This was favored both by natural circumstances and the spirit of the immigrants. For one thing, the abundance of land and the scarcity of labor made it impossible for companies, proprietors, or king to develop everywhere in the colonies a network of vast estates. In some sections, particularly in New England, the climate, the stony soil, the hills, and the narrow valleys conspired to keep the farms moderate in size. For another thing, many English, Scotch-Irish, and German peasants, even though they had been tenants in the Old World, did not propose to accept any kind of bondage in the New. If they could not get freeholds, they would not settle at all; thus they forced proprietors and companies to bid for their labor by selling land to them in small lots. So it happened that the freehold of modest size became the unit best liked by American farmers — all the better if it was free of quitrent. The people who tilled the farms were drawn from every quarter of western Europe; but in America they developed a patriotic bond of sympathy and independence on account of their ownership of the soil.

Social Effects of Land Tenure.   Although both were engaged in agriculture, the owner of a large estate and the owner of a small freehold differed widely in their ways of living, working, and

From Cook Studios, Richmond, Va.

"Westover," the Home of the Byrds, Built in Colonial Times

thinking.   The Southern planter, on his broad acres tilled by slaves, resembled the English landlord on his huge estate more than he did the colonial farmer who labored with his own hands in the fields and forests.   The planter sold his rice and tobacco in large amounts directly to British merchants who gave in exchange goods or cash.   His fine clothes, furniture, carpets, silverware, china, and cutlery came from English markets.   Loving the riper traditions of the mother country, he often sent his sons to Oxford or Cambridge for their education. In short he depended very largely for his prosperity and his forms of culture upon close relations with the Old World. He did not even need market towns in which to buy native goods, for they were made on his own plantation by his own artisans, who were usually gifted slaves.

The lot of the small farmer was totally different. His crops were not big enough to warrant direct trade with English merchants or the steady employment of a corps of artisans. He needed local markets, and they sprang up to meet his need. Smiths, hatters, weavers, wagon-makers, and potters at neighboring towns supplied him with the rough products of their skill. The finer goods bought by the rich planter in England, the small farmer ordinarily could not buy. His wants were limited to staples like tea and sugar, and between him and the European market stood the town merchant. His community was therefore more self-sufficient than the seaboard line of great plantations. It was more isolated, more provincial, more independent, more American. The planter faced the Old East. The farmer faced the New West, "the backwoods."

The Westward Movement. Yeoman and planter nevertheless were alike in one respect. Their land hunger was never appeased. Each had the eye of an expert for new and fertile soil; and so, north or south, as soon as a foothold was secured on the Atlantic coast, the current of migration set in westward, creeping through forests, along the rivers, and over the mountains. Many of the later immigrants, in their search for cheap lands, simply had to go to the border; but in the main the path to the West was broken by native Americans of the second and third generations. Explorers fired by curiosity and the lure of mystery, hunters, fur traders, and squatters, obeying their own sweet wills, blazed the trail; they opened routes and sent back stories of the fine regions they traversed. Then came the regular settlers with lawful titles to the lands they had purchased, sometimes singly and sometimes in companies.

This westward movement in Massachusetts was marked by the founding of Springfield in 1636 and Great Barrington in 1725. By the opening of the eighteenth century the pioneers of Connecticut had pushed north and west until their outpost towns adjoined the Hudson Valley settlements. The inland movement of New Yorkers followed the Hudson River to Albany, and from that old Dutch center it radiated in every direction, particularly westward through the Mohawk Valley. New Jersey was early filled to its borders, the beginnings of the present city of New Brunswick being made in 1681 and those of Trenton in 1685. For Pennsylvania, as for New York, the waterways pointed out the chief lines of advance. Pioneers, pushing up through the valley of the Schuylkill, spread over the fertile lands of Berks and Lancaster counties, laying out Reading in 1748. Another current of migration was directed by the Susquehanna and in 1726 the first farmhouse was built on the bank where Harrisburg later flourished. Along the southern tier of counties, a thin line of settlements stretched westward to Pittsburgh, reaching the upper waters of the Ohio while the colony was still under the Penn family.

In the South the westward march was equally swift. The seaboard was quickly occupied by planters and their slaves engaged in the cultivation of tobacco and rice. To the next area of settlement, the Piedmont plateau, lying back from the coast all the way from Maryland to Georgia, were turned two streams of migration, one westward from the sea and the other southward from the Middle colonies — Germans from Pennsylvania and Scotch-Irish furnishing the main supply. "By 1770, tide-water Virginia was full to overflowing and the 'back country' of the Blue Ridge and the Shenandoah was fully occupied. Even the mountain valleys . . . were claimed by sturdy pioneers. Before the Declaration of Independence, the oncoming tide of homeseekers had reached the crest of the Alleghenies."

Beyond these mountains pioneers had already ventured, heralds of an invasion that was about to break in upon Kentucky and Tennessee. As early as 1769 that intrepid frontiersman, Daniel Boone, curious to hunt buffaloes, of which he had heard weird reports, passed through the Cumberland Gap and brought back to North Carolina news of a wonderful country beyond the horizon. A hint was sufficient. Singly, in pairs, and in groups, settlers followed the path taken by Boone. A great land corporation, the Transylvania Company, adopting the example of the London

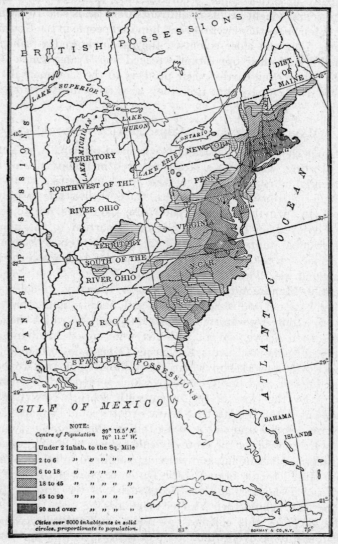

DISTRIBUTION OF POPULATION, 1790

Company in earlier times, secured a large grant of this western territory and sought profits in quitrents from lands sold to farmers. Within ten years there were several hundred people in the Kentucky region. Like the older colonists, they soon showed a dislike for quitrents, and their opposition wrecked the Transylvania Company. They even carried their protests to the Continental Congress in 1776, for by that time they were an "embryo fourteenth colony."

Manufacturing and Commercial Development

Though the labor of the colonists was spent principally in farming and planting, there was a steady growth in manufacturing and commercial pursuits. Most of the staple industries of to-day, particularly iron and textiles, can trace their start to colonial times. In turn this business enterprise soon gave rise to towns which enjoyed an importance out of proportion to the number of their inhabitants. In fact all the great centers of commerce and finance on the seaboard originated in the days when the king of England was "lord of these dominions."

Textile Manufacture as a Domestic Industry. One of the leading national industries, woolen and linen manufacture, was built up mainly by women, carrying on a work in which they had always been active. Wool and flax were raised in abundance. "Every farm house," says Katharine Coman, an economic historian, "was a workshop where the women spun and wove the serges, kerseys, and linsey-woolseys which served for the common wear." By the close of the seventeenth century New England turned out so much cloth that heavy exports could be made to the Southern colonies and to the West Indies. As the industry grew, mills were erected for the more difficult process of dyeing, carding, and fulling, but spinning and weaving continued to be done in the home. In all textile branches the Dutch of New Netherland, the Swedes of Delaware, and the Scotch-Irish of the interior "were not one whit behind their Yankee neighbors."

The effect of this colonial enterprise on England's economic life can hardly be overestimated. For many a century fine woolen cloth had been the chief staple in her foreign commerce, and the government at London made special efforts to increase and protect trade in it. When the colonies were established, English merchants and statesmen naturally expected to keep their monopoly. But in a little while Americans, instead of buying only cloth imported from England, were making it to sell. In the place of customers, they were becoming rivals. This was serious for England. Her merchants lost business, and Americans began to feel independent.

If British merchants themselves had not discovered the danger of American competition, sharp-eyed officers of the king in the provinces would have broken the news to them. Even in the early days of the eighteenth century the royal governor of New York, watching the Americans at wheel and loom, wrote to his

Courtesy of The Metropolitan Museum of Art
SPINNING IN COLONIAL TIMES

home government: "The consequence will be that if they can clothe themselves once, not only comfortably but handsomely too, without the help of England, they who are already not very fond of submitting to government will soon think of putting in execution designs they have long harboured in their breasts. This will not seem strange when you consider what sort of people this country is inhabited by."

The Iron Industry. Almost equally widespread was the art of ironworking — one of the first and most essential of colonial industries. Lynn, Massachusetts, had a forge and skilled artisans within fifteen years after the founding of Boston. The smelting of iron began at New London and New Haven about 1658; in Litchfield County, Connecticut, a few years later; at Great Barrington, Massachusetts in 1731; and near-by at Lenox some thirty years after that. New Jersey had iron works at Shrewsbury within ten years after the establishment of the colony. Early in the eighteenth

COLONIAL IRON POTS AND PANS

century forges appeared in the valleys of the Delaware and the Susquehanna, in a region destined to become one of the great iron centers of the world. Virginia began ironworking in the year that saw the introduction of slavery. Although the industry soon lapsed, it was renewed and flourished in the eighteenth century. Governor Spotswood was called the "Tubal Cain" of the Old Dominion because, like the famous Bible character, he took special pains to promote metal working. Indeed it seems that every colony except Georgia had its iron foundry. Nails, wire, metal wares, chains, anchors, bar and pig iron were made in large quantities; and Great Britain, by an act of 1750, encouraged the colonists to export rough iron to the British Isles.

Shipbuilding. Of all the specialized industries in the colonies, shipbuilding was perhaps the most profitable. The abundance of fir for masts, oak for timbers and boards, pitch for tar and turpentine, and hemp for rope made the way of the shipbuilder easy in the New World. By the middle of the seventeenth century

Courtesy of The Metropolitan Museum of Art

SHIPPING IN OLD SALEM

shipyards were scattered along the New England coast, at Newburyport, Salem, New Bedford, Newport, Providence, New London, and New Haven. Yards at Albany and Poughkeepsie in New York built ships for the trade of that colony with England and the Indies. Wilmington and Philadelphia soon entered the race and outdistanced New York, though unable to equal the pace set by New England. While Maryland, Virginia, and South Carolina also built ships, Southern interest was mainly confined to the business of producing ship materials: fir, cedar, hemp, and tar.

Fishing. The greatest single resource of New England, apart from agriculture, was the fisheries. Started by hardy sailors from

Europe long before the landing of the Pilgrims, fishing flourished under the indomitable seamanship of the Puritans, who labored with the net and the harpoon in almost every quarter of the Atlantic. "Look," exclaimed Edmund Burke, in the House of Commons, "at the manner in which the people of New England have of late carried on the whale fishery. Whilst we follow them among the tumbling mountains of ice and behold them penetrating into the deepest frozen recesses of Hudson's Bay and Davis's Straits, whilst we are looking for them beneath the Arctic circle, we hear that they have pierced into the opposite region of polar cold, that they are at the antipodes and engaged under the frozen serpent of the south. . . . Nor is the equinoctial heat more discouraging to them than the accumulated winter of both poles. We know that whilst some of them draw the line and strike the harpoon on the coast of Africa, others run the longitude and pursue their gigantic game along the coast of Brazil. No sea but what is vexed by their fisheries. No climate that is not a witness to their toils. Neither the perseverance of Holland nor the activity of France nor the dexterous and firm sagacity of English enterprise ever carried this most perilous mode of hard industry to the extent to which it has been pushed by this recent people."

A large and prosperous European trade was founded on the fisheries. The better quality of the fish caught for food was sold in the markets of Spain, Portugal, and Italy, or exchanged for salt, lemons, and raisins for the American market. Lower grades of fish were carried to the West Indies for slave consumption, and in part traded for sugar and molasses which furnished the raw materials for the thriving rum industry of New England. These activities in turn stimulated shipbuilding, steadily enlarged the demand for fishing and merchant craft of every kind, and thus kept the shipwrights, calkers, rope makers, and other artisans of the seaport towns rushed with work. They also increased trade with the mother country for, out of the cash collected in the fish markets of Europe and the West Indies, colonists could pay for the English manufactures imported. An ever-widening circle of American enterprise centered around this single industry, the nursery of seamanship and the maritime spirit.

Oceanic Commerce and American Merchants. All through the eighteenth century the commerce of the American colonies spread in every direction until it rivaled in the number of people employed, the capital engaged, and the profits gleaned the commerce of European nations. A modern historian has said: "The enterprising merchants of New England developed a network of trade routes that covered well-nigh half the world."

From an old print

BOSTON IN 1795

A part of this trade consisted in the export of raw materials and agricultural produce. The Southern colonies produced for transport tobacco, rice, tar, pitch, and pine; the Middle colonies, grain, flour, furs, lumber, and salt pork; New England, fish, flour, rum, furs, shoes, and small articles of manufacture. The variety of products was astounding. In fact a sarcastic writer once used it as an argument against the idea of an American union: "What sort of dish will you make? New England will throw in fish and onions. The Middle colonies, flaxseed and flour. Maryland and Virginia will add tobacco. North Carolina, pitch, tar, and turpentine. South Carolina, rice and indigo, and Georgia will sprinkle the whole composition with sawdust. Such an absurd jumble will you make if you attempt to form a union among such discordant materials as the thirteen British provinces."

Of course exports had to be exchanged for money or commodities. So as a balance to the export business, American commerce embraced an extensive import trade, principally in English and continental manufactures, tea, and "India goods." Sugar and molasses, brought from the West Indies, supplied materials for the distilleries of Massachusetts, Rhode Island, and Connecticut. The carriage of slaves from Africa to the Southern colonies employed hundreds of New England's sailors and added thousands of pounds to her capital.

Although the selling of imported goods was partly in the hands of British merchants, called "factors," located in America, it also engaged a large and imposing body of American merchants, such as the Willings and Morrisses of Philadelphia; the Amorys, Hancocks, and Faneuils of Boston; and the Livingstons and Lows of New York. In their zeal they were worthy rivals of their English competitors, so famous for world-wide commercial operations. While fully aware of the advantages they enjoyed in British markets and under the protection of the British navy, these American merchants were high-spirited and mettlesome, ready to contend with royal officers in order to shield American interests against outside interference.

Measured against the immense business of modern times, colonial commerce seems perhaps trivial. That however is not the proper test. Its significance lay in the fact that it was making the colonies rich and powerful in comparison with England. From small beginnings they had grown to national stature. In 1704 the entire export trade of England, including that to the colonies, was £6,509,000; in 1772, English exports to the American colonies alone amounted to £6,024,000; in other words, almost as much as the whole foreign business of England two generations before. At the first date colonial trade was but one-twelfth of the English export business; at the second date it was considerably more than one-third. In 1704 Pennsylvania bought in English markets goods to the value of £11,459; in 1772 the purchases of the same colony amounted to £507,909. In short, Pennsylvania imports increased fifty times within sixty-eight years, and in 1772 were almost equal to the entire export trade of England to the colonies at the opening of the century. It is small wonder that English merchants watched American business with eagle eyes.

Intercolonial Commerce. Although the bad roads of colonial America made overland transportation difficult and costly, the many rivers emptying into the sea and harbors along the coast favored a lively water-borne traffic. The Connecticut, Hudson, Delaware, and Susquehanna rivers in the North and several smaller rivers in the South made it practicable to carry goods to and from the interior regions in home-made sailing vessels with comparative ease. Sloops laden with American and foreign manufactures collected at some city, like Providence, New York, or Philadelphia, skirted the coasts and sailed up the navigable waters stopping at the chief towns where the factors on board traded with local merchants and gathered up the produce brought in from neighboring farms. Larger ships carried the grain, live stock, cloth, and hardware of New England to the Southern colonies where they were exchanged for tobacco, leather, tar, and ship timber. From the harbors along the Connecticut shores there were frequent sailings down through Long Island Sound to Maryland, Virginia, and the Carolinas.

Growth of Towns. In connection with this lively industry and intercolonial trade there grew up along the coast a number of prosperous marketing centers which were soon ranked among the first commercial towns of the British empire, comparing favorably in numbers and wealth with the ports of Liverpool and Bristol. Statistical records of that time are mainly guesses; but we know that Philadelphia stood first in size among these towns. Serving as the port of entry for Pennsylvania, Delaware, and western Jersey, it had within its borders, just before the Revolution, about 25,000 inhabitants. Boston was second in rank with somewhat more than 20,000 people. New York, the "commercial capital of Connecticut and old East Jersey," was slightly smaller than Boston, but growing at a steady rate. The fourth town in size was Charleston, South Carolina, with about 10,000 inhabitants. Newport in Rhode Island, a center of rum manufacture and shipping, stood fifth, with a population of about 7000. Baltimore and Norfolk were counted as "considerable towns."

Even back from the seaboard in the interior, Hartford, Connecticut, Lancaster and York in Pennsylvania, and Albany in New York, with growing populations and expanding trade, began to take on city airs. But other towns were generally straggling villages. Williamsburg, Virginia, for example, had about two hundred houses in which dwelt a dozen families of the gentry, a few tradesmen, and a number of mechanics. The inland county seat often consisted of nothing more than a log courthouse, a prison, and one wretched inn to house judges, lawyers, and litigants during the sessions of the court.

All the towns, whether large or small, exercised great influence on colonial opinion. They were the centers of wealth for one thing; of the press and political activity, for another. Living close together merchants and artisans could take concerted and quick action on public questions arising from their commercial operations. The towns were also centers for news, gossip, religious controversy, and political discussion. Moreover in the market places the farmers from the countryside learned of British policies and laws, and so, mingling with the townsmen, were drawn into the disputes over taxation, over the control of the colonies by the English Parliament, and over the efforts of British merchants to monopolize trade.

References

J. Bishop, *History of American Manufactures* (2 vols.).
E. L. Bogart, *Economic History of the United States*.
P. A. Bruce, *Economic History of Virginia* (2 vols.).
H. V. Faulkner, *American Economic History*.
E. Semple, *American History and Its Geographical Conditions*.
W. Weeden, *Economic and Social History of New England* (2 vols.).

Questions

1. Is land in your community parceled out into small farms? Contrast the system in your community with the feudal system of land tenure.

2. Are some things owned and used in common in your community? Why did common tillage fail in colonial times?

3. Describe the elements akin to feudalism which were introduced in the colonies.

4. Explain the success of freehold tillage.

5. Compare the life of the planter with that of the farmer.

6. How far had the western frontier advanced by 1776?

7. What colonial industry was mainly developed by women? Why was it very important both to the Americans and to the English?

8. What were the centers for ironworking? Shipbuilding?

9. Explain how the fisheries affected many branches of trade and industry.

10. Show how the American trade formed a vital part of English business.

11. How was interstate commerce mainly carried on?

12. What were the leading towns? Did they compare in importance with British towns of the same period?

Research Topics

Land Tenure. Coman, *Industrial History* (rev. ed.), pp. 32–38. Special reference: Bruce, *Economic History of Virginia.* Vol. I, Chap. VIII.

Tobacco Planting in Virginia. Callender, *Economic History of the United States,* pp. 22–28.

Colonial Agriculture. Coman, pp. 48–63. Callender, pp. 69–74. Special reference: J. R. H. Moore, *Industrial History of the American People,* pp. 131–162.

Colonial Manufactures. Coman, pp. 63–73. Callender, pp. 29–44. Special reference: Weeden, *Economic and Social History of New England.*

Colonial Commerce. Coman, pp. 73–85. Callender, pp. 51–63, 78–84. Moore, pp. 163–208. Lodge, *Short History of the English Colonies,* pp. 229–231, 312–314, 409–412.

CHAPTER IV

THE CULTURE OF COLONIAL AMERICA

People do not live by work alone, that is, merely to get food, clothing, and shelter. Men and women have other emotions besides hunger, cold, and thirst. They are social beings and join with their neighbors in common enterprises. They think as well as feel. They have curiosity about mankind, about life in general, about the mysteries of the world. They take part in great movements, such as the migration from Europe to America. They travel and write. They follow leaders of thought. They paint pictures, make beautiful objects, adorn buildings with a view to delighting the eye and the heart. Even the humblest persons like to mingle some charm and excellence with their work whenever they can. For reasons such as these, the history of industry and government alone cannot explain the growth and power of a nation. We must therefore go beyond the economics and politics of the colonies to examine their culture: that is, we must study matters of mind and spirit — what the churches were doing, what the schools were like, what books were being written and read, what was done to promote art, science, and letters.

THE CHURCHES

Compulsory Religion. At the time most of the colonies were founded in America, European rulers in general still thought that their subjects should be compelled to belong to their church — whether Protestant or Catholic — and should be forced to pay taxes to maintain it. Not until 1689 did the English government grant to Quakers, Baptists, and other Protestant sects the right to worship God in their own way. For a long period after that, it continued to refuse this privilege to Catholics and Unitarians and made everybody help the Established Church to meet its expenses.

The Church of England in America. When Virginia was founded in 1607, the religion of the Anglican Church was made by law the faith of the colony as a matter of course. The settlers had to attend that Church and pay tithes for its support. As in England, so in the first of her colonies, Catholics and Dissenters were subject to fines and punishments. Only slowly were they even admitted

From Cook Studios, Richmond, Va.

AN OLD PRINT OF WILLIAM AND MARY COLLEGE AT WILLIAMSBURG, VA., AS IT WAS PICTURED BY "E. J. P." IN 1840

to the province; but when once they were secretly or carelessly tolerated, they pressed in until they outnumbered the members of the Anglican Church.

The English Church was also established by law and supported by taxes in the Carolinas after 1704 and in Georgia when it became a royal province — this in spite of the fact that the majority of the population were actually Dissenters. Against the protests of the Catholics it was set up in Maryland as well. Notwithstanding the objections of the Dutch, the Church of England was established in a few New York communities. In reality however it was not possible to force everybody to pay taxes for its support

and there was a large measure of toleration in practice, whatever
the law, in the six colonies where the Anglican Church was supposed to be the only religious establishment.

Yet many things helped to strengthen the English Church
in the colonies. Since it represented the state religion of the
English government, the officials sent to America were nearly
always Anglicans. Its bishops and archbishops in England,
appointed by the king, naturally looked to the Anglican clergy in
the New World to check the movement for religious independence that was growing so powerful with time. Closely associated
with the monarchy, the Anglican Church also helped royal officers
in watching for any tendency to criticize the king's government.

Congregational Church Established in New England. Though
they came to America to found a colony where they could worship
God according to their consciences, the Puritans did not prefer
to allow anybody to think and act as he pleased in religious matters.
Far from it; they were much like Catholics and Anglicans in that
respect. Every person in Massachusetts, in the early days of
settlement, was supposed to belong to a Congregational Church
in one of the towns. Moreover, only church members could vote
in town meetings and everybody had to pay taxes to help support
the lawful religion. Thus in early Massachusetts the church
and state of the Puritans were united.

But as time passed people belonging to other sects migrated to
that colony and demanded a voice in the government as well as
toleration in religion. Naturally the demand of Anglicans in
Massachusetts for the vote won the support of the king and
Church of England. With an eye to breaking the Puritan monopoly, Charles II in 1684 actually annulled the old charter of the
Massachusetts Bay Company. When seven years later William
and Mary granted a new charter, they provided that henceforward
the king should appoint the governor of the colony, and they gave
the vote to every man who had certain property qualifications
whether he was a member of a Congregational Church or not.
Thus a royal governor and an official family, almost certain to be
Anglican in faith and monarchist in sympathies, were forced upon
Massachusetts; and members of all religious denominations, if

they had the required amount of property, were permitted to take part in elections. By this act in the name of the Crown, the Puritan monopoly was broken down in Massachusetts, but the Congregational Church remained "established" and the people had to pay taxes to support it. The same rule held in Connecticut and New Hampshire where Puritans also had a majority.

Growth of Religious Toleration. While in nine of the thirteen colonies churches were established by law, the novel principle of toleration spread everywhere. Under the system set up by Roger Williams and Anne Hutchinson, a wide liberty of religion was allowed in Rhode Island from the beginning. Most of the proprietors, wanting settlers to buy their lands, admitted people of various religious denominations.

Courtesy of The Metropolitan Museum of Art

THE BAPTIST MEETING HOUSE, PROVIDENCE, R. I., IN 1789

Lord Baltimore, a Catholic in spite of the English law, welcomed to Maryland Protestant immigrants as well as those of his own faith, and in 1649 the legislature of the colony declared that all who professed faith in Jesus Christ should enjoy freedom of worship, in this way excluding the Jews and Unitarians. True to the tenets of the Friends, Pennsylvania gave freedom of conscience to those "who confess and acknowledge the one Almighty and Eternal God to be the creator, upholder, and ruler of the world."

Thus the Middle colonies had the largest number of sects and the largest measure of toleration. Dutch Protestants, Huguenots, Quakers, Baptists, Presbyterians, New Lights, Moravians, Lutherans, Catholics, and other denominations became so numerous and so widely distributed that no single church could rule even if it wanted to. There were communities and indeed whole sections where one or another church was strongest but in no colony outside New England and Virginia was the legislature steadily controlled by any one religious group. Toleration encouraged the immigration of people of every faith and this very variety of settlers in turn helped to maintain toleration. On the whole America was ahead of Europe in religious freedom.

Leadership of the Clergy. But America was still like Europe in one respect: the clergy of all denominations were leaders of public opinion. In some communities they were almost the only persons who could read and write. They preached on Sundays and taught school on week days. They wrote most of the books and pamphlets. They often led in the debates in town meetings and helped to make popular sentiment about political questions, particularly the disputes between the colonists and the royal officers. They were supposed to guide their congregations in all matters pertaining to morals and right conduct. They helped to found and maintain colleges to train young clergymen so that their profession might not decline for want of numbers and talent.

Puritanism. Especially among the Puritans of New England did the clergy form a powerful class, powerful on account of their learning and their fearful sermons against the faithless and the wicked. They wrote the books for members of their sect to read — the famous preacher, Cotton Mather, having three hundred and eighty-three works to his account. In coöperation with the civil officers they enforced a strict observance of the Puritan Sabbath — a day of rest and religious worship that began at six o'clock on Saturday evening and lasted until sunset on Sunday. All work, all trading, all amusement, and all worldly conversation were absolutely prohibited during those hours. A thoughtless maid servant who for some earthly reason smiled in church was in danger of being banished as a vagabond. Robert Pike, a devout Puritan, thinking the sun had gone to rest, ventured forth on horseback one Sunday evening and was luckless enough to have a ray of light strike him through a rift in the clouds. The next day he was brought into court and fined for "his ungodly conduct." With persons accused of witchcraft the Puritans were ruthless. When a mania of persecution swept over Massachusetts in 1692, eighteen people were hanged, one was pressed to death, many suffered imprisonment, and two died in jail — most of them helpless women.

THE LAST PAGES OF THE "NEW ENGLAND PRIMER"

Religion and the American Spirit. But in spite of occasional frenzies, there was a general trend toward religious toleration and this favored the growth of an independent mind in politics. Presbyterians, Quakers, Baptists, and Puritans had no bishops and archbishops to bind them to London in matters of religious faith. Partly for this reason they did not turn to that city for guidance in political and business affairs. Local self-government in religion helped to train them for local self-government in politics. The spirit of independence which had led Dissenters to revolt in the Old World was thus nourished amid favorable circumstances in the

New World and it made them all the more zealous in the defense of every right against authority imposed by the British government.

Schools and Colleges

Religion and Local Schools. One of the first cares of each Protestant sect was the education of the children in its own faith. In this work the Bible — the King James translation into English — was the chief book for reading and study. Farmers, shopkeepers, and artisans, whose thinking had been bounded by the daily

Courtesy of The Metropolitan Museum of Art

Dutch-American Colonial Toys—Eighteenth Century

routine of labor before they learned to read, now found in the Scriptures not only an inspiration to right living, but also a book of romance, travel, and history.

For the authority of the religious creed imposed by the Church of England the Puritans substituted the authority of the Scriptures. They wrote a catechism or book of questions and answers based on the Bible, and very soon after their arrival in America they commanded all parents and masters of servants to see that their children and wards were taught to read the Holy Book and the catechism. Massachusetts was scarcely twenty years old when education of this character was made compulsory by law, and the towns were ordered to open public schools for children not taught at home.

Outside New England the idea of compulsory education was not regarded with the same favor; but the whole land was nevertheless dotted with little volunteer schools kept by "dames, itinerant teachers, or local parsons." Whether we turn to the life of Franklin in the North or of Washington in the South, we read of tiny schoolhouses where boys, and sometimes girls, were taught to read and write. Where there were no schools, fathers and mothers often gave their children the lessons in the alphabet at home and watched over their training till they were grown. Though illiteracy was widespread in the colonies, as it was at that time all over the earth, there is evidence to show that learning was making steady progress among the American people throughout the eighteenth century.

Religion and Higher Learning. Religious motives led to the creation of colleges as well as lower schools. Harvard founded in 1636 and Yale opened in 1718 were established primarily to train "learned and godly ministers" for the Puritan churches of New England. To the far north, Dartmouth, chartered in 1769, was started as a religious mission to the Indians but it developed into a college for the sons of New England farmers. The College of New Jersey, organized in 1746 and removed to Princeton eleven years later, was sustained principally by the Presbyterians. Two colleges looked to the Established Church as their source of inspiration and support: William and Mary founded in Virginia in 1693, and King's College, now Columbia University, chartered by King George II in 1754, on an appeal from the New York Anglicans, who hoped in this way to check the growth of religious dissent and the "republican tendencies" of the age. Two later colleges revealed a drift away from purely sectarian control. Brown, established in Rhode Island in 1764, and the Philadelphia Academy, forerunner of the University of Pennsylvania, organized by Benjamin Franklin, were so tolerant that they had members of several religious sects on their boards of trustees. It was Franklin's idea that his college should train young men for business and the professions and at the same time prepare them to serve in public office as leaders of the people.

Self-education in America. Important as were these institutions of learning, higher education was by no means confined within their walls. Private tutoring in the home was common and it was mainly in this way that colonial girls were introduced to the classics, history, and philosophy. Moreover the sheer struggle for a living against adversity trained many other young people so well that in every contest of mind and wit they could vie with the sons of Harvard, William and Mary, or any other college. Through this school of "hard knocks," for example, rose Benjamin Franklin, whose charming autobiography, in addition to being an American classic, is a fine record of self-education. His formal training in the classroom was limited to a few years at a local school in Boston; but his self-education continued throughout his life. As a boy, he loved to read and he devoured, he tells us, his father's dry library on theology, as well as Bunyan's works, Defoe's writings, and Plutarch's *Lives*. His literary style, perhaps the best of his time in the colonies, Franklin acquired by the diligent analysis of the English *Spectator*. By his own efforts he "attained an acquaintance" with Latin, Italian, French, and Spanish, which proved a great help to him later when he was to speak for all America at the court of the king of France. Self-trained, too, were the leaders among the colonial women. Colleges were not open to them, but they had a keen and intelligent interest in public affairs. This is evident in such records as the letters of Mrs. John Adams to her husband during the Revolution; the writings of Mrs. Mercy Otis Warren, the sister of James Otis, who measured her pen with the British propagandists; and patriot newspapers managed by women.

THE COLONIAL PRESS

The Rise of the Newspaper. American education and democracy were advanced by the open discussion of political questions in the press. Journalism, like education, was a matter of slow though sure growth. A printing press was brought to Massachusetts in 1639, but it was put in charge of an official censor and was limited to the publication of religious works. Forty years passed before the first newspaper appeared, bearing the curious title, *Publick Occurrences, Both Forreign and Domestick,* and it had not been running very long when the government of Massachusetts suppressed it for an article on politics. Publishing, indeed, seemed to be a precarious business.

Yet in 1704 there came a second venture in journalism, *The Boston News-Letter,* which proved to be a more lasting enterprise because it did not criticize the authorities. Still the public interest in the press was not very lively. When Franklin's brother, James, began to issue his *New-England Courant* in 1721, his friends

TOP OF THE FRONT PAGE OF THE "MASSACHUSETTS GAZETTE AND BOSTON NEWS-LETTER"

said that one newspaper was enough for America. Nevertheless he persisted and his confidence in the future was rewarded. Within thirty or forty years a gazette or chronicle appeared in nearly every colony, women as well as men taking a hand in editing and writing news stories. Benjamin Franklin was able to boast in 1771 that America had twenty-five newspapers. Boston led with five. Philadelphia had three: two in English and one in German.

Censorship and Restraints on the Press. The idea of printing without interference by government or church officials was however a radical one in that day. The founders of the American colonies had never known what it was to have free publication of books, pamphlets, broadsides, and newspapers. When the art of printing was first invented in Europe control of publishing was given to church authorities. After the establishment of the Anglican Church in England in the reign of Elizabeth, censorship of the press became a part of royal privilege. Moreover printing was restricted to Oxford, Cambridge, and London; and no one could publish anything without previous approval of the official censor. When the Puritans overthrew the English king, and assumed control of the government, they in turn sought to silence royalist and Anglican writers by a vigorous censorship of their own. On the restoration of the monarchy, control over the press was once more placed in royal hands where it remained until 1695, when Parliament, by failing to renew the licensing act, put an end to official censorship. By that time political parties were so active and powerful and printing presses were so numerous that official review of all published matter became almost impossible.

In America likewise exciting battles took place over freedom of the press. The Puritans of Massachusetts were no less anxious than King Charles or the Archbishop of London to shut out from the prying eyes of the masses all literature "not mete for them to read"; and so they established a system of official licensing for presses, which lasted until 1755. In other colonies where there was more diversity of opinion, publishers could go into this business without asking the consent of the government; but they were nevertheless liable to arrest for printing anything displeasing to colonial officers. In 1721 the editor of the *Mercury* in Philadelphia was called before the proprietary council and ordered to apologize for a political article, and for another offense of a similar character he was thrown into jail. A still more famous case was that of Peter Zenger, a New York publisher, who was arrested in 1735 for criticizing the colonial administration. Lawyers who ventured to defend the unlucky editor were deprived of their licenses to practice, and it became necessary to bring an attorney all the way from Philadelphia to defend the accused. By this time the tension of feeling was high, and the people cheered when the lawyer for the defense exclaimed to the jury that the very cause of liberty itself, not that of the poor printer, was on trial! The verdict in favor of Zenger, when it finally came, was the signal for an outburst of popular rejoicing. Already the subjects of King George in the province had learned how precious a thing is the freedom of the press.

Owing to the schools, few and scattered as they were, to the vigilance of parents, and to the natural curiosity of youths like Franklin, a very large number, perhaps nearly one-half, of the adult colonists learned to read. Through the newspapers, pamphlets, and almanacs that streamed from the types, the people could follow the course of public events and grasp the meaning of political arguments. An American opinion was thus in the process of making — an independent opinion matured by the press and enriched by debates around the fireside and in the taverns. When the day of resistance to British rule came, "government by the people" was at hand. For every person who could hear the voice of Patrick Henry and Samuel Adams, there were a thousand who could read their appeals on the printed page. Men who had spelled out their letters while poring over Franklin's *Poor Richard's Almanac* lived to read with ease Thomas Paine's call to arms.

LITERATURE, SCIENCE, AND ART

Works on American History. Although, as we have said, most of the books written in the colonies dealt with religious questions, the age produced many stories, histories, biographies, poems, and essays on manners and morals in general. A collection of all these volumes would make a library of considerable size. First among the story tellers was that man of amazing adventures, Captain John Smith, one of the leaders at Jamestown, Virginia. During the trying days when that colony was being started, Smith kept a simple record of events, which was carried to London and published in the year 1608 under the title *A True Relation of Virginia*. In these pages Captain Smith tells of quarrels among the settlers, sickness and famine, explorations in the wilderness, exploits with the Indians, and his visit to the great chief, "Emperor Powhatan." Later Smith wrote other books on America. If in some of his big yarns, such as the tale of his rescue by Pocahontas, his imagination was given too much range, still it is not fair to call him a "liar and braggart," as some writers have done. His works are valuable for the light they throw on the beginnings of the colonies.

Plymouth also had a chronicler and in no less a person than its Governor, William Bradford, who came over with the Pilgrims in 1620. After he had been in America about ten years, Bradford began to write an account of that great experience, and on his death in 1657 he left a large manuscript, *History of Plymouth Plantation*, written in a clear and interesting style. This was taken over to London, lost, then rediscovered in 1855, and printed. It is one of our most precious stories of colonial times. No less entertaining is Governor John Winthrop's *History of New England*, which gives us a word-painting of the days when Massachusetts was very young. As the colonists won more leisure, other writers compiled huge books on American history. In fact there were in 1776 eight or ten really important works on that subject, though some of them are frightfully dull to read.

Diaries and Travel Books. A favorite kind of writing was the diary or record of happenings jotted down from day to day, perhaps without any thought of printing. For nearly forty years Judge Sewall of Massachusetts kept such a memorandum of incidents in his life and his thoughts on various occasions. With the aid of this work we can piece together many colonial episodes and, what is better, gain an insight into the mind of a Puritan of those times. In his pages there are both wit and gravity. He had joined in condemning witches to death; but in after years he confessed his error publicly in church — a thing persecutors seldom do. "All men," he said, "as they are the sons of Adam, are co-heirs and have equal rights unto liberty and all other outward comforts of life." When he read that a British writer doubted whether there would be women in heaven, Sewall penned a long argument to prove that women, like men, will rise from the dead and go to paradise.

Less solemn was the journal kept by Sarah Kemble Knight telling about her plucky trip on horseback from Boston, through Rhode Island and Connecticut, to New York and back again. What a tale it is! With great gusto she describes the rough roads, jolting stages, bad rooms in the inns, crazy ferryboats, the rude manners of bystanders, and the strong language of ferrymen and hostlers. At one river she found the ferry so crowded that she did not dare to move her tongue from one side of her mouth to the other for fear she might upset the boat. She was astounded to find Connecticut customs so different from those of Boston. In Virginia Colonel William Byrd, a rich planter and cultivated gentleman, kept a report of his experiences which is full of humor and vivid pictures of the South during the early years of the eighteenth century.

Poetry. There were no Shakespeares in the American colonies and there was just one in England as a matter of fact — but there were several men and women who felt a strong urge to express themselves in "verse." Anne Bradstreet of Massachusetts, for example, brought out in London in 1650 a volume entitled "The Tenth Muse lately sprung up in America; or several poems compiled with great variety of wit and learning, full of delight . . ." which gave much pleasure to her readers. In lines somber and gay she described thoughts, feelings, and events in her life. At one time she rejoices in nature:

> Under the cooling shadow of a stately elm,
> Close sat I by a goodly river's side,
> Where gliding streams the rocks did overwhelm;
> A lonely place, with pleasures dignified.

At another she repels a criticism of women by referring to the mighty deeds of Queen Elizabeth:

> She hath wiped off the aspersion of her sex,
> That women wisdom lack to play the Rex.

If the poetry is a bit strained, the sentiment at least is loyal.

Indeed all the themes of public debate can be traced in colonial poetry. Lamenting "the good old days," Benjamin Thompson, who graduated from Harvard in 1662 while Anne Bradstreet was still living, wrote of the past:

> Under thatch'd huts, without the cry of rent,
> And the best sauce to every dish, content.

For a jolly Puritan this epitaph was composed:

> Here lies one,
> Whose life was whim, whose soul was pun;
> And if you go too near his hearse
> He'll joke you, both in prose and verse.

Essays and Almanacs. While the clergy were preaching their sermons on morals, laymen were writing essays on virtue for newspapers, magazines, and books. Benjamin Franklin's *Poor Richard's Almanac*, for instance, is full of wise and pithy sayings on correct conduct, thrift, manners, and money-making, mixed with witty "saws." He was fond of urging temperance, order, industry, frugality, cleanliness, moderation, justice, sincerity, and hard work on his readers, always pointing out the way to the happy and useful life. "Sloth, like rust, consumes faster than labor wears." "Dost thou love life, then do not squander time, for that's the stuff life is made of." "The sleeping fox catches no poultry." "Lost time is never found again." "He that riseth late must trot all day, and shall scarce overtake his business at night." "Experience keeps a dear school but fools will learn in no other and scarce in that." "If you will not hear reason, she'll surely rap your knuckles," wrote Franklin in summarizing the teachings of Poor Richard.

In his advice for the year, another colonial almanac-maker, Nathaniel Ames, entered under December 7–10:

> Ladies take heed,
> Lay down your fans,
> And handle well
> Your warming pans.

Under February 24–27, he gave this warning: "If you fall into misfortunes, creep through the bushes which have the least briers." Directed to humble people who could barely read and write, these almanac sayings were tuned to the popular wit of colonial times. They were designed to make men and women sober and industrious — the secret of good living in all ages.

Writing on Public Affairs. From essays on morals it was only a step to books on political problems. The question was soon asked:

REPRODUCTION OF THE KITCHEN OF THE PARSON CAPEN HOUSE IN TOPSFIELD, MASSACHUSETTS, BUILT IN 1683

REPRODUCTION FROM THE HOME OF THE MAYOR OF PHILADELPHIA, SHOWING
AMERICAN-MADE GOODS ON THE EVE OF THE REVOLUTION

"What kind of government is really the best?" In 1717 John Wise, a preacher of Ipswich, Massachusetts, answered by saying that nature had "set all men upon a level and made them equals" and that "a democracy in church and state is a very honorable and regular government according to the dictates of right reason." Then he added: "The end of all good government is to cultivate humanity and to promote the happiness of all." This was quite different from the inherited European idea that the end of government was to promote the happiness of a small class of rich people. In the same spirit as that of John Wise, another colonial writer, John Woolman, a Quaker tailor and preacher, opposed slavery as a wrong, deplored the poverty which he saw around him and the long hours of work for servants and laborers, and advocated freedom for slaves, shorter hours of work for all, and better wages in general. He thought America should be a land where all the people were free, could make a good living, and dwell together in friendship and peace. In other words the ferment of idealism and self-criticism was stirring in the colonies.

Natural Science. Theories about public welfare, such as those expressed in the writings of Wise and Woolman, were reinforced by the work of scientists who dealt directly with nature. In 1620, the very year in which the Pilgrims set sail for America, Sir Francis Bacon published in England his *Novum Organum* in which he urged the study of nature as well as of books. This, he said, would lead to an understanding of material things, to improvements in roads, canals, bridges, and other works for the benefit of all mankind. In 1660 a Royal Society was founded in London to encourage such studies in "the remotest parts of the earth," and several Americans became members.

Enthusiasm for science spread rapidly among the colonies. In Virginia, for example, John Banister, a botanist, made a careful study of local plants and wrote a work on the subject which was published in England. Another Virginian, Mark Catesby, spent sixteen years between 1710 and 1726 making a survey of plant and animal life in his province, the Carolinas, Florida, and the Bahamas. Somewhat later, better farming methods were explained and advocated by Jared Eliot, of Connecticut, in a book printed in 1748.

John Bartram of Pennsylvania did such wonderful work in local botany that he was appointed botanist to the king. About the same time his neighbor, Benjamin Franklin, was making more sensations for the city of Philadelphia by his scientific experiments and inventions. As early as 1727 he founded a literary and scientific club, known as the "Junto," which was later enlarged, and in 1769 changed into the American Philosophical Society. The avowed

Courtesy of The Metropolitan Museum of Art

BENJAMIN FRANKLIN

purpose of this Society was to encourage "experiments that let light into the nature of things, tend to increase the power of man over matter, and multiply the conveniences and pleasures of life."

Franklin himself was a scientist of great energy and skill. He invented an improved stove, called the Pennsylvania fireplace, which both saved fuel and kept rooms warmer. At the age of forty-one he began to study electricity. On discovering that lightning was the same thing as electricity, he sent a kite up into thunder clouds in 1752 "to draw the electric fire from them," thus making the test which was to extend his fame through America and all western Europe. Turning his discovery to a practical use, he invented a lightning rod. Among other things he studied water spouts at sea, phosphorous light in salt water, the temperature of the Gulf Stream, the effect of oil in stilling waves, heat and light, the evaporation of water, the causes of smoky chimneys, and the use of chemicals to fertilize the soil. Franklin also wrote about new researches in such a lively manner that interest in science spread far and wide among the colonies.

Handicrafts. The work of hands and heads took other forms. While the rich merchants and planters often bought their furniture, cloth, and utensils in the Old World, the public in general had to be content with goods made by local artisans and housewives. In reality this was fortunate. For all over colonial America lived workers in wood, iron, and textiles who showed skill in the things they made. Naturally in the beginning strength was the prime object. What was produced had to last. So the chairs and tables turned out by the craftsmen of Plymouth were strong enough to

Courtesy of The Metropolitan Museum of Art

A COLONIAL TABLE OF STURDY WORKMANSHIP

endure for centuries, as samples still in existence after three hundred years abundantly prove. In their very sturdiness lay a rugged beauty.

With increasing wealth, calls were made for more elaborate goods, and the craftsmen, especially of Connecticut, were given an opportunity to consider grace as well as strength in their handiwork. There was loveliness in some of the linens and rugs woven by colonial women, while in the pottery and glassware of New Jersey and Pennsylvania artistic feeling was also displayed. Although the names of the handicraft artists of colonial America are nearly all lost to history, hundreds of the products of their skill, preserved in private homes and public museums, bear witness to their talents.

Painting. Following Old World models more closely than did artisans, a few colonists turned to the painting of portraits. At first their pictures were stiff and awkward, of course, but near the close of the colonial period, four Americans began to exhibit work which was praised in the ruling circles of America and England. Two of these, Benjamin West born near Philadelphia, and John

Courtesy of The Metropolitan Museum of Art
Colonial Glassware

Singleton Copley, of Boston, spent their later years in London where they received royal honors and were classed among the leading artists of the age. To the other two, Charles Wilson Peale and Gilbert Stuart, we owe our best portraits of George Washington, Thomas Jefferson, and other leaders of those stirring years. Illustrations of their work are to be found in this book, pages 23, 126, 152, 212.

Architecture. Like paintings, the buildings of colonial times developed from crude beginnings to graceful beauty in the end. The first houses were made of logs because timber was abundant and there was a rush to get under shelter of any sort. Indeed throughout the colonial period, especially along the advancing frontier, a large proportion of the people continued to live in log cabins and huts. But as merchants and planters amassed wealth, they began to demand mansions, and as the towns grew in size the people went to great expense in erecting churches and other public buildings. In the South planters clung rather closely to English models and sometimes imported stones and bricks to insure correctness of style. In New England however carpenter-architects gave a distinct turn to English designs and built many houses of a modified type marked by a simplicity and grave dignity all their own. Moreover most of the New England villages were carefully planned and were controlled by town meetings instead of growing up haphazard; so the homes were fairly standardized in design. By the middle of the eighteenth century, says Lewis Mumford, in *Sticks and Stones*, "Boston was rich in public buildings, including four school houses, seventeen churches, a Town House, a Province House and Faneuil Hall — a pretty large collection for a town of twenty thousand inhabitants." The Dutch in New York clung to their European traditions and built their houses with ends to the streets and with gables notched like steps — a contrast to the style introduced by the English. Amid the rush and roar of modern Philadelphia stands Independence Hall, now two hundred years old, keeping its strong beauty against the wear of centuries. When the Declaration of Independence was announced from its portals, America was far on the way from the log cabins of early Jamestown and Plymouth.

References

A. M. Earle, *Home Life in Colonial Days*.
A. L. Cross, *The Anglican Episcopate and the American Colonies* (Harvard Studies).
E. G. Dexter, *History of Education in the United States*.
C. A. Duniway, *Freedom of the Press in Massachusetts*.
Benjamin Franklin, *Autobiography*.
Cambridge History of American Literature, Vol. I.
M. C. Tyler, *History of American Literature during the Colonial Times*.

Questions

1. Is leisure necessary for the production of art and literature? How may leisure be secured?
2. Explain the position of the churches in colonial life.
3. Contrast the political rôles of Puritanism and the Established Church.
4. How did diversity of opinion work for toleration?
5. Show the connection between religion and learning in colonial times.
6. Why is a "free press" such an important thing to American democracy?
7. Relate some of the troubles of early American publishers.
8. What branches of literature were developed in colonial times?
9. Name some of the leading writers and discuss the nature of their works.

10. Why are diaries and travel books especially useful for the study of the times?

11. What was the trend in the writings on public affairs?

12. Mention some of the advances made in natural science.

13. What was the nature of colonial handicrafts?

14. Can you name any good examples of colonial architecture?

Research Topics

Religious and Intellectual Life. Lodge, *Short History of the English Colonies:* (1) in New England, pp. 418–438, 465–475; (2) in Virginia, pp. 54–61, 87–89; (3) in Pennsylvania, pp. 232–237, 253–257; (4) in New York, pp. 316–321. Interesting source materials in Hart, *American History Told by Contemporaries*, Vol. II, pp. 255–275, 276–290. Beard, *Rise of American Civilization*, Vol. I, pp. 145–162.

Colonial Classes and Manners. Beard, *Rise of American Civilization*, Vol. I, pp. 125–145.

Colonial Education. Beard, Vol. I, pp. 166–184.

Colonial Literature. *Cambridge History of American Literature*, Vol. I, pp. 1–110.

Colonial Press. *Cambridge History of American Literature*, Vol. I, pp. 111–124. G. H. Payne, *History of Journalism in the United States*.

Colonial Life in General. John Fiske, *Old Virginia and Her Neighbors*, Vol. II, pp. 174–269; Elson, *History of the United States*, pp. 178–200.

Questions for Debate

1. The influence of the New England colonies before the Revolution was greater than that of the Middle (or the Southern) colonies in shaping American institutions.

2. The promotion of the arts is as important for a civilized people as the promotion of industry.

Historical Fiction

Beulah M. Dix, *The Making of Christopher Ferringham.*

CHAPTER V

THE RISE OF AMERICAN NATIONALISM

"There ought to be no New England man, no New Yorker, known on the continent; but all of us Americans!" exclaimed Christopher Gadsden at a colonial congress held in New York in 1765. By what steps had the inhabitants of thirteen separate colonies scattered along the Atlantic Coast come to think and feel as Americans? For one thing a common struggle for self-government against royal officers gave them kindred sentiments. Wars against the French and the Indians helped to weld them in spite of their differences. And finally they were drawn together in a mighty effort to resist the attempt of king and Parliament in London to control their taxes, trade, and industry in the interest of Great Britain.

THE CONTEST OVER SELF-GOVERNMENT

Early in the history of the colonies two distinct lines of development appeared in matters of government. One of them strengthened the Crown and the royal officers sent over to rule. The other, leading toward democracy and self-government, was the growth in the power of the popular legislative assemblies in which Americans themselves had the upper hand. Each movement gave impetus to the other, with increasing force during the passing years, until at last a collision ended in a war for American independence.

The Royal Provinces. Of the thirteen English colonies eight were royal provinces in 1776, with governors appointed by the king. Virginia passed under the direct rule of the Crown in 1624, when the charter of the London Company was annulled. The Massachusetts Bay Corporation lost its charter in 1684, and seven years later the right to choose its governor as heretofore. In the early eighteenth century both the Carolinas passed from ownership by proprietors to royal control. New Hampshire, severed from Massachusetts in 1679, and Georgia, surrendered by the trustees in 1752, went into the hands of the Crown. New York, transferred to the Duke of York on its capture from the Dutch in 1664, became a royal province when he took the title of James II in 1685. New Jersey, after remaining for nearly forty years under proprietors, was brought directly under the king in 1702. Maryland, Pennsylvania, and Delaware, although they retained their proprietary

THE ROYAL GOVERNOR'S PALACE AT NEW BERNE

character, were in some respects like the royal colonies, for the proprietors either governed directly or through agents of their own choice and were therefore independent of the people. Only two colonies, Rhode Island and Connecticut, retained full self-government. They alone had governors and legislatures entirely of their own choosing.

The chief officer of each royal province was a governor, who enjoyed high and important powers which he naturally sought to enlarge at every turn. He enforced the laws and, usually with the consent of a council, appointed civil and military officers. He granted pardons and reprieves; he was head of the supreme

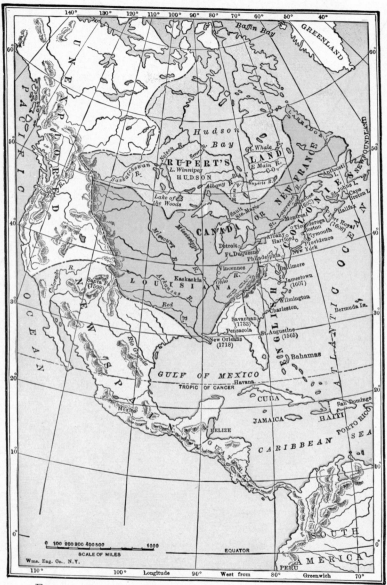

ENGLISH, FRENCH, AND SPANISH POSSESSIONS IN AMERICA, 1750

own before can be had for ready money. It is another addition to the value of money and of course another spur to industry. Every land is not so blessed."

It must not be thought however that every governor got off as lightly as Franklin's tale implies. On the contrary the legislatures, like Caesar, fed upon meat that made them great and steadily reduced royal control as they tried out and found their strength. Supporters of the governor in New York complained in 1747 that "the inhabitants of plantations are generally educated in republican principles; upon republican principles all is conducted. Little more than a shadow of royal authority remains in the Northern colonies." "Here," echoed the governor of South Carolina, the following year, "levelling principles prevail; the frame of the civil government is unhinged; a governor, if he would be idolized, must betray his trust; the people have got the whole administration in their hands; the election of the members of the assembly is by ballot; not civil posts only, but all ecclesiastical preferments are in the disposal or election of the people."

Yet the royal governors did not give up the case as hopeless. In stead they worked out a system of policy and action which they thought could bring the obstinate provincials to terms. That scheme, traceable in their letters to the government in London, consisted of three parts: (1) the royal officers in the colonies should no longer depend on voluntary payment of their salaries but should be made secure by acts of Parliament taxing the colonists for this purpose; (2) a British standing army ought to be maintained in America; (3) the remaining colonial charters should be revoked and government by direct royal authority strengthened.

Such a system seemed plausible enough to King George III and to many of his ministers in London. With governors, courts, and an army independent of the colonists, they fancied it would be simple to carry out both royal orders and acts of Parliament. This reasoning seemed both practical and logical. It was wanting in one respect only. It failed to take account of the fact that the American people were growing up in the practice of self-government and could manage their business without the aid of the British ministry, no matter how excellent it might be or how fine its intentions. In the promotion of colonial home rule, capable lawyers, such as Patrick Henry, trained in the courts, stood forth as popular leaders.

The Unifying Force of Foreign Conflict

While developing common habits of self-government under able leadership, the colonists were also drawn together through the necessity of dealing with ambitious and warlike neighbors. Along the frontiers of their tiny settlements roamed native Indians, growing more and more menacing as white men pressed into the interior, and sharp conflicts over land caused envy and hatred on both sides. In the south and to the west ruled Spain, holding tenaciously to her territory in America though crushed on the sea by the defeat of her Armada. North and west were the French, energetic, imperial in temper, and prepared to contest the advance of British power in America.

Indian Affairs. The several colonies had different experiences with the Indians. Their defense against the natives was not handled according to any uniform plan by the British government, which had the supreme authority in the matter. Neither did the proprietors and the governors who succeeded one another, in an irregular train, have the steady policy or the matured experience necessary for dealing wisely with Indian affairs. As the difficulties arose mainly on the frontiers, where the restless and pushing pioneers were making their way with gun and ax, nearly everything that happened was the result of chance rather than of deeds thought out in advance. A personal quarrel between a trader and an Indian, a jug of whisky, a keg of gunpowder, the exchange of guns for furs, treachery, or a flash of bad temper often set in motion destructive forces of the most appalling character.

On one side of the ledger may be set many pleasing items: Squanto and Samoset teaching the Pilgrims the ways of the wilds; Roger Williams buying his lands in a friendly fashion from the natives; and William Penn treating with them kindly on his arrival in America. On the other side of the ledger must be recorded several cruel and bloody affrays as the frontier rolled westward. The Pequods on the Connecticut border, sensing their

doom, fell upon the little settlements with awful fury in 1637
only to meet with dreadful punishment.   A generation later King
Philip, son of Massasoit, the friend of the Pilgrims, called his
tribesmen to a war of extermination which brought the strength of
all New England to the field and ended in his own destruction.
In New York the relations with the Indians, especially with the
Algonquins and the Mohawks, were marked by frequent and
desperate wars.   Virginia and her Southern neighbors suffered

From an old print

VIRGINIANS DEFENDING THEMSELVES AGAINST THE INDIANS

as did New England.   In 1622 Opecacano, a brother of Powhatan,
the friend of the Jamestown settlers, launched a general massacre;
in 1644 he too attempted a war of extermination.   In 1675 the
whole frontier was ablaze.   Nathaniel Bacon vainly attempted
to arouse the colonial governor to provide proper defense; failing
in that plea, he took the matter into his own hands, as we have seen,
and organized a successful expedition against the Indians.   As the
Virginia outposts advanced into the Kentucky country, a strife
with the natives opened on that "dark and bloody ground"; while
to the southeast, a savage struggle with the Tuscaroras called forth
the combined forces of the two Carolinas and Virginia.

From such horrors New Jersey and Delaware were saved on account of their geographical location. Pennsylvania, more willing to compromise with the natives, was likewise spared until her western vanguard came into full contact with the united French and Indians. Georgia, by clever dealings and treaties of alliance, managed to keep on fair terms with her belligerent neighbors, the Cherokees and Creeks. But neither diplomacy nor generosity could prevent fighting as the frontier advanced, especially after the French soldiers enlisted the Indians in their imperial enterprises. It was then that local battles became general warfare.

Early Relations with the French. During the first decades of French exploration and settlement in the St. Lawrence country, the English colonists gave little or no thought to their Canadian neighbors. Quebec, founded in 1608, and Montreal in 1642, were too far away, too small in population, and too slight in strength to awaken any interest in Boston, Hartford, or New York. It was the statesmen in France and England, clashing over the possession of the New World, who brought on the conflict, rather than the colonists in America. It was the ambition of Louis XIV of France, not the labors of his Jesuit missionaries and French rangers in the north and west, that sounded the first note of colonial alarm.

Evidence of this lies in the fact that three struggles between the English and the French occurred before their onrolling frontiers met at the Pennsylvania border. King William's War (1689–97), Queen Anne's War (1701–13), and King George's War (1744–48) were caused mainly by the intrigues and rivalries of European powers. Europe was fighting in America over territorial ambitions, and the colonies were caught in the trap, especially when the French drafted Indians into their service as allies against the English.

The Clash in the Ohio Valley. The second of these general wars had hardly closed, however, when the English colonists themselves began to be seriously worried by the rapid growth of French power in the West. Marquette and Joliet, who explored the Lake region, and La Salle, who in 1682 had gone down the Mississippi to the Gulf, had been followed by the builders of forts. In 1718 the

French founded New Orleans, thus taking possession of the gateway to the Mississippi as well as the St. Lawrence. A few years afterward they built Fort Niagara; in 1731 they occupied Crown Point; in 1749 they formally announced their dominion over all the territory drained by the Ohio River. Having asserted this lofty claim, they set out to make it good by constructing in the years 1752–54 Fort Le Bœuf near Lake Erie, Fort Venango on the upper waters of the Allegheny, and Fort Duquesne at the junction of the streams forming the Ohio. Though they were warned by George Washington, in the name of the governor of Virginia, to keep out of territory "so notoriously known to be property of the Crown of Great Britain," the French showed no signs of paying any attention.

The Final Phase — The French and Indian War. Thus it happened that the shot which started the Seven Years' War, known in America as the French and Indian War, was fired in the wilds of Pennsylvania. There began the onslaught that spread to Europe and even Asia and finally lined up England and Prussia on the one side and France, Austria, Spain, and minor powers on the other. On American soil the defeat of Braddock in 1755 and Wolfe's exploit in capturing Quebec four years later were the dramatic features. On the continent of Europe, England gave money to Prussia to hold France at bay. In India on the banks of the Ganges, as on the banks of the St. Lawrence, British arms were triumphant. Well could the historian write, "Conquests equaling in rapidity and far surpassing in magnitude those of Cortes and Pizarro had been achieved in the East." Well could the merchants of London declare that, under the administration of William Pitt, who labored to win for Britain more land and trade, commerce had been "united with and made to flourish by war."

From the point of view of the British empire, the results of the war were highly satisfactory. By the peace of 1763, Canada and the territory east of the Mississippi, except New Orleans, passed under the British flag. The remainder of the Louisiana territory was transferred to Spain and French imperial ambitions on the American continent were laid to rest. In exchange for Havana, which the British had seized during the war, Spain ceded to King

George the colony of Florida. Not without warrant did Macaulay write in after years that Pitt "was the first Englishman of his time; and he had made England the first country in the world."

WARFARE AND TRAINING IN GOVERNMENT

But while England was rejoicing, the very wars which caused her jubilation were preparing her colonies to break away from her. Circumstances beyond the control of the colonial assemblies which were always jealous of their local powers, compelled coöperation among them, grudging and stingy no doubt, but still coöperation. Eager as the American people were to be busy in their fields or at their trades, they were simply forced to raise and support armies, to learn the methods of warfare, and to practice, if in a small theater, the arts of association. These forces, all cumulative, drove the colonists to think of things beyond their local and personal needs — in the direction of common action or nationalism.

The New England Confederation. It was in their efforts to deal with the problems presented by the Indian and French menace that the Americans took the first steps toward union. Though there were many common ties among the settlers of New England, it required a deadly fear of the red men to produce in 1643 the New England Confederation, composed of Massachusetts, Plymouth, Connecticut, and New Haven. The colonies so united were bound together in "a firm and perpetual league of friendship and amity for offense and defense, mutual service and succor, upon all just occasions." They divided the burdens of wars among the members and provided for a congress of commissioners from each colony to decide on policies. For some twenty years the Confederation was active and it continued to hold meetings until the end of the Indian peril on the immediate borders.

Virginia, no less than Massachusetts, was aware of the importance of mutual aid. In the middle of the seventeenth century interest in trade and defense led her to make treaties of commerce and amity with New York and the colonies of New England. Delegates from Virginia met the agents of New York and Massachusetts at Albany in 1684 to discuss problems of general welfare.

And the Old Dominion, as Virginia was often called, coöperated loyally with the Carolinas in defense against Indian forays.

The Albany Plan of Union. An attempt at a general colonial union was made in 1754. On the suggestion of the Lords of Trade in England, a conference was held at Albany to consider Indian relations, to devise measures of protection against the French, and to enter into "articles of union and confederation for the general defense of his Majesty's subjects and interests in North America as well in time of peace as of war." New Hampshire, Massachusetts, Connecticut, Rhode Island, New York, Pennsylvania, and Maryland were represented. After much discussion a plan of union drafted mainly, it seems, by Benjamin Franklin was adopted and sent to the colonies and the Crown for approval. But the colonies, tenacious of their individual rights, refused to accept the scheme and the king disapproved it for the reason, Franklin said, that it had "too much weight in the democratic part of the constitution."

The Military Education of Americans. The same wars that showed the colonists the value of union instructed them in the art of defending their institutions. Particularly was this true of the last French and Indian conflict, which stretched all the way from Maine to the Carolinas and made heavy calls upon them for troops. In that struggle thousands of Americans got a taste, a strong taste, of actual fighting in the field. George Washington and Daniel Morgan, for instance, learned lessons that were not forgotten in after years. They saw what American militiamen could do under favorable circumstances and they watched British regulars operating on American soil. "This whole transaction," sagely remarked Franklin of Braddock's campaign, "gave us Americans the first suspicion that our exalted ideas of the prowess of British regular troops had not been well founded." It was no mere accident that the Virginia Colonel who drew his sword under the elm at Cambridge and took command of the army of the Revolution was the same Washington who had "spurned the whistle of bullets" at the memorable battle in Pennsylvania.

Financial Burdens and Commercial Disorder. While the provincials were learning lessons in warfare they were also paying its bills. All the battles were costly in treasure as in blood. The French and Indian struggle was especially expensive for the colonies because they had to support twenty-five thousand men in the field. Paper money was issued in huge amounts and debts were piled up. Commerce was driven from its usual markets and prices rose as a result. When the end came both England and America had heavy bills to pay, and to make matters worse a collapse of prices brought merchants face to face with ruin. It was in the

From an old print

BRADDOCK'S RETREAT

midst of this business panic that high taxes had to be laid to meet the cost of the war. Who was to pay and how? Over this question so much heat was generated that the colonies were welded into a coöperative unity.

THE WELDING INFLUENCE OF THE CONTEST WITH THE BRITISH GOVERNMENT

Neither the Indian wars nor the French wars wholly accounted for American patriotism. That was in a large measure the product of a long strife with the mother country over her ways of governing her colonies.   In other words the forces that created this nation did not operate in the colonies alone.   They were related to the character of the English monarchs, English domestic politics, the rivalry of American with English merchants, and English measures of control over the dominions.

The Last Stuart Kings.   For a while the struggles between Charles I (1625–49) and the Parliament and the turmoil of the Puritan republic (1649–60) gave the Englishmen so much trouble that they had little time to think of colonial policies or to interfere with colonial affairs.   But the restoration of the monarchy in 1660, accompanied by internal peace and the increasing power of the mercantile classes in the House of Commons, turned their attention again to America.   In the reign of Charles II (1660–85), himself an easy-going person, Parliament began the systematic regulation of trade and created special agencies to supervise the colonies.

Charles' successor, James II, though a man of sterner stuff and testy about his rights in the colonies as well as at home, accepted the policy thus inaugurated and even enlarged upon it.   If he could have kept his throne, he would have bent the Americans under a rigid rule or forced them into a revolution like that which he caused in England in 1688.   Determined to unite the Northern colonies, proud of their individual liberties, he made a martinet, Sir Edmund Andros, governor of all New England, New York, and New Jersey; and Connecticut only saved her charter by hiding it, tradition says, in a hollow oak tree.

For several months Andros gave the Northern colonies a taste of high-tempered despotism.   He wrung quitrents from landowners not accustomed to feudal dues; he seized the land of people who in his opinion had no lawful right to it; he forced the Episcopal service upon the Puritans' Old South Church in Boston; and he imprisoned a preacher who denounced taxation without representation.   In the middle of his arbitrary course, however, his hand was suddenly stayed.   When news came that Englishmen at home had dethroned King James, the people of Boston, kindling a fire on Beacon Hill, summoned the countryside to dispose of Andros, his agent in New England.   The response was prompt and hearty. The hated governor was arrested, cast into jail, and then sent back to the mother country under guard.

The overthrow of James, followed by the choice of William and Mary to reign in his stead, was a victory for Parliament, which was greeted with thanksgiving in New England. Massachusetts now received a new charter. It was not as liberal as the first, but it restored the spirit, if not the entire letter, of self-government. In the other colonies where Andros had been operating, a return was also made to the earlier liberties.

The Indifference of the First Two Georges. On the death in 1714 of Queen Anne, the successor of King William, the throne passed to a Hanoverian prince who, while grateful for English honors and revenues, was more interested in Hanover than in England. George I and George II, whose combined reigns extended from 1714 to 1760, never even learned to speak the English language, at least without an accent. Colonial affairs bored them both to weariness, and the stoutest defender of popular privileges in Boston or Charleston had no ground to complain of direct interference by the king. Moreover during a large part of this period, the real government of England was in the hands of the astute Sir Robert Walpole, who adopted as his motto: "Let sleeping dogs lie." He showed his understanding of popular sentiment by exclaiming: "I will not be the minister to enforce taxes at the expense of blood." Such kings and such a minister were not likely to cause a revolt in the thirteen colonies across the sea.

Control of the Crown over the Colonies. While no English ruler from James II to George III ventured to interfere with colonial matters personally, constant control over the colonies was exercised by the king's officers in London acting in his name. Strict watchfulness began in 1660, when a royal order created a committee of the king's council to meet twice a week to consider petitions and other papers dealing with colonial affairs. In 1696 a regular board, known as the "Lords of Trade and Plantations," was established and instructed to examine acts of colonial legislatures, recommend measures to them for their adoption, and hear petitions from the colonies or their agents in England.

Over colonial affairs this board had large powers. All bills passed by the American assemblies came before it for review. If it found an act unsatisfactory, it advised the king to apply the veto. Any individual who believed his personal or property rights injured by a colonial law could be heard by the board directly or through his own attorney, generally with an agent of the offending colony present.

Judicial Control. Besides the administrative control over the colonies exercised by royal governors and the board of trade, English courts of law had a broad authority over them. By virtue of his royal power the king was at the head of all tribunals in the empire. Any subject in England or America who felt aggrieved by any act of a colonial legislature or any decision of a colonial court, had the right, subject to certain regulations, to carry his case to the king in council acting as a court, forcing his opponent to follow it to London. In the course of such trials the king in council could, and frequently did, declare acts of colonial legislatures null and void, on the ground that they were contrary to English law.

Imperial Control in Operation. Day after day, week after week, year after year, the machinery for political and judicial control over colonial affairs worked without ceasing. At one time the British governors in the colonies were ordered not to approve any colonial law which laid a tax on European imports brought to America in English vessels; that is, the colonists could not have tariffs to protect their industry and trade. Again, when North Carolina laid a tax on peddlers, the British council in London objected to it as "restrictive upon the trade and dispersion of English manufactures throughout the continent." At other times, trade with the Indians was regulated in the interests of the whole empire and grants of lands by a colonial legislature were set aside.

In short the colonies were not free to trade among themselves in their own way, carry on commercial operations at sea at their will, or lay tariffs at their pleasure on imports in an effort to protect their own industries. A superior power, towering above that of the colonies, as the Supreme Court at Washington now towers above the states, kept the colonial legislatures within the metes and bounds of British law. In thousands of appeals, memorials, petitions, and complaints and in the rulings and decisions upon them were written the real history of British imperial dominion over the American colonies.

Parliamentary Control over Colonial Affairs. As Parliament gained in power at the expense of the king, it reached out to bring the American colonies also under its sway. Between the execution of Charles I and the accession of George III, it enacted scores of laws regulating the shipping, trade, and manufactures of America. Based on the "mercantile" theory then prevalent in the countries of Europe, these laws were designed to control the overseas plantations in such a way as to aid, first of all, the commercial and business interests of the mother country, where merchants and men of finance had got the upper hand. According to this theory, the colonies of the British empire were to be confined to agriculture and the production of raw materials, and forced to buy their manufactured goods of England.

The Navigation Acts. First among these measures were the navigation laws framed with the idea of building up the British merchant marine and navy as a means of defending commerce against the Spanish, Dutch, and French. The beginning of this type of legislation was made in 1651, and early in the reign of Charles II it was enlarged into a great system.

The Navigation Acts practically gave a monopoly of colonial commerce to British ships. No trade could be carried on between Great Britain and her dominions save in British vessels, manned mainly by British subjects, including the colonists. No European goods could be brought to America save in the ships of the country that produced them or in English-built ships, manned chiefly by Englishmen. Since the Dutch then carried to America a large amount of goods not of their own production, these laws were almost fatal to their shipping in the New World and injured the colonists as well by compelling them to pay higher freight rates. However the colonists got around this difficulty by building ships of their own for the carriage of their goods. Indeed the measures quickened shipbuilding in the colonies, where the abundance of raw materials gave the master builders of America many advantages over those of the mother country. Thus the colonists in the end actually profited from the restrictive policy written into the Navigation Acts.

Acts against Manufacture.   The second group of laws was aimed to prevent colonial industries from competing too sharply with those of England.   Among the earliest of these measures may be counted the Woolen Act of 1699, forbidding the export of woolen goods from the colonies and even the woolen trade between towns and colonies.   When Parliament learned as the result of an inquiry that New England and New York were making thousands of hats a year and sending large numbers annually to the Southern colonies and to Ireland, Spain, and Portugal, it passed a law in 1732, declaring that "no hats or felts, dyed or undyed, finished or unfinished" should be "put upon any vessel or laden upon any horse or cart with intent to export to any place whatever."   In effect this act almost wrecked the hat industry.

A few years later a similar attack was made on the iron industry. By an act of 1750 pig and bar iron from the colonies were given free entry to England, to encourage the production of the raw material; but coupled with it was a provision that "no mill or other engine for slitting or rolling of iron, no plating forge to work with a tilt hammer, and no furnace for making steel" should be erected in the colonies.   As for those already built, they were declared public nuisances and ordered closed.   Thus three important economic interests of the colonists, the woolen, hat, and iron industries, were put under a ban.

Trade Laws.   The third group of restrictive measures passed by the British Parliament related to the sale of colonial produce. An act of 1663 required the colonies to export certain articles to Great Britain or to her dominions alone; while sugar, tobacco, and ginger on their way to the continent of Europe had to pass through a British port, paying custom duties, and through a British merchant's hands, paying the usual profit.   At first tobacco was the only one of the "enumerated articles" which gave serious concern to the colonies.   In the course of time however other commodities were added to the list of articles, until by 1764 it embraced rice, naval stores, copper, furs, hides, iron, lumber, and pearl ashes. This was not all.   The colonies were compelled to bring their

European purchases back through English ports, paying more duties there and more profits to English merchants.

The Molasses Act. Not content with laws enacted in the interest of English merchants and manufacturers, Parliament sought to protect the British West Indies against competition from their French and Dutch neighbors. New England had been carrying on a good trade with the French islands in the West Indies and Dutch Guiana, where sugar and molasses could be obtained in large quantities at low prices. To this traffic English planters in the Barbadoes and Jamaica objected; so Parliament in 1733 passed the famous Molasses Act levying duties on the sugar and molasses which the colonists brought home. In fact it fixed such high rates that American commerce with the French and the Dutch would have been wrecked if the law had been obeyed. The duties however were not strictly collected by the king's officers and Americans kept up the trade with the foreigners by smuggling.

Effect of the Laws in America. Compared with the rigid monopoly of her colonial trade which Spain tried to maintain, the policy of England was both moderate and liberal. Moreover England even passed some acts which were intended to help colonial industry in cases where her own business men would not be injured.

Under the Navigation Acts, for example, American shipbuilders made positive gains and the producers of hemp, tar, lumber, and ship stores in general grew prosperous. Favors in British ports were granted to Americans as against foreign competitors and in some instances bounties were paid by England to encourage colonial enterprise. Taken all in all, there is much to be said in support of the argument that the colonists gained more than they lost by British trade and industrial legislation.

Be that as it may, it appears that the colonists felt little irritation against the mother country on account of the trade and navigation laws, when they were first enacted. Relatively few people were engaged in the hat and iron industries as compared with those in farming and planting, so that England's policy of confining America to agriculture did not bother the majority of the inhabitants. Furthermore the woolen industry, largely in the hands of women and carried on in connection with their domestic duties, was not their sole support.

As a matter of fact, the restrictive laws, especially those relating to trade, were not rigidly enforced at first. Cargoes of tobacco were boldly sent to continental ports by the colonists without so much as a bow to the English government, to which duties should have been paid. Sugar and molasses from the French and Dutch colonies were shipped into New England in spite of the law. Royal officers sometimes protested against smuggling and sometimes winked at it; at no time did they succeed in stopping it. But when the British government began to enforce its commercial laws more strictly after the French and Indian War, the shoe commenced to pinch and the colonists were drawn closer and closer together in the bonds of common resistance.

SUMMARY OF THE COLONIAL PERIOD

In the period between the landing of the English at Jamestown, Virginia, in 1607, and the close of the French and Indian War in 1763 — a period of a century and a half — a new nation was being prepared on this continent to take its place among the powers of the earth. It was an epoch of migration. Western Europe contributed emigrants of many races and nationalities. The English led the way. Next to them in numerical importance were the Scotch-Irish and the Germans. Into the melting pot were also cast Dutch, Swedes, French, Jews, Welsh, and Irish. Thousands of negroes were brought from Africa to till Southern fields or labor as domestic servants in the North.

Why did they come? The reasons are various. The Pilgrims and Puritans of New England, the French Huguenots, Scotch-Irish and Irish, and the Catholics of Maryland fled from intolerant governments that denied them the right to worship God according to the dictates of their own consciences. Thousands came to escape political tyranny and poverty in the Old World and to find free homes in America. Victims of kidnapers and negroes from Africa were dragged here against their will. The lure of adventure appealed to the restless and the lure of profits to the merchants.

How did they come? In some cases religious brotherhoods banded together and borrowed or furnished the funds necessary to pay the way. In other cases great trading companies were organized to found colonies. Again it was the wealthy proprietor, like Lord Baltimore or William Penn, who undertook to plant settlements. Many emigrants were able to meet their own expenses. Others bound themselves out to service for a term of years in exchange for the cost of the passage. Negroes were brought by traders for the purpose of making money.

Whatever their motive for coming, the colonists set to work with a will. They cut down forests, built houses, and laid out fields. They set up forges and workshops. They spun and wove. They fashioned ships and sailed the ocean. They bartered and traded. Here and there on favorable harbors they established centers of commerce — Boston, Providence, New York, Philadelphia, Baltimore, and Charleston. They founded churches, schools, colleges, and newspapers. They wrote histories, poems, and essays. With their growth in wealth they gave increasing attention to the arts — handicrafts, painting, and architecture. As soon as a firm foothold was secured on the shore line they pressed westward until, by the close of the colonial period, they were already on the crest of the Alleghenies.

Though they were widely scattered along a thousand miles of seacoast, the colonists were united in spirit by many common ties. They were mainly Protestant in religion. The language, the law, and the literature of England furnished a basis of national unity. Most of the colonists were engaged in the same hard task: that of conquering a wilderness. To bonds of kinship and language were added others created by necessity. They had to join in defense; first, against the Indians and then against the French. They were all subjects of the same sovereign — the king of England. The English Parliament made laws for them and the English government supervised their local affairs, their trade, and their manufactures. Common forces assailed them. Common grievances vexed them. Common hopes inspired them.

Many of the things which tended to unite them likewise tended to throw them into opposition to the British Crown and Parliament.

Most of them were freeholders; that is, farmers who owned their own land and tilled it with their own hands. A free soil nourished the spirit of freedom. Since the majority of the colonists were Dissenters, they were as a rule critics, not friends of the Church of England, that stanch defender of the British monarchy. Each colony in time developed its own legislature elected by the voters; it grew accustomed to making laws and laying taxes for itself. Here was a people learning self-reliance and self-government. The attempts to strengthen the Church of England in America and to transform all the colonies into royal provinces only fanned the independence which they were designed to quench.

Nevertheless, the Americans owed much of their prosperity to the assistance of the very government that irritated them. It was the protection of the British navy that had prevented Holland, Spain, and France from wiping out their settlements. Though their manufacture and trade were controlled in the interests of the mother country, they also enjoyed great advantages in her markets. Free trade existed nowhere upon the earth; but the broad empire of Britain was open to American ships and merchandise. It could be said, with good reason, that the disadvantages which the colonists suffered through British regulation of their industry and trade were in many respects offset by the privileges they enjoyed. Still that is somewhat beside the point, for mere economic advantage is not necessarily the determining factor in the fate of peoples. A thousand circumstances had helped to develop on this continent an American nation, to inspire it with a passion for independence, and to prepare it for a destiny greater than that of a prosperous dominion of the British empire. The economists, who tried to prove that America was richer and better off in every way under the British flag, could not change the spirit of Patrick Henry, Samuel Adams, Benjamin Franklin, or George Washington.

References

J. T. Adams, *Provincial Society, 1690–1763.*

C. M. Andrews, *Colonial Self-Government* (American Nation Series).

G. L. Beer, *Origin of the British Colonial System* and *The Old Colonial System.*

A. Bradley, *The Fight for Canada in North America.*
H. Egerton, *Short History of British Colonial Policy.*
F. Parkman, *France and England in North America* (12 vols.).
R. Thwaites, *France in America* (American Nation Series).
J. Winsor, *The Mississippi Valley* and *Cartier to Frontenac.*

Questions

1. Explain the terms: royal province, colonial assembly, and suffrage.
2. Give some of the undemocratic features of colonial governments. Also some of the democratic features.
3. How did the colonial assemblies help to create a spirit of self-reliance and independence?
4. Why were there continual contests between royal governors and colonial assemblies?
5. How would you define "nationalism"? "Patriotism"?
6. In what way may war promote nationalism?
7. Explain the failure to establish a uniform rule for dealing fairly with the Indians.
8. What was the outcome of the final clash with the French?
9. Enumerate the chief results of the wars with the French and the Indians. Discuss each in detail.
10. Explain why the character of the English king mattered to the colonists.
11. Contrast England under the Stuarts with England under the Hanoverians.
12. Explain how the English Crown, Courts, and Parliament controlled the colonies.
13. Name the three important classes of English legislation affecting the colonies. Explain each.
14. Do you think the English legislation was beneficial or injurious to the colonies? Why?

Research Topics

The Government of a Royal Province, Virginia. Lodge, pp. 43–50. Special Reference: E. B. Greene, *The Provincial Governor* (Harvard Studies).

The Government of a Proprietary Colony, Pennsylvania. Lodge, pp. 230–232.

Government in New England. Lodge, pp. 412–417.

Colonial Government in General. Beard, *Rise of American Civilization*, Vol. I, pp. 109–121.

Rise of French Power in North America. Special reference: Francis Parkman, *Struggle for a Continent.*

The French and Indian Wars. Special reference: W. M. Sloane, *French War and the Revolution*, Chaps. VI–IX. Parkman, *Montcalm and Wolfe*, Vol. II, pp. 195–299. Elson, *History of the United States*, pp. 154–177.

English Navigation Acts. Macdonald, *Documentary Source Book*, pp. 55, 72, 78, 90, 103. Coman, *Industrial History*, pp. 79–85.

British Colonial Policy. Callender, *Economic History of the United States*, pp. 102–108.

The New England Confederation. Analyze the document in Macdonald, *Source Book*, p. 45. Special reference: Fiske, *Beginnings of New England*, pp. 140–198.

The Administration of Andros. Fiske, *Beginnings*, pp. 242–278.

Biographical Studies. William Pitt and Sir Robert Walpole. Consult Green, *Short History of England*, on their policies, using the index.

Questions for Debate

1. Universal suffrage (for all free citizens) would have been unwise in colonial times.

2. The American unity was more a matter of necessity than of choice.

Historical Fiction

M. J. Canavan, *Ben Comee.*
Emerson Hough, *The Mississippi Bubble.*

PART II. CONFLICT AND INDEPENDENCE

CHAPTER VI

THE NEW COURSE IN BRITISH IMPERIAL POLICY

On October 25, 1760, King George II died and the British crown passed to his young grandson, George III. The first George, the son of the Elector of Hanover and Sophia the granddaughter of James I, was a thorough German who never even learned to speak the language of the land over which he reigned. The second George did not see England until he was a man. He spoke English with an accent and until his death preferred his German home. During the long years of their rule, the principle became well established that the king must always act through his ministers who spoke for the majority in Parliament.

GEORGE III AND THE BRITISH SYSTEM

The Character of the New King. The third George broke the German tradition of his family. He resented the charge that he was a foreigner and on all occasions made a display of his British sympathies. To the draft of his first speech to Parliament, he added the popular phrase: "Born and educated in this country, I glory in the name of Briton." Macaulay, the English historian, who was certainly no friend of high royal prerogative, said of George III: "The young king was a born Englishman. All his tastes and habits, good and bad, were English. No portion of his subjects had anything to reproach him with. . . . His age, his appearance, and all that was known of his character conciliated public favor. He was in the bloom of youth; his person and address were pleasing; scandal imputed to him no vice; and flattery might without glaring absurdity ascribe to him many princely virtues."

Nevertheless George III had been spoiled by his mother, his tutors, and his courtiers. Under their teachings he developed high and mighty notions about the sacredness of royal authority and his duty to check the power of Parliament and the ministers dependent upon it. His mother had dinned into his ears the slogan: "George, be King!" Lord Bute, his adviser, had told him that his honor required him to take an active part in governing and making laws. Thus educated, he surrounded himself with courtiers who encouraged him in his resolve to rule the country, to subdue all parties, and to make himself the real head of the nation and empire.

Political Parties and George III. The state of the political parties favored the plan of the king to revive some of the ancient glory of the Crown. One of these parties, called Whigs, consisting mainly of the smaller freeholders, merchants, and dissenters, had grown haughty and overbearing through long continuance in office and had raised up many critics even in its own ranks. The opposing party, known as Tories, had by this time given up all hope of restoring the direct Stuart line to the throne; but it still clung to old notions about the divine right of kings. With the accession of George III Tories seized the opportunity to rally around the throne again. George received them with open arms, gave them offices, and bought them seats in the Commons.

On the other hand they used him. Indeed it is well to remember that King George was not solely responsible for the acts of the British government which infuriated the colonists. All the vexatious laws were passed by Parliament and in general received the support of the landed and mercantile classes that ruled Great Britain. Since it was customary to transact official business in the king's name, George got far more blame than he really deserved.

The British Parliamentary System. The nature of the British Parliament at the time made smooth the way for the king and his allies to get the government into their hands. In the first place the House of Lords was composed mainly of nobles whose number the king could enlarge by appointing his favorites. Though the members of the House of Commons were elected by popular vote, they did not represent the masses of the people. Cities like Leeds, Manchester, and Birmingham, for example, had no representatives at all. While there were about eight million inhabitants in Great Britain, only about 160,000 could vote in 1768; that is to say, only about one in every ten adult males had a voice in the government. Many boroughs returned one or more members to the Commons although they had merely a handful of voters or in some instances not a single voter. Furthermore these tiny boroughs were often controlled by lords who frankly sold the seats in Parliament to the highest bidder. Such "rotten-boroughs," as they were called by reformers, were a public scandal, but George III and his faction made use of them to get their friends into the Commons.

GEORGE III's MINISTERS AND THEIR COLONIAL POLICIES

Grenville and the War Debt. Within a year after the accession of George III, William Pitt was turned out of office, the king treating him with "gross incivility" while the crowds shouted "Pitt forever!" The direction of affairs was then intrusted to ministers friendly to the king. Leadership in the House of Commons fell to George Grenville, half Whig and half Tory, a grave and laborious man who for years had groaned over the increasing cost of government.

The first task after the conclusion of war in 1763 was an adjustment of the finances and defenses of the empire. The national debt now stood at the highest point in the history of England. More taxes were absolutely necessary and the search for money finally led to America. With the support of the entire ministry, Grenville and his zealous colleague, Charles Townshend, set to work in February, 1763, to establish a stricter system of colonial government. Hitherto the Americans had paid the salaries of royal governors and judges, thus keeping them under a certain control. According to the new system the Crown was to pay these salaries, and Parliament was to tax the American people.

Restriction of Paper Money. The Grenville ministry also gave attention to complaints from English merchants about the way in which colonists were printing paper money and trying to pay their debts with it instead of the specie which was higher in value. To help these merchants out of their plight, the ministry in 1763 pushed through Parliament an act which declared void all colonial laws authorizing paper money or extending the time fixed for the payment of bills. Thus the first chapter was written in the long battle over "sound" *versus* "cheap" money.

Limitations on the American Movement Westward. In its new program the Grenville ministry touched another sore spot in America. As we have said, the king claimed all the land in his dominions and the right to grant it at his pleasure. In practice he and his colonial governors gave or sold at a low price to friends and favorites millions of acres of choice land in the colonies — some of which was held unused in huge estates simply to make money out of the increase in value. Finding good land near the sea rising in price, hardy American pioneers were always moving west and "squatting" on land bought from the Indians or taken without any authority whatever. The result was much confusion and bad temper. To put an end to misunderstandings, King George, by a royal proclamation of 1763, forbade the colonists to buy any more land from the Indians, and reserved to the Crown the sole right to acquire such lands and dispose of them for settlement. The same proclamation placed in the hands of royal officers the power of licensing trade with the Indians, which meant that they could control the profitable fur business. These two limitations on American freedom and enterprise were declared to be in the interest of the Crown and for the preservation of the rights of the Indians against fraud and abuse; but they were regarded by many Americans as wholly unwarranted.

The Sugar Act (1764). King George's ministers next turned their attention to taxation and commerce. Since the heavy debt under which England was laboring had been largely incurred in the defense of America, it seemed reasonable to them that the colonies should take some of the burden off the backs of English taxpayers. The Sugar Act of 1764 was the outcome. There was no doubt about the design of this law, for it was set forth plainly in the title: "An act for granting certain duties in the British colonies and plantations in America . . . for applying the produce of such duties . . . towards defraying the expenses of defending, protecting, and securing the said colonies and plantations." It also provided that smuggling was to be stopped. The old Molasses Act had been passed to check American trade but the Sugar Act was clearly intended to raise revenue from American commerce. That is, the British ministry now laid duties on sugar, indigo, calico, silks, and many other commodities imported into the colonies, for the purpose of bringing money into the royal treasury. The enforcement of the Molasses Act had been neglected; but this Sugar Act had "teeth in it." Shipmasters were registered in government books and were required to put up money or bonds as a guarantee that they would obey the customs law. For disobedience everybody concerned was liable to heavy punishment.

The strict terms of the Sugar Act were strengthened by other measures. Commanders of armed vessels stationed along the American coast were authorized to halt, search, and, on suspicion of smuggling, seize merchant ships approaching colonial ports. All British officers in America were instructed to be diligent in enforcing the trade and navigation laws. Revenue collectors, officers of the army and navy, and royal governors were curtly ordered to the front to do their full duty in this matter. Their sense of duty was quickened by an appeal to their selfishness, for naval officers who seized offenders against the law were rewarded by large prizes out of the forfeitures and penalties.

The Stamp Act (1765). While the Sugar Act was still being debated in Parliament, Grenville announced a plan for a stamp bill. The next year it went through both Houses with a speed that must have amazed its authors. The vote in the Commons stood 205 in favor to 49 against; while in the Lords it was not even necessary to go through the formality of a count. As George III was temporarily insane, a commission acting as a board of regency had to sign the bill for him. Against this measure the colonial agents in London were helpless. "We might as well have hindered the sun's progress!" exclaimed Benjamin Franklin. Protests of a few opponents in the Commons were equally vain. The ministry was firm in its course.

Like the Sugar Act, the Stamp Act declared that it was the purpose of the British government to raise revenue in America "towards defraying the expenses of defending, protecting and securing the British colonies and plantations in America." It was a long measure of more than fifty sections, carefully planned and skillfully drawn. By its provisions duties were laid in the colonies on practically all papers used in legal transactions —

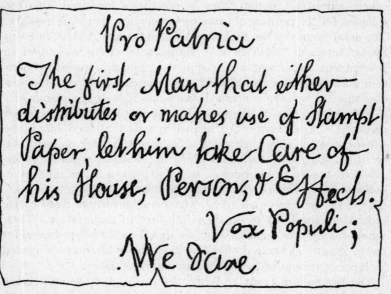

Pro Patria
The first Man that either
distributes or makes use of Stampt
Paper, let him take Care of
his House, Person, & Effects.
Vox Populi;
We Dare

STAMP ACT WARNING POSTED ON DOORS OF EVERY PUBLIC OFFICE AND ON
CORNERS OF STREETS IN NEW YORK CITY

deeds, mortgages, inventories, writs, bail bonds, on licenses to practice law and sell liquor, on college diplomas, playing cards,

 dice, pamphlets, newspapers, almanacs, calendars, and advertisements. The dragnet was closely knit, for scarcely anything escaped taxation.

STAMP ACT STAMPS

The Quartering Act (1765). The ministers were aware that the Stamp Act would rouse opposition in America — how great they did not suspect. Before the measure was passed, a friend of General Wolfe, Colonel Barré, who knew America well, gave them an ominous warning in the House of Commons. "Believe me — remember I this day told you so," he exclaimed, "the same spirit of freedom which actuated that people at first will accompany them still . . . a people jealous of their liberties and who will vindicate them, if ever they should be violated." The answer of the ministry to a prophecy of rebellion was a threat of force. Preparations were made to send a larger number of soldiers than usual to the colonies, and the ink was hardly dry on the Stamp Act when Parliament passed the Quartering Act ordering the colonists to provide food and housing for the soldiers who were to enforce the new laws. "We have the power to tax them," said one of the ministers, "and we will tax them."

COLONIAL RESISTANCE FORCES REPEAL

Popular Opposition. The Stamp Act was greeted in America by a sudden outburst of criticism from all classes. Merchants of the seaboard cities took the lead in making a dignified but emphatic protest and agreed not to import British goods while the hated law stood upon the books. Lawyers were incensed by the heavy taxes on legal papers or frightened by patriots who would not allow the use of stamped documents; so many of them joined the merchants in the outcry. Aristocratic colonial Whigs, who had long fretted about the doings of royal governors, now fumed against taxation without their consent, as the Whigs formerly had done in England. Without avail did the colonial Tories, including Anglican clergymen and royal officers, denounce the merchants, lawyers, and Whig aristocrats as "seditious, factious and republican." During the summer of 1765 the opposition to the Stamp Act and its accompanying measure, the Quartering Act, grew in strength and passion.

In a little while the cry against taxation by Parliament was taken up in the streets and along the countryside. All through the North and in some of the Southern colonies, there sprang up, as if by magic, committees and societies pledged to resist the Stamp Act to the bitter end. These popular societies were known as Sons of Liberty and Daughters of Liberty; the former including artisans, mechanics, and laborers; and the latter, patriotic women.

While the merchants and Whig gentlemen confined their efforts chiefly to writing well-phrased protests against British measures,

PATRICK HENRY MAKING THE "CAESAR HAD HIS BRUTUS" SPEECH
From an imaginative painting by P. F. Rothermel.

the Sons of Liberty rushed out into the streets and chose rougher measures. They stirred up riots in Boston, New York, Philadelphia, and Charleston when attempts were made to sell the stamps. They sacked and burned the residences of high royal officers. They organized committees of inquiry who by threats cut down the sale of British goods and the use of stamped papers. In fact the Sons of Liberty went to such excesses that mild opponents of the stamp tax drew back in fear at the forces they had unloosed. Meanwhile, the Daughters of Liberty reduced the trade in British goods by spurring on domestic industries, by manufacturing more cloth themselves, and by using substitutes for taxed foods.

Legislative Action against the Stamp Act. This widespread popular uprising was heartily applauded by leaders in the colonial assemblies, accustomed to battling against British policies. The Virginia House of Burgesses passed a set of resolutions declaring that the General Assembly of the colony alone had the right to lay taxes upon the inhabitants and that attempts to impose them otherwise were "illegal, unconstitutional, and unjust." It was in support of these resolutions that Patrick Henry, according to American tradition, uttered a daring threat: "Caesar had his Brutus, Charles I his Cromwell, and George III. . . ." Cries of "Treason" were calmly met by the orator who finished: "George III may profit by their example. If that be treason, make the most of it."

The Stamp Act Congress. The action of Virginia was answered by Massachusetts with an invitation calling upon the colonies to elect delegates to a Congress to be held in New York for the purpose of discussing their common problems. Nine colonies responded by sending representatives. After professing the warmest affection for the king's person and government, the Congress passed a series of resolutions that were clear as sunlight. They declared that taxes could not be imposed without their consent, given through their respective colonial assemblies; that the Stamp Act showed a tendency to subvert their rights and liberties; that the recent trade laws were burdensome and grievous; and that the right to petition the king and Parliament was their heritage. They thereupon made "humble supplication" for the repeal of the Stamp Act.

The Repeal of the Stamp Act and the Sugar Act. American resistance to the Stamp Act aroused England like an alarm bell.

British trade with the colonies had been effectively boycotted by the Americans; ships lay idly swinging at the wharves; bankruptcy threatened hundreds of merchants in London, Bristol, and Liverpool. Workingmen in the manufacturing towns were thrown out of employment. In place of the coveted revenue, the government was reaping rebellion.

Perplexed by the storm they had raised, the ministers summoned to the bar of the House of Commons, Benjamin Franklin, the agent for Pennsylvania in London. "Do you think it right," asked Grenville, "that America should be protected by this country and pay no part of the expenses?" The answer was brief: "That is not the case; the colonies raised, clothed, and paid during the last war twenty-five thousand men and spent many millions." Then came an inquiry whether the colonists would accept a modified Stamp Act. "No, never," replied Franklin, "never! They will never submit to it!" It was next suggested that military force might compel obedience to law. Franklin had a ready answer. "They cannot force a man to take stamps. . . . They may not find a rebellion; they may, indeed, make one."

A few days later repeal of the Stamp Act was moved in the House of Commons. The sponsor for the repeal spoke of commerce ruined, debts due British merchants placed in jeopardy, Manchester industries closed, workingmen unemployed, oppression instituted, and the loss of the colonies threatened. Pitt and Edmund Burke, the former near the close of his career, the latter just beginning his, argued cogently in favor of retracing the steps which the ministry had taken the year before. Grenville refused to retreat. "America must learn," he wailed, "that prayers are not to be brought to Caesar through riot and sedition." Nevertheless the Commons agreed to the repeal on February 22, 1766, amid the cheers of the victorious majority. It was carried through the Lords in the face of strong opposition and on March 18 reluctantly signed by the king, once more sane.

Although it repealed the Stamp Act, Parliament did not admit the claim of the Americans that it had no power to tax them. On the contrary, it passed at the same time a Declaratory Act which asserted that the colonies were subordinate to the Crown and Parliament of Great Britain; that the king and Parliament had undoubted authority to make laws binding the colonies in all cases whatsoever; and that the resolutions and proceedings denying such authority were null and void.

The repeal however was greeted by the colonists with great popular rejoicing. Bells were rung; toasts to the king were drunk; and trade resumed its normal course. The Declaratory Act, as a mere paper resolution, did not disturb the good humor of the crowds as they cheered the name of George III again. Their happiness was soon deepened by the news that even the Sugar Act had been repealed, thus practically restoring the condition of affairs before Grenville and Townshend commenced their policy of "thoroughness."

Resumption of British Revenue and Commercial Policies

The Townshend Acts (1767). The triumph of the colonists was brief. Though Pitt, the friend of America, was once more prime minister and seated in the House of Lords as the Earl of Chatham, his illness still gave to Townshend and the Tory party practical sway over Parliament. Learning nothing from the experience with the Stamp Act, Townshend now pushed through both Houses of Parliament three new laws affecting American trade. The first measure, issued on June 29, 1767, laid a tax on lead, glass, paint, tea, and a few other articles imported into the colonies, and provided that the money raised by such duties should be used in paying the salaries and other expenses of royal officials stationed there. The second measure, of the same date, declared that all duties on colonial goods were to be collected henceforward by British commissioners appointed by the king, paid from the British treasury, resident in the colonies, and independent of all control by the colonists. A third measure was the Tea Act of July 2, 1767, aimed at the tea trade which many Americans carried on illegally with foreigners. This law abolished the duty which the East India Company had to pay in England on tea exported to America, for it was thought that in this way the Company could undersell American tea smugglers.

Writs of Assistance Legalized by Parliament. Had Parliament not gone beyond imposing duties just to show its power and right, perhaps little would have been heard of the Townshend Acts. It arranged however for the strict, even harsh, enforcement of the law. It ordered customs officers to put an end to smuggling. In the revenue act of June 29, 1767, Parliament expressly authorized the superior courts of the colonies to issue "writs of assistance," empowering such officers to enter "any house, warehouse, shop, cellar, or other place in the British colonies or plantations in America to search for and seize" prohibited or smuggled goods.

Nothing could have been more irritating to defenders of American rights. To allow a "minion of the law" to enter at will a man's house and search his papers and premises was too much for the patience of people who had fled to America in a quest for self-government and free homes, who had braved such hardships to establish liberty, and who wanted to carry on their business without official interference.

The writ of assistance had been used in Massachusetts in 1755 to prevent unlawful trade with Canada and had aroused violent hostility at that time. It was again the subject of a hot dispute in 1761 when a customs officer asked a Massachusetts court for a writ "as usual." With great vigor the request was opposed by James Otis in a speech five hours long — a speech of such fire and eloquence that it sent every man who heard it away "ready to take up arms against writs of assistance." Otis denounced the practice as an exercise of arbitrary power which had cost one king his head and another his throne; he assailed it as a tyrant's device which placed the liberty of every man in jeopardy, allowed any petty officer to invade the home of an innocent citizen on the merest suspicion, and spread terror and desolation through the land. "What a scene," he exclaimed, "does this open! Every man, prompted by revenge, ill-humor, or wantonness to inspect the inside of his neighbor's house, may get a writ of assistance. Others will ask it from self-defense; one arbitrary exertion will provoke another until society is involved in tumult and blood." Such was the hated writ that Townshend proposed to put into the hands of customs officers in his grim resolve to enforce the law.

Then and there James Otis sounded the call to America to resist the exercise of arbitrary power by royal officers. "Then and there," wrote John Adams, "the child Independence was born."

The New York Assembly Suspended. In the very month that Townshend's Acts were signed by the king, Parliament took a still more drastic step. The scene of trouble was now New York. The legislature of that colony had failed to vote money for the care of British troops as ordered by the Quartering Act. Parliament therefore closed the assembly until it promised to obey the law. It was not until a third election was held that obedience could be wrung from the province. In the meantime all the colonies had learned on how frail a foundation their popular legislatures rested.

RENEWED RESISTANCE IN AMERICA

The Massachusetts Circular (1768). Under the leadership of Samuel Adams, Massachusetts resolved steadfastly to resist this renewed intervention in America. At his suggestion the assembly adopted a Circular Letter addressed to the legislatures of the other colonies informing them of the state of affairs in Massachusetts and roundly attacking the whole British policy. The Circular declared that Parliament simply had no right to lay taxes on Americans without their consent and that the colonists could not be represented in Parliament because it was too far away. The Letter went on shrewdly to ask whether any people could be called free, who were ruled by governors and judges appointed by the Crown and paid out of funds raised independently. Then in the most temperate tones, it invited the other colonies to take thought about the plight in which they were all placed.

The Dissolution of Assemblies. When he heard about the Circular Letter, the royal governor of Massachusetts ordered the assembly to withdraw it. On meeting refusal he promptly sent the members home. When the Maryland, Georgia, and South Carolina assemblies indorsed the Circular Letter they were also dissolved at once by their respective governors. Thoroughly aroused, the Virginia House of Burgesses passed resolutions on May 16, 1769, declaring that the sole right of imposing taxes in

Virginia was vested in its own legislature. In the same resolutions it proclaimed anew the right to petition the Crown, condemned the transportation of persons accused of crimes for trial in the mother country, and besought the king for a redress of the general grievances. Immediate dissolution was the answer of the royal governor to the appeal of the Virginia assembly.

SAMUEL ADAMS

After the portrait by J. S. Copley.

The Boston Massacre. American opposition to the British authorities kept steadily rising as assemblies were dissolved, the houses of citizens were searched, and troops were distributed in increasing numbers among the centers of discontent. Merchants again agreed not to import British goods, the Sons of Liberty resumed their agitation, and women once more resolved to promote and patronize domestic industries.

On the night of March 5, 1770, a crowd on the streets of Boston began to jostle and tease some British regulars stationed in the town. Things went from bad to worse until "a few boys and young fellows" started to throw snowballs and stones. Then the exasperated soldiers fired into the throng, killing five persons and wounding half a dozen more. The day after the "massacre," a rousing mass meeting was held and Samuel Adams was sent to demand the withdrawal of the soldiers. The governor hesitated and tried to compromise — but finding Adams relentless, he yielded and ordered the regulars away.

From New Hampshire to Georgia the country was stirred by the Boston Massacre. In Boston itself passions ran dangerously high. The guilty soldiers were charged with murder, but their defense was undertaken, in spite of the wrath of the populace, by John Adams and Josiah Quincy, who as lawyers thought even the gravest offenders entitled to their full rights at law. In his speech to the jury, however, Adams warned the British government against its course, saying that "from the nature of things, soldiers quartered in a populous town will always occasion two mobs where they will prevent one." When at the end only two of the soldiers were convicted and lightly punished, cries went up against "the failure of justice."

Resistance in the South. The year following the Boston Massacre some citizens of North Carolina, goaded by the conduct of the royal governor, openly resisted his authority. Many were killed as a result and seven who were taken prisoners were hanged as traitors. A little later royal troops and local militia met in a pitched battle near Alamance River, called the "Lexington of the South."

The *Gaspee* Affair and the Virginia Resolutions of 1773. On sea as well as on land, friction between the royal officers and the colonists developed into overt acts. While patrolling Narragansett Bay looking for smugglers one day in 1772, the armed ship, *Gaspee*, ran ashore and was caught fast. During the night several men from Providence boarded the vessel and after seizing the crew set it on fire. Yet when a royal commission was sent to Rhode Island to discover the offenders and bring them to account, it failed to find a single informer. The very appointment of this commission inspired the patriots of Virginia to call for general action; and in March, 1773, the House of Burgesses passed a resolution creating a standing committee of correspondence to aid in bringing about coöperation among the colonies against British measures.

The Boston Tea Party. Although the British government found the Townshend revenue act a failure and repealed in 1770 all the duties except that on tea, it kept on trying to enforce the other commercial regulations which it had imposed on the colonies.

In its twists and turns it decided to help the British East India Company out of the financial difficulties into which it had fallen partly by reason of the Tea Act mentioned above and the colonial boycott that followed. In 1773 Parliament provided that the Company would not have to pay the regular duties on any tea brought into England and then sent out to America. A small impost of three pence a pound, to be collected here, was left as a reminder of the principle laid down in the Declaratory Act that Parliament had the right to tax the colonists.

This arrangement with the East India Company was hateful to the colonists for several reasons. It was an act of favoritism to the English Company as a great monopoly. Moreover it promised to dump on the American market suddenly an immense amount of cheap tea and so cause heavy losses to American merchants who had large stocks of their own tea on hand. It threatened with ruin the business of all those who were engaged in secret commerce with the Dutch. It carried with it an irritating, if small, tax on imports, laid and collected by the British government.

In Charleston, Annapolis, and New York, sea captains who brought tea under this act were roughly handled. One night in December, 1773, a band of Boston citizens, disguised as Indians, boarded some tea ships and dumped their cargoes into the harbor. This was serious — open, flagrant, determined violation of the law. As such the British government viewed it.

Retaliation by the British Government

Reception of the News of the Tea Riot. The news of the tea riot in Boston confirmed King George in his idea that there should be no soft policy in dealing with his American subjects. "The die is cast," he declared. "The colonies must either triumph or submit. . . . If we take the resolute part, they will undoubtedly be very meek." Sharing this doctrine, Lord George Germain added that the acts of the tea party were "the proceedings of a tumultuous and riotous rabble who ought, if they had the least prudence, to follow their mercantile employments and not trouble themselves with politics and government, which they do not understand." This opinion was also held by Lord North, who had for three years been the king's chief minister; and even Pitt, now Lord Chatham, was willing to support the government in upholding its authority.

The Five Intolerable Acts. Aroused by colonial resistance, Parliament, beginning on March 31, 1774, passed five stringent laws known in American history as the "Intolerable Acts" — aimed at "curing the unrest in America." The first of them was a bill absolutely shutting the port of Boston to commerce with the outside world. The second, following closely, revoked the charter of Massachusetts and provided that henceforth her councilors should be appointed by the king, that all judges should be named by the royal governor, and that town meetings (except to elect certain officers) could not be held without the governor's consent. A third authorized royal agents to transfer to Great Britain or to other colonies the trials of officers or other persons accused of murder in connection with the enforcement of the law. The fourth act legalized the quartering of troops in Massachusetts towns. The fifth was the Quebec Act which granted religious toleration to the Catholics in Canada, extended the boundaries of Quebec southward to the Ohio River, and established in this western region government by a viceroy.

The Intolerable Acts went through Parliament with amazing speed. There was, it is true, an opposition, alert and informed. Burke spoke eloquently against the Boston Port Bill, assailed it for punishing the innocent with the guilty, and showed how likely it was to make uproar rather than bring peace. But his pleas were rejected. Without a roll call the bill passed both houses. The law destroying the charter of Massachusetts passed the Commons by a vote of three to one; and the third intolerable act by a vote of four to one. The victory of the ministry was complete. "What passed in Boston," exclaimed the great jurist, Lord Mansfield, "is the overt act of High Treason proceeding from our over lenity and want of foresight." The Crown and Parliament were united in resorting to punitive measures.

In the colonies the laws were received with dismay. By the American Protestants, the Quebec bill was especially criticized. This project they regarded not as an act of mercy to Catholics, but as a direct attempt to enlist French Canadians on the side of Great Britain. The British government did not grant religious toleration to Catholics either at home or in Ireland; so the Americans could see no good motive in granting it in North America. The Act was also attacked because Massachusetts, Connecticut, and Virginia had, under their charters, large claims in the territory thus annexed to Quebec.

To enforce these Acts the military strength of the British government was brought into play. The commander-in-chief of the armed forces in America, General Gage, was appointed governor of Massachusetts. More soldiers were shipped to the colonies, for now King George was to give "the rebels," as he called them, a dose of strong medicine. The majesty of his law was to be upheld by arms.

From Reform to Revolution in America

The Doctrine of Natural Rights. The dissolution of assemblies, the abolition of charters, and the use of troops certainly did not cure the unrest. They only made the struggle fiercer. In the early days of the contest with the British ministry, the Americans had emphasized their "rights as Englishmen" and objected to certain acts of Parliament as unlawful, as violating the principles of the English constitution under which all subjects lived. When they saw that such arguments had no effect on Parliament, they turned for support to revolutionary "natural rights."

The latter doctrine, in the form employed by the determined colonists, was also as English as the constitutional argument. John Locke had used it with good effect in defense of the English revolution in the seventeenth century; and American leaders, familiar with the writings of Locke, simply applied his teachings in the hour of their own distress. They now declared that their rights did not really depend on the English constitution or a charter from the Crown. "Old Magna Carta was not the beginning of all things," retorted Otis when the constitutional argument failed. "A time may come when Parliament shall declare every American charter void, but the natural, inherent, and inseparable rights of the colonists as men and as citizens will remain and, whatever becomes of charters, can never be abolished until the general conflagration." Of the same opinion was the young revolutionist, Alexander Hamilton. "The sacred rights of mankind," he exclaimed, "are not to be rummaged for among old parchments or musty records. They are written as with a sunbeam in the whole volume of human destiny by the hand of divinity itself, and can never be erased or obscured by mortal power."

Firm as the American leaders were in the statement and defense of their rights, there is every reason for believing that in the beginning they hoped to settle the issue by reason. They constantly vowed that they were loyal to the king when they protested in the strongest language against his policies. Even Otis, deemed a firebrand by the loyalists, was in fact trying to avert revolution by winning concessions from England. "I argue this cause with the greater pleasure," he urged in his speech against the writs of assistance, "as it is in favor of British liberty."

Burke Offers the Doctrine of Conciliation. The rising tide of American discontent was correctly measured by one Englishman at least, Edmund Burke, who early learned that attempts to restrain American democracy were like efforts to make water run uphill. He saw how fixed and rooted in the nature of things was the American ideal — how inevitable, how irresistible. He warned his countrymen that there were only three ways of handling the delicate situation. One was to remove the cause of trouble by changing the spirit of the colonists — an utter impossibility because that spirit was grounded in the very facts of American life. The second was to treat American leaders as criminals; of this he begged his countrymen to beware lest the colonists declare that "a government against which a claim of liberty is tantamount to high treason is a government to which submission is equivalent to slavery." The third and right way to meet the problem, Burke concluded, was to accept the American view, repeal the objectionable acts of Parliament, and treat the colonies as equal partners with England.

Events Produce the Great Decision. The right way, pointed out by Burke, was not pleasing to George III and the majority in Parliament. To their closed minds, American opinion was absurd and American resistance unlawful, riotous, and treasonable. The correct thing to do, in their view, was to dispatch more troops to crush the "rebels"; and that very act took the contest out of the realm of reason. As John Adams said, "Facts are stubborn things." Opinions were unseen, but marching soldiers were facts visible to the man in the street. "Now," said Gouverneur Morris, "the sheep, simple as they are, cannot be gulled as heretofore." It was too late to talk about the excellence of the British constitution.

References

G. L. Beer, *British Colonial Policy* (1754–63).
E. Channing, *History of the United States*, Vol. III.
R. Frothingham, *Rise of the Republic*.
J. K. Hosmer, *Samuel Adams*.
G. E. Howard, *Preliminaries of the Revolution* (American Nation Series).
J. T. Morse, *Benjamin Franklin*.
M. C. Tyler, *Patrick Henry*.
J. A. Woodburn (editor), *The American Revolution* (Selections from the English work by Lecky).

Questions

1. Show how the character of George III fitted the plans of the English governing classes.
2. Explain why the party and parliamentary systems of England favored their plans.
3. How did the state of English finances affect English policy?
4. Name five important measures of the English government affecting the colonies between 1763 and 1765. Explain each in detail.
5. Describe American resistance to the Stamp Act. What was the outcome?
6. Show how England renewed her policy of regulation in 1767.
7. Summarize the events connected with American resistance.
8. With what measures did Great Britain retaliate?
9. Contrast "constitutional" with "natural" rights.
10. What solution did Burke offer? Why was it rejected?

Research Topics

Powers Conferred on Revenue Officers by Writs of Assistance. See a writ in Macdonald, *Source Book*, p. 109.
The Acts of Parliament Respecting America. Macdonald, pp. 117–146. Assign one to each student for report and comment.

Source Studies on the Stamp Act.   Hart, *American History Told by Contemporaries*, Vol. II, pp. 394–412.

Source Studies of the Townshend Acts.   Hart, Vol. II, pp. 413–433.

American Principles.   Prepare a table of them from the Resolutions of the Stamp Act Congress and the Massachusetts Circular.   Macdonald, pp. 136–146.

An English Historian's View of the Period.   Green, *Short History of England*, Chap. X.

English Policy Not Injurious to America.   Callender, *Economic History*, pp. 85–121.

A Review of English Policy.   Woodrow Wilson, *History of the American People*, Vol. II, pp. 129–170.

The Opening of the Revolution.   Elson, *History of the United States*, pp. 201–226.

Questions for Debate

1. The British policy toward the American colonies was unwise.

2. The people of Great Britain and the people of the American colonies were generally friendly in the decade prior to the Revolution.

Historical Fiction

Robert W. Chambers, *Cardigan.*
Winston Churchill, *Richard Carvel.*
William M. Thackeray, *Henry Esmond.*

CHAPTER VII

THE AMERICAN REVOLUTION

Resistance and the British Answer

The Continental Congress. When the news of the "Intolerable Acts" reached America, everyone knew what strong medicine Parliament was prepared to give to everybody who resisted its authority. But in all the colonies there were persons ready to face danger without flinching. Soon therefore the cause of Massachusetts became the cause of thirteen united colonies. Opposition to British policy, hitherto local and fitful, now took on a national character. Town committees and provincial conventions were crowned by a Continental Congress, called by Massachusetts on June 17, 1774, at the suggestion of Samuel Adams.

The response to the summons was electric. By hurried and irregular methods delegates were elected during that summer, and on September 5 the Congress duly assembled in Carpenter's Hall in Philadelphia. Men destined to enduring fame were there — among them, George Washington and Patrick Henry from Virginia and John and Samuel Adams from Massachusetts. Every shade of opinion was represented but the majority favored compromise.

Under the influence of the moderate party Congress drew up a declaration of American rights and stated in temperate language the grievances of the colonists. It praised Massachusetts for opposing British measures and promised her the support of all sections. In an address to King George and another to the people of England, the Congress denied that it was seeking independence but in the same breath it attacked the policies pursued by the British government.

The Non-Importation Agreement. The Congress did not rest however with professions of faith and with petitions. It took a revolutionary step. It decided to block the importation of British goods into America, and the enforcement of this boycott

134

it placed in the hands of local "committees of safety and inspection" to be elected by the qualified voters. Thus the Congress threw itself athwart British law. It made a rule to bind all Americans to this course and arranged for this rule to be carried into effect by American officers. It set up a state within the British state and a test for American loyalty. Colonists, who up to this moment had been wavering, at last had to choose one authority or the other. They were for the boycott or they were against it. They either bought English goods or they did not. In the spirit of the toast — "May Britain be wise and America be free" — the first Continental Congress adjourned in October, having appointed the tenth of the following May for the meeting of a second Congress, should necessity require.

Lord North's "Olive Branch." Now the mother country was thoroughly aroused. When the report of the action of the American Congress reached England, the efforts of Pitt and Burke to secure a repeal of the obnoxious laws were simply howled down. All they could wring from the prime minister, Lord North, was a set of "conciliatory resolutions" proposing to relieve from taxation any colony that would assume its share of imperial defense and vote money to support the local officers of the Crown. And this "olive branch" was accompanied by a clear-cut resolution assuring the king that Parliament would back him up to the limit in suppressing the rebellion and by the Restraining Act of March 30, 1775, which in effect forbade all commerce with New England.

Bloodshed at Lexington and Concord (April 19, 1775). Meanwhile the royal officers in Massachusetts were watchful in upholding the king's government. General Gage, hearing that military stores had been collected at Concord, dispatched a small force from Boston to seize them. By this act he kindled the conflict he had sought to avoid. At Lexington, on the road to Concord, occurred the "little thing" that produced "the great event." An unexpected collision between British soldiers and American minutemen — a collision beyond the deliberate purpose of any person — transferred the contest from the forum to the battlefield.

The Second Continental Congress. Though blood had now been shed and war was actually at hand, the second Continental

Congress, which met at Philadelphia in May, 1775, still acted as if it thought that a peaceful solution was possible. It petitioned the king to use his influence in preventing the horrors of civil war. On the last day of July it made a calm but positive answer to Lord North's offer of conciliation; it declared that his plan was unsatisfactory because it did not renounce the right to tax and did not repeal the offensive acts of Parliament. But the Congress was still ready to negotiate on proper terms.

[3]

A PROCLAMATION.

By His **EXCELLENCY,**

The Honorable WILLIAM HOWE,

Major-General and Commander in Chief of all His Majefty's Forces within the Colonies laying on the Atlantic Ocean, from *Nova-Scotia* to *Weft-Florida* inclufive, &c. &c. &c.

WHEREAS it is become the indifpenfable Duty of every loyal and faithful Citizen, to contribute all in his Power for the Prefervation of Order and good Government within the Town of *Bofton* :

I DO hereby recommend, that the Inhabitants do immediately affociate themfelves, to be formed into Companies under proper Officers, felected by me, from among the Affociators, to be folely employed within the Precincts of the Town, and for the Purpofes abovementioned.

THAT this Affociation be opened in the Council Chamber, under the Direction of The Honorable PETER OLIVER, FOSTER HUTCHINSON and WILLIAM BROWN, Efquires, on Monday the thirtieth Day of October, 1775, and continued for four Days following, that no One may plead Ignorance of the fame.

OUT of the Number of Perfons voluntarily entering into this Affociation, all fuch as are able to difcharge the Duty required of them, fhall be properly Armed, and an Allowance of Fuel and Provifions be made to thofe requiring the fame, equal to what is iffued to His Majefty's Troops within the Garrifon.

GIVEN at Head-Quarters in Bofton, *this Twenty-eighth Day of October,* 1775.

Courtesy of the New York Public Library

GENERAL HOWE'S PEACE AND ORDER PROCLAMATION FOR BOSTON

Force, the British Answer. Just as the representatives of America were about to present the last petition of the Congress to the king on August 23, 1775, George III issued a proclamation of rebellion. This announcement declared that the colonists, "misled by dangerous and ill-designing men," were in a state of insurrection; it called on the civil and military powers to bring "the traitors to justice"; and it threatened with "condign punishment the authors, perpetrators, and abettors of such traitorous designs." It closed with the usual prayer: "God save the king." Later in the year Parliament passed a law intended to stop all trade and intercourse with America. It was useless for the Continental Congress to say anything more. Force was also America's answer.

AMERICAN INDEPENDENCE

Drifting into War. Indeed war had been foreseen and preparations made for it. Although the Congress had not given up all hope of compromise in the spring of 1775, it had definitely resolved to defend American rights by arms if necessary. It transformed the militiamen who had assembled near Boston after the battle of Lexington into a Continental army and selected Washington as commander-in-chief. It took upon itself the powers of a government, prepared to raise money, wage war, and carry on diplomatic relations with foreign countries.

Events followed thick and fast. On June 17, the American militia, by its stubborn defense of Bunker Hill, showed that it could make British regulars pay dearly for all they got. On July 3 Washington took command of the army at Cambridge. In January, 1776, after bitter disappointments in drumming up recruits for its army in England, Scotland, and Ireland, the British government made a contract with the Landgrave of Hesse-Cassel in Germany to hire thousands of soldiers and many pieces of cannon for use in America. This was the crowning insult to America, in the opinion of all friends of the colonies on both sides of the water at the time. And long afterward the English historian, Lecky, wrote of the bargain: "The conduct of England in hiring German mercenaries to subdue the essentially English population beyond the Atlantic made reconciliation hopeless and independence inevitable." The news of this deal in alien soldiers had scarcely reached America when there ran all down the coast the thrilling story that General Washington had taken Boston, on March 17, 1776, compelling the British commander, Lord Howe, to sail away with his entire army and many refugees for Halifax.

The Growth of Public Sentiment in Favor of Independence. Slowly and against their desires, prudent and honorable men, who dreaded with sincere horror the thought of revolution, were now drawn into the path that led to separation from England. In all parts of the country and among all classes, that question was being debated. "American independence," as the historian Bancroft says, "was not an act of sudden passion nor the work of one man or one assembly. It had been discussed in every part of the country by farmers and merchants, by mechanics and planters, by the fishermen along the coast and the backwoodsmen of the west; in town meetings and from the pulpit; at social gatherings and around the camp fires; in county conventions and conferences or committees; in colonial congresses and assemblies."

Paine's "Common Sense." In the midst of this ferment of opinion, a bold and eloquent pamphleteer, Thomas Paine, broke in upon the debating public with a program for absolute independence, without fears and without apologies. In the early days of 1776 he issued the first of his popular tracts, "Common Sense," which was a passionate attack upon the British Crown and an equally passionate plea for American liberty. Casting aside the language of petition with which Americans had hitherto addressed George III, Paine went to the other extreme and assailed him in violent words. He condemned monarchy itself as a system which had laid the world "in blood and ashes." Instead of praising the English constitution under which colonists had been claiming their rights, he brushed it aside as absurd and oppressive.

Having thus renounced loyalty to the old order, Paine went straight to the argument for immediate separation from Great Britain. There was no practical interest, he insisted, which should bind the colonies to the mother country. On the contrary allegiance to her had been responsible for the many wars in which they had been involved. Reasons of trade also favored independence. "Our corn will fetch its price in any market in Europe and our imported goods must be paid for, buy them where we will." As to matters of government, "it is not in the power of Britain to do this continent justice; the business of it will soon be too weighty and intricate to be managed with any tolerable degree of convenience by a power so distant from us and so very ignorant of us."

There was accordingly no alternative for America. "Everything that is right or natural pleads for separation. The blood of the slain, the weeping voice of nature cries ''tis time to part.' . . . Arms, the last resort, must decide the contest; the appeal was the

choice of the king and the continent hath accepted the challenge.
. . . The sun never shone on a cause of greater worth. 'Tis not
the affair of a city, a county, a province, or a kingdom, but of a
continent. . . . 'Tis not the concern of a day, a year, or an age;
posterity is involved in the contest and will be more or less affected
to the end of time by the pro-
ceedings now. Now is the
seed-time of Continental
union, faith, and honor. . . .
O! ye that love mankind! Ye
that dare oppose not only the
tyranny, but the tyrant, stand
forth. . . . Let names of
Whig and Tory be extinct.
Let none other be heard
among us than those of a good
citizen, an open and resolute
friend, and a virtuous supporter of the rights of mankind and of the free and independent states of America."
More than 100,000 copies of
Paine's pamphlet were scat-

From an old print

THOMAS PAINE

tered broadcast over the country, and as patriots read it they
exclaimed with Washington: "Sound doctrine and unanswerable
reason!"

The Drift of Events toward Independence. Official support
for the idea of independence soon began to come from many
quarters. On the tenth of February, 1776, Gadsden, in the convention of South Carolina, advocated a new constitution for that
colony and absolute independence for all America. The convention balked at a thoroughgoing revolution, but went halfway
by abolishing the royal administration and establishing a complete
plan of self-government. The next month, on April 12, its neighbor, North Carolina, took the daring step from which others
shrank. It empowered its representatives in the Continental
Congress to join the delegates of the other colonies in declaring

American independence. Rhode Island and Massachusetts quickly announced their approval. On May 15 the convention of Virginia instructed its delegates at Philadelphia to propose independence and to cast the vote of Virginia in favor of it.

Meanwhile the subject of independence was constantly being raised in the Continental Congress. "Are we rebels?" inquired Wythe of Virginia during a debate in February. "No: we must declare ourselves a free people." Others hesitated and spoke of waiting for the arrival of peace commissioners from England. "Is not America already independent?" asked Samuel Adams a few weeks later. "Why not then declare it?" Still there was uncertainty and delegates avoided the direct word. A few more weeks elapsed. At last on May 10 Congress resolved that the authority of the British Crown in America must come to an end and advised the colonies to set up state governments of their own.

Independence Declared. The way was fully prepared therefore when on June 7 the Virginia delegates in the Continental Congress moved that "these united colonies are and of right ought to be free and independent states." A committee was chosen at once to draft a formal document setting forth the reasons for the act, and on July 2 all the states save New York went on record in favor of breaking their political connection with Great Britain. On July 4, Jefferson's draft of the Declaration of Independence, changed in some details, was adopted. Couriers swiftly carried the news to the uttermost hamlet and farm. A new nation was announcing its arrival to the powers of the world.

To some documents is given immortality and the Declaration of Independence is among them. American patriotism is forever associated with it; but patriotism alone does not make it immortal. Neither does the vigor of its language or its summary of American grievances against King George give it a secure place in the records of time. The secret of its greatness lies in the simple fact that it is one of the landmarks in the history of a political ideal which for three centuries has been taking form and spreading throughout the earth, challenging kings and princes, shaking down thrones and aristocracies, and breaking the armies of irresponsible power on battle fields. That ideal, now so familiar, then so novel, is

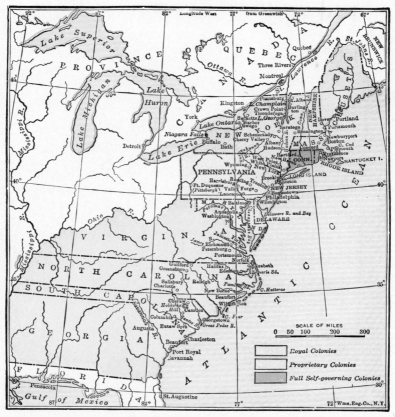

THE COLONIES OF NORTH AMERICA AT THE TIME OF THE DECLARATION
OF INDEPENDENCE

summed up in the single sentence: "Governments derive their just powers from the consent of the governed."

Written in a "decent respect to the opinions of mankind" to set forth the causes of the separation from Britain, the Declaration of Independence gave a long list of "abuses and usurpations" which had led the colonists to throw off the government of George III. That section of the Declaration has passed into "ancient" history and is seldom read. It is the part formulating a new basis for government and giving a new dignity to the common people that has become celebrated in the Old World as in the New — indeed in the Orient also.

In the more enduring passages there are four fundamental ideas which, from the standpoint of the old system of government, were the essence of revolution: (1) all men are created equal and are endowed by their Creator with certain inalienable rights, including life, liberty, and the pursuit of happiness; (2) the purpose of government is to secure these rights; (3) governments derive their just powers from the consent of the governed; (4) whenever any form of government becomes destructive of these ends it is the right of the people to alter or abolish it and institute new government, laying its foundations on such principles and organizing its powers in such form as to them shall seem most likely to effect their safety and happiness. Here was the prelude to the drama of modern democracy — a thrust at every form of political privilege not founded on popular consent.

THE ESTABLISHMENT OF GOVERNMENT AND THE NEW ALLEGIANCE

The Committees of Correspondence. As soon as debate had passed into a war for independence, the patriots found it necessary to set up their own governments. This was readily done, for they had the means at hand in town meetings, provincial legislatures, and committees of correspondence. The leading agencies of the Revolution were in fact the committees — small, local, unofficial groups of patriots formed to exchange views and arouse public sentiment. As early as November, 1772, such a committee had been created in Boston under the leadership of Samuel Adams. It held regular meetings, sent emissaries to neighboring towns, and carried on a campaign of education in the doctrines of liberty.

Upon local groups like the Boston committee were built county committees and then the larger colonial committees, congresses, and conventions, all representing those Americans who favored revolution. Finally upon these colonial assemblies was built the Continental Congress, the forerunner of union under the Articles of Confederation. Thus revolutionary government was set up within the British empire in America.

State Constitutions Framed. With the rise of these new assemblies of the people, the old colonial governments broke down. From the royal provinces the king's governor, judges, and high officers fled in haste, and patriots were chosen in their stead. The agents of proprietors likewise surrendered to popular will. Before the expiration of the year 1776, Virginia, New Jersey, Pennsylvania, Delaware, Maryland, Georgia, and New York had drafted their own constitutions as states, not as colonies uncertain of their destinies. Connecticut and Rhode Island, holding that their charters were equal to their needs, merely renounced their allegiance to the king and kept their old plans of government. South Carolina, which had drafted a temporary scheme early in 1776, drew up a new and more complete constitution in 1778. Two years later Massachusetts with much debate put into force its fundamental law, which in most of its essentials remains unchanged to-day.

In their broad outlines the first state constitutions followed colonial models. For the royal governor was substituted a governor or president chosen usually by the legislature; but in two instances, New York and Massachusetts, by popular vote. To take the place of the provincial council there was created a senate, except in Georgia; while the lower house, or assembly, was continued almost without change — in Pennsylvania without any senate to check it. Restrictions on the suffrage, though lowered slightly in some states, were kept in force, thus limiting the vote to property owners and taxpayers. Moreover the new state constitutions generally provided that governors, senators, and representatives must likewise be men of means. Without effect did voteless mechanics of the towns demand the suffrage for their class.

Protests of a few women, like Mrs. John Adams of Massachusetts and Mrs. Henry Corbin of Virginia, against their exclusion from political rights were also treated as mild curiosities of no significance, although in New Jersey women were allowed to vote for many years on the same terms as men.

Without any exceptions the state constitutions abolished the signs and symbols of royal power, vested all authority in "the people," and set up republican governments, hence opening a new era in politics. Copies of these documents were translated into French and widely circulated in Europe. There they served as a guide and inspiration to the agitators who were soon to begin the democratic revolution in the Old World with the overthrow of the French monarchy.

The Articles of Confederation. It was relatively easy for the revolutionary leaders to make state constitutions, for they could use their colonial governments as models. It was another matter to draw up a plan for a national union. Before 1776 the general government of the thirteen colonies had centered in London, and Americans had taken little or no part in it. When that general government was cast off, therefore, only a few patriot leaders had been trained to coöperate on a national scale.

Furthermore there were great difficulties in the way of common action. All Americans did not have the same economic interests by any means; for example, commerce and manufacturing in the North called for one policy and the planting system of the South for another. Besides it was difficult to decide on the amount of taxes each colony should pay and the number of soldiers it should furnish for the army. To very real divisions of interest were added local pride, the desire of state and village politicians to uphold their provincial dignity, and the scarcity of men with a large outlook upon national enterprise.

Nevertheless necessity compelled the revolutionists to consider some sort of federation. The second Continental Congress had hardly opened its sessions when the wisest leaders began to urge the formation of a lasting union. As early as July, 1775, Congress resolved to take up the question, and Franklin, undaunted by the fate of his Albany plan of twenty years before, once more wrote a draft of a common constitution. Prolix and desultory debates followed and it was late in 1777 when the Congress laid the Articles of Confederation before the states for their approval. Jealousies again delayed action; not until the spring of 1781 did the last of the states, Maryland, agree to the Articles. This plan of union, though it was all that could be wrung from the states, provided for neither a president nor a system of federal courts. It created simply a Congress of delegates in which all the states had an equal voice and gave it the right to call upon the state legislatures for money and soldiers.

The Application of Tests of Allegiance. As the successive steps were taken in the direction of independence, the revolutionary leaders sought to discover who were for and who were against the new nation in the process of making — who were patriots and who were not. When the first Continental Congress agreed to boycott British goods, it provided that local committees should be elected from among the voters to enforce the rules. Before these committees people who bought British goods were summoned and warned or punished according to circumstances. As soon as the state constitutions were put into effect, similar organizations set to work in the same way to ferret out everybody who did not support the new order of things.

These agencies bearing different names in different sections were sometimes ruthless in dealing with American "loyalists" who stood fast by King George. They called upon all men to sign a paper declaring their allegiance to the patriot cause, frequently known as the "association test." Those who refused were promptly branded as outlaws, and some were thrown into jail. The prison camp in Connecticut at one time held the former governor of New Jersey and the mayor of New York. Thousands of outlaws were enrolled on "black lists" and carefully watched by their neighbors. The list of Pennsylvania alone contained the names of nearly five hundred eminent persons who were under suspicion. Loyalists who were bold enough to speak and write against the Revolution were suppressed and their pamphlets were burned. In many places, especially in the North, the property of the loyalists was confiscated and the proceeds applied to the uses of the Revolution.

The work of the official agencies for putting down "Tories" — another name given to loyalists — was sometimes coupled with mob violence. A few of them were hanged without trial, and others were tarred and feathered. One was placed upon a cake of ice and held there "until his loyalty to King George might cool." Whole families were driven out of their homes to find their way as best they could within the British lines or into Canada, where the British government gave them lands. Although General Washington warned the people against excesses, rough methods of dealing with Tories were sometimes defended on the ground that the war for independence was also a civil war.

From an old print

MOBBING THE TORIES

Patriots and Tories. Thus by one process or another those who were to be citizens of the new republic were separated from those who wished to remain subjects of King George. Just how many Americans favored independence and how many were loyal to the British monarchy there is no way of knowing. No popular vote was taken directly on the question of revolution and hence the exact size of the patriot and loyalist parties cannot be known. On the one side we have the testimony of the cautious John Adams to the effect that two-thirds of the people were for the American cause and not more than one-third opposed the Revolution at all stages.

On behalf of the loyalists extensive claims were sometimes made. Joseph Galloway, who had been a member of the first

Continental Congress and later fled to England, testified before a committee of Parliament in 1779 that not one-fifth of the American people favored revolution and that "many more than four-fifths of the people prefer a union with Great Britain upon constitutional principles to independence." At the same time General Robertson, who had lived in America twenty-four years, declared that "more than two-thirds of the people would prefer the king's government to the Congress' tyranny." In an address to the king in that year a committee of American loyalists asserted that "the number of Americans in his Majesty's army exceeded the number of troops enlisted by Congress to oppose them."

The Character of the Loyalists. When General Howe was forced out of Boston, more than a thousand people fled with him. This great company, we are told, "formed the aristocracy of the province by virtue of their official rank; of their dignified callings and professions; of their hereditary wealth and of their culture." An act of banishment passed by Massachusetts in 1778, listing over 300 Tories, "reads like the social register of the oldest and noblest families of New England," more than one out of five being graduates of Harvard College. The same was true of New York and Philadelphia; namely, that the leading loyalists were high officials of the old order, clergymen, and the wealthiest merchants.

Tories Carp at the Patriots. Tories who remained in America joined the British army by the thousands or in other ways aided the royal cause. Those who were skillful with the pen scored the patriots in editorials, rhymed satires, and political catechisms. They declared that the members of the revolutionary Congress were "obscure, pettifogging attorneys, bankrupt shopkeepers, outlawed smugglers, etc." The people and their leaders they called "wretched banditti . . . the refuse and dregs of mankind." The generals in the American army they sneered at as "men of rank and honor nearly on a par with those of the Congress."

Patriot Writers Arouse the National Spirit. Attacked by fierce Tory pamphleteers, patriot writers had to work hard at the task of keeping up revolutionary temper among the people. Moreover they had to combat the discouragements due to American misfortunes in the early days of the war. A terrible disaster befell

Generals Arnold and Montgomery in the winter of 1775 when they attempted to bring Canada into the revolution. All through 1776 ill-luck dogged Washington's steps as he was defeated on Long Island, driven out of New York City, beaten at Harlem Heights and White Plains, and forced across the Hudson River. These reverses were almost too great for the stoutest patriots.

But pamphleteers, preachers, and publicists rose to meet the national needs. John Witherspoon, provost of the College of New Jersey, forsook the classroom to write and speak for the patriot cause. Philip Freneau, the poet, flung taunts at the Tories and praised the spirit of liberty in many a stirring poem. Songs, ballads, plays, and satires flowed from the press in an unending stream. Fast days, battle anniversaries, and celebrations of important steps taken by Congress gave patriotic clergymen opportunities for revolutionary sermons. "Does Mr. Wiberd preach against oppression?" anxiously inquired John Adams in a letter to his wife. The answer was decisive. "The clergy of every denomination, not excepting the Episcopalian, thunder and lighten every Sabbath. They pray for Boston and Massachusetts. . . . They pray for the American army."

Thomas Paine's pen seldom rested. He had been with the troops of Washington when they retreated from Fort Lee and were harried from New Jersey into Pennsylvania. He knew the effect of such reverses on the army as well as on the public. So in December, 1776, he made a second startling appeal to his country in a pamphlet entitled "The Crisis," the first part of which he had written while defeat and gloom were all about him. This tract was an anxious cry for unstinted support of the Revolution. "These are the times that try men's souls," he opened. "The summer soldier and the sunshine patriot will, in this crisis, shrink from the service of his country; but he that stands it now deserves the love and thanks of men and women." Paine poured out his scorn on the Tories, charging them with "servile, slavish, self-interested fear." He pointed out the shortcomings of the militia and called for a regular army of trained men enlisted for the duration of the war. He denied the charge that the retreat through New Jersey was a disaster and he promised victory soon. "By perseverance and fortitude," he insisted, "we have the prospect of a glorious issue; by cowardice and submission the sad choice of a variety of evils — a ravaged country, a depopulated city, habitations without safety and slavery without hope. . . . Look on this picture and weep over it." His ringing appeal was followed by another and another until the long contest was over.

How the War of Independence Was Waged

The Two Phases of the War. The war which started with the battle of Lexington on April 19, 1775, and closed with the surrender of Cornwallis at Yorktown on October 19, 1781, passed through two distinct phases — the first lasting until the treaty of alliance with France in 1778, and the second until the end of the struggle. During the first phase, the fighting was mainly in the North. Its outstanding features were the evacuation of Boston by the British, Washington's march to New York, the expulsion of American forces from New York, their retreat through New Jersey, the battle of Trenton, the seizure of Philadelphia by the British (September, 1777), the terrible winter at Valley Forge, the invasion of New York by Burgoyne, and his capture at Saratoga in October, 1777.

The final phase of the war, opening with the treaty of alliance with France on February 6, 1778, was confined chiefly to the Middle states, the West, and the South. In the first sphere of warfare the leading actions were the withdrawal of the British from Philadelphia, the battle of Monmouth, and the prevention of British excursions from New York City by deploying American forces from Morristown, New Jersey, up to West Point. In the West, George Rogers Clark, by his famous march into the Illinois country, secured Kaskaskia and Vincennes and laid a strong grip on the country between the Ohio and the Great Lakes. In the South, the British won many successes. They captured Savannah, conquered Georgia, restored the royal governor, seized Charleston in 1780, defeated Gates at Camden, and overran South Carolina, meeting severe reverses only at Cowpens and King's Mountain.

Then came the closing scenes as the British general, Cornwallis, began the last of his Southern operations. He pursued General Greene far into North Carolina, clashed with him at Guilford Court

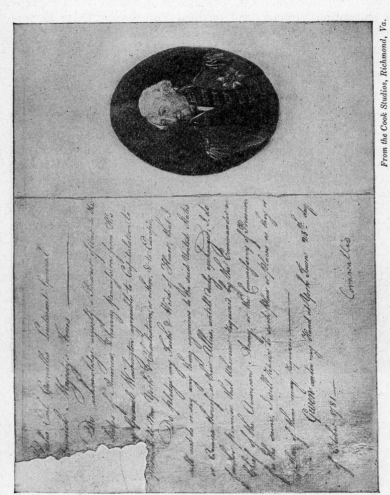

From the Cook Studios, Richmond, Va.

PAROLE OF LORD CORNWALLIS

House, retired to the coast, took charge of British forces engaged in plundering Virginia, and fortified Yorktown. There he was penned up by the French fleet from the sea and by the combined French and American troops on land. Caught in a trap, he was forced to surrender in the autumn of 1781.

The Geographical Aspects of the War. For the British the very land on which the war was fought offered many special

Courtesy of The Metropolitan Museum of Art

THE SURRENDER AT SARATOGA
From a painting by Fauvel.

obstacles. From first to last the theater of operations extended from Massachusetts to Georgia, a distance of almost a thousand miles. It was nearly three thousand miles from the main base of supplies in England, and behind the coast line was a seemingly endless wilderness into which Americans could retreat. Though the British held New York City until the close of the war, took Philadelphia and kept it until forced out by the French fleet, captured and occupied both Savannah and Charleston, they could not win by the mere conquest of ports.

Only a small portion of the American people lived in coastal towns. Countrymen in the interior were in no way dependent upon commerce for subsistence. They lived on the produce of the soil, not on the profits of trade, and this very fact gave them strength to endure. Whenever the British ventured far from the ports of entry, they met reverses. Burgoyne was compelled to surrender at Saratoga because he was surrounded and cut off from his base of supplies. As soon as the British ventured far from Charleston, they were harassed and worried by guerrilla warriors under Marion, Sumter, and Pickens. Cornwallis could technically defeat Greene at Guilford in the western part of North Carolina; but he could not grip the inland region he had invaded. Living by their own labor, holding the interior to which their armies could readily retreat, supplied mainly from native resources, the Americans could not be hemmed in, penned up, and destroyed by one fell blow or even by a series of battles.

The Sea Power. The British of course made good use of their fleet in cutting off American trade, but control of the sea did not seriously affect the United States at that time. It was still primarily an agricultural country and the ruin of its commerce was not a vital matter. It made little difference to a nation fighting for its very life, if silks, tea, and chinaware were cut off by the British blockade.

Moreover it had to make a virtue of necessity, for British supremacy on water could not be broken by American sea captains like John Paul Jones and John Barry, no matter how brilliant their exploits. They demonstrated the skill of American sailors and their courage as fighting men; they caused great losses to British shipping; but they did not dethrone the mistress of the seas. No more effective, though equally brave, were the deeds of the hundreds of privateers and minor captains who overhauled British supply ships and kept British merchantmen in constant anxiety. Not until the French fleet was thrown into the scale did the British have to reckon seriously with the perils of maritime disaster.

Commanding Officers. On the score of military leadership it is difficult to compare the contending forces in the revolutionary contest. There is no doubt that all the British commanders were

men of experience in fighting. Sir William Howe had served in
America during the French War and was widely known as a
competent officer. Nevertheless he loved ease, society, and good
living, and his failure to overwhelm Washington by sallies from
New York and Philadelphia destroyed every shred of his military
reputation. General John Burgoyne, to whom was given the task
of cutting a way into New York from Canada, had likewise seen
service in the French War both in America and Europe. He was
however more of an actor than an officer and, after the surrender
of his army in 1777, he spent his time largely in writing plays and
poetry. Sir Henry Clinton, who directed the campaign which
ended in the capture of Charleston in 1780, had "learned his
trade on the continent" and was regarded as a man of understanding in military matters. Lord Cornwallis, whose achievements at Camden and Guilford were blotted out by his surrender
at Yorktown, had seen service in the Seven Years' War and had
undoubted talents which he afterward displayed with great credit
to himself in India. Though none of the British generals were
perhaps men of first-rate ability, they all had training and experience to guide them.

On the other side Americans had a tower of strength in their
George Washington. He had long been interested in military
strategy and had tested his coolness under fire during the clashes
with the French nearly twenty years before. He had no doubts
about the justice of his cause, such as plagued some of the British
generals and put a drag on their activity. Stern, dogged, patient,
he drove straight ahead amid victory and defeat. "What held the
patriot forces together in the dark hour of the Revolution?"
This question is answered by Albert J. Beveridge in his *Life of
John Marshall:* "George Washington and he alone. Had he died
or been seriously disabled the Revolution would have ended. . . .
Washington was the soul of the American cause. Washington
was the government. Washington was the Revolution." The
delays of Congress in furnishing men and supplies, the selfishness
of civilians, who lived at ease while the army starved, the intrigues
of army officers against him, such as the "Conway Cabal," the
cowardice of Lee at Monmouth, even the treason of Benedict

PORTRAIT OF GEORGE WASHINGTON BY C. W. PEALE

THE SURRENDER OF CORNWALLIS
Painted by John Trumbull

Arnold, did not shake his iron will or his firm resolve to see the war through to the end. The weight of Washington's moral force was so immense that no mere study of his "strategy" reveals the secret of the man or his place in American history.

Of the generals who served under him, none could really be called experienced military men when the war opened. Benedict Arnold, unhappy traitor but brave and daring soldier, was a druggist, bookseller, and shipowner at New Haven when the news of Lexington called him to battle. Horatio Gates was looked upon as a "seasoned soldier" because he had entered the British army as a youth, had been wounded at Braddock's memorable defeat, and had served with credit during the Seven Years' War; but he was an outstanding failure of the Revolution. The triumph over Burgoyne was the work of other men; and his crushing reverse at Camden put an end to his military reputation. Nathanael Greene was a Rhode Island farmer and smith without military practice when he saw that war was coming; in a hurry he read Caesar's *Commentaries* and took up the sword. Francis Marion was a shy and modest planter of South Carolina whose sole passage at arms had been a brief but desperate brush with the Indians ten or twelve years earlier. Daniel Morgan, one of the heroes of Cowpens, had been a teamster with Braddock's army and had seen some fighting during the French and Indian War, but he had little or no knowledge of military tactics. John Sullivan was a successful lawyer at Durham, New Hampshire, and a major in the local militia when duty called him to lay down his briefs and buckle on some armor. Anthony Wayne was a Pennsylvania farmer and land surveyor who, on hearing the clash of arms, read a few books on war, raised a regiment, and offered himself for service. Such is the story of the chief American military leaders, and it is typical of them all. Some had seen fighting with the French and Indians, but none of them had seen warfare on a large scale. Courage, natural ability, and quickness of mind they had in abundance, and in battles such as were fought during the Revolution those qualities counted heavily in the balance.

Foreign Officers in American Service. Native genius was soon supplemented by military talent from beyond the seas — by soldiers who came for adventure, in hope of reward, or to aid in what they believed was a good cause. Baron Steuben, well schooled in the iron régime of Frederick the Great, King of Prussia, joined Washington at Valley Forge, and day after day drilled and maneuvered the men, laughing and cursing as he turned raw country boys into regular soldiers. From France came young Lafayette and the stern DeKalb; from Poland came Pulaski and Kosciusko — all educated in the arts of war as waged in Europe and fitted for leadership as well as for teaching recruits. Lafayette hurried over early in 1776 in a ship of his own, bringing several other trained officers, and he clung loyally to the American cause until the end, sharing all the hardships of army life. Pulaski fell at the siege of Savannah and DeKalb at Camden. Kosciusko survived the American war to fight in vain a few years later in Poland's war for independence against Russia. To these distinguished foreigners who freely threw in their lot with the revolutionists was due much of that spirit and discipline which fitted volunteers and militiamen to cope with British power.

The Soldiers. As far as the British soldiers are concerned, their annals are short and simple. The regulars from the standing army who were sent over at the opening of the contest, the recruits drummed up by special efforts in Britain, and the thousands of Hessians bought outright by King George gave little trouble in matters of discipline. These common soldiers were far away from home and enlisted for the duration of the war. Most of them had received some training and many of them had been in battle before. They fought bravely, as the records of Bunker Hill, Brandywine, and Monmouth show. Though many a private and subordinate officer of British blood and indeed some of the high officers did not like warring on their kin, they obeyed orders.

The Americans, on the other hand, while they fought for their hearths, were lacking at first in the training and experience of regular troops. When the war broke out, there were no common preparations to meet it. There was no continental army; there were only local bands of militiamen. Moreover these militiamen were all volunteers serving for a short time, unaccustomed to severe discipline and long campaigns. In fact many of them behaved about as they pleased. "The militia," lamented Washington, "come in, you cannot tell how; go, you cannot tell where; consume your provisions; exhaust your stores; and leave you at last at a critical moment."

Again and again Washington begged the Congress to provide for an army of regulars enlisted for the entire war, thoroughly trained, and paid according to some definite plan. But the civilians in the Congress were afraid that a standing army might set up a dictatorship, and it took much persuasion to make them grant half pay to all officers and a bonus to all privates who served until the end of the war. Even this scheme, which Washington thought far short of justice to the soldiers, did not produce quick results. It was near the close of the conflict before he had an army of well-disciplined veterans capable of meeting the British on an equal footing.

Though there were times when short-term volunteers did valiant fighting, it is due to truth to deny the time-honored tradition that a few "embattled farmers" easily downed the British regulars. They did nothing of the sort. With the victories of Bennington, Trenton, Saratoga, and Yorktown must be listed the defeats of Bunker Hill, Long Island, White Plains, Germantown, and Camden. "To bring men to be well acquainted with the duties of a soldier," wrote Washington, "requires time. . . . To expect the same service from raw and undisciplined recruits as from veteran soldiers is to expect what never did and perhaps never will happen."

How the War Was Won. Then how did the American army actually win the war? For one thing there were delays and blunders on the part of English generals who in 1775 and 1776 dallied in Boston and New York when they might have destroyed the scattered bands that made up the American army. "Nothing but the supineness or folly of the enemy could have saved us," said Washington in 1780.

Still it is fair to say that this delay was not all due to laziness of the British generals on the spot. Some of the ministers behind them in London believed that a large part of the colonists were really loyal to King George and that fighting would merely drive them over to Washington's side. Victory by masterly inactivity therefore seemed to them better than conquest — the slighter the wounds the quicker the healing. By the time the British awoke to the seriousness of the struggle, seasoned officers and troops from France were helping the American cause and the Americans themselves had learned many things about the conduct of campaigns. Moreover from the outset the British had trouble in getting supplies. Their soldiers could not forage with the skill of patriot militiamen, for they were foreigners in unfamiliar territory. Besides, the oversea voyages were always hazardous and doubly so after the warships of France joined American privateers in preying on British supply boats. The British were in fact worn down by a nagging guerrilla war and overcome on two important occasions by superior forces — at Saratoga and Yorktown.

MRS. MERCY OTIS WARREN

Women and the War. Throughout the Revolution patriot women worked hard for the American cause. When the dispute was limited to arguments they played a part in creating public sentiment for freedom. Mrs. Elizabeth Timothee, for example, founded in Charleston in 1773 a newspaper to champion the side of the province. In Massachusetts Mrs. Mercy Warren, the sister of James Otis, early begged her countrymen to rest their case upon their natural rights and later urged the leaders to stand fast in defending American liberties. While John Adams was still doubtful about the proper course for the Continental Congress, his wife was writing letters to him declaring her faith in "independency."

When war came down upon the country, women helped in every way. With a tireless pen Mrs. Warren wrote American plays and satires to offset loyalist propaganda. Almost every revolutionary leader had a wife or daughter who rendered service in the "second line of defense." Mrs. Washington managed the plantation while the General was at the front; she even went North to face the rigors of the awful winter at Valley Forge — an inspiration to her husband and his men. The daughter of Benjamin Franklin, Mrs. Sarah Bache, while her father was pleading the American cause as minister to France, organized the women of Pennsylvania to make clothes and collect other supplies for the soldiers. Near the firing line women were to be found, aiding the wounded, hauling powder, and carrying dispatches at the peril of their lives.

The work of women in furnishing food and clothing to soldiers and civilians was a necessary part of winning the war. They plowed, planted, and harvested crops. Experts in spinning and weaving, they now made a still larger proportion of the cloth used in America. And for their war work, the women of the Revolution were praised by high authorities on more than one occasion. They were given medals and public testimonials. Washington paid tribute to them for the encouragement and material aid which they had rendered to independence.

The Finances of the Revolution

When the Revolution opened, there were thirteen little treasuries in America but no common treasury, and from first to last the Congress was in the position of a beggar rather than a sovereign ruler. Having no authority to lay and collect taxes directly and knowing the dislike of the people for taxation anyway, it resorted mainly to loans and paper money to finance the war. "Do you think," cried one of the delegates, "that I will consent to load my constituents with taxes when we can send to the printer and get a wagon load of money, one quire of which will pay for the whole?"

Paper Money and Loans. Acting on this curious kind of reasoning, the Congress issued in June, 1776, two million dollars in bills of credit to be redeemed by the states on the basis of their respective populations. Other issues quickly followed. In all about $241,000,000 of Continental paper was printed, to which the several states added nearly $210,000,000 of their own notes. Then came interest-bearing bonds which were sold to patriots in ever increasing quantities. Several millions were also borrowed from France and small sums from Holland and Spain. Property of Tories was seized and sold, bringing in about $16,000,000.

Courtesy of the New York Public Library

CONTINENTAL CURRENCY — A FIVE-DOLLAR BILL DATED MAY 9, 1776, AND SIGNED BY W. MASTERS

Begging letters were sent to the states asking them to raise money for the Continental treasury, but the states, having vexations of their own, gave slight heed.

Inflation and Depreciation. As paper money flowed from the press, it fell rapidly in value until by 1779 the purchasing power of a dollar was worth only two or three cents in gold or silver. Attempts were made by the Congress and by the states to compel people to accept the notes at face value; but laws could not make water flow uphill. At once gambling in bonds and paper money began and great fortunes were made by lucky speculators, while the patriot army, half clothed, was freezing at Valley Forge. "Speculation, peculation, engrossing, forestalling," exclaimed Washington, "afford too many melancholy proofs of the decay of public virtue. Nothing, I am convinced, but the depreciation of our currency . . . aided by stock jobbing and party dissensions has fed the hopes of the enemy."

The Patriot Financiers. When the efforts of Congress failed to bring in enough money, private citizens shouldered the burdens. Haym Salomon, a merchant of Philadelphia, supplied members of Congress, including Madison, Jefferson, and Monroe, and army officers like Lee and Steuben with cash for their daily needs. All together he lent more than half a million dollars to the American cause, most of which was never paid back. Another Philadelphia merchant, Robert Morris, won for himself the name of the "patriot financier" because he labored night and day to find the funds to meet the bills which poured in upon the bankrupt government. When his own money gave out, he borrowed from his friends. Expert in the handling of merchandise, he set up warehouses at strategic points to furnish supplies to the troops, and in this way showed administrative as well as financial talents.

ROBERT MORRIS

Women organized "drives" for money, gave their plate and their jewels, and collected contributions from door to door. Farmers took certificates in return for their produce, and soldiers saw many a pay day pass without yielding them a penny. Thus by the issuance of paper notes, the floating of loans, borrowings in Europe, and the impressment of supplies, the Congress staggered through the Revolution like a pauper who knows not how his next meal is to be secured but is relieved at each crisis by a kindly fate.

THE DIPLOMACY OF THE REVOLUTION

Honor to the soldiers and civilians who waged the struggle at home must be shared with the American ministers in foreign countries who sought support there for the Revolution. The importance of winning friends in Europe was fully understood by leaders in the Continental Congress. They knew about the long struggle between Spain, France, Holland, and England over colonies and trade; and they were acquainted with the sympathies, interests, and prejudices of European nations and their rulers. So it was natural for them to seek money, supplies, and even military assistance from former enemies of Great Britain. To look after this delicate business, they created a secret committee on foreign correspondence as early as 1775 and prepared to send agents abroad.

American Agents Sent Abroad. Having heard that France was interested in the American issue, the Congress in March, 1776, sent a commissioner to Paris, Silas Deane of Connecticut, often styled the "first American diplomat." Later in the year a form of treaty to be presented to foreign powers was drafted, and Franklin, Arthur Lee, and Deane were selected as American representatives at the court of "His Most Christian Majesty the King of France." In 1779 John Jay of New York was chosen minister to Spain; John Adams was sent to Holland; and other agents were dispatched to Florence, Vienna, and Berlin. The representative selected for St. Petersburg spent two fruitless years there, "ignored by the court, living in obscurity and experiencing nothing but humiliation and failure." Frederick the Great, king of Prussia, was sympathetic but, fearing England's command of the sea, he refused to give direct aid to the Americans.

Early French Interest. The great diplomatic triumph of the Revolution was won at Paris, and Benjamin Franklin was the hero of the occasion, although many events prepared the way for his victory. Before the arrival of any representative, Louis XVI's foreign minister, Count de Vergennes, had brought to the attention of the king the opportunity offered by the war between England and her colonies. He showed Louis how France could "reduce the power and greatness of England" — the Empire that had forced upon her a humiliating peace in 1763, "at the price of our possessions, of our commerce, and our credit in the Indies, at the price of Canada, Louisiana, Isle Royale, Acadia, and Senegal." Equally successful with Vergennes in gaining the king's interest was a curious French adventurer, Beaumarchais, a man of wealth, a lover of music, and the author of two popular plays, "Figaro" and "The Barber of Seville." These two men were already urging upon the king secret aid for America when Deane appeared on the scene. Shortly after his arrival they quietly made plans to furnish money, clothing, powder, and other supplies to the United States through a private company, although official requests for such help were officially refused by the French government.

Franklin at Paris. When Franklin reached Paris, he was received only in private by the king's minister, Vergennes. The French people however made manifest their affection for the "plain republican" in "his full dress suit of spotted Manchester velvet." He was known among men of letters as an author, a scientist, and a philosopher of exceptional ability. His "Poor Richard" had thrice been translated into French and was scattered in numerous editions throughout the kingdom. People of all ranks — ministers, ladies at court, philosophers, peasants, and stable boys — knew of Franklin and wished him good fortune in his mission. The queen, Marie Antoinette, fated to lose her head in a French revolution, played with fire by encouraging "our dear republican."

For the king of France however the affair was no jest. England resented the presence of this "traitor" in Paris, and Louis had to be careful about plunging into another war that might also end in defeat. Moreover the early period of Franklin's stay in Paris was a dark hour for the American Revolution. Washington's brilliant exploit in surprising the British at Trenton on Christmas night, 1776, and the battle with Cornwallis at Princeton had been followed by the disaster at Brandywine, the loss of Philadelphia, the defeat at Germantown, and the retirement to Valley Forge for the winter of 1777–78. New York City and Philadelphia — two strategic ports — were in British hands; the Hudson and Delaware rivers were blocked; and General Burgoyne with his British troops was on the way down through the heart of northern New York, cutting New England off from the rest of the colonies. No wonder the French king was cautious. Then in a flash the unexpected happened. Burgoyne, hemmed in on all sides by the American forces, his foraging parties beaten back, his supplies cut off, surrendered on October 17, 1777, to General Gates, who had superseded General Schuyler in time to receive the honor.

Treaties of Alliance and Commerce (1778). News of this triumph, placed by historians among the fifteen decisive battles of the world, reached Franklin one night early in December while he and some friends sat gloomily at dinner. Beaumarchais, who was with him, saw at once the meaning of the American victory and set off to the court of Versailles with such haste that he upset his coach and dislocated his arm. At last the king and his ministers were convinced that the hour had come to aid the Americans. In February, 1778, they signed treaties of commerce and concord with the United States. France now frankly recognized American independence, made an alliance with the new republic to guarantee it, agreed to join in military and naval operations on Great Britain, and then declared war on King George.

Spain and Holland Involved. Within a few months Spain, hoping to drive the British out of Gibraltar, joined the concert of nations against England. Then Holland, after protesting against British interference with her ships on the high seas, united with Spain, France, and America in preying upon British commerce. To all this trouble for England was added the danger of a revolt in Ireland, where the flame of independence was also burning.

The British Offer Terms to America. Seeing that France was about to join America in a common war on the British Empire, Lord North proposed, in February, 1778, a renewal of amicable negotiations with the revolutionary colonists. By a solemn enactment Parliament declared that it did not intend to exercise the right of imposing taxes within the colonies; and authorized the sending of commissioners to America to arrange terms of peace and reunion. A truce was to be made, pardons granted, objectionable laws suspended, and the old imperial constitution, as it stood before the opening of hostilities, restored to full vigor. It was too late. Events had taken the destiny of America out of the hands of British commissioners and diplomats.

Effects of French Aid. The French alliance brought ships of war, huge sums of gold and silver, loads of supplies, and a large body of trained soldiers to the aid of the Americans. Timely as was this help, it meant no sudden change in the fortunes of war. It is true that the British evacuated Philadelphia in the summer following the alliance, and that Washington's troops, leaving Valley Forge, inflicted a heavy blow on the British at Monmouth. But the disloyal conduct of General Charles Lee prevented a triumph at Monmouth and the recovery of Philadelphia was more than offset by the treason of Benedict Arnold, by the loss of Savannah and Charleston (1780), and by the defeat of Gates at Camden.

In fact the full effect of the French alliance was not felt until 1781, when Cornwallis went into Virginia and settled at Yorktown. Accompanied by French troops Washington now marched rapidly southward and penned the British to the shore while a powerful French fleet shut off their escape by sea. It was this movement, which surely could not have been executed without French support, that put the finishing touches on British dominion in the United States. It was the surrender of Cornwallis at Yorktown that caused Lord North to pace the floor and cry out: "It is all over! It is all over!" What might have been done without the French alliance lies hidden from mankind. What was done with the help of French soldiers, sailors, officers, money, and supplies, is known to the whole earth. "All the world agree," exultantly wrote Franklin from Paris to General Washington, "that no expedition was ever better planned or better executed. It brightens the glory that must accompany your name to the latest posterity." Diplomacy as well as martial valor had its reward.

Peace at Last

British Opposition to the War. In explaining the defeat of the British government, we must remember that from start to finish it faced at home intelligent, informed, and merciless critics. These critics protested first against the Acts which had brought on the quarrel, then against the way in which war was waged, and finally against the futile struggle to retain a hold upon the American dominions. Among the members of Parliament who thundered against the ministry were some of the first statesmen and orators of the land. William Pitt, Earl of Chatham, though he deplored the idea of American independence until his death, flayed the British ministry as the aggressor and rejoiced in American resistance. Against every measure of coercion Edmund Burke spoke eloquently, and when the end came he strove for a peace which would give independence to America and work for reconciliation rather than ill-will. Charles James Fox openly said that he sympathized with the colonies and warmly defended their rights. Outside of the circle of statesmen there were stout advocates of a wiser colonial policy, like David Hume, the philosopher and historian, and Catherine Macaulay, a popular author who was bold enough to encourage Washington to keep on fighting for liberty.

Battered by such attacks the government enlisted a whole army of writers to pour out censure on the Americans and their English defenders. Dr. Samuel Johnson, who was employed in this business, was so savage that even the ministers had to tone down his pamphlets before printing them. Far more capable was Edward Gibbon, the famous author of *The Decline and Fall of the Roman Empire*. At first he was against British measures in America, but after he was given a good job in the government he lent his support to the ministry, causing critics to ridicule him in these lines:

> King George, in a fright
> Lest Gibbon should write
>   The story of England's disgrace,
> Thought no way so sure
> His pen to secure
>   As to give the historian a place.

Lord North Yields. British opponents of the government's course had said that the conquest of the colonies was impossible and that the granting of independence was the only hope for peace and reconciliation. Every day's news seemed to show that they were right. Moreover the war, which sprang out of an effort to relieve English burdens, actually made those burdens heavier than ever. Military expenses were daily increasing. Trade with the colonies, the greatest single outlet for British goods and capital, was ruined. The heavy debts due British merchants in America were not only unpaid but postponed into an indefinite future. Ireland was on the verge of revolution. The French had a dangerous fleet on the high seas. In vain did King George assert in December, 1781, that nothing would ever make him consent to a peace

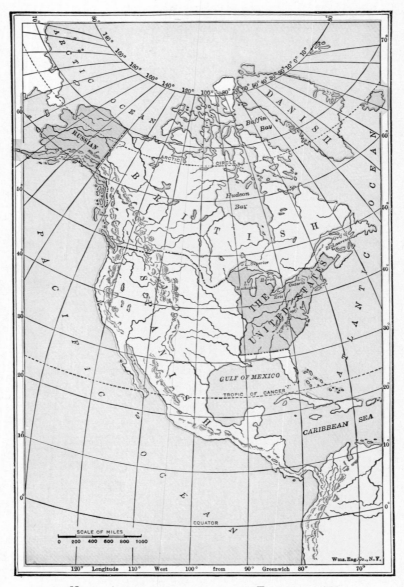

NORTH AMERICA ACCORDING TO THE TREATY OF 1783

conceding American independence. Parliament knew better and on February 27, 1782, the House of Commons adopted an address to the Crown against continuing the war. Lord North gave notice then that his ministry was at an end. The king moaned: "Necessity made me yield."

In April, 1782, Franklin received secret word from the English government that it was willing to discuss the terms of a settlement. This was awkward for him. In the treaty of alliance with France, the United States had promised not to arrange for peace without letting the French government know about it. Finding however that France was opposed to giving the Americans all the territory and fishing rights they demanded, the American commissioners conferred with the British agents at Paris without saying anything to the French minister. Indeed they actually signed a preliminary peace draft before they told him of their doings. When he was censured for this, Franklin replied that they "had been guilty of violating good manners but hoped that the great work would not be ruined by a single indiscretion."

The Terms of Peace (1783). The general settlement at Paris in 1783 was a triumph for America. King George recognized the independence of the United States, naming each state specifically, and agreed to boundaries extending from the Atlantic to the Mississippi and from the Great Lakes to the Floridas. But in spite of this heavy loss, England continued to hold Canada, Newfoundland, and the West Indies intact, made gains in India, and maintained her supremacy on the seas. Spain won Florida and Minorca, if not the coveted Gibraltar. France gained nothing important save the pleasure of seeing the British humbled, the colonies independent, and a new country created to offset England in the balance of power.

The generous terms won by the American commissioners at Paris called forth surprise and gratitude in the United States and smoothed the way for a renewal of trade with England. At the same time the settlement gave anxiety to European diplomats. "This federal republic is born a pigmy," wrote the Spanish ambassador to his royal master. "A day will come when it will be a giant; even a colossus formidable to these countries. Liberty of conscience and the facility of establishing a new population on immense lands, as well as the advantages of the new government, will draw thither farmers and artisans from all nations. In a few years we shall watch with grief the tyrannical existence of the same colossus."

SUMMARY OF THE REVOLUTIONARY PERIOD

The independence of the American colonies had been foreseen by many European statesmen as they watched the growth of their population, wealth, and power; but no one could fix the hour of the great event. Until 1763 the American colonists lived fairly happily under the British dominion. There were collisions from time to time, of course. Royal governors clashed with stiff-necked colonial legislatures. There were protests against the exercise of the king's veto power in specific cases. Nevertheless on the whole the relations between America and the mother country were more amicable in 1763 than at any period under the Stuart régime which closed in 1688.

The crash, when it came, was not deliberately willed by any one. It was the product of a number of forces that happened to draw together about 1763. Three years before, there had come to the throne George III, a young, proud, inexperienced, and stubborn king. For nearly fifty years his predecessors, Germans in language and interest, had let things drift in England and America. But George III decided that he would be king in fact as well as in name. About the same time England brought to a close the long and costly French and Indian war and began to stagger under a heavy burden of debt and taxes. The war had been fought partly in defense of the American colonies and nothing seemed more reasonable to English statesmen than the idea that the colonies should bear part of the cost of their own defense. While things were in this state there came into leadership in royal councils two men bent on serving England by taxing Americans and controlling their trade, Grenville and Townshend. The king was willing, the English taxpayers were thankful for any promise of relief, and most members of Parliament were ready to vote for the experiment. England therefore set out upon a new course. She imposed **taxes** upon the colonists, regulated their trade, and set royal officers over them to enforce the law. This action brought protests from the colonists. They held a Stamp Act Congress to declare their rights and petition for a redress of grievances. Some of the more restless provincials rioted in the streets, sacked the houses of the king's officers, and tore up the stamped paper.

Frightened by this uprising, the English government drew back and repealed the Stamp Act. Then it veered again and renewed its policy of interference. Intervention again called forth American protests. Protests aroused sharper action on the part of the British government. More British regulars were sent over to keep order. More irritating laws were passed by Parliament. Rioting again appeared; tea was dumped into the harbor of Boston and seized in the harbor of Charleston. The British answer was more force. The response of the colonists was a Continental Congress for defense. An unexpected and unintended clash of arms at Lexington and Concord in the spring of 1775 brought forth from the king of England a proclamation: "The Americans are rebels!"

The die was cast. The American Revolution had begun. Washington was made commander-in-chief. Armies were raised, money was borrowed, a huge volume of paper currency was issued, and foreign aid was summoned. Franklin plied his diplomatic arts at Paris until in 1778 he induced France to throw her sword into the balance. Three years later, Cornwallis surrendered at Yorktown. In 1783 by a formal treaty of peace, George III acknowledged the independence of the United States. The new nation, endowed with a vast domain of land stretching from the Atlantic Ocean to the Mississippi, began its career among the powers of the earth.

References

J. Fiske, *The American Revolution* (2 vols.).

H. Lodge, *Life of Washington* (2 vols.).

Allan Nevins, *The American States during and after the American Revolution.*

W. Sumner, *The Financier and the Finances of the American Revolution.*

O. Trevelyan, *The American Revolution* (4 vols.). A sympathetic account by an English historian.

M. C. Tyler, *Literary History of the American Revolution* (2 vols.).

C. H. Van Tyne, *The American Revolution* (American Nation Series) and *The Loyalists in the American Revolution*.

Questions

1. Why was the non-importation agreement revolutionary?
2. Contrast the work of the first and second Continental Congresses.
3. Why did efforts at conciliation fail?
4. Trace the growth of independence from opinion to action.
5. Why is the Declaration of Independence an "immortal" document?
6. What was the effect of the Revolution on governments?
7. Describe the contest between "Patriots" and "Tories."
8. What topics are considered under "military affairs"? Discuss.
9. Contrast the American forces with the British forces and show how the war was won.
10. Describe the work of women in the Revolutionary War.
11. How was the Revolution financed?
12. Describe the diplomatic triumph of the Revolution.
13. What was the nature of the opposition in England to the war?
14. Give the events connected with the settlement; the terms of peace.

Research Topics

American Rights. Draw up a table showing all the principles laid down by American leaders in (1) the Resolves of the First Continental Congress, Macdonald, *Documentary Source Book*, pp. 162–166; (2) the Declaration of the Causes and the Necessity of Taking Up Arms, Macdonald, pp. 176–183; and (3) the Declaration of Independence.

The Declaration of Independence. Fiske, *The American Revolution*, Vol. I, pp. 147–197. Elson, *History of the United States*, pp. 250–254.

Diplomacy and the French Alliance. Hart, *American History Told by Contemporaries*, Vol. II, pp. 574–590. Fiske, Vol. II, pp. 1–24. Callender, *Economic History of the United States*, pp. 159–168; Elson, pp. 251–256.

Biographical Studies. Consult an encyclopedia for Washington, Franklin, Samuel Adams, Patrick Henry, Thomas Jefferson.

The Tories. Hart, *Contemporaries*, Vol. II, pp. 470–480.

Valley Forge. Fiske, Vol. II, pp. 25–49.

The Battles of the Revolution. Elson, pp. 218–285.

An English View of the Revolution. Green, *Short History of England*, Chap. X, Sect. 2.

Historical Fiction

James Fenimore Cooper, *The Spy.*
Hallie E. Rives, *Hearts Courageous.*
P. L. Ford, *Janice Meredith.*

PART III. THE UNION AND NATIONAL LIFE

CHAPTER VIII

THE FORMATION OF THE CONSTITUTION

The rise of a republic in America was a great political sensation in a world ruled almost entirely by monarchs. Once subject to a king, thirteen states were now to be governed by officials elected by the "plain people," united peacefully in a confederation of their own making. Europe was amazed that the people were able to coöperate in this novel way instead of fighting among themselves to the injury of their common cause. And naturally sheer pride in the achievement filled the hearts and minds of many patriots whose labors and sacrifices had made independence and union possible. They pointed to the splendid phrasing of the Declaration of Independence, to their Confederation, and to the state constitutions drawn up by practical men. Surely now the republic could advance by its own momentum!

But there were then as always doubting Thomases who saw problems where others saw only glory. And a few such critics, who had themselves fought in the Revolution and made sacrifices for freedom, feared that the republic could not keep its independence or become great and prosperous unless vital changes were made in the scheme of government so recently adopted. They did not decry the work already done, but they were alarmed by the disorders in money matters, the bad state of commerce, the lack of foreign credit, and the backward condition of business.

THE GROUNDS OF DISCONTENT

Weakness of the Articles of Confederation. In fact the government of the United States under the Articles of Confederation had neither the strength nor the resources required to cope with the problems left by the war. The framers of that document had deliberately created a weak government. They remembered how the British king and Parliament had taxed the colonies, interfered in their affairs, controlled them by royal judges, and set a standing army over them. Having suffered from tyranny, they wanted no more of it. So the authors of the Articles did not provide for a strong executive officer — a president with kingly powers — or for a high court of judges, charged with law enforcement. They merely erected a Congress composed of from two to seven members from each state, chosen as its legislature might direct, and paid by the state. On all important questions in this Congress, each state had just one vote — little Delaware enjoying the same weight as the great dominion of Virginia. When decisions were made and laws passed, they were not carried out by any effective agency, executive or judicial. The Congress relied mainly on moral not physical force. It is true, the Congress could select a committee of thirteen — one from each state — to act as an executive body when it was not in session; but this scheme proved a failure.

Furthermore the two great powers of government, military and financial, were lacking. The Congress, to be sure, could authorize expenditures but it had to rely upon the states to provide voluntarily the money it voted to spend. It could also order the establishment of an army, but it could only request the states to supply quotas of soldiers. It could not lay any taxes at all. It had no means of touching directly a single citizen in the whole country. It could act only through the state governments. In short the first Congress of the republic was little more than an advisory committee for the thirteen states.

Financial and Commercial Disorders. With respect to such matters as the kinds of money in circulation, public debts, and trade, the Congress was powerless. It could not pay the interest on the huge debt piled up by the Revolution. Owners of government bonds were in despair, as the market value of their holdings sank to twenty-five or even ten cents on the dollar. The current bills of Congress were also unpaid. As some one complained, there was not enough money in the treasury to buy the pen and ink with which to write the minutes of this shadow legislature. The currency was utterly confused. Millions of dollars in Continental notes issued by the Congress had become mere trash worth but a cent or two on the dollar. There was no other expression of contempt so forceful as the popular saying: "Not worth a Continental." To make matters worse several states were pouring new paper money from their presses about as fast as they could print it. Even in using the gold and silver in circulation — mainly English, French, and Spanish coins — the public was often cheated because money changers were constantly clipping and filing away the metal. Another drag was placed on business by British trade discriminations directed against Americans as aliens, and the Congress was unable to get any favors from any foreign country because it could not regulate commerce and make retaliations. Even domestic trade was slowed down by the tariff barriers which some of the jealous states raised against their neighbors; New York, for example, placing customs duties on firewood imported from Connecticut! But the Congress could do nothing about it. As if to increase this economic chaos, some of the states passed laws making it difficult to collect debts within their borders.

Congress in Disrepute. With commercial treaties ignored, the laws unenforced, the treasury empty, and the public credit gone, the Congress of the young republic fell into disrepute at home and abroad: It called upon the states to pay their quotas of money into the treasury, only to be treated with disdain. Even its own members soon began to look upon it as a solemn farce. Some of the ablest men refused to accept election to it, and many who did take the doubtful honor failed to attend the sessions. Again and again it was impossible to secure a quorum in the Congress for the transaction of any business.

Troubles of the State Governments. "All power to the states!" was the popular cry in the beginning. They were free to pursue their own course without interference. Yet they too were loaded with revolutionary debts calling for heavy taxes. Oppressed by taxation and discouraged by the fall in prices which followed the return of peace, the farmers of several states compelled their legislatures to print large issues of paper money with which to pay the bills. This "cheap money" they tried to force upon unwilling creditors to square all accounts. In every part of the country laws were made one year only to be repealed the next and reënacted the third year.   Lands were sold by one legislature and the sales were canceled by its successor.   Uncertainty and distrust were the natural consequences.

So discontented had the farmers of New Hampshire become by 1786 that a crowd surrounded the legislature, demanding a repeal of burdensome taxes and the issue of more paper money.   With difficulty was an armed rebellion against the state government avoided.   Led by Daniel Shays, a former captain in the Revolutionary army, farmers of Massachusetts organized in the same year an open resistance to the authorities of their state.   Shays and his followers protested against the harsh action of creditors in foreclosing mortgages on farms, against lawyers for increasing the fees for their services, against heavy taxes, and against the refusal of the legislature to authorize paper money.   They seized the towns of Worcester and Springfield and broke up the courts of justice.   All through the western part of the state the revolt spread, sending a shock to every center and section of the young republic. Only by the most vigorous action was Governor Bowdoin able to quell the uprising; and even then the state government did not dare to deal severely with the prisoners because they had so many sympathizers.   Moreover Bowdoin and several members of the legislature who had been most active in suppressing the rebels were defeated at the next election.   For such reasons men who were opposed to revolution by Americans against Americans and others who wanted business put on its feet now talked of the necessity for a stronger central government to help restrain the populace.

Dangers to the Republic.   Watching the drift of affairs, many people were driven to the conclusion that the new ship of state, so proudly launched a few years before, was careening into anarchy.   "The facts of our peace and independence," wrote a friend of Washington, "do not at present wear so promising an appearance as I had fondly painted in my mind.   The prejudices, jealousies, and turbulence of the people at times almost stagger my confidence in our political establishments; and almost occasion me to think that they will show themselves unworthy of the noble prize for which we have contended."

Washington himself was profoundly discouraged. On hearing of Shays' rebellion, he exclaimed: "What, gracious God, is man that there should be such inconsistency and perfidiousness in his conduct! It is but the other day that we were shedding our blood to obtain the constitutions under which we now live — constitutions of our own choice and making — and now we are unsheathing our sword to overturn them." The same year he burst out in a lament over rumors that a royal government was to be restored: "I am told that even respectable characters speak of a monarchical government without horror. From thinking proceeds speaking. Hence to acting is often but a single step. But how irresistible and tremendous! What a triumph for our enemies to verify their predictions! What a triumph for the advocates of despotism to find that we are incapable of governing ourselves!"

Congress Attempts Some Reforms. The Congress was naturally excited by the events that disturbed George Washington and it tried many times to check tendencies so hostile to finance, commerce, industries, and the union itself. In 1781, even before the treaty of peace with England was signed, the Congress found out how trivial were its taxing powers and sent to the states a proposal to change the Articles of Confederation in such a way as to allow it to impose a slight tariff on imports. Yet this mild suggestion was rejected. , Two years later the Congress again asked for an amendment permitting the levy of duties on imports, to be collected this time by state officers and applied to the payment of the public debt. This more limited proposal, designed to save American credit, likewise failed. In 1786 the Congress made a third appeal to the states for help, declaring that they had been irregular and negligent in paying their quotas and that further trust in that mode of raising revenues was dishonorable and dangerous.

CALLING OF THE CONSTITUTIONAL CONVENTION

Hamilton and Washington Urge Reform. Outside Congress as well as within demands arose for reform. In 1780, a year before the Articles were adopted, the youthful Alexander Hamilton proposed calling a general convention for the purpose of drafting a new constitution on entirely different lines. With tireless energy he strove to bring his countrymen to his view. Agreeing with him on every point, Washington declared, in a circular letter to the governors, that the union would not last long unless there was lodged somewhere a supreme power "to regulate and govern the general concerns of the confederated republic." The governor of

Courtesy of The Metropolitan Museum of Art
PORTRAIT OF ALEXANDER HAMILTON BY
JOHN TRUMBULL
See page 219.

Massachusetts, frightened by the unrest all about him, suggested to the state legislature in 1785 the advisability of a national convention to enlarge the powers of the Congress. The legislature approved the idea, but did nothing to carry it out.

The Annapolis Convention. Action finally came from the South. It was the Virginia legislature that started the movement by calling a conference of delegates at Annapolis to consider matters of taxation and commerce. Yet when the convention assembled in 1786, it was found that only five states had been interested enough to send representatives. The leaders were deeply disappointed, but the resourceful Hamilton, a delegate from New York, turned the meeting to good account. He secured the adoption of a resolution inviting the Congress itself to summon a second convention, to meet at Philadelphia.

The Call at Last (1787). This step the Congress finally decided to take in February, 1787, by sending forth the call. But fearing that too many changes might be made, it restricted the new convention to "the sole and express purpose of revising the Articles of Confederation." Clinging to local liberties, it provided that all changes proposed must be referred to the Congress and then to the states for their approval.

Every state in the Union, except Rhode Island, responded to the call for the convention. Indeed some of the states, having the Annapolis resolution before them, had already selected delegates before the formal summons came. Thus by the pressure of governors, legislatures, and private citizens, the much discussed national convention became a fact. In May, 1787, it assembled in Philadelphia.

Eminent Men of the Convention. On the roll of that memorable convention were fifty-five men, at least half of whom were acknowledged to be among the foremost statesmen and thinkers in America. Every field of government was represented: war and administration in Washington, who was chosen president of the convention; diplomacy in Franklin, now old and honored both in his own land and in Europe; finance in Alexander Hamilton and Robert Morris; law in James Wilson of Pennsylvania; the philosophy of government in James Madison, soon to be called the "father of the Constitution."

They were not mere theorists. They were practical men whose rich political experiences had given them a deep insight into human behavior. Three had served in the Stamp Act Congress: Dickinson of Delaware, William Samuel Johnson of Connecticut, and John Rutledge of South Carolina. Eight had been signers of the Declaration of Independence: Read of Delaware, Sherman of Connecticut, Wythe of Virginia, Gerry of Massachusetts, Franklin, Robert Morris, George Clymer, and James Wilson of Pennsylvania. All but twelve had at some time served in the Congress and eighteen were members of that body at this very time. Washington, Hamilton, Mifflin, and Charles Pinckney had been officers in the Revolutionary army. Seven of the delegates had gained political experience as governors of states. "The convention as a whole," according to the historian Hildreth, "represented in a marked manner the talent, intelligence, and especially the conservative sentiment of the country." Above all things, the members were business-like. "Experience must be our only guide," said John Dickinson. "Reason might mislead us."

THE FRAMING OF THE CONSTITUTION

Problems Involved. The great problems before the convention were nine in number: (1) Shall the Articles of Confederation be revised or a different system of government constructed? (2) Shall the government be founded on states equal in power as under the Articles or on the broader and more democratic foundation of population? (3) What direct share shall the people have in the election of national officers? (4) What shall be the qualifications for the suffrage? (5) How shall the conflicting interests of the commercial and the planting states be balanced so as to safeguard the rights of each? (6) What shall be the form of the new government? (7) What powers shall be given to it? (8) How shall the state legislatures be restrained from attacks on property rights, such as the issuance of paper money? (9) Shall the approval of all the states be necessary, as under the Articles, for the adoption and amendment of the Constitution?

Revision of the Articles or a New Government? The moment the first problem was raised, that of a different kind of government, representatives of the small states, led by William Paterson of New Jersey, were on their feet for speeches. They feared that the equality and rights of the states would be in danger if the Articles of Confederation were overthrown. Their protest was therefore strenuous. They said that the Congress in summoning the convention had specifically stated that they were called together for "the sole and express purpose of revising the Articles of Confederation." They also cited their instructions from their state legislatures, ordering them to "revise and amend" the existing scheme of government, not to set up another. To depart from the order laid down by the Congress and the legislatures would be to exceed their powers, they argued, and to betray the trust given to them by their countrymen.

To their pleas, Randolph of Virginia replied: "When the salvation of the republic is at stake, it would be treason to our trust not to propose what we find necessary." Hamilton frankly said that on the point of their powers he had no scruples because the states would have to approve their work in the end. Hamilton's view won the day. The convention cast aside the Articles as if they did not exist and drew up a new constitution "laying its foundation on such principles and organizing its powers in such form" as to the delegates seemed "most likely to affect their safety and happiness."

A Government Founded on States or on People? The Compromise. Balked in their attempt to limit the convention to a mere revision of the Articles, the spokesmen of the smaller states redoubled their efforts to keep a voting equality with the larger states, a privilege then enjoyed in the single chamber of the existing Congress. The signal for a radical departure from the Articles on this point was given when Randolph presented "the Virginia plan." His project proposed that the new national congress consist of two houses instead of one and that the several states be allotted members according to wealth or free white population as the convention might decide. This plan was hotly challenged. Paterson of New Jersey declared that neither he nor his state would ever bow to such tyranny as unequal representation. He offered, instead, "the New Jersey plan" calling for a national congress of one house representing states as such, not wealth or people — a legislature in which all states, large or small, would still have equal voice. Wilson of Pennsylvania, on behalf of the more populous states, took an opposite position. It was absurd, he urged, for 180,000 men in one state to have the same weight in national councils as 750,000 men in another state. "The gentleman from New Jersey," he said, "is candid. He declares his opinion boldly . . . I will be equally candid . . . I will never confederate on his principles." So the controversy ran on through many tempestuous sessions.

At length the convention was deadlocked and about to break up — "scarce held together by the strength of a hair," as one of the delegates remarked. A crash was avoided only by a compromise — in the formation of a Congress of two houses. In the plan of the upper chamber, the Senate, the demands of the small states were partly met, for each state was given two members in that body. The larger states were then in a measure satisfied by a decision to distribute the members of the lower chamber, the House of Representatives, among the states on the basis of their population, counting three-fifths of the slaves as persons.

The Question of Popular Election. The question as to how federal officers and members of Congress should be elected also produced an angry debate which revealed in the convention a deep-seated distrust of the capacity of the people to govern themselves. Only a few delegates, it is true, believed that no branch of government should be elected directly by the voters; but still fewer desired to see all branches so chosen. One or two delegates even expressed a preference for a monarchy. The dangers of democracy were especially emphasized by Gerry of Massachusetts: "All the evils we experience flow from an excess of democracy. The people do not want virtue but are the dupes of pretended patriots. . . . I have been too republican heretofore but have been taught by experience the danger of a leveling spirit." It was to put a brake on democratic tendencies that Randolph proposed a "firm senate." To provide a further check on popular government Charles Pinckney of South Carolina declared that no one should be elected President who was not worth $100,000 and that high property qualifications should be placed on members of Congress and judges. But some members of the convention stoutly objected to such "high-toned notions of government." For example, Franklin and Wilson, both from Pennsylvania, heartily championed popular election in general; while men like Madison insisted that at least one part of the government should rest on the broad foundation of the people.

Out of this clash of opinion again came compromise. One branch, the House of Representatives, it was agreed, was to be elected directly by the voters, while the Senators were to be chosen less directly, by the state legislatures. The President was to be chosen in a still more complicated way — by electors selected as the legislatures of the states might determine for themselves. Judges of the federal courts were to be appointed by the President and Senate, not elected at all.

The Question of the Suffrage. Since the members of the House of Representatives were to be chosen by voters directly, a question of the suffrage arose in this connection, bringing on a sharp but brief battle in the convention. Gouverneur Morris proposed that only landowners should be permitted to vote. Madison replied that this would be no help because the state legislatures, which had made so much trouble, were already elected by farmers. Owing to disputes over the nature and amount of property qualifications to be imposed on the suffrage, no agreement could be reached. So the convention simply dodged the issue by deciding that the House of Representatives should be elected by voters having the "qualifications requisite for electors of the most numerous branch of the state legislature." Thus the suffrage provisions of the states were accepted for federal elections.

The Balance between Planting and Commercial States. After the debates had gone on for a few weeks, Madison came to the conclusion that the real division in the convention was not between the large and the small states as such but between the planting section founded on slave labor and the commercial North. The Southern states were not equal to the Northern states in free white population and wealth, which were proposed as the basis of power in the House of Representatives. Counting Delaware, there were six of the former as against seven commercial states. Dependent for their prosperity mainly upon the sale of tobacco, rice, and other staples abroad, they feared that a Congress controlled by ambitious traders might interfere with their exports and imports. Weaker in numbers, they were also afraid that the Northern majority would lay an unfair burden of taxes upon them.

Representation and Taxation. The Southern members of the convention were therefore very anxious to secure for their section the largest possible representation in Congress and also to check its taxing power. They thought of two ways to attain their goal. One was to count the slaves as people when distributing representatives in Congress among the states "according to their population"; the other was to provide that direct taxes should be apportioned among the states not on the basis of their wealth but the number of their free white inhabitants. These proposals ran against Northern interests and so encountered decided objections. Once more a compromise settled the issue between them. It was agreed that not all the slaves, but three-fifths, should be reckoned in both ways as people — when taxes were laid and when representatives were divided among the states.

Commerce and the Slave Trade. Southern interests were also reluctant to confer upon Congress the power to regulate interstate and foreign commerce. To the manufacturing and trading section this was essential. It would prevent the states from erecting tariff walls against one another, hampering the free flow of goods; it would also enable Congress to protect American manufacturers against European competition and to break down foreign discriminations against American commerce. To the South the proposal was menacing, because high import duties laid by Congress might restrain the free exchange of the produce of their plantations in European markets, and navigation acts might confine the carrying trade to American — in practice, Northern — ships at higher rates than the English charged. Anxiety about the slave traffic was still another worry, for some of the Southern states feared that the importation of negroes might be heavily taxed or immediately prohibited altogether.

By various routes, the morals of slavery came under review. Gouverneur Morris delivered his mind and heart on the subject, denouncing it as a wicked institution and the curse of heaven on the states in which it prevailed. Mason of Virginia, himself a slaveholder, was hardly less outspoken, saying: "Slavery discourages arts and manufactures. The poor despise labor when performed by slaves. They prevent migration of whites who really strengthen and enrich the country."

Slavery, on the other hand, had its apologists. Representatives from South Carolina argued that their entire economic life rested on negro labor and that the high death rate in the rice swamps made continuous importation necessary. Ellsworth of Connecticut took the ground that the convention should not meddle with slavery. "The morality or wisdom of slavery," he said, "are considerations belonging to the states. What enriches a part enriches the whole." To the future he turned an unruffled face: "As population increases, poor laborers will be so plenty as to render slaves useless. Slavery in time will not be a speck in our country." Virginia and North Carolina, already overstocked with slaves, were willing to prohibit the traffic; but South Carolina would not budge. She must have fresh supplies of slaves or she would not federate.

So it was agreed as a sectional compromise that, while Congress could regulate foreign trade, the importation of slaves should not be forbidden within twenty years and that meanwhile no import tax on them should exceed $10 a head. At the same time in providing for the regulation of foreign trade, it was decided that a two-thirds vote in the Senate should be necessary for the ratification of treaties. Thus Southern Senators could block a treaty which they did not like. A further concession to the South was made in the clause ordering the return of runaway slaves — a clause also useful to the North where indentured servants frequently escaped from their masters.

The Form of the Government. During the days when the branches of the new government — executive, legislative and judicial — were discussed, the sessions of the convention were naturally stormy. Opinion ran one way one day and another the next. How many branches should there be? Of how many persons should each branch be composed? How should they be elected? Such were the leading questions under this head.

The Executive. All members knew that the laws would have to be enforced but they did not want a dictator to do it. Clearly Congress could not be depended upon to carry its own orders into effect, for that theory had already been tried. So the New Jersey plan called for an executive council; while the Virginia plan proposed an executive branch elected by Congress, without stating whether it should consist of one or more persons. Respecting the form of the executive and methods of its election the delegates were torn by a fear of tyranny on the one side and popular unrest on the other. Finally to secure strength in law enforcement, the convention voted for a single executive, to be known as the President, gave him a four-year term, and endowed him with large powers in appointing civil officers and commanding the army and navy. To remove the President far from the populace, it provided that he should be elected indirectly by electors chosen as the legislatures of the several states might decide. Yet to put a check on him, it gave Congress the right to oust him by impeachment.

The Legislative Branch — Congress.   As we have already seen, the law-making power was vested in a Congress of two houses — one, the House of Representatives, to be elected by popular vote and the other, the Senate, to serve like the English House of Lords as a check on "the turbulence" of the more democratic chamber. Four means were selected to give the Senate a special position over against the House.   First, the Senators were not to be chosen directly by the voters but by the legislatures of the states, one degree removed from the populace.   Second, their term was fixed at six years instead of two, as in the case of the House.   Third, in order to avoid violent changes, only one-third of the Senators were to be elected at a time.   Finally, it was provided that Senators must be at least thirty years old while Representatives need be only twenty-five.   Age was supposed to be more cautious than youth.

The Judiciary.   The necessity for federal courts to help carry out the law was felt by all the members of the convention.   In a large measure the feebleness of the Articles of Confederation was due to the want of a judiciary, holding states and individuals in obedience to the laws and treaties of the union.   Nevertheless on this point the advocates of states' rights were extremely sensitive.   They did not like the idea of judges appointed at the national capital and freed entirely from local interests and traditions; they remembered how they had demanded from Britain the right of local trial by jury and how they had resented the English scheme for taking from colonial assemblies all their powers over the salaries of judges.   Yet grudgingly they yielded to the demand for federal courts, consenting at first only to a Supreme Court to review cases heard in lower state courts and finally to such inferior courts as Congress might deem necessary from time to time.

The System of Checks and Balances.   Thus the framers of the Constitution, in shaping the form of the new government for the United States, arranged to divide all the power of that government among three branches — executive, legislative, and judicial. Strictly speaking, we might say four branches, because the legislature, or Congress, was composed of two houses to check each other, and one of them, the Senate, was made a check on the

President through its right to ratify treaties and appointments. "The accumulation of all powers, legislative, executive and judicial, in the same hands," wrote Madison, "whether of one, a few, or many, and whether hereditary, self-appointed, or elective, may justly be pronounced the very definition of tyranny." In this manner the convention tried to distribute the power as widely as possible to prevent the tyranny of one man or many.

Henceforward laws were to be made by a legislature divided into two houses, the members of which were to be apportioned on a different basis, elected in different ways, and to serve for different terms. A veto on the acts of this Congress was vested in a President who was to be elected indirectly, to serve four years, not two like the members of the House or six like the Senators, and to be removed only by the difficult process of impeachment. After a law had run the gantlet of both houses and the President, it was subject to interpretation and annulment by federal judges appointed by the President with the consent of the Senate and serving for life. Thus it was made almost impossible for any political party to get hold of all branches of the government at a single popular election. As Hamilton remarked, the friends of sound government considered "every institution calculated to restrain the excess of law making and to keep things in the same state in which they happen to be at any given period as more likely to do good than harm."

The Powers of the Federal Government. On the question of the powers to be conferred upon the new government the members of the convention were fairly united. Even the delegates from the small states agreed with those from Massachusetts, Pennsylvania, and Virginia that the Articles of Confederation gave the Congress too little authority. The New Jersey plan as well as the Virginia plan recognized this fact. Some of the delegates, Hamilton and Madison, for instance, even proposed to give Congress the general right to make laws on all national matters; but others insisted on naming the powers to be conferred one by one, and finally their idea was accepted.

Taxation and Commerce. All agreed that revenue must be provided to pay the current expenses of government and discharge the public debt. When once the dispute over the apportionment of direct taxes among the slave states was settled, it was a simple matter to decide that Congress should have power to lay and collect taxes, duties, imposts, and excises. In this way the national government was freed from dependence upon stubborn and tardy legislatures and enabled to collect funds itself directly from citizens. No one contended that the anarchy created by state tariffs should be longer endured; hence, when the fears of the planting states were allayed and the "bargain" over the importation of slaves was reached, the convention vested in Congress full power to regulate both interstate and foreign commerce.

National Defense. The necessity for national defense was also realized, though the fear of a great army and militarism was strong in the minds of the delegates. The old practice of relying on quotas of soldiers furnished by the state legislatures found no advocate. As in the case of taxes, a direct authority over citizens was demanded. Therefore Congress was given full power to raise and support armies and build a navy. It could employ the state militia when desirable; but it could also maintain a regular army and call directly upon all able-bodied males for service if required by the nature of a crisis.

The "Necessary and Proper" Clause. In addition, there was included in the Constitution a general clause authorizing Congress to make all laws "necessary and proper" for carrying into effect each and every one of the powers that had been named. This clause was later interpreted by that master mind, Chief Justice Marshall, as granting to Congress an authority competent to meet the needs of a country spanning a continent.

Restraints on the States. Besides setting up a new central government endowed with such large powers, the convention sought to restrain the state legislatures in many ways. In every state, explains Marshall in his *Life of Washington*, was a party of men who had "marked out for themselves a more indulgent course. Viewing with extreme tenderness the case of the debtor, their efforts were unceasingly directed to his relief. To exact a faithful compliance with contracts was, in their opinion, a harsh measure which the people could not bear. They were uniformly in favor of relaxing the administration of justice, of according facilities for the payment of debts, or of suspending their collection and remitting taxes."

Under the dominance of this class, legislatures had enacted paper-money laws enabling debtors to pay their debts in "cheap money." The Constitution now put an end to such practices by providing that no state should emit bills of credit or make anything but gold or silver legal tender in the payment of debts. The state legislatures had passed laws allowing people to pay their debts by turning over to creditors land or personal property; they had repealed the charter of an endowed college and taken the management from the hands of the lawful trustees; and they had otherwise interfered with the enforcement of private agreements. With such events in mind, the convention put into the Constitution a clause forbidding states "to impair the obligation of contracts." Remembering how the farmers of Massachusetts had rioted against the state government, the convention added a brief sentence declaring that the President of the United States could send federal soldiers to suppress domestic insurrection whenever called upon by the legislature or, if it was not in session, by the governor of the state. To make sure that restraints on the states would not be dead letters, the convention made the federal Constitution, laws, and treaties the supreme law of the land, to be enforced by the President and national judges.

Provisions for Ratification and Amendment. When the frame of government had been determined, the powers to be vested in it had been enumerated, and the checks upon the states had been worked out, there remained three more questions to settle. How shall this Constitution be ratified? What number of states shall be necessary to put it into effect? How may it be amended in the future?

On the first point the call for the convention seemed to be decisive. The Articles of Confederation, still in effect, provided that amendments could be made only by unanimous vote in the existing Congress with the approval of all the states. As if to reinforce this rule the call for the convention had expressly stated that all changes proposed by the convention must be reported to the

Congress for adoption or rejection and then, if ratified, sent to the states for their review.

To have obeyed the strict letter of the law would have defeated the purposes of the delegates because the Congress and the state legislatures were openly hostile to such drastic changes as had been suggested. Unanimous ratification, as events proved, would have been impossible. Therefore the delegates decided that the Constitution should be sent to the old Congress with the recommendation that it in turn transmit the document, not to the state legislatures, but to a special convention in every state called for the purpose of passing upon it. This plan was carried out.

The convention was equally radical in dealing with the problem of how many states must vote for the new Constitution before it could be put into effect. Attempts to change the Articles in the past had failed because every amendment had to be approved by every state, and there was always at least one member of the Union unwilling to consent. The opposition to a new Constitution would no doubt be very great. Rhode Island had even refused to take part in framing it, and her antagonism to the whole procedure was well known. So the convention decreed that the Constitution should simply go into effect when ratified by nine states, leaving the others out in the cold.

Unanimous approval was also rejected in the arrangements for making future changes in the Constitution. The convention decided that an amendment could be made by a two-thirds vote of both houses of Congress with ratification by three-fourths of the states. All states would thus be bound by an amendment so adopted even in case a part of them objected to it. In this way America proposed to set out upon the high road that led beyond a league of jealous states to a unified nation.

THE STRUGGLE OVER RATIFICATION

On September 17, 1787, the Constitution was formally adopted. After nearly four months of debate in secret session the convention flung open the doors of the hall in which it met, and gave the public its finished plan for the new government. Now the great debate passed to the people.

The Opposition. Floods of criticism at once descended upon the Constitution. "Fraudulent usurpation!" cried Gerry, who had refused to sign it. "A monster" out of the "thick veil of secrecy!" declaimed a Pennsylvania newspaper. "An iron-handed despotism will be the result," prophesied a third. "We, 'the low born,'" sarcastically wrote a fourth, "will now admit the 'six hundred well-born' immediately to establish this most noble, most excellent, and truly divine constitution." The President will become a king; Congress will be as tyrannical as Parliament in the old days; the states will be swallowed up; the rights of the people will be trampled upon; the poor man's justice will be lost in the endless delays of the federal courts. Such was the tone of the protests against ratification.

Defense of the Constitution. Deeply moved by the outburst of opposition, Hamilton, Madison, and Jay vigorously used their

> In the PRESS,
> and speedily will be published,
>
> THE
> FEDERALIST,
>
> A Collection of Essays written in favor of the New Constitution.
>
> By a Citizen of New-York.
>
> Corrected by the Author, with Additions and Alterations.
>
> *This work will be printed on a fine Paper and good Type, in one handsome Volume duodecimo, and delivered to subscribers at the moderate price of one dollar. A few copies will be printed on superfine royal writing paper, price ten shillings.*
> *No money required till delivery.*
>
> *To render this work more complete, will be added, without any additional expence,*
>
> PHILO-PUBLIUS,
> AND THE
> *Articles of the Convention,*
> *As agreed upon at Philadelphia, September 17th, 1787.*

AN ANNOUNCEMENT THAT THE "FEDERALIST" IS TO BE PUBLISHED AS A BOOK

pens in defense of the Constitution. In a series of newspaper articles they discussed and argued for it with eloquence, learning, and dignity, explaining every important clause and provision of the proposed plan of government. These papers, afterward collected and published in a volume known as the *Federalist*, form the finest textbook on the Constitution that has ever been printed. It takes its place moreover among the wisest and greatest treatises on government written in any language in any time.

Other citizens, not so gifted, were no less earnest in their support of ratification. In private correspondence, editorials, pamphlets, and letters to the newspapers, they too urged their countrymen to forget local jealousies and accept a Constitution which, in spite of its defects great or small, was the only guarantee against confusion at home and dishonor abroad.

The Action of the State Conventions. Before the end of the year 1787, three states had ratified the Constitution: Delaware and New Jersey unanimously and Pennsylvania after a short though savage contest. Connecticut and Georgia followed early the next year. Then came the battle royal in Massachusetts, ending with ratification in February by the narrow margin of 187 votes to 168. In the spring came the report that Maryland and South Carolina were "under the new roof." On June 21, New Hampshire, where the sentiment was at first strong enough to defeat the Constitution, joined the new republic, influenced by the favorable decision in Massachusetts. Nine states had now accepted the Constitution and were cemented in the new commonwealth whether more saw fit to join or not. Swift couriers were sent to carry the glad tidings to New York and Virginia, where the question of ratification was still undecided.

By the time the news of New Hampshire's action arrived however, Virginia, after a long and searching debate, had given her approval by a narrow margin, leaving New York as the next seat of anxiety. In that state the popular vote for the delegates to the convention had been clearly and heavily against ratification. But events finally showed the futility of resistance, and Hamilton was at last able to marshal there a majority of thirty to twenty-seven members in favor of the Constitution.

The great campaign was over. All the states except North Carolina and Rhode Island had ratified. "The sloop Anarchy," wrote an excited journalist, "when last heard from was ashore on Union rocks."

The First Election. In the autumn of 1788 elections were held to fill the places in the new government. Popular opinion was overwhelmingly in favor of Washington for the first President. Yielding to pleas of advisers, he accepted the post in the spirit

of public service, and on April 30, 1789, took the oath of office at
Federal Hall in New York City. "Long live George Washington,
President of the United States!" cried Chancellor Livingston as

CELEBRATING THE RATIFICATION

soon as the General had kissed the Bible. The cry was caught
by the multitude and given back. The sensational experiment in
popular government was launched.

References

M. Farrand, *The Framing of the Constitution of the United States.*
P. L. Ford, *Essays on the Constitution of the United States.*
Federalist (in many editions).

G. Hunt, *Life of James Madison.*

A. C. McLaughlin, *The Confederation and the Constitution* (American Nation Series).

Questions

1. Account for the failure of the Articles of Confederation.
2. Explain the domestic difficulties of the individual states.
3. Why did efforts at reform by the Congress come to naught?
4. Narrate the events leading up to the constitutional convention.
5. Who were some of the leading men in the convention? What had been their previous training?
6. State the great problems before the convention.
7. In what respects were the planting and commercial states opposed? What compromises were reached?
8. Show how the "check and balance" system is embodied in our form of government.
9. How did the powers conferred upon the federal government help to cure the defects of the Articles of Confederation?
10. In what way did the provisions for ratifying and amending the Constitution depart from the old system?
11. What was the nature of the conflict over ratification?

Research Topics

English Treatment of American Commerce. Callender, *Economic History of the United States,* pp. 210–220.

Financial Condition of the United States. Fiske, *Critical Period of American History,* pp. 163–186.

Disordered Commerce. Fiske, pp. 134–162.

Selfish Conduct of the States. Callender, pp. 185–191.

The Failure of the Confederation. Elson, *History of the United States,* pp. 293–301.

Formation of the Constitution. (1) The plans before the convention, Fiske, pp. 236–249; (2) the great compromise, Fiske, pp. 250–255; (3) slavery and the convention, Fiske, pp. 256–266; and (4) the frame of government, Fiske, pp. 275–301; Elson, pp. 328–334.

Biographical Studies. Look up the history and services of the leaders in the convention in any good encyclopedia.

Ratification of the Constitution. Hart, *History Told by Contemporaries,* Vol. III, pp. 233–254; Elson, pp. 313–320.

Source Study. Compare the Constitution and Articles of Confederation under the following heads: (1) frame of government; (2) powers of Congress; (3) limits on states; and (4) methods of amendment. Every line of the Constitution should be read and reread in the light of the historical circumstances set forth in this chapter. See Appendix.

CHAPTER IX

POLITICS AND CULTURE OF THE YOUNG REPUBLIC

THE AMERICAN GOVERNMENT AT WORK

Friends of the Constitution in Power. The test of the Constitution came when the government created by it began to work under its provisions. This test it passed, partly because so many of its framers were members of the new government. In the first Congress that assembled after the adoption of the Constitution, there were eleven Senators, led by Robert Morris, the financier, who had been delegates to the national convention at Philadelphia in 1787. Several members of the House of Representatives, headed by James Madison, had also been there. George Washington, former member of that constitutional assembly and first President of the United States, strengthened the new system of government by every appointment he made. He chose as Secretary of the Treasury, Alexander Hamilton, who had been most zealous for its success; General Knox, head of the War Department, and Edmund Randolph, the Attorney-General, were enthusiastic supporters of the experiment. Every member of the federal judiciary whom Washington selected, from the Chief Justice, John Jay, down to the judges of the district courts, had favored the ratification of the Constitution, and a majority had served either as members of the constitutional convention or of the state ratifying conventions. Only one man of influence in the new government, Thomas Jefferson, the Secretary of State, was known to have doubts in the matter. He had been out of the country acting as minister at Paris when the Constitution was adopted, and he had written letters favoring some parts of it while criticizing others.

The Opposition. The inauguration of Washington amid the praise of his countrymen did not however set at rest all the political turmoil which had been aroused by the fierce contest over ratification. "The interesting nature of the question," wrote John Marshall, "the equality of the parties, the animation produced inevitably by ardent debate had a necessary tendency to embitter the dispositions of the vanquished and to fix more deeply in many bosoms their prejudices against a plan of government in opposition to which all their passions were enlisted." The leaders gathered around Washington were well aware of the excited state of the country. North Carolina and Rhode Island still refused to join the Union, the former holding out until November, 1789, and the latter until May, 1790. By small margins only had the Constitution been approved in the great states of Massachusetts, Virginia, and New York. And a majority of the state conventions had accompanied their ratifications with lists of amendments which they wanted Congress and the states to make at once.

From an old print

THE INAUGURATION OF WASHINGTON

The First Amendments — a Bill of Rights. To meet this opposition, Madison proposed, and the first Congress adopted a series of amendments to the document framed at Philadelphia. Ten were soon ratified by the states and became in 1791 a part of the Constitution itself. These amendments were very significant for they provided, among other things, that Congress could make no law respecting the establishment of religion or abridging the freedom of religious worship, speech, or the press or the right of the people peaceably to assemble and petition the government or a redress of grievances. They also guaranteed indictment by grand jury and trial by jury for all persons charged by federal officers with serious crimes. The tenth amendment went beyond this Bill of Rights for citizens and granted protection to the states by reserving to them power over all affairs not definitely given to Congress. Seven years later the eleventh amendment was added in the same spirit as the first ten, following a heated debate over the action of the Supreme Court in permitting a citizen to sue Georgia against her will. The new amendment forbade the federal courts to hear any suit brought against a state by a citizen.

Funding the National Debt. Declarations of rights on paper however paid no bills, and there was a huge public debt on which the interest was not being paid at all. To the solution of this problem Hamilton turned all his splendid genius. In a "Report on Public Credit" under date of January 9, 1790, one of the first and greatest of American state papers, he offered to Congress the outlines of his plan. He proposed that the federal government call in all the bonds, certificates of indebtedness, and other promises to pay which had been issued by the old Congress since the beginning of the Revolution. Then he urged that the entire amount be put into one consolidated federal debt and that the holders of the old paper receive from the government new bonds drawing interest at fixed rates. This process was called "funding the debt." Such a plan, Hamilton insisted, would satisfy creditors, restore landed property to its former value, and furnish money for agriculture and commerce in the form of credit and capital.

Assumption of State Debts. Hamilton next turned to the debts incurred by the several states in support of the Revolution. These, he said, should be added to the national debt; that is, "assumed" by the United States government. This project he defended not merely on grounds of national honor. It would, he believed, give strength to the new national government by making all public creditors — people of money and power in their several communities — look to Congress, rather than the states, for the payment of their claims.

Funding at Face Value. But should new bonds be given for old, dollar for dollar? This was a burning question. It was well known that thousands of patriots who had lent money to the government or served it in the hour of need had later sold their bonds and certificates at ruinous figures — ten, twenty, and thirty cents on the dollar. It was also well known that these bonds had been bought up by speculators who would be enriched if the government redeemed the old paper at face value. To many citizens this seemed unfair. Accordingly some people suggested that speculators be given new bonds equal to the amount they had laid out for their purchases and that the original holders be paid the balance. Seeing difficulties in carrying out this scheme, others urged the government to "scale the debt" by redeeming not at full value but at a figure reasonably above the market price. Against all such plans Hamilton set his face like flint. He insisted that the government was honestly bound to redeem every outstanding bond at its face value, no matter who held it.

Funding and Assumption Carried. Without much argument Congress voted in favor of funding the national debt at full value. The bill for the assumption of state debts however raised a sharp division of opinion. To the Southern members of Congress, assumption was a gross violation of states' rights, devised in the interest of Northern speculators who had bought up Southern bonds at very low prices. New England representatives, on the other hand, were strongly in favor of assumption; several of them threatened to break up the Union if the bill was voted down. In this sectional brawl was also involved a dispute over the permanent location of the national capital, then temporarily at New York City.

A deadlock, marked by the most surly feelings on both sides, brought the government to a standstill. Acting on an appeal from the Secretary of the Treasury, Jefferson then tried to see what he could do to make peace. By the use of tact he brought the opposing leaders together at a good dinner; once more, as on many other occasions, the Union was saved by compromise. According to the bargain made in Jefferson's dining room, enough Southern members voted for assumption to pass the bill, and they received in exchange Northern votes in favor of building the capital on the banks of the Potomac — after locating it for a ten-year period at Philadelphia to satisfy representatives from Pennsylvania.

The United States Bank. Another feature of Hamilton's program was a design for a great United States Bank. He proposed that Congress create a banking company, authorize it to

From an old print

FIRST UNITED STATES BANK AT PHILADELPHIA

raise a capital stock of $10,000,000 (three-fourths in new six per cent federal bonds and one-fourth in specie), and empower it to issue paper currency under certain rules. From this Bank, Hamilton believed, many advantages would flow. It would raise the price of government bonds, thus improving public credit. A common currency would be created, uniform in value from one end of the land to the other. Branches of the Bank in various cities would make it easy to send money anywhere in the country. Finally, through the issue of bank notes, the money capital available for agriculture and industry would be increased, stimulating the enterprise of all classes. To Hamilton's amazement, Jefferson hotly attacked the Bank scheme and declared that Congress had no power whatever under the Constitution to charter such a corporation. After weighing all opinions, Washington, however, decided in favor of Hamilton's plan and in 1791 the bill establishing the first United States Bank for a period of twenty years became a law.

The Protective Tariff. In connection with raising money to pay the interest on the debt and meet the expenses of the government, Hamilton proposed a third scheme — the protection of American industries by heavy duties on foreign manufactures. Indeed the first revenue act of 1789, though framed primarily to bring money into the empty treasury, declared in favor of the principle. Washington brought the subject before Congress in a message and Hamilton was instructed to prepare a definite plan. The result was his "Report on Manufactures," another state paper worthy of a place beside his "Report on the Public Credit." Hamilton based his argument on broad national grounds: the protective tariff, by encouraging the building of factories, would create a home market for the produce of farms and plantations. This in turn would make the United States independent of other countries in time of peace and double its security in time of war. The industries thus founded would employ women and children otherwise idle at least a part of the time. An increase in the trade between the manufacturing North and the planting South would strengthen the links of union by joining the ties of commerce to those of the new Constitution. Although Congress put only a few of Hamilton's suggestions into the tax law of 1792, his argument was read and discussed in all parts of the country.

THE RISE OF POLITICAL PARTIES

Division over Hamilton's Measures. As Hamilton laid his projects before Congress one after another, he awakened doubts and opposition as well as applause and support. Funding at face value, said his critics, was a government favor to speculators and an injustice to patriots who had been forced in time of need to sell their old bonds for anything they could get; the assumption of state debts was a deep design to undermine the state governments; Congress had no constitutional power to establish a bank; the law creating the Bank merely allowed a private corporation to make paper money and lend it at a high rate of interest; and the tariff was a tax on land and labor for the benefit of manufacturers.

Hamilton's reply was simple and straightforward. Some speculators, he admitted, had profited from the funding of the debt at face value but his policy was necessary to revive public credit. In view of the jealousies of the states it was a good thing to reduce their powers rather than increase them. The Constitution was to be interpreted in the full light of national needs, not strictly according to a narrow view. The Bank would enlarge the amount of capital so sorely needed to start up American industries, thus expanding the output of goods to be exchanged for the produce of farms and plantations. By protecting American industries and multiplying opportunities for employment, the tariff would benefit both land and labor. Out of such wise policies firmly pursued, he concluded, were bound to come strength for the new government at home, prosperity for the people, credit and power abroad. This view Washington fully indorsed, adding the magic of his name to the measures adopted under his administration.

Two Political Parties Appear. During this contest in opinion, voters gradually divided into two parties: Federalists and Anti-Federalists, the former led by Hamilton, the latter by Jefferson. The strength of the Federalists lay in the cities — Boston, Providence, Hartford, New York, Philadelphia, Charleston — among the manufacturing, financial, and commercial groups of the population who were impatient to extend their business operations. The strength of the Anti-Federalists lay mainly among the debt-burdened farmers in all sections of the country, who resented the growth of what they called "a money power," and among the planters who thought they might be overborne by the rapid rise of the commercial and manufacturing interests. In the course of time, the farming and planting South, outside the few towns, presented an almost solid front against the assumption of state debts, the Bank, and the protective tariff. In spite of Washington's efforts to keep peace, the conflict between the parties grew in rancor day by day.

Thomas Jefferson, Leader of the Opposition Party. The party fray had not gone far when the opponents of Washington's administration began to rally around Jefferson. Some of Hamilton's measures he approved at first but later renounced because, he said, he had not understood their dangers. Against others, particularly the Bank project, he took up the cudgels as soon as they were made known. More than once he and Hamilton, shaking violently with anger, attacked each other at Cabinet meetings, and nothing short of the calm pleas of Washington prevented an early and open break between them. In 1794 it finally came anyway. Jefferson resigned as Secretary of State and retired to Virginia to assume the leadership of the opposition.

Shy in manner, halting in speech, disliking the turmoil of public office, and deeply interested in science and philosophy, Jefferson was not very well fitted for the strenuous life of party politics. Nevertheless, he was ambitious and keen. And his ideal for America was by honest conviction exactly contrary to that of Hamilton. The latter believed in a strong, active, "high-toned," centralized government with power to carry out his program. Jefferson looked upon such a government as perilous to the liberties of "plain citizens." Hamilton was afraid of democracy. "Your people is a great beast," he is reported to have said. Jefferson professed a faith in the ability of the people to govern themselves and in their desire to do right.

On economic matters the opinions of the two leaders were also entirely different. Hamilton wanted America to become a great commercial and industrial nation. Jefferson was set against this course for his country. He feared the accumulation of riches and the growth of a large urban working class. He said that artisans are usually a dangerous element; that mobs of great cities are sores on the body politic; that workshops should stay in Europe; and that city crowds with their bad manners and morals should not be allowed to appear in America. The only substantial foundation for a republic, Jefferson believed, was in agriculture. Only by free farmers, owning the land they tilled and looking to the sun in heaven and the labor of their hands for their sustenance, could a strong nation be built and maintained. Trusting in the innate goodness of human nature when nourished on a free soil, Jefferson advocated measures to favor agriculture and to enlarge the rights of persons rather than the powers of government. Thus he became the champion of the individual against the government, and an ardent advocate of freedom of speech and scientific inquiry. It was no mere peevish spirit that drove him into opposition to Hamilton.

The Whisky Rebellion. While political strife was growing hotter, an armed revolt against the government took place in 1794. It grew out of one of Hamilton's measures — a law placing an excise tax on distilled spirits for the purpose of increasing the income applied to paying the interest on the funded debt. As it happened a very considerable part of the whisky manufactured in the United States was made by farmers, especially on the frontier, in their own stills. And under the new revenue law federal officers had the right to go into the homes of people, measure their liquor, and lay the tax on them. The bitterness which farmers had felt against Hamilton's measures from the beginning was now redoubled. In the western districts of Pennsylvania, Virginia, and North Carolina, they refused to pay the tax. In Pennsylvania some of them sacked and burned the houses of tax collectors, as the Revolutionists thirty years before had mobbed the agents of King George sent over to sell them stamps. Indeed the law was being violated in whole districts when Washington called out the troops to suppress "the Whisky Rebellion." Then the movement collapsed; but it left behind a deep-seated resentment which flared up in the election of several Anti-Federalist Congressmen to represent the angry farmers.

FOREIGN INFLUENCES AND DOMESTIC POLITICS

The French Revolution. In this exciting period when the young republic was distracted by its own party battle, a political cyclone broke in Europe — the epoch-making French Revolution — which not only rocked the thrones of the Old World but also aggravated the partisan passions then raging in the United States. The first scene in this dramatic affair opened in the spring of 1789, a few days after Washington was inaugurated. At that time the king of France, Louis XVI, driven into bankruptcy by royal extravagance and costly wars, was forced to ask his people for help. To

From an old print

LOUIS XVI IN THE HANDS OF THE MOB

lay his needs before them, he called a meeting of the French parliament, or "Estates General," which had not assembled for one hundred and fifty years. Acting under powerful leaders, the commoners, or "third estate," in this parliament, overthrew the other two estates, the clergy and the nobility, and as a national assembly assumed full authority. This was an act of revolution which stirred France from the Channel to the Mediterranean.

Amazing events followed in swift succession. On July 14, 1789, the Bastille, a royal prison and symbol of the king's absolute power over his subjects, was stormed by a Paris crowd and destroyed. On the night of August 4 the feudal privileges of the nobility were abolished by the national assembly to the great delight of the populace. Within a few days came the Declaration of the Rights of Man, proclaiming the rule of the people and equal privileges for all citizens. Then the assembly drew up a constitution which created a permanent parliament for France, and in 1791 forced Louis XVI to accept it. Little disorder accompanied these startling changes. To all appearances a peaceful revolution had stripped the king of his sovereignty and based the government on the consent of the governed — according to American principles.

American Influence in France. As a matter of fact, in making their revolution the French had been encouraged by the American example. French officers and soldiers who had served in the American war, on their return, told their countrymen marvelous tales about the United States. At the frugal table of General Washington in America and in council with the simple Franklin at Paris, French noblemen of ancient lineage had learned to respect both the talents and the character of the leaders of the republic beyond the seas. Travelers who had gone to see the American experiment with their own eyes carried back to the French king and the upper classes astounding stories of popular government.

On the other hand praising American democracy was regarded by French conservatives as playing with fire. "When we think of the false ideas of government and philanthropy," wrote one of Lafayette's aides, "which these youths acquired in America and propagated in France with so much enthusiasm and such deplorable success — for this mania of imitation powerfully aided the revolution, though it was not the sole cause of it — we are bound to confess that it would have been better, both for themselves and for us, if these young philosophers in red-heeled shoes had stayed at home in attendance on the court."

Early American Opinion of the French Revolution. So close were the ties between the two nations that every step in the first stage of the French Revolution was greeted with applause in the United States. "Liberty will have another feather in her cap," exultantly declared a Boston editor. "In no part of the globe," soberly wrote John Marshall, "was this revolution hailed with more joy than in America." To symbolize the friendship of the two countries, the main key to the Bastille was sent to Washington for a memento and he was glad to accept it as "a token of the victory gained by liberty." In the great events at Paris, Thomas Paine saw "the first ripe fruits of American principles transplanted into Europe." Federalists and Anti-Federalists, Hamiltonians and Jeffersonians looked on the new constitution of France as another proof that American ideals were sound.

The Reign of Terror. While warm congratulations were being exchanged, rumor began to say that all was not well in France. Enraged at the loss of their special privileges, many French noblemen fled into Germany where they plotted an invasion of their own country to overthrow government by commoners. Unhappy about his lot Louis XVI tried to get the help of neighboring kings in the same enterprise, and then attempted to escape from his kingdom, only to be captured and taken back to Paris in disgrace.

A new phase of the Revolution now unrolled. Working people, denied the right to vote by the first French constitution, became restless, especially in Paris. Assembling on the Champs de Mars, a large open field, they signed a petition calling for another constitution giving them the suffrage. When told to disperse, they refused and were fired upon by the national guard. This "massacre," as it was called, inflamed the populace; and a radical party known as "Jacobins" soon sprang up, taking its name from a Jacobin monastery in which it held its sessions. In September, 1792, another national convention, called to make a second constitution, abolished the monarchy, and set up a republic. On January 21, 1793, it sent Louis to the scaffold. To the war on Austria, already raging, it added a war on England. Then came a "reign of terror," during which the republicans in possession of the convention put to death a large number of people suspected of sympathy with the monarchy. They shot down peasants who rose in arms against their rule and established an iron dictatorship. Civil war ensued and terrible atrocities were committed on both sides — in the name of liberty and in the name of monarchy. To many Americans it now seemed that the French Revolution, begun with so much promise, had sunk into anarchy.

Burke Summons the World to War on France. By this great upheaval the ruling classes of England were frightened into a frenzy. Edmund Burke, fearing that French doctrines might spread to all Europe opened a verbal fight on them. In his *Reflections on the French Revolution,* written in 1790, he attacked with awful wrath the whole program of popular government; he called for war, relentless war, upon the French as monsters and outlaws; he demanded that they be brought to order by a restoration of the king to full power with the aid of foreign armies.

Paine's Defense of the French Revolution. To offset the campaign of hate against the French, Thomas Paine replied to Burke in another of his famous tracts, *The Rights of Man,* which was published in America with a letter of approval from Jefferson. Burke, said Paine, had been mourning about the glories of the French monarchy and aristocracy but had forgotten the starving people; had wept over the plumage and neglected the dying bird. Burke had denied the right of the French people to choose their own governors, blandly forgetting that the English government itself rested on two revolutions. He had boasted that the king of England held his own crown in contempt of the democratic societies. Paine answered: "If I ask a man in America if he wants a king, he retorts and asks me if I take him for an idiot." To Burke's charge that the doctrines of the rights of man were "newfangled," Paine replied that the question was not whether they were new or old but whether they were right or wrong. As to the French disorders and difficulties, he bade the world to be patient, to wait to see what would be brought forth in due time.

The Effect of the French Revolution on American Politics. The course of the French Revolution gave more rancor to the party argument already distracting America. Followers of Hamilton became more distressed than ever when they heard of the cruel deeds during the reign of terror. They denounced as "Jacobin" every American who did not condemn loudly enough the proceedings of the French republic. From his pulpit a Federalist preacher in Massachusetts berated "the atheistical, anarchical, and in other respects immoral principles of the French Republicans"; then with equal passion he attacked Jefferson and all the Anti-Federalists, charging them with spreading false French propaganda and betraying America. "The editors, patrons, and abettors of these vehicles of slander," he exclaimed, "ought to be considered and treated as enemies to their country. . . . Of all traitors, they are the most aggravatedly criminal; of all villains, they are the most infamous and detestable."

As a matter of fact, the Anti-Federalists were generally favorable to the French Revolution although they deplored many of the deeds committed in its name. Paine's pamphlet, indorsed by Jefferson, was widely read. Democratic societies, after the fashion of French political clubs, arose in the cities; the coalition of European monarchs against France was called a coalition against all republics; and the execution of Louis XVI was openly celebrated at a banquet in Philadelphia as a glorious event. Titles, such as "Sir," "The Honorable," and "His Excellency," were decried as aristocratic and the French title "Citizen" was adopted in their stead. Pamphlets in defense of the French multiplied, while the papers reported news from Paris with more detail.

The European War Disturbs American Commerce. This battle of wits, or rather contest in propaganda, might have gone on indefinitely in the United States without raising any practical questions if the country had not been caught in the war between England and France, now at white heat. Having command of the sea, the English claimed the right to seize American produce bound for French ports and to confiscate any American ships which carried French goods. Piling fuel on a fire already hot enough, they began to search American ships and seize British-born sailors found on board.

The French Appeal for Help. While the British were interfering with American trade and sailors, the French republic turned to the United States for aid in its war on England, sending over as its diplomatic agent "Citizen Genêt," an ardent supporter of the new régime. On his arrival at Charleston, he was greeted with fervor by the Anti-Federalists. As he made his way North he was wined and dined and given popular ovations that turned his head. So Genêt came to the conclusion that the whole country was ready to join France in her contest with England. He therefore attempted to use American ports as bases of operations for French privateers preying on British merchant ships; and he called on the United States to help France, according to promises contained in the treaty of 1778, in return for her assistance in the American Revolution.

Neutrality and the Jay Treaty. But Washington was unmoved by the popular sympathy for France. He received Genêt coldly. The demand for aid under the old treaty of alliance he answered by proclaiming the neutrality of America and warning American citizens against hostile acts toward either France or England. When Genêt continued to hold meetings, issue manifestoes, and stir up the people against England, Washington asked the French government to recall him. This act he followed up by sending the Chief Justice of the Supreme Court, John Jay, on a mission to England to make a pacific settlement of certain points in dispute.

The result was the celebrated Jay treaty of 1794. By its terms Great Britain agreed to withdraw her troops from the forts on the American frontier where they had remained since the war for independence and to grant a few trade concessions. Other sources of enmity toward Britain — her failure to return slaves carried off during the Revolution, the seizure of American ships, and the impressment of sailors — were not mentioned by the treaty, much to the annoyance of everybody in America, including Federalists. Nevertheless, dreading a second war with England, Washington induced the Senate to ratify the treaty.

At this outcome the hostility of the Anti-Federalists burst all bounds. Jefferson declared the Jay treaty "an infamous act which is really nothing more than an alliance between England and the Anglo-men of this country, against the legislature and the people of the United States." When Hamilton tried to defend it, he was stoned by a mob in New York and driven from the platform with blood streaming from his face. Jay was burned in effigy. Washington himself was criticized by a resentful House of Representatives. To display its feelings, it called upon him for papers dealing with the treaty, and then grew still more captious when he refused to send them on the ground that the House did not share in the treaty-making power.

Washington Retires from Politics. It was this political battle that confirmed the President in his determination to retire at the end of his second term in office. He did not believe that a third term was unconstitutional or improper; but he was worn out by his long and arduous labors in war and in peace and wounded by attacks from former companions.

Accordingly on the eve of the presidential election, in September, 1796, Washington issued his Farewell Address, another state paper to be treasured and read by generations of Americans to come. In this address he warned the people against sectional bickerings. He protested against the spirit of partisanship, saying that in government "of the popular character, in government purely elective, it is a spirit not to be encouraged." He cautioned Americans against "the insidious wiles of foreign influence," and told them that "Europe has a set of primary interests which to us have none or a very remote relation. Hence she must be engaged in frequent controversies, the causes of which are essentially foreign to our concerns. . . . It is our true policy to steer clear of permanent alliances with any portion of the foreign world. . . . Taking care always to keep ourselves, by suitable establishments, on a respectable defensive posture, we may safely trust to temporary alliances for extraordinary emergencies."

The Campaign of 1796 — Adams Elected. Washington's retirement gave great encouragement to the Anti-Federalists. In honor of France and in opposition to the "monarchical" tendencies of the Federalists, they adopted the name "Republican"; some radicals were even rash enough to call themselves "Democrats." Selecting Jefferson as their candidate for President, the Republicans carried on such a spirited campaign against John Adams, the Federalist nominee, that they came within four votes of electing their favorite.

The successful candidate, Adams, was not very well suited for leadership in a hot, political struggle. He was studious in habits and blunt in dealing with people. He was neither a good speaker nor a skillful peacemaker. In one of his books he had declared himself in favor of "government by an aristocracy of talents and wealth" — an offense which the Republicans never forgave. While John Marshall found him a "sensible, plain, candid, good-tempered man," Jefferson could see nothing in him but a "monocrat" and "Anglo-man." Had it not been for the conduct of the French government, Adams would have been unpopular during his entire administration.

The Quarrel with France. As the fates would have it however the French government managed to unite Republicans and Federalists in common anger against it. It regarded the Jay treaty between England and the United States as unfair and a violation of promises the Americans had made in the treaty with France in 1778. Accordingly it declined to receive the American minister, treated him with discourtesy, and finally told him to leave the country. As eager to maintain peace as Washington had been, Adams kept cool and sent to France a commission of eminent Americans with instructions to reach an understanding with the French republic. On their arrival they were surprised to find, instead of a welcome, an indirect request for an apology on the part of the American government, a payment in cash, and an annual tribute as the price of amity. When the report of the commission reached President Adams, he promptly laid it before Congress, referring to the Frenchmen who had made the demands, as "Mr. X, Mr. Y, and Mr. Z." So it was known as the "X.Y.Z. Affair."

This news, coupled with the fact that French privateers, like the British, were preying upon American commerce, offended even the Republicans who had been loudest in professing their French sympathies. They forgot their wrath over the Jay treaty and joined with the Federalists in shouting: "Millions for defense, not one cent for tribute!" Preparations for war were made on every hand. Washington was once more called upon to take his position at the head of the army. Indeed fighting actually began upon the high seas and went on without a formal declaration of war until the year 1800. By that time France had another government. Napoleon Bonaparte, as First Consul, had become head of the French republic, and the United States was able to make terms.

Alien and Sedition Laws. Perplexed by their experience with France, the Federalists resolved, if possible, to put an end to radical French influence in America and to silence Republican criticism in general. To accomplish this purpose they passed two harsh laws in the summer of 1798: the Alien and Sedition Acts.

The first of these measures gave the President the right to expel from the country or to imprison any alien whom he regarded as "dangerous" or "had reasonable grounds to suspect" of "any treasonable or secret machinations against the government."

An old cartoon

A QUARREL BETWEEN A FEDERALIST AND A REPUBLICAN IN THE HOUSE OF REPRESENTATIVES

The second, the Sedition Act, provided for fining and imprisoning everyone who tried to stir up an unlawful combination against the government and everyone who wrote, uttered, or published "any false, scandalous, and malicious writing . . . against the government of the United States, or either House of Congress, or the President of the United States, with intent to defame said government . . . to bring them or either of them into contempt or disrepute." This severe law was hurried through Congress in defiance of the opposition and in spite of the first amendment to the Constitution which clearly states that Congress shall make no law abridging freedom of speech or the press. Even many Federalists were dubious about the results of such action. When Hamilton read the bill he exclaimed: "Let us not establish a tyranny. Energy is a very different thing from violence." John Marshall told his friends in Virginia that, had he been in Congress, he would have opposed the two bills because he thought them "useless" and "calculated to create unnecessary discontents and jealousies."

The Alien law was not enforced; but it gave deep offense to the Irish and French in the United States who were reproaching the American government for dealing too gently with Great Britain. The Sedition law, on the other hand, was sternly applied. Several editors of Republican newspapers were soon put into jail or ruined by heavy fines for criticizing the Federalist President and his policies. Bystanders at political meetings who wished the President ill-luck or said that he was a disgrace to the country were rushed before Federalist judges and promptly fined and imprisoned. Although the prosecutions were not numerous, they caused a great furore. They led the Republicans to believe that the Federalists were going to use the courts and jails to stamp out all free political debate. In fact however the effort to check liberty of press and speech had exactly the opposite effect; instead of helping the Federalists, it sharpened criticism of their party.

The Kentucky and Virginia Resolutions. Of this situation Jefferson was quick to take advantage. He wrote out a set of resolutions declaring the Sedition law null and void, as violating the federal Constitution. These resolutions were passed by the Kentucky legislature late in 1798, signed by the governor, and sent to the other states for their consideration. Though unfavorable replies came from a number of Northern states, Kentucky the following year reaffirmed its position and declared that the states should refuse to obey, or nullify, any act of Congress which they deemed unconstitutional. It thus defied the federal government and announced a doctrine of *nullification* which was often used later by other states when they did not like laws passed by Congress. In Virginia, Madison led the attack on the Alien and Sedition laws. By careful maneuvering he got the legislature to pass resolutions condemning them and calling upon the other states to assert their rights and to adopt proper means to preserve them against violation; but by this action Madison did not mean to indorse nullification.

The Republican Triumph in 1800. In the presidential campaign of 1800 the Republicans, with Jefferson and Aaron Burr as their candidates for President and Vice President, did everything they could to put on the Federalist candidate, President Adams, all the blame for the Alien and Sedition laws. The Federalists, divided among themselves and having no love for Adams, could not make an enthusiastic fight. They tried to discredit opponents by calling them "Jacobins" and "Anarchists" but the public was tired of abuse. Therefore Adams was badly defeated in the election. The Republicans carried the entire South and New York, and won eight of the fifteen electoral votes in Pennsylvania. "Our beloved Adams will now close his bright career," lamented a Federalist newspaper. "Sons of faction, demagogues, and high priests of anarchy, now you have cause to triumph!"

Jefferson's election, however, was still uncertain. By a curious provision in the Constitution, presidential electors were instructed to vote for two persons without stating which office each was to fill; the person who received the highest number of votes was to be President and the candidate standing next was to be Vice President. Now it so happened that Burr, the Republican nominee for Vice President, won the same number of votes as Jefferson. Accordingly, as they were "tied," the election was thrown into the House of Representatives, where the Federalists held the balance of power. Although it was well known that Burr was not considered a candidate for President, his friends and many Federalists began scheming to elect him to that office. But at this stage Jefferson's strongest political foe, Alexander Hamilton, came out in his favor because he thought Burr was a more "dangerous" man. Hamilton's action turned the tide and on February 17, 1801, on the thirty-sixth ballot, Jefferson was victorious. To prevent a repetition of this unfortunate affair, the twelfth amendment to the Constitution was adopted in 1804, altering slightly the method of electing the President.

From Cook Studios, Richmond, Va.

PORTRAIT OF THOMAS JEFFERSON BY GILBERT STUART

BRUTON PARISH CHURCH, WILLIAMSBURG, VIRGINIA

A painting by A. Wordsworth Thompson.

Development in Culture

Social Changes Made by the Revolution. Naturally the great upheaval which marked the war for independence wrought many changes in the colonial culture described in the fourth chapter. The Revolution overthrew and drove from America the English ruling class made up of royal governors, judges, and other high officials. It likewise snapped some of the ties which united the Anglican Church in the colonies with the Established Church in England. During the war many large estates owned by Tories were seized, divided into small farms, and sold to patriots, thus increasing the number of freeholders. In the general process a new ruling class of native Americans — merchants, planters, and farmers — assumed the entire responsibility of government, which was something very different from merely sharing in a government with British officials having the upper hand. As colonists the Americans were only "provincials," that is, they were under the tutelage of the mother country whence came direction in literature, art, and social customs as well as affairs of state. Political independence however brought a large measure of social and intellectual independence. And the knowledge and interests of Americans were broadened by their own task of creating a republic and by closer relations with the Continent, especially with France.

Religious Toleration. One clear cultural change was the disestablishment of the Anglican Church in the six states where it had once enjoyed a special privilege. Besides placing this Church on an equal footing with all others, Virginia passed Jefferson's Statute for Religious Freedom in 1786 — a milestone in the history of liberty. This Act declared that no one should be compelled to attend any church or be taxed for the support of religion. It then provided that henceforward all persons were free to profess and by argument to maintain their own opinions in religious matters. The Constitution of the United States also promoted the growth of religious freedom because it did not place any religious qualifications on federal officers. In fact it specifically declared in Article VI that no religious test shall ever be applied to any office or public trust under the United States. Going a step further the first amendment to the Constitution forbade Congress to make any law respecting the establishment of religion or prohibiting the free exercise thereof.

Yet it would be a mistake to think that universal religious toleration was established in America at this time. Several state constitutions contained religious limitations on the right to vote and hold office; in some places Catholics and Jews were thus excluded from political affairs. Furthermore the Congregational Church continued to be the established church in New Hampshire until 1817, in Connecticut until 1818, and in Massachusetts until 1833. Many years were to pass before all citizens, regardless of their religion, were to enjoy the right of voting and holding office.

Few changes were made in the religious denominations inherited from colonial times. Some of the Congregational Churches however became Unitarian in faith and in 1790 the Catholic Church was given a bishop of its own, Father John Carroll of Baltimore. To these churches was added another. During the Revolution the Methodists, who had numbered only about three hundred in 1771, carried on a great evangelizing campaign and rapidly increased their membership. Shortly after the close of the war they founded an independent church, and under the leadership of the tireless missionary, Francis Asbury, stirred the country from the coast to the frontier with revival meetings. On his death in 1816 the Methodist Church claimed more than two thousand ministers and over two hundred thousand members.

Popular Education. Thrown upon their own resources by independence, Americans had to develop by education their native talents for self-government. All leaders of the age recognized the importance of the subject, and some wrote books and articles about it. Although there was nothing in the federal Constitution on education, Washington made a plan for a national university, urged Congress to vote funds for it, and on his death left a sum of money for that purpose. His Virginia neighbor, Thomas Jefferson, was especially alive to the need for popular education. He helped his old college, William and Mary, to frame a new course of study giving a larger place to science and modern languages; he worked out a complete system of public schools which he hoped to see established; and finally founded the University of Virginia.

But it took money to pay for buildings and teachers, and the young republic was not rich. About the only thing that the national government or the state governments could do was to grant land out of their respective public domains in aid of schools. This they did generously. In the second ordinance for the Northwest Territory, adopted by the Congress in 1785, one section of six

Courtesy of The Metropolitan Museum of Art

AN EARLY PRINT OF THE UNIVERSITY OF VIRGINIA

hundred and forty acres was set aside in each township for the support of public schools. This example in various forms was imitated by some of the states that owned public lands.

Since this land at first yielded little revenue and the people did not like to tax themselves for education, not much was done to promote public schools for more than fifty years after independence. The country continued to depend for elementary education on the little schools conducted by the various churches as in colonial times. These were supplemented however by academies — forerunners of high schools — sometimes founded by churches and sometimes by private interests. In both cases however students had to pay fees.

During this period the Sunday school was brought over from England and thousands of boys and girls learned their letters during the leisure of the Sabbath Day. At the same time an impetus was given to popular education by the adoption of another English scheme — the monitorial system. Under this plan a few pupils in each school were taught to read and write, and as quickly as they learned, they in turn taught younger pupils. It was a crude system, but at least it was a start.

Colleges. While the churches continued to found colleges, as they had done in colonial times, and doubled the number before the close of the eighteenth century, a new type of college now appeared. This was the state institution supported by grants of land and money made by state legislatures. Within a few years after the founding of the republic North Carolina, South Carolina, and Georgia had established such colleges. Tennessee and Ohio soon followed their example. And in 1825, while Jefferson was still living, the University of Virginia, which he had designed with such care, opened its doors to students.

The American Press. In response to the increasing interest of the people in public affairs, newspapers sprang up in all parts of the country. Forty-three papers, it is estimated, were being published at the end of the Revolution, and thirty years later every city and village of any size must have had its press, for there were then at least three hundred and sixty newspapers in the United States. In this period the daily paper made its bow, the first of them, *The Pennsylvania Packet and Daily Advertiser*, in 1784; twenty-five years afterward there were twenty-seven dailies scattered from Boston to New Orleans. As the party battle between the Federalists and the Republicans grew hotter, most of these papers became party organs, cheering one side and abusing the other. Hamilton and Jefferson each had a personal friend at the head of a journal and furnished him with materials to help keep the party fires burning.

To meet a growing demand for self-improvement new magazines were founded, popularizing literature, science, and art in an age when books were few and libraries scarce. Scores of magazines had their hour and died young. But a few were destined to a long life.

Matthew Carey's *Columbian Magazine* established in Philadelphia in 1786 was a staple in intellectual circles for more than half a century, and *The North American Review* first issued in Boston in 1815 is still published after the lapse of more than a century. The wide range of these early magazines is indicated by a descriptive note attached to one of the periodicals of the time: "A Monthly Museum of Knowledge and Rational Entertainment containing Poetry, Musick, Biography, History, Physics, Geography, Morality, Criticism, Philosophy, Mathematics, Agriculture, Architecture, Chemistry, Novels, Tales, Romances, Translations, News, Marriages, Deaths, &c., &c." One happy editor introduced to his readers "the elegant polish of the female pen" — a pen which was to become more active with every passing season.

Literature. Printing presses, newspapers, and magazines promoted all branches of literature, for they gave writers a market for plays, poems, and essays. Authors now tried to produce "the great American novel," often basing their plots on the contemporary political contest. For example a disciple of Jefferson, Hugh Brackenridge of western Pennsylvania, wrote a romance entitled *Modern Chivalry* in which he made fun of Federalists but warned working people to leave politics to "their betters." Another Anti Federalist, Charles Brockden Brown, who also published several novels, is noteworthy on account of "advanced" views on many subjects. In one of his works he makes a highly intelligent woman lament that women are excluded "from many professions which might afford us, in common with men, the means of subsistence and independence." On another page the same character complains that "We are excluded from all political rights without the least ceremony. Law-makers thought as little of comprehending us in their code of liberty as if we were pigs or sheep." These words Brown wrote in 1797. But this was not "a best seller." That honor seems to belong to *The Coquette*, a novel based on social life, by Hannah Webster Foster, printed in the same year, which went through thirteen editions before her death in 1840 and is still to be found in old bookshops.

Inspired by the debates on patriotic and political themes, playwrights tried to compose "the great American drama" for the theaters which were now permitted even in Puritan Boston. Royall Tyler's comedy, "The Contrast," produced in New York City in 1787, represented the protest of a stalwart farmer against the pride and soft manners of the city. In the course of the play the hero praises republican simplicity, decries luxury, and celebrates the glories of Greece in her early days when her people knew "no other tool than the ax and the saw." One of the Yankee characters boasts that "we don't make any great matter of distinction in our state between quality and other folks." A more versatile writer, William Dunlap, called the founder of the American theater, took up Tyler's refrain in his play, "The Father," and made one of his actors say:

> Then might, perhaps, one land on earth be found,
> Free from th' extremes of poverty and riches;
> Where ne'er a scepter'd tyrant should be known,
> Or tyrant lordling, curses of creation.

Sound Jeffersonian doctrine, this!

Poetry also reflected the strife of the republican age. A group of New England writers, known as the Hartford Wits, in a long poem called the "Anarchiad," published in 1787, ridiculed paper money, leveling democracy, and the general theories of such men as Daniel Shays who had led the farmers' rebellion in Massachusetts. On the other side Philip Freneau, "the poet of the Revolution," wrote with equal vigor in prose and verse in support of Jefferson's party. But he did not confine himself by any means to party affairs; for example he wrote a poem on Paul Jones, the naval hero of the Revolution. It is also appropriate to recall that William Cullen Bryant, whose "Thanatopsis" written in 1811 won immortality for him in American letters, began his career with politics in 1808 by a tirade against Jefferson, called "The Embargo."

With novelists, dramatists, and poets taking such a keen interest in American topics, it is not surprising to find historians engaged along the same lines. After playing her part as a penwoman in the war for independence, Mrs. Mercy Warren wrote a big three-volume history of the American revolution, published in 1805. Naturally the heroes of the war soon had biographers. Amid his

Architectural Suggestions of the Middle Period for Elaborating an
Old Home

READING THE NEWS
A painting by R. Caton Woodville

labors as Chief Justice of the Supreme Court, John Marshall took time to write a five-volume life of George Washington — which pleased the Federalists and made Jeffersonians mad by its treatment of party affairs. Leaving politics aside Mason L. Weems, better known as "Parson Weems," published in 1800 a life of the great General and President in which he told several doubtful stories, including the now famous yarn about little George, the hatchet, and the cherry tree.

Science. Carrying forward the practical side of science which had made Franklin noted in the colonial period, Americans now made a new chapter in the history of invention. In 1790 John Fitch launched a steam ferryboat which ran successfully between Philadelphia and Burlington. Having proved the soundness of his theory, Fitch tried in vain to raise money to build more ships, making a special point of their usefulness in navigating the Mississippi and Ohio rivers and opening up the West. "He is crazy, poor fellow," remarked bystanders when he explained his wild ideas. But his notions were developed by Colonel John Stevens who put a steamboat on the Hudson in 1798. They were fully realized when Robert Fulton built his *Clermont* which made its memorable voyage from New York City to Albany and back in 1807. A new era was opened in cotton raising by Eli Whitney when in 1792 he patented his gin which at one stroke made obsolete the thousand-year-old method of cleaning cotton by hand. It was by such inventions coupled with others made in Europe that "the Idea of Progress," created by French thinkers, was popularized and applied in America. Henceforward, it was said, the lot of all mankind can be steadily improved by the mastery of nature.

Painting. While historians were telling the stories of the Revolution and its heroes, artists were making famous scenes and actors live on canvas. John Trumbull of Connecticut painted portraits of Washington and Hamilton (p. 176) and pictures in the grand style of the battle of Bunker Hill, the signing of the Declaration of Independence, and the surrender of Cornwallis (p. 153). Gilbert Stuart, a son of Rhode Island, after studying in London with Benjamin West (p. 84), returned to the land of his birth after the Revolution and labored until his death in 1828 to preserve in paint and oil the features of the great and rich (p. 212). His portrayal of Washington is held by many critics to be the best, although it makes the General too severe in appearance.

Probably far truer to life were the portraits of Washington by Charles Wilson Peale of Maryland, an American patriot who took a loyal interest in the Revolution and had a genuine affection for its heroes. In all, Peale painted fourteen pictures of Washington (p. 152), representing a rugged soldier rather than a drawing-room gentleman, as the President was painted by Stuart. Moreover Peale worked hard to promote the fine arts in the United States and was instrumental in inducing Philadelphia to found an Art Academy in 1805, with faith in "the harvest of the future." Whatever place the painters of this period may occupy in the scale of criticism, we owe them a great debt for handing down to us concepts of the events and figures of that far-off time.

Architecture. Like painting and literature, architecture was affected by the republican ideal. Greece and Rome were now an inspiration to Americans, for these states too had once been self-governing commonwealths, as college students had learned from the classics. It is not strange therefore that federal buildings, banks (p. 197), and mansions were adorned with the columns and porticoes of the ancient designers. From the same source Major L'Enfant, the French engineer then resident in the United States, drew many of his ideas for the plan of the City of Washington, the capital of the republic, which he was commissioned to make. As orators now adopted the "fine style" of Cicero's orations, so architects depended for dignity and strength on the glory that was Greece and the power that was Rome.

References

J. S. Bassett, *The Federalist System* (American Nation Series).

C. A. Beard, *Economic Origins of Jeffersonian Democracy.*

E. P. Cubberley, *Public Education in the United States.*

S. Isham, *History of American Painting.*

J. F. Jameson, *The American Revolution Considered as a Social Movement.*

J. M. Lee, *History of American Journalism.*

H. Lodge, *Alexander Hamilton.*

J. B. McMaster, *History of the People of the United States*, Vol. I.
J. T. Morse, *Thomas Jefferson.*
T. Talmadge, *Story of Architecture in America.*

Questions

1. Who were the leaders in the first administration?
2. What step was taken to appease the opposition?
3. Enumerate Hamilton's great measures and explain each in detail.
4. Show that the parts of Hamilton's system were related.
5. Contrast the general political views of Hamilton and Jefferson.
6. What were the important results of the "peaceful" French Revolution (1789–92)?
7. Explain the interaction of opinion between France and the United States.
8. How did the "Reign of Terror" change American opinion?
9. What was the Burke-Paine controversy?
10. Show how the war in Europe affected American commerce and involved America with England and France.
11. What were American policies with regard to each of those countries?
12. What was the outcome of the Alien and Sedition Acts?
13. Enumerate the chief social changes brought about by the Revolution.
14. What advanced steps were taken in religious toleration?
15. What new ideas were introduced into lower schools?
16. What new type of college appeared?
17. Describe the novel features in journalism.
18. Give some of the ideas in current fiction, drama, and poetry.
19. Name two inventors and two painters of the period.
20. Why did architects turn to Greece and Rome for inspiration?

Research Topics

The French Revolution. Robinson and Beard, *Development of Modern Europe*, Vol. I, pp. 224–282; Elson, pp. 332–335.

The Burke-Paine Controversy. Make an analysis of Burke's *Reflections on the French Revolution* and Paine's *Rights of Man.*

The Alien and Sedition Acts. Macdonald, *Documentary Source Book*, pp. 259–267; Elson, pp. 348–355.

Kentucky and Virginia Resolutions. Macdonald, pp. 267–278.

Source Studies. Materials in Hart, *American History Told by Contemporaries*, Vol. III, pp. 255–343.

Biographical Studies. Alexander Hamilton, John Adams, Thomas Jefferson, and Albert Gallatin.

The Twelfth Amendment. Contrast the provision in the original Constitution with the terms of the Amendment. See Appendix.

Fiction and Drama. Beard, *Rise of American Civilization*, Vol. I, pp. 465–479. *Cambridge History of American Literature*, Vol. I, pp. 284–283, 215–232.

Science and the Idea of Progress. Beard, *Rise of American Civilization*, Vol. I, 441–447, 451–457.

Education. Beard, *Rise of American Civilization*, Vol. I, pp. 486–498.

The Painters. Beard, *Rise of American Civilization*, Vol. I, pp. 479–486. Consult also an encyclopedia under the names of the leading painters of the period.

Questions for Debate

1. Hamilton made a larger contribution than Jefferson to the establishment of American institutions.

2. The Federalists were justified in their hostility to Revolutionary France.

3. Literature and art are a part of the political and social life of a nation.

Historical Fiction

Gertrude Atherton, *The Conqueror*.
James Lane Allen, *The Choir Invisible*.
S. Weir Mitchell, *The Red City* (a sequel to *Hugh Wynne*).

CHAPTER X

HOW THE JEFFERSON PARTY GOVERNED AMERICA

REPUBLICAN PRINCIPLES AT STAKE

Opposition to Strong Central Government. Preferring open fields to commercial cities the Jeffersonian Republicans were in the beginning local-minded. Their love for America was certainly as strong as that of Hamilton; but they gave their thought and affection to the state rather than to the national government. Indeed a large number of the party members had been opponents of the Constitution in the days of its adoption. Jefferson had doubts about it and Monroe, who later became President, had been a foe of ratification. The former went so far in the direction of localism that he put the state above the nation in the Kentucky resolutions of 1798, declaring that the states could nullify federal law.

Republican Simplicity. Every act of the Jeffersonian party during its early days of power was in accord with its ideals of government. It had been against all pomp and ceremony for the chief executive of the nation, calling them signs of monarchy and tyranny. Appropriately therefore Jefferson's inauguration on March 4, 1801, the first at Washington, the new capital, was marked by simplicity. Thinking that Washington and Adams were too much like kings in reading presidential addresses to Congress, Jefferson sent his own message in writing — a custom that was continued until 1913 when Woodrow Wilson returned to the example set by the first President.

Republican Measures. The Republicans had complained about the great national debt — they said that the bondholders were a dangerous "money power"; so they began to pay it off as rapidly as possible. They had held commerce in low esteem and looked upon a large navy as a mere device to protect it; hence they reduced the number of warships. They had objected to excise taxes, particularly on whisky; these they quickly abolished, to the intense delight of the farmers. They had protested against the heavy cost of the federal government; they reduced expenses by discharging hundreds of men and closing offices.

They had criticized the Sedition Act; so they let it expire in 1801. Moreover Jefferson pardoned persons who had been sent to jail for disobeying it, and his party promptly impeached Samuel Chase, a judge of the Supreme Court, who had been especially severe in his attacks upon offenders under this law. Their failure to convict and oust Justice Chase was due to no lack of zeal on their part but to the opposition Federalist vote in the Senate where the trial was held. The Republicans had regarded the appointment of a large number of federal judges during the last hours of Adams' administration as an attempt of the Federalists to control the courts. Accordingly they at once repealed the law creating the new judgeships, depriving the "midnight appointees" of their posts. They knew that the federal offices, civil and military, had been sources of strength to the Federalist party; and Jefferson was careful to fill most of the vacancies as they occurred with members of his own party. To his credit however it must be said that he believed in giving places to worthy persons only and did not make wholesale removals to find room for political workers.

The Republicans thus hewed to the line of their general program of holding the national government within tight bounds. But they did not attempt to rewrite the Constitution as the Federalists feared they might do. They simply allowed critics of the federal system to express their opinions freely. "If there be any among us who wish to dissolve this union or to change its republican form," wrote Jefferson in his first inaugural, "let them stand undisturbed as monuments of the safety with which error of opinion may be tolerated where reason is left free to combat it." The future of America Jefferson believed to be full of promise. "A wise and frugal government which shall restrain men from injuring one another, shall leave them otherwise free to regulate their own pursuits of industry and improvement, and shall not take from the mouth of labour the bread it has earned. This is the sum of good government; and this is necessary to close the circle of our felicities."

But in spite of their theory that the central government must be weak for the sake of liberty, the Republicans made it strong for the sake of America. In a few short years that lay ahead it was their fate to double the territory of the United States; to give the Constitution a generous interpretation that shocked even many a Federalist by its breadth of view; to wage war against Great Britain in the name of commerce; to reëstablish the hated United States Bank; to enact a high protective tariff; to observe their Federalist opponents take their turn at defending the rights of the state; to announce that the central government was supreme in foreign affairs; and to see the Constitution upheld against the attacks of states by a son of agricultural Virginia, John Marshall, Chief Justice of the Supreme Court of the United States.

THE PROBLEM OF LAND IN THE WEST

Expansion and Land Hunger. The first measure which drove the Republicans out upon this new national course — the purchase of the Louisiana territory — surprised no one more than the Republicans themselves. It was not the lack of sufficient land for farmers that led Jefferson to add such an immense domain to the original possessions of the United States. The frontier was not crowded, for settlements in the Northwest Territory had not yet been pushed far beyond the north bank of the Ohio River. To the south, in Kentucky and Tennessee, there were still wide reaches of untilled soil. The Alabama and Mississippi regions were vast Indian frontiers of the state of Georgia, almost unoccupied and unexplored. Even to the wildest imagination there seemed to be soil enough to satisfy the land hunger of the American people for a century to come.

The Influence of the Mississippi River on Politics. At all events the East saw no good reason for expansion. The planters of the Carolinas, the manufacturers of Pennsylvania, the importers of New York, and the shipbuilders of New England looked to Europe for trade opportunities, refinements, and sometimes their very ideas of government; hence they were slow to appreciate the future of the West in national economy. The better educated the Easterners were, the less, it seems, they understood the destiny of the nation. Sons of Federalist fathers at Williams College, after a long debate, decided by a vote of fifteen to one that the purchase of Louisiana was undesirable.

On the other hand, the pioneers of Kentucky, Ohio, and Tennessee, if unlearned in books, saw with their very eyes the resources of the wilderness farther west. Many had been across the Mississippi and had beheld the rich lands so attractive to the white man — lands as fertile as could be found anywhere on the earth. Down the great river they were already floating their wheat, corn, and bacon to ocean-going ships bound for the ports of the seaboard or for Europe. Journeys over the mountain barriers to Eastern markets with their bulky farm produce, they knew from experience, were almost impossible, and costly at best. Nails, bolts of cloth, tea, and coffee could come that way on horseback, but corn and bacon could not be sent in return by any such route. A free outlet to the sea by the Mississippi was as essential to the pioneers of the Kentucky region as the harbor of Boston to the merchant princes of that metropolis.

Louisiana under Spanish Rule. But of this free outlet they were by no means sure. At the close of the Seven Years' War the Louisiana territory stretching from New Orleans to the Rocky Mountains had been given to the king of Spain. While he controlled the mouth of the Mississippi there was little to fear, for he had neither the army nor the navy competent to stop American trade. Moreover President Washington had been able, by great tact, to win from Spain in 1795 a trading privilege through New Orleans which for the moment met the demands of the frontiersmen, even if it did not allay their anxiety for the future. So things stood when a swift turn in events changed the whole situation.

Louisiana Transferred to France. In July, 1802, a royal order from Spain instructed the officials at New Orleans to close the port to American produce. Next, a dreadful rumor, long current, was confirmed — Napoleon had coerced Spain into returning Louisiana to France by a secret treaty signed in 1800. "Napoleon's soldiers, the scalers of the Alps and conquerors of Venice," now looked to the New World for adventure. Immediately of course the Western states were ablaze with excitement at the thought of French

From Ewing Galloway, New York

A COURTYARD IN OLD NEW ORLEANS

occupation of Louisiana. A call for war ran through the frontier; militiamen were collected to prevent the landing of French troops; and petitions for instant action flooded in upon Jefferson.

Jefferson Sees the Danger. Though a friend of France Jefferson was now urged to act in the interest of his own republic; and he did not wince. "The cession of Louisiana and the Floridas by Spain to France," he wrote to Livingston, the American minister in Paris, "works sorely on the United States. It completely reverses all the political relations of the United States and will form a new epoch in our political course. . . . There is on the globe one single spot, the possessor of which is our natural and habitual enemy. It is New Orleans through which the produce of three-eighths of our territory must pass to market. . . . France, placing herself in that door, assumes to us an attitude of defiance. Spain might have retained it quietly for years. Her pacific dispositions, her feeble state would induce her to increase our facilities there. . . . Not so can it ever be in the hands of France."

Louisiana Purchased. Acting on this belief but apparently seeing only the Mississippi outlet at stake, Jefferson sent his neighbor and companion, James Monroe, to France with the power to buy New Orleans and West Florida. Before Monroe arrived, the regular American minister, Livingston, had already convinced Napoleon that it would be wise to sell territory which might be wrested from him at any moment by the British navy. This was a telling plea, for the war between France and England, halted for a few months by the peace of Amiens, was once more raging in Europe. But clever as he was in his way, Livingston had at first no more thought of buying the whole Louisiana country than Jefferson had. He was dazed when Napoleon offered to sell the entire region as well as New Orleans. Amazing as the offer was, Livingston and Monroe decided to accept it for the United States. On April 30 they signed the treaty of cession, agreeing to pay $11,250,000 in six per cent bonds and to discharge certain claims filed against France by American citizens — making in all about fifteen millions. Spain protested; Napoleon's brothers fumed; but the deed was done.

Jefferson and His Constitutional Scruples. When the news of this event reached the United States, people were filled with astonishment, and no one more than Jefferson himself. He had thought of buying New Orleans and West Florida for a small sum, and now a vast domain had been dumped at his feet. He was puzzled. In the Constitution he found not a line authorizing the purchase of more territory by the government and so he drafted an

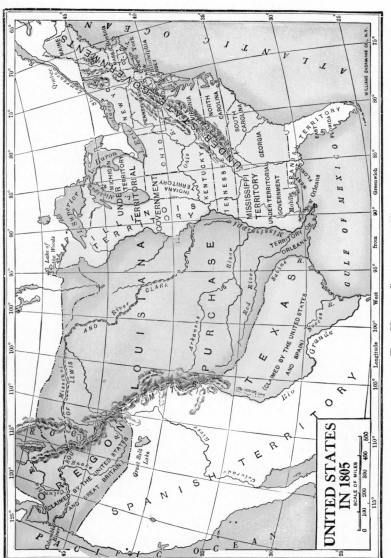

THE UNITED STATES IN 1805

amendment declaring "Louisiana, as ceded by France . . . a part of the United States." He had criticized the Federalists for piling up a big national debt and he could hardly endure the thought of issuing more bonds himself to pay for Louisiana.

In the midst of his quandary came the news that Napoleon might withdraw the bargain. That would be far worse than to change some of his theories; so Jefferson urged the Senate to approve the treaty of purchase at once. He still clung to his original idea that the Constitution did not warrant the step; but he finally surrendered, saying, "If our friends shall think differently, I shall certainly acquiesce with satisfaction; confident that the good sense of our country will correct the evil of construction when it shall produce ill effects." Thus the stanch advocate of "strict interpretation" cut loose from his own doctrine and left the explanation of the Constitution to "the good sense" of his countrymen.

The Treaty Ratified. This unusual action so favorable to the West provoked the ire of the seaboard Federalists. Some declared that it was unconstitutional, easily forgetting Hamilton's masterly defense of the Bank, also not mentioned in the Constitution. Others said that, if "the howling wilderness" ever should be settled, it would turn against the East, form new commercial ties with Europe through the port of New Orleans, and escape from federal control. Still others argued that the purchase would finally give a majority in Congress to "a hotch potch of wild men from the Far West." Federalists, who thought "the broad back of America" could readily bear Hamilton's big debt, now went into agonies over a bond issue of less than one-sixth of that amount. But in vain. Jefferson's party jammed the treaty through the Senate in spite of Federalist protests. In December, 1803, the French flag was hauled down from the old government buildings in New Orleans and the Stars and Stripes were hoisted in its place as a sign that the land of Coronado, De Soto, Marquette, and La Salle had passed to the United States.

By this single stroke, the original territory of the United States was more than doubled. At the time of the Purchase, Louisiana was a name applied to a vast region beyond the Mississippi which had never been surveyed. While its boundaries were vague, it is safe to say that the Louisiana territory included what is now Arkansas, Missouri, Iowa, Oklahoma, Kansas, Nebraska, South Dakota, and large portions of Louisiana, Minnesota, North Dakota, Colorado, Montana, and Wyoming. The farm land that the apostles of "a little America" on the seacoast called a hopeless wilderness was fully occupied within a hundred years and valued at nearly seven billion dollars, almost five hundred times the price paid to Napoleon.

Western Explorations. Having taken the fateful step, Jefferson wisely began to make the most of it. He got ready for the opening of the new country to settlers by sending the Lewis and Clark expedition to explore it, discover its resources, and lay out an overland route through the Missouri Valley and across the Great Divide to the Pacific. The story of this mighty exploit, which began in the spring of 1804 and ended in the autumn of 1806, was set down with skill and care in the journal of Lewis and Clark; when published even in a short form, the East began to take a more serious interest in the larger United States. The sources of the Mississippi also were explored by Zebulon Pike who made a series of trips along that river and later penetrated the Spanish territories of the far Southwest. In such ways, scouts and pioneers followed up the work of diplomats.

WAR FOR COMMERCIAL INDEPENDENCE

The English and French Blockades. Napoleon's cession of Louisiana was merely one outcome of the European war which was resumed that very year. By this war all the commercial troubles that had plagued America through the administrations of Washington and Adams were raised anew and multiplied for Jefferson. Republicans were plunged into a real hornets' nest. During the administration of the Federalists they had been critics only. Members of their party had burned Jay in effigy when he made a commercial treaty with England, stoned Hamilton for defending the treaty, jeered Washington's proclamation of neutrality, and spoken scornfully of "timid traders." Now Republican leaders could no longer take refuge in criticism. As the government in power they had to face similar problems of trade. In place of using words they had to act.

In an effort to bring France to her knees by starvation, England in 1806 declared the coast of Europe blockaded from Brest to the mouth of the Elbe River. Napoleon answered by his Berlin Decree of November, 1806, blockading in turn the British Isles. Great Britain countered with a second decree — the Orders in Council of 1807. By this action she modified her blockade a little bit, that is, she permitted American ships not carrying munitions of war to proceed to the Continent, on condition that they first stopped at a British port, secured a license, and paid a tax. To Napoleon the new British decree was the height of insolence and a gross violation of international law. In getting even with England he made things worse for Americans by his Milan Decree of December, 1807, which declared that any ship obeying the British rules would be subject to seizure and confiscation by the French.

The Impressment of Seamen. That was not all. In dire need of men for her navy, Great Britain again resorted to the practice of halting American ships at sea, searching them, and carrying away British-born sailors found on board. It was a fact that British sailors had fled in crowds to the American marine to escape from the floggings and other cruelties which they suffered in the British service. In many cases however it was difficult to tell whether seamen were English or American. Since they spoke the same tongue, language was no test. Rovers on the deep and stragglers in the ports of both countries, they frequently had no papers to show where they were born. Moreover Great Britain held to an ancient rule — "Once an Englishman, always an Englishman" — a doctrine rejected by the United States in favor of the principle that a man could choose the nation to which he would give his allegiance.

Taking full advantage of this situation, British sea captains, sometimes by mistake and often enough with utter indifference to all rights, carried away into service in their own navy genuine American citizens. Now the process of search and seizure, even when executed with all the civilities of law, was offensive enough, for it required American ships to "heave to," and rest under British guns until the searching party had pried into records, questioned seamen, seized and handcuffed victims.

Had such scenes of search and seizure been confined to the high seas and knowledge of them to rumors and newspaper stories, American anger might not have been so intense; but many occurred in sight of land. British and French vessels patrolled the coasts, firing on one another and chasing one another in American waters within the three mile limit. When in the summer of 1807 the American frigate *Chesapeake* refused to surrender men charged with desertion from King George's navy, the British warship *Leopard* opened fire, killing three men and wounding eighteen more — an act which even the British ministry could hardly excuse. If the French were less often offenders, it was not owing to their peculiar tenderness about American rights but because so few of their ships escaped the hawk-eyed British navy to operate in American waters.

Losses in American Commerce. Naturally this high-handed conduct on the part of the two warring navies was very injurious to the trade of the United States. By their enterprise American shippers had become the foremost carriers on the Atlantic Ocean. In a decade they had nearly doubled the tonnage of the merchant ships under the American flag. They had taken the place of the French marine which Britain swept from the seas and they were also supplying Britain with the sinews of war for the contest with Napoleon. Expressed in figures their shipping engaged in foreign trade amounted to 363,110 tons in 1791; 669,921 tons in 1800; and almost 1,000,000 tons in 1810. Such was the commerce placed in jeopardy by the British and French decrees. American ships bound for England were liable to be captured by stray French privateers which, in spite of the naval defeat at Trafalgar, still ranged the seas. On the other hand if American ships bound for the Continent failed to stop at British ports and pay tribute there, they were in danger of capture by the sleepless British navy and its swarm of auxiliaries. To cap the climax, American sea captains who in fear of British vengeance heeded the British Orders in Council were almost sure to fall a prey to French revenge, for their violation of the Milan Decree.

Jefferson's Policy. In short both the belligerents in Europe were guilty of injuring American commerce. The President's dilemma was certainly trying. War on both was out of the question. War on France was impossible because she now had no territory on this side of the water which could be invaded by American troops and her naval forces had been shattered. War on Great Britain was possible but not promising. Besides, Jefferson shrank from war itself. A man of peace, he disliked its brazen clangor; a humanist, he was haunted by the death and destruction which it brought in its train. So for six years Jefferson steered a neutral course, suggesting measure after measure with a view to avoiding bloodshed. To be sure, he sent Commodore Preble in 1803 to punish Mediterranean pirates for preying upon American commerce and enslaving American citizens; but a great war of doubtful outcome he evaded with steadfast earnestness, trying in its place every other means to protect American rights.

The Embargo and Non-Intercourse Acts. With the idea of bringing peaceful pressure to bear, Congress passed in 1806, with Jefferson's approval, a Non-importation Act closing American ports to certain products from British dominions. When this refusal to receive her goods failed to awe England, Jefferson took the lead in getting Congress to adopt in December, 1807, the Embargo Act which shut off foreign trade by ordering American vessels to stay at home. In a word France and England were to be brought to terms by cutting off their supplies from the United States.

The result of the embargo was mainly distressing to Jefferson's own country. It did not force England and France to promise to give up search and seizure. It merely paralyzed the business of American shipowners who had formerly been willing to run all risks for the sake of high profits. So foreign traffic simply collapsed and every section of the republic suffered. The South and West found their markets for cotton, rice, tobacco, corn, and bacon reduced. Shipmasters, shipbuilders, longshoremen, and sailors of New England were thrown out of employment. Prices of foreign goods mounted while incomes fell and wages ceased. Those who obeyed the law were ruined; those who tried to smuggle goods into Canada and Florida for shipment abroad were often caught and ruined too.

Jefferson's supporters accepted this medicine with wry faces as the only way out of submission or war. His opponents, without offering any solution of their own, called his program a contemptible plan that brought neither relief nor honor. Indeed the uproar against the scheme was so great that Congress, in the closing days of Jefferson's administration, repealed the Embargo law and substituted a Non-intercourse Act — a limited boycott — forbidding trade with England and France while permitting it with other countries. But this measure was equally futile in protecting American shipping.

Jefferson Retires in Favor of Madison. Tired of endless wrangling and wounded, as Washington had been, by merciless criticism, Jefferson welcomed the idea of retiring from office at the end of his eight years of service. Advisers urged him to "stay by the ship" and accept a third term. But he declined, saying that election for life might result from repeated reëlection. By reinforcing Washington's example, Jefferson made the "third term doctrine" a part of America's unwritten political law.

His close friend, James Madison, to whom Jefferson turned over the burdens of the presidency on March 4, 1809, was, like himself, a man of peace. Madison had been a leader since the days of the Revolution, but in legislative halls and council chambers, not on the field of battle. Small in stature, sensitive in feelings, studious in habits, he was no man for the rough and tumble of party politics. His chief service to the republic had been in the framing and the adoption of the Constitution. He was then elected a member of the first Congress and gave his support to many of Hamilton's measures. Later he joined Jefferson's party and served for eight years as his first counselor, the Secretary of State. At last as President he was called upon to apply in an hour of turmoil and peril the principles of the Constitution which he had helped to write and interpret. In keeping with his own ideals and walking in the footsteps of Jefferson, he sought to solve the foreign problem by peaceful negotiation.

The Trend of Events. While Madison was trying to avoid an armed conflict, events beyond his own control took the issue away from him. The country was drifting into war. In the spring of 1811 a British frigate held up an American ship near the harbor of New York and impressed a seaman claiming to be an American citizen. Burning with fury, the captain of the *President*, an American warship, acting under orders, poured several broadsides into the *Little Belt*, a British sloop, suspected of being the guilty party. The British also protected the Indian chief, Tecumseh, who was welding together the red men close to the western settlements and terrifying the frontier. Though Tecumseh's men were badly beaten at Tippecanoe by William Henry Harrison, the Indians still stood in the way of the pioneers, and it seemed to these Americans that Britain by her support of the natives was the true foe both on land and sea.

Clay and Calhoun. As such events moved swiftly, Congress came under the spell of a group of young Republicans, known as "War Hawks," led by Henry Clay of Kentucky and John C. Calhoun of South Carolina. The former boasted in a flair of folly that "the militia of Kentucky alone are competent to place Montreal and Upper Canada at your feet." The latter with a light heart spoke of conquering Canada — with its fertile fields — in a four weeks' campaign. "It must not be inferred," says Edward Channing, an eminent historian, "that in advocating conquest, the Westerners were actuated merely by desire for land; they welcomed war because they thought it would be the easiest way to abate Indian troubles. The savages were supported by the fur-trading interests that centered at Quebec and London. . . . The Southerners on their part wished for Florida and they thought that the conquest of Canada would obviate some Northern opposition to this acquisition of slave territory." Speaking for the West and South Clay and Calhoun ingeniously fanned into flame the old feelings against George III, who was still on the throne.

Madison Accepts War. Meanwhile the conduct of the British ministers with whom Madison had to deal made it almost impossible even for him to keep calm. One of them, a high Tory, believed that all Americans were alike "except that a few are less knaves than others" and his manners were as rough as his belief. On the recall of this minister the British government selected another no less haughty in his person and opinions. So Madison himself became thoroughly discouraged about the outcome of pacific measures. When the pressure from Congress became very heavy, he gave way and on June 18, 1812, signed the declaration of war on Great Britain. In official form Madison set forth the causes which justified the war, namely, British encouragement of

From a "Thistle" print — *Copyright Detroit Publishing Company*
THE BATTLE OF LAKE ERIE

the Indians to attack American citizens on the frontier; injuries to American trade by blockades; insults to the American flag by the search and seizure of ships flying it; and the impressment of American sailors into the British navy.

The Course of the War. This second American-English war lasted for over two years without yielding decided gains for either side. At one time the Americans were compelled to surrender Detroit to the British and to the end their invasion of Canada was a failure. On the other hand Captain Oliver H. Perry won a striking victory on Lake Erie and the British were prevented from invading New York by a brilliant action on the part of Lieutenant Thomas Macdonough on Lake Champlain. At the close of the war the triumph of General Jackson at New Orleans helped to offset the burning of public buildings in Washington by the British. On the Atlantic the stirring deeds of the *Constitution*, the *United States*, and the *Argus*, the heroic stand of Captain James Lawrence,

Courtesy of The Metropolitan Museum of Art

THE "CONSTITUTION"

The disabled ship is the British frigate *Java*.

and the exploits of a hundred privateers gave consolation to a nation suffering from the iron blockade finally established by the British government. As long as men love the annals of the sea, they will turn to the running battles, the narrow escapes, and the reckless daring of American sailors in that naval contest.

All this was exciting but it settled nothing whatever. In fact never was a government less prepared for warfare than was that of the United States in 1812. It had neither the disciplined troops, the battleships, nor the supplies for such a military task. Fortune alone favored the American cause. Harassed, worn, and financially embarrassed by nearly twenty years of fighting in Europe, Great Britain could do little in America even after Napoleon was overthrown and sent into exile at Elba in the spring of 1814. War clouds still hung on her European horizon — and in fact the tempest did break out there again in 1815. To be rid of American anxieties and free for European affairs, England was ready for peace, especially as the Americans insisted on no surrender of her claims.

The Treaty of Peace. Both countries were in truth sick of a war that offered neither glory nor profit. So after an exchange of notes they sent representatives to Ghent to discuss a settlement. Long negotiations were finally ended by an agreement on Christmas Eve, 1814, a few days before Jackson's victory at New Orleans. When the treaty reached America the people were surprised to find that it said nothing about the seizure of American sailors, the destruction of American trade, the searching of American ships, or the support of Indians on the frontier. Nevertheless, we are told, the public "passed from gloom to glory" on the arrival of the news of peace. Bells were rung; schools were closed; flags were displayed; and many a rousing toast was drunk in tavern and private home. The rejoicing could continue. With Napoleon definitely beaten at Waterloo in June, 1815, Great Britain had no more need to impress sailors, search ships, and seize American goods bound to the Continent. Once more the terrible sea power sank into the background and the ocean was again white with the sails of merchantmen.

REPUBLICANS BECOME NATIONALISTS

Federalists Have a Turn at Localism. By a strange whirl of fortune's wheel, the party of Hamilton, Washington, and Adams, the party of strong nationalism, became the party of localism and began to exalt the states above the Union. Finding its shipping interests crippled in the European conflict and then penalized by embargoes, New England opposed the declaration of war on Great Britain, which threatened the completion of the harm already begun. At all events the second war against England promised

more to farmers and planters than to merchants. After it was
started the Federalist leaders came perilously near to treason in
their efforts to hamper the national government in waging it. Then
in their despair they fell back upon the doctrine of nullification —
states' rights — so recently condemned by them when it came from
Kentucky on another issue.

Taking this tack the Senate of Massachusetts resolved that the
war was being prosecuted against Great Britain "without justifiable

From an old cartoon

New England Jumping into the Arms of George III

cause," and refused to approve military and naval projects not
connected with "the defense of our seacoast and soil." In the
same spirit a Boston newspaper declared that the Constitution
was nothing but a treaty among sovereign states, that states could
decide for themselves whether they would obey federal law, and
that armed resistance to the national government on the part of
a state would not be rebellion or treason. Not a whit behind
Massachusetts, the general assembly of Connecticut informed
President Madison that "the state of Connecticut is a free, sovereign, and independent state." Over in New York Gouverneur
Morris, a member of the convention which had drafted the Con-

stitution, suggested a conference to consider whether the Northern states should remain in the Union.

At length on the call of Massachusetts, in October, 1814, a convention of delegates from Connecticut, Massachusetts, Rhode Island, and certain counties of New Hampshire and Vermont was held at Hartford to discuss the rights of New England in the Union. Although extreme theories were rejected, the convention resolved that acts of Congress contrary to the Constitution are void; that in case of deliberate, dangerous, and clear-cut violations by Congress the state is duty bound to interfere for the protection of its citizens; and that when crises occur the states must be their own judges and execute their own decisions. Thus New England answered the war cry of Calhoun and Clay. Fortunately its actions were not so rash as its words. The Hartford convention merely proposed certain amendments to the Constitution and adjourned. At the close of the war its proposals were forgotten; and the men who made them never became dominant in national politics.

The Second United States Bank. In driving the Federalists toward nullification and waging a national war themselves, the Republicans lost their former taint of localism. Moreover their new acts, made necessary by the war, were modeled after the old national laws of the Federalists. For example, with a view to helping untangle their war finances, they chartered in 1816 for a period of twenty years a second United States Bank — the very kind of bank which Jefferson and Madison had once declared unconstitutional. The Constitution remained unchanged; but times and circumstances had changed Republican ideas about it. Calhoun dismissed the question of legality with a few words as if it were a negligible matter, while Madison set aside his own scruples and signed the bill for the charter.

The Protective Tariff of 1816. To the law creating the Bank, the Republicans added another Federalist measure — a high protective tariff. Clay regarded it as the beginning of his "American system" of protection. Calhoun defended it on national principles. For this sudden shift in policy the young Republicans were taunted by some of the older party members with betraying the "agricultural interest" which Jefferson had fostered; but Calhoun refused to listen to their charges. He declared that he was in fact trying to help agriculture. "When the seas are open," he said, "the produce of the South may pour anywhere into the markets of the Old World. . . . What are the effects of a war with a maritime power — with England? Our commerce annihilated . . . our agriculture cut off from its accustomed markets, the surplus of the farmer perishes on his hands. . . . The recent war fell with peculiar pressure on the growers of cotton and tobacco and the other great staples of the country; and the same state of things will recur in the event of another war unless prevented by the foresight of this body. . . . When our manufacturers are grown to a certain perfection, as they soon will be under the fostering care of the government, we shall no longer experience these evils." With Republicans taking this stand, the Federalist party had nothing particular to offer the country and it disappeared from national politics after a crushing defeat in the presidential campaign of 1816.

Monroe and the Florida Purchase. To the victor in that political contest, James Monroe of Virginia, fell two tasks which added to the prestige of the national government and deepened the sense of patriotism that weaned men away from mere allegiance to states. The first of these was the purchase of Florida from Spain. If the acquisition of Louisiana let the Mississippi flow "unvexed to the sea," it left territory east of the river cut off from the Gulf, thus affording grounds for American discontent. Furthermore owing to uncertainty about the boundaries of Louisiana, the United States had a claim to West Florida, which gave it some warrant for the occupation of that region. In any case the Florida swamps were a base for Indian marauders who now and then swept into American settlements.

On the occasion of one such Indian outbreak, President Monroe ordered General Jackson to capture the offenders, within the Floridas if necessary. Taking his order as a hint that he was to seize the region, this doughty warrior replied that, if possession was the object of the invasion, he could occupy the Floridas within sixty days. Without waiting for an answer to this letter, he launched his expedition, and in the spring of 1818 was master of the Spanish king's domain.

There was nothing for the king to do but to make the best of the fact by ceding his Florida territory to the United States in return for five million dollars to be paid to American citizens who had claims against his government. On Washington's birthday, 1819, the treaty was signed. Besides transferring the Floridas, it defined the boundary between Spanish Mexico and the United States by a line drawn from the mouth of the Sabine River in a northwesterly direction to the Pacific. Even Monroe, still a Jeffersonian, now forgot to inquire whether Congress had the power to buy new territory. The Republicans seemed further away than ever from the days of "strict construction."

The Missouri Compromise. The Republicans also took a broad view of the Constitution when they made the Missouri Compromise in 1820. Although they insisted that Missouri be admitted to the Union as a slave state, balanced against the free state of Maine, they agreed to prohibit slavery in the Louisiana territory north of the line 36° 30'. During the debate on the subject it had been said that Congress had no constitutional right to abolish slavery in the territories. To this argument the Northwest Ordinance ratified by Congress in 1789 seemed an answer out of experience, but Monroe laid the Missouri question before his cabinet, which included Calhoun of South Carolina, Crawford of Georgia, and Wirt of Virginia, all supposed to favor the early Jeffersonian principle of strict construction. From them he received a unanimous verdict that Congress did have the power to prohibit slavery in the territories it governed. Acting on this advice he approved, on March 6, 1820, the bill establishing freedom north of the compromise line, thus writing a loose interpretation of the Constitution into law.

The Monroe Doctrine. Still more effective in making Americans think nationally was Monroe's announcement of the doctrine that bears his name. The occasion was another European crisis. During the Napoleonic era, while Europe was centered on its own affairs, the Spanish colonies in America, following the example set by their English neighbors in 1776, declared their independence.

Unable to conquer them alone, the king of Spain turned for help to the rulers of Europe who viewed republics with horror.

The Holy Alliance. He found them sympathetic. Indeed Austria, Prussia, and Russia, under the leadership of the Czar, Alexander I, had already entered into a Holy Alliance to uphold royal authority. Although the language of this triple understanding was vague, the alliance was later regarded as a union of monarchs to prevent the rise and growth of popular government. The outlook for democracy was dark in 1822 when a conference of delegates from Russia, Austria, Prussia, and France met at Verona to consider, among other things, revolutions that had just broken out in Spain and Italy. In fact the Czar, who coveted the west coast of North America, proposed to send an army to aid the king of Spain in his domestic troubles — perhaps a step toward intervention in Spanish America. But a lack of money and troops prevented the grand association of monarchs from making a general war on popular government, if indeed they could ever have agreed on details of action.

The Peculiar Position of England. Moreover England refused to coöperate. Her merchants, having built up a large business with Latin-American republics, had no desire to see Spanish rule restored and with it Spain's former trade monopoly. Besides, the divine right doctrine had been exploded in England and the representative principle of government established in its stead. Already there were signs of the coming popular flood which was soon to carry through Parliament the first English reform bill of 1832, extending the suffrage and promising more democracy. British statesmen therefore had to be cautious about aiding absolute monarchs on the Continent. In such circumstances, the astute prime minister, Canning, proposed to the American minister in London that England and the United States unite in declaring their unwillingness to see the Spanish republics overthrown by European intervention.

Jefferson's Advice. The proposal for joint action was declined; but President Monroe consulted Madison, Jefferson, and his Secretary of State, John Quincy Adams, about issuing a warning to Europe on the subject of interference in American affairs.

They favored the plan.   Grateful for England's coöperation, Jefferson exclaimed: "One nation, most of all, could disturb us in this pursuit of freedom; she now offers to lead, aid, and accompany us in it.   By acceding to her proposition we . . . bring her mighty weight into the scale of free government and emancipate a continent at one stroke. . . .   With her on our side we need not fear the whole world.   With her then we should most sedulously cherish a cordial friendship."

Monroe's Statement of the Doctrine.   Acting on the advice of such political counsellors, President Monroe sent a message to Congress, on December 2, 1823, which included a statement now famous throughout the world as the Monroe Doctrine.   To the autocrats of Europe he announced that the United States would regard "any attempt on their part to extend their system to any portion of this hemisphere as dangerous to our peace and safety." While he did not propose to interfere with any colony still ruled by a European power, he ranged himself squarely on the side of those that had declared their independence.   Any effort of a European government to oppress them or control their destiny in any manner, he said, would be viewed as "a manifestation of an unfriendly disposition toward the United States."   Referring in another part of his message to a recent claim to the Pacific Coast made by the Russian Czar, Monroe warned the Old World that "the American continents, by the free and independent condition which they have assumed and maintained, are henceforth not to be considered as subjects for future colonization by any European powers."   This was a sudden and startling announcement to the rulers of the earth that the young republic in the New World was ready to take a hand in shaping international relations at least with respect to this hemisphere.   It made even Monroe's countrymen think of themselves more as a nation and less as a mere collection of states.

The National Decisions of Chief Justice Marshall

John Marshall, the Nationalist.   Republicans in state politics, who did not at first catch the grand national style of their leaders at the capital of the United States, were assisted in their education by John Marshall, a Federalist from Virginia. While Chief Justice of the Supreme Court of the United States from 1801 to 1835, he lost no chance to exalt the Constitution above the claims of the states. Even his fiercest opponents have never denied Marshall's superb legal ability or his sincere devotion to the national idea. All likewise admit that for talents, native and acquired, he was an ornament to the humble democracy that brought him forth. His whole career was American.

Born on the frontier of Virginia, reared in a log cabin, granted only the barest rudiments of school education, inured to hardship and rough surroundings, he yet rose by masterly efforts to the highest judicial honor.

On Marshall the experience of the Revolution and of its aftermath made a lasting impression. He was no "summer patriot." He had been a soldier in the Revolutionary army. He had suffered with Washington at Valley Forge. He had seen his comrades in arms starving and freezing because the

From a painting by Henry Inman

JOHN MARSHALL

Continental Congress had neither the power nor the will to force the states to do their full duty. To him the Articles of Confederation were the symbol of futility. Into the struggle for the formation of the Constitution and its ratification in Virginia, he had therefore thrown himself with the ardor of a true soldier. Later, as a member of Congress, a commissioner to France, and Secretary of State, he had aided the Federalists in establishing the republic. When they were driven from power in the executive and legislative branches of the government, he was chosen for their last stronghold, the Supreme Court. By historic irony he administered the oath of office to his political foe, Thomas Jefferson; and long after Jefferson had retired to private life, the stern Chief Justice continued to announce the old Federalist principles from the Supreme Bench.

Marbury *vs*. Madison — an Act of Congress Annulled. Marshall had been in his high office about two years when he laid down for the first time in the name of the entire Court the doctrine that judges have the power to declare an act of Congress null and void when in their opinion it violates the Constitution. Now the Constitution did not say that in so many words. Though many able men held that the judicial branch of the government enjoyed this right, the issue was not settled until 1803 when the case of Marbury *vs*. Madison was decided. In rendering the opinion of the Court, Marshall cited no precedents. He did not build his argument on history, but rested it on the general nature of the American system. The Constitution, he argued, is the supreme law of the land; it limits and binds all who act in the name of the United States; it limits the powers of Congress and defines the rights of citizens. If Congress can ignore its rules and trespass upon the rights of citizens, Marshall argued, then the Constitution disappears and Congress is supreme. Since the Constitution is actually supreme it is the duty of judges under their oath of office to see that legislators do not violate it. Therefore from the nature of the American system the courts must declare null and void all acts which are not authorized by the Constitution. "A law repugnant to the Constitution," he said, in clinching the matter, "is void and the courts as well as other departments are bound by that instrument."

This doctrine that the courts stand above law-makers was received by Jefferson and many of his disciples with dismay. If the idea was sound, he exclaimed, "then indeed is our Constitution a complete *felo de se* [legally, a suicide]. For, intending to establish three departments, coördinate and independent that they might check and balance one another, it has given, according to this opinion, to one of them alone the right to prescribe rules for the government of the others, and to that one, too, which is unelected by and independent of the nation. . . . The Constitution, on this hypothesis, is a mere thing of wax in the hands of the judiciary, which they may shape and twist into any form they please. It should be remembered, as an axiom of eternal truth in politics, that whatever power in any government is independent, is absolute also. . . . A judiciary independent of a king or executive alone is a good thing; but independence of the will of the nation is a solecism, at least in a republican government." But Marshall was mighty and his doctrine prevailed, though from time to time other men sharing Jefferson's views likewise opposed the exercise of this power to pass upon the measures of Congress.

Acts of State Legislatures Declared Unconstitutional. Had Marshall stopped with declaring a law of Congress invalid, he would have heard less criticism from Republican quarters; but in the same cool manner he set aside acts of state legislatures as well, whenever in his opinion they too violated the federal Constitution. In 1810 in the case of Fletcher *vs.* Peck, he overturned an act of the Georgia legislature and bluntly told the state that it was not sovereign and independent but was "a part of a large empire . . . a member of the American union; and that union has a constitution . . . which imposes limits to the legislatures of the several states." Applying the same ruling to the case of McCulloch *vs.* Maryland decided in 1819, Marshall declared null and void an act of the Maryland legislature designed to close the branches of the United States Bank in that state.

In the same year by his still more memorable Dartmouth College decision, Marshall annulled a law of the New Hampshire legislature which made serious changes in the charter received by the college long before from King George. That charter, he declared, was a contract between the state and the college which the legislature under the federal Constitution could not violate. Two years later he stirred the wrath of Virginia by calling her to the bar of the Supreme Court to answer a charge that one of her laws was unconstitutional and then he read the state a lecture on her place in the Union in a powerful opinion rendered in the case of Cohens *vs.* Virginia.

These decisions of course aroused the legislatures of the states. They passed resolutions protesting and condemning; but Marshall never turned and never stayed. The Constitution of the United States, he fairly thundered at them, is the supreme law of the land; the Supreme Court is the proper tribunal to pass finally upon the validity of the laws of the states; and "those sovereignties" are irrevocably bound by the decisions of that Court, no matter what they say. This was a strong dose for the Southern authors of the Kentucky and Virginia Resolutions and for Northern members of the Hartford convention; but both had to swallow it.

The Doctrine of Implied Powers. While holding Congress by the leash in the Marbury case and the state legislatures in a score of cases, Marshall by other decisions championed the liberal view of the Constitution rather than the narrow construction. In McCulloch *vs.* Maryland he was as broad in theory as Alexander Hamilton had been. This case involved, among other things, the question whether the Act of 1816 establishing the second United States Bank was authorized by the Constitution. Marshall said it was. He pointed to the words in the Constitution which stated that Congress may do what is "necessary and proper" to carry its powers into effect. He called attention to the fact that Congress can lay taxes and coin money and then quickly added that a bank is useful in the exercise of these rights; if not absolutely necessary, at least it is entirely proper and constitutional. "With respect to the means by which the powers that the Constitution confers are to be carried into execution," he said, Congress must be allowed "to perform the high duties assigned to it in the manner most beneficial to the people." In short the Constitution of the United States, according to Chief Justice Marshall, was not a straitjacket for the government but a flexible instrument vesting in Congress the authority necessary to meet problems as they rise.

SUMMARY OF THE UNION AND NATIONAL LIFE

During the strenuous period which followed American independence the experiment in republican government was under the direction of the men who had launched it. All the Presidents in that era had taken part in the Revolution. This was therefore the "age of the American Fathers." It saw the ruin of the country threatened under the Articles of Confederation, the drafting of a Constitution for the republic, the rise of political parties, the expansion of the territory of the United States beyond the Mississippi, a second war with England, the Florida purchase, and the apparent triumph of the national spirit over sectionalism and localism.

The government, founded under the Articles of Confederation. was not adequate to the needs of an independent nation. It was not empowered to raise directly money with which to pay its debts or even its running expenses. It could not protect American manufactures and commerce against foreign competition. It could not put an end to the flow of paper money printed by the various states. It could not send troops into states to suppress riots that menaced their very existence. Without money, an army, or courts of law, the government of the United States seemed to be breaking into pieces. Merchants and some veterans of the war for independence even ventured to talk of setting up a king, but Washington, Hamilton, and Madison insisted that the republic could be saved by the adoption of a new constitution.

At last the Congress of the United States was persuaded to call a national convention to take into account the state of America. In May, 1787, this convention assembled at Philadelphia and for months it debated and wrangled. The small states demanded equal rights with the large states. The large states vowed they would never grant it. But a spirit of conciliation, fair play, and compromise finally brought agreement and peace. In addition there were jealousies between the planting states and the commercial states. Here too compromises had to be worked out. Some of the delegates feared the growth of democracy and others hoped for it. These factions also had to be mollified. Finally a plan of government was drafted — the Constitution of the United States — and submitted to the states for approval. After a long and exciting campaign enough states ratified the Constitution to make it the law of the land. On April 30, 1789, George Washington was inaugurated first President.

The new government proceeded to fund the Continental debt, assume the revolutionary debts of the states, found a national bank, lay taxes to pay the bills, and pass laws protecting American industry and commerce. Hamilton led in this movement, but he had not gone far when he met opposition. Jefferson was his most powerful antagonist. In time the followers of these men formed two political parties, known as the Federalists and the Republicans. For ten years they filled the country with political turmoil. In

1800 the Federalists were defeated by the Republicans and Jefferson became President.

In theory the Republicans favored the states rather than the federal government, but in practice they added to the prestige and power of the nation. They purchased Louisiana from France, they waged a war against England, they created a second United States Bank, they enacted the protective tariff of 1816, they declared that Congress had power to abolish slavery north of the Missouri Compromise line, and they lifted the shield of the Monroe Doctrine between the Western Hemisphere and Europe.

Yet America was still a part of European civilization. Currents of opinion flowed to and fro across the Atlantic. Advocates of popular government in Europe looked to America as a great model. Events in Europe also reacted upon thought in the United States. The French Revolution directly influenced the course of American politics. While it was in the stage of mere reform all America favored it. When the French king was executed and a radical democracy was set up, American sympathy wavered and divided. When France fell under the military rule of Napoleon and preyed upon American commerce, the United States made ready for war.

The conduct of England likewise affected events in America. In 1793 war broke out between England and France and raged with only a slight intermission until 1815. England and France both preyed upon American commerce, but England was the more serious offender because she had command of the seas. Though Jefferson and Madison strove for peace, the country was swept into war by the vehemence of the "Young Republicans" headed by Clay and Calhoun.

When the armed conflict was closed, one in diplomacy opened. The monarchs of Europe seemed ready to help Spain recover possession of her Latin-American colonies. Their threat to America brought forth the Monroe Doctrine in which the powers of Europe were warned not to interfere with the independent countries in this hemisphere or to attempt to get any new colonies in it. It appeared that nationalism was to have a peaceful triumph over localism.

In this period as in colonial times, the American people were by no means absorbed in politics, agriculture, and business. They made progress in religious toleration; they gave encouragement to schools and founded state colleges. Newspapers flourished and hustling dailies now took their place beside the old, easy-going weeklies. Popular magazines sprang up in the leading cities, spreading interest in literature and the arts. Poets, novelists, and dramatists drew pen-pictures of all phases of American life. Fitch, Stevens, Fulton, and Whitney applied science to invention and by showing how nature might be mastered advanced the idea of progress — the continual improvement of the lot of mankind. Artists, such as Stuart, Peale, and Trumbull, gave to posterity pictures of heroes and great scenes. A civilization distinctively American was in process of making.

References

H. Adams, *History of the United States, 1800–1817* (9 vols.).
K. C. Babcock, *Rise of American Nationality* (American Nation Series).
E. Channing, *The Jeffersonian System* (Same Series).
D. C. Gilman, *James Monroe.*
J. S. Penman, *The Irresistible Movement of Democracy.*
J. W. Pratt, *The Expansionists of 1812.*
W. Reddaway, *The Monroe Doctrine.*
T. Roosevelt, *Naval War of 1812.*

Questions

1. What were the leading features of Jefferson's political theory?
2. Enumerate the chief measures of his administration.
3. Were the Jeffersonians able to apply their theories? Give the reasons.
4. Explain the importance of the Mississippi River to Western farmers.
5. Show how events in Europe forced the Louisiana Purchase.
6. State the constitutional question involved in the Louisiana Purchase.
7. Show how American trade was affected by the European war.
8. Compare the policies of Jefferson and Madison.
9. Why did the United States become involved with England rather than with France?
10. Contrast the causes of the War of 1812 with the results.
11. Give the economic reasons for the attitude of New England.
12. Give five "nationalist" measures of the Republicans. Discuss each in detail.
13. Sketch the career of John Marshall.

14. What was the main point decided by the case of Marbury *vs.* Madison?

15. Summarize Marshall's views on: (*a*) states' rights; and (*b*) a liberal interpretation of the Constitution.

Research Topics

The Louisiana Purchase. Text of Treaty in Macdonald, *Documentary Source Book*, pp. 279–282. Source materials in Hart, *American History Told by Contemporaries*, Vol. III, pp. 363–384. Narrative, Henry Adams, *History of the United States*, Vol. II, pp. 25–115; Elson, *History of the United States*, pp. 360–365.

The Embargo and Non-Intercourse Acts. Macdonald, pp. 282–288; Adams, Vol. IV, pp. 152–177; Elson, pp. 394–405.

Congress and the War of 1812. Adams, Vol. VI, pp. 113–198; Elson, pp. 400–436.

Proposals of the Hartford Convention. Macdonald, pp. 293–302.

Manufactures and the Tariff of 1816. Coman, *Industrial History of the United States*, pp. 184–194.

The Second United States Bank. Macdonald, pp. 302–306.

Effect of European War on American Trade. Callender, *Economic History of the United States*, pp. 240–250.

The Monroe Doctrine. Macdonald, pp. 318–320.

Lewis and Clark Expedition. R. G. Thwaites, *Rocky Mountain Explorations*, pp. 92–187. Schafer, *A History of the Pacific Northwest* (rev. ed.), pp. 29–61.

Questions for Debate

1. The Constitution must be strictly interpreted.

2. John Marshall's assertions of the authority of the Supreme Court have been beneficial in their effect.

Historical Fiction

Irving Bacheller, *D'ri and I.*
James Barnes, *Midshipman Farragut.*
Herman Melville, *Moby Dick.*

PART IV. THE WEST AND JACKSONIAN DEMOCRACY

CHAPTER XI

THE FARMERS BEYOND THE APPALACHIANS

Alexander Hamilton favored a strong national government but he did not trust the people. Thomas Jefferson had faith in the people but feared a strong national government. The work of uniting Hamilton's nationalism and Jefferson's democracy was in time undertaken by new leaders from the region beyond the mountains — Henry Clay of Kentucky, Andrew Jackson of Tennessee, and Abraham Lincoln of Illinois. In the main the people for whom they spoke came from all sections of the seaboard but in their frontier home they forgot most of the quarrels that had made trouble among the original thirteen states. They thought of themselves as Americans and their country as a nation; rather than of themselves as New Englanders or Southerners with their government a mere league of states. How this New West grew up is our next theme.

PREPARATION FOR WESTERN SETTLEMENT

The West and the American Revolution. Strange as it may seem, the distant frontier as well as the coast towns had figured in the American Revolution. The action of Great Britain in closing western land to easy settlement in 1763 helped to bring on the war for independence. When Indians were used by England to defend that land against advancing Americans, zeal for the patriot cause set the border aflame. Men who had seen the west with their own eyes — Daniel Boone, John Sevier, and George Rogers Clark, for example — thoroughly understood the value of the far-away country beyond the mountains. It was they who gave the East no rest until their vision was shared by leaders on the coast, directing the government of the United States. And one of their number, a seasoned Indian fighter, George Rogers

Clark, with aid from Virginia, seized Kaskaskia and Vincennes during the Revolution, thus securing the whole Northwest for the Union while the fate of Washington's army was still in doubt.

Western Claims and Land Surveys. The treaty of peace, made with Great Britain in 1783, ceded to the United States all the coveted territory west to the Mississippi, but conditions were not yet ripe for settlement. Massachusetts, Connecticut, and Virginia had conflicting claims to land in the Northwest, based on old charters and other contentions, while Virginia, North Carolina, South Carolina, and Georgia had even more definite rights in the territory below the Ohio River. Only after a severe contest did Virginia, Massachusetts, and Connecticut turn over to the Union their rights in the Northwest, the last completing its transaction in 1786; and many years passed before the region to the south was finally cut loose from the seaboard owners.

From Brown Brothers, New York

GEORGE ROGERS CLARK

From an original miniature ascribed to J. W. Jarvis.

Whatever the claims of the states, no regular settlement of the Northwest could take place until the region was surveyed by civil engineers and official maps were made so that land grants could be definitely located and titles accurately entered in government records. To solve this problem the Congress under the Articles of Confederation passed an ordinance in 1785 ordering a survey of the Northwest Territory, laying it out into rectangular townships each six miles square, each township with thirty-six internal sections — each section containing 640 acres which in turn could be readily subdivided.

The Northwest Ordinance of 1787. With claims of the states out of the way and provisions for land surveys duly made, the next question was that of the form of government for the Northwest Territory. Pioneers were longing for a chance to till the fertile soil of the new country, and veterans of the Revolution were eager to exchange for titles to good land the paper warrants which they had received for their military services. Under pressure from such prospective settlers, the Congress finally passed in 1787 the Northwest Ordinance which provided a temporary system of control by the Confederation and arranged that a local assembly for self-government should be established as soon as there were five thousand free males in any district. When these districts became populous enough, the Ordinance provided, they were to be admitted to the Union on an equal footing with the original states. Religious freedom was proclaimed. The safeguards of trial by jury and regular law courts were guaranteed and in fact established, thus assuring order to settlers peaceably disposed. To crown it all, slavery and involuntary servitude were forbidden. This charter of the Northwest, so well planned in all its details, was continued in force by the first Congress under the Constitution in 1789. Later its main provisions, except the ban on slavery, were extended to the territory south of the Ohio ceded to the United States by North Carolina and Georgia.

Final Preparations for Settlement. When the problems of land claims, surveys, and government were squarely met, there yet remained two barriers to free action in the Northwest. First of all, after the peace with Great Britain, a number of forts in the Lake region were still occupied by British soldiers as a pledge that the terms of the treaty would be fulfilled by the United States. Not until the Jay treaty was duly ratified in 1795 were these soldiers withdrawn from American soil. Even then tribes of Indians remained, roaming the frontier and ready to resist with all their might the advance of the white men into their hunting grounds. But after the adoption of the Constitution a well-equipped army was raised to maintain peace on the border.   At last the way was entirely clear for pioneers.

The Land Companies, Speculators, and Western Land Tenure. As in English colonization so in the American settlement of the West, great companies and single proprietors possessing large grants of land sometimes took the lead in starting migrations. The very year that the Northwest Ordinance was adopted, the Ohio Land Company, a New England concern, bought from the Congress a million and a half acres on the Ohio and began operations by planting the town of Marietta.   About the same time J. C. Symmes got a million acres lower down on the river where the city of Cincinnati was founded.   Other individuals bought up soldiers' claims and so obtained enormous holdings for speculative purposes.   Indeed, there was such a rush to make fortunes quickly by real estate "deals" that President Washington remonstrated against the "rage for speculating in and forestalling of land on the North West of the Ohio" and urged Congress to fix a reasonable price per acre so as to favor small buyers and discourage big manipulators.

Congress, however, was not yet willing to use the public domain for the sole purpose of developing a body of small freeholders in the West.   It still looked upon the sale of public lands as a way of raising money with which to pay off the public debt; hence it thought more of instant income than of helping people to get farms of moderate size.   Although it fixed the price of land at $2 an acre in 1796, it put no limit on the amount which one could buy.   It also aided the professional dealer by allowing the purchase of land on an installment plan — paying a small sum down and the balance later.   On such terms a speculator with a few thousand dollars could get possession of an enormous plot of land. If he was lucky in selling it, he could meet the installments out of sales and make a handsome profit for himself.   Even when the installment feature was given up in 1821 and the price of the land lowered to a cash price of $1.25 an acre, the custom of selling to adventurers in large lots was continued.

Development of the Small Freehold.   Nevertheless, the cheapness of land and the difficulty of getting laborers for great estates

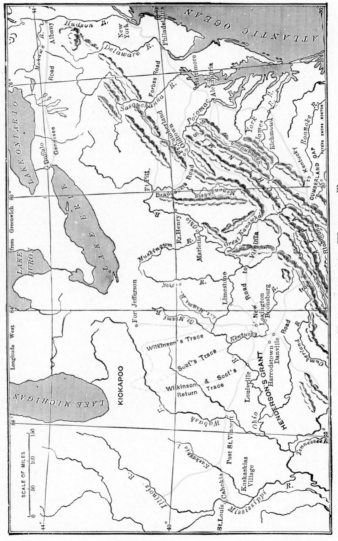

ROADS AND TRAILS INTO THE WESTERN TERRITORY

once more favored the growth of small farms. With a capital of from two to three hundred dollars a family could embark on a land venture. If it had good crops, it could meet the deferred payments as they fell due. Although many people lost their property by failing to pay their final installments, in the end the freehold of about a hundred and sixty acres or less became the typical unit of agriculture over an immense area of the West. Usually the domains of the great companies were broken up in a little while and sold in small lots.

This tendency toward small farms was also aided by a clause in the Northwest Ordinance declaring that the land of any person dying intestate — that is, without leaving a will disposing of it — should be divided equally among his heirs. In this way the law promoted equality in the ownership of property.

The Western Migration and New States

The People. With government established, a federal army to deal with the Indians, and lands mapped for sale, the way was prepared for immigrants. And they came with a rush, under company leadership and on their own initiative. Young New Englanders, weary of tilling the stony soil of their native states, poured through New York and Pennsylvania, some settling on the northern bank of the Ohio but most of them in the Lake region. Sons and daughters of German farmers in Pennsylvania and many a redemptioner who had served out his time with his master pressed on into Ohio, Kentucky, Tennessee, or beyond. From the worn fields and the clay hills of Southern states came pioneers of English and Scotch-Irish descent, the latter in great numbers. Indeed, one historian of high authority goes as far as to say "that the rapid expansion of the United States from a coast strip to a continental area is largely a Scotch-Irish achievement." While native Americans of mixed stocks led the way into the West, it was not long before immigrants direct from Europe, under the stimulus of company enterprise, began to filter into the new settlements.

The types of people were soon as various as the nations they represented. A New England missionary, Timothy Flint, who published entertaining *Recollections* in 1826, found the West an astonishing medley of races and classes. Some, he relates, had been hunters in the upper world of the Mississippi, above the falls of St. Anthony. Some had been still farther north, in Canada. Still others had wandered from the South — the Gulf of Mexico, the Red River, and the Spanish country. French boatmen and trappers, Spanish traders from the Southwest, Virginia planters with their droves of slaves mingled with English, German, and Scotch-Irish farmers. Hunters, forest rangers, restless bordermen, and squatters, like the foaming combers of an advancing tide, arrived first. Then came the farmers, masters of the ax and plow, with their wives who shared every burden and hardship while together they struggled to obtain the comforts and advantages of civilized life. Hunters and rangers passed on to fresh scenes; the homemakers built for all time.

The Number of Immigrants. There were no official stations on the frontier to record the number of immigrants who entered the West during the years immediately following the Northwest Ordinance. But travelers of the time report that every road was "crowded" with pioneers, wagons, and cattle; and that they were seldom out of the sound of the snapping whip of the teamster urging forward his horses or the crack of the hunter's rifle as he brought down his evening meal. "During the latter half of 1787," says Coman, "more than nine hundred boats floated down the Ohio carrying eighteen thousand men, women, and children, and twelve thousand horses, sheep, and cattle, and six hundred and fifty wagons." Other lines of travel were also popular and with the years the flooding tide of home seekers rose higher and higher.

The Western Routes. Four chief routes led into the country beyond the Appalachians. The Genesee road, beginning at Albany, ran almost due west through a level country to the present site of Buffalo on Lake Erie. In the dry season, wagons laden with goods could easily pass along it and then into northern Ohio. A second route, through Pittsburgh, was fed by three eastern branches, one starting at Philadelphia, one at Baltimore, and another at Alexandria. A third main route wound through the mountains from Alexandria to Boonesboro in Kentucky and then westward across the Ohio to St. Louis. A fourth, the most famous of all, passed through the Cumberland Gap and by branches extended into the Cumberland Valley and the Kentucky country.

Of these four lines of travel, the Pittsburgh route was for a long time the best. When pioneers were once safely on the headwaters of the Ohio and in possession of a flatboat, they could find a quick passage into all parts of the West and Southwest. Whether they wanted to settle in Ohio, Kentucky, or western Tennessee, they could readily find their way down the river to their journey's

FLATBOAT ON THE OHIO RIVER

end or at least to some spot near-by. Naturally people from the South, as well as the Northern and Middle states, chose this route; so it came about that the sons and daughters of Virginia and the Carolinas mingled with those of New York, New Jersey, Pennsylvania, and New England in the settlement of the Northwest territory.

The Methods of Travel into the West. Many stories telling of travel into the West in the early days have been preserved. The country was scarcely opened when visitors from the Old World and from the Eastern states, driven by curiosity, made their way to the frontier and wrote books about it to inform or amuse the public. One of these "tourists," Gilbert Imlay, an English traveler, has given us an account of the Pittsburgh route as he found it in 1791. "If a man . . ." he writes, "has a family or goods of any sort to remove, his best way, then, would be to purchase a waggon and team of horses to carry his property to Redstone Old Fort or to Pittsburgh, according as he may come from the Northern or Southern states. A good waggon will cost, at Philadelphia, about £10 . . . and the horses about £12 each; they would cost something more both at Baltimore and Alexandria. The waggon may be covered with canvass, and if it is the choice of the people, they may sleep in it of nights with the greatest safety. But if they dislike that, there are inns of accommodation the whole distance on the different roads. . . . The provisions, I would purchase in the same manner [that is, from the farmers along the road]; and by having two or three camp kettles and stopping every evening when the weather is fine upon the brink of some rivulet and by kindling a fire they may soon dress their own food. . . . This manner of journeying is so far from being disagreeable that in a fine season it is extremely pleasant."

The Admission of Kentucky and Tennessee. When the eighteenth century drew to a close, Kentucky had a population larger than Delaware, Rhode Island, or New Hampshire, and Tennessee claimed 60,000 inhabitants. In 1792 Kentucky finally declared her independence from Virginia and took her place as a state in the Union. Eastern Federalists did not like the newcomer and they were glad to offset the growth of the West a little bit by the admission of Vermont about the same date.

As if to assert their emancipation from traditions, the makers of Kentucky's first constitution did not adopt the Virginia plan of restricting the vote to landowners but gave it to all free males — later restricted to whites. Kentucky's neighbor to the south, Tennessee, took a similar step toward a wider democracy and in the face of another Federalist explosion was accepted as the sixteenth state in 1796.

Ohio. Tennessee had scarcely found its way into the Union when another appeal was made to Congress, this time from the pioneers in Ohio. Little posts started at Marietta and Cincinnati had become flourishing centers of trade, to which the stream of immigration, flowing down the river, daily added inhabitants, while the expanding farms all around poured produce into the markets to be exchanged for "store goods." North as well as south the white population increased. After the Indians were overcome by federal troops in 1794 and the last British soldier left the frontier forts under the terms of the Jay treaty of 1795, settlements appeared on Lake Erie in the "Western Reserve" —

a region that had been kept by Connecticut when she gave up her other rights in the Northwest.

At the close of the century, Ohio, claiming a population of more than 50,000, felt that it had outgrown its territorial status. Indeed, some Ohio pioneers had wanted self-government from the first. Two years before the enactment of the Northwest Or-

From Ewing Galloway, New York
EARLY MISSISSIPPI STEAMBOAT

dinance, squatters in that region had been invited by one John Emerson to assemble after the fashion of men of Hartford, Windsor, and Wethersfield in old Connecticut and frame a government for themselves. This true son of New England declared that men "have an undoubted right to pass into every vacant country and there to form their constitution" and then added that Congress could not keep them out of the Confederation. This grand convention was never held because the government forbade it; but the spirit of John Emerson lived on. In November, 1802, a convention chosen by voters met under the authority of Congress at Chillicothe, and drew up a constitution which was duly approved at the polls. On the roll of this convention were such names as Abbott, Baldwin, Cutler, Huntington, Putnam, and Sargent, and the list of counties from which they came included Adams, Fair-field, Hamilton, Jefferson, Trumbull, and Washington. Obviously this new state in the West was peopled and led by the old stock. In 1803 Ohio was admitted to the Union.

Indiana and Illinois. As in Ohio, so in Indiana, the frontier crept steadily northward from the river, mainly under the leader-ship of settlers from the South — restless pioneers from Virginia, North Carolina, and Kentucky hoping for better luck in a new country. As soon as they had formed a tier of counties against Ohio on the east and in the Wabash Valley on the west, they began to shout for statehood. At length with the consent of Congress the Indianians drafted a constitution in 1816 and inaugurated their government at Corydon. "The majority of the members of the convention," we are told by a local historian, "were frontier farmers who had a general idea of what they wanted and had sense enough to let their more erudite colleagues put it into shape."

The story of Illinois was much the same. It too was settled by an upward migration from the river and just as soon as a few counties were occupied the men insisted on electing delegates to draw up a constitution. The leader of the convention was a man born in New York and reared in Tennessee; and the Illinois con-stitution itself was copied largely from the constitutions of Ken-tucky, Ohio, and Tennessee. In 1818 Illinois was taken "under the roof" as a state.

Louisiana, Mississippi, and Alabama. Meanwhile to the far South across the Mississippi, clearing and planting had gone on with bustle and enterprise. The cotton and sugar lands of Louisi-ana, opened by French and Spanish settlers, were expanded in every direction by planters from the older states with their armies of slaves. New Orleans, a good market and a center of culture, grew apace. In 1810 the population of lower Louisiana was over 75,000. The time had come, said the leaders of the people, to fulfill the promise made to France in the treaty of cession; namely, to grant to the inhabitants of the territory statehood and the rights of American citizens.

Once more Federalists from New England, still having a voice in Congress, if somewhat weaker, spoke up in tones of horror. "I am compelled to declare it as my deliberate opinion," said Josiah Quincy of Massachusetts in the House of Representatives, "that if this bill [to admit Louisiana] passes, the bonds of this Union are virtually dissolved . . . that as it will be the right of all, so it will be the duty of some [states] to prepare definitely for a separation; amicably if they can, violently if they must. . . . It is a death blow to the Constitution. It may afterwards linger; but lingering, its fate will, at no very distant period, be consummated." Federalists from New York, like those from New England, also opposed admitting more Western states; but the party of Madison and Jefferson had the necessary majority in Congress and granted the coveted statehood to Louisiana in 1812.

When Mississippi and Alabama knocked at the doors of the Union a few years later, the Federalists had still less influence on account of their attempts to obstruct the government during the second war with England; hence politicians from the Southwest met a kindlier reception at Washington. Mississippi in 1817 and Alabama in 1819 took their places among the United States of America.

Missouri. By this time yet another commonwealth was rising to power in the Louisiana Purchase. It was peopled by immigrants who came down the Ohio in fleets of boats or crossed the Mississippi from Kentucky and Tennessee. Thrifty Germans from Pennsylvania, hardy farmers from Virginia ready to work with their own hands, freemen seeking freemen's homes, and planters with their slaves moving on from exhausted fields on the seaboard all mingled in the widening settlements of the Missouri country. Peoples from the North and South came together; small farmers and big planters merged in one community. When their numbers had reached sixty thousand or more, they started a contest in Congress by demanding admission to the Union as a slave state, thereby "ringing an alarm bell in the night," as Jefferson phrased it. After the excitement subsided, Missouri was brought into the Union with slavery; but more than offsetting this concession to the South, Maine was admitted as a free state and a line dividing servitude from freedom was drawn westward through the rest of the Louisiana territory.

THE SPIRIT OF THE FRONTIER

Land Tenure and Liberty. Throughout an immense area of this new West the democracy of freehold farmers prevailed. In the Gulf states and the lower Mississippi Valley, it is true, the slave system flourished; but in large sections of Tennessee, Kentucky, and Missouri, upper Alabama, and the entire Northwest territory, the mass of the people belonged to free white families engaged in tilling the soil. In these regions there was no caste or class. Nearly all were fairly equal in riches and earned their living by the labor of their own hands. The Northwest territory was almost as large as the original thirteen states combined, excepting Georgia, and it had no great slave plantations or feudal estates. "In the subdivision of the soil and the great equality of condition," as Daniel Webster once said, "lay the true basis, most certainly, of popular government." There was the undoubted source of the democracy which was soon to make itself heard in the White House.

The Characteristics of Western People. Travelers into the Northwest during the early nineteenth century agreed that the people of the region were generally alike in their manners and customs. In the following words a visitor once wrote of them: "A spirit of adventurous enterprise, a willingness to go through any hardship to accomplish an object. . . . Independence of thought and action. They have felt the influence of these principles from their childhood. Men who can endure anything; that have lived almost without restraint, free as the mountain air or as the deer and the buffalo of their forests, and who know they are Americans all. . . . An apparent roughness which some would deem rudeness of manner. . . . Where there is perfect equality in a neighborhood of people who know little about each other's previous history or ancestry but where each is lord of the soil he cultivates. Where a log cabin is all that the best of families can expect to have for years and of course can possess few of the external decorations which have so much influence in creating a diversity of rank in society. These circumstances have laid the foundation for that equality of intercourse, simplicity of manners, want of deference, want of reserve, great readiness to make acquaintances, freedom of speech,

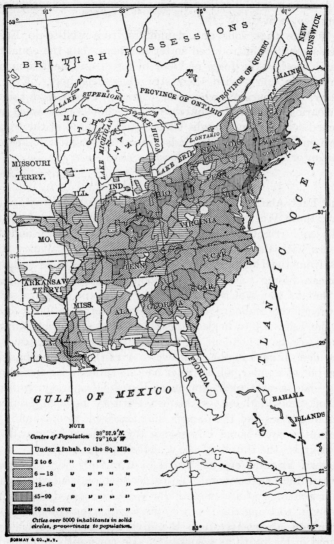

DISTRIBUTION OF POPULATION, 1830

indisposition to brook real or imaginary insults which one witnesses among people of the West."

It is true that sons and daughters from well-to-do Eastern homes sometimes introduced softer manners; but the equality of life and the leveling force of labor in forest and field soon made them one in spirit with their struggling neighbors. Even the ministers and teachers, who came when the cabins were raised in the clearings and rude churches and schoolhouses were built, preached sermons and taught lessons that savored of the frontier, as any one may know who reads Peter Cartwright's *A Muscular Christian* or Eggleston's *The Hoosier Schoolmaster*.

THE WEST AND THE EAST MEET

The East Alarmed. Bent on having their own way in local affairs, these Westerners gave the conservative East many rude shocks and frightened gentlemen in powdered wigs and knee breeches with the idea that the whole Mississippi Valley might break from the Union, and possibly make connections with some European power. Not without good grounds did Washington hint that "a touch of a feather would turn" the Western settlers away from the seaboard to the Spaniards; and seriously did he urge the East not to neglect them, lest they be "drawn into the arms of, or be dependent upon foreigners." Taking advantage of the deep unrest in the Southwest, Aaron Burr, who had been forced out of regular politics after he killed Alexander Hamilton in a duel, laid a wild plan, known as Burr's Conspiracy, to form a state of some kind out of Spanish territory next to Louisiana. Such enterprises and the danger that the West would finally rule the country made some Federalists try to block its growth and keep it under the thumb of the seaboard states.

Eastern Friends of the West. Fortunately for the nation, however, there were several political leaders, particularly from the coastal South, who understood the West, welcomed its progress, and sought to bring the two sections together by common bonds. Washington always retained the love for the West which he acquired in his youth as a surveyor. He constantly reminded his Eastern colleagues that the lands beyond the mountains were highly important to the nation. He put before the governor of Virginia a project for a wagon road connecting the seaboard with the Ohio country and was active in schemes for improving the navigation of the Potomac. In season and out he advocated strengthening the ties of commerce between the East and the West. "Smooth the roads," he said, "and make easy the way for them, and then see what an influx of articles will be poured upon us; how amazingly our exports will be increased by them; and how amply we shall be compensated for any trouble and expense we may encounter to effect it." On the issue of the West Jefferson saw eye to eye with Washington. He too was interested in every phase of its development — survey of lands, exploration of waterways, opening of trade, and even the discovery of the bones of prehistoric animals. Robert Fulton, the inventor of the steamboat, was another man of vision who for many years urged his countrymen to unite East and West by a canal and thus cement the Union, raise the value of the public lands, and extend the principles of republican government.

The Difficulties of Early Transportation. Naturally those who wished to bind the seaboard with the frontier had to think of ways to improve communication, that is, travel and the carriage of goods and mails. The produce of the West — wheat, corn, bacon, hemp, cattle, and tobacco — was so bulky, the way was so long, and the roads were so bad that overland transportation was very costly. Consequently the inhabitants of the Mississippi Valley were at first forced to ship most of their produce to the East over a long water route through New Orleans and up the Atlantic coast. In exchange, salt, iron, guns, powder, and other necessities were brought back across the mountains over narrow wagon trails that were almost impassable in the rainy season.

The National Road. To farsighted men, like Jefferson's Secretary of the Treasury, Albert Gallatin, "the father of internal improvements," the solution of the problem of trade with the West lay in roads and canals. Early in Jefferson's administration, Congress voted that part of the money from the sale of lands should be used to build highways running westward from headwaters of the Eastern rivers to the Ohio River and beyond into the

Northwest territory. In 1806, after many misgivings, it authorized a great national highway binding the East and the West. This Cumberland Road, as it was called, began in northwestern Maryland, wound through southern Pennsylvania, crossed the narrow neck of Virginia at Wheeling, and then shot almost straight across Ohio, Indiana, and Illinois into Missouri. By 1817, stagecoaches were running between Washington and Wheeling; by 1833 contractors had carried their work to Columbus, Ohio; and by 1852,

THE CUMBERLAND ROAD

to Vandalia, Illinois. Over this ballasted road mail and passenger coaches could go at high speed and heavy freight wagons at a steady pace.

Canals and Steamboats. A second epoch in the union of the East and the West opened with the completion of the Erie Canal in 1825, offering an all-water inland route from New York City to the Great Lakes and the Mississippi Valley. Not to be outdone by her neighbor, Pennsylvania then started to construct a system of canals and portages from Philadelphia to Pittsburgh, finishing the last link in 1834. Extending the network, Ohio herself built a canal uniting Lake Erie with the Ohio River, making a water route through a rich wheat belt. Passengers could at last travel into the West by inland waterways with safety and comfort, if not at a rapid speed, and the bulkiest of freight could be easily handled. Moreover, the charge for carrying goods was reduced by the Erie Canal from $32 a ton per hundred miles to $1.

The turning of traffic from the New Orleans route was also aided by steamboats. In the early days twenty men had to work hard with sail and oar to drive a five-ton scow up the river at a rate ranging from ten to twenty miles a day, but when the steamer appeared on the Ohio River about 1810 "speed" became the watchword. In 1825, Timothy Flint traveled a hundred miles a day on the new steamer *Grecian* "against the whole weight of the Mississippi current." Three years later the round trip from Louisville

GOVERNOR CLINTON SYMBOLIZES THE OPENING OF THE ERIE CANAL

"Clinton lifted one of these kegs high in the air and in full view of the assembled multitude poured its contents into the briny ocean saying, 'This solemnity, at this place [the New York City harbor], on the first arrival of vessels from Lake Erie, is intended to indicate and commemorate the navigable communication which has been accomplished between our Mediterranean seas and the Atlantic Ocean.'"

to New Orleans was cut to eight days. Heavy produce that once had to float down to New Orleans could be carried upstream and sent to the East by way of the canal systems.

Thus the far country was brought near to the Old East. Timid souls no longer shrank from the thought of a perilous journey to Ohio, and soon all routes were more thickly crowded than ever with immigrants. Before their axes the forests fell like grain before the sickle. Clearings through the woods spread out into a vast mosaic of farms, stretching from the Southern Appalachians to Lake Michigan. The national census of 1830 gave 937,000 inhabitants to Ohio; 343,000 to Indiana; 157,000 to Illinois; 687,000 to Kentucky; and 681,000 to Tennessee.

With the rise in population and the growth of agriculture came greater political influence at the national capital. Men who had hitherto been content with Presidents from the seaboard now showed a spirit of independence by giving only three electoral votes for John Quincy Adams of Massachusetts in 1824; and at the very next election they sent to Washington a son of the soil from Tennessee, Andrew Jackson, to serve as the chief executive of the nation — the first of a long line of Presidents from the Mississippi basin.

References

W. G. Brown, *The Lower South in American History*.

B. H. Hibbard, *History of the Public Land Policies*.

B. A. Hinsdale, *The Old North West* (2 vols.).

A. B. Hulbert, *Great American Canals* and *The Cumberland Road*.

F. L. Paxson, *History of the American Frontier*.

T. Roosevelt, *Thomas H. Benton*.

F. J. Turner, *Rise of the New West* (American Nation Series).

J. Winsor, *The Westward Movement*.

Questions

1. How did the West come to play a rôle in the Revolution?
2. What preparations were necessary to settlement?
3. Give the principal provisions of the Northwest Ordinance.
4. Explain how freehold land tenure happened to predominate in the West.
5. Who were the early settlers in the West? What routes did they take? How did they travel?
6. Explain the Eastern opposition to the admission of new Western states. Show how it was overcome.
7. Trace a connection between the economic system of the West and the spirit of the people.
8. Who were among the early friends of Western development?
9. Describe the difficulties of trade between the East and the West.
10. Show how trade was promoted.

Research Topics

Northwest Ordinance. Analysis of text in Macdonald, *Documentary Source Book.* Roosevelt, *Winning of the West*, Vol. V, pp. 5–57.

The West before the Revolution. Roosevelt, Vol. I; Paxson, *History of the American Frontier*, pp. 1–32.

The West during the Revolution. Roosevelt, Vols. II and III; Paxson, pp. 32–42.

Tennessee. Roosevelt, Vol. V, pp. 95–119 and Vol. VI, pp. 9–87.

The Cumberland Road. A. B. Hulbert, *The Cumberland Road.*

Early Life in the Middle West. Callender, *Economic History of the United States*, pp. 617–633; 636–641.

Slavery in the Southwest. Callender, pp. 641–652.

Early Land Policy. Callender, pp. 668–680; Paxson, pp. 43–76.

Westward Movement of Peoples. Roosevelt, Vol. IV, pp. 7–39.

Lists of books dealing with the early history of Western states are given in Hart, Channing, and Turner, *Guide to the Study and Reading of American History* (rev. ed.), pp. 62-89.

Kentucky. Roosevelt, Vol. IV, pp. 176–263.

Historical Fiction

J. A. Braden, *Far Past the Frontier.*
Edward Eggleston, *The Hoosier Schoolmaster.*

CHAPTER XII

JACKSONIAN DEMOCRACY

When seaboard Federalists tried to prevent the admission of new Western states to the Union, they were not merely "playing politics." Far from it. They honestly feared, as they often said, that the farming regions would "overbalance" the commercial sections by getting a majority of the presidential electors and members of Congress. Besides this specter hinting of the future, they had to face immediately at home the propertyless masses who were threatening to overbalance the property-classes by winning the right to vote. In other words while a farming democracy loomed on the Western horizon, an urban democracy was rising ominously in the Eastern cities. Out of the union of these two forces came the Democracy of Andrew Jackson's party.

Rise of Democracy in the East

Rule by Property Owners. Although it was the habit of the Revolutionary fathers to speak of government as founded on the consent of the governed, they did not give the vote to all men when they framed the first state constitutions. On the contrary they thought that only property owners or at least taxpayers should be granted the ballot, and so they put definite limits on the right to the suffrage.

Broadly speaking, these limits fell into three classes — taxpaying, freehold, and general property. Three states, Pennsylvania (1776), New Hampshire (1784), and Georgia (1798) gave the ballot to all who paid taxes, without reference to the nature or value of their property. Three, Virginia, Delaware, and Rhode Island, clung to the old theory that only freeholders — owners of land — could be intrusted with the ballot. Still other states, while restricting the suffrage, allowed property owners in general, as well as landowners, to vote. In Massachusetts, for instance, the ballot was conferred on all men who owned land yielding an annual income of three pounds or other property worth sixty pounds outright.

But the men who were thus permitted to vote could not choose anybody they liked for office. In many states they could vote only for persons of wealth, because the law limited public offices to large property owners. In New Hampshire, the governor had to be worth five hundred pounds, one half in land; in Massachusetts, one thousand pounds, all freehold; in Maryland, five thousand pounds, one thousand of which was freehold; in North Carolina, one thousand pounds freehold; and in South Carolina, ten thousand pounds freehold. A state senator in Massachusetts had to be the owner of a freehold worth three hundred pounds or personal property worth six hundred pounds; in New Jersey, one thousand pounds' worth of property; in North Carolina, three hundred acres of land; in South Carolina, two hundred pounds freehold. For members of the lower house of the legislature lower qualifications were required.

In most of the states the suffrage or office-holding or both were further limited to people of certain religious views. No single sect was strong enough to rule after the Revolution, but frequently Catholics and Jews were either denied the ballot or the right to hold office. North Carolina and Georgia would not allow anyone to vote who was not a Protestant. Delaware withheld it from all who did not believe in the Trinity and the inspiration of the Scriptures. Massachusetts and Maryland limited it to Christians. Affording a striking contrast, Virginia and New York, advanced for their day in this respect, placed no religious limits on voting and office-holding.

The Defense of the Old Order. It must not be supposed that property qualifications on voters and officers were just thoughtlessly adopted by the Revolutionary fathers. By no means; they were regarded as right and necessary. Indeed as towns grew in size and the number of landless citizens multiplied, the restrictions were defended with increasing vigor. In Massachusetts, the mighty Daniel Webster upheld the rights of property in government in a memorable speech delivered in 1820: "It is entirely just that property should have its due weight and consideration in political arrangements. . . . The disastrous revolutions which the world has witnessed, those political thunderstorms and earthquakes which have shaken the pillars of society to their deepest foundations, have been revolutions against property." In Pennsylvania, a leader in local affairs cried out against a plan to remove the tax-paying limitation on the suffrage: "What does the delegate propose? To place the vicious vagrant, the wandering Arabs, the Tartar hordes of our large cities on the level with the virtuous and good man?" In Virginia, Jefferson himself had long believed in the rule of property owners and had scorned urban masses as "mobs of the great cities." It was near the end of the eighteenth century before he accepted the idea of manhood suffrage and even then he was unable at once to convert the lawmakers of his own state. "It is not an idle chimera of the brain," said one of them, "that the possession of land furnishes the strongest evidence of permanent, common interest with, and attachment to, the community. . . . It is upon this foundation I wish to place the right of suffrage."

Attacks on the Restricted Suffrage. The changing conditions of American life, however, soon led to protests against the limits on political rights laid down in the first state constitutions. Where the freehold qualification was in force, business men could not vote or hold office unless they happened to own land. In New York, for example, the most illiterate farmer who had one hundred pounds' worth of land could vote for governor while a landless city banker or merchant could not. It is not surprising, therefore, to find business men objecting to freehold limitations on the suffrage. Lawyers, doctors, and other members of the professional classes were also active in breaking down the barriers which excluded them from public affairs unless they had the right property qualifications. It was a schoolmaster, Thomas Dorr, who led the popular uprising in Rhode Island which brought the rule by freeholders to an end in the state government.

Besides the business and professional classes, the mechanics of the towns were especially hostile to laws which barred them from voting or holding office. Though usually a minority, they had early begun to influence the course of public affairs. They had made the riots against the Stamp Act, they had overturned King George's statue, and they had "crammed stamps down the throats of collectors."

When the state constitutions were framed they held meetings, and drew up "demands," particularly in New York City and Philadelphia. In June, 1776, the "mechanics in union" in New York protested against putting the new state constitution into

THOMAS DORR AROUSING HIS FOLLOWERS

effect without their approval and declared that the ballot in such a case "is the birthright of every man to whatever state he may belong." Though their petition was rejected at the moment, victory lay ahead. When, a few years later, the federal Constitution was being discussed, mechanics were generally in favor of it, because they knew that one of its main objects was to promote trade and commerce, closely related to their daily bread. Accordingly during the struggle over ratification, they organized meetings, passed resolutions praising the Constitution, and often joined in parades to stir up favorable sentiment even though they could not vote in the election and so express their will directly. Finally after the rise of trade unions, workingmen were sometimes imprisoned or fined for uniting to demand higher wages, for calling strikes, or throwing down their tools. Thus they became interested in the election of judges and lawmakers and lifted their voices in a louder shout for the ballot.

Those who attacked the old system of class rule found a strong moral support in the Declaration of Independence. Was it not stated that all men are created equal? Was it not declared that governments derive their just power from the consent of the governed? Having applied these principles with effect to George III in 1776, it seemed proper to apply them to the privileged classes of Massachusetts or Virginia in the years that followed. "How do the principles thus proclaimed," asked the non-freeholders of Richmond, in petitioning for the ballot, "accord with the existing regulation of the suffrage? A regulation which, instead of the equality nature ordains, creates an odious distinction between members of the same community . . . and vests in a favored class, not in consideration of their public services but of their private possessions, the highest of all privileges."

Abolition of Property Qualifications. By many small victories rather than by a single stroke did the advocates of manhood suffrage carry the day. Slight gains were made during the Revolution or shortly afterward. By taking an active part in the contest over the constitution of 1776, the mechanics of Pennsylvania were able to force the qualification on voting down to the payment of a small tax. Vermont came into the Union in 1792 without any property restrictions. In the same year Delaware gave the vote to all men who paid taxes. Maryland, reckoned one of the most conservative of states, adopted manhood suffrage in 1809; nine years later, Connecticut, by no means extreme in its views, extended the ballot to all taxpayers.

Five states, Massachusetts, New York, Virginia, Rhode Island, and North Carolina, clung to their restrictive laws while these reforms were going on around them; but they too had to yield in time. The last great struggle in Massachusetts took place in the constitutional convention of 1820, where Webster, in the prime of his manhood, and John Adams, in the closing years of his old age, combined against such radical ideas as manhood suffrage. In spite of their orations, the property test was given up and a small tax-paying qualification was put in its place. New York surrendered the next year and, after trying some minor restrictions for five years, went completely over to white manhood suffrage in 1826. To Rhode Island the agitation soon spread and brought about Dorr's Rebellion. As a result, in 1843, taxpayers as well as landowners were given the ballot for state elections. Virginia held fast to the freehold qualifications until 1830 and then admitted to the suffrage all white males who were householders and heads of families and also paid taxes to the state. Broadly speaking, property tests for officeholders and religious tests in general were abolished when the suffrage was extended.

At the end of the first quarter of the nineteenth century, most of the white male industrial workers and mechanics in the Northern cities had won the ballot and could at last enjoy with the free farmers a voice in the government of their common country. "Universal democracy," sighed Thomas Carlyle, who closely watched the course of events in the United States, "whatever we may think of it has declared itself the inevitable fact of the days in which we live; and he who has any chance to instruct or lead in these days must begin by admitting that. . . . Where no government is wanted, save that of the parish constable, as in America with its boundless soil, every man being able to find work and recompense for himself, democracy may subsist; not elsewhere." Amid grave misgivings on the part of the passing generation, America was started out on a great adventure in popular rule, in the populous towns of the East as well as in the forests and fields of the West.

THE NEW DEMOCRACY ENTERS THE ARENA

The Spoils System and Rotation in Office. Once granted the ballot, the new voters wanted offices in addition. They therefore insisted on extending the custom of rewarding party workers with public positions, until everybody who labored hard in elections felt entitled to a government job. Closely connected with this custom was the practice of fixing a short term for officers and changing them every year or two. "Long continuance in office," explained a champion of this idea in Pennsylvania in 1837, "unfits a man for the discharge of its duties, by rendering him arbitrary and aristocratic, and tends to beget, first life office, and then hereditary office, which leads to the destruction of free government." Such was the origin of the doctrine of "rotation in office." Besides making the terms of officers short, the new democracy insisted that more officers should be elected instead of appointed either by the governor or the legislature. Even geologists, veterinarians, surveyors, and engineers were sometimes made elective on the plea that appointment "smacked of monarchy."

Popular Election of Presidential Electors. In a short time democracy made its way upward from the state governments into the federal system. The framers of the Constitution had provided that presidential electors should be chosen as the state legislatures might decide. And the legislatures, greedy of power, at first decided to choose the electors themselves; but they did not long enjoy this right in peace. Democracy, thundering at their doors, demanded that the right be given to the people. Grudgingly they yielded, sometimes granting it and occasionally withdrawing it again — with the drift decidedly in the direction of popular election. In 1824, Vermont, New York, Delaware, South Carolina, Georgia, and Louisiana left the choice of electors with the state legislature, but by 1832 South Carolina alone held to the original practice.

The Nominating Convention. As the suffrage widened and the popular choice of presidential electors spread, another democratic agitation arose, demanding a change in the methods used by the political parties in selecting their candidates. After the retirement of Washington, both the Republicans and the Federalists found it necessary to agree upon their presidential nominees before the election and adopted a colonial device — a preëlection caucus or party meeting. That is, the Federalist members of Congress held a conference at the national capital and chose their candidates, and the Republicans did the same. In a short time the nomination of candidates for President and Vice President by congressional party caucuses became a regular custom. The election still remained with the people; but the power of naming candidates for them to elect passed into the hands of a small body of Senators and Representatives.

Objections to this were bound to come. To a friend of "the plain people," such as Andrew Jackson proclaimed himself to be, the caucus was especially tyrannical because it never gave him the nomination. More conservative men also objected to it. They pointed out that the Constitution had intended to make the President an independent officer and that he had now fallen under the control of a caucus of congressmen. In other words, by a party practice Congress had become supreme over the President. A big quarrel over the matter was started in 1824 when the congressional caucus of the Republican party overlooked the obvious hero, General Jackson, and selected as the candidate, William H. Crawford, of Georgia, a man of distinction but no such popularity. The followers of the General were enraged and demanded nothing short of the death of "King Caucus." Their clamor was effective and under their attacks the caucus came to an end.

Its place was taken in 1831 by the national nominating convention, composed of delegates elected by party voters. Senators and Representatives were not ousted from party affairs but they were now outnumbered by hundreds of delegates "fresh from the people," as Jackson was wont to say. In fact, each convention was made up mainly of officeholders and office seekers — an outcome which caused the new scheme to be denounced as hotly as King Caucus had been, particularly by ambitious politicians who failed to obtain a nomination by the new route. Yet it gained in popular favor and by 1840 was well established.

The Last Stand of the "Aristocracy." In the election of 1824 the "aristocracy" waged its last successful skirmish. Until then leadership by men of "wealth and talents" had been almost unquestioned. There had been five Presidents — Washington, John Adams, Jefferson, Madison, and Monroe — and all had belonged to families of wealth. Not one had ever worked with his hands for a livelihood. Four of them had been slaveholders in Virginia, the "mother of Presidents." Jefferson was a scholar, interested in natural science, familiar with foreign languages, a gentleman of dignity and grace of manner, if queer in his efforts at simplicity. Madison, it was said, was armed "with all the culture of his century." Monroe was a graduate of William and

Mary and, if not rich, was certainly not to be classed as poor. Jefferson and his two successors called themselves Republicans and professed a faith in the people but they were not "of the people" themselves. They were not sons of the soil or the workshop.

Monroe was the last of the Presidents belonging to the heroic epoch of the Revolution. He had served in the war for independence, in the Congress under the Articles of Confederation, and in official capacity after the adoption of the Constitution. In short, he was of the age that had wrought American independence and set up the republic — a great but a passing age. Washington had died in 1799, preceded a few months by Patrick Henry and followed within four years by Samuel Adams. Hamilton had been killed in a duel with Aaron Burr in 1804. Thomas Jefferson and John Adams were still alive in 1824 but they were soon to leave the scene. While Madison survived them ten years, he was too old to take an active part in campaigns and elections.

The Election of John Quincy Adams (1824). The bridge between this generation and the new, between rule by property owners and rule by "the people," was held for a time by John Quincy Adams, son of a former President, John Adams. But the campaign which brought about his election marked the close of the "era of good feeling" that had followed the collapse of the Federalist party. The democracy of farmers and mechanics had now entered the lists. In that campaign, four leading candidates offered themselves to the voters — John Quincy Adams, Andrew Jackson, Henry Clay, and W. H. Crawford — but no one received a majority of the electoral votes. As provided by the Constitution, therefore, the selection of the President passed to the House of Representatives. Jackson's supporters called attention to the fact that he had received the largest vote and argued that he was entitled to the office. But Clay, as Speaker of the House, threw his influence to Adams, assuring the latter's election, much to the chagrin of the Hero of New Orleans. Jackson shook hands with the victor on the day of his inauguration but never forgave him or Clay.

While Adams called himself a Republican in politics and often spoke of the "rule of the people," he was generally regarded by farmers and mechanics as "an aristocrat" — that is, not of their kind. He was not a son of the soil or the bench. Neither was he acquainted at first hand with the labor of field and shop. He had

ANDREW JACKSON

After a painting by Thomas Sully. — Stipple engraving by J. B. Longacre.

been educated at Harvard and in Europe. Like his illustrious father, he was a stern man, little given to seeking favor with the masses. Moreover he was from the East and all true Jacksonians from the West thought him too "high-toned" for them. Their dislike for Adams was deepened when he appointed Clay Secretary of State; and they set up a cry that there had been a "deal" by which Clay had helped to elect Adams just to get office for himself.

Though Adams carried on his administration in a fine spirit of public service, he was unable to overcome the ill-will raised by the method of his election. On the contrary, by favoring government aid in building roads and canals and public grants of money to promote education, the arts, and sciences, he ran counter to the current which had set in against the use of federal funds for internal improvements. By signing the Tariff Bill of 1828, soon known as the "Tariff of Abominations," he made new enemies in the South and West without adding many friends in New York, Pennsylvania, and Ohio where he sorely needed them. Charged with making a "corrupt bargain" with Clay to secure his election, attacked for advocating a high protective tariff, called an "aristocrat" in an age of democracy, Adams could not hope to remain in office.

The Triumph of Jackson in 1828. Probably no candidate for President ever had such passionate acclaim as Andrew Jackson in 1828. He was truly a man of the people. Born of poor parents in the upland region of South Carolina, schooled in poverty, he was devoid of the hauteur which often goes with a formal education. He seemed to be the very symbol of the young democracy. Early in his youth he had gone to the frontier of Tennessee where he soon won a name as a brave Indian fighter. On the march and in camp, he endeared himself to his men by sharing their hardships, sleeping on the ground with them, and eating parched corn when nothing better could be found for the privates. From local honor he sprang into national fame by his exploit at the battle of New Orleans. His standing as a military hero was strengthened by the feeling that he had been a martyr to political treachery in 1824. Farmers of the West and South claimed him as their own. Mechanics of the Eastern cities, recently enfranchised, also looked upon him as their comrade. Though his views on the tariff, internal improvements, and other issues before the country were either vague or unknown, he was readily elected President.

The returns of the electoral vote in 1828 showed the sources of Jackson's power. In New England he received only one ballot — that one from Maine. But he got a majority of the electors in New York and all of them in Pennsylvania; and he carried every state south of Maryland and beyond the Appalachians. On the other hand, Adams did not get a single electoral vote in the South and West and stood low in the opinion of the Eastern mechanics.

So the onrushing democracy swept over the bridge where Adams had stood on guard. When Jackson took the oath of office on March 4, 1829, the government of the United States changed in character. Until this time the election of a President — even that of Jefferson, who took a special pride in simple habits — had given no rude shock to the city of Washington. Hitherto the inauguration of a President meant that an old-fashioned gentleman, accompanied by a few servants, had driven to the government mansion in his own coach, taken the oath with quiet dignity, appointed a few new men to the higher posts, retained in office nearly all civil employees, and begun his work without uproar. The arrival of Jackson was more like a hurricane. When he was installed, men and women came hundreds of miles to see the ceremony. Great throngs crowded into the White House, "upset the bowls of punch, broke the glasses, and stood with their muddy boots on the satin-covered chairs to see the people's President." If Jefferson's inauguration was "the great revolution," as he called it, Jackson's was a riot.

THE NEW DEMOCRACY AT WASHINGTON

The Spoils System. This influx of farmers and frontiersmen drove "the old residents" in Washington to cover. To speak of politics became "bad form" among fashionable women. And of course the clerks and other civil servants of the government at once realized that they were in mortal peril of losing their positions to the office seekers who now flooded the capital. Doubtless the major portion of them had opposed the election of Jackson and looked with feelings akin to contempt upon him and his followers. And he returned their scorn. With a hunter's instinct, Jackson scented his prey. Determined to have none of his enemies in office, he discharged hundreds of employees to make room for men "fresh from the people." This was a novel custom. No such wide sweep had been made before. Other Presidents had expelled a few officers for taking part in opposition politics, and in making appointments they had been careful not to choose actual foes; but they had not looked on government offices mainly as jobs for their party.

By making wholesale removals and by putting party workers into the vacancies — a practice already flourishing in New York — Jackson set up a new order of things at Washington. The famous slogan "To the victor belong the spoils of victory" he adopted as a rule for the federal government. Statesmen like Calhoun denounced the practice and writers like James Russell Lowell laughed at it; but it held sway for half a century, growing worse and worse in its effects. If any one ventured to say that training and experience were necessary for officials. Jackson answered: "The duties of any public office are so simple or admit of being made so simple that any man can in a short time become master of them."

The Tariff and Nullification. Jackson had not been in power very long when the old issue of states' rights against nationalism reappeared, forcing him to turn his attention a little from the distribution of spoils. The immediate occasion of the trouble was the tariff — a matter on which Jackson had no very decided views. His mind did not naturally run to difficult economic questions; and owing to the divided opinion of the country it was "good politics" to be vague in talking about protection for American industries. Especially was this true because the tariff issue was threatening to split the country into parties again.

The Development of the Policy of "Protection." As a matter of fact the question could not possibly be avoided, for the industrial progress of the country since the War of 1812 had been accompanied by corresponding demands for "protection." During that conflict, the United States, cut off from English manufactures as during the Revolution, built up home industries to meet the unusual call for iron, steel, cloth, and other military and naval supplies, as well as ordinary needs. Iron foundries and textile mills sprang up as in the night; hundreds of business men invested their

money in industrial enterprises so essential to the military requirements of the government; and the people at large fell into the
habit of buying American-made goods again. As the London
Times said of the Americans, "Their first war with England
made them independent; their second war made them formidable."

To deal with this state of affairs, the tariff of 1816 was especially
designed. It was intended, first, to prevent England from ruining
"infant industries" by dumping accumulated stores of goods
suddenly upon American markets; and, secondly, to increase
the demand for American agricultural produce by promoting
manufactures. It realized the purposes of its framers. It kept in
operation the mills and furnaces so recently built. It multiplied
the number of industrial workers and raised the home demand for
farm products.

The tariff of 1816 brought about another very important result.
It turned the capital and business enterprise of New England from
shipping to manufacturing, and converted her statesmen into
ardent advocates of protection. In the early years of the nineteenth century, the Yankees had put their money and energy
into building and operating ships to carry produce from America
to Europe and manufactures from Europe to America. For this
reason, they were against the tariff of 1816 framed for the purpose
of encouraging domestic industries and cutting down the carrying
trade to and from Europe. Defeated in their efforts, they made
the best of the situation and began to put more money into manufacturing. Soon they, too, were in favor of heavier taxes on
European commodities imported into the United States. As the
money invested and the labor employed in the favored industries
increased, the demand for heavier protection grew stronger. Even
the farmers who furnished raw materials, like wool, flax, and hemp,
began to clamor for it like the manufacturers. So the textile interests of New England, the ironmasters of Connecticut, New
Jersey, and Pennsylvania, the wool, hemp, and flax growers of
Ohio, Kentucky, and Tennessee, and the sugar planters of Louisiana gradually united in support of a high protective tariff. That
was one side of the story.

The Planting States Oppose the Tariff.   There was also another side.   In the meantime, the cotton and tobacco states forgot about the havoc wrought during the Napoleonic wars when their produce could not be sold because there were no ships to carry it to Europe. The seas were now free and the South had more goods to ship. The area devoted to cotton had swiftly expanded as Alabama, Mississippi, and Louisiana were opened up.   Cotton was in fact becoming "king" in the South and planters had reached the conclusion that they could make money easiest by selling their staple direct to English mill-owners and buying their manufactured goods in English markets in exchange.   Taxes on imports, they argued, raised the price of goods they had to buy.

The Tariff of Abominations.   They were overborne, however, in 1824, and again in 1828, when Northern manufacturers and Western farmers forced Congress to make an "upward revision" of the tariff, that is, increase the rates.   The Act of 1828, known "as the Tariff of Abominations," slightly changed later, was "the straw which broke the camel's back."   Southern leaders now turned absolutely against the whole protective system.   The legislatures of Virginia, North Carolina, South Carolina, Georgia, and Alabama denounced it; at a general conference held at Augusta a chorus of protest rang out against it; and South Carolina, weary of verbal battles that ended in smoke, decided to prevent the collection of protective duties on imports.

South Carolina Nullifies the Tariff.   And this is the way South Carolina proceeded.   On October 26, 1832, the state legislature passed a bill calling for a state convention, which was elected by the voters and duly assembled in the following month.   After a few days' debate it adopted a bill now famous as the Ordinance of Nullification.   Every line of this document was clear and firm. The tariff, it alleged, gives "bounties to classes and individuals . . . at the expense and to the injury and oppression of other classes and individuals"; it violates the Constitution of the United States and is therefore null and void; its enforcement in South Carolina is unlawful; if the federal government attempts to coerce the state into obeying the law, "the people of this state will thenceforth hold themselves absolved from all further obligations to maintain or preserve their political connection with the people of the other states and will forthwith proceed to organize a separate government and do all other acts and things which sovereign and independent states may of right do." In short, it threatened a declaration of independence, in the language used by the authors of the Kentucky resolutions in 1798–99 and the New England Federalists during the War of 1812.

Southern States Condemn Nullification. But other planting states were not yet ready to go that far. The Georgia legislature replied to South Carolina: "We abhor the doctrine of nullification as neither a peaceful nor a constitutional remedy." Alabama found it "unsound in theory and dangerous in practice." North Carolina resolved that it was "revolutionary in character, subversive of the Constitution of the United States." Mississippi answered: "It is disunion by force — it is civil war." Virginia spoke more softly; she condemned the tariff and upheld again the principles of the Virginia resolutions but denied that South Carolina could find in them any sanction for her proceedings.

Jackson Upholds the Union. Still South Carolina stuck by her guns, warning the federal government not to try to collect its taxes in her ports. So the eyes of the country were turned upon Andrew Jackson, the head of the government thus defied. It was known that he had no sympathy with nullification for, at a Jefferson dinner in the spring of 1830 while the subject was in the air, he had proposed a toast: "Our federal union; it must be preserved." Now that a flat refusal to obey a national law had come from South Carolina, Jackson replied that he would enforce it with all the power at his command. And he added with his frontier directness: "If a single drop of blood shall be shed there in opposition to the laws of the United States, I will hang the first man I can lay my hands on engaged in such conduct upon the first tree that I can reach." He made ready to keep his word by preparing to use military and naval forces in carrying the law into execution. Then in a long and eloquent proclamation to the people of South Carolina, he declared that the Union was a nation, not a mere league of free states, and that he would preserve it by all legal means. Nullification he branded as "incompatible with the existence of the Union, contradicted expressly by the letter of the Constitution, unauthorized by its spirit, inconsistent with every principle on which it was founded, and destructive of the great objects for which it was formed."

A Compromise. In his message to Congress, however, Jackson used gentler words. A few days before his proclamation was issued, he suggested that protective duties should be laid only on the articles of domestic manufacture necessary to safety in war-time, and shortly afterward he asked Congress to pass a new act to aid him in enforcing the laws. Thus Congress had two propositions before it: one to remove the chief grounds for South Carolina's complaints and the other to compel her to obey if she tried to stop the collection of customs duties in her ports. On February 12, 1832, Henry Clay laid before the Senate a compromise bill which provided that the tariff should be lowered year by year until in 1842 it reached the level of the law which South Carolina's representative, Calhoun, had favored in 1816. About the same time a "force bill" giving the President more power in executing the federal laws was taken up. After a brief but very spirited debate, both measures were passed and they were signed by President Jackson on the same day, March 2. Looking upon the reduction of the customs duties as a victory, South Carolina repealed her ordinance against the tariff and to express her contempt enacted another nullifying the force bill — a futile gesture.

The Hayne-Webster Debate. Where the actual victory lay in this contest, long a subject of logic-chopping, need not concern us. Perhaps the chief result of the whole affair was to define the issues between North and South — to make clear the principles for which men on both sides were years afterwards to lay down their lives. Indeed South Carolina on her part and Jackson on his had merely given wide publicity to doctrines laid before the Senate in the Hayne-Webster debate of 1830. On that occasion, Senator Hayne, of South Carolina, a skilled lawyer and courtly orator, had set forth with learning and eloquence the opinion that the Union was a compact among sovereign states from which the parties could lawfully withdraw at will. This address, lending support to nullification and secession, called to his feet Daniel Webster, Senator from Massachusetts, and inspired him to deliver a reply that the North has placed among the powerful orations of all time. In direct opposition to Hayne's view, Webster argued that the Constitution was supreme over the states, that the Union was eternal, and that states could not lawfully withdraw from it. Thus the two theories — states' rights and national supremacy — were outlined in a fashion which everybody could understand.

The War on the United States Bank. Before the Nullification battle in South Carolina was over, Jackson had another fight on his hands, one of his own making. He did not like the United States Bank which had been established in 1816 and his followers called it "a dangerous money power." They accused it of using money in elections, making loans to its favorites, and having politicians on its payroll.

DANIEL WEBSTER

In his very first message to Congress, President Jackson discussed the Bank in unmistakable language. He declared that it was doubtful whether Congress had power to create it and alleged that it had failed to accomplish its prime purpose, that is, to establish a sound and uniform currency. If such a bank was necessary, he continued, it should be a public bank, owned and managed by the government, not a private concern granted special privileges by Congress. In his second and third messages, Jackson came back to the subject, leaving the decision, however, to "an enlightened people and their representatives."

Made anxious about the future by Jackson's tactics, the Bank applied to Congress for a new charter in 1832, four years before the one it held was to expire. With his mind upon the presidency and an issue for the campaign, Henry Clay took the side of the Bank. Under his leadership, Congress passed the bill granting a new charter and sent the measure to Jackson for his signature. The President's response was an instant veto.

In his veto message, Jackson hinted that the Bank was corrupt and assailed it as unconstitutional. He refused to agree that the Supreme Court had settled the question when it had declared in 1819 that the Constitution gave Congress power to establish the Bank. "Each public officer," he argued, "who takes an oath to support the Constitution swears that he will support it as he understands it, not as it is understood by others." And Jackson's veto held good because the advocates of the Bank could not muster a two-thirds vote in Congress to carry the bill over his head.

A mere veto of the new charter for the Bank did not satisfy Jackson. He declared war on the existing Bank by ordering the Secretary of the Treasury to withdraw from it all the government deposits. This action he followed up by charging the Bank with using money to secure the election of its supporters to Congress. Stung by this accusation, the Senate passed a resolution that Jackson "had assumed upon himself authority and power not conferred by the Constitution and laws, but in derogation of both." But Jackson heedlessly crashed ahead.

When the Bank's charter expired in 1836, banking once more returned to the control of the states. Then the state legislatures, under a decision rendered by the Supreme Court after the death of Marshall, began to charter banks under state ownership and control, with full power to issue paper money. This they did deliberately in spite of the provision in the Constitution forbidding the states to issue bills of credit or make anything but gold and silver coin legal tender in the payment of debts. Once more the country was flooded by paper currency of uncertain value. To make matters worse, Jackson deposited huge sums of government money in state banks, especially those which supported him in politics — "pet banks," as they were styled at the time. In 1837, partly as a result of the abolition of the federal Bank, the country was plunged into one of the most devastating panics which it ever experienced.

Internal Improvements Checked. The United States Bank had presented to Jackson a very plain problem — that of destruction. But he was not so sure of his way in dealing with the subject of federal grants of money in aid of highways and other internal improvements. Jefferson had strongly favored such grants but his successors did not share his views. Both Madison and Monroe vetoed acts of Congress appropriating money for public roads, giving as their reason the argument that the Constitution had not authorized laws of this nature. Jackson, though puzzled by bickerings on both sides, followed their example by vetoing similar bills, but he was not certain just what the Constitution said on the point. Congress, he thought, might lawfully build highways for national and military purposes, and yet it was not easy to decide when any particular road fell within that class.

The Triumph of the Executive Branch. Jackson's reëlection in 1832 proved to him that he was the chosen leader of the people, instructed to ride roughshod over Congress and even the Courts. No President before or since ever held in times of peace such lofty notions of his rights and duties. He looked on all the government employees simply as servants of his wishes; a sign or a nod from him made or unmade the fortunes of the humble and the mighty. His lawful cabinet of advisers, filling all the high posts in the government, he treated with scant courtesy; he preferred rather to rely on the advice of an unofficial body of intimates, who became known as "the kitchen cabinet" on account of their backstairs methods. Under the leadership of an astute politician, Amos Kendall, this secret clique carried out decrees and orders by sending the President's lightest wish or strictest command to the uttermost part of the country. Willfully and in spite of all opposition, Jackson removed the deposits from the United States Bank. When the Senate protested against his conduct, he did not rest until he forced it to "expunge," that is, repeal, its resolution of censure; in time one of Jackson's lieutenants, with his own hands, tore it from the records. When Chief Justice Marshall issued a decree against

Georgia which did not suit him, Jackson, according to tradition, blurted out that Marshall could go ahead and enforce his own orders. To the end of his second term, he dominated the scene and not yet satisfied he chose his successor.

THE RISE OF THE WHIGS

Jackson's Measures Arouse Opposition. Conduct so high-handed could not fail to produce a counterblast. The truth

AN OLD CARTOON RIDICULING CLAY'S TARIFF AND INTERNAL IMPROVEMENT PROGRAM

is Jackson's measures upset the business and finances of the country. The United States Bank was destroyed; and state paper money, some of it almost as worthless as the notes of revolutionary days, deluged the country, hindering the transaction of business. The use of federal funds to build roads and improve waterways, so helpful to commerce, was blocked by executive vetoes. The Supreme Court, which had long held states to their duties under the Constitution, was openly flouted; states' rights judges, deliberately appointed by Jackson, began to overthrow the rulings of Marshall. The protective tariff, under which the textile industry of New England, the iron mills of Pennsylvania, and the wool, flax, and hemp farms of the West had flourished, received a severe blow in the compromise of 1832, which provided for a steady reduction of duties. To heap up the measure, Jackson's party cast aside the now reputable name of Republican as too mild and boldly chose for its title "Democratic" — challenging everybody who doubted the wisdom of the people. All these things worked together to raise up against the Jacksonians a stanch party of opposition.

Clay and the National Republicans. In this movement leadership fell to Henry Clay, a son of Kentucky, rather than to Daniel Webster of Massachusetts, for Clay had qualities which endeared him to both masses and classes. Like Jackson, Clay was born in a home haunted by poverty. Left fatherless early and forced to make his own living, he went from Virginia into Kentucky where by sheer force of intellect he rose quickly to the top as a lawyer and was elected to Congress. In all sections he became immensely popular. Farmers of Ohio, Indiana, and Kentucky loved him; financiers and business men of New York and Philadelphia trusted him.

In due time, Clay collected under his banner most of Jackson's foes — united by one tie only, dislike for "Old Hickory." Nullifiers and advocates of states' rights were yoked with Unionists of Webster's school; ardent protectionists were bound together with equally ardent free traders; all were known as "National Republicans." Thus adroitly changed, the old title selected by Jefferson for his party, now given up by Jacksonian Democracy, was adopted to cover the supporters of Clay. The platform of the National Republican party, however, favored Federalist rather than Jeffersonian principles: protection for American industry; internal improvements; respect for the Supreme Court; and denunciation of the spoils system. Jackson was not overthrown at once, but the popular vote cast for Clay in 1832 was large enough to serve as a warning for the future.

Van Buren and the Panic of 1837. Nothing, however, could shake Jackson's belief in himself. Near the end of his second term, he named his successor; at a national convention, chosen by party voters, but packed with his officeholders and supporters, he nominated for the presidency Martin Van Buren of New York. Once more he proved his strength by carrying the country for the Democrats. With a fine flourish, he attended the inauguration of Van Buren and then retired, amid the applause and tears of his devotees, to the Hermitage, his home in Tennessee.

This was just in time for Jackson to escape the odium of an industrial panic which struck the country with terrible force in the very next summer. Among the causes of the crisis, no doubt, were the destruction of the Bank and the issuance of the "Specie Circular" of 1836 which made the purchasers of public lands pay for them in coin, instead of the paper notes of state banks. Whatever the cause, the disaster was widespread. Bank after bank went under; boom towns in the West collapsed; Eastern mills shut down; and working people in the industrial centers, starving from unemployment, begged for relief. In this storm President Van Buren simply drifted about offering no measure of reform or public assistance to the suffering people. He did, it is true, seek to make the funds of the government safe by proposing that its deposits be taken out of private banks and put into government vaults for security, and this plan for "an independent treasury system" was finally accepted by Congress in 1840. But it scarcely pleased anybody, because it did nothing to solve the paper-money problem.

Had Van Buren been popular at the outset he might have lived down the discredit of the panic unjustly placed at his door; unhappily for him, he was not a general favorite. Though a man of many talents, he owed his position to Jackson rather than to his own personal qualities. People on the frontier had no enthusiasm for him. He came from the center of the "money power" and they even suspected that he ate from "gold plate" and could not be a real Democrat after all. Yet Van Buren was Jackson's choice and so the Democratic party renominated him for President in 1840.

The Whigs and General Harrison. Since Jackson had behaved like a king, the National Republicans decided to call themselves "Whigs" — the title of an old English party which had once set itself against the Crown. Taking a leaf out of the Democratic book, they nominated, not Clay of Kentucky, well known for his attitude toward the Bank, the tariff, and internal improvements, but a military hero, General William Henry Harrison — a man as much like Jackson as possible — whose political opinions were also decidedly foggy. The son of a Virginia signer of the Declaration of Independence, Harrison sprang into public notice by winning a battle more sensational than important, "Tippecanoe," a brush with the Indians in Indiana. He added to his laurels by rendering praiseworthy services during the War of 1812. When peace returned, he was rewarded by a grateful people with a seat in Congress. At the end of his term he retired to quiet life in a little village near Cincinnati.

Like Jackson, Harrison was claimed as a product of the South and the West. He was also a military hero, a lesser light but still a light. Like Old Hickory, he rode on a tide of popular feeling against an Eastern man, Van Buren, accused of being an aristocrat. His personal renown was sufficient, for the Whigs in selecting him as their candidate shrewdly refused to adopt a platform or declare their belief in anything. When some Democrat said that Harrison was a backwoodsman whose sole wants were a jug of hard cider and a log cabin, the Whigs treated the remark as proof positive that Jackson men ought to vote for him. The jug and the cabin they proudly accepted as their symbols for the campaign, and won for their chieftain 234 electoral votes, while Van Buren got only sixty.

Harrison's Death. The Hero of Tippecanoe was not long to enjoy the fruits of his victory. A hungry horde of Whig office seekers descended upon him like wolves upon the fold. If he went out, they waylaid him; if he stayed indoors, he was besieged; not even his bedchamber was spared. None too strong at best he took a deep cold on the day of his inauguration and, exhausted by driving out Democrats and trying to satisfy the Whigs, he fell mortally ill. Before the end of a month Harrison lay dead at the capital.

Tyler's Administration. Harrison's successor, John Tyler of Virginia, the Vice President, whom the Whigs had nominated to catch the votes in the South, was more of a Democrat than anything else, though he was not partisan enough to satisfy either side. Whigs railed at him because he would not approve the founding of another United States Bank. Democrats fumed at him for refusing, until near the end of his term, to favor the annexation of Texas, which had declared its independence of Mexico in 1836.

Tyler's entire administration, marked by unseemly wrangling, produced only two measures of significance. His party, the Whigs, flushed by victory, with the aid of a few protectionist Democrats, enacted in 1842 a new tariff law destroying the compromise made between the North and the South in the days of nullification. Later, the distinguished leader of the Whigs, Daniel Webster, as Secretary of State, negotiated with Lord Ashburton, representing Great Britain, a treaty which settled a long-standing dispute between the two countries over the Maine boundary. A year after closing this chapter in American diplomacy, Webster withdrew to private life, leaving the President to endure alone the buffets of political fortune.

To the end, the Whigs regarded Tyler as disloyal to their cause; but the judgment of history is that it was a case of the biter bitten. Tyler had not deceived them. They had nominated him for the vice presidency for the purpose of winning Democratic votes, little reckoning with the chances of his becoming President. But when the campaign of 1844 arrived they turned against him and selected Henry Clay as their candidate. Once more the Democratic party was returned to power, this time under President James K. Polk, a friend of General Jackson, from Tennessee — an ardent advocate of slavery extension.

References

J. S. Bassett, *Life of Andrew Jackson.*
C. G. Bowers, *The Party Battles of the Jacksonian Epoch.*
J. W. Burgess, *The Middle Period.*
H. Lodge, *Daniel Webster.*
W. Macdonald, *Jacksonian Democracy* (American Nation Series).
Ostrogorski, *Democracy and the Organization of Political Parties,* Vol. II.
C. Schurz, *Henry Clay.*
J. S. Penman, *The Irresistible Movement of Democracy.*

Questions

1. By what devices was democracy limited in the first days of our republic?

2. On what grounds were the limitations defended? Attacked?

3. Outline the rise of political democracy in the United States.

4. Describe three important changes in our political system.

5. Contrast the Presidents of the old and the new generations.

6. Account for the unpopularity of John Q. Adams' administration.

7. What had been the career of Andrew Jackson before 1829?

8. Sketch the history of the protective tariff and explain the theory underlying it.

9. Explain the growth of Southern opposition to the tariff.

10. Relate the leading events connected with nullification in South Carolina.

11. State Jackson's views and tell the outcome of the controversy.

12. Why was Jackson opposed to the Bank? How did he finally destroy it?

13. The Whigs complained of Jackson's "executive tyranny." What did they mean?

14. Give some of the leading events in Clay's career.

15. How do you account for the triumph of Harrison in 1840?

Research Topics

Jackson's Criticisms of the Bank. Macdonald, *Documentary Source Book*, pp. 320–329; Penman, *The Irresistible Movement of Democracy*, pp. 111–118.

Financial Aspects of the Bank Controversy. Dewey, *Financial History of the United States*, Sections 86–87; Elson, *History of the United States*, pp. 481–484.

Jackson's View of the Union. See his proclamation on nullification in Macdonald, pp. 333–340.

Nullification. McMaster, *History of the People of the United States*, Vol. VI, pp. 153–182; Elson, pp. 476–481.

The Webster-Hayne Debate. Analyze the arguments. Extensive extracts are given in Macdonald's larger three-volume work, *Select Documents of United States History, 1776–1781*, pp. 239–260.

The Character of Jackson's Administration. Woodrow Wilson, *History of the American People*, Vol. IV, pp. 1–87; Elson, pp. 487–490.

The People in 1830. From contemporary writings in Hart, *American History Told by Contemporaries*, Vol. III, pp. 509–530.

Manhood Suffrage in New York. Penman, *The Irresistible Movement of Democracy*, pp. 94–100.

CHAPTER XIII

THE MIDDLE BORDER AND THE GREAT WEST

"We shall not send an immigrant beyond the Mississippi in a hundred years," exclaimed Livingston, the principal author of the Louisiana Purchase. He believed he was speaking the truth, for doubtless he had in his mind's eye a picture of great stretches of land scattered from the Appalachians to the Mississippi, still unoccupied. He also knew that it had taken two whole centuries to settle the seaboard region; so, to practical men like himself, this prophecy seemed perfectly sound. And yet before the lapse of half that time there arose beyond the Mississippi a tier of new states reaching from the Gulf of Mexico to the southern boundary of Minnesota and a commonwealth on the Pacific coast where American emigrants had raised the Bear flag of California.

THE ADVANCE OF THE MIDDLE BORDER

Missouri. When the middle of the nineteenth century arrived, the Mississippi River, which Daniel Boone had crossed during Washington's administration "to escape from civilization" in Kentucky, had become the waterway for a mighty empire. The center of population of the United States had now passed to the Ohio Valley. Missouri, with its wide reaches of rich soil had drawn to its borders thousands of planters from the old Southern states — from Virginia and the Carolinas as well as from Kentucky and Tennessee. When the great compromise of 1820 admitted her to the Union with slavery, wearing "every jewel of sovereignty," as a florid orator declaimed, slave owners could migrate to Missouri with every assurance that their property would be safe there. Soon the western shore of the Mississippi and both banks of the Missouri, to the uttermost limits of the state, were lined by plantations tilled by bondmen. In the neighborhood of Jefferson City the slaves numbered more than a fourth of the population.

Into this stream of migration from the planting South flowed another current of land-tilling farmers; some from Kentucky, Tennessee, and Mississippi, driven out by the onrush of the planters buying small farms and uniting them into vast estates; and still more from the East and the Old World. To the northwest over against Iowa and to the southwest against Arkansas, these yeomen laid out farms to be tilled by their own labor. In such regions the number of slaves seldom rose above five or six per cent of the population. St. Louis, enriched by the fur trade of the Far West and the steamboat traffic of the river, grew into a thriving commercial city; by 1850 it had among its seventy-five thousand inhabitants nearly forty thousand foreigners, German immigrants from Pennsylvania and Europe forming the largest single group.

Arkansas. Below the Missouri lay the territory of Arkansas, which had long been the paradise of swarthy hunters and restless frontiersmen fleeing from the advancing borders of farm and town. Searching for a life wild and free, where the rifle supplied game and a few acres of ground, an abundance of corn and potatoes, they filtered into the territory to "squat" on the land. Without so much as asking the leave of any government, territorial or national, they claimed as their own the soil on which they first planted their feet. Like their neighbors, the Cherokee Indians, whose very habits and dress they sometimes imitated, the squatters spent their days in the midst of rough plenty, if beset by chills, fevers, and other ills of the flesh. For many years they lived in this way unvexed by politics or civilization.

Unfortunately for them, however, the valleys of the Mississippi and Arkansas rivers were well suited to the cultivation of cotton and tobacco and their sylvan peace was soon broken by an invasion of planters. These newcomers, with their slaves, spread upward in the valley toward Missouri and along the southern border westward to the Red River. In time the slaves in the tier of counties against Louisiana ranged from thirty to seventy per cent of the population. This marked the doom of the small farmer, swept Arkansas into the sphere of planting politics, and brought on an agitation at Washington in favor of admission to the Union — a boon granted in 1836.

Michigan. But for every new slave state taken into the Union, a free state was demanded by the North to maintain the balance of power — a custom which now encouraged the people of Michigan in their belief that the time had come for them to enjoy the privilege of statehood. Along the southern border of that territory, the land had been occupied largely by pioneers from New England, who built prim farmhouses and adopted the town-meeting plan of self-government after the fashion of their old home. The famous trading post of Detroit was growing into a flourishing city as the boats plying on the Great Lakes brought travelers, settlers, and freight through the narrows. In all, according to the census of 1830, there were more than ninety thousand inhabitants in the territory; so they felt justified in asking permission to join the Union. When Congress delayed in granting their request, they lost all patience, called a convention, drew up a constitution, and in an effort to determine the southern boundary of their state started a lively argument with Ohio. The hand of Congress was now forced. After much debate the dividing line was finally fixed, and Michigan, though shorn of some of the land she claimed, came into the Union in 1837.

Wisconsin. To the west lay the territory of Wisconsin which shared with Michigan an interesting history running back into the heroic days when French hunters and missionaries were planning an empire for the great monarch, Louis XIV. It will not be forgotten that French rangers of the woods, black-robed "Fathers" prepared for sacrifice, even death, trappers of the French agencies, and French explorers — Marquette, Joliet, and Menard — were the first white men to paddle their barks through the northern waters. They first blazed trails into the black forests and left traces of their wanderings in the names of portages and little villages. It was from these forests that red men in full war paint journeyed far to fight under the banner of France when the soldiers of King Louis made their last stand at Quebec and Montreal against the imperial arms of Britain.

When, a generation afterward, the Stars and Stripes supplanted the British flag in the Northwest territory, the French were still almost the only white people in the region. But they were soon joined by hustling Yankee fur traders bent on keeping out all British rivals. These traders cut wilderness roads and selected routes through lake and stream and over portages for settlers and their families from the states "back East." It was the forest rangers who discovered the waterfalls later used to turn the mills that ground the grain from the expanding farm lands. In the wake of the fur hunters, forest men, and farmers came miners from Kentucky, Tennessee, and Missouri to exploit the lead ores of the Northwest, some bringing slaves to work their claims, in spite of the law. Had it not been for the gold fever of 1849 that drew the wielders of pick and shovel to the Far West, Wisconsin would early have taken a high rank as a mining region.

At a favorite point of vantage on Lake Michigan, the village of Milwaukee became a thriving center for lumber and grain shipments and a place of entry for goods and immigrants from the East bound to various points in Wisconsin. With much pride the town claimed twenty thousand inhabitants at the middle of the century. By that time Germans, Irish, and Scandinavians had found their way into all parts of the territory. Accustomed to hard work, they joined Americans from the older states in clearing forests, building roads, erecting mills, and connecting streams with canals to make a network of routes for the traffic that poured to and from the Great Lakes. In 1848 Wisconsin closed a chapter in the history of the Northwest by entering the Union.

Iowa and Minnesota. Southwest of Wisconsin beyond the Mississippi, where the tall grass of the prairies waved like the sea, farmers from New England, New York, and Ohio had prepared Iowa for statehood. A tide of immigration that might have flowed into Missouri went northward; for freemen, disliking slavery and slave markets, preferred the open country above the Compromise line. With astonishing swiftness they opened up farms westward from the Mississippi. True to Yankee customs, some of these pioneers turned to trading on the river and before 1836 they had built three prosperous business centers: Dubuque, Davenport, and Burlington. That both religion and learning might flower on the frontier as in the states from which they came, they founded colleges and academies. So in a short time the Iowans came to feel that they had outgrown the dependence of a territory. Congress agreed, and Iowa was admitted to the Union in 1846.

Above Iowa, on the Mississippi, lay the territory of Minnesota — wide-reaching home of the Dakota and Ojibway Indians. Like Michigan and Wisconsin, it had been early explored by French scouts, and the first white settlement was the little French village of Mendota. To the people of the United States, the resources of the country were revealed by the official visit of Zebulon Pike, in 1805, and by American fur traders always on the lookout for pelts. In 1839 an American settlement was planted at Marina on the St. Croix, as an outpost of the frontier. Within twenty years Minnesota, boasting a population of 150,000, applied for admission to the Union, and in 1858 her plea was granted.

On to the Pacific — Texas and the Mexican War

The Uniformity of the Middle West. There was a certain monotony about pioneering in the Northwest and on the middle border. As the stretches of level land were cleared for the plow, they were divided like checkerboards into squares — of forty, eighty, one hundred sixty, or more acres, each the seat of a homestead. A striking uniformity appeared in the endless succession of fertile fields. No majestic mountains relieved the sweep of the prairie. Few monuments of other races and antiquity remained to awaken curiosity about the ancient history of the region. No sonorous bells in old missions rang out the passing day. The red man bartering blankets and furs for powder and whisky had moved farther west. Everywhere the population was simply made up of farming families engaged in severe and unbroken labor — chopping down trees, draining fever-breeding swamps, breaking new ground, and planting from year to year the same kind of crops. The very nature of their work made it possible for the native Americans to receive Irish, Germans, and other nationalities into their midst with little friction. All were alike frugal and industrious tillers of the soil, doing their work from sun to sun in a similar routine.

A Contrast in the Far West and Southwest. A little farther west, however, there were more variety and excitement. Once George Rogers Clark and Daniel Boone had urged the smug Americans of the seaboard to seek their fortunes beyond the Appalachians. Now Kit Carson, James Bowie, Sam Houston, Davy Crockett, and John C. Frémont were to lure them into a stranger land, only a part of which was at the moment under the American flag. This inviting region rolled in a wide sweep from the headwaters of the Mississippi to the banks of the Rio Grande; from the valleys of the Sabine and Red rivers to Montana and the Pacific slope. In comparison with the middle border, it offered such startling novelties that it hardly seemed possible to bring it into unity with the other sections of the country. What contrasts

SANTA BARBARA MISSION

indeed! The blue-grass region of Kentucky or the rich, black soil of Illinois — the painted desert, the home of sage brush and coyote! The level prairies of Iowa — the mighty Rockies shouldering themselves high against the horizon! The long bleak winters of Wisconsin — California of endless summer! The log churches of Indiana or Illinois — the quaint missions of San Antonio, Tucson, and Santa Barbara! The little state of Delaware — the empire of Texas, one hundred and twenty times its area! And most amazing of all, scattered about through the Southwest were the signs of an ancient civilization — fragments of four- and five-story dwellings, pieces of ruined dams and canals — reminders of a departed people which had once overcome the aridity of the desert and lifted itself above the roaming tribes of the plains.

The settlers of this vast empire were to be more diverse in race and habits than those of the original British colonies on the Atlantic coast. While Americans of English, Irish, Scotch-Irish, and German descent were still represented as usual by wanderers from the Eastern states, now for the first time great throngs of Scandinavians joined in the work of developing the land. And though some of the makers of the Western history were to establish their homes on quiet farms as the border advanced against the setting sun, others were to be Indian scouts, hunters, fur trappers, miners, cowboys, planters, keepers of lonely posts on the plain and the desert, stage drivers, pilots of wagon trains, pony riders carrying mails, fruit growers, "lumber jacks," and smelter workers. Nevertheless one bond united them. Different as they were in race and occupation, they became, in some strange way, Americans all.

Southern Planters and Texas. While the farmers of the North apparently had before them boundless acres of unoccupied Western prairies over which they could advance at their pleasure, this was not true of Southern planters. After the restless subjects of King Cotton had exhausted the virgin soil of the coastal states and pushed on to new lands at the frontier of Louisiana, they reached a barrier in their path. At this point where the fertile soil of Texas beckoned them onward, they came face to face with foreign authority — first Spanish and then Mexican. But for a time even this barrier was easily forced. Little realizing the perils of a "peaceful penetration," the government at Mexico City opened wide the doors to aliens and made huge grants of land to contractors in exchange for promises to bring immigrants into Texas. One of these contractors, Moses Austin, an adventurous Yankee from Connecticut, acting under an agreement made with Mexico in 1820, undertook to found a large American settlement near Bexar. Though he died soon, the commission was faithfully carried out by his son, Stephen F. Austin, and a new way was broken into the Southwest. Within a decade about twenty thousand Americans had crossed the border into the Mexican territory.

Mexico Closes the Door. Unaccustomed to enterprise like this, Mexico was frightened by the size of the invasion. To make matters worse, quarrels broke out between the Americans and the natives of Texas.   Then President Jackson gave Mexico a terrible shock by offering to buy Texas for the United States — a broad hint of what was coming.   Thoroughly upset by this turn in events the Mexican government tried to close the doors tight.   It stopped all American colonizing schemes, canceled many land grants, put a tariff on farming implements, and abolished slavery.   But its efforts to block migration availed nothing.   From Texas was sent a call for help which ran through the western border of the United States.   And the sentinels of the frontier answered it.   Davy Crockett, noted bear hunter and backwoods politician, James Bowie, skillful wielder of the knife that to this day bears his name, and Sam Houston, warrior and pioneer, rushed to the aid of their countrymen in Texas.   Soon they made it known that in spite of Mexican sovereignty, they would be their own masters.

The Independence of Texas Declared.   Numbering about one-fourth of the population in Texas, they raised the standard of revolt in 1836.   Following in the footsteps of their ancestors, they summoned a convention, stated their grievances, and finally issued a declaration of independence.   Knowing that the government of Mexico would not quietly accept their decree as final, they dispatched a force to repel the "invading army," as General Houston called the troops advancing under the command of Santa Ana, the Mexican president.   A portion of the Texan soldiers took their stand in the Alamo, an old Spanish mission amid the cottonwood trees on the edge of San Antonio.   Instead of obeying orders to blow up the mission and retire, they held their ground until they were completely surrounded by Mexicans and cut off from all help.   Refusing to surrender, they fought to a finish, the last man falling a victim to the sword.   But American vengeance was swift.   Within three months General Houston overwhelmed Santa Ana at the San Jacinto, took him prisoner of war, and crushed all hopes in Mexico for a recovery of Texas.

With Houston at the head, the Lone Star Republic, as the leaders named independent Texas, then sought admission to the United States.   All that was necessary appeared to be a treaty annexing their country to the Union.   And this seemed at first a simple matter.   President Jackson had a warm regard for General

Houston, and with his usual sympathy for rough and ready ways of accomplishing results, approved what the Americans had done in Texas. In fact, through his agent in Mexico Jackson had long labored, by means none too delicate, to win from the Mexican republic the cession of the coveted territory. So when the Texans took matters into their own hands, he was more than pleased himself; but he knew that he could not obtain the consent of two-thirds of the Senators to a treaty of annexation and he went out of office in 1837, leaving Texas uncertain as to her future.

Northern Opposition to Annexation. In many parts of the North, opposition to annexation was clear and strong. Anti-slavery agitators could hardly find words fiery enough to express their feelings. "Texas," exclaimed W. H. Channing, the famous Boston preacher, in a letter to Clay, "is but the first step of aggression. I trust indeed that Providence will beat back and humble our cupidity and ambition. I now ask whether as a people we are prepared to seize on a neighboring territory for the end of extending slavery? I ask whether as a people we can stand forth in the sight of God, in the sight of nations, and adopt this atrocious policy? Sooner perish! Sooner be our name blotted out from the record of nations!" William Lloyd Garrison, the abolitionist, called for the secession of the Northern states if Texas was brought into the Union with slavery. Henry Clay, Whig candidate for President, taking into account shifting public sentiment, blew hot and cold and finally lost the election of 1844 by giving a halfway indorsement of annexation. But in spite of all criticisms the Democrats in their campaign of that year called for the "Reannexation of Texas," basing their demand on claims which the United States once had to Spanish territory beyond the Sabine River.

Annexation. During the year following the declaration of independence by Texas, the chief politicians had to walk very warily. Van Buren of New York, at heart opposed to slavery extension, refused to press the issue of annexation. Tyler, a proslavery man from Virginia, by a strange fling of fortune carried into office as a Whig, let the troublesome matter rest until the end of his term was in sight. He then listened with favor to the voice of the Southern planters. He was, no doubt, impressed by Calhoun's clever argument which ran in this vein: All good Americans want to uphold the Constitution; the admission of Texas is absolutely essential to the preservation of the Union, for it will maintain the balance of power by aiding the South as against the North now growing so swiftly in wealth and population.

Impressed by such pleas, Tyler appointed Calhoun to the office of Secretary of State in 1844 and told him to arrange with Texas a treaty of annexation — a task at once executed. But this scheme was blocked in the Senate where once more the necessary two-thirds vote could not be mustered. Balked but not defeated, annexationists then drew up a joint resolution which required only a majority vote in both houses, and in February of the next year, just before Tyler

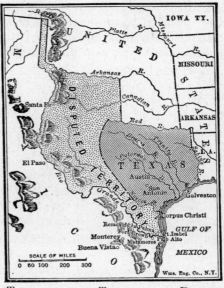

TEXAS AND THE TERRITORY IN DISPUTE

yielded office to Polk, they were able to push it through Congress. So Texas, amid the groans of Boston and the hurrahs of Charleston, folded up her Lone Star flag and came under the Stars and Stripes as a member of the Union.

The Mexican War. But this was not the end of the story. A war with Mexico foretold by the abolitionists and dreaded by Henry Clay followed annexation. The apparent cause was a dispute over the boundaries of the new state. Texans claimed all the land down to the Rio Grande. Mexicans placed the border of Texas at the Nueces River and a line drawn thence in a northerly direction. Accepting the Texan view of the argument, President Polk ordered General Zachary Taylor to move beyond the Nueces in defense of the American claim.   This act the Mexicans deemed an invasion of their territory, and within a short time they attacked the American troops.

Thereupon President Polk declared that American blood had been "spilled on American soil" and that war existed "by the act of Mexico."   A great many leading Whigs asserted that the President's conduct was a shameful aggression on a weaker nation but Congress, in a great outburst of patriotic fervor, granted money and supplies to carry on the struggle.   Although a few Whigs in

Photograph by Ewing Galloway, New York

CHAPULTEPEC PALACE, MEXICO CITY, MEXICO

the House of Representatives refused to vote in favor of Polk's policy, the war was popular throughout the South and West. After grumbling a little, New England gave loyal, if not enthusiastic, support to a conflict it had not desired.   Only a handful of objectors refused to be reconciled.   James Russell Lowell, in the Biglow Papers, flung scorn and sarcasm at the federal government to the end, and William Lloyd Garrison was even more indignant.

The Outcome of the War.   There had never been any doubt, of course, about who would be victor in the war.   General Taylor might have won it in northern Mexico if politics had not intervened.   But Polk, in an effort to avoid making the General another military hero for the Whigs to nominate for President, decided to divide honors by sending a second officer, General Winfield Scott, to strike a blow at the enemy's capital, Mexico City. The deed was done with speed and pomp — and two heroes, instead of one, were presented to the nation. Moreover a third military candidate was made in the Far West when John C. Frémont, in coöperation with Commodores Sloat and Stockton and General Kearny, planted the Stars and Stripes on the Pacific slope.

In February 1848, the Mexicans came to terms, yielding to the victor California, Arizona, New Mexico, and more — a domain greater in extent than the combined areas of France and Germany. As a salve to their wound, the vanquished received fifteen million dollars in cash and the cancellation of many claims held by American citizens. Five years later, through the negotiations of James Gadsden, the United States won from Mexico another cession of lands along the southern border of Arizona and New Mexico in return for a payment of ten million dollars.

General Taylor Elected President. The ink was barely dry on the treaty that closed the war when the "rough and ready" General Taylor, a slave owner from Louisiana, "a Whig," as he said, "but not an ultra Whig," was put forward as the Whig candidate for President. He himself had not voted for years and had little knowledge of political affairs. With a gesture of generosity he referred such questions as the tariff, currency reform and internal improvements to the people's representatives in Congress and offered to enforce the laws as made, if elected. The admirers of Henry Clay, who wanted him for President, were grieved to have their leader pushed aside for a military man, but they had to surrender. Polk thought that he deserved a second term but the Democrats would not even nominate him. Instead they put up Governor Lewis Cass of Michigan and lost the election. So it came about that the hero of Buena Vista, celebrated for his laconic order, "Give 'em a little more grape, Captain Bragg" became President of the United States.

THE PACIFIC COAST AND UTAH

Oregon. Closely associated in the popular mind with the contest over Texas was a dispute with Great Britain about Oregon. In their presidential campaign of 1844, the Democrats had coupled with the slogan, "The Reannexation of Texas," two other cries, "The Reoccupation of Oregon" and "Fifty-four Forty or Fight." Like the first, they too were based on American claims to land. Their use by politicians showed that the distant Oregon country, larger in area than New England, New York, and Pennsylvania combined, was now to be a subject of public excitement.

THE OREGON COUNTRY AND THE DISPUTED BOUNDARY

Joint Occupation and Settlement. Both England and the United States had long laid claim to Oregon and in 1818 they had agreed to occupy the territory jointly — a contract which was renewed in 1828 for an indefinite period. Under this plan, citizens of both countries were free to hunt and settle anywhere in the region. Soon there was a rush of British fur traders and Canadian priests into Oregon, with Americans not far behind them. In 1811 John Jacob Astor, a resourceful merchant of New York, sent out an expedition to establish a post at Astoria and his vanguard was quickly followed by prospectors and trappers. About twenty years later, American missionaries — among them two very remarkable men, Jason Lee and Marcus Whitman — were preaching the gospel to the Indians of Oregon.

Through reports from fur traders and missionaries, Eastern farmers heard of fertile lands on the Pacific slope. And those with the pioneering spirit made ready to transport themselves, their families, and their plows to the far-off West. In 1839 a group went forward by the tedious route around Cape Horn. Four years later a great expedition went overland. The way once broken, migration became heavy. As soon as a few settlements were made the chief pioneers held a mass meeting and agreed upon a plan of self-government. "We, the people of Oregon territory," runs the preamble to their plan, "for the purposes of mutual protection and to secure peace and prosperity among ourselves, agree to adopt

COVERED WAGONS ON A WESTERN TRAIL

the following laws and regulations until such time as the United States of America extend their jurisdiction over us." Thus American tradition swept on its course across the Rocky Mountains.

The Boundary Dispute with England Adjusted. By this time it was evident that the boundaries of Oregon must be fixed. Even before the Mexican dispute reached the stage of warfare, President Polk had made the question of Oregon an issue in the campaign of 1844 and after he was elected he pressed it upon the attention of the country. In his inaugural address and his first message to Congress he dwelt upon the claim of the Democratic platform that "our title to the whole territory of Oregon is clear and unquestionable." But he knew very well that English statesmen did not accept this view at all.

Having the war with Mexico on his hands, Polk sought a compromise with Great Britain. Moved by a hint from the American minister, the British government offered a settlement which fixed the boundary of Oregon at the forty-ninth parallel and gave it Vancouver Island. In spite of his flaming talk about "fifty-four forty," Polk at once chose this way out of the dilemma. After a sharp debate, the treaty, duly drawn in 1846, was ratified by the Senate, surrendering the bigger claim. "Oh! mountain that was delivered of a mouse," exclaimed Senator Benton of Missouri, referring to the outcome, "thy name shall be fifty-four forty!" In 1859, the southern part of the Oregon country was admitted to the Union as the state of Oregon, leaving the northern and eastern sections still in the position of a territory.

California. Notwithstanding the growth of freedom in the Northwest, the planting interests might have been content had fortune not wrested from them the fair country of California. The Far North was no place for slaves anyway but upon the latter many Southerners had set their hearts. Its mild climate and fertile soil seemed well suited to slavery, and leaders among the planters naturally expected to extend their sway to that whole territory. California was more than 155,000 square miles in area — about seventy times the size of the state of Delaware. It could readily be divided into five or six large states, if that became necessary to preserve the Southern balance of power at Washington.

Early American Relations with California. Time and tide, it seems, were not on the side of the planters. Already Americans of a far different type were invading the Pacific slope. Long before Polk could have dreamed of California, the Yankee with his cargo of notions had gone around the Horn to search for profitable trade. In fact, since the days of President Washington, daring skippers had been sailing out of New England harbors on the cruise around South America to California, then to China and around the world, trading as they went and leaving pots, pans, woolen cloth, guns, boots, shoes, salt fish, naval stores, and rum in their wake. "Home from Californy!" rang the cry in many a New England port as the good captain let go his anchor on his return from the Pacific.

The Overland Trails. Not to be outdone by mariners of the deep, western scouts searched for overland routes to the Pacific. Zebulon Pike, explorer and pathfinder, by his expedition into the Southwest during Jefferson's administration, had discovered the resources of the region and had showed his countrymen how easy

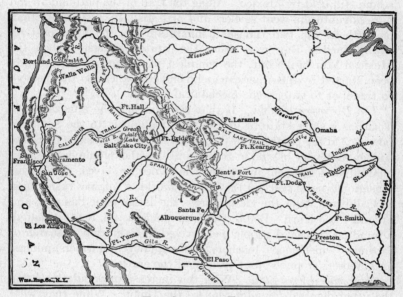

THE OVERLAND TRAILS

it was to reach Santa Fé from the upper waters of the Arkansas River. In a little while, traders formally opened the route, with Franklin, Missouri, and later Fort Leavenworth, as the starting point. Along the trail thus surveyed moved caravans heavily guarded by armed men against marauding Indians. Sand storms often wiped out all signs of the route; hunger and thirst drove bands of wagoners to death; but the lure of the game and the profits at the end kept the business going. Huge stocks of cottons, glass, hardware, and ammunition were drawn almost across the continent to be exchanged at Santa Fé for furs, Indian blankets, silver, and mules; and many fortunes were made out of the traffic.

Americans in California. Why stop at Santa Fé? The question was quickly answered: in 1829, Ewing Young opened the path onward to Los Angeles. Then in 1842 Frémont made the first of his celebrated expeditions across plain, desert, and mountain, arousing the interest of the entire country in the Far West — a land still held by Mexico. Along the trail of the pathfinders and pure adventurers went settlers and artisans. By 1847 more than one-fifth of the two thousand inhabitants in the little post on San Francisco Bay were from the United States. When the Mexican War broke out, the conquest of California had already been started by the Americans who had gone there to till the soil, to trade, or to enter some mechanical pursuit.

The Discovery of Gold. If that war clinched the annexation of Texas as a slave state, it did not add California to the Southern power. On the contrary, in the very year of the cession, 1848, the sudden discovery of gold at Sutter's Mill in the Sacramento Valley guaranteed settlement by people who owned no slaves. When this sensational news reached the outside world, a mighty rush began to California, over the trails, across the Isthmus of Panama, and around Cape Horn. Before two years had passed, it is estimated, a hundred thousand people had arrived in California in search of fortunes — mechanics, teachers, doctors, lawyers, farmers, miners, and laborers from the four corners of the earth.

California a Free State. With this increase in population came the usual demand for admission to the Union. While they were waiting for word from Washington, the Californians held a convention in 1849 and framed their constitution. With impatience, the delegates waved aside the plea that "the balance of power between the North and the South" required the adoption of slavery in California. Unanimously, they voted in favor of freedom and applied for statehood on that condition. Though a Southern man, President Taylor advised Congress to admit the applicant. Robert Toombs of Georgia, on the other hand, vowed to God that he would rather have the South withdraw from the Union. In the compromise of 1850 California was admitted as a free state.

From an old print

SAN FRANCISCO IN 1849

Utah. On the long road to California, in the midst of sandy and barren wastes, a religious sect, the Mormons, had planted a colony to which the government of the United States now had to give attention. Founded in 1830 under the leadership of Joseph Smith of New York, the sect had suffered from many cruel buffets of fortune. In search of liberty bands of Mormons had migrated to Missouri where they were set upon and beaten. Indeed some of them were murdered by their neighbors. Others, harried out of Missouri, went into Illinois only to see their director and prophet, Smith, first imprisoned and then shot by a mob. Having raised up a cloud of enemies on account of their religious faith and finally the practice of polygamy — that is, allowing a man to have more than one wife — many of them gladly accepted the suggestion of a new leader, Brigham Young, that they go into the Far West beyond the plains of Kansas. With a company of picked men, Young then searched far and wide until in 1847 he found for his people a suitable home overlooking the Salt Lake Valley. In one mighty wagon caravan, his followers, now numbering several thousand, moved out to their distant haven.

Brigham Young and His Economic System. In Brigham Young the Mormons had a chieftain of remarkable power, who gave direction to the irrigation of the arid soil, the management of property, and the upbuilding of industry. He promised them to make the desert blossom as the rose, and verily he did it. He shaped the enterprise of the colony along coöperative lines, holding down the profiteer with one hand and encouraging the energetic poor with the other. With the shrewdness befitting a clever business man, he knew how to draw the line between public and private interest. Land was given outright to each family, but care was exercised in the distribution so that none should have great advantage over another. The purchase of supplies and the sale of produce were carried on through a coöperative store and the profits were devoted to the general welfare. Irrigation works were built by common labor and water rights were granted to all families on generous terms.

The Growth of Industries. Though farming long remained the major interest of the colony, the Mormons wanted to be self-supporting in every possible way and so they bent their efforts to manufacturing as well and later to mining. Their missionaries, who hunted in the highways and byways of Europe for converts to join the colony, never failed to point out its economic advantages as indicated by President Young: "We want a company of woolen manufacturers to come with machinery and take the wool from the sheep and convert it into the best clothes. We want a company of potters; we need them, the clay is ready and the dishes wanted. . . . We want some men to start a furnace forthwith; the iron, coal, and molders are waiting. . . . We have a printing press and any one who can take good printing and writing paper to the Valley will be a blessing to themselves and the church." Recruits poured in. Roads and bridges were built; millions were spent on experiments in agriculture and manufacturing; missionaries were maintained at a huge cost in the East and in Europe; an army was kept for defense against the Indians; and settlements were planted in the outlying regions.

Polygamy Forbidden. The hope of the Mormons that they might forever remain undisturbed was however dashed to earth, for hundreds of farmers and artisans belonging to other religious sects came to live among them. In 1850 the colony was so populous and prosperous that Congress organized it into a territory and brought it under the supervision of the federal government. Now protests against polygamy were made both in the colony itself and in the country at large. In 1856 the new Republican party proclaimed it "the right and duty of Congress to prohibit in the territories those twin relics of barbarism, polygamy and slavery." In time the Mormons had to give up their custom of "plural marriages" which was condemned by the public opinion of all western civilization; but they kept the other features of their religious faith. Monuments to their enterprise are seen in their Temple and Tabernacle, their irrigation works, and the great wealth of their Church.

SUMMARY OF WESTERN DEVELOPMENT AND NATIONAL POLITICS

While the statesmen of one generation were solving the problems of their coastal settlements, hunters, pioneers, and home seekers were preparing new problems for the next generation. The West was rising in population and wealth. Between 1783 and 1829, eleven states were added to the original thirteen. All but one were in the West. Here the familiar process of colonization was repeated. Hardy frontier people cut down forests, built log cabins, laid out farms, and blazed trails through the wilderness. They started a new civilization just as the immigrants to Virginia or Massachusetts had done two centuries earlier.

Like the seaboard people before them, they too loved independence and self-government. After they had founded several states, they wanted to send a President from their part of the country to the White House. And in 1829 they had the pleasure of seeing one of their own leaders, Andrew Jackson of Tennessee, elected to the presidency. Again in 1840, in 1844, in 1848, and in 1860, the Mississippi Valley could boast that one of its sons had been chosen to that high office. In its democratic views the West now got support from the mechanics in the towns of the East where the old aristocracy had been forced to extend the suffrage.

Under Jackson's leadership the second United States Bank was destroyed. When he attacked nullification in South Carolina, the West gave him lusty cheers. It approved his policy of dividing government offices among party workers — "the spoils system" in all its fullness. On only one point did it fail to follow him. It heartily favored internal improvements — the appropriation of federal funds for highways, canals, and railways. Jackson's misgivings on this question and his veto of a road-improvement bill raised against him much criticism in the Mississippi Valley.

From the point of vantage on the Middle Border, pioneers pressed onward. They pushed into Texas, which belonged to Mexico. There they created a state, declared their independence, demanded a place in the Union, and won their point, bringing on, as a consequence, a war with Mexico. With the same energy pioneers crossed the trackless plain and desert, opening trails to Sante Fé, to Oregon, and to California. In the sandy waste of Utah, the Mormons began to reclaim the desert and to make it a garden spot. Americans from the East were upon the scene when victory in the Mexican War brought California under the Stars and Stripes. They had staked out farms in the Willamette Valley when the slogan "Fifty-four Forty or Fight" forced a settlement of the Oregon boundary. Before the half century mark had been reached, the United States had begun its career on the Pacific Ocean. From Jamestown to San Francisco — what a brief span of time! And yet what a movement of peoples!

References

E. C. Barker, *Life of Stephen F. Austin.*
G. P. Brown, *Westward Expansion* (American Nation Series).
R. C. Cleland, *A History of California.*
K. Coman, *Economic Beginnings of the Far West* (2 vols.).
W. J. Ghent, *The Road to Oregon.*
F. Parkman, *California and the Oregon Trail.*
R. S. Ripley, *The War with Mexico.*
W. C. Rives, *The United States and Mexico, 1821-48* (2 vols.).

Questions

1. Give some of the special features in the history of Missouri, Arkansas, Michigan, Wisconsin, Iowa, and Minnesota.
2. Contrast the climate and soil of the Middle West and the Far West.
3. How did Mexico at first encourage American immigration?
4. What produced the revolution in Texas? Who led in it?
5. Narrate some of the leading events in the struggle over annexation.
6. How was the war started?
7. Give the details of the peace settlement with Mexico.
8. What is meant by the "joint occupation" of Oregon?
9. How was the Oregon boundary dispute finally settled?
10. Compare the American "invasion" of California with the migration into Texas.
11. Explain how California became a free state.
12. Describe the early economic policy of the Mormons.

Research Topics

The Independence of Texas. McMaster, *History of the People of the United States*, Vol. VI, pp. 251–270. Woodrow Wilson, *History of the American People*, Vol. IV, pp. 102–126.

The Annexation of Texas. Source materials in Hart, *American History Told by Contemporaries*, Vol. III, pp. 637–655; Elson, *History of the United States*, pp. 506–510, 515.

The War with Mexico. Elson, pp. 515–527.

The Oregon Boundary Dispute. Schafer, *History of the Pacific Northwest* (rev. ed.), pp. 88–104; 173–185.

The Migration to Oregon. Schafer, pp. 105–172. Coman, *Economic Beginnings of the Far West*, Vol. II, pp. 113–166.

The Santa Fé Trail. Coman, *Economic Beginnings*, Vol. II, pp. 75–93.

The Conquest of California. Coman, Vol. II, pp. 297–319.

Gold in California. McMaster, Vol. VII, pp. 585–614.

The Mormon Migration. Coman, Vol. II, pp. 167–206.

Biographical Studies. Frémont, Generals Scott and Taylor, Sam Houston, and David Crockett.

The Romance of Western Exploration.   J. G. Neihardt, *The Splendid Wayfaring; The Song of Hugh Glass; The Song of Three Friends;* and *The Song of the Indian Wars.*

PART V. DEMOCRACY AND CONFLICT

CHAPTER XIV

THE RISE OF THE INDUSTRIAL SYSTEM

If Jefferson could have lived to see the Stars and Stripes planted on the Pacific Coast, the broad empire of Texas added to the planting states, and the valley of the Willamette waving with wheat sown by farmers from New England, he would have rejoiced in the triumph of agriculture. Even a stanch old Federalist like Gouverneur Morris, who tried so hard to maintain the supremacy of "the commercial states," would have accepted defeat as final.

Indeed the party of Jefferson, merely renamed by Jackson, grew stronger year by year as farmers of the Northwest and planters from the Southwest poured in upon the floor of Congress. Its candidate in 1852, General Franklin Pierce, carried every state except Massachusetts, Vermont, Kentucky, and Tennessee. This victory for the Democracy was all the more striking because Pierce was a minor figure in the Mexican War and yet won against a distinguished general, Winfield Scott, whom the Whigs had nominated in the hope that "a big military man" would sweep the country. In celebrating the victory of agriculture, President Pierce told the people soon after he took office that, in their interest, the tariff on imports was to be reduced to afford little or no protection for industries, thus cutting the prices of many goods they had to buy. To the planters he gave extra encouragement by dismissing the slavery agitation as a trivial uproar scarcely worth noticing. The party of Hamilton and Clay — the party of protection for American industries — seemed dead and buried.

THE INDUSTRIAL REVOLUTION

A Turn in Affairs. But pride often goeth before a fall, as the proverb warns us. For a time the confidence of the Democrats was supreme. Jackson had destroyed the United States Bank — that "great money power." Polk had signed the tariff bill of 1846

325

which struck a heavy blow at protection for manufactures. Pierce now promised to reduce the tariff to a lower point and silence the abolitionists — by belittling their doctrines. His successor was to take a long stride toward free trade — no protection at all for American industries. But during all these years while farmers and planters were in power at Washington, new factories were being built, new mines opened, new railways constructed, and new cities peopled. Even then America was already in the process of becoming the greatest industrial nation on earth. She had inventors, business enterprise, vast natural resources, and the free labor supply of Europe to draw upon.

The Inventors. While statesmen were publicly discussing political questions, a number of ingenious men were quietly inventing machines that were to revolutionize industry and destroy forever the social order based on the stagecoach and tallow candle, in which politicians had been brought up. In England, James Watt brought the steam engine to a high degree of perfection. In the United States John Fitch and Robert Fulton applied the steam engine to the driving of boats; John Stevens and Peter Cooper tried out "the iron horse" on iron highways; John and Samuel Slater built spinning mills on English models; Elias Howe attached the thread and needle to the flying wheel to make the sewing machine; Samuel F. B. Morse spanned continents with the telegraph; Cyrus Field linked the New World with the Old by a cable laid along the bed of the Atlantic; and Cyrus McCormick offered farmers a reaper in place of the sickle and the scythe. If less celebrated in the pages of the older histories, these men did more to transform the face of the earth and alter the course of human affairs than all the statesmen of their time. Steel and steam were to become masters of the world. Manufacturing in the United States was to employ more people and larger capital than agriculture, and to win its victories in politics.

Industry Outstrips Planting. Though fascinating as a romance, the story of invention cannot be told in detail in a book as small as this. Moreover it is the effects of invention on American life rather than the nature of machinery itself which we must consider. Neither the conflict between North and South at the middle of the century nor the problems of the later age can be understood without reference to the social changes wrought by steam engines and machines. The first sign of the modern industrial era was the uprush of mills managed by aggressive business leaders and manned by labor drawn from native and foreign sources. For every planter who bought land in the Southwest and gathered an army of slaves around him to till it, there now rose in the North a magician of steel and steam who collected under his factory roof an army of free workers.

In seven-league boots this new industrial giant strode ahead of the agricultural giant. Between 1850 and 1860, to use dollars and

LOWELL, MASSACHUSETTS, IN 1838, AN EARLY INDUSTRIAL TOWN

cents as the measure of their march, the value of domestic manufactures, including the output of mines and fisheries, rose from $1,019,106,616 to $1,900,000,000 — an increase of eighty-six per cent in ten years. Meanwhile the total production of naval stores, rice, sugar, tobacco, and cotton, the staples of the South, moved only from $165,000,000, in round figures, to $204,000,000. At the halfway point of the century, the capital invested in industry, commerce, and city property in general far exceeded the value of all the farm land between the Atlantic and the Pacific. Each year the captains of industry turned out goods worth nearly twenty times all the bales of cotton picked on Southern plantations. Indeed the iron, boots and shoes, and other leather goods pouring annually from Northern mills surpassed in value the entire yield of cotton.

The Agrarian West Turns to Industry. Nor was this vast enterprise confined to the old Northeast where, as Madison had once pointed out, commerce was early dominant. "Cincinnati," runs an official report in 1854, "appears to be a great central depot for ready-made clothing and its manufacture for the Western markets may be said to be one of the great trades of that city." "There," wrote a traveler, "I heard the crack of the cattle driver's whip and the hum of the factory: the West and the East meeting." Louisville and St. Louis were already noted for their clothing trades and the manufacture of cotton bagging. Five hundred of the two thousand woolen mills in the country in 1860 were in the Western states. Of the output of flour and grist mills, which almost reached in value the cotton crop in 1850, the Ohio Valley furnished a rapidly growing share. Consequently the center of Jackson's agricultural democracy, where Federalists had been almost as scarce as monarchists, turned surely as the needle to the pole toward the principle of protection for domestic industry, espoused by Hamilton, the Federalist, and defended by Clay, the Whig.

The Extension of Canals and Railways. As necessary to great industry as machinery itself was a great market spread over a wide and varied area and knit together by efficient means of transportation. In other words, manufacturers had to exchange their goods for food supplies. Such a market was opened to them in their own country by the steamship which began its career in 1807 on the Hudson, by the canals starting with the Erie in 1825, and by the railways which came into practical operation a few years afterward.

With unerring instinct Eastern merchants and manufacturers reached out for the trade of the Northwest Territory where free farmers were producing every season staggering crops of corn, wheat, bacon, and wool. To turn these crops away from the Mississippi route and bring them more directly to its cities, Eastern enterprise built two big canal systems — the Erie connecting New York City with the waterways of the Great Lakes and the Pennsylvania chain linking Philadelphia with the headwaters of the Ohio. Soon the routes cut by the canal builders were paralleled by railways. By 1860, New York had rail connections with Chicago and St. Louis, one of the lines running through the Hudson and Mohawk valleys and along the Great Lakes, the other through Philadelphia and Pennsylvania and across the rich wheat fields of Ohio, Indiana, and Illinois. Not to be outdone by her two rivals for the Western trade, Baltimore also engaged in railway construction and by 1857 had trains running into St. Louis.

With the East and the West drawing together in this fashion, Southern leaders had to give attention to railways themselves. To

AN EARLY TRAIN NAMED THE DE WITT CLINTON

offset the magnet pulling business away from New Orleans, they took part in building a line to connect the Gulf with Chicago, and gave cordial support to the project of the Democratic leader, Stephen A. Douglas, for the Illinois Central Railway as one feature of a unified program. To assure a swifter movement of cotton and tobacco to market, lines were laid down along the coast linking Richmond, Charleston, and Savannah. Other railways struck inland from the coast, giving an outlet to the sea for Raleigh, Columbia, Atlanta, Chattanooga, Nashville, and Montgomery. Nevertheless, in spite of this achievement, the mileage of all the Southern states in 1860 did not equal that of Ohio, Indiana, and Illinois.

Banking and Finance. Largely on account of business activity, money became more plentiful in the North. In 1860 the banks of the four industrial states of Massachusetts, Connecticut, New York, and Pennsylvania had funds greater than those of the banks in all the other states combined. New York City had in truth become the money market of America — the center to which industrial companies, railway promoters, and even farmers and planters turned for capital to start and carry on their operations. The banks of Louisiana, South Carolina, Georgia, and Virginia were rich of course, but they were not to be compared with the financial institutions of the East.

The Growth of the Industrial Population. Such a revolution in industry, transport, and finance, overturning the agricultural civilization inherited from the past, could not fail to bring in its train amazing consequences. Some were sudden and obvious. Others we are just beginning to understand. One of the clear and striking changes was the growth of an industrial population, detached from the land, concentrated in cities, and, to use Jefferson's phrase, dependent upon "the caprices and casualties of trade" for a livelihood. This was a result, as the great Virginian had foreseen, which was sure to come from public and private efforts to stimulate industry in preference to agriculture.

It was estimated in 1860, on the basis of the census figures, that mechanical production gave employment to 1,100,000 men and 285,000 women, making, if the average number of their dependents be reckoned, nearly 6,000,000 people — about one-sixth of the entire population of the country — sustained by manufacturing. "This," runs the official record, "was exclusive of the number engaged in the production of many of the raw materials and of the food for manufacturers; in the distribution of their products, such as merchants, clerks, draymen, mariners, the employees of railroads, expresses, and steamboats; of capitalists; various artistic and professional classes, as well as carpenters, bricklayers, painters, and the members of other mechanical trades not classed as manufacturers. It is safe to assume then that one-third of the whole population is supported, directly, or indirectly, by manufacturing industry." The statistics of labor alone were an omen of the future: by 1860 the free workers employed by business enterprise already exceeded the number of slaves on Southern farms and plantations.

Immigration. How was it possible to obtain so quickly such a huge number of free laborers? This is an interesting question, especially when we remember how hard it was for colonial leaders to secure immigrants — and how in their efforts they resorted to slavery, indentured servitude, and kidnaping. The answer to the question is to be found partly in European conditions, partly in the cheapness of transportation after the opening of the steamship era, and partly in the increasing use of women and children in industry. Time was about to fulfill Oliver Ellsworth's prophecy of 1787: white labor would become so abundant that slavery would disappear as the more costly of the two labor systems.

The Coming of the Irish. About 1845 the migration from Ireland to America suddenly became a torrent. For centuries the Irish had chafed at the bonds imposed on them by the English government under which they had to live. Thoroughly loyal to their own race, they were ruled by the Parliament at London, in which their small minority of representatives had little influence. Catholic in religion, they had been compelled to support the Anglican church. Tillers of the soil, they were forced to pay enormous rents to absentee landlords who resided in England. To their ancient woes a potato famine in 1846 added physical distress beyond description. In cottages and fields and along the highways victims of starvation lay dead by the hundreds, while thousands of survivors suffered the agonies of hunger. At this hour of misery America offered a haven to those who were lucky enough to have the money to pay their passage over the sea, and between 1850 and 1860 at least 750,000 Irish immigrants entered the United States.

The German Migration. To political discontent and economic misfortune may likewise be traced the origins of a great Germanic migration which began about the same time. The potato blight that fell upon Ireland also visited the Rhine Valley and southern Germany with results as pitiable if less extensive. This calamity inflicted by nature was made worse a little later by another inflicted by despotic German kings and princes. In 1848 a popular

uprising in favor of republics and democratic government swept
through Europe. For a time it rode on a full tide of success.
Monarchs were overthrown, or compelled to promise better government, and tyrannical ministers fled from their palaces. Then
came reaction. Those who had championed democracy were imprisoned, shot, or harried into exile. Men of great ability, whose
sole offense was opposition to kings and princes, now fled to
America, bringing with them to the land of their adoption the
spirit of liberty. In 1847 over fifty thousand Germans came, the
forerunners of political refugees and a general migration that increased, almost steadily, for many years. The census of 1860
showed that in the previous twenty years nearly a million and a
half Germans had found homes in the United States. Far and wide
they scattered, from the mills and shops of the seacoast towns to
the uttermost frontiers of Wisconsin and Minnesota.

The Labor of Women and Children. If the industries were
"manned" and the canals and railways of the country were constructed largely by foreigners, important native sources of labor
must not be overlooked; above all, the women and children of New
England. Spinning and weaving, by a tradition that runs far
beyond the written records of mankind, belonged especially to
women. Indeed it was dexterous wives, spinsters, and boys and
girls who laid the foundations of the textile industry in America,
in the households of colonial times. When spinning and weaving
were taken from homes to factories operated by water power or
steam engines, women and children followed as a matter of course,
for they had to go on working for a living. "The cotton manufacture alone employs six thousand persons in Lowell," wrote a
French observer in 1836; "of this number nearly five thousand are
young women from seventeen to twenty-four years of age, the
daughters of farmers from the different New England states."
It was not until after the middle of the century that foreign immigration began to supply most of the workers for the factories of
New England.

The Rise of Organized Labor. Spreading mill towns of New
England, New York, and Pennsylvania and growing cities like
Columbus, Cincinnati, Louisville, St. Louis, Detroit, and Chicago

in the West, naturally brought changes, as Jefferson had prophesied, in "manners and morals." One of these was the formation of labor unions and an increasing interest in politics on the part of industrial workers.

Even before the coming of steam and machinery, in the "good old days" of handicrafts, workers in many trades — printers, shoemakers, and carpenters, for example —had begun to draw together in societies to demand higher wages, shorter hours, and milder laws. With the rise of the factory system local labor unions multiplied rapidly in manufacturing centers, and federations of several crafts appeared in the chief cities. By 1860 the plumbers, printers, mule spinners, iron molders, and stonecutters had formed national trade unions. Women likewise began to organize, make de-

From Brown Brothers, New York

FIRST MODEL OF HOWE'S SEWING MACHINE

mands, and strike for shorter hours and higher wages. All over the North labor leaders pressed to the front — forceful characters who forged links binding individual workers into a number of brotherhoods. Indeed they advanced so fast that they made an attempt in 1834 to federate all the crafts into one national organization; but their project soon failed because it was ahead of its time. Fifty years were to elapse before the American Federation of Labor accomplished this task.

However by the middle of the century the labor movement had

developed certain well-defined features: unions in specific crafts, labor leaders, strikes, lockouts, a labor press, labor political programs, and labor political parties. In every great city disputes over wages and hours were frequent; the newspapers recorded about four hundred local strikes in two years, 1853–54. Labor journalism seems to have begun with the founding of the *Mechanics' Free Press* in Philadelphia in 1828 and the establishment of the New York *Workingman's Advocate* shortly afterward. The mill girls of Lowell published a paper called *The Lowell Offering*. Such scattered efforts were in later years followed by regular trade papers designed to weld together and advance the interests of particular crafts.

Labor and Politics. It early became the practice for labor unions to frame political programs and ask the voters to support their planks. Among the reforms they sought were: abolition of imprisonment for debt, manhood suffrage in states still having property qualifications, free and universal education, laws protecting the safety and health of workers in mills and factories, abolition of lotteries, repeal of laws requiring militia service, and free land in the West.

Into the labor papers and platforms sometimes crept a note of hostility to employers. For instance in issuing a call for a local convention, Philadelphia workmen invited "all those of our fellow citizens who live by their own labor and none other." In Newcastle county, Delaware, a labor organization in 1830 complained: "The poor have no laws; the laws are made by the rich and of course for the rich." Here and there an extremist went to the length of advocating an equal division of wealth among the people — the plainest kind of communism.

Agitation of this character in labor circles of course led to criticism of Whigs and Democrats, who talked so much about tariffs and banks and so little about conditions of labor. It also resulted in attempts to found independent labor parties. In Philadelphia, Albany, New York City, and several New England cities, labor candidates were put up for elections in the early thirties and in a few cases were victorious at the polls. "The balance of power has at length got into the hands of the working people, where it properly belongs," exclaimed the *Mechanics' Free Press* of Philadelphia in 1829. But such triumphs were short-lived. Quarrels broke out among labor leaders themselves. Newspapers denounced "trade union politicians" as "demagogues," "levellers," and "rag, tag, and bobtail"; and a few editors, looking on labor unrest as the sour fruit of manhood suffrage, suggested as a remedy for unrest that the vote be taken from the masses.

Clever political leaders, however, especially the managers of Tammany Hall, a Democratic organization in New York City, made terms with dissatisfied labor, offering reforms in exchange for votes. Under the double influence of attacks and concessions the political fever quickly died away, and the end of the thirties saw no remnant of labor parties left. Leaders of industrial workers then turned to a task which seemed more practical, that of organizing the rank and file into craft unions bent upon raising wages and reducing hours.

THE INDUSTRIAL REVOLUTION AND NATIONAL POLITICS

Southern Plans for Union with the West. Well aware that an industrial revolution was taking place in the Northeast, Southern statesmen like Calhoun sought to hold the West and the South together in the same political party as long as possible. The theory on which they operated was simple: both sections were primarily agricultural — producing raw materials and buying manufactured goods; the interests of the two sections were one; and by standing together in favor of low tariffs, they could force down the price of manufactures.

The East Forms Ties with the West. On the other hand Eastern statesmen also saw the importance of forming strong ties with the agricultural West and directing the produce of the Ohio Valley to Philadelphia and New York. It was to effect this economic union that the railways and canals, which we have described, were built. By the middle of the century, Southern writers noted a marked shift in the course of trade. "The great cities of the North," lamented one of them, De Bow, "have severally penetrated the interior with artificial lines until they have taken from the open and untaxed current of the Mississippi the commerce produced on its borders." To this observer it was astounding to behold "the number of steamers that now descend the upper Mississippi River, loaded to the guards with produce, as far as the mouth of the Illinois River and then turn up that stream with their cargoes to be shipped to New York via Chicago. The Illinois canal has not only swept the whole produce along the line of the Illinois River

From Brown Brothers, New York

A MODEL OF THE McCORMICK THIRD REAPER, 1851

to the East, but it is drawing the products of the upper Mississippi through the same channel; thus depriving New Orleans and St. Louis of a rich portion of their former trade."

This drift of business from New Orleans to the Atlantic seaboard was also favored by the credit which Eastern bankers were able to extend to the produce buyers and to the farmers on the soil. The acute Southern thinker just quoted, De Bow, admitted with evident regret, in 1852, that "last autumn, the rich regions of Ohio, Indiana, and Illinois were flooded with the local bank notes of the Eastern States, advanced by the New York houses on produce to be shipped by way of the canals in the spring. . . .

These moneyed facilities enable the packer, miller, and speculator to hold on to their produce until the opening of navigation in the spring and they are no longer obliged, as formerly, to hurry off their shipments during the winter by the way of New Orleans in order to realize funds by drafts on their shipments. The banking facilities at the East are doing as much to draw trade from us as the canals and railways which Eastern capital is constructing." Thus canals, railways, and financial credit were swiftly forging bonds of practical advantages between the home of Jacksonian Democracy in the West and the home of Federalism in the East — foretelling strange political events. The idea of Nationalism to which Webster paid eloquent tribute became more and more real with the passing of time.

The West and Manufacturers. In addition to the commercial bonds between East and West there was growing up a similarity in economic life. As skilled white labor increased in the Ohio Valley, industries sprang up there as if by magic. Cities became larger and customs more like those of the industrial East. And for the new factories, the Western states produced some important raw materials, notably, wool, hemp, and flax, which had to face foreign competition. This was a vital matter. Since the South had no such competition in its cotton and tobacco, the East could not make a bargain with the planters by giving them protection on their raw materials in exchange for heavy duties on manufactured goods. With the West, however, it was now possible to deal on a basis of give and take in tariffs; that is, for example, New England could offer to trade Ohio a high rate on raw wool for a high rate on cotton cloth.

The South Dependent on the North. While East and West were drawing together, the distinctions between North and South were becoming steadily more pronounced, and so pushing them further apart in sympathy. The planting states possessed few industries and produced little save raw materials, and they wanted to escape from high tariffs on the goods they had to buy. Furthermore nearly all the commodities which they bought in Europe came overseas to Northern ports, to be transshipped by rail and water to Southern points of distribution. That part of their rice, cotton, and tobacco, which was not carried to Europe in European vessels, was transported by Northern masters. In these ways, a large share of the business connected with the sale of Southern produce and the purchase of wares in exchange passed into the hands of Northern merchants and bankers who, following the rules of trade, made profits out of it. Even planters who wanted to buy more land and more slaves on credit often borrowed money in the North where the rate of interest was lower than the smaller banks of the South could afford.

The South Reckons the Cost of Economic Dependence. At this stage when Southern dependence upon Northern capital had become a striking reality, Southern leaders began to say openly that the planters had become tribute-bearers to Northern manufacturers and financiers. "The South," complained De Bow, "stands in the attitude of feeding . . . a vast population of [Northern] merchants, shipowners, capitalists, and others who, without claims on her progeny, drink up the life blood of her trade. . . . Where goes the value of our labor but to those who, taking advantage of our folly, ship for us, buy for us, sell to us, and, after turning our own capital to their profitable account, return laden with our money to enjoy their easily earned opulence at home?"

Southern statisticians even attempted to figure out how great this tribute actually was in dollars and cents. They estimated that the planters annually lent to Northern merchants the full value of their exports, a hundred millions or more, to be used in trading operations. They calculated that no less than forty millions all told had been paid to shipowners in profits. They reckoned that if the South manufactured her raw cotton into cloth she would realize from seventy to one hundred millions a year in profits that otherwise went to the North. As a climax to their figuring they attacked the planters for spending some fifteen millions a year pleasure-seeking in the cities and summer resorts of the North.

Southern Opposition to Northern Policies. The logical outcome of this line of thinking was that the laws demanded by the North to promote business enterprise were injurious to Southern planting and also to certain farming groups in the West, especially the corn and wheat producers. A protective tariff raising the prices of manufactures for the tiller of the soil, subsidies increasing the tonnage of the ships owned in the North, internal improvements such as roads and canals forging new economic links between East and West, and a United States Bank increasing the "money power" of the North — all these things were generally regarded in the South and West as contrary to the cotton, tobacco, corn, and wheat interests. They were constantly compared by Southern orators to the restrictive measures used by Great Britain more than half a century before to check American colonial enterprise.

Oppression had justified a war for independence against Great Britain, they argued, and it could justify another such struggle for liberty. "It is curious as it is melancholy and distressing," came a broad hint from South Carolina, "to see how striking is the analogy between the colonial vassalage to which the manufacturing states have reduced the planting states and that which formerly bound the Anglo-American colonies to the British empire. . . . England said to her American colonies: 'You shall not trade with the rest of the world for such manufactures as are produced in the mother country.' The manufacturing states say to their Southern colonies: 'You shall not trade with the rest of the world for such manufactures as we produce.' " So the writer concluded that the South must either control the national government and prevent laws contrary to its interests, or it must declare its political and economic independence as the colonies had done.

Efforts to Start Industries Fail.   Facing this crisis a few Southern leaders sought another remedy — the establishment of factories in their section. To effect this purpose they formed societies for the encouragement of mechanical industries and they invited capitalists to invest in Southern undertakings. But the results were slight. Natural resources, coal, and water power were abundant; but planters could not become business men over night and slaves were not accustomed to managing machinery. Moreover the stream of European immigration flowed North and West, not South. To Irishmen and Germans slavery was a strange, if not a repelling institution. They did not take to it kindly nor care to make their homes where it existed. While slavery lasted,

therefore, the South could not become industrial; it was bound
to remain agricultural.

The Southern Theory of Sectionalism. As time went on,
Southern statesmen became more and more convinced that the
industrial system was their deadly enemy. Their theory of
American politics was stated in a few words by George McDuffie,
a spokesman for South Carolina: "Two great interests have sprung
up, standing directly opposed to each other. One of these consists
of those manufactures which the Northern and Middle states are
capable of producing but which, owing to the high price of labor
and the high profits of capital in those states, cannot hold competition with foreign manufactures without the aid of bounties,
directly or indirectly given, either by the general government or
by the state governments. The other of these interests consists of
the great agricultural staples of the Southern states which can find
a market only in foreign countries and which can be advantageously
sold only in exchange for foreign manufactures which come in
competition with those of the Northern and Middle states. . . .
These interests then stand diametrically and irreconcilably opposed
to each other. The interest, the pecuniary interest of the Northern
manufacturers, is directly promoted by every increase of the taxes
imposed upon Southern commerce; and it is unnecessary to add
that the interest of the Southern planters is promoted by every
diminution of taxes imposed upon the productions of their industry.
If, under these circumstances, the manufacturers were clothed
with the power of imposing taxes, at their pleasure, upon the
foreign imports of the planter, no doubt would exist in the mind of
any man that it would have all the characteristics of an absolute
and unqualified despotism." Whether right or wrong, this opinion
was widely held in the South and became the prevailing doctrine
of the planters and their representatives in Congress.

Their antagonism to the North was deepened by a belief that
Northern manufacturers and bankers formed an "aristocracy of
wealth," bent on attaining supreme power in the government at
Washington. "By the aid of various associated interests," continued McDuffie, "the manufacturing capitalists have obtained a
complete and permanent control over the legislation of Congress

on this subject [the tariff]. . . . Who ever knew the tariff men to divide on any question affecting their confederated interests? . . . The watchword is, stick together, right or wrong upon every question affecting the common cause. Such, sir, is the concert and vigilance and such the combinations by which the manufacturing party, acting upon the interests of some and the prejudices of others, have obtained a decided and permanent control over public opinion in all the tariff states." Thus, in the minds of Southern statesmen, the North, to put it bluntly, was ruled by a "confederated interest" which threatened the planting interest with ruin. Whether the theory was sound or not a host of Southern statesmen had become convinced by 1860 that it was, and were ready to act upon it.

References

M. Beard, *Short History of the American Labor Movement.*
E. L. Bogart, *Economic History of the United States.*
J. R. Commons, *History of Labour in the United States* (2 vols.)
H. V. Faulkner, *American Economic History.*
C. D. Wright, *Industrial Evolution of the United States.*

Questions

1. What signs pointed to a complete Democratic triumph in 1852?
2. What is the explanation of the extraordinary industrial progress of America?
3. Compare the planting system with the factory system.
4. In what sections did industry flourish before the Civil War? Why?
5. Show why transportation is so vital to modern industry and agriculture.
6. Explain how it was possible to secure so many people to labor in American industries.
7. Trace the steps in the rise of organized labor before 1860.
8. What political and economic reforms did labor demand?
9. Why did the East and the South seek closer ties with the West?
10. Describe the economic forces which were drawing the East and the West together.
11. In what way was the South economically dependent upon the North?
12. State the national policies generally favored in the North and condemned in the South.

13. Show how economic conditions in the South were unfavorable to industry.

14. Give the Southern explanation of the antagonism between the North and the South.

Research Topics

The Inventions. Assign one to each student. Satisfactory accounts are to be found in any good encyclopedia, especially the Britannica.

River and Lake Commerce. Callender, *Economic History of the United States*, pp. 313–326.

Railways and Canals. Callender, pp. 326–344; 359–387. Coman, *Industrial History of the United States*, pp. 216–225.

The Growth of Industry, 1815–1840. Callender, pp. 459–471. **From 1850 to 1860.** Callender, pp. 471–486.

Early Labor Conditions. Callender, pp. 701–718.

Early Immigration. Callender, pp. 719–732.

Clay's Home Market Theory of the Tariff. Callender, pp. 498–503.

The New England View of the Tariff. Callender, pp. 503–514.

Questions for Debate

1. The growing differences between North and South were due mainly to slavery.

2. The Industrial Revolution made possible the settlement of the West.

Historical Fiction

Mary S. Watts, *Nathan Burke.*
Charles Dickens, *Martin Chuzzlewit.*
Stephen Crane, *The Red Badge of Courage.*

CHAPTER XV

THE PLANTING SYSTEM AND NATIONAL POLITICS

Efforts on the part of Southern statesmen to unite all agricultural interests in a solid party against the manufacturing interests were hampered by diversities in labor systems. Had the soil of the cotton states been tilled by farmers it would have been easier to maintain connections with the wheat and corn belts where freeholders were in an overwhelming majority. But the soil of the planting states was tilled mainly by slaves and the proud master of bondmen was quite a different person from the simple owner of a small farm who plowed and reaped with his own hands. To keep them in harmony was difficult. Inevitably a controversy over the slave system itself was drawn into the sectional conflict.

SLAVERY — NORTH AND SOUTH

The Decline of Slavery in the North. When the Constitution was adopted, slavery was lawful in all the Northern states except Massachusetts. There were almost as many bondmen in New York as in Georgia. New Jersey had more than Delaware or Tennessee, indeed nearly as many as both combined. All told, however, there were only about forty thousand in the North as against nearly seven hundred thousand in the South and most of the Northern slaves were domestic servants, not laborers necessary to keep the mills going or fields under cultivation.

Moreover, slavery was declining rather than growing in the North. Without a struggle Massachusetts gave it up in 1780. In the same year Pennsylvania provided for gradual emancipation. New Hampshire, where there had been only a handful, Connecticut, with a few thousand domestics, and New Jersey early followed these examples. New York, in 1799, declared that all children born of slaves after July 4 of that year should be free, though held for a term as apprentices; and in 1827 it swept away the last signs of the system of slavery.   So with the passing of the generation that had framed the Constitution, slavery disappeared in the leading commercial states.

The Growth of Northern Sentiment against Slavery.   In both sections of the country there had long existed a strong opposition to slavery both on moral and on economic grounds. In the constitutional convention of 1787, Gouverneur Morris had condemned it and proposed that the whole country bear the cost of abolishing it.   Soon afterward a society for promoting abolition, established under the presidency of Benjamin Franklin, laid before Congress a petition asking that liberty be given to "those unhappy men who alone in this land of freedom are degraded into perpetual bondage."   When Congress, acting on the recommendations of President Jefferson, provided for the abolition of the foreign slave trade on

Courtesy of The Metropolitan Museum of Art

HENRY CLAY

From a painting by Theodore Sidney Moise.

January 1, 1808, several Northern members joined with Southern members in declaring that not only the slave trade but slavery itself was an evil.   Later, colonization societies were formed to encourage the emancipation of slaves and their return to Africa.   James Madison was president and Henry Clay vice president of such an organization.

This antislavery sentiment, however, bore no trace of ill-will toward masters.   "We consider slavery your calamity, not your crime," wrote a distinguished Boston clergyman to his Southern brethren, "and we will share with you the burden of putting an end to it. We will consent that the public lands shall be appropriated to this object. . . . I deprecate everything which shows discord and exasperating sectional animosities."

Uncompromising Abolition. Gradually this spirit of generosity vanished. Just as Jacksonian Democracy rose to power a new kind of antislavery doctrine was heard in the land. For mild theories about the way to solve the problem was now substituted a clear-cut demand for instant abolition at any price. This was the note struck in 1831 when William Lloyd Garrison founded in Boston his antislavery paper, *The Liberator*. With singleness of purpose and utter contempt for all opposing opinions, he pursued a course of passionate abolition agitation. He apologized for having ever "assented to the popular but pernicious doctrine of gradual abolition." He chose for his motto: "Immediate and unconditional emancipation!" He assured his readers that he would be "harsh as truth and uncompromising as justice"; that he would not "think or speak or write with moderation." Then he flung out his defiant slogan: "I am in earnest — I will not equivocate — I will not excuse — I will not retreat a single inch — and I will be heard. . . . 'Such is the vow I take, so help me God.' "

Though Garrison complained that "the apathy of the people is enough to make every statue leap from its pedestal," he soon learned how alive the masses were to the meaning of the issue. Abolition orators were stoned in the streets and hissed from the platforms. Their meeting places were often attacked and sometimes burned to the ground. Garrison himself was assaulted in the streets of Boston and had to take refuge from the angry mob behind prison bars. Lovejoy, a publisher in Alton, Illinois, merely for willingness to give abolition a fair hearing, was brutally murdered; and his printing press was broken to pieces as a warning to those who tried to disturb the nation's peace of mind. The South, doubly frightened by Garrison's temper and a slave revolt in 1831, which ended in the murder of a number of white people, closed all discussion of slavery in its section of the country. "Now," declared Calhoun, "it is a question which admits of neither concession nor compromise."

As both sides grew reluctant to listen to argument, the antislavery agitation gathered in force and intensity. It won to the cause the poet, Whittier, who blew a blast from the New England hills:

"No slave-hunt in our borders — no pirate on our strand;
No fetters in the Bay State — no slave upon our land."

It inspired James Russell Lowell to condemn slavery in prose and poetry. Other abolitionists, not gifted as speakers or writers, signed petitions against slavery and showered them upon Congress. In fact the stream was so great that the House of Representatives, forgetting its traditions about the right of petition, adopted in 1836 a "gag rule" which prevented the reading of appeals and consigned them to the waste basket. Not until the Whigs were in power nearly ten years later was John Quincy Adams able to carry a motion removing the bar to petition.

How deep was the impression made upon the country at large by this agitation for immediate and unconditional emancipation? There is no way of telling exactly. If the popular vote for those candidates who simply opposed the extension of slavery to the Western territories be taken as a standard, abolition sentiment was slight indeed. In 1844, the Free Soil candidate, Birney, polled only 62,000 votes out of over a million and a half; the Free-Soil vote of the next campaign went beyond a quarter of a million, but the increase was due to the personality of the candidate, Martin Van Buren; four years afterward it fell to 156,000, apparently showing that the pleas of the abolitionists found no widespread response among the people.

Yet the agitation undoubtedly ran further than the ballot box indicated. Young statesmen of the North, in whose hands the destiny of frightful years ahead was to lie, were shaken out of indifference to slavery and their consciences were stirred by the continuous appeal to destroy the institution as a disgrace to the republic. In a little while positive rivalry began among Northern leaders in the effort of each to prove himself the first abolitionist. Thus Senator Charles Sumner of Massachusetts boasted that he read *The Liberator* two years before Wendell Phillips, the youthful Boston lawyer who cast aside his profession to devote himself entirely to abolition.

Early Southern Opposition to Slavery. In the early years of the republic many Southern people likewise believed that slavery was morally wrong and would come to an end in due time through natural causes. Washington disliked it and directed in his will that his own slaves should be set free after the death of his wife. Jefferson, looking into the future, condemned the system in words that showed deep feeling: "Can the liberties of a nation be thought secure when we have removed their only firm basis, a conviction in the minds of the people that their liberties are the gift of God? Are they not to be violated but with His wrath? Indeed I tremble for my country when I reflect that God is just; that His justice cannot sleep forever." Furthermore, Southern men accepted in 1787 the

From Brown Brothers, New York

ELI WHITNEY'S FIRST COTTON GIN

Ordinance which excluded slavery from the Northwest territory, and also the Missouri Compromise which shut it out of a vast section of the Louisiana territory.

The Revolution in the Slave System. Among the representatives of South Carolina and Georgia, however, the antislavery views of Washington and Jefferson were by no means approved. Furthermore, certain developments in Southern agriculture began to work in favor of extending rather than abolishing the system of chattel servitude. The invention of the cotton gin and textile machinery created such a lively market for cotton that the planters, with all their skill and energy, could hardly meet its demands. With feverish energy they called for more land to till and more slaves to till it. In their search for additional acres they drove the small farmers who had few or no slaves steadily from the seaboard into the less fertile uplands or to the Northwest where freedom reigned.

With the increasing demand for slaves, the number of bondmen rose from 700,000 in Washington's day to more than three millions in 1850. Meanwhile, the nature of slavery itself was changed. Instead of the homestead where the same family of masters kept the same families of slaves from generation to generation, now came the plantation system of the Far South and Southwest where masters were ever moving, ever extending their holdings of lands, and ever buying more slaves. This in turn reacted on the older South where the raising of slaves for the market became a regular and highly profitable business. So all parts of the South were linked together in a great slave trade.

Slavery Defended as a Positive Good. Consequently, apologies for slavery became fainter and fainter in the South. Finally they gave way to claims that slavery was actually beneficial. Calhoun, in a famous speech in the Senate in 1837, sounded this new Southern note by declaring slavery "instead of an evil, a good — a positive good." His reasoning was as follows: in every civilized society one portion of the community must live on the labor of another; learning, science, and the arts are built upon leisure; the African slave, kindly treated by his master and mistress and looked after in his old age, is better off than the free laborers of Europe; and under the slave system conflicts between capital and labor are avoided. The advantages of slavery in this respect, he concluded, "will become more and more manifest, if left undisturbed by interference from without, as the country advances in wealth and numbers."

Slave Owners Powerful in Politics. This doctrine was eagerly seized by the planters as they came more and more to overshadow the small farmers of the South and as they watched the menace of abolition growing upon the horizon. They felt warranted in coöperating for the protection of an institution so necessary, so natural, so perfectly good.

Though in 1850 the slave owners were only about three hundred and fifty thousand in a national population of nearly twenty million whites, they had enormous power. They were knit together by the bonds of a common interest. They had leisure and wealth for their own defense. They often went in person to the Congress of the United States as representatives of the South. They could travel and attend conferences and conventions. Throughout the South the press, the schools, and the pulpits were on their side, for the small farmers who owned no slaves were often illiterate as well as poor. The planters formed, as it were, a mighty union for the protection and advancement of their cause. Aided by those mechanics and farmers of the North who stuck by Jacksonian Democracy through thick and thin, they almost became masters of the federal government. "We nominate Presidents," exultantly boasted a Richmond newspaper; "the North elects them."

In fact this jubilant Southern claim was admitted by William H. Seward, a Republican Senator from New York, in a speech describing

JOHN C. CALHOUN

the power of slavery in the national government. "A party," he said, "is in one sense a joint stock association, in which those who contribute most direct the action and management of the concern. . . . The slaveholders, contributing in an overwhelming proportion to the strength of the Democratic party, necessarily dictate and prescribe its policy." He went on: "The slaveholding class has become the governing power in each of the slaveholding states and it practically chooses thirty of the sixty-two members of the Senate, ninety of the two hundred and thirty-three members of the House of Representatives, and one hundred and five of the two hundred and ninety-five electors of President and Vice President of the United States." Then he spoke of the slave power in the Supreme Court. "That tribunal," he asserted "consists of a chief justice and eight associate justices. Of these, five were called from slave states and four from free states. The opinions and bias of each of them were carefully considered by the President and Senate when he was appointed. Not one of them was found wanting in soundness of politics, according to the slave-holder's exposition of the Constitution."

Slavery in National Politics

How Slavery Became Involved in Politics. Had there been no antislavery agitation, Congress would have been compelled to discuss the subject from time to time and to make important decisions concerning it. Under the Constitution, Congress had to make all needful rules for the government of the territories, the District of Columbia, the forts and other property under national authority; so it was compelled to determine whether slavery should exist in these places. Upon Congress also was conferred the power to admit new states; whenever a territory wished to come into the Union as a state, Congress had to decide whether it should be a slave or a free state. Moreover, the Constitution gave Congress the power to enforce the clause which called for the return of runaway slaves to their owners. And since the control of the post office was vested in the federal government, it faced the problem of permitting abolition literature to pass through the mails. Finally the right of citizens to petition the government made it legal for abolitionists to carry their complaints against slavery straight to the houses of Congress. It was thus impossible, constitutionally, to draw a boundary around the slavery issue and confine the debate to the states.

The Territorial Question. In no way could Congress avoid dealing with one vital question: "When any new territory is acquired how much of it shall be given over to slavery?" This issue was raised with respect to the territory between the Appalachians and the Mississippi before the end of the eighteenth century and was settled by a division along the Ohio River. And with the Louisiana Purchase and then the acquisition of an immense area at the close of the Mexican War, Congress had to deal with it again. Yet for a long time it was possible for the North and the South to arrive at a compromise of some kind whenever the question came up for debate.

The Missouri Compromise. It was over the application of Missouri for admission to the Union that the first menacing clash came in Congress over bondage and freedom. By 1818 slavery sentiment had become so strong on the one side and the antislavery sentiment so keen on the other that Missouri's quest for

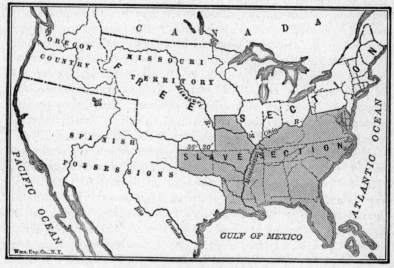

MAP OF MISSOURI COMPROMISE

admission as a state brought both houses of Congress into a deadlock. The South, having half the Senators, could prevent attempts to force Missouri to disown slavery; while the North, powerful in the House of Representatives, could keep Missouri with slavery out of the Union.

To break this political deadlock a compromise had to be reached. So Maine, separated from the parent state of Massachusetts, was brought into the Union as a free state and Missouri with slavery. At the same time it was agreed that the remainder of the vast Louisiana territory north of the parallel of 36° 30' should be, like the old Northwest, forever free; while the southern portion was given over to bondage. In reality this bargain was an immense gain for liberty, because the area dedicated to free farmers was many times greater than that left to the planters and the principle was once more asserted that Congress had full power to prevent slavery in the territories.

The Wilmot Proviso. Later the annexation of Texas with slavery gave to the planting interest a feeling of greater security against the increasing wealth and population of the North. Texas, it was said, could be divided into four slave states. The far western territories secured by the treaty of peace with Mexico contained the promise of at least three more. Thus, as each new free-soil state knocked for admission to the Union, the South could demand as the price of its consent a new slave state. Abolitionists and moderate opponents of slavery alike were in despair. Texas, they groaned, would fasten it upon the country more tightly. "No living man," cried one, "will see the end of slavery in the United States!"

It so happened, however, that the events which, it was thought, would strengthen slavery let loose a popular storm against it. The first cloud appeared in the sky on August 6, 1846, only a few months after war was declared on Mexico. On that day, David Wilmot, a Democrat from Pennsylvania, introduced into the House of Representatives a resolution to the effect that slavery should be excluded from every part of the territory taken away from Mexico. "The Wilmot Proviso," as the resolution was called, was defeated but it was a challenge to the South and it fanned the abolitionist flame kindled by Garrison.

Instead of ignoring the challenge the South quickly accepted it. Speaking in the House of Representatives, Robert Toombs of Georgia declared: "In the presence of the living God, if by your legislation you seek to drive us from the territories of California and New Mexico . . . I am for disunion." South Carolina announced that the day for talk had passed and the time had come to join her sister states in resisting the application of the Wilmot Proviso "at any and all hazards." A general conference was called at Nashville for the frank purpose of arresting "the course of aggression" and, if that was not possible, providing for their "separate welfare by the formation of a compact and union that will afford protection to their liberties and rights." States that had spurned South Carolina's plea for nullification in 1832 responded to this new appeal with alacrity — an omen of the secession to come.

The Great Debate of 1850. Challenge and counter-challenge had lifted the temper of the country to white heat when Congress

A Cartoon Representing Webster "Stealing Clay's Thunder"

convened in December, 1849. It was a memorable session, memorable for the distinguished men who took part in the debates and for the Compromise of 1850 which it produced. In the Senate sat for the last time three heroic figures: Webster from the North, Calhoun from the South, and Clay from the borderland. For nearly forty years these three had been leaders of men. All had grown old and gray in political service. Calhoun was already broken in health and in a few months was to be borne from the public arena forever. Clay and Webster had but two more years to live.

Experience, learning, statecraft — all these things they now marshaled in a mighty effort to solve the slavery problem. On January 29, 1850, Clay offered to the Senate a sectional compromise intended to yield something to each side and a few days later, in a powerful oration, he made a passionate appeal for a union of American hearts through mutual sacrifices. But Calhoun demanded for the South the full measure of its claims: equal rights in the territories bought by common blood; the return of runaway slaves as required by the Constitution; the suppression of abolitionists; and the restoration of the balance of power between the North and the South. Webster, of Massachusetts, to the amazement of many New Englanders who expected him to uphold liberty as stanchly, in his notable "Seventh of March Speech," condemned the attempt of Wilmot to forbid slavery in the regions taken from Mexico, agreed with the South that the fugitive slave provision should be enforced, denounced the abolitionists, and made a fervid plea for the Constitution, the Union, and liberty.

The Compromise of 1850. When the debates were closed, the results were totaled in a series of laws which were signed in September, 1850, by President Fillmore, who had taken office a few months earlier, on the death of Zachary Taylor. By these acts, known as the Great Compromise, both sides won certain concessions. In deference to the North, trade in slaves in the District of Columbia was forbidden, although slavery itself was allowed to exist there as before. To the South was given a new fugitive slave law, drastic in letter and spirit, to be enforced by federal officers instead of local authorities, such as sheriffs and constables. The act provided that masters or their agents, merely by filing claims, might seize escaped slaves without granting the alleged fugitives the right to have a jury trial, to give testimony on their own behalf, or to have witnesses. Anybody who interfered with the enforcement of the law was liable to heavy fine and imprisonment. So far the South had the better of the bargain.

Now what was done with the new territory in the West? Here neither side won definitely. Congress did not decide for or against slavery there. It merely organized the territories of New Mexico and Utah and added that when states were formed in these regions they might come into the Union "with or without slavery as their constitutions may provide at the time of their admission." Thus the Wilmot doctrine was rejected, while slavery was not guaranteed to the planters. And California was at the same time taken into the Union as a free state.

Proslavery Triumph in the Election of 1852. Judging by the election in 1852, the people were tired of slavery agitation and wanted the subject dropped. Both parties, Whigs and Democrats, indorsed the fugitive slave law and approved the Great Compromise. The Democrats, with Franklin Pierce as their candidate for President, swept the country against the war hero, General Winfield Scott, on whom the Whigs had staked their hopes. Even Webster, broken with grief at his failure to receive the nomination, advised his friends to vote for Pierce and turned away from politics to meditate upon approaching death. The election results seemed to prove that everybody, save a handful of agitators, looked upon the recent compromise as the end of the trouble. "The people, especially the business men of the country," says the historian Elson, "were utterly weary of the agitation and they gave their suffrages to the party that promised them rest." The Free Soil party, which attacked slavery as "a sin against God and a crime against man," and advocated freedom for the territories, failed to carry a single state. In fact it polled fewer votes than it had four years earlier — 156,000 as against nearly 3,000,000, the combined vote of the Whigs and Democrats. It is not surprising, therefore, that President Pierce, surrounded in his cabinet by strong Southern sympathizers, should promise an end to slavery agitation.

Antislavery Agitation Renewed. But the promise was easier to make than to fulfill. Indeed the attempt to execute one measure included in the Compromise — the fugitive slave law — actually added to the uproar over slavery. Framed to aid the planters, it helped to overthrow them by bringing slavery to the very doors of Northern homes. Slavery five hundred miles away on a Louisiana plantation was so remote from the North that only the most excitable abolitionist could keep up a constant rage against it. On the other hand "slave catching," "man hunting" by federal officers on the streets of Philadelphia, New York, Boston, Chicago, or Milwaukee and in the hamlets and villages of the wide-stretching country districts of the North was another matter. It carried the most odious aspects of slavery straight to thousands of men and women who would otherwise have remained indifferent to the system. Law-abiding merchants, mechanics, farmers, and women now saw peaceful negroes, who had resided in their neighborhoods perhaps for years, torn away by federal officers and borne back to bondage; and immediately mere spectators were transformed into enemies of the law. They helped slaves to escape; they snatched them away from officers who had captured them; they broke jails open and sent fugitives off to Canada.

Assistance to runaway slaves, always more or less common in the North, was by this time organized into a system. Regular routes, known as "underground railways," were laid out across the free states into Canada, and trusted advocates of freedom maintained "underground stations" where fugitives were concealed in the daytime between their long night journeys. Funds were raised and secret agents sent into the South to help negroes to flee. One negro woman, Harriet Tubman, "the Moses of her people," with headquarters at Philadelphia, is accredited with nineteen such invasions into slave territory and the emancipation of three hundred negroes. Those who worked at this business were in constant peril. One underground operator, Calvin Fairbank, spent nearly twenty years in prison for aiding fugitives to escape from the South. Yet perils and prisons did not stay those determined men and women who, in obedience to their consciences and their sympathies with human suffering, set themselves to this lawless work.

From thrilling stories of adventure along the underground railways came some of the scenes and themes of the novel by Harriet Beecher Stowe, *Uncle Tom's Cabin*, published in 1852, two years after the Compromise. Her stirring tale set forth the worst features of slavery in vivid word-pictures that caught and held the attention of millions of readers. Though the book was in many ways unfair to the South and was denounced by Southerners as a hideous distortion of the truth, it was quickly dramatized

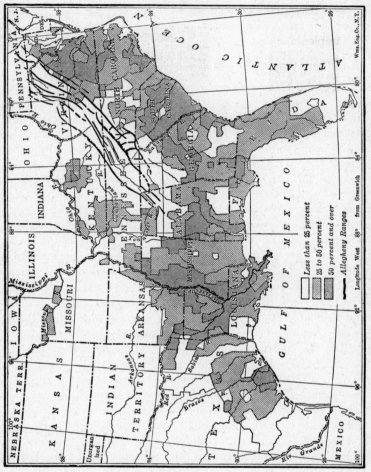

DISTRIBUTION OF SLAVES IN THE SOUTHERN STATES

Less than 25 percent
25 to 50 percent
50 percent and over
Allegheny Ranges

Longitude West   from Greenwich

and played in every city and town throughout the North. Topsy,
Little Eva, Uncle Tom, the fleeing slave, Eliza Harris, and the
cruel slave driver, Simon Legree, with his baying bloodhounds,
became living specters in many a home that sought to bar the door
to the "unpleasant and irritating business of slavery agitation."

The Drift of the Irrepressible Conflict

Repeal of the Missouri Compromise.   Nevertheless, to practical
men, the "rub-a-dub" uproar of a few abolitionists, an occasional
riot over fugitive slaves, and the vogue of a popular novel seemed
hardly worthy of notice.   In fact, encouraged by the election of
1852, the proslavery statesmen grew so bold that they now dared
to repeal the Missouri Compromise prohibiting slavery in the
northern part of the Louisiana territory.   The leader in this fateful
enterprise was Stephen A. Douglas, Democratic Senator from
Illinois, and the occasion for his action was a demand for the formation of territorial governments in the regions west of Iowa and
Missouri.

Like Clay and Webster before him, Douglas was consumed by
an ambition to become President of the United States and to
reach his goal it was necessary to win the support of the South.
This he undertook to do by paving the way for slavery in a great
section dedicated to freedom by a compromise more than thirty
years old.   On January 4, 1854, he introduced in Congress a bill
organizing the Nebraska territory on the understanding that the
people might decide for themselves whether they would have
slavery or not.   This was the doctrine of "squatter sovereignty" —
let the "squatters" or settlers have slavery or freedom as they will.

After a heated debate, in which Douglas was forced to accept
amendments to his proposal, a bill known to history as the Kansas-
Nebraska Act became a law on May 30.   This act created two
territories, Kansas and Nebraska, and then provided that they or
territories formed out of them could come into the Union "with or
without slavery as their constitution may prescribe at the time of
their admission."   Not content with this halfway measure, the
law then went on expressly to declare the Missouri Compromise
null and void.   Thus by a single stroke the very heart of the

American continent, devoted to freedom by a solemn agreement between North and South, was thrown open to slavery, and at once a desperate struggle began between slave owners and the advocates of liberty to see which side could get possession of Kansas first.

If Douglas fancied that Northern people would receive the overthrow of the Missouri Compromise in silence, he quickly learned his error. A blast of rage, terrific in its fury, swept from Maine to Iowa. Staid Boston hanged him in effigy with an inscription — "Stephen A. Douglas, author of the infamous Nebraska bill: the Benedict Arnold of 1854." City after city burned him in effigy until, as he himself said, he could travel from the Atlantic coast to Chicago in the light of the fires. Thousands of Whigs and Free-Soil Democrats declared that the startling measure showed an evident resolve on the part of the planters to rule the whole country, and they deserted the parties which had sanctioned the Kansas-Nebraska Bill. By the abolitionists it was viewed as an act of defiance. It set an issue even for the moderate and timid who had been unmoved by the orations over slavery in the Far South. The time had come to settle the question whether slavery was to be confined within its existing boundaries or be allowed to spread all over the West, perhaps everywhere in the United States. Within that question was hidden another: Shall the planting South or the industrial and farming North govern the nation?

Rise of the Republican Party. Events of terrible significance, coming swiftly, lashed the country like a ship before a gale straight into civil war. The Kansas-Nebraska bill made breaches in the old parties and called into being the Republican party. While that bill was pending in Congress, many Northern Whigs and Democrats had come to the conclusion that the formation of a new party determined to keep slaves out of the territories must follow the repeal of the Missouri Compromise. Several places claim to be the Republican birthplace; but most historians agree that it was Ripon, Wisconsin. In that town a mass meeting of Whigs and Democrats assembled in February, 1854, and resolved to form an independent party if the Kansas-Nebraska Bill should pass. At a second meeting called after Congress enacted the law, a fusion committee representing Whigs, Free Soilers, and Democrats was formed and the name Republican — the name of Jefferson's party — was once more selected. All over the country similar meetings were held and political committees were organized.

When the presidential campaign of 1856 opened, the Republicans entered the contest. They held a national convention in Philadelphia, drew up a platform opposing the extension of slavery in the territories, and nominated for the presidency, John C. Frémont, the distinguished explorer. Prominent men like Longfellow, Washington Irving, William Cullen Bryant, Ralph Waldo Emerson and George William Curtis went over to the new party and 1,341,-264 votes were rolled up for "free labor, free speech, free men, free Kansas, and Frémont." Although this was many times the Free-Soil vote of four years before, the Democrats won a decisive victory. Their candidate, James Buchanan of Pennsylvania, was elected by a vote of 174 to 114 electors.

The Dred Scott Decision (1857). In his inaugural address, Buchanan vaguely hinted that the Supreme Court of the United States would soon settle one of the questions affecting slavery in the territories. This was a reference to the Dred Scott case then pending. Scott was a slave who had been taken by his master into the upper Louisiana territory where freedom had been established by the Missouri Compromise, and then carried back into his old state of Missouri. He brought suit for his liberty on the ground that residence in the free territory made him free. This raised the question whether the Missouri Compromise prohibiting slavery north of 36° 30′ was really legal after all — that is, authorized by the federal Constitution. The Court might have avoided answering it by saying that even though Scott was free in the territory he became a slave again in Missouri by virtue of the law of that state. The Court, however, faced the issue squarely. It held that Scott had not been free anywhere and that, besides, the Missouri Compromise violated the Constitution and was null and void.

The decision was a triumph for the South. It declared that Congress had no power to prevent slavery in the territories. Under the decree of the highest court in the land, that could be done only by an amendment to the Constitution which required a two-thirds vote in Congress and the approval of three-fourths of the states. Obviously such an amendment was impossible — the Southern states had too many votes; but the Republicans were not daunted. "We know," said Lincoln, "the Court that made it has often over-ruled its own decisions and we shall do what we can to have it overrule this." Legislatures of Northern states passed resolutions condemning the decision and the Republican platform of 1860

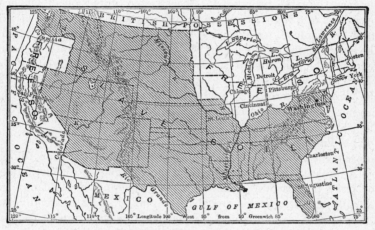

SLAVE AND FREE SOIL ON THE EVE OF CIVIL WAR

characterized the theory that the Constitution permitted slavery in the territories as "a dangerous political heresy at variance with the explicit provisions of that instrument itself . . . with legis-lative and judicial precedent . . . revolutionary in tendency and subversive of the peace and harmony of the country."

The Panic of 1857. In the midst of the dissension over the Dred Scott decision, came one of the worst business panics which ever afflicted the country, to add to the excitement. In the spring and summer of 1857, fourteen railroad corporations including the Erie, Michigan Central, and the Illinois Central failed to pay their bills; banks and insurance companies, some of the largest and strongest institutions in the North, closed their doors; stocks and bonds fell in a crash on the markets; manufacturing was paralyzed; tens of thousands of working people were thrown out of employment; "hunger meetings" of idle men were held in the cities and banners bearing the inscription: "We want bread" were flung out. New York workingmen threatened to invade the chamber of the city council, to demand "work or bread," and the frightened mayor called for the police and soldiers. For this distressing state of affairs many remedies were offered; none with more zeal and persistence than the proposal for the stricter protection of business by means of a higher tariff on European goods. Those who attributed the panic to foreign undercutting of American prices placed the entire blame on the law of March, 1857, a Democratic measure reducing the customs rates. In the manufacturing districts of the North this was called a "Democratic assault on business." So the same commercial issue which had rent the country since the origin of the republic raised its scare-head again — at a time when the slavery fever was most acute.

The Lincoln-Douglas Debates. The following year this sectional strife found expression in a series of debates held in Illinois by Abraham Lincoln and Stephen A. Douglas, both candidates for the United States Senate. At the opening of his campaign Lincoln had uttered his trenchant saying that "a house divided against itself cannot stand. I believe this government cannot endure permanently half slave and half free." In another address he had accused Douglas, Buchanan, and the Supreme Court of acting in secret to spread slavery over the continent. This daring statement aroused Douglas, who was making his campaign on the doctrine of squatter sovereignty; that is, the right of the people of each territory "to vote slavery up or down." After a few long-distance exchanges, the candidates agreed to meet face to face and discuss the issues before the people. Never had such crowds been seen at political meetings in Illinois. Farmers deserted their plows, smiths their forges, and housewives their baking to hear "Honest Abe" and "The Little Giant" talk on the slavery question.

During the discussion Lincoln clearly defined his position. He accepted the idea that the South was entitled under the Constitution to a fair fugitive slave law. He hoped that there might be no new slave states; but he did not believe that Congress could exclude the people of a territory from the Union merely because they saw fit to adopt a constitution legalizing the ownership of slaves. Such were Lincoln's concessions to the South. On the other hand, he favored the abolition of slavery in the District of Columbia and in the territories by act of Congress.

Moreover, he drove Douglas into a corner by asking him how he squared "squatter sovereignty" with the Dred Scott decision; how, in other words, the people of a territory could vote slavery down when the Court had declared that even Congress, which had superior powers in governing territories, could not do it under the Constitution. To this question Douglas lamely replied that the inhabitants of a territory, by "unfriendly legislation," might make property in slaves insecure and thus destroy slavery itself. In spite of his weak argument on this point Douglas won the election to the Senate; but Lincoln, lifted into national fame by the debates, beat him in the campaign for President two years later.

John Brown's Raid. Not long after the debaters closed their battle of words, the country was startled by something more serious than verbal disputes. Inflamed by a hatred for slavery in itself, John Brown, a grim and resolute man, turned from agitation to violence. "These men are all talk; what is needed is action — action!" he once exclaimed after listening to oratory on slavery. During the struggle over Kansas, he had hurried to the frontier, gun and dagger in hand, to help expel slave owners from the free soil of the West. There he committed deeds of such ferocity that he was outlawed and a price put on his head. Still he kept on the path of "action."

Aided by funds from Northern sympathizers, he gathered a small band of his followers around him, saying to them: "If God be for us, who can be against us?" In the autumn of 1859 he went into Virginia, hoping, as he explained, "to effect a mighty conquest even though it be like the last victory of Samson." He seized the government armory at Harper's Ferry, declared free the slaves whom he found there, and called upon them to take up arms in defense of their liberty. But his hope was as forlorn as it was desperate. Armed troops came down upon him and, after a hard battle, captured him. Tried for treason, Brown was sentenced to death. To pleas for clemency based on the ground that the prisoner was simply a lunatic, the governor of Virginia turned a deaf ear. "This is a beautiful country," said the condemned man, glancing upward to the eternal hills on his way to the gallows, as calmly as if he were returning home from a long journey. "So perish all such enemies of Virginia. All such enemies of the Union. All such foes of the human race," solemnly announced the executioner as he fulfilled the judgment of the law.

John Brown's raid and its grim ending made a national sensation. Abolitionists looked upon Brown as a martyr and tolled funeral bells on the day of his execution. Longfellow wrote in his diary: "This will be a great day in our history; the date of a new revolution as much needed as the old one." Southerners such as Jefferson Davis saw in the affair "the invasion of a state by a murderous gang of abolitionists bent on inciting slaves to murder helpless women and children" — a crime for which the leader had met a felon's death. Lincoln spoke of the raid as absurd, the deed of an enthusiast who had brooded over the oppression of a people until he fancied himself commissioned by heaven to liberate them — an attempt which ended in "little else than his own execution." To Republican leaders as a whole, the event was very embarrassing. They were taunted by the Democrats with responsibility for the deed. Douglas declared it to be his "firm and deliberate conviction that the Harper's Ferry crime was the natural, logical, inevitable result of the doctrines and teachings of the Republican party." So persistent were attacks of this character that the Republicans in 1860 denounced Brown's raid "as among the gravest of crimes."

The Democrats Divided. When the Democratic convention met at Charleston in the spring of 1860, a few months after Brown's execution, its members knew that there was danger ahead. Between the extreme slavery advocates of the Far South and the so-called proslavery Democrats of the Douglas type, a chasm yawned which no appeals to party loyalty could bridge. Coming from the West, Douglas knew that, while the North was not abolitionist, it stood positively against an extension of slavery into the territories by act of Congress; that squatter sovereignty was the mildest kind of compromise acceptable to the farmers whose votes could decide the election. But Southern leaders would not accept his opinion. Yancey, of Alabama, refused to palter with any plan built on the proposition that slavery was in itself an evil. He ridiculed Northern Democrats for taking the ground that slavery was wrong, and then saying that nothing could be done about it. That, he said, was the fatal error — the cause of all discord, the source of "Black Republicanism," as well as squatter sovereignty. The command was thus given to the Northern delegates: "You must not apologize for slavery; you must declare it right; you must advocate its extension." The demand, so bluntly put, was as bluntly answered. "Gentlemen of the South," responded a delegate from Ohio, "you mistake us. You mistake us. We will not do it."

For ten days the Charleston convention wrangled over a platform and balloted for the nomination of a candidate. Though in the lead, Douglas could not get the two-thirds vote required for victory. For more than fifty times the roll of the delegates was called without a decision. Then in sheer desperation the convention adjourned to meet later at Baltimore. But the interval did not cool the temper of its members. When they again assembled, passions ran as high as ever; so finally the uncompromising delegates from the South withdrew to Richmond, nominated John C. Breckinridge of Kentucky for President, and put forth a platform favoring the extension of slavery to the territories and asserting the duty of the federal government to protect it there. The delegates who stayed at Baltimore nominated Douglas and indorsed his doctrine of squatter sovereignty. Thus the Democratic party was split wide open.

The Constitutional Union Party. While the Democratic party was being disrupted, a fragment of the former Whig party, known as the Constitutional Unionists, held a convention at Baltimore and selected its national candidates: John Bell from Tennessee and Edward Everett from Massachusetts. No hot heads were in control of this political assembly. It was mainly composed of aged men whose views were those of Clay and Webster, admired compromisers of the past. In their platform they sought to extinguish the evil spirit of sectionalism by inviting their fellow citizens to "support the Constitution of the country, the Union of the states, and the enforcement of the laws." The party that campaigned on this pacific sentiment drew only laughter from the Democrats and scorn from the Republicans. It polled less than one-fourth of the votes.

The Republican Triumph. With the Democrats split into factions the Republican party that had led a forlorn hope four years before thought it was on the high road to success at last. New and powerful recruits were found when it held its convention at Chicago. Advocates of a high protective tariff and friends of free homesteads for farmers and workingmen mingled with enthusiastic foes of slavery. Still firm in their opposition to slavery in the territories, the Republicans also took a stand at this hour on the homestead issue, which had long been merely a matter of debate. They declared definitely in favor of giving the public lands away to actual settlers in farms of moderate size. They also approved customs duties designed "to encourage the development of the industrial interests of the whole country." Their platform was greeted with cheers which, according to the stenographic report of the convention, became especially loud when the protective tariff and homestead planks were read.

Having skillfully made a platform to unite the North in opposition both to slavery and to the planting system, the Republicans were careful in their selection of a candidate. The tariff plank might carry Pennsylvania; but Ohio, Indiana, and Illinois were equally essential to success at the polls. The southern counties of these states were filled with immigrants from Virginia, North Carolina, and Kentucky who, even if they had no love for slavery, certainly had none for abolition. Moreover, having taken part in the fight on the United States Bank in Andrew Jackson's day, they were suspicious of men from the East who wanted to reëstablish the Bank. Accordingly, they did not favor the candidacy of William H. Seward, the Republican Senator and "favorite son" of New York.

After much discussing and trading of votes, the convention

came to the conclusion that Abraham Lincoln of Illinois was the most "available" candidate. He was of Southern origin, born in Kentucky in 1809 — a fact that helped him in the campaign in the Ohio Valley. He was a man of the soil, the son of poor frontier parents, a pioneer who in his youth had labored in field and forest, celebrated far and wide as "honest Abe the rail-splitter" — a good point in appealing to Jackson Democrats. It was well known that, while he disliked slavery, he was no abolitionist. He had come dangerously near to radicalism in his "house-divided-against-itself" speech but he had never committed himself to Seward's doctrine that there was a "higher law" than the Constitution, dedicating the territories to freedom. Slavery in the South he tolerated as a fact; slavery in the territories he opposed with all his strength. So moderates could accept him, while abolitionists, too few to be taken seriously, could be disregarded. Of Lincoln's sincerity there could be no doubt. He was a speaker and writer of singular power. By the use of simple and homely language, he commanded the hearts and minds of those who heard him speak or read his printed words. He had gone far enough in his opposition to slavery; but not too far. He was the man of the hour! Amid lusty cheers from ten thousand throats, Lincoln was nominated for the presidency by the Republican convention. In the ensuing election, he carried all the free states except New Jersey.

References

F. E. Chadwick, *Causes of the Civil War* (American Nation Series).

W. E. Dodd, *Statesmen of the Old South; Expansion and Conflict* (Riverside Series).

E. Engle, *Southern Sidelights* (Sympathetic account of the Old South).

A. B. Hart, *Slavery and Abolition* (American Nation Series).

J. F. Rhodes, *History of the United States*, Vols. I and II.

T. C. Smith, *Parties and Slavery* (American Nation Series).

Questions

1. Trace the decline of slavery in the North and explain it.
2. Describe the character of early opposition to slavery.
3. What was the effect of abolition agitation?
4. Why did antislavery sentiment practically disappear in the South?

5. On what grounds did Calhoun defend slavery?

6. Explain how slave owners became powerful in politics.

7. Why was it impossible to keep the slavery issue out of national politics?

8. Give the leading steps in the long controversy over slavery in the territories.

9. State the terms of the Compromise of 1850 and explain its failure.

10. What were the startling events between 1850 and 1860?

11. Account for the rise of the Republican party. What party had used the title before?

12. How did the Dred Scott decision become a political issue?

13. What were some of the points brought out in the Lincoln-Douglas debates?

14. Describe the party division in 1860.

15. What were the main planks in the Republican platform?

Research Topics

The Extension of Cotton Planting. Callender, *Economic History of the United States*, pp. 760–768.

Abolition Agitation. McMaster, *History of the People of the United States*, Vol. VI, pp. 271–298.

Calhoun's Defense of Slavery. Harding, *Select Orations Illustrating American History*, pp. 247–257.

The Compromise of 1850. Clay's speech in Harding, *Select Orations*, pp. 267–289. The compromise laws in Macdonald, *Documentary Source Book of American History*, pp. 383–394. Narrative account in McMaster, Vol. VIII, pp. 1–55; Elson, *History of the United States*, pp. 529–538.

The Repeal of the Missouri Compromise. McMaster, Vol. VIII, pp. 192–231; Elson, pp. 559–569.

The Dred Scott Case. McMaster, Vol. VIII, pp. 278–282. Compare the opinion of Taney and the dissent of Curtis in Macdonald, *Documentary Source Book*, pp. 405–420; Elson, pp. 581–585.

The Lincoln-Douglas Debates. Analysis of original speeches in Harding, *Select Orations*, pp. 309–341; Elson, pp. 585–590.

Biographical Studies. Calhoun, Clay, Webster, A. H. Stephens, Douglas, W. H. Seward, William Lloyd Garrison, Wendell Phillips, and Harriet Beecher Stowe.

CHAPTER XVI

DEMOCRATIC VISTAS

The upheaval of Jacksonian Democracy and swift spread of American dominion to the Pacific caused a commotion comparable to that created by the American Revolution and in some respects more alarming to conservative people both in the United States and in Europe. The fathers of the republic had not put the "plain people" into the saddle but the Jacksonian revolution gave the vote to practically all white male citizens and in a few states also to free colored men. It went further by placing in the White House, at the center of power, "a man of the people."

To European defenders of monarchy as well as to most Federalists in the United States something more dangerous had happened than setting up parliaments controlled by property owners and unchecked by kings. Naturally there was a rush of foreigners to inspect the new and strange social order in America. For instance, from France came Alexis de Tocqueville who, after traveling widely, published a description of what he observed, in two remarkable volumes called *Democracy in America*. From England came Harriet Martineau who in her book, *Society in America*, wrote favorable comments on the democratic experiment of the United States, hoping thereby to convince her own country that its democratic tendencies were not a peril. But Charles Dickens, then very young, journeyed as far west as Columbus, Ohio, and issued a terrific blast against this country, entitled *American Notes*. There were ever so many more observers whom we cannot mention here. Whether friends or foes, these foreign visitors were right in their conclusion that America in the age of Jackson and Lincoln represented a social revolution. Many phases of republican culture known to the era of Washington and Hamilton had been transformed by new machines, industries, ideas, and customs.

RELIGIOUS AND INTELLECTUAL LIFE

Changes among the Churches. Democracy did not mean irreligion, however. As a matter of fact, growth of population was accompanied by an extraordinary rise in church membership. Among Methodists and Baptists, particularly, this natural increase was stimulated by tumultuous revival meetings in the West and South, which brought converts to their churches in throngs. On the other hand the Catholics drew their new strength mainly from the European immigrants of their denomination who poured through the gates opened so generously; during the forty years between 1820 and 1860, the number of Catholics mounted from 244,500 to 3,000,000. Besides an upswing in membership, the Protestant churches continued to show the old tendencies to division and subdivision. Presbyterians and Baptists broke into several branches and the Methodists split over the slavery question into Northern and Southern wings. New sects also appeared. Calling for "a return to primitive Christianity," Alexander Campbell marshaled a host of followers as Disciples of Christ, sometimes known simply as "Christians" or "Campbellites." Prophesying the second coming of Christ and an end of the world, William Miller enrolled a faithful band who dressed in white robes and awaited the heralded advent in 1843. It was in this period too that the Mormons came on the scene.

The Swing from Puritanism. Throughout New England, a strong movement was bearing Americans away from the type of Christianity that had prevailed in colonial times. More Congregational preachers and churches went over to the Unitarian faith. Ralph Waldo Emerson, finding himself unable to accept current religious doctrines, left the pulpit entirely to become a free writer and lecturer. Other ministers, such as Horace Bushnell, Mark Hopkins, and Henry Ward Beecher turned in the "liberal" direction, placing more stress on the teachings of Christ and less on the creed of their churches. Meanwhile the Puritan Sabbath was gradually relaxed until it became lawful to travel on Sunday and even to engage in mild forms of amusement after religious services closed.

Growth of Religious Toleration. In keeping with the spirit of the age many changes were made in the laws so that the members of all churches might be on an equality in their rights as citizens. As we have said, the Congregational Church was disestablished in Massachusetts in 1833, marking the end of direct state support for religion. By the extension to Catholics and Jews of the right to vote and hold office in the states which had formerly excluded them, the last of the legal discriminations among religious denominations were abandoned. It is true that near the middle of the century a Native American party, opposed to giving Catholics full rights as citizens, was formed and flourished for a time, but its early death showed that the people at large had no particular interest in it. It could be said, therefore, that by 1850 the spirit of Jefferson's Statute for Religious Freedom had become the ideal

RALPH WALDO EMERSON

and the actual practice. If some persons wanted to restore the colonial order, the general drift of opinion was against them.

Ferment of Secular Ideas. Turning from religious to secular, or worldly, affairs, we find a bewildering whirl of novel ideas, or perhaps old ideas in different garb. Startled by the terrible poverty in the industrial cities and by the agitations of trade unionists, writers sought solutions for the "problem of misery." Ralph Waldo Emerson, a philosopher, Horace Greeley, an editor, and Albert Brisbane, a social reformer, spoke and wrote continually on this theme. By their studies of the question many humane people

became convinced that poverty was to be abolished by the formation of small colonies combining agriculture with manufacturing
and operating on a communistic basis. This remedy is now called
"utopian socialism," because it proved so much of a dream. It
was tried in several places in the United States but where the
colonies did not fail, they usually lost their original character.

Besides economic experiments, the woman's rights movement,
foreshadowed in the early republic, got into full swing. Women
began to lecture, publish, and teach with more freedom and enthusiasm and, as we shall see in chapter XXV, they finally won the
civil and political equality with men which they now earnestly
demanded. A temperance movement likewise grew into a tremendous agitation at this time, marked by mass meetings at which
"demon rum" was denounced, while thousands signed pledges
never to touch intoxicating liquors again. Starting with pleas
for individual abstinence, it developed into a prohibition campaign
and in 1846 Maine passed a law forbidding the sale of intoxicating
liquors for beverage purposes within the borders of the state. If
the uprising against slavery had not submerged all other reforms,
more would have been heard of utopias, feminism, and prohibition in the days of Abraham Lincoln.

EDUCATION AND JOURNALISM

Popular Education for Democracy. Since all free male citizens
were to vote and women were to enter industries which called for
the rudiments of learning at least, it followed that everybody must
know how to read and write. So there were practical as well as
religious reasons for promoting elementary schools. Moreover
working people, through their trade-union organizations, insisted
that education should be both general and free. As democracy
advanced, the demand for free elementary schools supported by
taxation grew loud enough to be heard in the state legislatures,
especially of the North. Far and wide this great popular need was
discussed and urgency of action was emphasized by Horace Mann
and Henry Barnard, Emma Willard and Mary Lyon, democratic
educators, who wrote and traveled and lectured up and down and
to and fro across the country advocating tax-supported schools.

By this time the population was so large that church schools, Sunday Schools, and monitorial schools — supported by charity and tuition fees — simply could not educate the masses. That was clearly a government task. But the states were slow to assume the burden and when they did they chose to take it up in piecemeal fashion. Hence there is not a single law, event, or date in the history of popular education which serves as a recording milestone. One scheme after another was tried.

First there were laws permitting charitable societies to raise money for education by various means, including lotteries. Then there was state aid in the form of money grants to private schools. A third step was legislation allowing, but not requiring, counties and cities to tax their inhabitants to maintain schools, first for pauper children and then for all children. After a difficult campaign many states were next induced to require local districts

Courtesy of the New York Public Library
MARY LYON

to establish a minimum education for all children, supported by local taxes, by aid from the state treasury, and by tuition fees. Succeeding steps were the abolition of fees and the withdrawal of state aid from private religious schools. Thus by several stages the free and secular common school was created in America. "By 1850," writes E. P. Cubberley, "it may be said that the question of providing a common school education for all children at public expense had been settled, in principle at least, in every Northern state." Many Southern states as well had started along this road. It has been calculated by the Bureau of Education that in 1800 each individual in the nation, on an average, received during his lifetime 82 days of education and in 1860 at least 454 days —

figures which tell of awakening humanity. During this span of years public high schools were founded here and there but their true development belongs to a later period.

Colleges. There were some striking collegiate departures in the era which saw the rise of the public elementary school. Religious denominations continued to erect institutions of higher learning in the East and to plant them on the frontier in the path of the pioneer. With the admission of new states beyond the Appalachians, state colleges and universities were established, carrying forward a work already begun on the seaboard by the Carolinas, Georgia, and Virginia. But beside the historic colleges for instruction in the classics and the Bible now rose schools especially appropriate to the more industrial age. The Rensselaer Polytechnic, founded in 1824 in New York State, developed into a regular engineering college by the middle of the century.

Photograph from Brown Brothers, New York

HORACE MANN

Harvard and Yale added scientific schools and Michigan University opened an agricultural college. American college boys and, in a few places such as Oberlin, college girls were now given an opportunity to study something besides Greek, Latin, mathematics, and "literary" subjects.

Changing Conditions for Journalism. All things worked together to serve democracy and nothing more effectively than the press. By a strange kind of fortune just as the suffrage was being extended and the masses were learning to read, a number of mechanical inventions came along to multiply newspapers, books, and magazines and reduce their cost. Railways and the easy carriage of mails extended by hundreds of miles the area which each editor could reach. When Horace Greeley first saw a telegraph instrument he exclaimed to the inventor, Morse: "You are going to turn the newspaper office upside down with your invention." And the prophecy came true. By means of the telegraph the news of the nation could be quickly sent to every city and in a few hours given out to the people through the papers. On top of these marvels

Courtesy of the New York Public Library

THE FIRST EDITION OF "THE NEW YORK SUN"

came the invention of presses which could be driven by steam engines; in 1846 *The Philadelphia Public Ledger* installed the first rotary machine in the United States. This model was soon so improved by its builder, Robert Hoe, that it could turn out ten thousand copies an hour — as contrasted with the former rate of a few hundred by hand.

At last there were to be newspapers for "the people." In the days of the Fathers only the rich could afford to buy them. But in 1833 a penny paper, *The New York Sun*, made its appearance in the streets and working people as well as merchants were included in its big audience. The example was contagious and, with the development of advertising, cheap newspapers became possible everywhere, in Western mining camps no less than Eastern cities. According to a rough estimate there were 366 newspapers in the United States in 1810; forty years later their number, including weeklies and dailies, had mounted to 2625, with a combined circulation of about four million copies. Every village of any size had its weekly and every city one or more dailies, but the overwhelming majority were in the North. In 1839 New York and Pennsylvania had more periodicals than all the Southern states together.

Technical advance in printing and illustrating led to countless experiments in the line of weeklies and monthlies. Most of them could not survive because the age was not rich enough to support all the literary, religious, temperance, labor, antislavery, feminist, reform, scientific, and technical journals that burst into life. *Godey's Lady's Book*, founded in 1830, and made a success later by Sarah J. Hale as editor, lasted many decades as a messenger bearing to homes near and far poetry, romances, household recipes, and fashions, intermixed with articles on higher education for women. Among the literary monthlies, *Harper's Magazine*, established in 1850, and the *Atlantic Monthly*, floated seven years afterward, have lived on beside the still older *North American Review* into the twentieth century.

LITERATURE AND DRAMA

"In the four quarters of the globe, who reads an American book?" asked the English critic, Sydney Smith, in 1820. Thus, as James Russell Lowell put it, John Bull held up Brother Jonathan by the roadside and cried out to him: "Stand and deliver a literature!" And Brother Jonathan, after fumbling in his pockets, had to admit that he hadn't one about him. However, within a few years, there was a positive deluge of American books, with readers in all quarters of the globe. Authors wrote with such power that the Middle Period is often called the "golden age" of American literature.

American Fiction. In this literary awakening all phases of the national life were chosen as themes for story and novel. Nathaniel Hawthorne immortalized the Puritan New England of his ancestors;

The Scarlet Letter and *The House of Seven Gables* are genuine
American classics. James Fenimore Cooper, whose first novel
appeared in the very year that Sydney Smith asked his scornful
question, specialized in stories of the frontier and red men, but
he did not confine himself to them. He portrayed the whole
American scene: the Revolutionary War, pioneers, Indians, spies,
pirates, slave traders, soldiers, sailors, planters, farmers, hunters,
trappers, merchants, women, mountain, plain, lake, and ocean.
And he drew his pictures in a style so vivid that the English
novelist, Thackeray, placed Cooper on the level with Sir Walter
Scott while the French novelist, Victor Hugo, ranked him above
Scott.

Choosing American themes also, Cooper's New York neighbor,
Washington Irving, started with humorous tales and a comical
"Knickerbocker" history of New York and then wrote serious
biographies of Christopher Columbus and George Washington.
But Irving loved Spanish history so much that his tales of Spain
are said in that country to be "the American discovery of Spain."
Life in the planting South found its enthusiast in William Gilmore
Simms, of South Carolina, who described aristocratic society, with
its fighting men and fair women. Naturally he defended slavery
as a wise, moral, and beneficent institution, good for slaves and
masters. On the other side, slavery was assailed in a terrific
onslaught by Harriet Beecher Stowe, whose *Uncle Tom's Cabin*
ran into many editions. "So you are the little woman who caused
this great war!" exclaimed Lincoln when he met her in the midst
of the crisis. The sea, by which so many New Englanders lived,
no less than the land, had its interpreter in Herman Melville,
author of *Moby Dick*, undoubtedly one of the best novels of the
nineteenth century and still multiplying the number of its devoted
admirers.

The Poetry of Americanism. In verse, as in fiction, can be
traced the early history of America and the course of the Middle
Period. Heroic colonial days live again in the lines of Henry W.
Longfellow's *Courtship of Miles Standish*, for he was a talented
story-teller. Phases in the struggle with Mexico and over slavery
stand forth in the realistic poems of James Russell Lowell. The

smiling fields, the grassy lanes, the cold gray winters of New England, critical views of Daniel Webster, and abolition agitations are all mirrored in the rhymed sketches of John Greenleaf Whittier. The swing of the Congregationalists to the Unitarian faith appears in the philosophic poems of William Cullen Bryant, especially in the awe of Nature that pervades *Thanatopsis*. A severe English critic admitted that there were "few pieces in the works of even the very first of our living poets" that exceeded Bryant's ode to death "for sublimity and compass of poetical thought."

Courtesy of The Metropolitan Museum of Art

WALT WHITMAN

A portrait by John W. Alexander

Then came one who sang wholly of the people, Walt Whitman, of New York. As he said himself, he was "Not a dilettante democrat." He was in truth a Jackson and Lincoln democrat — "a man who is a double part with the common people and with immediate life—who adores streets—loves docks— loves to talk with free men — loves to be called by his given name and does not care that any one calls him Mister." Whitman not only loved the common people but he had an unlimited faith in America — in its capacity to do great things, not by copying Europe or borrowing plumage, but by working honestly at the tasks in hand, with sympathy and intelligence. While he could rejoice in action, Whitman could also weep in hours of affliction — to which his poem on the death of Lincoln bears moving witness. Bold in thought, stanch in his democracy, loyal in his Americanism, striking new notes in "free verse," Whitman has made a deeper and more lasting impression than any American poet of the period. But Edgar Allan

Poe also won renown for his tales and weird, sonorous rhymes — his musical verse loved by all who enjoy sheer tones.

Historical Writings. With something like Whitman's enthusiasm for America, George Bancroft devoted himself to writing a history of the country from the founding of the colonies to the making of the Constitution, publishing his first volume in 1834 and completing the series in 1882. A Democrat in politics, Bancroft displayed a natural pride in the growth of American democracy. Yet in spite of this "bias" he wrote a work of permanent value, especially because he devoted great industry to the collection and use of original documents, papers, letters, and memoirs. In a less exalted strain, one of Bancroft's contemporaries, Richard Hildreth, a disillusioned Federalist from New England, retold the American story from the discoveries of Columbus to the Missouri Compromise. With perfect frankness, Hildreth declared that the country had had enough Fourth of July Orations and that the time had come to portray the Fathers as they were, without rouge, tinsel, and apologies. Colder than Bancroft in his judgments, Hildreth was more accurate in his statements; and when his first volume was printed in 1849 he was acclaimed a historian of a more "scientific" temper.

Not attracted by American themes, other historians turned abroad for inspiration. W. H. Prescott found delight in Spain; his *Life of Ferdinand and Isabella* and his stories of the conquest of Mexico and Peru, done with great thoroughness, have not been superseded by newer works. Another son of Massachusetts, John Lothrop Motley, educated at Harvard like Prescott, went to Holland for materials and wrote three huge volumes on the rise of the Dutch Republic, which even the leading Dutch historians warmly commended to their countrymen. Looking beyond the United States but not so far, Francis Parkman chose for his subjects French explorations and colonization in Canada and recounted the adventures in many entertaining volumes.

Ralph Waldo Emerson. Without question the supreme intellectual figure of the Middle Period was Ralph Waldo Emerson. Born in Puritan Boston in 1803 and educated at Harvard for the church, he entered the ministry only to leave it shortly. Retiring to Concord, he served as a kind of philosopher-at-large to America until his death in 1882. Though he wrote some poetry, his chief rôle was that of essayist and lecturer on religion, conduct, and life. With his pen he discussed every issue of his time — education, science, travel, democracy, slavery, women's rights, war, and politics. Everything he handled he illuminated, and everyone seeking to understand the age of Jackson and Lincoln must study Emerson's numerous works. Nothing was ever written in that generation more profound than his lecture on "The Conservative" delivered in Boston in 1841. Nothing revealing contemporary thought excels his lecture on "Poetry and Imagination" written in 1854.

The Drama. As the new printing machinery transformed publishing, so new mechanical appliances altered the theater. Railways, for example, enabled famous actors to travel over the continent and thus encouraged capitalists to build playhouses with assurance that talent would not be wanting. With the help of the railway, Charlotte Cushman, Edwin Forrest, Joseph Jefferson, and James H. Hackett, and all the leading actors and actresses "toured the country," at least east of the Mississippi, with American plays in their list. According to estimates more than one hundred and fifty dramas were constructed between 1825 and 1860, from the events and personages of the Revolution alone. Moreover all the current political battles were interpreted on the stage — the struggle over the Bank, the triumph of Andrew Jackson, campaigns of Whigs and Democrats, the Oregon boundary, the annexation of Texas, the gold rush, and the Mexican War. *Rip Van Winkle* gave joy as a comedy. Indeed all American life was mirrored in the drama; Yankees, planters, farmers, slaves, townspeople, and sailors. Plays written about masses throwing off classes in ancient Rome were particularly successful in the age of Jacksonian democracy.

NATURAL SCIENCE

The Leading Scientists. Slowed down somewhat by the Revolution and the troubles that followed it, natural science now took on new vitality, and five or six thinkers did work of outstanding importance. At Yale College, Benjamin Silliman collected minerals, assembled a chemical laboratory, and founded the *American Journal of Science*. Besides this he instilled a love of science into a generation of students. Matthew Maury of Virginia studied the weather, ocean currents, and the bed of the sea; in valuable treatises he pointed out the safest routes for captains and solved problems for inventors dreaming of transatlantic cables. In New

Courtesy of Smithsonian Institution

THE SMITHSONIAN INSTITUTION IN 1871

York, Joseph Henry labored as a tireless experimenter in physics; as early as 1831 he devised an apparatus for ringing a small bell by means of an electric current — called "the earliest example of a true magnetic telegraph." To the end of his long life in 1878, Henry continued to make contributions to various branches of physics. Nor were the flora and fauna of America neglected. By the middle of the century, American botanists, with Asa Gray of Harvard in the forefront, were well advanced in the study and classification of American plants. And John James Audubon, after wandering with his wife for years in the forests to study and paint plants and birds, had built for himself an international reputation as an ornithologist.

Scientific Institutions. Owing to the immense mass of materials required for scientific studies, the necessity for museums and laboratories became generally recognized. Moved to action by a gift from an Englishman, James Smithson, the federal government established in 1846 the Smithsonian Institution, the foundation of the enormous collection which makes the United States National Museum one of the first of its kind in the world. To foster their several special branches the geologists, geographers, ethnologists, and mathematicians formed national societies and these fellowships were crowned in 1847 by the establishment of the American Association for the Advancement of Science to "promote intercourse between American scientists, to give a strong and more systematic impulse to research, and to procure for the labors of scientific men increased facilities and wider usefulness."

The Triumph in Anæsthetics. It was in the midst of this scientific ferment that American doctors first successfully applied chemicals to the prevention of pain in surgical operations. No doubt the use of leaves and drugs to reduce physical suffering had been known since ancient times, but near the middle of the nineteenth century four American experimenters, working separately carried vague theories into practical realization — C. J. Jackson, Crawford Long, Horace Wells, and W. T. Morton. It was in 1844 that Wells, then a dentist at Hartford, Connecticut, used nitrous oxide to make himself insensible while a tooth was pulled. News of this development spread around the earth and within a few years scientists, by improving anæsthetics, had done more to relieve physical pain than all the soothsayers and medicine men had done in ten centuries.

Applied Science. Carrying forward the tradition established by Franklin and advanced by Fulton and Whitney, an army of inventors extended science to other practical uses in the form of machines. The age of Jackson and Lincoln produced such things as the electric telegraph, the sewing machine, the reaper, the rubber boot, and the transatlantic cable. Indeed the Patent Office in Washington was literally crammed with "newfangled" implements designed to increase the wealth, convenience, happiness, and power of mankind. In 1832 Matthew Baldwin began to build locomotives in Philadelphia; by 1851 the works of Cyrus McCormick in Chicago were turning out a thousand reapers a year; in 1858 the first "electric word" passed over the cable connecting the United States and England. On account of the social changes

From Brown Brothers, New York

THE FIRST TELEGRAPH

wrought by these achievements, it would be well to treat such dates with as much respect as the years of most battles and political events!

THE ARTS

Painting and Drawing. All the arts in turn showed the influences of democracy, westward expansion, and industrialism. There were, to be sure, artists to keep up the styles of Stuart, Peale, and Trumbull. Portraits of Webster, Clay, Calhoun, Marshall, and Daniel Boone were painted by Chester Harding, the son of a Massachusetts farmer, reared on the frontier. An English boy, John Wesley Jarvis, brought to Philadelphia at the age of five, after an apprenticeship painting fire buckets and flags, turned to portraiture and soon had rich clients North and South. To his brush is due the picture of Henry Clay which hangs in the City Hall in New York. Another English lad who came to America as a child, Thomas Sully, early employed as a clerk in an office in Charleston, South Carolina, and discharged for incompetence, turned to the arts and became a national figure. To him we owe one of our striking portraits of General Andrew Jackson (p. 283).

This work by Harding, Jarvis, and Sully and other artists, similarly inspired, mainly represented "the rise of a native school." But so excited were Americans by the "great out of doors" which they had acquired that they tried to put it on canvas in as much detail as possible. As a critic wrote in 1853: "The future of our art must be inherently vast like our western plains, majestic like our forests, generous like our rivers." It was this ambition and this view of art which inspired the paintings of a large group

Courtesy of the New York Public Library

YOSEMITE VALLEY
A painting by Albert Bierstadt.

of landscape artists, known as the Hudson River School. Was it not fitting that, in an age when pioneers were winning a continent, artists should paint the scenes of their labors? While John F. Kensett, a son of Connecticut, reproduced on canvas the glories of the White Mountains, Albert Bierstadt, born in Germany and reared in America, found in the Yosemite Valley the grandeur for his scenes.

Still more in keeping with the democratic movement was the development of "the graphic arts" — cartooning, drawing, and engraving on wood, copper, and stone. Magazines and popular books, pouring from the presses for the turbulent democracy, were enlivened by illustrations — some bad but many excellent. If all the printed words of the period were destroyed, it would be possible to reconstruct large sectors of the political and social life of the time from drawings such as those of Thomas Nast (p. 454).

Handicrafts and Architecture. Naturally the advent of the machine was blighting to the handicrafts, for the artisans who worked in wood, metal, and textiles could not compete with the tireless and swift steam engines. But while machine-made goods swamped the market, attempts were made to retain some artistic skill and taste. This was the motive behind the founding of the National Academy of Design in New York in 1825 and a similar school for women in Philadelphia in 1853. How to nourish the love of beauty and talent became one of the major problems of the arts and indeed of American civilization itself.

Architecture like the crafts suffered a kindred decay at the outset of industrialism. The country was big and young and the people were in a hurry. They could buy machine-made decorations and cover up the lack of craftmanship in the houses they rushed up so quickly. Besides, democracy began to boast wildly about the right of everyone to do as he pleased — not only in politics but in building. So architecture became a riot of styles and no styles — often very ugly. In fact many artists despaired of beauty in the reign of democracy and machines. Yet what they thought was an incurable disease others called "a passing fever."

References

The Cambridge History of American Literature, Vols. I and II.
Allan Nevins, *American Social History as Recorded by British Travellers.*
E. P. Cubberley, *Public Education in the United States.*
J. M. Lee, *History of American Journalism.*
Samuel Isham, *The History of American Painting* (1927 ed.).
Lewis Mumford, *Sticks and Stones.*
F. Weitenkampf, *American Graphic Art.*

Questions

1. Give some of the leading changes in religious life.
2. What new ideas were most widely discussed?

3. By what steps were public schools finally established?
4. What were the departures in higher education?
5. How did inventions affect the "democracy" of the press?
6. Name a few of the prose writers and give their chief themes.
7. How many poets and poems of the period do you know?
8. Who were the leaders in natural science?
9. What was the greatest American medical discovery of the age?
10. List the distinctive features of the period in the arts.

References

The Ferment of New Ideas. Beard, *Rise of American Civilization*, Vol. I, pp. 725–736.

Promotion of Science. Beard, Vol. I, pp. 737–748. Consult any encyclopedia for biographies of the leaders mentioned in the text.

Leading Ideas in Literature. Beard, Vol. I, pp. 749–794.

Painting. S. Isham, *History of American Painting*, pp. 107–296.

Education. Consult an encyclopedia under Henry Barnard, Emma Willard, Mary Lyon, and Horace Mann.

Press. Consult an encyclopedia under Horace Greeley.

CHAPTER XVII

THE CIVIL WAR AND RECONSTRUCTION

"The irrepressible conflict is about to be visited upon us through the Black Republican nominee and his fanatical, diabolical Republican party," ran an address to the voters of South Carolina during the campaign of 1860. If that calamity comes to pass, replied the governor of the state, our answer will be a declaration of independence. In a few days the suspense was over; news of Lincoln's election came speeding along the wires. Prepared for the event, the editor of the Charleston *Mercury* unfurled the flag of his state amid loud cheers from throngs in the streets. Then he seized his pen and wrote: "The tea has been thrown overboard; the revolution of 1860 has been initiated." Echoing such sentiments the legislature called on the voters to elect delegates to a convention for the purpose of deciding whether the state should remain any longer in the Union.

THE SOUTHERN CONFEDERACY

Secession. Soon after the convention of South Carolina assembled in December, it voted as one man to withdraw from the Union. Bells were rung exultantly, the roar of cannon carried the word to outlying counties, fireworks lighted up the heavens, and champagne flowed. The crisis so long expected had come at last; even the conservatives who had prayed that they might escape the dreadful crash greeted it with a sigh of relief.

South Carolina then sent forth an appeal to her sister states — states that had in Jackson's day repudiated nullification as leading to "the dissolution of the Union." The answer which came this time was in a different tone. Scarcely a month had elapsed when five other states — Florida, Georgia, Alabama, Mississippi, and Louisiana — had broken their tie with the North. In February, Texas followed. Virginia, hesitating until the bombardment of

Fort Sumter forced a decision, seceded in April; but fifty-five of her one hundred and forty-three delegates voted against this action and prepared the way for the creation of the new state of West Virginia, which Congress admitted to the Union in 1863. In May, North Carolina, Arkansas, and Tennessee announced their independence.

Secession and the Nature of the Union. Secession, of course, was contrary to the Northern theory of the Constitution — a theory worked out by Webster and enlarged by Lincoln. According to this belief, the Union was older than the states; it was created before the Declaration of Independence by the formation of the Continental Congress for the purpose of common defense. The Articles of Confederation strengthened the national bond and the Constitution simply sealed it forever. The federal government was not established by a mere agreement among states as such; it was established by the people and derived its powers directly from them. "It is," said Webster, "the people's Constitution, the people's government; made for the people; made by the people; and answerable to the people. The people of the United States have declared that this Constitution shall be the supreme law." When a state questions the lawfulness of any act of the federal government, it cannot nullify or disobey that act or withdraw from the federation; it must abide by the decision of the Supreme Court of the United States with respect to the issue. The Union of these states is perpetual, ran Lincoln's argument in his first inaugural; the federal Constitution has no provision for its own destruction; it can be destroyed only by some action which it does not authorize; even if it is nothing but an agreement or compact among the states, the consent of all is necessary to its dissolution; therefore, no single state can lawfully leave the Union and acts of violence against the United States are insurrectionary or revolutionary. This was the political system which Lincoln believed himself bound to defend by his oath of office "registered in heaven."

All this reasoning Southern statesmen flatly rejected. In their opinion, the thirteen original states won their independence as separate and sovereign powers. The treaty of peace with Great

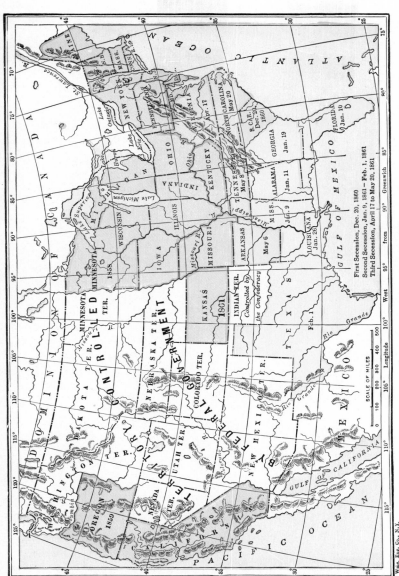

THE UNITED STATES IN 1861

The border states (in purple) remained loyal.

First Secession, Dec. 20, 1860
Second Secession, Jan. 9, 1861 – Feb. 1, 1861
Third Secession, April 17 to May 20, 1861

Wm. Eng. Co., N.Y.

Britain named them all and acknowledged them "to be free, sovereign, and independent states." In specific language the Articles of Confederation declared that "each state retains its sovereignty, freedom, and independence." The Constitution merely formed a "league of nations" — an alliance of thirteen separate countries. Acting through conventions elected by the voters, the states had voluntarily entered the Union by ratifying the Constitution; in the same manner they could voluntarily leave it. Such was the doctrine of Hayne, Calhoun, and Jefferson Davis. Secession was to them, therefore, right and lawful.

The Formation of the Confederacy. Replying to a call from Mississippi, a congress of delegates from the seceded states met at Montgomery, Alabama, early in 1861, and adopted a temporary plan of union. It selected, as provisional president, Jefferson Davis of Mississippi, a man well fitted for leadership, a graduate of West Point, who had rendered distinguished services in the Mexican War, in public office, and as a member of Congress.

JEFFERSON DAVIS

In March, a permanent constitution of the confederate states was drafted. It was quickly ratified by the states; elections were held in November; and the government under it went into effect the next year. In form, this new constitution was very much like that of the United States. It provided for a President, a Senate, and a House of Representatives along almost identical lines. It did not, however, confer the same powers upon them. Indeed, it forbade the use of government money for internal improvements. It also prohibited the granting of bounties from the public treasury and the laying of duties on imports in such a way as to promote or foster any branch of industry. Deeming secession lawful, the confederate constitution declared that each state acted "in its sovereign and independent character" in joining the Southern union.

Financing the Confederacy. No government ever set out upon its career facing more perplexing tasks than did the Southern Confederacy. The North had a monetary system; the South had to create one. The North had a scheme of taxation that produced large revenues from numerous sources; the South had to make a new financial plan. Like the North, the Confederacy hoped to secure a large income from customs duties on foreign goods, easily collected and little felt among the masses. To this hope the blockade of Southern ports ordered by Lincoln in April, 1861, soon put an end by cutting down foreign trade. Then the Southern Congress levied a direct property tax apportioned among the states, only to be disappointed in the small amount of money collected.

Besides resorting to taxation, the Confederacy sold bonds to its citizens and the first issue brought into the treasury nearly all the gold and silver available in the Southern banks. Large issues were also floated in London, Paris, and Amsterdam — at first bringing better prices than the bonds of the North. The next recourse of the Confederacy was to print huge quantities of paper money. In all approximately one billion dollars streamed from its presses. To the issues of the confederate Congress were added untold millions poured out by the states and by private banks. Before long, this paper money began to fall in value; in January, 1863, one gold dollar was worth fifty in confederate paper. No laws could stop its headlong plunge.

Human and Material Resources. When we measure strength for strength in men, money, and supplies, it is difficult to see how the South could expect to win. In the Confederacy there were eleven states in all, to be pitted against twenty-three in the Union; a population of nine millions, more than one-third slave, was arrayed against twenty-two millions, mainly free; a land without great industries for producing war supplies and without vast capital to furnish war finances was joined in battle with a nation already largely industrial and owning property worth eleven billion dollars. How, therefore, could the Confederacy think for a moment of sustaining itself against such a combination of men, money, and materials as the North could marshal?

Southern Expectations. The answer to this question is to be found in the ideas that were held by Southern leaders. First of all, they planned to carry the Confederacy up to the Ohio River; and, with the aid of Missouri, to gain the Mississippi Valley, the granary of the nation. With greater assurance, they counted upon a steady trade with England — the exchange of cotton for war materials. They likewise placed some reliance on open aid from the monarchical governments of Europe that would look with satisfaction upon the break-up of the American republic. Finally, they thought that they could bring on an industrial crisis in the manufacturing states by cutting off their supplies. "I firmly believe," wrote Senator Hammond of South Carolina, in 1860, "that the slaveholding South is now the controlling power of the world; that no other power would face us in hostility. Cotton, rice, tobacco, and naval stores command the world; and we have the sense to know it and are sufficiently Teutonic to carry it out successfully. The North without us would be a motherless calf, bleating about, and die of mange and starvation."

There were other grounds for the confederate faith in victory. Southern leaders had long controlled the national government and they left it weak in military and naval resources when they turned it over to Lincoln in 1861. Moreover, they had experienced generals to lead their armies. Hence most of them looked to a swift war, if it came at all, to put the finishing stroke to independence. "The greasy mechanics of the North," it was repeatedly said, "will not fight." Though outnumbered, Southerners took comfort in the history of the American Revolution. "Our fathers, a mere handful, overcame the enormous power of Great Britain," a saying of ex-President Tyler, ran current to cheer up the doubtful. If everything else was to be discounted, the South was sure that internal divisions would cripple the Union. It knew that many abolitionists and Southern sympathizers were ready to let the confederate states go in peace; that Lincoln spoke for only one-third of the people; and that the vote for Douglas, Bell, and

Breckinridge meant a strong opposition to the Republicans and their policies.

Efforts at Compromise. Reviewing the same facts, Republican leaders were themselves uncertain as to the outcome of a civil war and they made many efforts to avoid it. Thurlow Weed, an Albany politician who had helped to carry New York for Lincoln, proposed to extend the Missouri Compromise to the Pacific — with freedom on one side and slavery on the other. Jefferson Davis, warning his followers that a war if it broke out would be terrible, was willing to accept the offer; but Lincoln, who had pledged himself to the abolition of slavery in all the territories, stood like a rock against it. His followers in Congress took the same position with regard to a similar plan made by Senator Crittenden of Kentucky.

Though he adhered to his promise to oppose slavery in the territories, Lincoln gave his word to Southern leaders that he would not meddle in any way with slavery in the states. Anxious to reassure the South on this point, the Republicans in Congress agreed that the Constitution should be so amended as to forbid forever the abolition of slavery or any interference with it in any state. Indeed a resolution to this effect, duly passed, was sent forth on March 4, 1861, with the approval of Lincoln and it was actually ratified by three states before the storm of war destroyed it. By the irony of fate, the thirteenth amendment was to abolish, not guarantee, slavery.

THE WAR MEASURES OF THE FEDERAL GOVERNMENT

Raising the Union Armies. The bombardment of Fort Sumter by confederate forces on April 12–14, 1861, led President Lincoln and Congress to turn from negotiations to problems of warfare. Little did they realize the size of the task before them. Lincoln's first call for volunteers, issued on April 15, 1861, limited the number to 75,000 and put their term of service at three months. A rude awakening swiftly followed. A terrible defeat of the Federals at Bull Run on July 21 revealed the grave character of the work before them; and by a series of measures Congress put the entire man power of the country at the President's command. Under these acts, he issued new calls for volunteers. Early in August, 1862, he ordered a draft of militiamen numbering 300,000 for nine months' service. The results were disappointing — ominous — for only 87,000 soldiers were added to the army. Something more drastic was necessary.

So in March, 1863, Lincoln signed a thoroughgoing draft law. This measure made liable to military duty all able-bodied male citizens and persons of foreign birth who had declared their intention to become citizens, between the ages of twenty and forty-five years — with certain exceptions. From the men enrolled were drawn by lot those destined to active service. Unhappily

THE DRAFT RIOTS IN NEW YORK CITY

the law struck a mortal blow at the principle of equality by allowing any person to escape the army if he found a substitute for himself or paid to the government a sum, not exceeding $300, to be fixed by general order. This provision, so obviously favoring people with money, sowed seeds of bitterness which sprang up a hundred-fold in the North.

As a matter of fact the very beginning of the drawings under the draft law in New York City, on Monday, July 13, 1863, was marked by desperate rioting. In the course of this uprising, the draft headquarters were destroyed; the office of the *Tribune* was sacked; negroes were seized, hanged, and shot; the homes of several Unionists were burned down; and pitched battles were fought in the streets between objectors and the police. Business stopped and a large part of the city passed into the hand of rioters.

Not until late the following Wednesday did enough federal troops arrive to establish order and permit the draft to go on.

In the end the results of the draft were disappointing to the government. The exemptions were numerous and the number who paid $300 rather than serve was larger than anybody had expected. Volunteering, it is true, increased but even that could hardly keep the thinning ranks of the army filled. Then with reluctance Congress struck out the $300 clause while still permitting the well-to-do to hire substitutes if they could find them. With all this power in its hands the federal government was able by January, 1865, to construct an army that outnumbered the Confederates two to one.

Financing the Union. In spite of the advantages which it had over the South in money matters, the North confronted difficulties in securing revenues to pay its heavy bills. When Lincoln took office the Treasury was almost empty and before long he had to face huge military and naval expenditures, rising from $35,000,-000 in the first year of the war to $1,153,000,000 in the last year. Hence Congress had to tap every available source of income. The duties on imports were raised, not once but many times, producing huge returns and also meeting the demands of manufacturers for protection. Direct taxes were imposed on the states according to their respective populations. Stamp taxes and taxes on luxuries, trades, employments, and the earnings of companies were laid with a weight that, in ordinary times, would have produced a terrible outcry. In fact, the whole gamut of taxation was run. A tax on incomes and gains by the year, the first in the history of the federal government, was included in the long list.

Revenues from taxes were supplemented by revenues from bond issues, mounting in size until in October, after the end of the war, the debt stood at $2,208,000,000. To the ordinary debt was added nearly half a billion dollars in "greenbacks" — paper money authorized by Congress in despair as the income from bond sales and taxes failed to meet rising expenditures. But this currency, like all such paper, quickly began to decline until, in the darkest days of the Union in 1864, one dollar in gold was worth nearly three in greenbacks.

The Blockade of Southern Ports. Four days after his call for volunteers, April 19, 1861, President Lincoln ordered the Union navy to stop up the ports of the Southern Confederacy. Vessels attempting to enter or leave these harbors, if they disregarded the warnings of a blockading ship, were to be captured and brought as prizes to the nearest convenient port. To make the order effective, steps were taken to enlarge the naval forces, depleted by neglect; finally the entire coast line was so closely patrolled that few blockade runners could break through the net. The collision between the two iron-clads, *Merrimac* and *Monitor*, in March, 1862, sealed the fate of the Confederacy: the South could not smash the blockade by her "iron monster." The success of the Union navy in reducing Southern trade is recorded in the falling export of cotton: $202,000,000 in 1860; $42,000,000 in 1861; and $4,000,000 in 1862.

A BLOCKADE RUNNER

The effect of the blockade upon Southern war power was deadly. Confederate bonds could not be sold abroad when it was discovered that cotton could not be safely sent over the sea to pay the interest on them. Even when supplies were obtained on credit in England or France, they could seldom be carried through the blockade. Only with great difficulty could the confederate government get paper with which to make money and bonds. Publishers, in despair, were finally driven to the use of brown wrapping paper and wall paper. As the railways, engines, and cars wore out, it became impossible to renew them from Europe. Thus, while the North could freely import war supplies from the Old World and export grain to pay for them, the South was bottled up and forced to rely mainly on her own meager industries for guns, munitions, and other materials necessary to victory. Southern manufacturers showed great energy but they could not catch up with their Northern rivals.

Diplomacy. The struggle had not advanced far when both governments turned to European countries for aid. Almost at the very beginning of the war, the Confederacy asked England and France to lend it money and to treat it as an independent nation. Later when the blockade cut down cotton shipments, President Davis urged the two countries to interfere in order to get this staple for their mills. But the scheme failed. It is true that the reduction in cotton imports threw thousands of English textile workers out of employment; yet while on the very point of starvation, they held meetings to condemn slavery and pledge their support to the North. Never did they petition their government to aid the South by breaking the blockade.

With the ruling classes of the Old World it was far otherwise. Napoleon III, Emperor of the French, was eager to help in destroying the American republic; if he could have won England's assistance, he would have done it. As things turned out, he secured plenty of sympathy across the Channel but no official coöperation. According to the historian, James Ford Rhodes, "four-fifths of the British House of Lords and most members of the House of Commons were favorable to the Confederacy and anxious for its triumph." On the other hand, the North had many supporters in England — like John Bright — who carried on an earnest agitation against all plans for aiding the South. In the end the attacks of such critics, together with Northern victories at Vicksburg and Gettysburg, kept the governments of England and France from recognizing the independence of the Confederacy and lending it open assistance.

While stopping short of this action, England and France took several steps, however, that were in favor of the South. They early declared that they would treat the Confederates as "belligerents" and accord them the rights of a people at war — a measure which aroused anger in the North but was afterward admitted to be sound. Later in 1861, Napoleon III proposed to Russia that the European powers unite against the North, only to meet a refusal. The next year he suggested to Great Britain that the time had come to interfere in the war and was told to wait awhile. Not daunted by these rebuffs, he tendered his services as a mediator to Lincoln. This time he received in reply a polite letter declining his offer and a sharp resolution from Congress suggesting that he had better attend to his own affairs.

Beyond a doubt, the English and French governments were friendly to confederate agents throughout the war. The British ministry allowed British shipyards to build war vessels and rams for the Confederacy and coolly let them escape to play havoc with Northern commerce. One of these vessels, the *Alabama*, built in Liverpool and paid for by bonds sold in England, did enormous damage before it was sunk by the *Kearsarge*. From the start, the American minister in London, Charles Francis Adams, protested warmly against the course pursued by the British government and after tedious pleading finally induced it to put a stop to such practices.

JOHN BRIGHT

In all fairness it should be said that the North was partly to blame for the ill-will which arose in London. Seward, the Secretary of State, was needlessly harsh in his dealings with Great Britain; and had it not been for the good temper of Lincoln, controversy might have led to an open break. Moreover, New York and Boston papers were severe in their attacks on England. On one occasion, at least, words were backed up by an act akin to hostility. In November, 1861, Captain Wilkes, commanding a Union vessel, overhauled the British steamer *Trent* and carried off by force two confederate agents, Mason and Slidell, sent by President Davis to represent him at London and Paris respectively. Clearly this was a case of search and seizure, and when Great Britain demanded the release of the two men, the United States promptly admitted that it was in the wrong. It surrendered the prisoners to a British vessel for safe conduct abroad and made fitting apologies. Nothing but careful management enabled the Union to keep England and France at bay.

Emancipation. Besides waging war, blockading ports, and warding off foreign interference, the federal government finally decided to strike a formidable blow at the South by freeing the slaves in the states in arms against the Union. This step was early and repeatedly urged upon Lincoln by the abolitionists, but he steadily refused to take it. He knew that the abolitionists were merely a handful, that emancipation might drive the border slave states into secession, and that the Northern soldiers had enlisted to preserve the unity of the nation rather than to destroy slavery. Moreover, he had before him a resolution passed by Congress on July 22, 1861, which declared that the sole purpose of the war was to save the Union and that there would be no interference with the Southern labor system.

Though pledged to safeguard slavery, the federal government soon found itself upon a new course. Before a year had elapsed, namely, on April 10, 1862, Congress offered to give financial aid to any state that would adopt gradual emancipation. Six days later it abolished slavery in the District of Columbia. Two short months passed. Then on June 19, 1862, it abolished slavery in the territories of the United States. Chief Justice Taney still lived, the Dred Scott decision stood as written in the book, but the Constitution had been reread in the light of war.

While these measures were pending in Congress, Lincoln was slowly making up his mind to go still further. By July of that year he had come to a great decision. Near the end of the month he read to his cabinet the draft of a proclamation of emancipation which he intended to issue as soon as a victory at arms would make it more than an idle gesture. In September, the golden opportunity seemed at hand, when the Confederates, who had invaded Maryland under General Lee, were forced back at the battle of Antietam by Union troops commanded by General McClellan. Although this was not a grand victory, if a victory at all, Lincoln, on September 22nd, issued his proclamation announcing that, unless the confederate states returned to their allegiance by January 1, 1863, the slaves in all districts under arms against the Union would be freed. By Southern leaders the idea was simply treated as absurd, and on the date set Lincoln carried

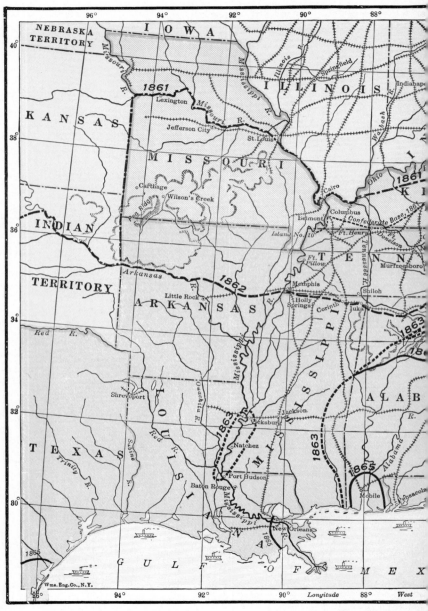

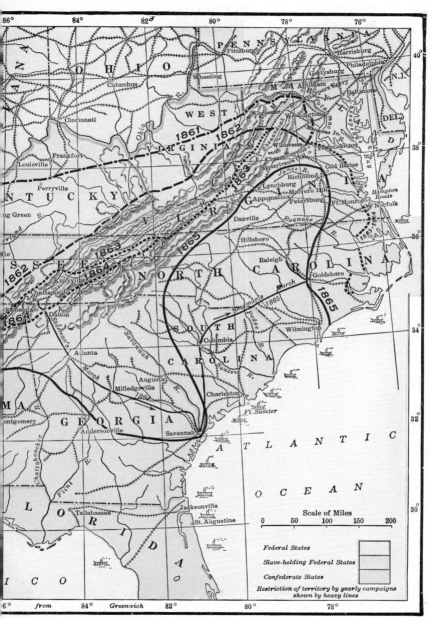

out his promise. The Emancipation thus proclaimed was a war-measure, taken by the President as commander-in-chief of the armed forces, on grounds of military necessity. It did not abolish slavery. It only emancipated slaves in places then offering resistance to federal authority. Everywhere else, as far as the Proclamation was concerned, slavery remained lawful.

But to seal emancipation forever and to extend freedom to the whole country, Congress, in January, 1865, on the urgent advice of Lincoln, sent to the states the thirteenth amendment, destroying slavery throughout the United States. By the end of 1865 the amendment was ratified. The nation was no longer divided against itself; it did not fall; it was all free.

Restraints on Civil Liberty. Like other governments in all great wars, particularly those in the nature of a civil strife, Lincoln's administration adopted strong measures to create a public opinion favorable to its plans and to block the schemes of its opponents. Within two weeks after his first call for volunteers, the President empowered General Scott to suspend the writ of habeas corpus along the line of march between Philadelphia and Washington. By this suspension army officers were given the right to arrest and hold any person they regarded as "dangerous," without any interference by the civil courts. At a later date, the area ruled by military officers was extended by executive proclamation. By an act of March 3, 1863, Congress authorized the President to suspend the writ anywhere and everywhere in the United States; and in the autumn of that year he established military rule throughout the length and breadth of the land. The power of the government was also strengthened by an act of July 31, 1861, which imposed heavy penalties on those who by force or threat interfered with the execution of the law.

Thus doubly armed, the Union authorities suppressed active sympathy with the Southern cause. Editors who criticized the government too severely were arrested and imprisoned, their papers suspended, and their newsboys locked up. People who organized "peace meetings" were sent to jail. Members of the Maryland legislature, the mayor of Baltimore, and certain local editors supposed to favor the South were imprisoned on military orders, although charged with no offense, and were denied the privilege of a hearing on their guilt before a civil magistrate. These severe measures were not confined to the theater of war nor to the border states where the spirit of secession was strong enough to endanger the cause of the Union. They were applied in the Northern states up to the very boundaries of Canada.

THE FEDERAL MILITARY HOSPITAL AT GETTYSBURG

Such drastic actions on the part of military authorities were so foreign to the normal course of American life that they awakened widespread hostility. Meetings of protest were held throughout the North. Thirty-six members of the House of Representatives tried, in vain, to put their names on record against suspending the habeas corpus act. When the case of a man arrested under the

President's military authority was brought before Chief Justice Taney, of the Supreme Court, the Justice declared that the President had no power under the Constitution to suspend the writ of habeas corpus. In Congress and out, Democrats, abolitionists, and champions of civil liberty denounced Lincoln and his Cabinet in unsparing terms. A Democratic leader of Ohio, C. L. Vallandigham, afterward banished to the South for his opposition to the war, repeatedly called Lincoln "Cæsar"; while Wendell Phillips declared that he was "a more unlimited despot than the world knows this side of China."

Sensitive to such thrusts, Lincoln tried to soften the rigors of the law by paroling many political prisoners. His general policy, however, he defended in homely language, very different in tone from the big words of the lawyers. "Must I shoot a simple-minded soldier boy who deserts, while I must not touch a hair of the wily agitator who induces him to desert?" he asked in a quiet way of some citizens who objected to arresting people for "talking against the war." This statement summed up his theory of his duties. He was engaged in a war to save the Union, and in his opinion all measures necessary and proper to accomplish that purpose were warranted by the Constitution which he had sworn to uphold.

Military Strategy — North and South. The broad outlines of the military program followed by the commanders of the opposing armies are clear, even though it is hard for one who is not a soldier to master the details of a campaign or, for that matter, the maneuvers of a single great battle. For the South, the problem was mainly that of defense, though even for defense swift strokes at the North were later thought indispensable by General Lee. The problem of the North, to put it baldly, was one of invasion and conquest. Northern armies had to go into Southern territory and beat the Southern armies on their own ground or wear them down to exhaustion.

In the prosecution of the war, geography, as usual, played a significant part. The Appalachian ranges, stretching through the Confederacy to northern Alabama, divided the campaigns of the Union armies into Eastern and Western enterprises. Each offered special advantages. Victory in the East promised the capture of Richmond, the confederate capital — an event which would encourage the North and raise its standing abroad. Victory in the West would split the Confederacy all the way to New Orleans.

As it turned out, the Western forces of the Union accomplished their task first. In February, 1862, General Ulysses S. Grant captured Fort Donelson on the Cumberland River, rallied wavering Unionists in Kentucky, forced the evacuation of Nashville, and drove a wedge two hundred miles into the Confederacy. At Shiloh, Murfreesboro, Vicksburg, Chickamauga, Chattanooga, desperate fighting followed and, in spite of varying fortunes, resulted in the withdrawal of confederate forces into Georgia. By the middle of 1863, Vicksburg had been captured and the Mississippi Valley was open to the Gulf. The way was now prepared for Sherman's final stroke — the march from Atlanta to the sea — made with needless severity in the autumn of 1864.

GENERAL ULYSSES S. GRANT

Instead of a corresponding series of advances, the Union forces in the East could offer little more than misfortunes and disasters. Far from capturing Richmond, they were early thrown on the defensive. General after General — McClellan, Pope, Burnside, Hooker, and Meade — was tried and found wanting. None could administer a crushing defeat to the confederate troops and more than once Union armies were beaten in a fair battle. They did succeed, however, in checking the advancing Confederates under General Lee — first at Antietam in September, 1862, and then at Gettysburg in July, 1863 — checks reckoned as victories, although in each instance the Confederates escaped ruin. Not until the beginning of the next year, when General Grant, well supplied with men and munitions, began his hammering at the confederate army in Virginia, did the triumph of the Union become certain. The pitiless drive told at last. On April 9, 1865, General Lee, seeing the futility of further conflict, laid down his arms at Appomattox, not far from the capital of the Confederacy.

Abraham Lincoln. The services of Lincoln to the cause of the Union were so great that no complete record of them can be made. His thought and planning appear in every part of the varied activities that finally crowned Northern arms with victory. Is it in diplomacy? Does Seward, the Secretary of State, suggest measures likely to turn England against the United States? Lincoln counsels moderation. He takes Seward's caustic message and with his own hand strikes out words that sting and substitutes words that merely call for fair play. Is it a matter of compromise with the South, so often urged by men on both sides sick of bloodshed? Lincoln is always ready to listen but he stands without flinching for the maintenance of the Union and after 1863 for the abolition of slavery. Is it a question of the General best fitted to win Gettysburg — Hooker, Sedgwick, or Meade? Lincoln goes in person to the War Department in the dead of night to take counsel with his Secretary and to make the fateful choice.

Is it a complaint from a citizen, deprived, as he believes, of his civil liberties unjustly or in violation of the Constitution? Lincoln is prepared to hear it and anxious to afford relief, if warrant can be found. Is a mother begging for the life of a son sentenced to be shot as a deserter? Lincoln receives her petition, and often grants it even against the protests made by his Generals in the name of military discipline. Do politicians stir up troubles in the army and among civilians? Lincoln waves aside their petty quarrels and invites them to think of the greater cause. Does a New York newspaper call him an ignorant Western boor? Lincoln's reply is an address at Gettysburg, which will live as long as the language in which it was written.

Throughout the entire span of his service, however, Lincoln was beset by merciless critics. Abolitionists called him a coward when he delayed the stroke at slavery. Antiwar Democrats lashed out at every step he took. Even in his own party he found no peace.

Charles Sumner complained: "Our President is now dictator, *imperator* — whichever you like; but how vain to have the power of a god and not to use it godlike." Leaders among the Republicans sought to put him aside in 1864 and elect Salmon P. Chase in his place. "I hope we may never have a worse man," was Lincoln's quiet answer.

In the end the Republicans nominated Lincoln again, but they cast off their old name and called themselves the "Union

WILLIAM H. SEWARD

Party." Moreover, they chose a Southern Democrat, Andrew Johnson, of Tennessee, as their candidate for Vice President. To meet the Union party appeal, the Northern Democrats selected as their candidate General McClellan and demanded peace. "After four years of failure to restore the union by the experiment of war, during which, under the pretense of military necessity or war power higher than the Constitution, the Constitution itself has been disregarded in every part and public liberty and private right alike trodden down . . . justice, humanity, liberty, and public welfare demand that immediate efforts be made for a cessation of hostilities, to the end that peace may be restored on the basis of the federal union of the states." It is true that General McClellan tried to soften this platform by saying that he could not look his old comrades in the face and pronounce their efforts vain; but the Democratic call to the nation to repudiate Lincoln and restore peace had gone forth. The response came, giving Lincoln 2,200,000 votes against 1,800,000 for McClellan. The cruel things said about him during the campaign, he forgave and forgot. When in April, 1865, he was shot by a Southern sympathizer, John Wilkes Booth, he above all others in Washington was planning measures of moderation and healing.

PRESIDENT LINCOLN AND "TAD" IN 1861

From the original negative made in Brady's studio in Washington

GENERAL LEE ON "TRAVELER"

Taken at Lexington, Virginia, after the war

THE RESULTS OF THE CIVIL WAR

There is a natural tendency on the part of writers to lay stress on the dramatic and heroic aspects of war; but the long judgment of history requires us to include other significant phases as well. Like every great armed conflict, the Civil War outran the purposes of those who took part in it. Waged over the nature of the Union, it made a revolution in the Union itself, changed public policies, and gave a new direction to agriculture and industry.

The Supremacy of the Union. First and foremost, the war settled for all time the question whether states could lawfully withdraw from the Union. The doctrine of state sovereignty was laid to rest. Men might still speak of the rights of states but those rights were not to include nullification and secession any more. The nation was supreme in fact and in theory.

The Destruction of the Slave Power. Besides upholding the Union, the war destroyed the planting aristocracy of the South — which had furnished so many leaders of undoubted ability and had tried so hard to check the industrial and commercial ambition of the North. The first effective blow at the planters was struck by the abolition of slavery. The second came with the fourteenth amendment in 1868 and the third with the fifteenth in 1870 — two measures which gave the ballot to freedmen and excluded from public office the confederate leaders — driving from the work of rebuilding the South the finest talents of the section. As if to add bitterness to that kind of gall and wormwood, the fourteenth amendment forbade the United States or any state to pay any debts incurred in aid of the Confederacy or in the emancipation of the slaves. So Southern planters found themselves stripped of their property in slaves, shut out of the government, and ruled by their former bondmen directed by Republican chiefs. Their labor system was wrecked and their money and bonds were as worthless as waste paper. The South was at last subject to the North. That which neither the Federalists nor the Whigs had been able to accomplish by politics was done by war.

The Triumph of Industry. While the planting system was being ruined, Northern industry was making such a rapid upswing that the old Whigs of Massachusetts and Pennsylvania were fairly bewildered by it. The war itself pushed it forward, for the demands of the federal government for manufactured goods at high prices more than replaced the lost markets of the South. Between 1860 and 1870 the number of manufacturing establishments increased 79.6 per cent as against 14.2 for the previous decade; while the number of persons employed in them almost doubled. There was no doubt about the future of industry in the United States.

Victory for the Protective Tariff. Manufacturing was henceforth to be well protected by high tariffs on imported goods. For many years before the war advocates of protection had been losing ground. The tariff act of 1857 imposed duties so low as to give few favors to American business enterprise. Secession changed all that. In securing money to pay its current war bills the federal government raised the duties on foreign goods so high that the surviving followers of Clay or Webster must have gasped with astonishment. When the war was over a big debt was left, with interest and principal to be paid. So arguments for protective tariffs based on economic reasoning were now supported by the plain necessity of the government for revenue, which admitted no dispute.

A Liberal Immigration Policy. Linked with the growth of industry was the labor supply. The problem of manning the new and growing business undertakings became a pressing matter with which Republican leaders had to grapple. As their guide they had the platform, adopted by their Union party in 1864, declaring "that foreign immigration, which in the past has added so much to the wealth, the development of resources, and the increase of power to this nation — the asylum of the oppressed of all nations — should be fostered and encouraged by a liberal and just policy." That very year Congress created a bureau of immigration and authorized a form of indentured labor, by making it legal for immigrants to pledge their wages in advance for the payment of their passage to the United States. Though the law was soon repealed, the practice of importing laborers under bond was long continued. The cheapness of steamship travel shortened the term which the indentured immigrant had to serve, but while it lasted he was bound by his contract.

The Homestead Act of 1862. To some extent the immigration law was an offset to the Homestead Act of two years before, giving away federal lands to settlers. For a long time free homesteads had been stoutly opposed by both manufacturers and planters. The former were against it because it might lure men away from the factories or encourage them in demanding higher wages as the condition of remaining at work. Planters on the other hand had feared free homesteads for the very good reason that free farms meant more free states and more power to the North. Together these two classes were strong enough to defeat homestead bills for a generation, in spite of the growing demand on the part of farmers and mechanics. At last in 1862, with nearly all the Southern statesmen out of Congress and with manufacturers mollified by various favors, Congress passed the Homestead Act — a law which provided for the free distribution of land in 160-acre lots among the men and women of strong arms and willing hearts, who were ready to build their serried lines of homesteads to the Rockies and beyond.

Internal Improvements. Though they divided on the matter of free homesteads, farmers and manufacturers readily agreed on the desirability of government aid to waterways and highways. The Western tiller of the soil was impatient for some easy way of sending his produce to market and the manufacturer himself was eager for the same means to transport his goods to the consumer on the farm. So while confederate leaders were writing into their constitution of 1861 a clause forbidding the government to spend any money for internal improvements, the Republican leaders at Washington were beginning to make vast grants of public lands to railways — a new kind of "internal improvement."

Sound Finance — National Banking. Equally indispensable to economic enterprise was the creation of a better monetary system. From Hamilton's day to Lincoln's, business men in the East had demanded a sound national currency. But they did not always get their way. The Constitution, it is true, did forbid states to emit bills of credit — issue paper money — but in the age of Jacksonian Democracy, politicians got around this provision. Under their direction many states enacted laws chartering banking companies and authorizing them to issue paper notes. After the death of Chief Justice Marshall, the Supreme Court declared that these laws were not contrary to the Constitution, and soon banks in Western and Southern states were printing huge quantities of paper notes to help borrowers pay their debts.

While dealing with war finance, the Republicans attacked this state paper money. By an act of Congress in 1864, they provided for the creation of national banks under the control of the federal government and gave these fiscal institutions the right to issue currency based on federal bonds. The next year Congress laid a heavy tax on state bank notes and thus put a stop to them. In this way, by two measures, Congress restored federal control over the monetary system, without reëstablishing the United States Bank so hated by Jacksonian Democracy.

Destruction of States' Rights by the Fourteenth Amendment. These acts and others not cited here gave strength to the Union, at the expense of the powers and dignity of the states. They were all very significant, but the crowning act of nationalism was the fourteenth amendment which, among other things, forbade states to "deprive any person of life, liberty, or property without due process of law." The reason given for this provision was the need for protecting the rights of freedmen against hostile legislatures in the South. The chief result of the amendment, as was foretold in protests loud and long from all quarters of the Democratic party, was to make every act of every state, municipal, and county authority liable to be annulled by the Supreme Court at Washington. The expected happened.

Few negroes ever brought cases under the fourteenth amendment to the attention of the courts; but thousands of state laws, municipal ordinances, and acts of local authorities were set aside as null and void under it. Laws of states regulating railway rates, fixing hours of labor in bakeshops, and taxing corporations were in due time declared void as conflicting with an amendment supposed to be designed solely to uphold the rights of negroes. A state could be haled before the Supreme Court at Washington whenever it was duly charged with depriving any person or company of lawful rights and liberties. Thus the old federation of "independent states," all equal in powers and dignities, each wearing the "jewel of sovereignty" so celebrated in Southern oratory, had gone the way of all flesh under the withering blast of civil war.

RECONSTRUCTION IN THE SOUTH

Theories about Position of the Seceded States. On the morning of April 9, 1865, when General Lee came to terms with General Grant, eleven states stood in a strange relation to the federal government against which they had been fighting. Lawyers and politicians were very uncertain as to what should be done with these members of the former Confederacy. Radical Republicans argued that they were "conquered provinces" at the mercy of Congress, to be governed under its laws until it decided to readmit any or all of them to the Union. But men of milder views maintained that the war had been waged by the North on the theory that no state could legally secede from the Union, and therefore the confederate states had merely tried to withdraw and failed. The upshot of this reasoning was simple: "The Southern states are still in the Union and it is the duty of the President, as commander-in-chief, to remove the federal troops as soon as order is restored and the state governments are ready to function as usual."

Lincoln's Proposal. Some such moderate plan of reconstruction had been suggested by Lincoln in a proclamation of December 8, 1863. He proposed to pardon nearly all who had shared in "the existing rebellion," whenever they would take an oath of loyalty to the Union. He then said that when, in any of the states named, this oath was taken by a number of lawful voters equal to one-tenth the votes cast in 1860, they should be allowed to set up a state government again. Such a government, he added, should be treated as the lawful authority of the state and given its old rights under the federal Constitution. With reference to the former slaves Lincoln made it clear that their freedom must be recognized, but added that he would not object to any laws "which may yet be consistent as a temporary arrangement with their present condition as a laboring, landless, and homeless class."

Andrew Johnson's Plan — His Impeachment. Lincoln's successor, Andrew Johnson, who had been the Vice President, soon made it known that he wished to pursue a somewhat similar course. In a number of states he appointed military governors and told them at the earliest possible moment to call conventions, chosen "by that portion of the said states who are loyal to the United States." Such conventions were then to proceed with forming regular state governments. Immediately however Johnson, who was a Southern man and a Democrat, was charged by the Republicans with being too ready to restore the confederate states to their old places in the Union and with violating various national laws. As the months went by, the opposition in Congress to his measures and policies grew in size and ferocity. Finally President Johnson was impeached by the House of Representatives in March, 1868, and was acquitted by the Senate only because his foes lacked one vote of the two-thirds necessary to find him guilty of any high crimes or misdemeanors.

Congress Enacts "Reconstruction Laws." In fact Congress was in a position to have its own way with the confederate states. Under the Constitution, each House could decide whether to admit or exclude members, that is, whether they were properly elected and entitled to their seats. Southern Senators and Representatives could therefore be kept out at will. Congress was also the law-making body of the country and had the power to admit states to the Union. So it began to pass a series of reconstruction acts — carrying them all over Johnson's veto. And these measures, the first of which became a law on March 2, 1867, showed little mercy to the secessionists.

They laid off the ten states — the whole Confederacy with the exception of Tennessee — still outside the pale, into five military districts, each commanded by a military officer appointed by the President. They ordered the commanding general to make a list of voters for the election of delegates to state conventions for the purpose of drafting new constitutions. Such voters, however, were not to be, as Lincoln had suggested, loyal persons entitled to vote under the law existing in 1860 but "the male citizens of the said state, twenty-one years old and upward, of whatever race, color, or previous condition . . . except such as may be disfranchised for participation in the rebellion or for felony at common law."

This was the death knell to the idea that the leaders of the Confederacy and their white supporters were to share in setting up the new order. Power was instead thrust into the hands of the emancipated male negroes and the handful of whites who alone could show a record of loyalty. That was not all. Each state was forced to ratify the fourteenth amendment to the federal Constitution before it could be restored to the Union.

The membership of the conventions may be easily imagined. Men who had been slaves a few years before suddenly found themselves a force in government. An army of adventurers from the North — "carpetbaggers" as they were called because they carried all their possessions in traveling bags made of carpet — poured in upon the scene to aid in "reconstruction." Undoubtedly, many honorable people took part in restoring state governments in the South, but enough rascals had a hand in it to discredit even the good that was done. Under such conditions, the Southern states were one after another brought back into the Union by the grace of Congress, the last in 1870. Not until seven years later, however, were all Northern soldiers withdrawn from Southern capitals and not until many years after that was federal control over state elections finally ended.

The Status of the Freedmen. Even more troublesome than the issues connected with the return of the seceded states to the Union, was the question of what to do with the newly emancipated slaves. That problem, often put to abolitionists before the war, now had to be squarely faced. The thirteenth amendment abolishing slavery had not touched it at all. It declared bondmen free, but did nothing to provide them with work or homes and did not mention the subject of their political rights. All these matters were left to the states, and some legislatures, by laws known as "black codes," reëstablished a form of slavery under the guise of punishing negroes for vagrancy and "apprenticing" them to masters. Such methods in fact partly explain the reaction that led Congress to give up Lincoln's milder policies and undertake a harsher program of reconstruction.

Still no serious effort was made to solve by law the economic problems of the freedmen. Radical abolitionists had contended that the slaves, when emancipated, should be given outright the fields of their former masters; but Congress steadily rejected the very idea of any seizure of land. It did try to give immediate aid by creating, in 1865, the Freedmen's Bureau and charging it with the duty of looking after refugees. It authorized the issue of food and clothing to the destitute and the renting of certain lands under federal control to former slaves at low rates. But the larger question of how these people were to make a living, it left to time.

Against many protests, particularly from Democrats, Congress did insist, however, on granting freedmen certain rights by national law. These rights fell into two broad divisions, civil and political. By an act passed in 1866, Congress gave to former slaves the privileges of white citizens with respect to making contracts, giving testimony in courts, and purchasing, selling, and leasing property. Doubtful whether it had the power to enact this law, Congress then passed and submitted to the states the fourteenth amendment which gave citizenship to all persons born or naturalized in the United States, assured them the privileges and immunities of citizens, and declared that no state should deprive any person of life, liberty or property without due process of law. Furthermore, Congress tried to give social equality to negroes by the second Civil Rights Bill of 1875 which promised them, among other things, the full and equal enjoyment of inns, theaters, public conveyances, and places of amusement — a law later declared unconstitutional by the Supreme Court.

The question of political rights for freedmen was still more thorny; but radical Republicans, like Charles Sumner, asserted that no person's civil liberty was secure unless he could vote for the government officers who enforced it. Hence in this same fourteenth amendment they attempted to compel the states to give the ballot to all negro men, leaving the women to take care of themselves. The amendment declared in effect that when any state deprived adult male citizens of the right to vote, its representation in Congress should be reduced in the proportion which such persons bore to the voting population. If, for example, the state excluded half the men from voting, it was to lose half its members in the House of Representatives.

But this provision failed to accomplish its purpose and thereupon the fifteenth amendment was passed and ratified. The new amendment, adopted in 1870, stated very clearly that no citizen could be deprived of the right to vote "on account of race, color, or previous condition of servitude." To make certain the execution of this rule, Congress, beginning in 1870, enacted three drastic laws, sometimes known as "force bills," which provided for the use of federal officers, civil and military, as supervisors of elections in all parts of the Union. So the federal government, after abolishing chattel slavery, sought to sweep away its signs and badges, civil, social, and political. Never, save perhaps in some of the civil conflicts of Greece or Rome, had there taken place in the affairs of a nation a social revolution so complete, so profound, and so far-reaching in its consequences.

SUMMARY OF THE SECTIONAL CONFLICT

Just as the United States, under the impetus of Western enterprise, rounded out the continental domain, its very existence as a nation was threatened by conflict between two sections. This storm had been long gathering upon the horizon. From colonial times there had been a marked difference between the South and the North. The former by climate and soil was suited to a planting system — the cultivation of tobacco, rice, cotton, and sugar cane — and in the course of time slave labor became the foundation of that system. The North, on the other hand, added trade and manufacturing to its agriculture. Slavery, though lawful, did not thrive there. An abundant supply of free labor kept the Northern wheels turning.

This difference between the two sections was intensified with the advent of the steam engine and the factory. Between 1815 and 1860 an industrial revolution took place in the North. Its signs were gigantic factories, great numbers of industrial workers, immense cities, flourishing commerce, and prosperous banks. By canals and railways New York, Boston, and Philadelphia were linked with the wheatfields of Ohio, Indiana, and Illinois. A steel net drew North and Northwest together. Business ties bound them still closer. Western trade was turned from New Orleans to the East and Eastern money was lent to upbuild Western enterprise.

In time, the industrial North and the planting South worked out different ideas about politics. The former looked with favor on protective tariffs, ship subsidies, a national banking system, and internal improvements. Moreover the farmers of the West urged the federal government to give its Western land away in free homesteads. Meanwhile, the South steadily swung around to the opposite view. Its spokesmen came to look on most of these policies as injurious to the planting interests.

Into economic questions a moral issue was drawn. The Northern states, in which slavery was not important, had early abolished it. In the course of a few years advocates of universal emancipation, led by William Lloyd Garrison, began to agitate for the abolition of slavery throughout the Union. Far and wide the agitation spread. Thoroughly frightened, the South called on the North to stop the agitators, to guarantee the return of runaway slaves, and to allow slavery in the Western territories.

With the passing years the conflict between the two sections grew in intensity. It flamed up in 1820 and was quenched by the Missouri Compromise. It took on the form of a tariff controversy and nullification in 1832, and was once more allayed by mutual concessions. It appeared after the Mexican war when the question of slavery in the new territories was raised. Again compromise — the great settlement of 1850 — seemed to restore peace, for a moment. Then a series of startling events swept the sections into war: the repeal of the Missouri Compromise in 1854, the rise of the Republican party pledged to prohibit slavery in the territories, the Dred Scott decision, the Lincoln-Douglas debates, John Brown's raid, the election of Lincoln, and secession.

The Civil War, lasting for four years, tested the strength of both North and South — in leadership, in finance, in diplomatic skill, in material resources, in industry, and in armed forces. By the blockade of Southern ports, by an overwhelming weight of men and materials, and by relentless hammering on the field of battle, the North was victorious.

The consequences of the war were revolutionary. Slavery was

abolished and the freedmen given the ballot. Southern planters who had once been the leaders of their section were nearly all ruined in purse and deprived of political power. The Union was declared to be perpetual, the right of a state to secede having been forever settled by battle. Federal control over the affairs of states, counties, and cities was assured by the fourteenth amendment. The power and prestige of the national government were increased beyond all expectations. The North was now free to adopt a protective tariff, a national banking system, land grants for railways, and free lands for farmers. For nearly a generation planting had been the greatest economic interest in the country. Business enterprise was to take its place in rank.

References

NORTHERN ACCOUNTS

J. K. Hosmer, *The Appeal to Arms* and *The Outcome of the Civil War* (American Nation Series).

J. Ropes, *History of the Civil War* (best account of military campaigns).

J. F. Rhodes, *History of the United States*, Vols. III, IV, and V.

J. T. Morse, *Abraham Lincoln* (2 vols.).

SOUTHERN ACCOUNTS

W. E. Dodd, *Jefferson Davis.*

Jefferson Davis, *Rise and Fall of the Confederate Government.*

E. Pollard, *The Lost Cause.*

A. H. Stephens, *The War between the States.*

Questions

1. Contrast public opinion of secession in 1860 with that on nullification in 1832.

2. Compare the Northern and Southern views of the Union.

3. What were the peculiar features of the confederate constitution?

4. How was the Confederacy financed?

5. Compare the resources of the two sections.

6. On what foundations did Southern hopes rest?

7. Describe the attempts at a peaceful settlement.

8. Compare the raising of armies for the Civil War with the methods employed in the World War. (See below, chapter xxvii.)

9. Compare the financial methods of the government in the two wars.

10. Explain why the blockade was such a deadly weapon.
11. Give the leading diplomatic events of the war.
12. Trace the growth of antislavery sentiment.
13. What measures were taken to restrain criticism of the government?
14. What part did Lincoln play in all phases of the war?
15. State the principal results of the war.
16. Compare Lincoln's plan of reconstruction with that adopted by Congress.
17. What rights did Congress attempt to confer upon the former slaves?

Research Topics

Was Secession Lawful? The Southern view by Jefferson Davis in Harding, *Select Orations Illustrating American History*, pp. 364–369. Lincoln's view, Harding, pp. 371–381.

The Confederate Constitution. Compare with the federal Constitution in Macdonald, *Documentary Source Book*, pp. 424–433 and pp. 271–279.

Federal Legislative Measures. Prepare a table and brief digest of the important laws relating to the war. Macdonald, pp. 433–482.

Economic Aspects of the War. Coman, *Industrial History of the United States*, pp. 279–301. Dewey, *Financial History of the United States*, Chaps. XII and XIII. Tabulate the economic measures of Congress in Macdonald.

Military Campaigns. The great battles are fully treated in Rhodes, *History of the Civil War*, and teachers desiring to emphasize military affairs may assign campaigns to members of the class for study and report. A briefer treatment in Elson, *History of the United States*, pp. 619–750.

Biographical Studies. Lincoln, Davis, Lee, Grant, Sherman, and other leaders in civil and military affairs, with reference to local "war governors."

English and French Opinion of the War. Rhodes, *History of the United States*, Vol. IV, pp. 337–394.

The South during the War. Rhodes, Vol. V, pp. 343–382.

The North during the War. Rhodes, Vol. V, pp. 189–342.

Reconstruction Measures. Macdonald, *Source Book*, pp. 500–511, 514–518, 529–530; Elson, pp. 751–764.

The Force Bills. Macdonald, pp. 547–551, 554–564.

PART VI. NATIONAL GROWTH AND WORLD POLITICS

CHAPTER XVIII

THE POLITICAL AND ECONOMIC EVOLUTION OF THE SOUTH

The outcome of the Civil War in the South was nothing short of a revolution — an overthrow of the ruling class, the labor system, and the government. As if this were not enough, agriculture, business, and transportation were badly damaged by the war itself. And filling the cup of Southern sorrow to the brim, political leaders from the North, strangers to the life and traditions of the South, took charge of affairs.

THE SOUTH AT THE CLOSE OF THE WAR

A Ruling Class Disfranchised. The transformation in the South was in many respects unlike that which followed the war for American independence or the French upheaval begun in 1789. It did not bring power to a new class that had sought it and understood the art of government, as those revolutions had done. This "second American revolution," on the contrary, gave the ballot to freedmen who had played little part in the struggle for their liberty. Furthermore it took away from the Southerners who had directed secession not only their leadership but also their right to share in the government of state and nation. By the fourteenth amendment all civil and military places were closed to every man who had once taken an oath to support the Constitution as a member of Congress, as a state legislator, or as a government officer, and had afterward engaged in "insurrection or rebellion" or "given aid and comfort to the enemies" of the United States. This sweeping rule, made stronger by the federal reconstruction acts, laid under the ban most of the talent, energy, and experience of the South.

The Condition of the State Governments. For a long time after peace was restored a part of the South was occupied by Union troops. Many state governments now passed largely into the control of former slaves, led principally by Northern carpetbaggers or Southern adventurers, known as "Scalawags." The result was a carnival of waste, folly, and corruption. The "reconstruction" legislature of South Carolina, for example, bought clocks at $480 apiece and chandeliers at $650. To purchase land for freedmen the sum of $800,000 was appropriated; and then swamps worth seventy-five cents an acre were bought by the state at five times the value. Between 1868 and 1873, the debt of that state rose from about $5,800,000 to $24,000,000, and nobody could tell what went with millions of the money.

Economic Ruin — Urban and Rural. No matter where Southerners turned in 1865 they found devastation — in the towns, in the fields, and along the highways. Atlanta, the city to which Sherman applied the torch, lay in ashes; Nashville and Chattanooga had been partially wrecked; Richmond and Augusta had suffered severely from fires. Charleston was described by a visitor as "a city of ruins, of desolation, of vacant houses, of rotten wharves, of deserted warehouses, of weed gardens, of miles of grass-grown streets. . . . How few young men there are, how generally the young women are dressed in black! The flower of their proud aristocracy is buried on scores of battlefields."

Those who journeyed through the country reported desolation widespread and equally pathetic. An English traveler who made his way along the course of the Tennessee River in 1870 wrote: "The trail of war is visible throughout the valley in burnt-up gin houses, ruined bridges, mills, and factories . . . and large tracts of once cultivated land are stripped of every vestige of fencing. The roads, long neglected, are in disorder and, having in many places become impassable, new tracks have been made through the woods and fields without much respect to boundaries." Here a great plantation had been confiscated by the federal authorities while the owner was fighting for the Confederacy. There fields lay in waste as the result of invasion and battle. In the wake of the armies the homesteads of rich and poor alike, if they escaped flames, had been despoiled of the stock and seeds necessary to renew agriculture.

Railways Dilapidated. Highways, canals, and other means of transportation were war-shocked. From Pocahontas to Decatur, Alabama, a distance of 114 miles, we are told, the railroad was "almost entirely destroyed, except the roadbed and iron rails, and they were in very bad condition — every bridge and trestle destroyed, crossties rotten, buildings burned, water tanks gone, tracks grown up with weeds and bushes, not a sawmill near the line, and the labor system of the country gone. About forty miles of the

From Harper's Weekly, January 7, 1865

DESTRUCTION SCENE IN THE SOUTH

track were burned, the crossties entirely destroyed, and the rails bent and twisted in such a manner as to require great labor to straighten and a large portion of them requiring renewal."

Capital and Credit Destroyed. Money and banking were likewise in confusion. The confederate currency, inflated to the bursting point, had blown up and was as worthless as waste paper. Bonds of the confederate government were just as valueless. Gold and silver coins were seldom seen. Furthermore the fourteenth amendment to the federal Constitution made null and void all confederate war bonds; while Southern debtors were now pressed by their Northern creditors to pay the millions of dollars they had borrowed before the war. Such debts were often secured by mortgages on plantations and the federal courts stood ready to help the creditors seize the land in case of default in payments.

The Restoration of White Supremacy

Intimidation. In spite of all their handicaps, however, former Southern leaders resolved to recover their position of power and to check the rule of freedmen. The opening battle in their political contest for white supremacy was waged, in the main, by secret organizations, among which the Ku Klux Klan and the White Camelia were the most prominent. The first of these societies appeared in Tennessee in 1866 and held its initial national convention the following year. It was in origin a social club. According to its program, its objects were "to protect the weak, the innocent, and the defenseless from the indignities, wrongs, and outrages of the lawless, the violent, and the brutal; and to succor the suffering, especially the widows and orphans of the confederate soldiers." The whole South was called "the Empire" and its monarch a "Grand Wizard." Each state was a realm and each county a province. In secret orders of one kind or another over half a million men were enrolled.

The methods of the Ku Klux and the White Camelia were similar. Solemn parades of masked men on horses bedecked in long robes were held, sometimes in open daylight and sometimes in the dead of night. Notices were sent about, warning persons to quit certain practices — particularly to stay away from polling booths. If the warning failed, something more frightful was tried. For instance, at the hour of midnight a horseman would ride up to the house of some man marked for "a lesson," lift his headgear, take off a skull, and hand it to the trembling victim with the request that he hold it for a few minutes. Actual violence was employed in some cases either officially or unofficially by members of the Klan. Tar and feathers were freely applied; the whip was often laid on unmercifully; and occasionally a brutal murder was committed. If Klan members were fired upon from bushes or behind trees, swift revenge followed. The situation became so terrifying that Congress in 1870 forbade citizens to go about in disguise for the purpose of interfering with elections or the rights guaranteed to citizens by federal law.

Foreseeing such a step on the part of the federal government, the central Ku Klux was officially dissolved by the "Grand Wizard" in 1869. Nevertheless local societies retained their organizations and methods, for the spirit survived the national association. "On the whole," says a Southern writer, "it is not easy to see what other course was open to the South. . . . Armed resistance was out of the question. And yet there must be some control had of the situation. . . . If force was denied, craft was inevitable."

The Struggle for the Ballot Box. Very soon such strong-arm practices had an effect on the elections. The freedman, into whose hand the ballot had been thrust, ordinarily did not care to risk his head in trying to exercise his political rights. A mere show of force, a mere threat kept thousands of ex-slaves away from the polls. Thus the whites steadily regained their former power in the state government in spite of the laws. Nothing could prevent it. Congress enacted bill after bill setting up federal supervision of elections; Northern politicians tried to hold down the Southern leaders in every way; but all such efforts were like resistance to the course of nature.

Amnesty for Southerners. The recovery of white supremacy was quickly felt in Washington and in national politics. The Democratic party in the North welcomed it as a sign of its own recovery. Moderate Republicans, anxious to heal the sharp hostility between the North and the South for the sake of peace, encouraged it. Indeed, complete pardon or amnesty for Confederates was soon widely advocated. Yet the struggle to remove the stamp of secession from them and to restore them to all the rights of citizens was slow and difficult. Lincoln, with his usual generosity, in the midst of the war, had offered a general amnesty to all who had been in arms against the Union, on condition that they then take an oath of loyalty; but Johnson, who was bent on making "treason infamous," deprived still more Confederates of their rights.

For a long time, Congress seemed relentless toward secessionists.

In vain did men like Carl Schurz plead with their colleagues to crown their victory in battle with a noble act of universal pardon and oblivion. Congress would not yield. It would grant amnesty in individual cases; but not to everybody on the proscribed list. When finally in 1872, seven years after the surrender at Appomattox, it did pass a general amnesty bill, it insisted on certain exceptions. Confederates who, before the war, had been members of Congress or had served in other high posts, civil or military, under the federal government, were still excluded from important offices. Not until the summer of 1898, when the war with Spain had begun, did Congress forgive all and abolish the last of the disabilities imposed on supporters of the "lost cause."

The Force Bills Attacked. The granting of a large measure of amnesty in 1872 encouraged the Democrats to attack federal supervision of elections. Within two years they won a majority in the House of Representatives and at once moved to repeal the "force bills." But the Republicans, having control in the Senate, blocked this direct action. So the Democrats sought to carry their point by attaching a "rider," or condition, to the appropriation bill for the support of the army, providing that no troops should be used to sustain the federal government in Louisiana. The Senate defeated this scheme, too. As a result, Congress adjourned without voting money for the army and this satisfied the Democrats for the moment. The next session, they let the army finance bill pass but kept up their fight on the force laws until they wrung from President Hayes a measure forbidding the use of United States troops as guards at polling booths. The following year they again placed a rider on the army bill and carried it through, putting an end to the use of money for any kind of military control over elections. Clearly the reconstruction program was going to pieces; and the Supreme Court helped along the process by declaring parts of the reconstruction laws invalid. In 1878 the Democrats even won a majority in the Senate and returned to power a large number of men once prominent in the confederate cause.

By this time a new generation was coming on the scene. The supremacy of the whites in the South, if not yet complete, was at least assured. United States marshals, deputies, and supervisors still watched over elections but they could not call on federal troops for aid. When in 1894 the last fragment of the force bills was swept away, the country took little note; so far was opinion ahead of the action.

New State Constitutions Confirm White Supremacy. Having reëstablished white supremacy in fact, Southern leaders now decided to confirm it by law. Hence they framed new state constitutions so worded as to deprive negroes of the ballot. Mississippi took this step in 1890; South Carolina in 1895; Louisiana in 1898; North Carolina in 1900; Alabama and Maryland in 1901; and Virginia in 1902.

The authors of these measures made no attempt to conceal their purposes. "The intelligent white men of the South," said Governor Tillman, "intend to govern here." Since however the fifteenth amendment to the federal Constitution forbade them to deprive any citizen of the right to vote on account of race, color, or previous condition of servitude, they had to achieve their ends in other ways. The means they chose were few, simple, and effective. The first and most easily applied was the provision which required each prospective voter to read a section of the state constitution or "understand and explain it" when read to him. Many negroes could not pass this examination as conducted by white election officers.

Among the other tests was the rule that only taxpayers or the owners of property could vote. Unwilling thus to disfranchise any poor white man who had stood by them "in the dark days of reconstruction," Southern leaders sometimes inserted into their suffrage laws a provision known as "the grandfather clause." This clause gave the ballot to any man who did not have either the property or the educational qualifications, provided he had voted on or before 1867 or was the son or grandson of such a person. Of course, no colored man in the South could qualify under this scheme.

Before long these new laws accomplished their purpose. Of the 147,000 negroes in Mississippi above the age of twenty-one, approximately 8600 registered under the constitution of 1890. Louisiana had 127,000 colored voters enrolled in 1896; under the constitution drafted two years later the registration fell to 5300. An analysis of the figures for South Carolina in 1900 indicates that about one negro out of every hundred adult males of that race took part in elections.

The Supreme Court Refuses to Intervene. Numerous efforts were made to persuade the Supreme Court of the United States to declare such laws unconstitutional; but the Court never made a direct decision on the merits of the issue. In one case the Court remarked that it could not take charge of the election machinery of Alabama; it said that relief, in case of injustice, would have to come from the President or the Congress of the United States. Only one of the several methods used to exclude negroes from voting, namely, the "grandfather clause," was held to be a violation of the federal Constitution. This decision, rendered in 1915, in the Oklahoma and Maryland cases, did not, however, touch the chief measures of exclusion.

Proposals to Reduce Southern Representation in Congress. In fact, these measures did not in so many words deprive any one of the vote on account of race or color. They did not, therefore, run counter to the letter of the fifteenth amendment, any more than the educational qualifications imposed on the suffrage in some Northern states. But they did make the states which adopted them subject to the terms of the fourteenth amendment. This amendment very explicitly says that whenever any state deprives adult male citizens of the right to vote (except in certain minor cases) its representation in Congress shall be reduced.

Accordingly those who protested against negro disfranchisement demanded the enforcement of the fourteenth amendment. Indeed in their platform of 1908 the Republicans promised to take this step, but after they won the election they did not carry their pledge into effect. Henceforward Southern leaders were able to regard such Republican threats as idle gestures in no way endangering the laws which assured white supremacy.

The Solid South. Out of the long conflict over reconstruction there emerged what was known as the "solid South" — a block of Southern states that never gave an electoral vote to a Republican candidate for President. Before the Civil War, the Southern people had been divided on political questions. Take, for example, the election of 1860. In nine of the slave states — Delaware, Virginia, Tennessee, Missouri, Maryland, Louisiana, Kentucky, Georgia, and Arkansas — a majority of the votes was cast against the representative of the extreme Southern point of view, John C. Breckinridge. Each of the six states carried by Breckinridge

Photograph by Ewing Galloway, New York

ALAMO PLAZA, SAN ANTONIO, TEXAS

registered a heavy vote against him. North Carolina gave Breckinridge only 849 votes more than Bell and Douglas. In every Southern state the vote for Bell, the candidate who stood firmly for the Constitution, the Union, and silence on slavery, was large. Virginia, Kentucky, Missouri, and Tennessee recorded more votes for Bell than for Breckinridge; in Georgia, Bell's vote was 42,000 against 51,000 for his opponents; in Louisiana, 20,000 against 22,000; in Mississippi, 25,000 against 40,000.

But when war came, men who had voted on opposite sides joined hands in defense of their homes. And after the armed conflict was over they remained side by side working, they said, against "Republican misrule and negro domination." By 1890, with Northern control definitely broken, the boast was made that there were at least twelve Southern states in which no Republican candidate for President could win a single electoral vote.

Dissent in the Solid South. Though it was the custom to speak of the South as "solid," as a matter of fact there were always independents in that section. In 1892, for instance, the Populists made heavy inroads upon the Democratic vote there. At other times contests between factions within the Democratic party over the choice of candidates proved that the South was far from a unit in its opinions. In some places, moreover, a normal Republican minority of considerable size appeared at the opening of the twentieth century. By way of illustration we may cite the case of Georgia where Taft polled 41,000 votes in 1908 against 72,000 for Bryan; in North Carolina 114,000 against 136,000. In 1920, Harding, the Republican candidate, broke the record by carrying Tennessee as well as Kentucky, Oklahoma, and Maryland. In 1928, Herbert Hoover brought even Virginia, North Carolina, and Texas into his column, leaving only South Carolina, Georgia, Alabama, Mississippi, Louisiana, and Arkansas "solid" for Alfred E. Smith, the Democratic candidate.

THE ECONOMIC ADVANCE OF THE SOUTH

The Break-up of the Great Estates. With the overthrow of chattel slavery, the great estate frequently gave way to the small farm. The plantation was indeed founded on slavery. Before the war, the prosperous planter, either by desire or necessity, generally used his savings to buy more land. As his slaves increased in numbers, he was forced to sell them or enlarge his acreage and he usually chose the latter plan, especially in the Far South. Other things had also favored the growth of large estates. Slave labor quickly wore out the soil by crude tillage and compelled the cutting of forests to extend the area under cultivation. Then of course the planter took pride in his great estate — a sign of his wealth and power.

But the war and emancipation, which drove the planter from political life for such a long time, permanently destroyed the very foundation of the system by which he lived. With heavy debts to pay and his credit ruined, he found it hard to borrow money with which to start cultivation again. Moreover, he faced a new problem in getting laborers to till his fields. Rather than work

A SOUTHERN COTTON MILL IN A COTTON FIELD

now under supervision, a great many former slaves chose to rent plots of land or buy them on installments and live in a way more in keeping with emancipation. White farmers on the other hand would rarely hire themselves out to planters, for they wanted to own land, not to work for someone else. Hence thousands of plantations had to be broken up and sold, making the small farm the general unit of cultivation in the South as in the North. Between 1870 and 1900 the number of such holdings doubled in every state south of a line drawn west along the Potomac and Ohio rivers, except Arkansas and Louisiana. From year to year the process continued, sweeping away the great estates which had once distinguished the planting section from the rest of the country.

The Diversification of Crops. No less significant was a change which came in the methods of farming in the South. Under slavery, tobacco, rice, and sugar were staples and "cotton was king." The cultivation of these crops was simple and quickly learned. It called for little skill on the part of overseers or slaves. For a time after slavery was abolished the same crops remained staples, but far-sighted agriculturists at length began to see the dangers of risking everything on one or two products such as tobacco or cotton. The mild climate all the way around the coast from Virginia to Texas and the richness of the soil invited them to experiment with crops. Peaches, oranges, peanuts, and other fruits and vegetables were found to grow luxuriantly. Then markets were extended by refrigeration on steamships and freight cars which put great cities within easy reach of Southern gardeners. Hence wide areas of the old South were turned from the historic staples to the production of foodstuffs. Between 1880 and the close of the century the value of its farm crops increased from $600,000,000 to $1,270,000,000.

The Industrial and Commercial Revolution. With the radical changes in agriculture also came an industrial and commercial revolution. The South had always been rich in natural resources but under the slave system they had been little used. Rivers that would have turned millions of spindles tumbled unheeded to the seas. Coal and iron beds lay unopened. Timber on the lands cleared for planting had been burnt or allowed to fall to earth in decay. Southern enterprise and energy were all turned to planting. Furthermore, slavery discouraged the immigration of white artisans who might have supplied the skill for industry.

Under the new régime of emancipated labor, however, planters were simply forced to try other lines of activity, and the South began to catch the industrial spirit that had conquered the agricultural North. Before many years had passed enormous strides were taken in exploiting mineral wealth. Iron ore of every quality was found, the chief beds being in Virginia, West Virginia, Tennessee, Kentucky, North Carolina, Georgia, Alabama, Arkansas, and Texas. Five important coal basins were uncovered: in Virginia, North Carolina, the Appalachian chain from Maryland to Northern Alabama, Kentucky, Arkansas, and Texas. Oil pools were found in Kentucky, Tennessee, and Texas. Within the twenty years from 1880 to 1900, the output of mineral wealth

STEEL MILLS — BIRMINGHAM, ALABAMA

multiplied tenfold. At the end of the century the iron industries of West Virginia and Alabama had begun to rival those of Pennsylvania. Birmingham became the Pittsburgh and Atlanta the Chicago of the South.

In other lines Southern enterprise made amazing gains. Huge sawmills were built in the timber districts, particularly in Louisiana, Arkansas, and Mississippi. When the second decade of the twentieth century opened, leadership in the lumber business had passed from the Great Lakes region to the South. In 1913 eight

Southern states produced nearly four times as much lumber as the Lake states and twice as much as the vast forests of Washington and Oregon.

In the meantime, the rise of the cotton industry was equally astounding. In 1865, cotton spinning was almost negligible in the Southern states. By 1880 they had one-fourth of the mills in the country. At the end of the century they had one-half the mills, the two Carolinas taking the lead by working up at home more than one-third of their entire cotton crop — which they had formerly sent away to New and Old England. Having both raw materials and power at hand, they enjoyed many advantages over Northern rivals in manufacturing, and at the opening of the new century were outstripping the latter in the proportion of spindles annually put into operation. Moreover, since the cotton planters now had a market at neighboring mills, they began to look forward to a day when the price of their staple would no longer be fixed on the cotton exchanges of New York, New Orleans, and Liverpool.

Transportation kept pace with industry. In 1860, the South had about ten thousand miles of railway. By 1880 the figure had doubled. During the next twenty years over thirty thousand miles were added, most of the increase being in Texas. About 1898, a period of consolidation opened, in which scores of short lines were united, mainly under the leadership of Northern capitalists. Once the union of Southern lines was effected, a through service was provided to the North and West. Thus Southern industries were given outlets to the markets of the whole country and brought within the currents of national business enterprise.

The Social Effects of the Economic Changes. As long as the slave system lasted and planting was the major interest, the South was bound to be sectional in character. With slavery gone, crops diversified, natural resources developed, industries promoted, and communication with the rest of the country improved, the social order of the ante-bellum days rapidly passed. The South became more like the North in its agriculture and business.

One of the first signs of the resemblance to come lay in the rise of farmers to a place of social and political importance. There had always been in the South a large class of white yeomen who held no slaves and tilled the soil with their own hands, but they labored under severe handicaps in the days of slavery. Since the fertile fields of the coast and river valleys were nearly all monopolized by planting, they had been driven into the uplands where the soil was thin and the crops were light. Still, though their lot was hard, they increased in numbers and zealously worked their freeholds.

When at last emancipation forced the break-up of plantations, these farmers were able to buy land more worthy of their plows. By good management they restored much of the worn-out soil to its original fertility, and raised themselves in the scale of prosperity. It soon became a common thing for their sons to enter the professions, as only planters' sons had done before; while their daughters went away to college to prepare themselves for teaching. So a more democratic tone was given to the white society of the South. Moreover the migration to the North and West, which had formerly carried away thousands of energetic young people of yeoman stock, was reduced and their talents were turned to rebuilding the South.

The growth in the number of farmers was followed by the multiplication of small towns and villages — rather a novel feature in the South. Before 1860 it was possible to travel through endless stretches of cotton and tobacco without seeing a single city. The mansion of the plantation, not the town, was the center of social life for the dominant class of the "Old South" — of amusements and recreation. Carpentry, bricklaying, and blacksmithing were usually done on each estate by slaves skilled in simple handicrafts. Supplies were bought wholesale. Such modes of living did not require numerous villages and towns with shops, schools, and offices.

But the abolition of slavery altered these habits and requirements. Small farms now spread out where plantations had formerly stood. The emancipated negroes turned more to agriculture than to handicrafts; and white mechanics and storekeepers began to serve the needs of farming communities. Soon a class of local merchants and artisans grew to be an important element in the Southern social system; a native industrial class appeared; and in the county seats, once dominated by planters, business and professional men asserted themselves as leaders.

Another result of civil crisis was the transfer of many families from planting to business. Philip A. Bruce, a Southern historian, has described this trend from land to trade in a single paragraph: "The higher planting class that under the old system gave so much distinction to rural life has, as far as it has survived at all, been concentrated in the cities. The families that in the time of slavery would have been found only in the country are now found, with a few exceptions, in the towns. The transplantation has been practically universal. The talent, the energy, the ambition that formerly sought expression in the management of great estates and the control of hosts of slaves, now seek a field of action in trade, in manufacturing enterprises, or in the general enterprises of development. This was for the ruling class of the region the natural outcome of the great economic revolution that followed the war."

As in other parts of the world, the growth of business in the South was attended by a great increase in the number of industrial workers dependent upon wages for their livelihood. When Jefferson Davis was inaugurated President of the Southern Confederacy, there were scarcely one hundred thousand persons employed in Southern manufacturing as against more than a million in Northern mills. Fifty years later, Georgia and Alabama alone had more than one hundred and fifty thousand wage-earners. Necessarily this meant the rise of industrial cities in the South. In 1910, New Orleans, Atlanta, Memphis, Nashville, Houston, and San Antonio stood in the same relation to the New South that Cincinnati, Chicago, Cleveland, and Detroit had stood to the New West fifty years before. The problems of labor and capital and municipal government that, earlier writers boasted, would never perplex their section, had come in full force.

The Revolution in the Status of the Slaves. No element of Southern society, of course, was so shaken up by the Civil War and its aftermath as the slaves. On the day of emancipation, they stood free but empty-handed, the owners of no tools or property, generally the masters of no trade and wholly inexperienced in the arts of self-help that the whites as a rule possessed. They had never been accustomed to looking out for themselves. The plantation bell had called them to labor and released them at the close of the day.   Doles of food and clothing had been regularly handed to them in given quantities.   They did not understand wages, ownership, renting, contracts, mortgages, leases, bills or accounts.

Now that they were "free," they generally chose one of four courses.   In many cases they remained with their former masters in their cabins, pre-sumably working for daily wages in-stead of food, cloth-ing, and shelter as before.   But as few masters had cash to dispense, the new relation was in truth much like the old. The planters still offered only food, clothing, and shel-ter; the freedmen gave their labor in return.   That was the best many could do.   On the other

Courtesy of The Metropolitan Museum of Art
In Gayer Hours
A water color by Thomas Eakins.

hand, thousands who did not want to remain in this condition fled from the plantation to the nearest town or city, or to the distant North, to seek employment and pay.   This was the second choice.

A third course open to freedmen was that of renting land from the former master, paying him usually with a share of the crops produced.   On such terms a large number became tenants.   Be-sides offering him a chance to acquire land in time, this method meanwhile gave to the renter, to a certain extent at least, a control over his own hours of labor.   The fourth and most difficult path for freedmen was that which led to actual ownership of land.   Often a generous master helped his ex-slaves to purchase small holdings on easy terms.   The more enterprising and the more fortunate, who started as wage-earners or tenants, made their way upward to ownership and by the end of the century one-fourth of the colored laborers on the land at last owned the soil they tilled, but frequently subject to mortgage.

Though relatively poor, the South finally started to educate the colored population. The slaves had been almost wholly illiterate and a great many spoke only curious dialects more akin to African tongues than to English. So the task of teaching them to read and write was difficult, but by the end of the century schools had been provided for more than one-half the colored children. And from year to year the proportion of negro children in attendance steadily rose.

Yet in spite of all that was done, negroes continued to stand on a peculiar footing in the South and indeed in all parts of the country. They were almost entirely excluded from voting in the Far South. Throughout the Southern states, special rooms were set aside for them in the railway stations and special cars on the trains. When they tried to enter industry, they were often blocked by trade unions, if they were not defeated by their woeful lack of skill and technical training. Indeed, it seems that they actually lost ground in machine industries between 1890 and 1900.

During the opening years of the twentieth century, however, their position changed in many ways. By that time, owing to the great emigration from the South, they were in a majority in only two states, South Carolina and Mississippi. The proportion of the colored population was also declining in Arkansas, Virginia, West Virginia, and North Carolina. Every train from the South carried emigrants, traveling singly and in families, to hunt the opportunities which rumor had told them about. And after Congress cut down European immigration by the drastic act of 1924, the demand for negro labor in the North rose rapidly, speeding up the movement from Southern fields. As whole counties were stripped of their colored population, the negro quarters of Northern cities grew into cities themselves.

Thus the negro question entered into more modern phases. For the purpose of checking the loss of labor and promoting better relations, Interracial Committees, composed of white and colored citizens, sprang up in the South; while in the North an Association for the Advancement of the Condition of Colored People undertook to aid negroes in their efforts at self-help. Meeting stronger competition from negroes, some labor unions began to push organization among them and to admit them to membership more cordially. With the shifting of the colored population, the race question became less sectional and more national.

In many other ways the South was brought into the main currents of nationalism. By studying together in schools and colleges, boys and girls from South and North rubbed off the sharp angles of sectionalism. Southern writers — Ellen Glasgow, Mary Johnston, James Branch Cabell, and Du Bose Heyward, to mention just a few — found a hospitable reception in the North; while favors were fully reciprocated on the other side. As Southern economic enterprise spread, Northern capital was turned to the South and Northern capitalists joined Southerners in the direction of their industries. Moreover, Southerners went North to enter business or the professions, and before long the Georgia and Virginia Societies in New York were friendly rivals of the New England Society. Thus the sectionalism that produced the terrible Civil War sank into the background of American memories.

References

W. G. Brown, *The Lower South.*

H. W. Grady, *The New South* (1890).

A. B. Hart, *The Southern South* and R. S. Baker, *Following the Color Line* (two works by Northern writers).

H. A. Herbert, *Why the Solid South.*

Edwin Mims, *The Advancing South* (1926).

E. G. Murphy, *Problems of the Present South.*

T. N. Page, *The Negro, the Southerner's Problem.*

B. T. Washington, *The Negro Problem; The Story of the Negro; The Future of the Negro.*

Questions

1. Give the main subdivisions of the chapter.
2. Compare the condition of the South in 1865 with that of the North.
3. How does money capital contribute to prosperity? Describe the plight of Southern finance.

4. Give the chief steps in the restoration of white supremacy.

5. Give Lincoln's plan for amnesty. What principles do you think should govern the granting of amnesty?

6. How were the "force bills" overcome?

7. Compare the fourteenth and fifteenth amendments with regard to the suffrage provisions. Explain how they may be circumvented.

8. Account for the Solid South. What was the situation before 1860?

9. In what ways did Southern agriculture tend to become like that of the North? What were the social results?

10. Name the chief results of an "industrial revolution" in general. In the South, in particular.

11. What courses were open to freedmen in 1865?

12. Give the main features in the economic and social status of the colored population in the South.

Research Topics

Amnesty for Confederates. Study carefully the provisions of the fourteenth amendment in the Appendix. Macdonald, *Documentary Source Book of American History*, pp. 470 and 564. A plea for amnesty in Harding, *Select Orations Illustrating American History*, pp. 467–488.

Political Conditions in the South in 1868. Dunning, *Reconstruction, Political and Economic* (American Nation Series), pp. 109–123; Hart, *American History Told by Contemporaries*, Vol. IV, pp. 445–458, 497–500; Elson, *History of the United States*, pp. 764–770.

Movement for White Supremacy. Dunning, *Reconstruction*, pp. 266–280; Paxson, *The New Nation* (Riverside Series), pp. 39–58; Beard, *American Government and Politics*, pp. 499–502.

The Withdrawal of Federal Troops from the South. Sparks, *National Development* (American Nation Series), pp. 84–102; Rhodes, *History of the United States*, Vol. VIII, pp. 1–12.

Southern Industry. Paxson, *The New Nation*, pp. 192–207; T. M. Young, *The American Cotton Industry*, pp. 54–99.

Questions for Debate

1. The policy of the Republican Congress toward the South after the Civil War was justifiable.

2. The Fourteenth and Fifteenth Amendments should have been and should be enforced by legislation.

Historical Fiction

G. W. Cable, *John March, Southerner*.
Ellen Glasgow, *The Voice of the People*.
Thomas Nelson Page, *Red Rock*.

CHAPTER XIX

BUSINESS ENTERPRISE AND THE REPUBLICAN PARTY

The presidency of Lincoln was an era of war and sorrow. It was followed by the rush and roar of "business enterprise" — the tremendous, tireless energy of a virile people applied to the developing of natural resources of unparalleled richness. The chief goal of this effort was high profits for the captains of industry, on the one hand; and high wages for the workers, on the other. Its signs, to use the language of a Republican orator in 1876, were golden harvest fields, whirling spindles, turning wheels, open furnace doors, flaming forges, and chimneys filled with eager fire. The slogan written over factory doors was "prosperity." A Republican President was its "advance agent." Released from obstruction by Southern planters and the confusing issue of slavery which had checked the growth of the West, business enterprise sprang forward to the task of conquering the entire country. It even flung its outposts to the uttermost parts of the earth — Europe, Africa, and the Orient — where there were markets for American goods and more resources for American capital to develop.

RAILWAYS AND INDUSTRY

The Outward Signs of Enterprise. There are writers, fond of figures, who try to picture this business enterprise of their countrymen in terms of miles of railways constructed, factories built, men and women employed, fortunes made, wages paid, cities founded, rivers spanned, boxes, bales and tons produced. Historians, however, naturally contrast it with the past. Against the slow and leisurely stagecoach, they set the swift express rushing from New York to San Francisco in less time than Washington consumed in his triumphal tour from Mt. Vernon to New York for his inaugural. Against the lazy sailing vessel drifting before a genial breeze, they place the turbine steamer crossing the

439

Atlantic in five days or the still swifter airplane piloted by Colonel Charles Lindbergh making the journey in less than thirty-four hours. For the tiny workshop where a master and a dozen workmen and apprentices wrought by hand, they offer the giant factory where ten thousand persons or more attend revolving wheels driven by steam. Phrases, such as the "romance of invention" and "captains of industry," they see creeping into literature.

The Service of the Railway. All this is fitting in its way. Figures and contrasts, however, cannot describe the whole business adventure. Take, for example, the extension of railways. It is easy to say that there were 30,000 miles in 1860; 166,000 in 1890; and 242,000 in 1910. It is simple to show upon the map how a few straggling lines became a perfect mesh of railways; or how, like the tentacles of a great monster, the roads ending in the Mississippi Valley in 1860 were extended until they tapped every wheat field, mine, and forest beyond the Valley. Eloquent of enterprise as such an account truly is, it leaves out of the story some of the most important points. For example it does not tell that railways turned all America into one great market for goods; that they standardized the United States until cities on the Pacific had all the leading features of cities on the Atlantic; that in the West they were indeed the forerunners of civilization, the makers of homesteads, the builders of states. No other nation has a railway romance like that.

Government Aid for Railways. Still the story is not ended, for railways became almost as great an issue in American politics as slavery had been. After a long siege in Congress, government bounty was granted to make possible the building of western lines. By the year 1872 the federal government had given to railway promoters 155,000,000 acres of land — an area estimated as almost equal to that of Pennsylvania, New York, Connecticut, Rhode Island, Massachusetts, Maine, New Hampshire, and Vermont. The Union Pacific Company alone secured a free right of way through the public domain, twenty sections of land with each mile of railway, and a loan up to fifty millions of dollars secured by a second mortgage on the Company's property. More than half of the northern tier of states lying against Canada from Lake Michi-

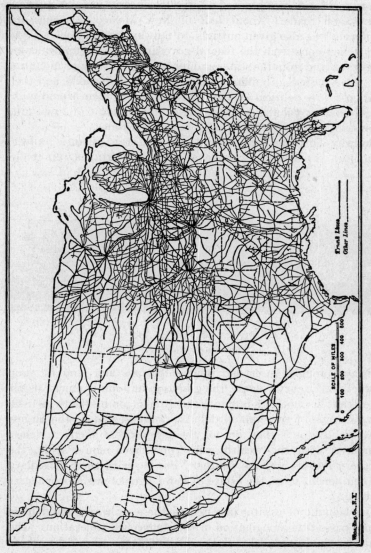

SCALE OF MILES
0 100 200 300 400 500

Trunk Lines
Other Lines

Wim. Eng. Co., N.Y.

RAILROADS OF THE UNITED STATES

gan to the Pacific was granted to private concerns in aid of railways and wagon roads. About half of New Mexico, Arizona, and California was also given outright to railway corporations. These vast concessions from the federal government were supplemented by gifts of land from the states and by stock subscriptions mounting into the hundreds of millions. The history of these gifts and their relation to the political leaders that engineered them would make an astounding volume to place beside the account of royal gifts of land in America to Englishmen in colonial times.

Railway Fortunes and Capital. Out of this gigantic railway promotion, the first really immense American fortunes were made.

Courtesy of Union Pacific System

UNION PACIFIC 4–12–2 TYPE LOCOMOTIVE
Built by the American Locomotive Company.

Railways brought surer and quicker profits than land for crop production. Henry Adams, the grandson of John Quincy Adams, stated that his mother's father, Peter Brooks, on his death in 1849, left a fortune of two million dollars, "supposed to be the largest estate in Boston," then one of the few centers of great riches. Compared with the wealth won from the Union Pacific, the Northern Pacific, and the Southern Pacific, with their subsidiary and component lines, the estate of Peter Brooks was a poor man's heritage.

The amount of capital invested in these railways would have simply passed the imagination of the stagecoach generation. The total Revolutionary debt of the United States — a debt which men of little faith thought the country could never pay — was reckoned at a figure well under $75,000,000. When the Union Pacific Railroad was completed, there were outstanding against it $27,000,000 in first-mortgage bonds, $27,000,000 in second-mortgage bonds held by the government, $10,000,000 in income bonds, $10,000,000 in land-grant bonds, and, on top of that huge bonded indebtedness, $36,000,000 in stock — making $110,000,000 in all. This sum far exceeded the whole funded debt of early days whose holders Jefferson feared as "a great money power." What would he have thought about the financial significance of railways?

Growth and Extension of Industry. In the field of manufacturing, mining, and metal working, business enterprise, if measured in mere dollars, far outstripped the results of railway construction. By the end of the century there were about ten billion dollars invested in factories alone and five million wage-earners employed in them; while the total value of the output, fourteen billion dollars, was fifteen times the figure for 1860. Industries multiplied in the Eastern states. They spread westward also until by the close of the century, Ohio had almost reached and Illinois had surpassed Massachusetts in the annual value of their manufactured goods.

Meanwhile tremendous wealth in the form of natural resources was disclosed in the South and West. Coal deposits were found in the Appalachians from Pennsylvania to Alabama, in Michigan, in the Mississippi Valley, and in the Western mountains from North Dakota to New Mexico. In nearly every coal-bearing region, iron was also discovered and the great fields of Michigan, Wisconsin, and Minnesota soon rivaled those of the Appalachian area. Copper, lead, gold, and silver in fabulous quantities were unearthed by prospectors who left no plain or mountain fastness unexplored. Petroleum, first pumped from the wells of Pennsylvania in the summer of 1859, made new fortunes matching those derived from trade, railways, manufacturing, and land speculation. It scattered its treasure with a lavish hand through Oklahoma, Texas, and California.

The Trust — An Instrument of Industrial Progress. Soon there appeared upon the scene business leaders with plans for gigantic companies. Their constructive genius brought together under one management hundreds of factories or thousands of miles of railways. For countless small undertakings competing with one another and so holding down the gains for all, they substituted great combinations checking such rivalry and controlling prices. As early as 1879, undercutting in oil, threatening disaster to everybody in the industry, led a number of companies in Cleveland, Pittsburgh, and Philadelphia to unite in saving themselves by price-fixing. Three years later groups of oil concerns joined forces and placed all their stocks in the hands of trustees, among whom was John D. Rockefeller. The trustees, in turn, issued to each shareholder a certificate for his stock, and took over the direction of the entire business themselves. Such was the nature of the "trust," soon to become a big issue in politics.

JOHN D. ROCKEFELLER

Gradually competition gave way to combination in iron and steel, copper, lead, sugar, cordage, and other commodities. Soon after they were formed, these giant trusts or corporations controlled, if not most of the output, at least enough to determine in a large measure the prices charged to consumers. Railways, mills, mines, and other business concerns followed in this change from individual to corporation control. At the end of the nineteenth century, three-fourths of the output of manufactures came from industries under corporate management and only one-fourth from individual and partnership undertakings.

The Banking Corporation. In former times a person who saved money either used it in his own enterprise, lent it to a neighbor, or hid it away where it set no industry in motion. Even in the early stages of modern business, it was common for a manufacturer to rise from small beginnings by financing extensions out of his earnings and profits. But the huge new corporations required millions and even billions of capital. The savings of a single person or of a few persons were so inadequate for the financing of trusts that banks had to be enlarged to meet demands.

In the process the banks became real directors of business. They undertook to sell the stocks and bonds issued by corporations and trusts, and to supply them with credit for operations. Indeed, many great mergers were brought about by bankers with millions and billions under their control. The United States Steel Corporation, for example, was formed by J. P. Morgan and Company. Through ties with one another, the banks made a perfect network of agencies all over the country, gathering up the pennies and dollars of the masses as well as the thousands of the rich and pouring them all into the channels of business. In the growth of banking on a national scale, a few great money centers, notably Wall Street in New York and State Street in Boston, took the leadership and the chief trusts established their offices close to this money market.

The Significance of the Corporation. The corporation thus became the striking feature of American business — comparable in its wealth and power and the number of its servants with kingdoms and states of old. It made possible gigantic enterprises once entirely beyond the reach of any individual, no matter how rich he might be. It stopped many of the costly wastes of competition in manufacturing, advertising, and selling. It studied the cheapest methods of production and shut down mills that were poorly equipped or badly located. It built laboratories for research in industry, chemistry, and mechanical invention. Through the sale of stocks and bonds in small lots, it enabled tens of thousands of people to become little capitalists interested in the success of business enterprise. The corporation made it possible for one person to own, for instance, a $50 share in a million-dollar concern — a thing entirely out of the question under a system of individual owners and simple partnerships.

There was, of course, another side to the picture. Many corporations tried to become monopolies and to make profits, not so much by good management as by charging high prices or taking advantage of their rivals. Sometimes they mercilessly crushed their competitors, bribed members of legislatures to secure favorable laws, and gave money to both political parties for the purpose of influencing elections. Wherever a trust got hold of most of the business in its field, it was able to check even the strongest trade unions in their efforts to raise wages or reduce hours. In short, the power of the trust in finance, in manufacturing, in politics, and in the field of labor control became a mighty factor in politics.

The Corporation and Labor. When master and workmen labored side by side in the era of small industries, the owner could not ignore his employees even if he would. He saw them day by day and all the day. They let him know when they thought he was taking unfair advantage of them. But for this more sympathetic tie between owner and employee, the trust brought another kind of relation. The owner disappeared from the corporation's giant factory and his place was taken by a manager sent by the trustees — first of all to make profits for the invisible owners of the stock. In this arrangement the corporation was called "soulless," for labor was apt to be viewed as a "commodity" to be bought and sold like material things without regard for the human element.

Cities and Immigration. As factories expanded, the cities which sheltered them and their employees naturally increased in size. In Washington's time nine-tenths of the American people were engaged in agriculture and lived in the country; in 1890 about one-third of them dwelt in towns of 2500 and over; in 1920 more than half were in towns of that rank. Forty years, between 1860 and 1900, saw Greater New York grow from 1,174,000 to 3,437,000; San Francisco from 56,000 to 342,000; Chicago from 109,000 to 1,698,000. The miles of city tenements began to rival, in the number of their inhabitants, the farm homesteads of the West. The time so dreaded by Jefferson had arrived. The republic of small farmers had passed away and people were "piled up on one another in great cities."

To the new industrial nation flowed annually an ever-swelling tide of immigration from all parts of the world, reaching the half million point in 1880; rising to three-quarters of a million three years later; and passing the million mark in a single year at the opening of the new century. Of course immigration was as old as America but its character was now materially altered. In the

BESSEMER BLAST IN ACTION
Bethlehem Steel Company's Mill at Buffalo, N. Y.

first place, there were marked changes in the nationality of the newcomers. Migration from Northern Europe — England, Ireland, Germany, and Scandinavia — diminished; that from Italy,

Russia, and Austria-Hungary multiplied until in the ten years
between 1900 and 1910 more than three-fourths of the immigrants
came from these three lands. Italians, Poles, Magyars, Czechs,
Slovaks, Croats, Russians, and Jews outnumbered the English,
Irish, and Germans.

In the second place, these newcomers could not be received
as well as earlier immigrants had been. There was no more free
land to provide them with homesteads. Besides, captains of
industry had encouraged them to come to America to work in the
mills and mines; so they pressed into labor camps or the great
industrial centers. They were crowded — nay, overcrowded —
into racial colonies where they preserved their languages, their
newspapers, and their old-world customs, views, and loyalties.

So eager were business men to get a cheap and abundant labor
supply that they asked few questions about the effect of this
"alien invasion" on the people already in America or the laborers
themselves. They even encouraged it by importing huge armies
of foreigners under contract to work in their industries. There
seemed to be no limit to the factories, forges, refineries, and railways that could be built, to the multitudes that could be employed
in conquering a continent, to the money that could be made by
captains of industry. As for the future, that was left to Providence!

Business Theories of Politics. Like the planters of the old
South, business men had their special theory of politics. And the
theory was very simple. "It is the duty of the government,"
they said, "to protect American industry against foreign competition by means of high tariffs on imported goods, to help this
industry flourish at home by encouraging the immigration of
European labor, to aid railways by generous grants of land, to
sell mineral and timber lands at low prices to energetic men ready
to develop them, and then to leave the rest to the initiative and
drive of private individuals and companies." As Calhoun had
called the slave system a perfect good, so business men in the North
now thought that their methods were perfectly good. Just as the
planters resented interference with their affairs so business men
opposed government interference with the management, prices,

rates, charges, and conduct of industry.   Judging from their
speeches and writings, they thought the nation was just a great

Copyright by Underwood and Underwood, N. Y.

BROAD STREET, NEAR WALL STREET, NEW YORK CITY

collection of individuals, companies, and labor unions mainly
struggling for profits or high wages, with the government serving
as a kind of policeman keeping the peace.

THE SUPREMACY OF THE REPUBLICAN PARTY (1861–1885)

Business Men and Republican Policies. Most of the leaders in industry were found in the Republican ranks. They worked in the North and the Republican party was essentially a Northern product. In its platforms, moreover, it indorsed the business program: protective tariffs, a sound monetary and banking system, promotion of railways and industry by land grants, and the development of internal improvements. It was generous in its immigration policy. It proclaimed America an asylum for the oppressed of all countries and flung wide the doors to all comers.

Sources of Republican Strength. For various reasons the Republican party grew into a political organization of great power. It had started in a wave of moral enthusiasm against slavery and had attracted to itself, if not the abolitionists, certain idealists like James Russell Lowell and George William Curtis, who had opposed slavery when it was neither safe nor popular to do so. With moral principles the party combined practical considerations. Business men believed in it. Workingmen who longed to become farmers owed to it their chance to get free homesteads in the West while the land lasted. Under a Republican administration, besides, the Union had been saved. To the Republican party veterans of the Union army were indebted for their pensions — rewards for military service surpassing in liberality anything that the world had ever seen. To the Republican party every investor in government bonds looked for the full payment of the interest and principal of the huge debt created in defense of the Union. In Republican hands were all the federal offices which the spoils system had made the property of the party in power. Federal employees could thus be relied upon to support the party that employed them.

Of all these things Republican leaders made full use. Sometimes they went too far in their party claims, as politicians of all parties often do. Particularly was this true in the case of saving the Union. "When in the economy of Providence, this land was to be purged of human slavery . . . the Republican party came into power," ran a declaration in one of their platforms. "The Republican party suppressed a gigantic rebellion, emancipated four million slaves, decreed the equal citizenship of all, and established universal suffrage," ran another. It so happened that aid was also rendered by millions of Northern Democrats who stood by the Union and by tens of thousands of Democrats who actually fought in the Union army. But the Republicans in their zeal were apt to forget this.

Republican Control of the South. To their natural strength in the North, the Republicans for a long time added the advantages due to control over the South where the newly enfranchised negroes gave a grateful support to the party mainly responsible for their freedom. These advantages they were unwilling to surrender — all the more because they believed control over the South was justified. Many of them were sincere friends of the freedmen and wanted to win for them complete civil and political equality, wiping out not only slavery but all its badges of servitude. Others had fought in forum and field to save the Union and regarded Republican supremacy after the war as necessary to prevent the leaders of secession from coming back to power. At the same time there were undoubtedly men of the baser sort who looked on politics as a mere game and who made use of federal military occupation of the South to "feather their own nests." At all events, both by laws and presidential acts, the Republicans for many years maintained their dominion in the South. Even South Carolina, where reposed the ashes of John C. Calhoun, went Republican in 1872 by a vote of three to one!

Republican rule was made easy by the force bills described in a previous chapter — measures which vested the supervision of elections in federal officers appointed by Republican Presidents. These drastic laws, the Republican authors claimed, were necessary to safeguard the polls in the South where timid freedmen might be frightened from using their votes, and also in the North, particularly in New York City where, it was alleged, Democrats were guilty of frauds.

The Democrats on their side hotly denied the charges, and replied that the force bills were nothing but schemes of the Republicans to keep themselves in office by interfering with elections. Likewise their measures of reconstruction, such as giving the suffrage to freedmen, were looked upon by Democratic leaders as so many tricks for establishing Republican supremacy throughout the country. "Nor is there the slightest doubt," exclaimed Samuel J. Tilden, spokesman of the Democrats in New York and candidate for President in 1876, "that the paramount object and motive of the Republican party is by these means to secure itself against a reaction of opinion adverse to it in our great populous Northern commonwealths. . . . When the Republican party resolved to establish negro supremacy in the ten states in order to gain to itself the representation of those states in Congress, it had to begin by governing the people of those states by the sword. . . . The next was the creation of new electoral bodies for those ten states, in which, by exclusions, by disfranchisements and proscriptions, by control over registration, by applying test oaths . . . by intimidation and by every form of influence, three million negroes are made to predominate over four and a half million whites."

The War as a Campaign Issue. Even the repeal of force bills could not allay the sectional feelings born of the war. The Republicans long insisted on calling the men who had so recently been in arms against the Union "traitors" and "rebels." The Southerners on the other hand regarded their opponents as political oppressors and applied to them epithets none too gentle — "Black Republicans," "blatherskites," and "renegades," for example. The passions of the war had been too strong; the distress too deep to be soon forgotten. The generation that went through it all remembered it all. For twenty years the Republicans made "a straight appeal to the patriotism of the Northern voters." They maintained that their party had saved the Union, emancipated the slaves, and was alone worthy of governing the nation.

Though the Democrats resented this policy and called it "waving the bloody shirt," the Republicans kept on "talking about the War of the Rebellion." As late as 1884 one of them expressed the hope that they might "wring one more President from the bloody shirt." They declared that the Democratic candidate, Grover Cleveland, had avoided serving in the war for the Union by hiring a substitute; and they complained that he had "insulted the Union veterans" by going fishing on Memorial Day.

Three Republican Presidents. Owing to their great strength, the Republicans were able to hold the presidency from 1869 to 1885. The three Presidents elected in this period, Grant, Hayes, and Garfield, had certain popular characteristics in common. They were all of origin humble enough to please the most exacting Jacksonian Democrat; that is, they sprang from "the people," as the phrase ran. They had all been officers in the Union army. Next to Lincoln, Grant was regarded as the savior of the Constitution. Hayes and Garfield, though lesser stars in the military heavens, had honorable records duly appreciated by Union soldiers, now organized into the Grand Army of the Republic and active in every campaign in fact if not in theory. It is true that Grant was not a politician and had never voted the Republican ticket; but this was overlooked, for he was glad to have the Republican nomination. Hayes and Garfield were loyal Republican party men. The former had served in Congress and for three terms as governor of his state. The latter had long been a member of the House of Representatives and was Senator-elect when he was called to the presidency.

They all possessed still another asset emphasized by their political managers. They were from Ohio, and Ohio was a strategic state. It lay between the manufacturing East and the agrarian West. With growing industries and wool to sell, it benefited from the protective tariff loved by the East. Yet being mainly agricultural still, it had some sympathy for the Western farmers who showed low-tariff or free-trade tendencies. Hence good strategy gave to the East a large share in shaping laws and framing policies and to the West the candidates. This division in privileges — very general in politics — was accompanied by a careful selection of the candidate for Vice President, no less than the President. With Garfield, for instance, was associated a prominent New York politician, Chester A. Arthur, who, as fate decreed, became President on the assassination of his superior.

The Disputed Election of 1876. Whether one of these three Presidents, Hayes, was actually the winner in the election of 1876 was a question. His Democratic opponent, Samuel J. Tilden, received a safe majority of the popular vote and had a claim to a majority of the electoral votes. Four states sent in double returns, one set for Tilden and another for Hayes. In these circumstances, both parties claimed the victory and the rivalry ran so high that there was actual talk of civil war again. Fortunately, in the end, peace prevailed. Congress provided for an electoral commission of fifteen members which, after reviewing the contested returns, decided in favor of Hayes. And Tilden was himself so temperate in the matter that the Democrats accepted the judgment though they did not think that Hayes was really entitled to the office.

THE GROWTH OF OPPOSITION TO REPUBLICAN RULE

Political Abuses. Their long tenure of power was not wholly creditable to the Republican party because many of its members were guilty of wrongdoing in office. For that matter neither did the Democrats manage to avoid such evils in states and cities where they had the majority. In New York City, for instance, the local Democratic organization, known as Tammany Hall, passed under the sway of "Boss" Tweed who plundered the treasury until public-spirited citizens rose in revolt, drove the ringleader from power, and sent him to jail — Samuel J. Tilden taking direction in this

"THAT'S WHAT'S THE MATTER."

Boss Tweed. "As long as I count the Votes, what are you going to do about it? say?"

ONE OF THE ANTI-TWEED CARTOONS IN "HARPER'S WEEKLY" BY THOMAS NAST

cleansing of his own party. On the other hand, in Philadelphia, Republican bosses were guilty of offenses as odious as those committed by New York Democrats. Indeed, just after the Civil War there were so many political scandals that one editor asked: "Are not all the great communities of the Western World growing more corrupt as they grow in wealth?"

In national politics, where the opportunities were greater, betrayals of public trust were especially flagrant. Members of Congress, it was found, accepted stocks and bonds in exchange for votes in favor of land grants and other concessions to railway companies. Revenue officers permitted whisky distillers to evade their taxes, in return for heavy bribes. A probe into the post-office department unearthed the malodorous "star route frauds" — the deliberate overpayment of favored mail carriers whose lines were marked in the official record by asterisks or stars. Even cabinet officers came under suspicion, for the trail of the serpent led straight to the door of a Secretary of War.

In the lower ranges, the spoils system became worse as the number of federal employees multiplied. Holders of offices and seekers of office were so numerous that they formed a regular political army. They crowded into Republican councils, hunting for favors from the government in power. They filled positions in the party ranging from the lowest township committee to the national convention. They became professional experts making politics their daily business. They helped to nominate candidates and draft platforms, elbowing aside the ordinary citizen who could only give a day now and then to political affairs. Even the Civil Service Act of 1883, wrung from Congress two years after the assassination of President Garfield by an office seeker made little change at first. It is true, the Act took away from the spoilsmen a few thousand government positions, but it did not stop the practice of rewarding party workers with government jobs.

This state of affairs discouraged many distinguished citizens. James Russell Lowell, for example, thought he saw a steady decline in public morals. In 1865, hearing of Lee's surrender, he had exclaimed: "There is something magnificent in having a country to love!" But in 1876, when asked to write an ode for the centennial of American independence, he could think only of a biting satire on the nation:

> "Show your state legislatures; show your Rings;
> And challenge Europe to produce such things
> As high officials sitting half in sight
> To share the plunder and fix things right.

If that don't fetch her, why, you need only
To show your latest style in martyrs — Tweed:
She'll find it hard to hide her spiteful tears
At such advance in one poor hundred years."

When critics abused him for his "attack upon his native land," Lowell replied sadly: "These fellows have no notion of what love of country means. It was in my very blood and bones. If I am not an American who ever was? . . . What fills me with doubt and dismay is the degradation of the moral tone. Is it or is it not a result of democracy? Is ours a 'government of the people, by the people, for the people,' or a Kakistocracy [a government of the worst], rather for the benefit of knaves at the cost of fools?"

A Reform Movement within the Republican Ranks. Views set forth by Lowell, himself a Republican, were shared by others in his party. In fact, very soon after the close of the Civil War members of the rank and file began to protest against the conduct of their chiefs. In 1872 a group, calling themselves Liberal Republicans, broke away from the party, nominated a candidate of their own, Horace Greeley, and put forward a platform criticizing the Republican President fiercely enough to please the stoutest Democrat. They accused Grant of using "the powers and opportunities of his high office for the promotion of personal ends." They charged him with retaining "notoriously corrupt and unworthy men in places of power and responsibility." They alleged that the Republican party kept "alive the passions and resentments of the late civil war . . . for their own advantage" and employed the "public service of the government as a machinery of corruption."

There were not enough Liberals, however, to elect Greeley; he was defeated even though the Democrats indorsed him. As a result most Republican reformers decided that independent action was useless. So, at least, it was regarded by the younger men of the rising generation, like Henry Cabot Lodge of Massachusetts and Theodore Roosevelt of New York — until the latter attempted it himself in after years. Pointing to Greeley's failure they insisted that reformers who desired to rid the party of abuses should do their work "on the inside."

The Mugwumps and Cleveland Democracy in 1884. In spite of Republican dissensions, the Democrats were slow to make headway themselves. They no longer had the capable direction of planters, such as Calhoun, Davis, and Toombs; they were charged by their opponents with being "guilty" of secession; and they were stripped of the support of the South while it was under Republican control. Not until the last Southern state was restored to the Union, not until a general pardon for Confederates was wrung from Congress, not until white supremacy was regained at the polls and the last federal soldier withdrawn from Southern capitals did the Democrats succeed in capturing the presidency.

Their return to power came in 1884 when a number of circumstances favored them. They were especially lucky in finding a candidate who had no political enemies in national politics, Grover Cleveland, then governor of New York and widely celebrated as a man of "sterling honesty." They were aided in their cause by the fact that the Republican nominee, James G. Blaine, of Maine, was under fire from the reformers in his own party. Indeed, a number of dissatisfied Republicans openly deserted Blaine and supported Cleveland — among them Carl Schurz, George William Curtis, and William Everett, men of fine ideals and undoubted integrity. Though the "regular" Republicans called them "Mugwumps" and laughed at them as the "men milliners, the dilettanti, and carpet knights of politics," they threw many votes to the Democratic side.

The campaign which took place that year was one of the most savage in American history. Issues were thrust into the background. Even the tariff was not taken seriously. Personal abuse was the favorite weapon of party orators. On their part the Democrats insisted that "the Republican party so far as principle is concerned is a reminiscence. In practice it is an organization for enriching those who control its machinery." For Blaine, they could hardly find words biting enough. The Republicans answered in kind. They praised their own good works and denounced the "fraud and violence practised by the Democracy in the Southern states." They attacked Cleveland's character in revenge for attacks upon Blaine. Perhaps never in the record of political campaigns did speakers and editors sink to so low a level. Decent people were sickened. Moreover, nothing was decided by the balloting. Cleveland was elected, but his victory was a narrow one. A shift of a few hundred votes in New York City would have sent his opponent to the White House instead. His majority was too small to give him the backing for a strong administration.

Changing Political Fortunes (1886–96).   In his message of 1887 he attacked the tariff as "vicious, inequitable, and illogical"; as a system of taxation that laid a burden upon "every consumer in the land for the benefit of our manufacturers." This tariff message the Republicans called a free-trade assault upon the industries of the country.   Largely on that issue they elected to the presidency, in 1888, Benjamin Harrison of Indiana, a shrewd lawyer, descendant of the hero of Tippecanoe, and son of the old Northwest.   Thinking that victory was an order from the people to protect American industries, the Republicans, under the leadership of William McKinley in the House of Representatives, enacted in 1890 a tariff law imposing the highest duties on imports yet laid in the United States.   But their judgment of what was popular was wrong.   That very autumn they lost seats in the congressional elections, and two years later they were beaten in the presidential campaign. With Cleveland as their candidate again in 1892, the Democrats carried the country with a bigger vote than in 1884.

References

W. Kaempffert, *A Popular History of American Invention.*

L. H. Haney, *Congressional History of Railways* (2 vols.).

J. P. Davis, *The Union Pacific Railway.*

J. M. Swank, *History of the Manufacture of Iron.*

M. T. Copeland, *The Cotton Manufacturing Industry in the United States* (Harvard Studies).

Allan Nevins, *Emergence of Modern America* (1865–1878).

Ida Tarbell, *History of the Standard Oil Company* (Critical).

G. H. Montague, *Rise and Progress of the Standard Oil Company* (Friendly).

H. P. Fairchild, *Immigration*, and F. J. Warne, *The Immigrant Invasion* (Both works favor exclusion).

I. A. Hourwich, *Immigration* (Against exclusionist policies).

J. F. Rhodes, *History of the United States*, 1877–1896, Vol. VIII.
Edward Stanwood, *A History of the Presidency*, Vol. I, for the presidential elections of the period.

Questions

1. Contrast the state of industry and commerce at the close of the Civil War with its condition at the close of the Revolutionary War.
2. Enumerate the services rendered to the nation by the railways.
3. Explain the peculiar relation of railways to government.
4. What sections of the country have been industrialized?
5. How do you account for the rise and growth of the trusts? Explain some of the economic advantages of the trust. The disadvantages.
6. Are the people in cities more or less independent than the farmers? What was Jefferson's view?
7. State some of the problems raised by unrestricted immigration.
8. What was the theory of the relation of government to business in this period?
9. State the leading economic policies sponsored by the Republican party.
10. Why were the Republicans especially strong immediately after the Civil War?
11. What illustrations can you give showing the influence of war in American political campaigns?
12. Account for the strength of middle-western candidates.
13. Enumerate some of the abuses that appeared in American politics after 1865.
14. Sketch the rise of the reform movement.
15. How was the fluctuating state of public opinion reflected in the elections from 1880 to 1892?

Research Topics

Invention, Discovery, and Transportation. Sparks, *National Development* (American Nation Series), pp. 37–67; Bogart, *Economic History of the United States*, Chaps. XXI, XXII, and XXIII.

Business and Politics. Paxson, *The New Nation* (Riverside Series), pp. 92–107; Rhodes, *History of the United States*, Vol. VII, pp. 1–29, 64–73, 175–206; Wilson, *History of the American People*, Vol. IV, pp. 78–96.

Immigration. Coman, *Industrial History of the United States* (2d ed.), pp. 369–374; E. L. Bogart, *Economic History of the United States*, pp. 420–422, 434–437; Jenks and Lauck, *Immigration Problems;* Commons, *Races and Immigrants*.

The Disputed Election of 1876. Haworth, *The United States in Our Own Time*, pp. 82–94; Dunning, *Reconstruction, Political and Economic* (American Nation Series), pp. 294–341; Elson, *History of the United States*, pp. 800–806.

Abuses in Political Life. Dunning, *Reconstruction*, pp. 281–293; see criticisms in party platforms in Stanwood, *History of the Presidency*, Vol. I; Bryce, *American Commonwealth* (1910 ed.), Vol. II, pp. 136–167; 379–448.

Studies of Presidential Administrations. (*a*) Grant, (*b*) Hayes, (*c*) Garfield-Arthur, (*d*) Cleveland, and (*e*) Harrison, in Haworth, *The United States in Our Own Time*, or in Paxson, *The New Nation* (Riverside Series), or still more briefly in Elson.

Cleveland Democracy. Haworth, *The United States*, pp. 164–183; Rhodes, *History of the United States*, Vol. VIII, pp. 240–327; Elson, pp. 843–870.

Analysis of Modern Immigration Problems. *Syllabus in History* (New York State, 1919), pp. 110–112.

Questions for Debate

1. The "trusts" have been a beneficial factor in our industrial development.

2. The Civil Service System secures the best conduct of government business.

Historical Fiction

Irving Bacheller, *Cricket Heron.*
Winston Churchill, *Coniston.*
W. Allen White, *A Certain Rich Man.*

CHAPTER XX

THE DEVELOPMENT OF THE GREAT WEST

When the new era of business enterprise opened in 1865, Kansas and Texas were sentinel states on the middle frontier. Beyond the Rockies, California, Oregon, and Nevada stood guard — the last of them admitted to the Union in 1864. Between the middle and the far frontiers lay a vast reach of plain, desert, plateau, and mountain, almost wholly undeveloped. This huge domain, extending from Canada to Mexico, had fewer than half a million inhabitants. No railway line stretched across it. St. Joseph on the Missouri was the terminus of the Eastern lines. Twenty-five days were required for the overland journey from Missouri to California by the stage-coach system, established in 1858, and more than ten days for the swift pony express, organized in 1860. Indians still roamed the plain and desert and more than one powerful tribe disputed the white man's title to the soil.

THE RAILWAYS AS TRAIL BLAZERS

Building Railways to the Pacific. For many years before the crisis of 1861 the importance of a rail connection between the East and the Pacific Coast had been well understood. Advocates of the plan had already asked Congress to pass a law authorizing such a railroad and to grant land and money in its aid. Democrats and Republicans both approved the idea, but they could not agree on the place where the road should be built. Southern statesmen wanted to run the line from the Gulf through Texas to the Pacific, while Northerners stood out for a central route. Neither side would yield an inch.

The North had its way during the war. By legislation begun in 1862, Congress provided for the organization of companies to build a railroad from the Missouri River to California and, as we

461

have seen, granted land and money to aid in the enterprise. The western end, the Central Pacific, was built, in the main, by Chinese labor under the direction of Leland Stanford. A large part of the money for it was furnished by the Mormons of Utah and by the state government, ranchmen, miners, and business men of California. The eastern end, the Union Pacific, starting at Omaha, was financed chiefly by Eastern capital and was constructed principally by veterans of the Civil War and immigrants from Ireland and Germany. When the two companies met near Ogden, Utah, in 1869, the last spike uniting the Atlantic and the Pacific was driven amid a great demonstration of thanksgiving.

Courtesy of The Metropolitan Museum of Art
A Railway Builder
A Sculpture by Mahonri Young.

Other lines to the Pacific were now proposed; but the business panic of 1873 checked railway building for a while. When prosperity returned, however, construction was renewed and the year 1883 saw a series of railway triumphs. In February trains were running from New Orleans through Houston, San Antonio, and Yuma to San Francisco, as the result of a union of the Texas Pacific with the Southern Pacific and other companies. In September the finishing touch was given to the Northern Pacific at Helena, Montana. Lake Superior was now united with Puget Sound. That same year a third line was opened to the Pacific by way of the Atchison, Topeka, and Santa Fé, making connections through Albuquerque and Needles with San Francisco. All parts of the Far West were accessible to settlement and business enterprise.

UNITED STATES IN 1870

Western Railways Precede Settlement. Everywhere in this region promoters went to work at the task of bringing immigrants to occupy the great open spaces. Empire builders bought railway lands in huge tracts; they acquired more from the government; they planned new cities. With towns on maps and railway and steamboat connections established with the rest of the world, they sent out missionaries to tell the people "back East" about the wonderful farming land and business opportunities in the West. Their converts they carried west bag and baggage in long trains. The spirit of this enterprise speaks through the following advertisement of the time, telling about a proposed railway to cut through a new region: "This extension will run 42 miles from York, northeast through the Island Lake country, and will have five good North Dakota towns. The stations on the line will be well equipped with elevators and will be constructed and ready for operation at the commencement of the grain season. Prospective merchants have been active in securing desirable locations at the different towns on the line. There are still opportunities for hotels, general merchandise, hardware, furniture, and drug stores, etc."

Among the railway promoters and builders of the West, James J. Hill, of the Great Northern and allied lines, was one of the most forceful figures. He knew that tracks and trains were useless without passengers and freight; without a population of farmers and town dwellers to furnish business for them. He therefore advertised the advantages of the new West widely in the Virginias, Iowa, Ohio, Indiana, Illinois, Wisconsin, and Nebraska especially. To prospective settlers his agents said: "You see your children come out of school with no chance to get farms of their own because the cost of land in your older part of the country is so high that you can't afford to buy land to start your sons out in life around you. They have to go to the cities to make a living or become laborers in the mills or hire out as farm hands. There is no future for them there. . . . You farmers talk of free trade and protection and what this or that political party will do for you. Why don't you vote a homestead for yourself? That is the only thing Uncle Sam will ever give you. Jim Hill hasn't an acre of land to sell you. We are not in the real estate business. We don't want you to go

out West and make a failure of it because the rates at which we
haul you and your goods make the first transaction a loss. . . .
We must have landless men for a manless land."

Unlike steamship companies drumming up emigrants in Europe
just to get the fares, Hill was seeking permanent settlers who
would raise farm produce, manufacture goods, and use the railways
as the means of exchange. Hence he fixed low rates for the railway
journey to the West and let his passengers take some cattle and
furniture free. His plan was so reasonable that thousands of
families answered his call. In 1894, a vanguard of home seekers
left Indiana in fourteen passenger coaches, filled with men, women,
and children, accompanied by forty-eight freight cars carrying
household goods and live stock. In the next ten years 100,000
people from the Middle West and the South, responding to Hill's
appeals, went to the Western country where they brought millions
of acres of prairie land under cultivation.

When Hill got his people on the land, he took an interest in
everything that related to their prosperity. Was the output of
produce for his freight cars kept down by bad drainage on the
farms? He then concerned himself with ditching and tiling.
Were farmers hampered in hauling their goods to his trains by bad
roads? In that case, he urged the states to build better highways.
Did the traffic slacken because the food shipped was not of the
best quality? Then live stock must be improved and scientific
farming promoted. Did the farmers need money to get started?
Banks must be founded close at hand to advance it.

Indeed, Hill neglected no opportunity to increase the traffic
on his railway lines. He wanted no empty cars running in either
direction and no wheat stored in warehouses for the lack of markets.
Seeking an outlet for the surplus of the farms he looked to the
Orient as well as to Europe. He sent agents to China and Japan
to discover what American goods and produce those countries
might buy and what manufactures they had to offer to Americans
in exchange. To open the Pacific trade he bought two great steamships, the *Minnesota* and the *Dakota*. When some Japanese agents
came to the United States on their way to Europe to buy steel
rails, Hill showed them how easy it was for them to make their

purchases in this country and ship by way of American railways and American vessels. So the railway builder and promoter, who helped to break the virgin soil of the prairies, lived through the pioneer epoch and into the age of great finance. Before he died he saw the wheat fields of North Dakota linked with the spinning jennies of Manchester and the docks of Yokohama.

The Evolution of Grazing and Agriculture

Indians in the West. Unlike the frontier of New England in colonial days or that of Kentucky later, the advancing line of home builders in the Far West had little difficulty with warlike natives. It is true, Indian attacks were made on railway construction gangs; General Custer had his fatal battle with the Sioux in 1876 and there were minor brushes; but none of them checked the westward march of the white people. Indeed from first to last, the United States Army made the way smooth for oncoming settlers. The former practice of dealing with the Indians as independent nations was given up by Congress in 1871 and many tribes were removed to special reservations where they were mainly supported by the government. Control over their affairs was vested in 1869 in a board of commissioners with orders to treat the Indians as wards of the nation — a trust which unhappily was too often betrayed. A further step in policy was taken in 1887 when individual Indians were allowed to acquire government land, become citizens, and settle down among their white neighbors as farmers or cattle raisers. The disappearance of the buffalo, the chief source of food supply for the wild Indians, had made them more and more willing to surrender the freedom of the hunter for the routine of the reservation, ranch, or wheat field. At last in 1924 Congress declared that all Indians born within the United States were American citizens.

The Cowboy and Cattle Ranger. Between the frontier of farms and the mountains were plains and semi-arid regions in vast reaches suitable for grazing. As soon as the railways were open into the Missouri Valley, affording an outlet for shipments, cattle and sheep raising began on an immense scale. In this scene the far-famed American cowboy was the hero. Great herds of cattle were bred in Texas and as spring came on they were driven northward across the plains and over the buffalo trails. In a single year, 1884, it is estimated that nearly one million head of cattle were moved out of Texas to the North by four thousand cowboys, supplied with thirty thousand horses and ponies.

From 1870 to 1890 cattle men and sheep raisers had an almost free run of the country; they used public lands without paying for the privilege; and they often waged war on one another over the possession of ranges. At length, however, both lost this large liberty, for homesteaders and land companies fenced in the plain with endless lines of barbed wire. In 1893 a writer familiar with the frontier lamented that the age of the cowboys was about over: "Towns are growing up on their pasture lands; irrigation schemes of a dozen sorts threaten to turn bunch-grass scenery into farm-land views; farmers are preëmpting valleys and the sides of waterways;

Courtesy of The Metropolitan Museum of Art
A SINGING COWBOY
Another water color by Eakins.

and the day is not far distant when stock-raising must be done mainly in small herds, with winter corrals, and then the cowboy's days will end. Even now his condition disappoints those who knew him only half a dozen years ago. His breed seems to have deteriorated and his ranks are filling with men who work for wages rather than for love of the free life and bold companionship that once tempted men into that calling. Splendid Cheyenne saddles are less and less numerous in the outfits; the distinctive hat that made its way up from Mexico may or may not be worn; all the civil authorities in nearly all towns in the grazing country forbid the wearing of side arms; nobody shoots up these towns any more. The fact is the old simon-pure cowboy days are gone."

Settlement under the Homestead Act of 1862. The rapid settlement of Western lands which swept away the Indians and the cowboys was encouraged by railway companies and the federal government. The former adopted the policy of selling large blocks of their land at low prices to induce immigration. Congress helped on the process in 1862 by passing the Homestead law which, as we have indicated, provided that public lands should be given away in lots of 160 acres. The applicant for a homestead merely had to pay a small entrance fee and then occupy his farm for five years in order to get outright ownership. Even this five-year rule was waived in the case of the Union veterans, who were allowed to count their term of military service as a part of the period of residence required. As the soldiers of the Revolutionary and Mexican wars had advanced in large numbers to the frontier in earlier days, so now veterans of the Civil War led in the occupation of the New West. With them went thousands of Germans, Irish, and Scandinavian immigrants, fresh from the Old World. Between 1867 and 1874, 27,000,000 acres were staked out in quarter-section farms. In twenty years (1860–80) the population of Nebraska leaped from 28,000 to almost half a million; Kansas from 100,000 to a million; Iowa from 600,000 to 1,600,000 and the Dakotas from 5000 to 140,000. By 1890 free land had passed.

The Diversity of Western Agriculture. In soil, produce, and methods of tillage, Western agriculture presented many contrasts with that of the East and South. To be sure the typical American unit — the small farm tilled by the owner — appeared as usual in the arable and well-watered regions; but by its side was often staked out a huge domain owned by Eastern or foreign companies and cultivated by hired labor. Sometimes the great estate took the shape of a "bonanza farm" devoted mainly to wheat and corn, raised on a large scale by machinery. At other times, it assumed the form of a cattle ranch embracing tens of thousands of acres over which roamed enormous herds of horses, cows, and sheep. Again it was a vast holding of diversified uses, such as the Santa Anita ranch near Los Angeles, a domain of 60,000 acres "cultivated in a glorious sweep of vineyards and orange and olive orchards, rich sheep and cattle pastures and horse ranches."

Irrigation. In another respect agriculture in the Far West was unique. Over a large area spreading through eight states — Montana, Idaho, Wyoming, Utah, Colorado, Nevada, Arizona, New Mexico, and parts of adjoining states — the rainfall was so slight that the ordinary crops known to American farmers could not be produced at all. The Mormons were the first Anglo-Saxons to tackle aridity and they were baffled for a time; but after studying the problem, they solved it for themselves by building great irrigation works. Other settlers pouring into the West also attacked the desert with a will, some of them saying that it was easier to scoop out an irrigation ditch than to cut forests and wrestle with stumps and stones. Private companies bought immense desert areas at low prices, built irrigation works, and then sold their lands in small plots at a good profit. Ranchers with an instinct for water, like that of the miner for metal, sank wells into the dry sand and were rewarded with gushers that "soused the thirsty desert and turned its good-for-nothing sand into good-for-anything loam." In 1894, Congress came to the aid of the farmers by granting federal lands to the states to be used for irrigation purposes. In this work Wyoming took the lead by passing a law which encouraged capitalists to invest in irrigation and at the same time provided for the sale of redeemed lands to actual settlers. Finally in 1902 Congress joined in the conquest of the desert by passing the Reclamation Act providing federal funds for the construction of dams and water canals.

"Nowhere," writes E. A. Powell, in his picturesque *End of the Trail*, "has the white man fought a more courageous fight or won a more brilliant victory than in Arizona. His weapons have been the transit and the level, the drill and the dredge, the pick and the spade; and the enemy which he has conquered has been the most stubborn of all foes — the hostile forces of Nature. . . . The story of how the white man within the space of less than thirty years penetrated, explored, and mapped this almost unknown region; of how he carried law, order, and justice into a section which had never had so much as a speaking acquaintance with any one of the three before; of how, realizing the necessity for means of communication, he built highways of steel across this territory from east to west and from north to south; of how, undismayed by the savageness of the countenance which the desert turned upon him, he laughed and turned up his sleeves, and spat upon his hands, and slashed the face of the desert with canals and irrigating ditches, and filled those ditches with water brought from deep in the earth or high in the mountains; and of how, in the conquered and submissive soil, he replaced the aloe with the alfalfa, the mesquite with maize, the cactus with cotton, forms one of the most inspiring chapters in our history. It is one of the epics of civilization, this reclamation of the Southwest, and its heroes, thank God, are Americans. . . .

"The Arizonians, mindful of the fact that God, the government, and Carnegie help those who help themselves, spent their days wielding the pick and shovel, and their evenings in writing letters to Washington with toil-hardened hands. After a time the government was prodded into action and the great dams of Laguna and Roosevelt are the result. Then the people, organizing themselves into coöperative leagues and water-users' associations, took up the work of reclamation where the government left off; it is to these energetic, persevering men who have drilled wells, plowed fields, and dug ditches through the length and breadth of that great region which stretches from Yuma to Tucson, that the metamorphosis of Arizona is due."

The effect of irrigation was amazing. Wastes of sand and sagebrush gave way to fertile fields bearing crops of wheat, corn, fruits, vegetables, and grass. Huge ranges grazed by sheep were divided into small plots for farming. In the man-made garden spots rose prosperous communities — communities unlike the townships of Iowa and the industrial centers of Massachusetts. Their intensive tillage left little room for hired labor. Their small holdings drew families together in close social life instead of dispersing them on the lonely plain. Often water-power plants were built in connection with irrigation works to supply electricity for labor-saving devices, thus carrying many a burden that in other days fell heavily upon the shoulders of the farmer and his family.

Mining and Manufacturing in the West

Mineral Resources. In yet another striking feature the Far West differed from the Mississippi Valley at least — that was in the supremacy of mining over agriculture throughout a huge portion of its area. Indeed it was the minerals rather than the land that attracted the first pioneers. The discovery of gold in California in 1848 was the signal for a great rush of prospectors, miners, and promoters who explored the valleys, climbed the hills, washed the sands, and dug up the soil in their feverish search for gold, silver, copper, coal, and other ores. In Nevada and Montana a development of mineral resources went on during the Civil War helping the North to finance its campaigns. Alder Gulch became Virginia City in 1863; Last Chance Gulch was named Helena in 1864; and Confederate Gulch was christened Diamond City in 1865. At Butte miners began operations in 1864 and within five years had washed out eight million dollars' worth of gold. Under the gold they found silver; under silver, copper.

Even at the end of the nineteenth century, after cattle raising and agriculture were well advanced, minerals continued to be the chief source of wealth in a number of states. This was revealed by the figures for 1910. The gold, silver, iron, and copper of Colorado were worth more than the wheat, corn, and oats combined; the copper of Montana sold for more than all her cereals and four times the price of her wheat. The interest of Nevada was also mainly mining, the annual receipts from that source being $43,000,000 or more than one-half the national debt of Hamilton's day. The yield of the mines of Utah was worth four or five times the wheat crop; the coal of Wyoming brought twice as much as her great wool clip; the minerals of Arizona were totaled at $43,000,000 as against a wool clip reckoned at $1,200,000; in Idaho alone of this group of states did the wheat crop exceed in value the output of the mines.

Timber Resources. The forests of the great West, unlike those of the Ohio Valley, proved a boon to the pioneers rather than a foe to be attacked. In Ohio and Indiana, for example, frontier homemakers had to cut, roll, and burn thousands of trees before they could put out a crop of any size. Beyond the Mississippi, however, all ready for the breaking plow were broad reaches of almost treeless prairie, where every stick of timber was precious. In the other parts, often rough and mountainous, stood primeval forests of the finest woods which furnished business for the railroads, besides supplying them with ties, bridge timbers,

Photograph from Underwood and Underwood, N. Y.
LOGGING

and telegraph poles. Surplus lumber, such as had burdened the pioneers of the Northwest territory a hundred years before, they carried to markets, East and West.

Western Industries. Certain peculiar conditions of the Far West led to a rise of industries more rapid than is usual in a new country. For instance the mining activities, which in many sections preceded agriculture, called for sawmills to furnish timber for the mines and for smelters to reduce and refine ores. Huge ranches supplying sheep and cattle suggested the construction of the packing houses at Kansas City and other shipping centers.

The waters of the Northwest afforded salmon for 4000 cases of canned fish in 1866 and for 1,400,000 cases in 1916. The very abundance of California's fruits and vegetables made necessary the quick erection of numerous canneries. The lumber industry, starting with crude sawmills to provide rough timbers for railways and mines, ended in special factories for paper, boxes, and furniture. Moreover, the railways, built in many regions previous to settlement, offered an advance outlet for manufactures, and so encouraged the establishment of industries long before there were enough farmers to create a local market.

Social Effects of Western Economy. In many respects the social life of the Far West also was unlike that of other regions of the United States. Treeless prairies, though open to homesteads, were often occupied by great estates tilled in part by tenants and in part by migratory laborers who came from all sections of the country especially in harvest time. From the mineral resources of the Far West were derived huge mining fortunes which made the riches of Eastern mercantile families look trivial by comparison. Other millions were won in the railway business and from the cattle and sheep ranges. In fact in certain districts the "cattle king," as he was called, was as dominant as the planter had been in the old South, though he usually had different political views. Everywhere in the grazing country he was an important person. He "sometimes invested money in banks, in railroad stocks, or in city property. . . . He had his rating in the commercial reviews and could hobnob with bankers, railroad presidents, and metropolitan merchants. . . . He attended party caucuses and conventions, ran for the state legislature, and sometimes defeated a lawyer or metropolitan 'business man' in the race for a seat in Congress. In proportion to their numbers, the ranchers . . . have constituted a highly impressive class."

Although many of the early capitalists of the Far West, especially from Nevada, spent much of their money in the East, others tried to do something for the sections in which they had made their fortunes. A railroad pioneer, General Palmer, built his home at Colorado Springs, founded the town, and encouraged local improvements. Denver owed its first big buildings to the civic patriotism of Horace Tabor, a wealthy mine owner. Leland Stanford paid his tribute to California by endowing a university. Colonel W. F. Cody, better known as "Buffalo Bill," after starting his career with a "boom town" which collapsed, made a large sum of money supplying buffalo meat to construction hands (hence his popular name), raised it to a fortune by his famous Wild West Show, and used it chiefly in promoting a Western reclamation scheme.

While business enterprise was advancing rapidly in the Far West, an industrial population was following in its train. Even cattle ranges and hundreds of farms were carried on very much like factories, for they were managed by overseers who hired plowmen harvesters, and cattlemen at regular wages — often merely for a few weeks in the year. Mining, lumbering, and fruit-growing also employed thousands of workers during rush months and turned them off in the "slack" season. The inevitable result of such conditions was armies of migratory laborers wandering from camp to camp, from town to town, and from ranch to ranch, without homes or fixed habits of life. Owing principally to this state of affairs many long and lawless conflicts were waged between capital and labor in the Far West, giving peculiar features to the trade union and labor movement.

THE ADMISSION OF NEW STATES

The Spirit of Self-Government. Whenever a few residents were settled permanently in any Western region, they usually took steps to form a regular government. If federal officers were at hand to help in the undertaking they were welcomed, but if no such aid was forthcoming, then the people on the ground simply arranged some plan for managing community affairs themselves. To assist in the process of self-government, Congress, from time to time, divided the federal domain in the West into territories — each with a governor appointed by the President and a legislature elected by the voters.

As long as a region was nothing but a territory, however, the selection of the governor and other officers was controlled by politics at Washington. Moreover the disposition of land, mineral

A Town on the Prairie

rights, forests, and water power was also in the hands of federal authorities. Thus practical reasons united with the spirit of independence in the demand for statehood. The moment a territory had more than a handful of people a cry went up for admission to the Union.

Nebraska and Colorado. Two regions, Nebraska and Colorado, had little difficulty in securing that privilege. The first, Nebraska, had been organized as a territory by the famous Kansas-Nebraska bill which did so much to bring on the Civil War. Lying to the north of Kansas, which had been admitted in 1861, it escaped an invasion of slave owners from Missouri and was settled largely by farmers from the North. Though it claimed a population of only 67,000 it was regarded with kindly interest by the Republican Congress at Washington and, reduced to its present boundaries, it was given the coveted statehood in 1867.

This transaction was scarcely completed when Congress heard from the people of Colorado to the southwest. Though numbering only a few thousand they had been organized under territorial government in 1861 and within ten years they could point to an astonishing growth. Silver and gold deposits in the Leadville and Cripple Creek districts had attracted an army of miners and prospectors. The city of Denver, founded in 1858 and named after the governor of Kansas, whence came many of the early settlers, had grown from a straggling camp of log huts into a prosperous center of trade. By 1875 it was reckoned that the population of the territory was not less than 100,000; accordingly in the following year Congress bowed to the popular appeal and made Colorado a member of the Union.

Six New States (1889–90). For many years afterward a deadlock in Congress prevented the admission of any more states. Not until 1889 was the spell broken on petitions from the Dakotas. The Dakota territory, organized in 1861, had been looked upon as the home of the Sioux Indians whose huge reservation lay in the path of the advancing frontier. But discovery of gold in the Black Hills marked their doom. Even before Congress could open their lands to miners, pioneers in search of fresh soil to till commenced to swarm over the Dakota country. Farmers from adjoining Min-

nesota and from the Eastern states, Scandinavians, Germans, and
Canadians came in swelling waves to occupy the fertile Dakota
regions, famous even as far away as the fjords of Norway. Seldom
had the plow of man cut through richer soil than was found in the
bottoms of the Red River Valley, and its lure became still stronger
after 1883 when the completion of the Northern Pacific afforded a
means of transportation east and west. The population of Dakota,
which had numbered 135,000 in 1880, passed the half million mark
before ten years had elapsed.

Remembering that Nebraska had been admitted with only
67,000 inhabitants, the Dakotans could not see why they should
be kept under territorial government. At the same time Washington, far away on the Pacific Coast, Montana, Idaho, and Wyoming, boasting of their populations and their riches, put in their
own eloquent pleas. But Congress delayed until 1889, when it
finally received into the Union North and South Dakota, Washington, and Montana. The next year it admitted Idaho and
Wyoming, the latter with woman suffrage which had been granted
by the territorial legislature.

Utah. Although Utah was a well-settled and industrious community, its admission was put off on account of popular hostility
to polygamy. The custom, it is true, had been prohibited by act
of Congress in 1862; but the law had been evaded. In 1882 Congress made another effort to stamp out polygamy. Five years later
it even went so far as to authorize federal officers to seize the property of the Mormon Church in case the practice of plural marriages
was not stopped. Meanwhile, the Gentile or non-Mormon population was steadily increasing, and, at length, the leaders in the
Church saw that it was useless to struggle any more against the
sentiment of the majority of the American people. So they gave
up the battle in 1896 and Utah was admitted as a state under a
constitution which forbade plural marriages absolutely and forever. Horace Greeley, who visited Utah in 1859, had prophesied
that the Pacific Railroad would work a revolution in the land of
Brigham Young and his prophecy came true.

Rounding out the Continent. Only three continental territories
now remained out of the Union. Oklahoma, once an Indian

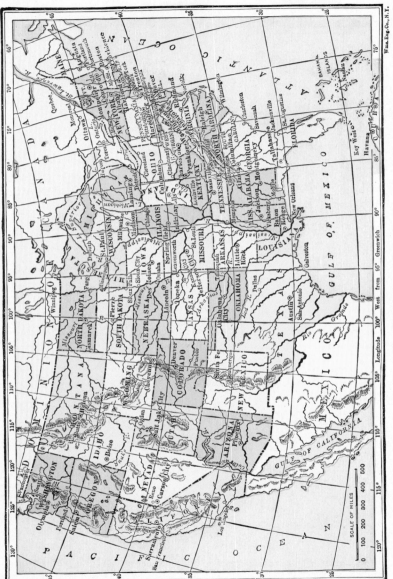

THE FORTY-EIGHT STATES

reservation, had been opened for settlement to white men in 1889. The rush upon the fertile lands of this region was marked by all the frenzy of the final, desperate chance.   At a signal from a bugle

THE CANADIAN BUILDING AT THE PANAMA-CALIFORNIA INTERNATIONAL EXPOSITION, SAN DIEGO, 1915

a monster procession of families in wagons and people on horse-back and on foot burst into the territory.   During the first night a city of tents was raised at Guthrie and Oklahoma City.   In ten days wooden houses rose on the plains.   In a single year there were schools, churches, business blocks, and newspapers.   Within fifteen years there was a population of more than half a million.

To the southwest, Arizona with a population of about 125,000 and New Mexico with 200,000 inhabitants now joined Oklahoma in asking for statehood. But Congress, then Republican, naturally did not look with pleasure on the addition of more Democratic states. It was literally compelled by public opinion and a sense of justice to admit Oklahoma in 1907. Three years later the Democrats won a majority in the House of Representatives and so Arizona and New Mexico were soon taken "under the roof." Thus the continental domain was rounded out with states.

The Influence of the Far West on National Life

The Last of the Frontier. When Horace Greeley made his trip west in 1859, he recorded the progress of civilization in his journal in this fashion:

> "May 12th, Chicago. Chocolate and morning journals last seen on the hotel breakfast table.
> "23rd, Leavenworth (Kansas). Room bells and bath tubs make their final appearance.
> "26th, Manhattan. Potatoes and eggs last recognized among the blessings that 'brighten as they take their flight.'
> "27th, Junction City. Last visitation of a bootblack, with dissolving views of a board bedroom. Beds bid us good-by."

Within thirty years travelers were riding across that country in Pullman cars and enjoying at the hotels all the comforts of a modern civilization. The "wild west" had disappeared, and with it the frontier of pioneers that had given such a peculiar tone to America and had "poured in upon the floor of Congress" so many "backwoods politicians," as they were scornfully styled.

Free Land and Eastern Labor. It was not only the picturesque features of the frontier that had vanished. Nearly all the arable land in the public domain had been granted away. For more than a hundred years any man or woman of moderate means had been able to secure a farm and by hard labor an independent livelihood. For a hundred years America had been in a position to supply land to all the immigrants who cared to till the soil. After 1862 it had given farms to all qualified applicants. Every new pair of strong arms meant more fields under cultivation and more wealth. Work-

The Collieries, as Etched by Joseph Pennell

A MODERN CORN-CUTTING MACHINE IN IOWA

men in Eastern factories, mines, or mills, who did not like their hours, wages, or conditions of labor, could simply move out into the country. Now all that was over. By 1890 most of the desirable land had been occupied, and industrial workers faced a more difficult situation.

Grain Supplants King Cotton. In the meantime a revolution was taking place in agriculture on account of Western developments. Until 1860 the chief staples sold abroad by the United States were Southern cotton and tobacco. With the advance of the frontier, corn and wheat overtook them both, and the West became the granary of the East and of Western Europe. In place of the scoop shovel once used to handle grain came the towering elevator, loading and unloading thousands of bushels every hour. The refrigerator car and ship made the packing industry as stable as the production of cotton or corn, and gave an immense impetus to cattle raising and sheep farming. So the meat of the West appeared on the English dinner table by the side of bread baked from Dakotan wheat.

International Results of Western Development. Billions of dollars' worth of American grain, dairy produce, and meat were now poured into European markets where their sale paid off American debts due to money lenders or raised more capital to expand American economic enterprises. Thus Western produce aided in the progress of America toward financial independence. The country which once had timidly turned to the Old World to borrow money at high rates of interest moved swiftly toward the time when it was to lend money abroad by the billions; that is, become a creditor instead of a debtor among the nations. Every grain of wheat and corn pulled the balance down on the New World side of the scale.

Eastern Agriculture Affected. In the East as well as in Europe the opening of the Western granary produced great economic changes. Whole sections of the poorest land went entirely out of cultivation, abandoned farms in the New England hills bearing solemn witness to the competing power of Western wheat fields. Sheep and cattle raising, as well as wheat and corn production, suffered at least a relative decline. Thousands of farmers engaged in tilling land of the lower grade were forced to go West or were driven to the margin of subsistence. At last even the herds of cows that supplied Eastern cities with milk were fed upon grain brought halfway across the continent.

The Expansion of the American Market. Industry also was affected in many ways by the development of food-producing regions. The demand for farm machinery, clothing, boots, shoes, and other commodities gave to American manufacturers a market bigger than Alexander Hamilton had ever imagined in his boldest dreams. Moreover, it brought into the Mississippi Valley giant manufacturing plants, once confined to the seaboard states, and helped to transform the region of the Great Lakes into an industrial empire. Herein lies the explanation of the growth of mid-western cities after 1865. Chicago, with its thirty-five railways, tapped every locality of the West and South, while its water connections afforded routes in other directions, making it a highly strategic center for industries. Long foresight led Cyrus McCormick to build his reaper works in Chicago before 1860. From Troy, New York, came a large stove plant. That was followed by a shoe factory from Massachusetts. As a matter of course, the packing industry flourished at this city — so accessible to cattle raisers and shippers and so well united with Eastern markets.

To the opening of the Far West the Lake region was indebted for a large part of the water-borne traffic which made it "the Mediterranean basin of North America." The produce of the West and the manufactures of the East flowed through it in a continuous stream. On this account there was a swift rise of shipyards on the Great Lakes which helped to offset the decline of the American marine on the high seas. In response to the stimulus Detroit turned to shipbuilding, and in time could boast that her mechanics were able to turn out a ten-thousand ton leviathan for ore or grain about "as quickly as carpenters could put up an eight-room house." Thus in its relation to the Far West, the old Northwest — the wilderness of Jefferson's time — had taken the position once held by New England: it was supplying money and manufactures for a vast agricultural empire stretching toward the setting sun.

America on the Pacific. It has been said that the Mediterranean Sea was the center of ancient civilization; that modern civilization has developed on the shores of the Atlantic; and that the future belongs to the Pacific. At any rate, the sweep of American migration to the western coast was followed by a rapid growth of American interest in the affairs of the Pacific and the Far East.

From an old print

COMMODORE PERRY'S MEN MAKING PRESENTS TO THE JAPANESE
Note the model train and grindstone.

Indeed before California was annexed, regular traffic sprang up between American ports and the Hawaiian Islands and China. Two years previous to the settlement of the dispute with England over Oregon, namely, in 1844, the United States had begun official relations with the government at Peking. Just a decade later and four years after the admission of California to the Union, the barred door of Japan was forced open by Commodore Perry. Now commerce flourished under federal protection. In 1865, a ship from

Honolulu carried sugar, molasses, and fruits from Hawaii to the Oregon port of Astoria. The next year a vessel from Hongkong brought rice, mats, and tea from China. An era of profitable business was inaugurated. The annexation of Hawaii in 1898, the addition of the Philippines at the same time, and the use of American troops in helping to put down a rebellion in Peking in 1900, were signs of American interest and power on the Pacific.

Conservation and the Land Problem. Among its many consequences, the rounding out of the continent brought new and serious problems to the governments of the states and the nation. Suddenly the people of the whole country were forced to realize that there was a limit to the rich land available and to the forests and minerals awaiting the ax and the pick. Hitherto the government had pursued the easy course of giving away arable land and selling forest and mineral lands at low prices. Now it had difficult problems of conservation to solve. It even had to consider questions relative to land ownership again, especially if the tradition of small farms was to be maintained. As long as there was an abundance of land for every man or woman who wanted a home on the soil, it mattered little whether single landlords or companies held millions of acres, or a hundred men in one western river valley owned 17,000,000 acres. But when the good land for small homesteads was all distributed, then fundamental matters had to be faced. At the opening of the twentieth century the nation, which for a hundred years had been granting land and natural resources with a lavish hand, was forced to enact law after law conserving its forests and minerals. And at that very time the state of California on the utmost border of the continent was moved to pass a land-settlement law authorizing government aid in breaking up large estates into small lots and making it possible for actual settlers to buy homesteads on liberal terms. Such issues and such policies showed that America had passed out of the pioneer stage forever.

References

Henry Inman, *The Old Santa Fé Trail*.
R. I. Dodge, *The Plains of the Great West* (1877).
C. H. Shinn, *The Story of the Mine*.

Cy Warman, *The Story of the Railroad*.
Emerson Hough, *The Story of the Cowboy*.
W. E. Smythe, *The Conquest of Arid America*.
E. S. Meany, *History of the State of Washington*.
Hamlin Garland, *A Son of the Middle Border*.
T. Dennett, *Americans in Eastern Asia*.

Questions

1. Name the states west of the Mississippi in 1865.
2. In what manner was the rest of the western region governed?
3. How far had settlement been carried?
4. What were the striking physical features of the West?
5. How was settlement promoted after 1865?
6. Why was admission to the Union so eagerly sought?
7. Explain how politics became involved in the creation of new states.
8. Did the West rapidly become like the older sections of the country?
9. What economic peculiarities did it retain or develop?
10. How did the federal government aid in Western agriculture?
11. How did the development of the West affect the East? The South?
12. What relation did the opening of the great grain areas of the West bear to the growth of America's commercial and financial power?
13. Discuss the significance of American expansion to the Pacific Ocean.

Research Topics

The Passing of the Wild West. Haworth, *The United States in Our Own Times*, pp. 100–124.

The Indian Question. Sparks, *National Development* (American Nation Series), pp. 265–281.

The Chinese Question. Sparks, *National Development*, pp. 229–250; Rhodes, *History of the United States*, Vol. VIII, pp. 180–196.

The Railway Age. Schafer, *History of the Pacific Northwest*, pp. 230–245; E. V. Smalley, *The Northern Pacific Railroad*; Paxson, *The New Nation* (Riverside Series), pp. 20–26, especially the map on p. 23, and pp. 142–148.

Agriculture and Business. Schafer, *Pacific Northwest*, pp. 246–289.

Ranching in the Northwest. Theodore Roosevelt, *Ranch Life*, and *Autobiography*, pp. 103–143.

Historical Fiction

Helen Hunt Jackson, *Ramona*.
Emerson Hough, *The Girl at the Half-Way House*.
Mark Twain, *Roughing It*.

CHAPTER XXI

THE ISSUES OF DOMESTIC POLITICS (1865–1897)

For thirty years after the Civil War, the two leading political parties, although they were arrayed against each other in presidential campaigns, were not sharply divided over many definite issues. Before 1860 the Democrats had attacked protective tariffs, federal banking, internal improvements, and heavy taxes; now they spoke softly on all these points. On the other hand, the Republicans remembered that they had been a minority of the voters in 1860 and were warned by the loss of the House of Representatives in 1874 against being too confident. So they were very careful about taking a bold stand on too many questions. Again and again the votes in Congress showed that no clear line separated all the Democrats from all the Republicans. There were Republicans who favored tariff reductions, and there were Democrats who approved high protection. Only on laws dealing with the South was the division between the parties fairly precise; and this could be explained on practical as well as sentimental grounds.

Perhaps, the vagueness of party platforms was due to the fact that the people were not certain as to what they wanted. Out of the eighteen years between 1875 and 1892, the Democrats had a majority in the House of Representatives for fourteen years while the Republicans carried every presidential election but one. Hayes had a Democratic House during his entire term and a Democratic Senate for two years of the four. During his first administration Cleveland faced a hostile Republican majority in the Senate and was often in conflict with the Democratic majority in the House. Throughout his four years Harrison was supported by a Republican Senate, but in the lower chamber his party had a bare majority from 1889 to 1891 and lost that at the election held in the middle of his term. Evidently, the sympathies of the country were constantly veering from one direction to another.

THE CURRENCY QUESTION

Debtors and the Fall in Prices. Nevertheless, during these years of confusion in public sentiment, a number of great issues were vehemently debated in Congress and outside. For many reasons the currency question came first. As of old, the farmers and planters of the West and South were heavily in debt to the East for borrowed money; and they relied on the sale of cotton, corn, wheat, and hogs to get the funds to pay what they owed. During the Civil War, the Western farmers had been able to sell their produce at high prices and thus discharge their debts with ease; but after the war prices fell rapidly. Wheat that sold at two dollars a bushel in 1865 brought sixty-four cents twenty years later. The meaning of this for farmers in debt — and nearly three-fourths of them were in that class — can be shown by a single example. A thousand-dollar mortgage on a Western farm could be paid off by five hundred bushels of wheat when wheat was selling at two dollars a bushel; but it took about fifteen hundred bushels to pay the same debt when wheat was at the bottom of the scale. For the farmer, wheat was the measure of his labor, his toil under the summer sun; and he looked to the government for a currency that would uphold its price.

Creditors and Falling Prices. For a bondholder or creditor, on the other hand, falling prices were better. If, for instance, with the annual interest of sixty dollars on a thousand-dollar bond, he could buy seventy or eighty bushels of wheat instead of twenty or thirty, he made just that much gain. Moreover the gain seemed to him entirely just. Creditors had suffered heavy losses when the Civil War carried prices skyward while the interest rates on their old bonds remained stationary. For example if a man had a $1000 bond issued before 1860 and paying interest at five per cent, he received fifty dollars a year from it. Before the war each dollar would buy a bushel of wheat; in 1865 it would buy only half a bushel. When prices — that is, the cost of living — began to go down, creditors therefore were pleased with the course of things.

Causes of Falling Prices. This drop in prices after 1865 was due, no doubt, to many causes. The government ceased buying supplies for war purposes, new wheat-growing regions were opened, and the use of labor-saving machinery on farms increased, raising the output of crops for sale. The currency too was a factor in the situation. Whatever the cause the less fortunate farmers believed that the way to enhance the prices of their produce was to issue more money. They viewed it as a case of supply and demand; that is, if there was little currency in circulation, prices would be less; if there was a lot of money going round, prices would be high. Consequently they looked with favor upon all plans to enlarge the amount of money issued by the federal government. On the other hand, the creditors naturally thought that it would be a good thing to cut down the volume of money in circulation in order to get better returns on loans.

The Battle over the Greenbacks. This century-old contest over the currency once more became acute when Congress in 1866 passed a law authorizing the Treasury to withdraw from circulation the "greenbacks," as legal-tender notes were called, as fast as they were collected in payment of taxes and other dues. Immediately the paper-money party launched a counter movement and after years of agitation forced Congress in 1878 to keep on reissuing legal-tender notes as they came in. Then the friends of "easy money" rejoiced:

> Thou, Greenback, 'tis of thee,
> Fair money of the free,
> Of thee we sing.

Resumption of Specie Payment. The victory however had a sting in it. When the opponents of greenbacks found that they could not stop the circulation of this currency altogether, they got Congress to pass a law in 1875 placing paper money on a specie basis. This law provided that on and after January 1, 1879, the Secretary of the Treasury must redeem in coin legal-tender notes presented at the proper office in sums of not less than fifty dollars. When the hour for redemption arrived, a large hoard of gold was on hand. "On the appointed day," wrote the assistant secretary, "anxiety reigned in the office of the Treasury. Hour after hour passed; no news from New York. Inquiry by wire showed that all was quiet. At the close of the day this message came: '$135,000

of notes presented for coin — $400,000 of gold for notes.' . . .
By five o'clock the news was all over the land, and the New York
bankers were sipping their tea in absolute safety."

The Specie Problem — the Parity of Gold and Silver. Now
the people who believed in expanding the amount of currency
afloat in the country began to demand that the government mint
more silver into coin. This introduced a novel element into the
historic monetary question and started one of the most strenuous
battles in the history of American politics. The issue turned on
legal as well as economic points. By the Constitution Congress
was given the power to coin money while the states were forbidden
to make anything but gold and silver legal tender in the payment
of debts. Evidently the use of both metals was contemplated.
Such at least was the view of many statesmen, including James
G. Blaine, an outstanding Republican leader. The difficulty however lay in keeping gold and silver on the same level so that they
would circulate equally. Obviously if the gold in a gold dollar
exceeds in market value the silver in a silver dollar, people will
hoard gold coins and use silver in buying and selling. For example,
Congress in 1792 fixed the ratio of the two metals at one to fifteen
— declared one ounce of gold worth fifteen of silver — but it soon
found that gold had been undervalued. When again in 1834 the
ratio was put at one to sixteen, silver was undervalued. Then
silver was not brought in for coinage and almost dropped out of
circulation. Indeed many silver dollars were melted down in
factories to make jewelry and plate.

Silver Demonetized in 1873. There things stood in 1873. In
that year Congress stopped the coinage of standard silver dollars,
which seemed a natural thing to do. Although the act was later
called "the crime of '73," secretly committed against the people,
the debates in Congress do not sustain the charge. In the course of
the argument on the law it was clearly stated by one speaker at
least: "This bill provides . . . for substituting as legal tender,
coin of only one metal instead of two as heretofore."

The Decline in the Value of Silver. In any case little was said
at the time about the "crime." It was changing circumstances
that forced the silver issue to the front. New silver lodes, dis-

covered in the Far West, were pouring into the market great streams of the white metal, bearing down its price. Moreover Germany, having given up the silver standard in 1871, steadily increased her demand for gold, and several Latin-American countries followed this example, thereby helping to raise the market value of the yellow metal. Then came the resumption of specie payment which, in effect, placed the paper money on a gold basis. Within twenty years an ounce of silver was worth in gold only about half what it was in 1870.

That there had been a real decline in silver was denied by the advocates of that metal. They said that gold had gone up because governments had given it a monopoly in their mints — a monopoly which, they claimed, sprang from a conspiracy against the people framed by the bankers of the world. Furthermore they declared that the Resumption Act really cut down the amount of money in the country, lowered the prices of labor and produce, and favored the holders of bonds and mortgages bearing a fixed rate of interest. When wheat sold at sixty-four cents a bushel, their search for relief became desperate, and they at last united in demanding that the government coin silver free of charge and treat sixteen ounces of silver as worth one of gold.

Republicans and Democrats Divided. On this question Republicans and Democrats both were divided; the line was drawn between the East on the one hand and the South and West on the other, rather than between the two major parties. Such a trusted Republican leader as James G. Blaine stated, in a speech delivered in the Senate in 1878, that the Constitution required Congress to make gold and silver the money of the land and that the only question left was the one of fixing the ratio between them. Moreover, Blaine admitted the main argument of the silver advocates, namely, that a reopening of the government mints of the world to silver would bring it up in price to its old relation with gold. He also agreed that their warnings of coming troubles were well founded, for he said: "I believe the struggle now going on in this country and in other countries for a single gold standard would, if successful, produce widespread disaster throughout the commercial world. The destruction of silver as money and the establishment of gold as the sole unit of value must have a ruinous effect on all forms of property, except those investments which yield a fixed return."

Blaine's speech exactly suited the silver party. "Three-fourths of the business enterprises of this country are conducted on borrowed capital," said Senator Jones, of Nevada. "Three-fourths of the homes and farms that stand in the names of the actual occupants have been bought on time and a very large proportion of them are mortgaged for the payment of some part of the purchase money. Under the operation of a shrinkage in the volume of money, this enormous mass of borrowers, at the maturity of their respective debts, . . . are in reality, in the amount of the principal alone, returning a percentage of value greater than they received — more in equity than they contracted to pay . . . . In all discussions of the subject the creditors attempt to brush aside the equities involved by sneering at the debtors."

The Silver Purchase Act (1878). Even before the actual resumption of specie payment, the advocates of free silver were numerous, particularly in the Democratic party. They had a majority in the House of Representatives in 1878 and they carried a silver bill through that chamber. Blocked by the Republican Senate they accepted a compromise in the Bland-Allison bill, which ordered the government to buy a large amount of silver every month and coin it into dollars. But this action did not halt silver on its downward course or force it out into circulation in large quantities. Thereupon the silver faction pressed through Congress in 1886 a bill which ordered the Treasury to issue paper certificates based on the silver that was piling up in its vaults. Still silver kept falling. Then the advocates of more money declared that the government simply must adopt the free and unlimited coinage of silver, at the ratio of sixteen to one.

The Sherman Silver Purchase Act and the Bond Sales. For a time Republican leaders, particularly from the East, staved off extreme action by another compromise: the Sherman Act of 1890 providing for more purchases of silver and for the issue of notes redeemable in gold or silver at the discretion of the Secretary of the Treasury. In vague words they said that it was "the established policy of the United States to maintain the two metals on a parity with each other upon the present legal ratio or such other ratio as may be provided by law." For a while silver rose. Then it turned once more on its downward course.

In the meantime the Treasury was in trouble. To maintain a gold reserve in its vaults, President Cleveland sold government bonds; and to his dismay he found that, as soon as the gold was brought into the Treasury, paper notes were presented for redemption and the gold was quickly carried out again. Seeing no other way to end the vicious circle thus created, he urged Congress to repeal the Sherman Silver Purchase Act. While many of the Democrats rejected the proposal as "treason to the party," a group of Republicans came to his rescue in 1893 and struck from the law its principal sections. Defeated in Congress, the silver faction now made ready to submit the silver question to the voters in the next presidential campaign.

The Protective Tariff and Taxation

Fluctuation in Tariff Policy. Like the silver issue, the tariff tended to align the manufacturing East against the agricultural West and South rather than to cut directly between the parties. Yet on the whole the Republicans stood squarely by the rates laid on foreign imports during the Civil War. Except for some reductions in 1872, which were soon offset by increases, the customs rates stood at about the same level for nearly twenty years. When a revision was made, it was undertaken by the Republicans. Confronted by a huge surplus of revenue in the Treasury in 1883, they modified the tariff a little on the theory that it ought to be reformed by its friends rather than by its enemies. On the other hand, it was the Republicans also who passed the McKinley tariff bill of 1890 which carried protection far above all previous levels.

Although they usually voted against Republican measures, Democrats on their part were not all free traders or even advocates of tariff for revenue only. In Cleveland's first administration they did attack the protective system in the House, where they had a majority, and in this they had the help of the President. The assault failed, for it was blocked by the Republicans in the Senate.

After the sweeping victory of 1892, the Democrats in the House again tried to bring down the tariff by the Wilson bill of 1894, but they were checkmated by members of their own party in the upper chamber. In the end they agreed to a compromise which was more protectionist than free-trade. The Republicans taunted them with being "babes in the woods." President Cleveland so disliked the bill that he refused to sign it, and merely allowed it to become a law, on the lapse of ten days, without his approval.

The Income Tax of 1894. Supporters of tariff reform often joined with their plans for reducing import duties a proposal for a tax on incomes. Most of the great industries, they argued, were in the East; the protective tariff taxed consumers for the benefit of Eastern manufacturers; in reality it levied a tribute upon the rest of the country. As an offset they therefore urged the federal government to lay a tax on large incomes, that is, in effect, principally on the rich people of the East who got most of the benefit of protective tariff. "We propose," said one of them, "to place a part of the burden upon the accumulated wealth of the country instead of placing it all upon the consumption of the people." In this spirit Congress, when it passed the Wilson tariff bill in 1894, put a tax upon all incomes of $4000 a year or more.

But the Democrats were not united as one man on this action. Senator Hill, of New York, turned fiercely upon his party colleagues, exclaiming: "The professors with their books, the socialists with their schemes, the anarchists with their bombs are all instructing the people in the . . . principles of taxation." Even the Eastern Republicans were hardly as savage in attacking the tax. However all this criticism was wasted. The next year the Supreme Court of the United States declared the income tax in general null and void as a direct tax laid on incomes wherever found and not apportioned among the states according to population as the Constitution required. The fact that four of the nine judges dissented from this decision reflected the divided state of public opinion.

RAILWAYS AND TRUSTS

State Regulation. A similar dissension over the railways and trusts also ran through both parties. With respect to the railways, the demand for government regulation, like the call for free silver, came chiefly from the West. There farmers got control in state legislatures, in the early seventies, particularly in Iowa, Wisconsin, and Illinois, and enacted drastic laws prescribing the maximum charges which companies could make for carrying freight and passengers. The range of such laws was limited, however, because the state could not fix the rates for transporting goods and passengers beyond its own borders. Control over interstate commerce, under the Constitution, belonged to Congress.

The Interstate Commerce Act of 1887. Taking the next logical step, farmers and business men began to demand federal regulation of interstate railway lines. In 1887, the pressure became so heavy that Congress enacted a law forbidding many abuses on the part of railways; such as making lower rates for one shipper than another and granting secret rebates of money to favored persons and companies. At the same time it created the Interstate Commerce Commission to enforce the new rules. Though a substantial beginning, this Act did not settle the question of rate-fixing, or remove the railway question from politics.

The Sherman Anti-Trust Law of 1890. As in the case of the railways, attacks upon the trusts were first made in state legislatures where it became the fashion to lay severe penalties on individuals and trusts that formed monopolies and "conspired to raise prices." Republicans and Democrats united in voting for measures of this kind. From state capitals, plans to curb the trusts were soon carried to Washington. Though the Republican leader, Blaine, had once said that "trusts were largely a private affair with which neither the President nor any private citizen had any particular right to interfere," a Republican Congress enacted in 1890 its first measure against great business concerns — the Sherman Anti-Trust Act. This law declared illegal "every contract, combination in the form of trust or otherwise, or conspiracy in restraint of trade and commerce among the several states or with foreign nations."

The Futility of the Anti-Trust Law. Whether the Sherman law was aimed at all combinations or merely those which placed an "unreasonable restraint" on trade was not clear. Indeed

Senator O. H. Platt of Connecticut hinted that it was sheer non-sense. "The questions of whether the bill would be operative, of how it would operate, or whether it was within the power of Congress to enact it," he said, "have been whistled down the wind in this Senate as idle talk and the whole effort has been to get some bill headed 'A bill to punish trusts,' with which to go to the country." Whatever its purpose, the Sherman Anti-Trust Act had little or no effect on existing trusts or on the formation of new combinations. It was practically unenforced by Harrison and Cleveland, in spite of the constant cry for action against "monopolies." It was patent that neither the Republicans nor the Democrats wanted to wage a war on trusts to a finish.

MINOR PARTIES AND UNREST

The Demands of Dissenting Groups. From the election of 1872 onward, there appeared in each presidential campaign one, sometimes two or more parties, that appealed mainly to wage-earners and farmers. Whether they chose to call themselves Labor Reformers, Greenbackers, or Anti-Monopolists, their slogans and their platforms all pointed in one direction. Even the Prohibitionists, who in 1872 started on their national career with a single issue, the abolition of the liquor traffic, soon began to take sides on other questions. In fact they were split into two factions over the free-silver issue in 1896.

Among the schemes favored by these minor political parties the following were the most important: the earliest possible payment of the national debt; government regulation of the rates of railways and telegraph companies; repeal of the specie resumption act of 1875; the issue of legal-tender notes by the government, convertible into interest-bearing obligations on demand; unlimited coinage of silver as well as gold; a tax on inheritances; legislation to take from "land, railroad, money and other gigantic corporate monopolies . . . the powers they have so corruptly and unjustly usurped"; popular or direct election of United States Senators; woman suffrage; and an income tax, "placing the burden of government on those who can best afford to pay instead of laying it on the farmers and producers."

Criticism of the Old Parties.   To this program of concrete measures the minor parties usually attached criticism of the major parties and sometimes, it must be said, of the federal government itself. "We denounce," exclaimed the Labor Party in 1888, "the Democratic and Republican parties as hopelessly and shamelessly corrupt and, by reason of their affiliation with monopolies, equally unworthy of the suffrages of those who do not live upon public plunder." "The United States Senate," insisted the Greenbackers, "is a body composed largely of aristocratic millionaires who according to their own party papers generally purchased their elections in order to protect the great monopolies which they represent."

The Grangers.   Behind these charges were generally arrayed, it seems, farmers of the West.   Always active in politics before the Civil War, they had cast their lot as a rule with one or the other of the leading parties.   In 1867, however, there grew up among them an association known as the "Patrons of Husbandry" which soon moved in the direction of independent politics.   Agents of this society formed secret lodges or "granges" in various parts of the country, and told the farmers that they ought to look out for their own interests.   At first the granges took no part in politics but before long some of their ardent members were urging farmers to use their organization in party affairs, on the theory that where a few votes are marshaled together in a democracy there is power.

The Greenback Party.   The first important political action of the Grangers was the attack on the railways in the Middle West which forced several state legislatures to reduce freight and passenger rates by law.   Encouraged by this success, some leaders in the movement launched in 1876 a new political party, popularly known as the Greenbackers because it favored the reissue of the legal tenders or greenbacks.   They polled few votes in the presidential election, but two years later, in the congressional elections, they swept whole sections of the country.   Their candidates received more than a million ballots and fourteen were returned to the House of Representatives.   To all outward signs a third party had come to stay.

The hopes of the promoters were quickly dashed.   The revival of industry from a severe panic which had set in during 1873, the

Silver Purchase Act, and the reissue of greenbacks removed some of the causes of discontent. There was also a rush of farmers into the camp of the faction that promised relief through the free coinage of silver. At all events the Greenback vote fell to about 300,000 in the election of 1880. A still greater drop came in 1884, and the party disappeared.

Rise of the Populist Party. The funeral of the Greenback party was hardly over when two new political groups appeared in the agrarian sections: The National Farmers' Alliance and Industrial Union, particularly strong in the South and West; and the Farmers' Alliance, operating in the North. Boasting a membership of more than three millions the two orders entered politics in 1892. They held a national convention, nominated a candidate for President, and adopted the name of "People's Party," from which they became known as Populists. Their platform, in every line, reflected radicalism. They declared that "the newspapers are largely subsidized or muzzled; public opinion silenced; business prostrate; our homes covered with mortgages; and the land concentrating in the hands of capitalists. . . . The fruits of the toil of millions are boldly stolen to build up colossal fortunes for a few." After this general indictment, the Populists named their remedies: free coinage of silver, a graduated income tax, postal savings banks, and government ownership of railways and telegraphs. They also favored the initiative, referendum, and popular election of United States Senators, and declared that federal troops should not be used in labor disputes. On this platform, the Populists polled over a million votes, won twenty-two presidential electors, and sent a powerful delegation to Congress.

Industrial Distress Adds to the Ferment. During the next four years many events helped to strengthen Populism. By giving whole-hearted support to the gold standard and urging the repeal of the Silver Purchase Act, President Cleveland drove many of his own party over to the Populist side. Unrest was then aggravated by an industrial crisis that fell upon the land: banks and business houses went into bankruptcy; factories were closed; idle men thronged the streets hunting for work; and labor disputes broke out in manufacturing districts. In 1894 a strike at the Pullman car works in Chicago widened to the railways, tying up big trunk lines and involving disorders. Against the protests of the governor of Illinois, John P. Altgeld, federal troops were sent to the scene of action by the President. Supplementing this executive action, the United States district court at Chicago issued an injunction, or order, forbidding the president of the railway union, Eugene V. Debs, or his assistants to interfere with the carriage of the mails or with interstate commerce in any form. For refusing to obey the order, Debs was arrested and imprisoned and at last the strike was broken, leaving sullen feelings in its wake. On top of this came the decision of the Supreme Court of the United States, the next year, declaring null and void the income tax law just enacted by Congress. By all these events the ire of the Populists was fanned to flame in every part of the West and South.

The Sound Money Battle of 1896

Conservative Anxiety. Conservative men in both parties looked upon the rise of populism and the spread of labor disputes as signs of a revolutionary spirit — indeed as a danger to American institutions and ideals. "The income tax law of 1894," exclaimed the distinguished New York advocate, Joseph H. Choate, in his high-tempered speech before the Supreme Court, "is communistic in its purposes and tendencies and is defended here upon principles as communistic, socialistic — what shall I call them — populistic as ever have been addressed to any political assembly in the world." Mr. Justice Field in the name of the Court replied: "The present assault upon capital is but the beginning. It will be but the stepping stone to others larger and more sweeping till our political conditions will become a war of the poor against the rich." As for the free coinage of silver, conservatives were almost unanimous in calling it sheer robbery; an effort of the debtors to pay their debts with money worth fifty cents on the dollar; a challenge to law, order, and honor.

Republicans Favor the Gold Standard. It was among the Republicans that such opinions were most generally held. As a party they were prepared to face Populists in an almost solid phalanx while the Democrats were divided among themselves.

When their national convention assembled in 1896, the position of the Republicans was soon made clear: a declaration against the adoption of free silver by the United States alone was carried by a vote of eight to one. The party, to use the language of one of its leaders, Henry Cabot Lodge, stood entrenched against "not only that organized failure, the Democratic party, but all the wandering forces of political chaos and social disorder . . . in these bitter times when the forces of disorder are loose and the wreckers with their false lights gather at the shore to lure the ship of state upon the rocks." Yet the truth is that William McKinley, whom the Republicans nominated for President, had voted in Congress for the free coinage of silver, was widely known as a bimetallist, and was only with difficulty persuaded to approve the flat indorsement of the gold standard made by his party. Having accepted it, however, he became its valiant champion although his prime interest was in the protective tariff. Nothing was worse, he said, than attempts "to array class against class, 'the classes against the masses,' section against section, labor against capital, 'the poor against the rich,' or interest against interest." The whole program of Populism he called a "sudden, dangerous, and revolutionary assault upon law and order."

The Democratic Convention at Chicago. If the Republicans were furious, so were the Democrats. From the opening prayer in their convention at Chicago to the last motion before the house, every act, every speech, every scene, every resolution displayed deep passions. Departing from long party custom, they voted down with indignation a proposal to praise the Democratic President, Cleveland. When the platform, with its radical planks indorsing free silver and the income tax, was laid before the convention, emotions ran riot. Senator Hill, of New York, trembling with wrath, protested against principles that must drive out of the party men who had grown gray in its service; against "unusual, unwise, and revolutionary steps." Senator Vilas, of Wisconsin, cried out that there was no difference in principle between the free coinage of silver — "the confiscation of one-half of the credits of the nation for the benefit of debtors" — and communism itself — "a universal distribution of property."

The "Crown of Thorns" Speech. The champions of free silver replied in equally militant tones. They accused the gold advocates of being the aggressors who had assailed the labor and the homes of the people. William Jennings Bryan, of Nebraska, voiced their views in an oration that brought shouts of applause from the excited delegates. He declared that their cause "was as holy as the cause of liberty — the cause of humanity." He exclaimed that the contest was between the idle holders of idle capital and the toiling millions. Then he named those for whom he spoke — the wage-earner, the country lawyer, the small merchant, the farmer, and the miner. "The man who is employed for wages is as much a business man as his employer. The attorney in a country town is as much a business man as a corporation counsel in a great metropolis. The merchant at the crossroads store is as much a

Copyright by Underwood and Underwood, N. Y.

WILLIAM J. BRYAN IN 1898

business man as the merchant of New York. The farmer . . . is as much a business man as the man who goes upon the board of trade and bets upon the price of grain. The miners who go a thousand feet into the earth or climb two thousand feet upon the cliffs . . . are as much business men as the few financial magnates who in a back room corner the money of the world. . . . It is for these that we speak. We do not come as aggressors. Ours is not a war of conquest. We are fighting in defense of our homes, our families, and our posterity. We have petitioned and our petitions have been scorned. We have entreated and our entreaties have been disregarded. We have begged and they have mocked when our calamity came. We beg no longer; we entreat no more; we petition no more. We defy them. . . . We shall answer their demands for a gold standard by saying to them: 'You shall not press upon the brow of labor this crown of thorns. You shall not crucify mankind upon a cross of gold.' "

Bryan Nominated. Never in the history of national conventions had an orator more completely swayed a multitude. After cheering Bryan until they could cheer no more, his supporters tore the standards from the floor and gathered around the Nebraska delegation. The platform as reported was carried by a vote of two to one and the young orator from the West, hailed as America's Tiberius Gracchus, was nominated as the Democratic candidate for President. Delegates from the South and West were victorious over the East.

The Democratic Platform. The platform on which Bryan stood, unlike most party documents, was a clear-cut manifesto. It denounced the practice of allowing national banks to issue notes intended to circulate as money, recalling Jackson's famous attack on the Bank in 1832. It declared that tariff duties should be laid "for the purpose of revenue" — Calhoun's doctrine. It demanded the free coinage of silver at the ratio of sixteen to one. An indorsement of the income tax came next on the program. Moreover the platform alleged that the Democratic income-tax law of 1894 was "in strict pursuance of the uniform decisions of the Supreme Court for nearly a hundred years." As if recalling the position of the Republicans on the Dred Scott case forty years before, it hinted that the decision which annulled the law might be reversed by the same Court, "as it may hereafter be constituted."

The appeal to labor voiced by Bryan in his "crown of thorns" speech was reinforced in the platform. "As labor creates the wealth of the country," ran one plank, "we demand the passage of such laws as may be necessary to protect it in all its rights." Referring to the recent Pullman strike, the platform condemned "arbitrary interference by federal authorities in local affairs" and called it "a violation of the Constitution of the United States and a crime against free institutions." It likewise struck at "government by injunction as a new and highly dangerous form of oppression by which federal judges, in contempt of the laws of states and rights of citizens, become at once legislators, judges, and executioners." The remedy offered was a federal law assuring trial by jury to persons arrested for disobeying the orders of federal judges in labor disputes — contempt of court. Having made this declaration of faith, the Democrats, with Bryan at the head, raised their standard of battle, and marched into the political arena.

The Heated Campaign. The campaign which followed outdid in speeches, fireworks, and bitterness of tone all other presidential conflicts, not excepting the fateful struggle of 1860. Huge sums of money were collected by both parties. Railway, banking, and other corporations gave generously to the Republicans; the silver miners, less lavishly but with the same anxiety, supported the Democrats. The nation was flooded with pamphlets, posters, and handbills. Every public forum, from the great halls of the cities to the "red schoolhouses" in the country, was occupied.

Bryan took the stump himself, visiting all parts of the land in special trains and addressing literally millions of people in the open air. But McKinley adhered to the older and more formal plan. He received delegations at his home in Canton, Ohio, and spoke on the issues of the campaign from his front porch, leaving to an army of lesser orators in his party the task of talking to the crowds in their home towns. Parades and monster mass meetings filled the air with politics. Manufacturers, frightened by pictures of a disordered public credit, put up notices that they would close their doors if the Democrats won the election. Men were dismissed from public and private places on account of their political affiliations, one eminent college president being forced to resign because he favored free silver.

The Republican Victory. At the election the verdict of the nation was decisive. McKinley received 271 of the 477 electoral votes, and 7,111,000 popular votes as against Bryan's 6,509,000. The Republicans also won a safe majority of the seats in the House of Representatives and carried the Senate by a narrow margin. Thus they got control over the entire federal government, which they were to hold for fourteen years. A great issue had been fought to a finish and the party of "sound" finance and protective tariffs set out upon its course with confidence.

REPUBLICAN MEASURES AND RESULTS

The Gold Standard and the Tariff. Yet owing to their weakness in the Senate, the Republicans did not at once pass a law making the gold dollar the standard for national currency. Not until 1900 did they take that positive step. In his first inaugural President McKinley placed the tariff, rather than the money question, in the forefront. "The people have decided," he said, "that such legislation should be had as will give ample protection and encouragement to the industries and development of our country. . . . With adequate revenue secured, but not until then, we can enter upon changes in our fiscal laws." As the Republicans had only forty-six of the ninety Senators, and at least four of them were known advocates of free silver, the President was wise in selecting protection for the first congressional debate.

Congress gave heed to the warning. Under the direction of Nelson P. Dingley, whose name was given to the bill, a tariff measure levying the highest rates yet laid in the history of the country was carried through the House of Representatives. Many attacks were made on the Dingley bill in the Senate, especially by members from the West, but in the end enough favors were given that section to win a majority. Duties on sugar, tin, steel, lumber, hemp, and in fact all of the prime commodities handled by combinations and trusts, were materially raised and the protective principle thoroughly entrenched.

Growth of Combinations. The years that followed the enactment of the Dingley law were, whatever the cause, the most prosperous the country had enjoyed for a long time. Industries of every kind were soon running full blast; labor was employed; foreign commerce flourished as never before. While business was increasing, new and bigger companies were being formed. In 1899 the smelters formed a trust with a capital of $65,000,000 and in the same year the Copper Trust was incorporated under the laws of New Jersey, with a par value capital fixed shortly afterward at $175,000,000. A year later the National Sugar Refining Company, of New Jersey, started with a capital of $90,000,000 and adopted the policy of issuing to its stockholders no public statement about

PRESIDENT McKINLEY AND HIS CABINET — WITH JOHN HAY AND ELIHU ROOT SEATED
IN THE FOREGROUND TO THE RIGHT.

its earnings. Before another twelvemonth had passed the country was surprised to learn that the famous Morgan banking house of New York had created the United States Steel Corporation with a capital of more than a billion dollars.

Through connections with these huge undertakings, the great leaders in finance were welded into a single group. To use the language of an authority: "They are all allied and intertwined by their various mutual interests. For instance, the Pennsylvania Railroad interests are on the one hand allied with the Vanderbilts and on the other with the Rockefellers. The Vanderbilts are closely allied with the Morgan group. . . . Viewed as a whole we find the dominating influences in the trusts to be made up of a network of large and small capitalists, many allied to one another by ties of more or less importance, but all being appendages to or parts of the greater groups which are themselves dependent on and allied with the two mammoth Rockefeller and Morgan groups. These two mammoth groups jointly . . . constitute the heart of the business and commercial life of the nation." Such was the picture of triumphant business enterprise drawn by a financier within a few years after the memorable campaign of 1896.

America had become one of the chief workshops of the world. The capital of the United States Steel Corporation alone was more than ten times the total national debt of Hamilton's day, which, the apostles of calamity declared, the people could never pay. Having filled domestic markets to overflowing, American industry was looking abroad for new outlets for its goods. Moreover, since American business men and bankers were closely united in great trusts, they were well prepared to meet foreign competitors in the rivalry over the trade of five continents and seven seas.

References

F. W. Taussig, *Tariff History of the United States*.

J. L. Laughlin, *Bimetallism in the United States*.

A. B. Hepburn, *History of Coinage and Currency in the United States*.

E. R. A. Seligman, *The Income Tax*.

S. J. Buck, *The Granger Movement* (Harvard Studies).

F. H. Dixon, *State Railroad Control*.

H. R. Meyer, *Government Regulation of Railway Rates.*
W. Z. Ripley (editor), *Trusts, Pools, and Corporations.*
R. T. Ely, *Monopolies and Trusts.*
J. B. Clark, *The Control of Trusts.*

Questions

1. What proof have we that the political parties were not clearly divided over issues between 1865 and 1896?

2. Why is a fall in prices a loss to farmers and a gain to holders of bonds?

3. Explain the theory that the quantity of money determines the prices of commodities.

4. Why was it difficult, if not impossible, to keep gold and silver on a parity?

5. What special conditions favored a fall in silver between 1870 and 1896?

6. Describe some of the measures taken to raise the value of silver.

7. Explain the relation between the tariff and the income tax in 1894.

8. How did it happen that the farmers led in regulating railway rates?

9. Give the terms of the Sherman Anti-Trust Act. What was its immediate effect?

10. Name some of the minor parties. What were the reforms they advocated?

11. Describe briefly the experiments of the farmers in politics.

12. How did industrial conditions increase unrest?

13. Why were conservative men disturbed in the early nineties?

14. Explain the Republican position in 1896.

15. Give Bryan's doctrines in 1896. Enumerate the chief features of the Democratic platform.

16. What were the leading measures adopted by the Republicans after their victory in 1896?

Research Topics

Greenbacks and Resumption. Dewey, *Financial History of the United States* (6th ed.), Sections 122–125, 154, and 378; MacDonald, *Documentary Source Book of American History*, pp. 446, 566; Hart, *American History Told by Contemporaries*, Vol. IV, pp. 531–533; Rhodes, *History of the United States*, Vol. VIII, pp. 97–101.

Demonetization and Coinage of Silver. Dewey, *Financial History*, Sections 170–173, 186, 189, 194; MacDonald, *Documentary Source Book*, pp. 174, 573, 593, 595; Hart, *Contemporaries*, Vol. IV, pp. 529–531; Rhodes, *History*, Vol. VIII, pp. 93–97.

Free Silver and the Campaign of 1896. Dewey, *National Problems* (American Nation Series), pp. 220–237, 314–328; Hart, *Contemporaries*, Vol. IV, pp. 533–538.

Tariff Revision. Dewey, *Financial History*, Sections 167, 180, 181, 187, 192, 196; Hart, *Contemporaries*, Vol. IV, pp. 518–525; Rhodes, *History*, Vol. VIII, pp. 168–179, 346–351, 418–422.

Federal Regulation of Railways. Dewey, *National Problems*, pp. 91–111; MacDonald, *Documentary Source Book*, pp. 581–590; Hart, *Contemporaries*, Vol. IV, pp. 521–523; Rhodes, *History*, Vol. VIII, pp. 288–292.

The Rise and Regulation of Trusts. Dewey, *National Problems*, pp. 188–202; MacDonald, *Documentary Source Book*, pp. 591–593.

The Grangers and Populism. Paxson, *The New Nation* (Riverside Series), pp. 20–37, 177–191, 208–223.

General Analysis of Domestic Problems. *Syllabus in History* (New York State, 1920), pp. 137-142.

Historical Fiction

Winston Churchill, *Mr. Crewe's Career.*

CHAPTER XXII

AMERICA AS A WORLD POWER (1865–1900)

Shortly after the war with Spain in 1898 it became the fashion to say that America had now attained the position of a "world power." But in fact ever since the Declaration of Independence, the United States had been a world power influencing by its commerce, its wealth, and its arms the course of events in two hemispheres. Before the Constitution was adopted, American ships were plowing the waters of the Pacific, developing the China trade. When the Mediterranean pirates preyed on American merchantmen at the beginning of the nineteenth century, American vessels of war compelled them to stop the practice. When Great Britain, at the close of the "Opium War," ordered China to open certain ports to British commerce, the government of the United States at once insisted that its citizens should also have the same rights, and in 1844 negotiated a treaty with China which gave official sanction to our commerce in that ancient empire. Then Japan was "gently coerced" into amicable relations ten years later by Commodore Perry at the head of a small but adequate naval force. It was only for a short time during our Civil War that the attention of the American nation was centered almost entirely on domestic affairs and even then the government was continually confronted by grave international questions. In dealing with the modern phases of our world politics, therefore, we are merely carrying forward an old story.

AMERICAN FOREIGN RELATIONS (1861–1898)

Blocking French Intervention in Mexico. Besides keeping on the alert against European intervention in our own Civil War, President Lincoln had another foreign menace to watch. When he was inaugurated, Mexico was in the midst of a revolution involving American interests. Indeed some members of Congress were considering the use of troops to establish order beyond the Rio Grande but Americans were soon so occupied with their own fighting that they had no soldiers to spare for distant battlefields.

At this point however France, England, and Spain decided to intervene in Mexico, using as an excuse the fact that the Mexican government had ceased paying the interest on its debt held by their subjects. They made an agreement to work together in collecting this money and in protecting their citizens who resided in Mexico. In spite of the refusal of the United States to join in their enterprise, they went ahead with military and naval preparations. But they had not gone very far when England and Spain discovered that Napoleon III had plans for seizing power in Mexico and, unwilling to play his game, withdrew their ships and soldiers, leaving the field to him.

Unquestionably the French Emperor dreamed of setting up in the western hemisphere an imperial power to offset the strength of the United States. Collecting debts in Mexico was only a cloak for deeper designs. Throwing off his disguise in 1864, Napoleon aided Mexican monarchists in turning their country into an empire and helped them to place on the throne the Archduke Maximilian, a brother of the ruler of Austria. He also sent French soldiers to support the puppet monarch.

Although this attack upon the Mexican republic was resented in the United States, the federal government could do little more than protest until 1865. But when our own war drew to a close, General Sheridan was at once dispatched to the Mexican border with a large armed force. Believing in drastic action, General Grant urged the immediate use of the American troops to expel the French from this continent. As it happened, this was rendered unnecessary because the Secretary of State, Seward, was able to prevail upon Napoleon III to withdraw his expedition by making him understand that the Americans now had soldiers to spare. Without the backing of French arms, the sham empire in Mexico fell down like a house of cards. The unlucky Maximilian was shot by a Mexican firing squad and his wife, Carlotta, then in Europe seeking aid, became insane from the horrors of the tragedy.

Alaska Purchased. While winding up the dispute with Napoleon, Seward was also starting out on the realization of his dream for American expansion in the Pacific by attempting to purchase Alaska from Russia. Finally by a treaty signed on March 30, 1867, the deed was accomplished, bringing to the United States a domain of nearly six hundred thousand square miles — a territory larger than Texas and nearly three-fourths the size of the Louisiana Purchase. But the House of Representatives was with difficulty persuaded to vote the $7,200,000 to pay for Alaska in the face of cries that the government was merely buying "an iceberg."

American Interest in the Caribbean. Having won this diplomatic triumph, Seward turned to another phase of expansion. He negotiated with Denmark a treaty for the purchase of the Islands of St. John and St. Thomas in the West Indies, strategic points in the Caribbean for sea power. But the Senate refused to ratify the proposal.

Not at all discouraged by Seward's failure in this case, President Grant tried his best to get possession of Santo Domingo. This little republic had found it impossible to maintain an orderly government and in the course of its troubles an agent sent out by Grant induced its president in 1869 to sell his country to the United States.

Immediately Grant sent the treaty of sale to the Senate with his enthusiastic approval, only to have it rejected. Confident nevertheless that his policy was correct Grant continued to advise Americans to acquire Santo Domingo. In his last message to Congress he still referred to the matter, saying that time had only proved the wisdom of his early project for annexation.

The *Alabama* Claims Arbitrated. Meanwhile the State Department undertook to settle more urgent questions, such as a quarrel with Great Britain growing out of civil-war diplomacy. For her breach of neutrality in permitting confederate cruisers to be built in her ports and launched to prey on the commerce of the North, a bill of damages had been presented by the United States. At first the British government refused to listen to any such claims but President Grant insisted on keeping the issue alive. At length in 1871, the Secretary of State, Hamilton Fish, reached an agreement with Great Britain in the Treaty of Washington which provided that the *Alabama* claims and several other points in dispute between the two countries should be settled by a high court of arbitration appointed for the purpose.

This tribunal of arbitration sat at Geneva in Switzerland, and after listening to long arguments on both sides awarded to the United States the lump sum of $15,500,000 to be divided among American claimants. The damages thus allowed were large, larger than strict justice required and the decision consequently excited much adverse comment in England. Nevertheless, the British government promptly paid the bill. The world was given a demonstration that two powerful nations could avoid war in settling a serious controversy.

Samoa. If the Senate had its doubts at first about the wisdom of acquiring naval bases in distant seas, the same could not be said of the State Department and naval officers. In 1872 Commander Meade, of the United States navy, while cruising around in the Pacific, visited Tutuila, one of the Samoan Islands, far below the equator and nearer to Australia than to California. Pleased with the spot, he made an agreement with a local chieftain, providing among other things that the United States could use the harbor of Pago Pago as a naval port. This agreement was changed six years later into a formal treaty which the Senate was induced to ratify.

Such enterprise could not escape the vigilant eyes of England and Germany, both mindful of the course of the sea power in history. The German emperor, taking advantage of a row between his consul in Samoa and a native king, announced that he had an interest in the islands. Aware of the dangers arising from German outposts in the southern seas so near to Australia, England put in her claims too. So it happened that the three countries sent battleships to Samoan waters, threatening a triangular naval war. A terrible storm however destroyed most of the ships and suggested a compromise rather than a fight.

At all events they arranged in 1889 for a three-cornered control over the islands. But the scheme did not work out well, owing to continual wrangling and jealousy among them, and at the end of ten years it was given up. England withdrew altogether, leaving Germany all the islands except Tutuila and certain minor points which were ceded outright to the United States. In this way the American navy got one of the finest harbors in the Pacific.

Cleveland and the Venezuela Affair. Nearer home, the federal government had to deal with a controversy arising under the Monroe Doctrine. For some time Great Britain and Venezuela had been arguing with each other over the western boundary of British Guiana and, on appeal for help from Venezuela, President Cleveland was forced to make a decision.

When he found that Great Britain stood fast by her claims, he had his Secretary of State, Richard T. Olney, write a note to London asking whether the British government would arbitrate the points at issue. This note Olney accompanied by a warning to the effect that the United States could not permit any European power to contest its mastery in this hemisphere. "The United States," said the Secretary, "is practically sovereign on this continent and its fiat is law upon the subjects to which it confines its interposition. . . . Its infinite resources, combined with its isolated position, render it master of the situation and practically invulnerable against any or all other powers."

To this defiant note asserting the power of the United States under the Monroe Doctrine, the British government made a stiff reply. It denied that the Monroe Doctrine was binding in international law. It maintained that the dispute with Venezuela was a matter of interest merely to the two parties. It declared that arbitration of the question was impossible. By way of rejoinder President Cleveland now made two startling proposals. He asked Congress to create a commission for the purpose of finding out what was the true boundary between Venezuela and British Guiana. Then he announced to the world that it would be the duty of this country, "to resist by every means in its power, as a willful aggression upon its rights and interests, the appropriation by Great Britain of any lands or the exercise of governmental jurisdiction over any territory which, after investigation, we have determined of right belongs to Venezuela." Cleveland realized that this was a serious threat but he declared that he knew what he

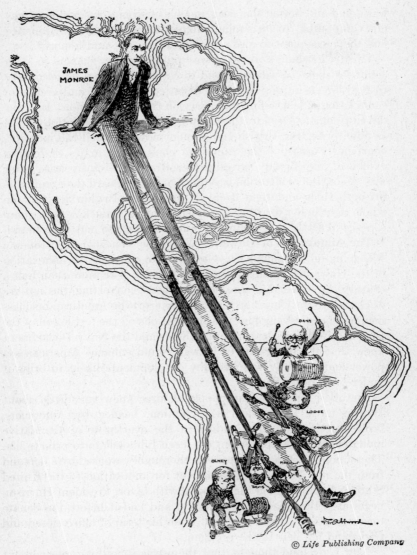

STRETCHING THE MONROE DOCTRINE

A contemporary cartoon by F. G. Attwood.

was doing and hinted that war, much as it was to be deplored, was not comparable to "a supine submission to wrong and injustice and the consequent loss of national self-respect and honor."

When Cleveland's message was published, newspapers in both countries spoke of war as bound to come. Congress voted money to pay for an inquiry into the disputed boundary and created a commission of learned men to carry on the investigation. But war did not come. Deaf to the clamor of the militant section of the London press, the British government now deplored the incident, courteously assisted the American commission in its search for evidence, and finally agreed to arbitrate the entire case after all. A court of arbitration was duly set up; it heard the arguments on both sides and then decided that Great Britain was on the whole right in her territorial claims against Venezuela. Once more a peaceful settlement of an international dispute had been found.

The Annexation of Hawaii. While the Venezuela controversy was going on, President Cleveland had to consider the annexation of the Hawaiian Islands in the mid-Pacific. For more than half a century American missionaries had been converting the natives of Hawaii to the Christian faith and enterprising American business men had been developing sugar plantations on the fertile soil of the islands. Both the Department of State and the Navy Department knew that the possession of Hawaii would enhance American sea power and carefully watched any developments likely to bring it under some other flag.

Doubtless the American people at large knew very little about Hawaii until 1893, when a revolution, headed by Americans, broke out in Honolulu, ending in the overthrow of the native monarchy and the retirement of Queen Liliuokalani to private life. Thereupon American interest was thoroughly aroused by a demand from the new Hawaiian government for annexation to the United States. Looking upon the proposal with favor, President Harrison negotiated the treaty of annexation and laid it before the Senate for ratification. There it rested when his term of office closed and Cleveland fell heir to the problem.

Now Cleveland thought that there was something queer about the Hawaiian revolution. So he sent a special commissioner to the islands to make a study of the whole situation and report to him directly. On the basis of his agent's findings, Cleveland came to the conclusion that the revolution in the island kingdom had been accomplished by the improper use of the armed forces of the United States and that the wrong should be righted by a restoration of the queen to her throne. He then withdrew the treaty of annexation from the Senate.

In the minds of Republicans this reverse action on the part of Cleveland was an attack on the motives of Harrison, the former Republican President, and a rank "betrayal of American interests." In their platform of 1896 they stated their own position: "Our foreign policy should be at all times firm, vigorous, and dignified and all our interests in the western hemisphere carefully watched and guarded. The Hawaiian Islands should be controlled by the United States and no foreign power should be permitted to interfere with them." As the popular vote in the election of that year was decidedly in favor of the Republicans, Congress by a joint resolution, passed on July 6, 1898, annexed the islands to the United States and later conferred upon them a territorial form of government — a legislature elected locally by the voters and a governor appointed by the President of the United States with the approval of the Senate.

GROVER CLEVELAND

CUBA AND THE SPANISH WAR

Early American Relations with Cuba. The year that brought Hawaii under the American flag likewise drew to an end another struggle over a similar outpost in the Atlantic, one of the last remnants of the once glorious Spanish empire — the island of Cuba.

For a century the Department of State had kept an eye upon this base of power, knowing full well that both France and England, already owning islands in the West Indies, were also watching Cuba. In the administration of President Fillmore these two countries had united in proposing to the United States a treaty guaranteeing Spain in her possession of Cuba. But to this suggestion the American government replied that the affair was one between Spain and the United States alone.

During the long contest in the United States over the balance of power between the North and the South, the planters often thought of bringing Cuba into the Union as a slave state to offset a free state. Such a project was publicly announced in 1854 when three American ministers abroad, stationed at Madrid, Paris, and London respectively, held a conference and issued the celebrated "Ostend Manifesto," favoring the annexation of Cuba by the United States. In this notice to the world they declared that Cuba, by her geographical position, formed a natural part of the United States, that possession by a foreign power would be dangerous to American interests, and that an effort should be made to buy the island from Spain. In case the owner refused to sell, they concluded, with a flourish, "by every law, human and divine, we shall be justified in wresting it from Spain if we possess the power." This strange proclamation was however promptly disowned by the United States government.

Revolutions in Cuba. For nearly twenty years the Cuban question rested. Then it was revived in another shape during President Grant's administration, when the natives revolted against their Spanish rulers and started a guerrilla warfare which raged for ten years — until 1878. Remembering their own struggle for independence many American citizens sympathized with the Cubans. Expeditions to help them were fitted out secretly in American ports; arms and supplies were smuggled into Cuba; and American soldiers of fortune joined the insurgents. But the American government talked officially about neutrality and for-

mally called on Spain to protect American lives and property in the
revolutionary area. President Grant refused to recognize Cuban
independence on any terms.

When a lull in Cuban disorders came it proved to be brief,
for in 1895 there was a renewal of revolutionary outbreaks. In
every phase the contest between the rebels and the Spanish troops
was marked by extreme
cruelty and a total disre-
gard for life and property.
Once more the questions
that had tormented
Grant's administration
were presented in familiar
forms to President Cleve-
land. Hoping to win by
forcing American intervention, Gomez, the leader of
the revolt, laid waste the
island with fire and sword.
By a proclamation of No-
vember 6, 1895, he ordered
his men to destroy plantations, tear up railways, and
shut the sugar factories.
His work of havoc was
completed on the other
side by the Spanish general,
Weyler, who concentrated
the inhabitants from rural
regions in military camps,

An old cartoon

A SIGHT TOO BAD

Struggling Cuba. "You must be awfully
near-sighted, Mr. President, not to recognize
me." *U. S. Grant.* "No, I am far-sighted:
for I can recognize France."

where they died by the hundreds of disease and starvation.
Stories of atrocities, bad enough in simple truth, became lurid
when told by American newspapers. All over the United States
sermons were preached about Spanish misdeeds; orators demanded
that the Cubans be upheld "in their heroic struggle for independence"; editors spurned mediation and called for intervention, if
necessary with war.

Cleveland's Policy. Unmoved by this agitation, President Cleveland chose the way of peace. He declared that the United States would refuse to take sides in the quarrel between Cuba and Spain and would observe strict neutrality. He declined to act on a resolution of Congress in favor of giving to the Cubans the rights of belligerents. Indeed, anxious to bring order quickly to the distracted island, he offered the services of the United States as mediator — a tender declined by the Spanish government with the broad hint that he had better make American citizens quit sending unlawful aid in money, arms, and supplies to the insurgents. Accordingly Cleveland left "the public nuisance" to his successor, President McKinley, inaugurated on March 4, 1897.

Republican Policies. Now the Republicans were in a position to employ that "firm, vigorous, and dignified" foreign policy which they had approved in their platform. They had declared: "The government of Spain having lost control of Cuba and being unable to protect the property or lives of resident American citizens or to comply with its treaty obligations, we believe that the government of the United States should actively use its influence and good offices to restore peace and give independence to the island." The American property in Cuba to which the Republicans referred in their platform was by this time worth more than fifty million dollars; the commerce with the island amounted to more than one hundred millions annually; and the claims of American citizens against Spain for property destroyed totaled sixteen millions. To the pleas of suffering humanity, which made such a popular propaganda in favor of American intervention in Cuba, there were thus joined economic considerations of great weight.

President McKinley Negotiates. In face of a growing public opinion in favor of instant action, McKinley first chose the path of diplomacy. A short time after his inauguration he made a dignified protest to the Spanish government against its policies in Cuba. In the exchange of notes which resulted, Spain granted many concessions. General Weyler was recalled to Madrid; a governor-general less bloodthirsty in methods was appointed in his stead; a change was made in the policy of concentrating civilians in military camps; and finally "home rule" was promised to Cuba. There seemed to be no doubt that the Spanish government wanted to avoid a war which could have but one outcome. Indeed the American minister at Madrid, General Woodford, reported that firm and patient pressure by the United States would result in the peaceful surrender of Cuba by the Spanish government.

The De Lome and the *Maine* Incidents. Such a policy was upset by events. In February, 1898, a private letter written by Señor de Lome, the Spanish minister at Washington, expressing contempt for the President of the United States, was filched from the mails and published to the world by a powerful journalist, William R. Hearst. Owing to the sensation caused by this news few citizens thought about the breach of courtesy committed in breaking open a personal letter. The Spanish government however did what it could to make amends by officially condemning De Lome and recalling him to Madrid.

At this point a far more serious event put the pacific relations of the two countries in dire peril. On February 15, the American battleship, *Maine*, riding in the harbor of Havana, was blown up and sunk, carrying to death two officers and two hundred and fifty-eight members of the crew. Immediately the tragedy was ascribed by the American papers to Spanish officials, and the effect on the readers can be imagined. When, on March 21, a commission of inquiry reported that the ill-fated ship had been blown up by a submarine mine which had in turn set off some of the ship's magazines, blame for the disaster was promptly laid on Spain. Any American who said that the Cuban revolution was not our affair was now silenced by the cry: "Remember the Maine!"

Spanish Concessions. Still the State Department, under McKinley's hand, kept on negotiating with Madrid and the Spanish government on its part made more promises of reform in the island. Early in April however there came a sudden and decided change in the trend of American diplomacy. On the 4th, McKinley instructed the American minister at Madrid to warn the Spanish government that he was getting ready to lay the Cuban business before Congress. This decision, every one knew, from the

CUBAN REVOLUTIONISTS

temper of Congress, meant war — a prospect which, of course, excited all the European nations. The Pope showed his interest by urging a peaceful solution of the problem. England, France, and Germany, foreseeing an increase of American power, sought to prevent war. Conscious of her weakness, Spain at last dispatched to the President a note promising to stop the fighting in Cuba, to call a Cuban parliament, and to grant all the autonomy that could be reasonably asked.

President McKinley Calls for War. For reasons of his own — reasons which have never yet been fully explained — McKinley ignored Spain's final offers. At the very moment when his patience seemed to bear fruit, he veered sharply from his course and launched his country into war by sending to Congress a militant message on April 11, 1898. Without making public the last note he had received from Spain, he declared that he was at the end of his resources and that the case was in the hands of Congress. He pointed out the sufferings of the Cubans, the injuries done to American citizens and business, and the inability of Spain to bring about peace. Then he asked for authority to employ military and naval forces in restoring order in Cuba.

The Resolution of Congress. There was no doubt of the outcome when the issue was placed in charge of Congress. Resolutions were soon introduced in the House of Representatives authorizing the President to use armed might in bringing peace to Cuba and "establishing by the free action of the people thereof a stable and independent government of their own." To the form and spirit of this proposal some Democrats and Populists took exception. In the Senate, where they were stronger, they compelled the narrow Republican majority to change the wording of the war resolutions. In the final form, these recognized the independence of Cuba, called on Spain to withdraw from the island, and empowered the President to use force to the extent necessary to carry the decision into effect. But in making these demands the United States disclaimed "any disposition or intention to exercise sovereignty, jurisdiction, or control over said island except for the pacification thereof." This action was taken by Congress on April 19, 1898, and approved by the President on the next day.

War and Victory. Military events then followed in swift succession. The navy, as a result in no small measure of the previous activity of Theodore Roosevelt, assistant secretary of the Department, was ready for the trial by battle. Wherever Spanish power lay, attacks were made upon it. On May 1, Commodore Dewey at Manila Bay shattered the Spanish fleet stationed there, marking the doom of Spanish dominion in the Philippines. On July 3, the Spanish fleet under Admiral Cervera, in attempting to escape from Santiago, Cuba, was destroyed by American forces under Commodore Schley. On July 17, Santiago itself, invested by American troops under General Shafter and shelled by American ships, gave up the struggle. On July 25 General Miles landed in the neighboring island of Porto Rico. On August 13, General Merritt and Admiral Dewey carried Manila by storm. The war was over.

The Peace Protocol. Spain had already accepted the stern facts. As early as July 26, 1898, it asked the French ambassador in Washington, M. Cambon, to get from President McKinley his terms of peace. On August 12, a preliminary protocol was signed, providing three fundamental conditions: Cuba was to be free, Porto Rico was to be ceded to the United States, and American troops were to hold Manila pending the final treaty of peace. On October 1, the commissioners of the two countries met at Paris to bring about the settlement.

Peace Negotiations. When the day for the first session of the peace conference arrived, the government at Washington apparently had not yet made up its mind on the Philippines. Perhaps, before the battle of Manila Bay, not ten thousand people in the United States knew or cared where the Philippines were. Certainly in the autumn of 1898 there was no decided opinion as to what should be done with the fruits of Dewey's victory. President McKinley doubtless spoke for the general public when he told the peace commissioners on the eve of their departure that there had originally been no thought of conquest in the Pacific.

It was the march of events, he said, which had imposed new duties on the country: "Incidental to our tenure in the Philippines . . . is the commercial opportunity to which American statesmanship cannot be indifferent. It is just to use every legitimate means for the enlargement of American trade." On this ground he told the commissioners that the United States must have at least the island of Luzon, the chief of the Philippine group, with its harbor of Manila. Not until the latter part of October did he definitely instruct them to demand the entire Philippine archipelago. Though

SCENE IN THE PHILIPPINES
Showing a Home of a Native of the Wealthier Class.

stunned by this order the Spanish agents had to yield; and with heaviness of heart they surrendered the last sign of Spain's long rule in the Pacific.

Final Terms of Peace. The treaty of peace, as finally agreed upon, included the following terms: independence of Cuba; cession of Porto Rico, Guam, and the Philippines to the United States; settlement of claims filed by the citizens of both countries; payment of twenty million dollars to Spain by the United States for the Philippines. A great decision to accept colonial possessions had been made by the American peace commissioners directed by

McKinley. Would the United States Senate, where the Democrats and the Populists held the balance of power, approve this new form of territorial expansion? That was the next question.

The Contest over the Treaty of Peace. The publication of the treaty annexing distant colonies divided the American people into two camps: for and against the policy. In Republican opinion the trend in favor of annexation became open and strong. Perhaps a majority of the men standing highest in that party had undergone the change of heart reflected in the letters of John Hay, Secretary of State. In August of 1898 he had hinted, in a friendly letter to Andrew Carnegie, that he sympathized with the latter's opposition to "imperialism"; but he had added quickly: "The only question in my mind is how far it is now possible for us to withdraw from the Philippines." In November of the same year he wrote to Whitelaw Reid, one of the peace commissioners at Paris: "There is a wild and frantic attack now going on in the press against the whole Philippine transaction. Andrew Carnegie really seems to be off his head. . . . But all this confusion of tongues will go its way. The country will applaud the resolution that has been reached and you will return in the rôle of conquering heroes with your 'brows bound with oak.' "

Republican Senators, such as Beveridge of Indiana and Platt of Connecticut, now appealed to the country to approve annexation. "Every expansion of our territory," said the latter, "has been in accordance with the irresistible law of growth. We could no more resist the successive expansions by which we have grown to be the strongest nation on earth than a tree can resist its growth. The history of territorial expansion is the history of our nation's progress and glory. It is a matter to be proud of, not to lament. We should rejoice that Providence has given us the opportunity to extend our influence, our institutions, and our civilization into regions hitherto closed to us, rather than contrive how we can thwart its designs."

On the other hand the plan for annexing the Philippines was earnestly attacked by opponents, and a few stanch Republicans joined the majority of Democrats in denouncing the treaty as a departure from the ideals of the American republic. George G.

Vest, a Democrat from Missouri, introduced in the Senate a resolution that "under the Constitution of the United States, no power is given to the federal government to acquire territory to be held and governed permanently as colonies." George F. Hoar, a Republican Senator from Massachusetts, whose long and honorable career gave weight to his lightest words, criticized annexation as "a new imperialism," and to the end of his days believed that the drift into rivalry with European nations as a colonial power was fraught with danger to democratic civilization. "Our imperialistic friends," he said, "seem to have forgotten the use of the vocabulary of liberty. They talk about giving good government. 'We shall give them such a government as we think they are fitted for.' 'We shall give them a better government than they had before.' Why, Mr. President, that one phrase conveys to a free man and a free people the most stinging insult. In that little phrase, as in a seed, is contained the germ of all despotism and of all tyranny. Government is not a gift. Free government is not to be given by all the blended powers of earth and heaven. It is a birthright. It belongs, as our fathers said, and as their children said, as Jefferson said, and as President McKinley said, to human nature itself."

With opinion so divided, the Senate was slow in coming to a decision on the peace treaty, containing the plans for annexing colonies. In general Democrats and Populists were against it. Nevertheless William Jennings Bryan finally hurried to Washington and brought his personal influence to bear in favor of approval. "Patriotism requires ratification," some persons argued. "The country desires peace and the Senate should not delay," others insisted. On February 6, 1899, the requisite majority of two-thirds was mustered, but many a Senator who voted for the treaty shared the misgivings of Senator Hoar as to the "dangers of imperialism." Indeed at the time, the Senators passed a resolution declaring that the policy to be adopted in the Philippines was still an unsettled question. In this way the question of their independence was left open, satisfying Bryan for the moment.

The Change in Foreign Relations. The war against Spain, while it brought about Cuban independence, like all armed conflicts, produced additional results wholly unforeseen by the mass of the people who had urged and supported it. Among other things it had a great influence on the attitude of European countries toward the American republic. Good will for the United States was from the first positive and outspoken in England. "The state of feeling here," wrote John Hay, then ambassador to London, "is the best I have ever known. From every quarter the evidences of it come to me. The royal family by habit and tradition are most careful not to break the rule of strict neutrality, but even among them I find nothing but hearty kindness and — so far as is consistent with propriety — sympathy. Among the political leaders on both sides I find not only sympathy but a somewhat eager desire that 'the other fellows' shall not seem more friendly."

The distinguished English statesman, Joseph Chamberlain, frankly said in a political address at the very beginning of the war that the next duty of Englishmen "is to establish and maintain bonds of permanent unity with our kinsmen across the Atlantic. . . . I even go so far as to say that, terrible as war may be, even war would be cheaply purchased if, in a great and noble cause, the Stars and Stripes and the Union Jack should wave together over an Anglo-Saxon alliance." To the American ambassador Chamberlain confided significantly that he did not "care a hang what they say about it on the continent," which was another way of hinting that Germany and France had better heed his warning. At any rate this friendly English opinion was perhaps useful to the United States in keeping European powers from coming to the aid of Spain. But Henry Adams, recalling humiliations in London during the Civil War when his father was the American minister, coolly remarked that "the sudden appearance of Germany as the grizzly terror" had simply "frightened England into America's arms." Whatever the cause Great Britain and the United States seemed to be drawing closer together, as if in preparation for the mighty struggle with Germany that was to come.

AMERICAN POLICIES IN THE PHILIPPINES AND THE ORIENT

The Filipino Revolt against American Rule. On turning from the war with Spain to take up their new tasks the Americans were confronted by perplexing questions. How were the possessions to be governed? Were the inhabitants to become American citizens? How was trade with them to be regulated? But they had scarcely stated these issues when a native uprising against American rule broke out in the Philippines. The leader of this revolt, Aguinaldo, had aided the American forces in overthrowing Spanish dominion, and he had assumed that as a result of their joint operations the islands would be made independent like Cuba.

When the news reached him that the American flag was to be raised in place of the Spanish flag, he naturally felt a great deal of resentment. Early in 1899 smoldering embers were set ablaze by a slight collision between his followers and American soldiers. In a flash, this incident developed into serious fighting which finally widened into a general guerrilla warfare lasting three years and costing heavily in men

Copyright by Underwood and Underwood, N. Y.
ANOTHER PHILIPPINE HOME

and money. Without effect did McKinley assure the Filipinos that the government to be set up in the islands would be designed "not for our satisfaction or for the expression of our theoretical views, but for the happiness, peace, and prosperity of the people of the Philippine Islands."

Attacks on Republican "Imperialism." The Filipino insurrection inspired American opponents of McKinley's colonial policies to put a keener edge on their criticism of his "imperialism." Senator Hoar spared no words in his censure of the new political course. The revolt against American rule was to him one more proof that annexation had been a mistake and the beginning of injustice. "I have failed to discover in the speeches, public or private, of the advocates of this war," he exclaimed in the Senate, "or in the press which supports it and them, a single expression anywhere of a desire to do justice to the people of the Philippine Islands, or of a desire to make known to the people of the United States the truth of the case. . . . The catchwords, the cries, the pithy and pregnant phrases of which their speech is full, all mean dominion. They mean perpetual dominion. . . . There is not one of these gentlemen who will rise in his place and affirm that if he were a Filipino he would not do exactly as the Filipinos are doing; that he would not despise them if they were to do otherwise. So much at least they owe of respect to the dead and buried history — the dead and buried history so far as they can slay and bury it — of their country." In the way of practical suggestions, the Senator proposed the recognition of Filipino independence, American aid in establishing self-government, and an invitation to all nations to join in a guarantee of freedom to the islands.

The Republican Answer. To McKinley and his supporters, engaged in a struggle to maintain American supremacy in the Philippines by arms, such talk seemed positively treasonable. They pointed out the obstacles in the way of democracy for a collection of seven million people ranging in civilization from ignorant hill men to the cultured inhabitants of Manila. The incidents of the uprising and its repression, they admitted, were painful enough; but minor as compared with the disorders that would follow the attempt of the Filipinos to manage their own affairs. They preferred, they explained, to put down the insurrection and gradually prepare the inhabitants of the islands for self-government. So they applied force without stint to quelling the revolt. Then they devoted their attention to the development of civil government, commerce, and industry.

The Boxer Rebellion in China. On the mainland of Asia as well as in the Philippines the McKinley administration used force in protecting American interests. In 1900 when a native uprising against foreigners, known as the Boxer revolt, broke out in China, the United States joined several other powers in a military expedition and in a diplomatic settlement at its conclusion. The Boxers, a patriotic secret society, had for some time carried on a campaign of hatred against all aliens in the Celestial empire, who were, it was alleged, "lacerating China like tigers." In the summer of 1900 their revolt ran riot with vengeful fury. Missionaries and traders were murdered in the provinces; foreign legations were stoned; the German ambassador was killed in the streets of Peking; and to all appearances a war of extermination had begun. In the month of June nearly five hundred men, women, and children, representing all the alien nations, were besieged in the British quarters in Peking, where they had taken refuge.

Intervention in China. But the arrival of armed forces, made up of Japanese, Russian, British, American, French, and German soldiers and marines saved them from capture. When once these foreign troops were in possession of the Chinese capital however fresh problems arose to be solved. For more than half a century, the powers of Europe had been in truth, as the Boxers claimed, carving up the Chinese empire, taking territory, railway concessions, mining rights, ports, and commercial privileges at the expense of the huge but helpless victim. The United States alone among the great nations, while as zealous as any in the pursuit of trade, had refrained from seizing Chinese territory or ports. Moreover, the Department of State had been urging European countries to respect Chinese territorial integrity, and to allow China to trade equally with all nations.

The American Policy of "the Open Door." On this basis, which he called "the Open Door" plan, John Hay, as Secretary of State, offered his suggestions for peace in China. "The policy of the government of the United States," he said to the great powers, in the summer of 1900, "is to seek a solution which may bring about permanent safety and peace to China, preserve Chinese territorial and administrative entity, protect all rights guaranteed to friendly powers by treaty and international law, and safeguard for the world the principle of equal and impartial trade with all parts of the Chinese empire." This was a clear warning to the world that the United States would not join in a scramble to punish the Chinese by tearing away more territory. In the end damages were collected by the Western nations from China for injuries inflicted upon their citizens by the Boxers; but the United States, finding the sum awarded in excess of legitimate claims, returned the balance in the form of a fund to be applied to the education of Chinese students in American colleges. By this action, the hold of the United States upon the affections of the Chinese people was strengthened and, in the long run, Hay remarked himself, "our great commercial interests in that Empire were safeguarded."

Imperialism in the Presidential Campaign of 1900. Believing that they had pursued a right policy in foreign and domestic affairs, the Republicans renominated McKinley for the campaign of 1900 and set forth their position in ringing phrases: "In accepting by the treaty of Paris the just responsibility of our victories in the Spanish war, the President and Senate won the undoubted approval of the American people. No other course was possible than to destroy Spain's sovereignty throughout the West Indies and in the Philippine Islands. That course created our responsibility, before the world and with the unorganized population whom our intervention had freed from Spain, to provide for the maintenance of law and order, and for the establishment of good government and for the performance of international obligations. Our authority could not be less than our responsibility, and wherever sovereign rights were extended it became the high duty of the government to maintain its authority, to put down armed insurrection, and to confer the blessings of liberty and civilization upon all the rescued peoples. The largest measure of self-government consistent with their welfare and our duties shall be secured to them by law." In a whirlwind of enthusiasm, the Republicans nominated for the vice presidency, against his protest, Theodore Roosevelt, governor of New York and the hero of the Rough Riders, who had been a popular figure in the Cuban war.

Arraying themselves against Republican policies, the Democrats again selected William Jennings Bryan as their candidate, and drafted a platform criticizing "the imperialistic program" of McKinley's administration. "As we are not willing," ran one of the planks, "to surrender our civilization or to convert the republic into an empire, we favor an immediate declaration of the nation's purpose to give to the Filipinos, first, a stable form of government; second, independence; third, protection from outside interfer-

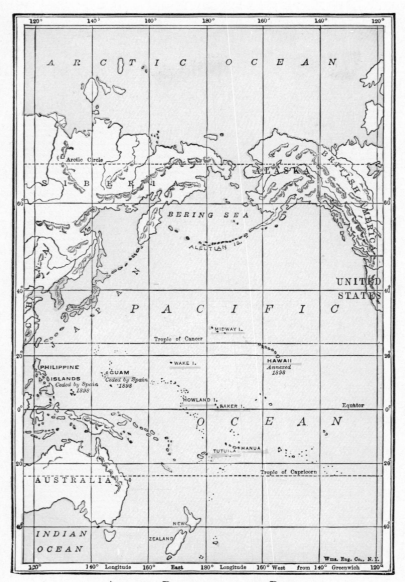

AMERICAN POSSESSIONS IN THE PACIFIC

ence. . . . The greedy commercialism which dictated the Philippine policy of the Republican administration attempts to justify it with the plea that it will pay, but even this sordid and unworthy plea fails when brought to the test of facts. The war of 'criminal aggression' against the Filipinos entailing an annual expense of many millions has already cost more than any possible profit that could accrue from the entire Philippine trade for years to come. . . . We oppose militarism. It means conquest abroad and intimidation and oppression at home. It means the strong arm which has ever been fatal to free institutions. It is what millions of our citizens have fled from in Europe. It will impose upon our peace-loving people a large standing army, an unnecessary burden of taxation, and would be a constant menace to their liberties."

With the issues growing out of the Spanish war explained and discussed in the open, the people rejected Bryan, the Democratic candidate, even more decidedly than four years before. Victorious at the polls, McKinley turned with renewed confidence to promoting the program he had thus far advanced. But fate cut off his leadership. In September, 1901, shortly after his second inauguration, he was shot by an anarchist while attending the Buffalo Exposition. "What a strange and tragic fate it has been of mine," wrote John Hay, on the day of the President's death, "to stand by the bier of three of my dearest friends, Lincoln, Garfield, and McKinley, three of the gentlest of men, all risen to the head of the state and all done to death by assassins." On September 14, 1901, the Vice President, Theodore Roosevelt, took up the reins of power that had fallen from the hands of his distinguished chief, and promised to continue "absolutely unbroken" the policies he had inherited.

Summary of National Growth and World Politics

The economic aspects of the period between 1865 and 1900 may be readily summed up: recovery of the South from the ruin of the Civil War, extension of railways, development of the Great West, and triumph of industry and business enterprise. In the South many great plantations were broken up and sold in small farms, crops were diversified, the small farming class was raised in the scale of social importance, cotton manufacturing was launched, and coal, iron, timber, and other resources were brought into use. In the West the free arable land was practically exhausted by 1890 under the terms of the Homestead Act; gold, silver, copper, coal, and other minerals were discovered in abundance; numerous rail connections were formed with the Atlantic seaboard; the cowboy and the wild Indian disappeared with the advance of a standardized civilization of electric lights and bathtubs. By the end of the century the American frontier was no more. The primitive life so long associated with America was a thing of the past. The cultural unity of the continental United States was established.

Progress was most marked in the field of business enterprise. The industrial system, which had risen and flourished before the Civil War, grew into immense proportions and industries spread from the Northeast into all parts of the country. Small business concerns often grew into huge corporations. Individual plants were merged under the management of gigantic trusts. Short railway lines were united to form national systems. The population of industrial wage-earners rose into the tens of millions. Immigration increased by leaps and bounds. Cities now overshadowed the country. The nation that had once depended upon Europe for most of its manufactured goods became a competitor of Europe in the markets of the earth.

Political changes accompanied the sweep of business enterprise. White supremacy was restored in the South; to the discussion of the old questions, such as the currency, the tariff, and national banking were added new issues like the trusts and labor problems. Foreign affairs took on novel phases. Alaska was purchased from Russia; attempts were made to extend American naval control to the Caribbean region; a Samoan island was brought under the flag; and the Hawaiian Islands were annexed. The Monroe Doctrine was applied with vigor in the dispute between Venezuela and Great Britain.

In 1898 aid was given to the Cubans in their revolutionary struggle against Spain, thus starting a war which ended in the annexation of Porto Rico, Guam, and the Philippines by the

United States. American influence in the Orient was enlarged by business men and missionaries, and the American government took an active part in discussions among the world powers over the state of China. Questions connected with foreign and "imperial" policies were united with domestic issues to make up the substance of politics. In the direction of these affairs, the Republicans took the leadership, for they held the presidency during all the years, except eight, between 1865 and 1900.

References

J. W. Foster, *A Century of American Diplomacy; American Diplomacy in the Orient.*
W. F. Reddaway, *The Monroe Doctrine.*
J. H. Latané, *The United States and Spanish America.*
A. C. Coolidge, *The United States as a World Power.*
A. T. Mahan, *Interest of the United States in the Sea Power.*
Parker T. Moon, *Imperialism and World Politics.*
F. E. Chadwick, *Spanish-American War.*
D. C. Worcester, *The Philippine Islands and Their People.*
M. M. Kalaw, *Self-Government in the Philippines.*
L. S. Rowe, *The United States and Porto Rico.*
F. E. Chadwick, *The Relations of the United States and Spain.*
W. R. Shepherd, *Latin America; Central and South America.*
D. Y. Thomas, *One Hundred Years of the Monroe Doctrine.*

Questions

1. Tell the story of the international crisis that developed soon after the Civil War with regard to Mexico.
2. Give the essential facts relating to the purchase of Alaska.
3. Review the early history of our interest in the Caribbean.
4. Amid what circumstances was the Monroe Doctrine applied in Cleveland's administration?
5. Give the causes that led to the war with Spain.
6. Tell the leading events in that war.
7. What was the outcome as far as Cuba was concerned? The outcome for the United States?
8. Discuss the attitude of the Filipinos toward American sovereignty in the islands.
9. Describe McKinley's colonial policy.
10. How was the Spanish War viewed in England? On the Continent?
11. Was there a unified American opinion on American expansion?

12. Was this expansion a departure from our traditions?
13. What events led to foreign intervention in China?
14. Explain the policy of "the open door."

Research Topics

Hawaii and Venezuela. Dewey, *National Problems* (American Nation Series), pp. 279–313; Macdonald, *Documentary Source Book*, pp. 600–602; Hart, *American History Told by Contemporaries*, Vol. IV, pp. 612–616.

Intervention in Cuba. Latané, *America as a World Power* (American Nation Series), pp. 3–28; Macdonald, *Documentary Source Book*, pp. 597–598; Roosevelt, *Autobiography*, pp. 223–277; Haworth, *The United States in Our Own Time*, pp. 232–256; Hart, *Contemporaries*, Vol. IV, pp. 573–578.

The War with Spain. Elson, *History of the United States*, pp. 873–879.

Terms of Peace with Spain. Latané, pp. 63–81; Macdonald, pp. 602–608; Hart, *Contemporaries*, Vol. IV, pp. 588–590.

The Philippine Insurrection. Latané, pp. 82–99.

Imperialism as a Campaign Issue. Latané, pp. 120–132; Haworth, pp. 257–277; Hart, *Contemporaries*, Vol. IV, pp. 604–611.

Biographical Studies. William McKinley, M. A. Hanna, John Hay; Admirals, George Dewey, W. T. Sampson, and W. S. Schley; and Generals, W. R. Shafter, Joseph Wheeler, and H. W. Lawton.

General Analysis of American Expansion. *Syllabus in History* (New York State, 1920), pp. 142–147.

Questions for Debate

1. All international disputes can be settled by arbitration.
2. It would have been wiser to give the Philippines independence in 1899.

PART VII: PROGRESSIVE DEMOCRACY AND FOREIGN RELATIONS

CHAPTER XXIII

THE EVOLUTION OF REPUBLICAN POLICIES
(1901–1913)

Theodore Roosevelt. When Theodore Roosevelt took the oath of office, September 14, 1901, the presidency passed to a novel type of leader. Roosevelt was brusque, hearty, restless, and fond of action — "a young fellow of infinite dash and originality," as John Hay remarked of him; combining the spirit of his college, Harvard, with the breezy freedom of the plains; interested in everything — a new species of game, a new book, a diplomatic riddle, or fresh theory of history or biology. Though only forty-three years of age he was experienced in the art of practical politics. Coming upon the political scene in the early eighties, he had associated himself with the reformers in the Republican party; but he was no "Mugwump." From the first he vehemently preached the doctrine of party loyalty; if beaten in the convention, he voted the straight ticket in the election. For many years he strictly adhered to this rule, winning in recognition of his talents and fidelity important public offices. He served in the New York legislature, as head of the New York City police force, as federal civil service commissioner under President Harrison, as assistant secretary of the navy under President McKinley, and as governor of the Empire State. If political managers of the old school spoke of him as "brilliant but erratic," they soon found him equal to the shrewdest in negotiation and action.

FOREIGN AFFAIRS

The Panama Canal. The paramount foreign question before President Roosevelt on the day of his inauguration, that of the Panama Canal, was a heritage from his predecessor. The idea of a water route across the isthmus, long a dream of navigators, had become a living issue with the voyage of the battleship *Oregon* around South America during the Spanish War. But before the United States could act it had to undo the Clayton-Bulwer treaty, made with Great Britain in 1850, which provided for the construction of the canal under their joint supervision. Though it raised knotty problems the change was at length effected by the Hay-Pauncefote treaty of 1901 authorizing the United States to proceed alone, on condition that there should be no discrimination against other nations in the matter of rates and charges.

This accomplished, it was necessary to decide just where the canal should be built. One group in Congress advocated the route through Nicaragua; in fact, two official commissions had already approved that location. Another group favored cutting the channel through Panama, after purchasing the rights of a defunct French company which, under the direction of De Lesseps, hero of the Suez Canal, had made a costly failure some twenty years before. At the close of a heated argument over the merits of the two plans, preference was given to the Panama project. As the isthmus was then a part of Colombia, President Roosevelt proceeded to negotiate with the government of that country a treaty empowering the United States to build the canal in its territory. Without a hitch the treaty was framed, but it was rejected by the Colombian senate, much to the President's annoyance. "You could no more make an agreement with the Colombian rulers," he exclaimed, "than you could nail jelly to a wall." He was spared the necessity by a timely revolution. On November 3, 1903, Panama threw off its allegiance to Colombia and in about seventy-two hours the United States recognized its independence.

An immediate sequel to this amazing incident was the signature of a treaty between Panama and the United States in which the latter secured the right to construct the long-discussed canal in return for a guarantee of Panamanian independence and certain payments in money. The concessions and property of the French concern were then bought, and the final details settled. A lock rather than a sea-level canal was agreed upon and the task of building it was assigned to the government, instead of to private contractors. Next, a corps of doctors of medicine, headed by Colonel W. C. Gorgas, was employed to stamp out the tropical diseases that had made Panama a continuous plague spot. Finally, in 1904, as President Roosevelt said, "the dirt began to fly." After surmounting formidable difficulties — engineering, labor, and sanitary — the American forces in 1913 joined the waters of the Atlantic and the Pacific, reducing the sea voyage from New York to San Francisco by nearly eight thousand miles. Exulting in the achievement, Congress passed, in President Taft's administration,

PANAMA: A SHIP PASSING THROUGH THE GATUN LOCKS

a tolls bill discriminating in rates in favor of American ships — notwithstanding the equality clause in the treaty with Great Britain. But on the insistence of the next President, Woodrow Wilson, this measure was repealed.

The Conclusion of the Russo-Japanese War. While Roosevelt was trying to get the Panama Canal started, another difficult task in foreign affairs fell to his lot. In the winter of 1904 a terrible conflict broke out between Japan and Russia over the division of spoils in Manchuria. The fortunes of war were on the whole with the agile forces of Nippon and, it seems, President Roosevelt's sympathies were largely with the Japanese, although he was careful to maintain official neutrality. At all events, Secretary Hay wrote in his diary on New Year's Day, 1905, that the President was "quite firm in his view that we cannot permit Japan to be robbed a second time of her victory," referring to the fact that ten years before, after defeating China, Japan had been compelled by Russia, Germany, and France to give up the fruits of conquest.

Whatever the President's personal feelings may have been, he was aware that Japan, despite her triumphs over Russia, was staggering under a heavy burden of debt and he believed that the world balance of power needed a Japan strong in finance and arms. At a suggestion from Tokyo he invited both belligerents in the summer of 1905 to stop fighting and hold a peace conference. If they had any doubts as to the wisdom of this counsel they were soon convinced by European bankers who had already come to an agreement that the conflict could not go on any longer. After some delay the two warsick powers consented to send delegates to a conference at Portsmouth, New Hampshire, for the purpose of discussing a settlement. With fine urbanity Roosevelt presided over the opening ceremonies and at the close he had the satisfaction of seeing his efforts crowned by a treaty of peace and amity.

The Monroe Doctrine Applied Again to Venezuela. Less spectacular than the Russo-Japanese settlement but not less perplexing was a diplomatic exchange with Germany over the Monroe Doctrine. This clash grew out of the inability or unwillingness of the Venezuelan government to pay certain debts due foreign creditors. Having exhausted their patience in trying to collect, England, Germany, and Italy in December, 1902, sent battleships to Venezuelan ports. Their action was followed by the rupture of diplomatic relations, with a possibility that war and the occupation of Venezuelan territory might result.

Now Roosevelt was as determined as Cleveland had been that on no account should European countries be allowed to seize South American territory. But he won his point with less friction. He urged an arbitration of the dispute, winning the assent of England and Italy. After a little hesitation Germany in turn agreed to that solution of the thorny problem and the incident was closed. In this fashion another chapter was written in the history of the Monroe Doctrine. Thus interpreted by Roosevelt, the Doctrine meant that the United States would not help Latin-American countries evade their debts, although it would block any action on the part of European powers that might lead to the temporary or permanent occupation of Latin-American territory.

The Santo Domingo Protectorate. The same issue was involved in a tangle over Santo Domingo which emerged in 1904. The Dominican republic, like Venezuela, was heavily in debt, and certain European governments declared that, unless the United States undertook to look after the finances of the debtor, they would resort to armed coercion. What was the United States to do? The danger of having some European power intrenched in Santo Domingo was too real to be denied. Thoroughly aware of this peril Roosevelt acted with characteristic speed, and in spite of strong opposition in the Senate was able to secure a treaty in 1907 which placed Dominican finances under American supervision.

In the course of the debate over this settlement, a number of interesting questions arose. Should the United States approve the practice of European governments in using armed force to collect debts owed to private citizens? Was the American navy to be used to help creditors collect their debts anywhere in Latin-America? Would it not be best to refer all such matters to the Hague Court or to special international commissions for arbitration? To the last question the answer was made that the United States could not surrender any issue coming under the terms of the Monroe Doctrine to the decision of an international tribunal. "The country," said Roosevelt emphatically, "would certainly decline to go to war to prevent a foreign government from collecting a just debt; on the other hand, it is very inadvisable to permit any foreign power to take possession, even temporarily, of the customs houses of an American republic in order to inforce the payment of its obligations; for such a temporary occupation might turn into a permanent occupation. The only escape from these alternatives may at any time be that we must ourselves undertake to bring about some arrangement by which so much as possible of a just obligation shall be paid." The Monroe Doctrine was negative in its original form: it denied to European states the right to do certain things in this hemisphere. That it imposed positive duties on the United States was the point now affirmed and developed.

The Hague Conference. Controversies over Latin-American relations naturally turned Roosevelt's mind to the consideration of permanent methods for the peaceful settlement of international quarrels. Indeed the possibility of preventing warfare was now being earnestly discussed among the civilized peoples in general. As if conscious of coming calamity, a few statesmen of the Old World seemed to be searching for a way to reduce armaments and avoid the trial of international cases by the cruel and costly process of battle. At all events the Russian Czar, Nicholas II, fated to die in one of the terrible holocausts which he helped to bring upon mankind, invited the nations of the earth to send delegates to a peace convention at The Hague in 1899. Although this conference did nothing to reduce military burdens or to outlaw war, it did recognize the right of neutral nations to offer their services as mediators to countries at war. Moreover it established a court at The Hague for the voluntary arbitration of international disputes.

Encouraged by this experiment, feeble as it had been, President Roosevelt himself proposed a second conference, yielding to the Czar the honor of issuing the call. At this next international assembly, held at The Hague in 1907, the representatives of the United States offered a plan for the compulsory arbitration of certain matters of international strife, but the scheme was not adopted, partly on account of opposition from the German delegates. Reduction of armaments was again deferred. In fact, all that was accomplished this time was an agreement upon a few rules for the conduct of "civilized warfare."

The World Tour of the Fleet. As if to assure the world then that the United States placed no more reliance on peace conferences than other nations, Roosevelt made a display of American power the following year by sending a fleet of sixteen battleships on a tour around the globe. On his own authority, he ordered the ships to sail out of Hampton Roads and circle the earth by way of the Straits of Magellan, San Francisco, Australia, the Philippines, China, Japan, and the Suez Canal. This enterprise was not, as some critics claimed, a "mere boyish flourish." It was an exhibition of sea power indicating that the wide empire of American trade and dominion had a force adequate to sustain it. The voyage around the world therefore served a double purpose. It interested Roosevelt's countrymen in his naval program and it reminded other governments that the American giant was not sleeping in the midst of international rivalries.

COLONIAL ADMINISTRATION

A Constitutional Question Settled. In colonial administration, as in foreign policy, Roosevelt advanced with confident strides in a

Photograph from Underwood and Underwood, N. Y.

A SUGAR MILL, PORTO RICO

path already marked out by his predecessor. President McKinley had defined the principles that were to control the development of Porto Rico and the Philippines. The Republican party had announced a program of pacification, gradual self-government, and commercial improvement. The only remaining question of importance, "Does the Constitution follow the flag?" — to use the popular phrase — had been answered by the Supreme Court of the United States in 1901.   Although it was well known that the framers of the Constitution had not thought of governing any such dependencies as the Philippines and Porto Rico, the Court found a way for Congress to apply to these possessions any reasonable rules required by the circumstances.

Porto Rico.   The government of Porto Rico was a relatively simple matter.   It was a single island with a fairly united population, apart from the Spanish upper class.   For a time after the occupation in 1898, it was managed under military rule. This régime was succeeded by the establishment of civil government under the "organic act" passed by Congress in 1900, which assured to Porto Ricans American protection.   It provided for a governor and six executive secretaries appointed by the President of the United States with the approval of the American Senate; and for a legislature of two houses — one elected by popular vote, and an upper chamber composed of the executive secretaries and five other persons appointed in the same manner.   In this fashion, the United States turned back to the political system maintained by England in her provinces in colonial days.   The natives were given a voice in their government and the power of initiating laws; but the final word both in legislation and administration was vested in officers appointed in Washington.   Such was the plan under which the affairs of Porto Rico were conducted by President Roosevelt.   Indeed, it lasted until the new organic act of 1917, which gave the Porto Ricans American citizenship and changed the plan of government.

The Philippines.   The administration of the Philippines presented far more difficult problems.   The number of islands, the variety of languages and races, the grades of civilization all combined to test the skill of the American officials who undertook to rule them.   In coping with the situation, the American government advanced by three stages.   At first the islands were managed directly by the President of the United States under his supreme military power.   In 1901 a civilian commission, headed by William Howard Taft, was selected by President McKinley and charged with the administration of all the provinces in which the revolt against American authority had been suppressed. Under the terms of an organic act, passed by Congress in 1902, the third

W. H. TAFT [THIRD FROM RIGHT] IN THE PHILIPPINES

stage was reached by granting the Filipinos a share in their government in 1907. The islands now passed under the rule of a governor and commission, appointed by the President and Senate, and a legislature — one house elected by popular vote and an upper chamber composed of the commission. This scheme, like that obtaining in Porto Rico, remained intact until a Democratic Congress under President Wilson's leadership carried the colonial administration into its fourth phase by making both houses elective. Self-government was thus extended to the islands; but it encouraged rather than dampened the movement among the Philippine natives for complete freedom.

Cuban Relations. Though nominally independent, Cuba also presented some puzzles for the government at Washington to solve. In the enthusiasm that greeted the declaration of war on Spain, Congress, as we have seen, recognized the independence of Cuba and disclaimed "any disposition or intention to exercise sovereignty, jurisdiction or control over said island except for the pacification thereof." Before withdrawing American troops from the island however Congress in March, 1901, enacted, and required Cuba to approve, a series of restrictions known as the Platt Amendment. These provisions limited Cuba's power to borrow money, gave the United States the right to intervene whenever necessary to protect life and property, and reserved to the United States coaling stations at certain points to be agreed upon. The Cubans made strong protests against what they deemed "infringement of their sovereignty"; but finally accepted their fate. Even when in 1906 President Roosevelt landed American troops in the island to quell a domestic dissension, they acquiesced in the action, evidently regarding it as a distinct warning that they should learn to conduct their elections in an orderly manner.

THE ROOSEVELT DOMESTIC POLICIES

Social Questions to the Front. In affairs at home, as well as abroad, Roosevelt was always at the forefront. From the day of his inauguration to the close of his service in 1909, by means of messages, speeches, and interviews, he kept up a lively discussion of trusts, capital, labor, poverty, riches, lawbreaking, good citizenship, and kindred themes. Many a subject previously touched upon only by the minor parties, such as the Greenbackers and

Populists, he dignified in a presidential message or by a public address. That he did this with any clear-cut design or policy in his mind does not seem to be the case. He admitted himself that when he became President he did not have in hand any settled or far-reaching plan of social betterment. He did have however decided opinions on general principles. "I was bent upon making the government," he wrote, "the most efficient possible instrument in helping the people of the United States to better themselves in every way, politically, socially, and industrially. I believed with all my heart in real and thoroughgoing democracy and I wished to make the democracy industrial as well as political, although I had only partially formulated the method I believed we should follow." At least he had departed a long way from the traditional idea of the government as nothing but a big policeman keeping order among people fighting over the distribution of the nation's wealth and resources.

Roosevelt's View of the Constitution. Equally significant was Roosevelt's attitude toward the Constitution and the office of President. He held that the Constitution "should be treated as the greatest document ever devised by the wit of man to aid a people in exercising every power necessary for its own betterment, not as a strait-jacket cunningly fashioned to strangle growth." He viewed the presidency as he did the Constitution. Strict constructionists of the Jeffersonian School, of whom there were many even in the Republican party, maintained that the President could do nothing that he was not specifically authorized to do by the Constitution. Roosevelt took exactly the opposite position. He believed that it was not only the President's right but his duty "to do anything that the needs of the nation demanded unless such action was forbidden by the Constitution or the laws." He declared that he acted "for the common well-being of all our people whenever and in whatever manner was necessary, unless prevented by direct constitutional or legislative prohibition."

Trusts and Railways. To the trust question, Roosevelt devoted special attention. This was unavoidable. By far the major part of the business of the country was by this time brought under the control of corporations. Indeed, their growth had been the leading feature in American industrial development at the turn of the century. In this conquest of business by trusts and "the resulting private fortunes of great magnitude," the Populists and the Democrats had seen a peril to the republic. "Plutocracy has taken the place of democracy; the tariff breeds trusts; let us therefore destroy the tariff and the trusts" — this was the campaign slogan used by Bryan and his disciples.

With such reasoning Roosevelt had little patience. He rejected the idea that the trusts were the product of the tariff or of governmental action of any kind. He insisted that they were the outcome of "natural economic forces": (1) destructive competition among business men compelling them to avoid ruin by coöperation in fixing prices; (2) the growth of markets on a national scale and even international scale, calling for vast accumulations of capital to carry on such business; (3) the possibility of immense savings by the union of many plants under a single management. Unregulated competition he regarded as "the source of evils which all men concede must be remedied if this civilization of ours is to survive." The notion, therefore, that mammoth business concerns should be or could be broken up by a decree of law, Roosevelt treated as absurd.

Nevertheless, he believed that "evil trusts" should be prevented from "wrongdoing of any kind"; that is, punished for plain swindling, for making agreements to limit output, for refusing to sell to customers who dealt with rival firms, and for conspiracies with railways to destroy competitors by charging high freight rates, and for similar abuses. Accordingly, he proposed, not the destruction of the trusts, but their regulation by the government. This, he contended, would preserve the good features of business on a large scale while putting a stop to the evils that it entailed. The railway company he declared to be a public servant. "Its rates should be just to and open to all shippers alike." In such language he answered those who thought that trusts and railway combinations were private concerns to be managed solely by their owners as they pleased and for personal profit. Such likewise was his reply to those who thought trusts and railway combinations could be abolished by tariff reduction or criminal prosecution.

The Labor Question. On the labor question, then pressing to the front in public interest, Roosevelt also took advanced ground

Copyright by Underwood and Underwood, N. Y.

ROOSEVELT TALKING TO THE ENGINEER OF A RAILROAD TRAIN

for his time. He declared that the workingman, single-handed, empty-handed, and threatened with starvation if unemployed, was no match for the employer who was able to bargain and wait.

This inequality between the two contracting parties led him to accept the principle of the trade union; namely, that only by collective bargaining can labor be put on a footing to measure its strength fairly with capital. While he severely arraigned labor leaders who advocated violence and extreme doctrines, he held that "the organization of labor into trade unions and federations is necessary, is beneficent, and is one of the greatest possible agencies in the attainment of a true industrial, as well as a true political, democracy in the United States." The last resort of trade unions in labor disputes, the strike, he approved in case negotiations failed to secure "a fair deal."

Yet Roosevelt thought that labor organizations, even if wisely directed, could not solve all the pressing social questions of the age. The aid of the government at many points he believed necessary to avoid undeserved poverty, industrial diseases, unemployment, and the sad consequences of industrial accidents. In his first message of 1901, for instance, he urged that workers injured in industry should have definite and ample compensation. From time to time he advocated other legislation to obtain what he called "a larger measure of social and industrial justice."

Great Riches and Taxation. Even the charge of the radicals, such as the Populists, that the "toil of millions is boldly stolen to build up colossal fortunes for a few" — a charge which his predecessors considered beneath contempt — Roosevelt treated as worthy of an answer. In his first message he denied the truth of the common saying that the rich were growing richer and the poor were growing poorer. He asserted that, on the contrary, the average man, wage-worker, farmer, and small business man, was better off than ever. That there had been abuses in the heaping up of private riches he did not pretend to ignore, but he believed that the men who won immense fortunes, on the whole, conferred positive benefits upon the country. Nevertheless, he felt that grave dangers to the safety and the happiness of the people lurked in gross inequalities of wealth. In 1906 he wrote that he wished it were in his power to prevent the growth of enormous fortunes. The next year, to the astonishment of many leaders in his own party, he told Congress in a message that he approved both income and inheritance taxes, then generally viewed as Populist or Democratic measures. He took the stand that such taxes should be levied in order to bring about a more equitable distribution of wealth and wider equality of opportunity among citizens.

LEGISLATIVE AND EXECUTIVE ACTIVITIES

Economic Legislation. When Roosevelt turned from expressing his opinions to the work of trying to get his bills through Congress, he found himself faced with strong opposition in both parties. Many of his views were too advanced for the Republicans and the making of laws to apply them was slow. But in his administrations several measures were enacted that bore the stamp of his theories, although it could hardly be said that he controlled Congress to the same degree as did some other Presidents. The Hepburn Railway Act of 1906 enlarged the interstate commerce commission; it extended the commission's power over oil pipe lines, express companies, and other interstate carriers; it gave the commission the right to reduce rates found to be unreasonable and discriminatory; it forbade "midnight tariffs," that is, sudden changes in rates favoring certain shippers; and it prohibited common carriers from transporting goods owned by themselves, especially coal, except for their proper use. Two important pure food and drug laws, passed during the same year, were designed to protect the public against diseased meats and harmful foods and drugs. His labor legislation included an act making interstate railways liable to damages for injuries sustained by their employees and the law of 1908 limiting the hours of railway employees engaged as trainmen or telegraph operators.

Reclamation and Conservation. The open country — deserts, forests, waterways, and public lands — interested Roosevelt no less than railway and industrial questions. Indeed, in his first message to Congress he placed the conservation of natural resources among "the most vital internal problems" of the age, and brought before the people more forcibly an issue that had been discussed in a casual way since Cleveland's first administration. The suggestion called forth an immediate response from Congress. Under the leadership of Senator Newlands, of Nevada, the Reclamation Act of 1902 was passed, providing for the irrigation of desert areas in the West. By this Act proceeds from the sale of public lands were set aside for the construction of dams and sluiceways to hold water and divert it as needed to the thirsty sands. Furthermore it arranged that the rents paid by water users should go into a reclamation fund to continue the good work forever. Construction was started immediately under the terms of the law. Within seventeen years about 1,600,000 acres had been reclaimed and more than a million were actually irrigated. In the single year 1918, the crops of the irrigated districts were valued at approximately $100,000,000.

In his first message, also, Roosevelt urged the transfer of all control over national forests to trained men in the Bureau of Forestry — a recommendation carried out in 1907 when the Forestry Service was created. In every direction progress was made in the administration of the national domain. The science of forestry was improved and public interest in the subject awakened. Lands in the national forest available for agriculture were opened to settlers. Water-power sites on the public domain were leased for a term of years to private companies instead of being sold outright. The area of the national forests was enlarged from forty-three million acres to one hundred and ninety-four million acres by presidential proclamation — more than forty-three million acres being added in one year, 1907. Men who turned sheep and cattle to graze on the public lands were compelled to pay a fair rental in return for this privilege. Fire prevention work on a large scale was undertaken in the forests, reducing the appalling annual destruction of timber. Millions of acres of mineral land, such as the government had been almost giving away to mining companies, were withdrawn from sale. Lawsuits were started in the courts against those who had obtained public lands by fraud and vast tracts were recovered for the government. An agitation was begun, which bore fruit under the administrations of Taft and Wilson, in favor of reserving to the federal government the ownership of coal, water power, phosphates, and other natural resources while authorizing corporations to develop them under leases for a fixed period of years.

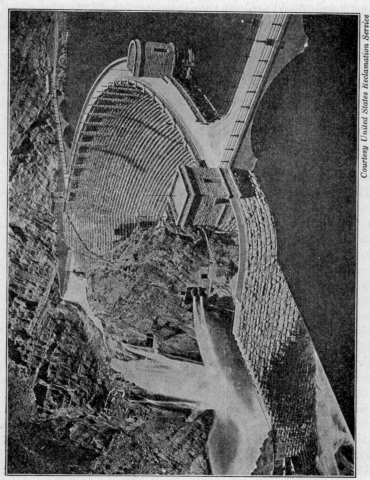

THE ROOSEVELT DAM, PHOENIX, ARIZONA

The Prosecution of the Trusts. As an executive, President Roosevelt was a distinct "personality." Discriminating between "good" and "bad" trusts he prosecuted some of the latter with much energy. On his initiative, the Northern Securities Company, formed to obtain control of certain great Western railways, was dissolved by order of the Supreme Court. Proceedings were instituted against the American Tobacco Company and the Standard Oil Company as monopolies conducted in violation of the Sherman Anti-Trust Law. The Sugar Trust was found guilty of cheating the New York customs house and some of the minor officers were sent to prison. Frauds in the Post Office Department were uncovered and the offenders brought to book. In fact hardly a week passed without news of "wrongdoers" and "malefactors" being haled into federal courts.

The Great Coal Strike. The Rooseveltian theory that the President could do anything for public welfare not forbidden by the Constitution and the laws was put to a severe test in 1902. A strike of the anthracite coal miners, which started in the summer, ran on late into the autumn, paralyzing industries and threatening cities with the menace of a winter without heat. Governors and mayors were powerless and appealed for aid. Although John Mitchell, leader of the miners, repeatedly urged conciliation, the mine owners rejected the demands of the men and refused to arbitrate the points in dispute. At length Roosevelt made up his mind that the situation was intolerable. He arranged to have the federal troops, if necessary, take possession of the mines and operate them until the strike could be settled. He then invited the contestants to the White House and by dint of hard labor induced them to accept, as a substitute or compromise, arbitration by a commission which he appointed. Thus, by stepping outside the Constitution and acting as the first citizen of the land, Roosevelt averted a crisis of great magnitude.

The Election of 1904. Inevitably the views and measures which he advocated with such gusto aroused hostility within his party as well as without. There were rumors of a movement among the Republicans to defeat his nomination in 1904 and it was said that the "financial and corporation interests" were in arms against him.

A prominent Republican paper in New York City accused him of having "stolen Bryan's thunder" by attacking great riches, harrying the trusts, and favoring labor unions. But when the Republican convention assembled in Chicago, the opposition melted away and Roosevelt was nominated by acclamation.

This action brought a curious reversal in the tactics of Democratic leaders. They now denounced the President as erratic, dangerous, and radical and assumed the moderate rôle themselves. Turning from the Populistic Bryan, they selected as their candidate, Judge Alton B. Parker, of New York, a man who had repudiated free silver, and they made a direct appeal for conservative support. But public opinion was not so conservative as they thought. Judge Parker's vote fell more than a million below that cast for Bryan in 1900; and of the 476 electoral votes he received only 140. In addition to sweeping the Republican sections, Roosevelt invaded Democratic territory, carrying the state of Missouri. With this vindication at the polls, his leadership in the party was so widely recognized that he virtually selected his successor.

THE ADMINISTRATION OF PRESIDENT TAFT

The Campaign of 1908. Long before the close of his elective term, Roosevelt let it be known that he favored for the next President, William Howard Taft, of Ohio, his Secretary of War. To attain this goal he used every shred of his enormous influence and in the end won the nomination for Mr. Taft. Though the Republican party adopted a platform that was conservative in tone, Taft gave it a progressive tinge by expressing his personal belief in the popular election of United States Senators, an income tax, and other liberal measures. Roosevelt announced his faith in the Republican candidate and appealed to the country to elect him.

Since Roosevelt had awakened so much interest in old Populistic doctrines, Bryan thought that the signs were favorable for a third attempt to win the presidency. At all events, Parker's disaster had taught his party that victory did not lie in a conservative policy. With little difficulty, therefore, the veteran leader from Nebraska once more rallied the Democrats around his standard, won the nomination, and wrote a platform attacking the tariff, trusts, and monopolies. But for a third time Bryan was "snowed under," though he polled almost a million and half more votes than did Parker in 1904. Taft was victorious.

Tariff Revision and Party Dissensions. At the very outset of his term, President Taft had to face the tariff issue which had been raised in the campaign. Moved by the Democratic demand for a drastic reduction in the rates, he had expressed an opinion implying that he approved a "downward revision." Of this opinion Democrats made much and Republicans from the Middle West rejoiced in it. As a matter of fact pressure for tariff reform was coming from all sides. More than ten years had elapsed since the enactment of the Dingley bill, new industries had grown up, and old processes of manufacture had changed. Evidently the day for revision — at best a thankless task — had arrived. Without shirking, Taft faced the responsibility by calling Congress in a special session. Until the midsummer of 1909, Republican Senators and Representatives wrangled among themselves over tariff schedules, and when on August 5 the Payne-Aldrich tariff bill became a law, a critical breach had been made in their ranks. Powerful Senators from the Middle West had delivered threatening speeches against many of the high rates imposed by the bill and at the finish had broken away from their party to vote against it.

The Income Tax Amendment. This rift in party harmony was widened by another serious difference of opinion. During the debate on the tariff bill, a concerted effort was made to include in it a clause laying a tax on incomes — in spite of the decision of the Supreme Court in 1895 declaring such a tax unconstitutional. Conservative men, shocked by this proposal to ignore the solemn decree of that great tribunal, would not listen to the idea. Yet an influential combination of Republicans and Democrats was bent upon shifting at all costs some of the burden of taxation from consumers to the possessors of large incomes. The upshot was a compromise. For the moment the income tax bill was dropped; but Congress passed the sixteenth amendment to the Constitution authorizing it to levy taxes on incomes — later. A sufficient number of states ratified the amendment and early in 1913 it was proclaimed.

President Taft's Policies. After the enactment of the tariff bill, Taft continued to push forward his legislative program. He recommended and Congress created a chain of postal savings banks in connection with the post office — a scheme which had long been opposed by private savings banks. With his encouragement two years afterward, Congress defied the lobby of the express companies and supplemented the savings banks with a system of parcels post. Aware that the business methods of the federal government were not up-to-date, the President obtained from Congress an appropriation for an economy and efficiency commission charged with the duty of inquiring into wasteful practices and recommending improvements. The chief result of this investigation was an urgent report in favor of a national budget program to take the place of the hit-and-miss methods of spending money which had hitherto prevailed at Washington.

Long an advocate of the peaceful settlement of controversies among nations, Taft now tried to realize his ideals. He negotiated with England and France general treaties providing for the arbitration of disputes which were "justiciable" in character even though they might involve questions of "vital interest and national honor." But they were coldly received in the Senate and so amended that he abandoned them altogether. With greater determination he made an agreement with Canada providing mutual concessions in tariff rates and he drove it through Congress in the face of strong opposition from his own party. Having risked and produced a serious breach in Republican ranks, Taft was chagrined to see the whole scheme come to naught when its sponsors in Canada were overthrown in the elections of 1911.

Prosecution of the Trusts. To make matters worse the party schism was extended by what appeared to be the successful prosecution of several strong corporations under the Sherman Anti-Trust Act of 1890. In two important cases, the Supreme Court ordered the dissolution of the Standard Oil Company and the American Tobacco Company on the ground that they violated the law. But in taking this step Chief Justice White was at some pains to state that the law did not apply to any corporations which did not "unduly" restrain trade. At once his remark was construed to mean that the Court would not interfere with trusts as such, and it became the subject of a popular outcry against the President and the judges.

PROGRESSIVE INSURGENCY AND THE ELECTION OF 1912

Growing Dissensions. All in all, Taft's administration from the first day had been marked by party discord. High words had passed over the tariff bill and they still rankled in the minds of disgruntled members of Congress. Differences over economic issues were complicated by strife between youth and old age. In the House of Representatives there developed a group of young "insurgent" Republicans, who rebelled against the dominance of the Speaker, Joseph G. Cannon, and other members of the "Old Guard," as they named the men of long service and conservative inclinations. In 1910 the insurgents went so far as to join with the Democrats in a movement to break the Speaker's sway by ousting him from the rules committee and depriving him of the power to appoint its members. Since the rules committee really directed business in the House of Representatives, this was in effect an attack on the Republican "machine," weakening the party from within. In the autumn of that year the Democrats won a clear majority in the House of Representatives and opened a drive on President Taft by demanding an immediate downward revision of the tariff — a blow aimed at the industrial wing of the Republican party.

Rise of the Progressive Republicans. Not satisfied with their victory over Speaker Cannon, certain insurgents, calling themselves "Progressive Republicans," started a movement to prevent Taft's renomination. As early as January 21, 1911, they formed a Progressive Republican League at the home of Senator La Follette of Wisconsin and launched an attack on the Taft measures and policies in general. In October they indorsed La Follette as "the logical Republican candidate" for President, and appealed to the whole party for support.

Roosevelt in the Field. From a fray of this character Roosevelt could not abstain. Soon after his return in 1910 from a hunting trip in Africa and a tour in Europe, he delivered a series of addresses

Photograph by Underwood and Underwood

THEODORE ROOSEVELT SPEAKING AT BELLOWS FALLS, VERMONT

Woodrow Wilson Speaking from His Summer Home at Long Branch, New Jersey

in which he formulated a progressive program of his own. In a speech in Kansas, he favored regulation of the trusts, a graduated income tax bearing heavily on great fortunes, tariff revision schedule by schedule, conservation of natural resources, labor legislation, the direct primary, and the right of the voters to recall unsatisfactory officials. In an address before the Ohio state constitutional convention in February, 1912, he indorsed the initiative and referendum and announced a doctrine known as the "recall of judicial decisions." This was a novel and radical note in American politics. An ex-President of the United States proposed that the people be given the right to reverse at the polls the decision of a judge who set aside any act of a state legislature passed in the interests of social welfare. Impressed by these addresses, the Progressive Republicans turned from La Follette to Roosevelt and induced him to come out himself as a candidate against Taft for the Republican nomination.

The Split in the Republican Party. The country then witnessed the spectacle of former friends — one of whom really put the other into office — engaged in rivalry to secure a majority of the delegates to the Republican convention to be held at Chicago. When the convention assembled, about one-fourth of the seats were disputed by two sets of claimants. After the usual hearings the national committee settled the contests in such a way as to give Taft a safe majority of delegates. Unable to change this ruling, Roosevelt and his followers "bolted" the Republican party. Most of his supporters withdrew from the convention and the few who remained behind refused to answer the roll call. Undisturbed by this formidable revolt, the regular Republicans renominated President Taft and put forth a platform condemning many Progressive doctrines, especially the recall of judges.

Formation of the Progressive Party. Roosevelt now declared that the Republican convention did not represent the voters of the party; that any candidate named by it would be "the beneficiary of a successful fraud"; and that it would be deeply discreditable to any man to accept the convention's approval in such circumstances. Since this opinion was widely held among his followers, a call was sent forth for a "Progressive" convention to be held in

Chicago on August 5.   When this conference assembled it had the appearance of a civic mass meeting rather than that of a typical collection of politicians.   Women delegates were prominent, while the regular "war horses" of politics were notably absent.   Cheered as a conquering hero, Roosevelt made an impassioned speech setting forth his "confession of political faith."   He was nominated by acclamation and Governor Hiram Johnson of California was selected as his companion candidate for Vice President.   With a great flourish of trumpets the convention adopted a platform indorsing such striking reforms as woman suffrage, direct primaries, the initiative, referendum, and recall, popular election of United States Senators, and the short ballot.   It also favored a program of social legislation, including minimum wages for women and the prohibition of child labor.   It approved the regulation, rather than the dissolution, of the trusts.   Like the fiery apostles of a lofty cause, the Progressives entered upon the campaign for the election of their distinguished leader.

Woodrow Wilson and the Election of 1912.   With the Republicans divided, victory loomed up as a possibility before the Democrats and a terrific contest over the nomination occurred at their convention in Baltimore.   Champ Clark, Speaker of the House of Representatives, and Governor Woodrow Wilson, of New Jersey, were the favorites.   After tossing to and fro for seven long, hot days, and taking forty-six ballots, the delegates, under the still potent sway of Bryan, finally gave the honor to the Governor.   As a professor, a writer on historical and political subjects, and the president of Princeton University, Wilson had become well known among educators and students.   While governor of New Jersey he had attracted the support of progressives in both parties and become a figure in national life.   With grim determination he had "waged war on the bosses" and pushed through the legislature measures establishing direct primaries, regulating public utilities, and creating a system of workmen's compensation.   During the presidential campaign, Governor Wilson toured the country and aroused immense enthusiasm by a series of critical addresses, later published under the title of *The New Freedom.*   Like Roosevelt he attacked "malefactors of great wealth" and declared that "the government of the United States is at present the foster child of the special interests." He proposed to free the country by breaking the dominance of "the big bankers, the big manufacturers, the big masters of commerce, the heads of railroad corporations and of steamship corporations."

In the election Governor Wilson easily secured a majority of the electoral votes, and his party, besides retaining possession of the House of Representatives, captured the Senate as well. But his popular vote was far from a victory, for the combined Progressive and Republican total exceeded it by 1,300,000. In addition the Socialists, with Eugene V. Debs as their candidate again, polled about 900,000 votes — more than double the number received four years before. Thus, as the result of factional fights, the Republicans, after holding the office of President for sixteen years, lost control over the federal government, and power passed to the Democrats under the direction of a man destined to be another outstanding personality of the modern age — Woodrow Wilson.

General References

J. B. Bishop, *Theodore Roosevelt and His Time* (2 vols.).

Theodore Roosevelt, *Autobiography; New Nationalism; Progressive Principles*.

W. H. Taft, *Popular Government*.

Walter Weyl, *The New Democracy*.

H. Croly, *The Promise of American Life*.

J. B. Bishop, *The Panama Gateway*.

J. B. Scott, *The Hague Peace Conferences*.

W. B. Munro (ed.), *Initiative, Referendum, and Recall*.

C. R. Van Hise, *The Conservation of Natural Resources*.

Gifford Pinchot, *The Fight for Conservation*.

W. F. Willoughby, *Territories and Dependencies of the United States* (1905).

Research Topics

Roosevelt and "Big Business." Haworth, *The United States in Our Own Time*, pp. 281–289; F. A. Ogg, *National Progress* (American Nation Series), pp. 40–75; Paxson, *The New Nation* (Riverside Series), pp. 293–307.

Our Insular Possessions. Elson, *History of the United States*, pp. 879–886.

Latin-American Relations.   Haworth, pp. 294–299; Ogg, pp. 254–257.

The Panama Canal.   Haworth, pp. 300–309; Ogg, pp. 266–277; Paxson, pp. 286–292; Elson, pp. 888–893.

Conservation.   Haworth, pp. 331–334;   Ogg, pp. 96–115;   Beard, *American Government and Politics* (5th ed.), pp. 414–429.

Republican Dissensions under Taft's Administration.   Haworth, pp. 351–360; Ogg, pp. 167–186; Paxson, pp. 324–342; Elson, pp. 901–907.

The Campaign of 1912.   Haworth, pp. 360–379; Ogg, pp. 187–208.

Questions

1. Compare the early career of Roosevelt with that of some other President.

2. Name the chief foreign and domestic questions of the Roosevelt-Taft administrations.

3. What international complications were involved in the Panama Canal problem?

4. Review the Monroe Doctrine.   Discuss Roosevelt's applications of it.

5. What is the strategic importance of the Caribbean to the United States?

6. What is meant by the sea power?   Trace the voyage of the fleet around the world and mention the significant imperial and commercial points touched.

7. What is meant by the question: "Does the Constitution follow the flag?"

8. Trace the history of self-government in Porto Rico.   In the Philippines.

9. What is Cuba's relation to the United States?

10. What was Roosevelt's theory of our Constitution?

11. Give Roosevelt's views on trusts, labor, taxation.

12. Outline the domestic phases of Roosevelt's administrations.

13. Account for the dissensions under Taft.

14. Trace the rise of the Progressive movement.

15. What was Roosevelt's progressive program?

16. Review Wilson's early career and explain the underlying theory of *The New Freedom.*

Questions for Debate

1. Our recognition of Panama was justifiable.

2. Immediate independence should be granted the Philippines.

3. The income tax is a just and wise form of taxation.

CHAPTER XXIV

THE SPIRIT OF REFORM IN AMERICA

An Age of Criticism

Attacks on Abuses in American Life. The Progressive uprising just described was not a sudden and unexpected crisis. It came as the climax to a revolt against corruption in politics which produced the Liberal Republican outbreak in the seventies and the Mugwump movement of the early eighties, followed by continuous criticism of political and economic affairs. From 1870 until his death in 1892, George William Curtis, president of the Civil Service Reform Association, kept up a running fire upon the evils of the spoils system. In a book called *The American Commonwealth*, published in 1888, James Bryce, an English student of politics, gave the whole country a shock by his picture of the corrupt "rings" and "machines" which dominated the cities of the United States. Six years later Henry D. Lloyd, a Chicago journalist, in a volume entitled *Wealth against Commonwealth*, attacked in scathing language certain trusts which had destroyed competitors and bribed public officials. In 1903 Ida Tarbell, a writer of history, gave to the public an account of the ruthless methods of the Standard Oil Company in crushing its rivals. About the same time another journalist, Lincoln Steffens, exposed the sordid character of politics in several municipalities in a series of articles bearing the painful heading: *The Shame of the Cities*. The critical spirit appeared in other forms: in weekly and monthly magazines, in essays, pamphlets, editorials, and news stories, in novels such as Churchill's *Coniston* and Sinclair's *The Jungle*. It became so violent and so wanton that the opening years of the twentieth century were well named "the age of the muckrakers."

The Subjects of the Criticism. In this outburst of invective, nothing was spared. It was charged that each of the great political parties had fallen into the hands of professional politicians who cared nothing for the public welfare but devoted their time to managing conventions, making platforms, and nominating candidates, just to wring money out of the game. It was alleged that mayors and councils had actually sold street-railway and other franchises to private companies. It was asserted that many powerful labor unions owed their gains to leaders who blackmailed employers. Some critics specialized in descriptions of the poverty, slums, and misery of the cities. Others took up "frenzied finance" and accused financiers of selling worthless stocks and bonds to an innocent populace. Still others saw in the accumulations of millionaires the downfall of the republic — democracy giving way to an aristocracy of wealth.

The Attack on "Invisible Government." The burden of all this criticism was that the control of public affairs had passed from the people to an "invisible government." So eminent and conservative a statesman as the Hon. Elihu Root lent the weight of his name to such a view. Speaking of his native state, New York, he said in 1915: "What is the government of this state? What has it been during the forty years of my acquaintance with it? The government of the Constitution? Oh, no; not half the time or half way. . . . From the days of Fenton and Conkling and Arthur and Cornell and Platt, from the days of David B. Hill down to the present time, the government of the state has presented two different lines of activity: one, of the constitutional and statutory officers of the state and the other of the party leaders; they call them party bosses. They call the system — I don't coin the phrase — the system they call 'invisible government.' For I don't know how many years Mr. Conkling was the supreme ruler in this state. The governor did not count, the legislature did not count, comptrollers and secretaries of state and what not did not count. It was what Mr. Conkling said, and in a great outburst of public rage he was pulled down. Then Mr. Platt ruled the state; for nigh upon twenty years he ruled it. It was not the governor; it was not the legislature; it was Mr. Platt. And the capital was not here [in Albany]; it was at 49 Broadway; Mr. Platt and his lieutenants. It makes no difference what name you give, whether you call it Fenton or Conkling or Cornell or Arthur or Platt or by the names of men now living. The ruler of the state during the greater part of the forty years of my acquaintance with the state government has not been any man authorized by the constitution or by law. . . . The party leader is elected by no one, accountable to no one, bound by no oath of office, removable by no one."

The Nation Aroused. But with this critical mood came also the spirit of reform. The charges were often exaggerated, if not positively false; but there was on the whole enough truth in them to demand the remedying of many abuses. Roosevelt doubtless summed up the sentiment of the large majority of citizens when he declared in 1907 that all the wrongdoers should be punished, and added: "It makes not a particle of difference whether these crimes are committed by a capitalist or by a laborer, by a leading banker or manufacturer or railroad man or by a leading representative of a labor union. Swindling in stocks, corrupting legislatures, making fortunes by the inflation of securities, by wrecking railroads, by destroying competitors through rebates — these forms of wrongdoing in the capitalist are far more infamous than any ordinary form of embezzlement or forgery." The time had come, he urged, to stop "muckraking" and abolish the evils which had grown up.

Political Reforms

The Public Service. On no issue, perhaps, were reformers more thoroughly united than that of reducing the evils of the spoils system. And after fifty years of agitation they won a great victory in the federal Civil Service Act of 1883, establishing five vital principles in law: (1) government officials must be chosen, not on the recommendation of party workers, but on the basis of competitive examinations testing their qualifications; (2) promotions are to be made for serving the government well rather than aiding a political party; (3) government employees do not have to contribute to campaign funds; (4) officers shall hold their positions during good behavior; and (5) there shall be no dismissals merely for political reasons. The Civil Service Act itself at first applied only to 14,000 federal offices, but by other acts of Congress and presidential orders it was extended until in 1916 it covered nearly 300,000 employees out of an executive force of approximately 414,000. While gaining steadily at Washington, civil-service reformers carried their agitation into the states and cities. By 1920 they were able to report ten states with civil-service commissions and the merit system well intrenched in more than three hundred cities.

In excluding spoilsmen from public office, the reformers were, in a sense, engaged in a negative work: that of "keeping the rascals out." But there was a second and larger phase to their movement, one constructive in character: that of putting skilled, loyal, and efficient servants into places of responsibility. Changes in the work of government made this absolutely necessary. Everywhere on land and sea, in town and country, new burdens were laid upon public officers. They were called upon to supervise the ships sailing to and from our ports; to inspect the water and milk supplies of our cities; to construct and operate great public works, such as the Panama Canal, irrigation dams, and harbor improvements; to regulate the complicated rates of railway companies; to safeguard health and safety in a thousand ways; to climb the mountains to fight forest fires; and to descend into the deeps of the earth to combat the deadly coal gases that assail the miners. In a word, those who labor to master the secrets and the powers of nature were summoned to the aid of the government: chemists, engineers, architects, nurses, surgeons, foresters — the skilled in all the sciences, arts, and crafts. This was no task for mere "politicians."

Keeping rascals out of office was a simpler task than finding competent people to meet these high demands. "Now," said the reformers, "we must make attractive careers in the government work for the best American talent; we must train those applying for admission and increase the skill of those already in positions of trust; we must see to it that those entering at the bottom have a chance to rise to the top through merit; in short, we must work for a government as skilled and efficient as it is strong, one commanding all the wisdom and genius of America that public welfare requires."

The Australian Ballot. Side by side with this effort to prevent mere party control of offices and to raise the standards of public officials ran a movement to make the voters more independent of machine politics. In the early days elections were frequently held in the open air and the poll was taken by a show of hands or by the enrollment of the voters under names of their favorite candidates. When this ancient practice was abandoned in favor of the printed ballot, there was still no secrecy about elections. Each party prepared its own ballot, often of a distinctive color, containing the names of its candidates. On election day, these papers were handed to the voters by party workers; and any one could tell from the color of the ballot dropped into the box, or from some mark on the outside of the folded ballot, just how each man voted. Those who bought votes were sure that their purchases were "delivered." Those who intimidated voters could know when their brow-beating brought results. In this way the party ballot strengthened the party machine.

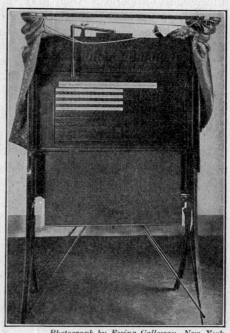

Photograph by Ewing Galloway, New York

A VOTING MACHINE USED BY VOTERS IN NEW YORK CITY

To remedy these abuses, reformers urged the adoption of the "Australian ballot" which had the following features. It was official, that is, furnished by the government, not by party workers; it contained the names of all candidates of all parties; it was given out only in the polling places; and it was marked in secret.

In short it permitted the voter to express his own will in his own way. The first state to introduce it was Massachusetts. The year was 1888. Before the end of the century it had been adopted by nearly all the states in the Union. Then came experiments with a mechanical apparatus which kept the chief features of the Australian ballot and automatically counted the results. The good effect of the change in reducing the amount of cheating and bribery in elections was beyond all question.

The Direct Primary. In connection with the general uprising against machine politics, came a war on the old method of nominating candidates by conventions. These time-honored party assemblies, which had originated in the days of Andrew Jackson, were now accused of being merely "gangs" of party workers living on the spoils system and taking orders from an inner circle or "ring" of bosses. The remedy offered in this case was again "more democracy," namely, the abolition of the party convention and the adoption of the direct primary. Candidates were no longer to be chosen by secret conferences. Any member of a party was to be allowed to run for any office, to present his name to his party by securing signatures to a petition, and to submit his claims to his fellow partisans at a direct primary — an election within the party. In this movement Governor La Follette of Wisconsin was very active and his state was the first in the Union to adopt the direct primary for state-wide purposes. The idea spread, rapidly in the West, steadily if more slowly in the East. In nearly every section the public grasped eagerly at this scheme for checking the power of "the bosses." Governor Hughes pressed it upon the legislature of New York. State after state accepted it until by 1918 there were only four — Rhode Island, Delaware, Connecticut, and New Mexico — which had not bowed to the winds.

Popular Election of Federal Senators. While the movement for direct primaries was still advancing, a demand for the popular election of Senators, like it in purpose and spirit, swept to complete success. The constitutional provision giving the state legislatures the right to elect Senators had worked out in practice in such a way as to vest the selection in secret party caucuses in the legislatures. And growing out of these caucuses there had been many scandals, some direct proofs of brazen bribery and corruption, and dark hints also. The Senate was called by its critics "a millionaires' club," and it was looked upon as the "citadel of conservatism." The prescription in this case was likewise "more democracy" — direct election of Senators by popular vote.

This reform was not a new idea. It had been proposed in Congress as early as 1826. President Johnson, an ardent advocate, made it the subject of a special message in 1868. Later it came up from time to time in congressional debates. At last, in 1893, the year after the great Populist upheaval, the House of Representatives, by the requisite two-thirds vote, definitely provided for it in an amendment to the federal Constitution. Again and again the amendment passed the House; but the Senate voted it down. Many of the ablest Senators spoke eloquently against it. Senator Hoar of Massachusetts, for example, declared that it would transfer the seat of power to the "great cities and masses of population"; that it would "overthrow the whole scheme of the Senate and in the end the whole scheme of the national Constitution as designed and established by the framers of the Constitution and the people who adopted it."

Failing in the Senate, advocates of popular election made a rear assault through the states. They induced state legislatures to enact laws requiring the nomination of candidates for the Senate by the direct primary, and then they bound the legislatures to abide by the popular choice. Nevada took the lead in 1899. Shortly afterward Oregon practically ordered its legislators to accept the nominee who received the highest popular vote; and the country witnessed the spectacle of a Republican legislature "electing" a Democrat to represent the state in the Senate at Washington. By 1910 three-fourths of the states had applied the direct primary in some form to the choice of Senators. Men selected by that method began to pile up votes in the United States Senate, until in 1912 the two-thirds majority was secured for an amendment to the federal Constitution providing for the popular election of Senators in all the states. It was so quickly ratified that it went into effect the following year.

The Initiative and Referendum.   While taking away from state legislatures their right to elect United States Senators, the reformers also attempted to restrain their lawmaking power because their acts were frequently contrary to the public interest.   The proposal in this case was the introduction of a Swiss plan known as the initiative and referendum.   The initiative permits any one to draw up a bill and, when he has got a certain number of voters to sign a petition favoring it, to compel its submission to the people at the polls.   If the bill thus initiated receives a sufficient majority, it becomes a law — without going to the legislature at all.   The referendum allows citizens who disapprove any act passed by the legislature to get up a petition against it and require a vote on it in the same manner at the polls.   These two practices constitute a form of "direct government."

They were prescribed "to restore the government to the people." The Populists favored them in their platform of 1896.   Bryan, two years later, made them a part of his program, and in the same year South Dakota adopted them.   In 1902 Oregon, after a strenuous campaign, added a direct legislation amendment to the state constitution.   Within ten years all the Southwestern, Mountain, and Pacific states, except Texas and Wyoming, had followed this example.   To the east of the Mississippi, however, direct legislation met a chilly reception.   By 1920 only five states in this section had accepted it: Maine, Massachusetts, Ohio, Michigan, and Maryland, the last approving the referendum only.

The Recall.   Executive officers and judges, as well as legislatures, had come in for their share of criticism, and it was proposed that they should in turn be subjected to a closer scrutiny by the public. For this purpose a scheme known as the recall was advanced — which permitted a certain percentage of the voters to draw up a petition, secure signers, and compel any officer, at any time during his term, to face at a new election the judgment of the people on his conduct.   This feature of direct government, tried out first in the city of Los Angeles, was extended to state-wide uses in Oregon in 1908.   It failed, however, to capture popular imagination to the same degree as the initiative and referendum.   At the end of ten years' agitation, only ten states, mainly in the West, had adopted it for general purposes, and four of them did not apply it to the judges of the courts. It was nevertheless extensively advocated in cities and incorporated in hundreds of municipal laws and charters, giving voters larger control over mayors and other local officials.

Direct government in all its forms was bitterly opposed by gentlemen of the old school of government. It was denounced by Senator Henry Cabot Lodge of Massachusetts as "nothing less than a complete revolution in the fabric of our government and in the fundamental principles upon which that government rests." In his opinion, it promised to break down the representative principle and "undermine and overthrow the bulwarks of ordered liberty and individual freedom." President Taft shared this belief and spoke of direct government with similar scorn.

Commission Government for Cities. The quest for better government led to more study of the management of cities as a science. City government, Bryce had remarked, was the one conspicuous failure in America. This sharp thrust, though resented by some Americans, was accepted as a proper warning by others, and many remedies were offered by doctors of the body politic. Chief among them was the idea of simplifying the city government so that the people could understand it and control it more effectively. "Let us elect only a few men and make them clearly responsible for the city government!" was the new cry in municipal reform. So, generally speaking, city councils were reduced in size; one of the two houses, which several cities had adopted in imitation of the federal government, was abolished; and in order that the mayor could be held to account, he was given the power to appoint all the chief officials. This made the mayor, in some cases, the only elective city executive and wholly responsible for the local administration.

A further step in municipal reform was taken in Galveston, Texas, after a devastating storm had laid waste the city in 1901, and raised difficult questions of reconstruction to be solved. Confronted by a real crisis the citizens decided that they needed a more businesslike management of city affairs in the future. Consequently they abolished the mayor and council scheme and vested all power in five commissioners, one of whom was assigned to the office of "mayor president." In 1908, the commission form of government, as this plan was soon named, was adopted by Des Moines, Iowa. The attention of all municipal reformers was drawn to it and it was hailed as the guarantee of a better city administration in every respect. By 1920, more than four hundred cities, including Memphis, Spokane, Birmingham, and Newark, had accepted commission government.

The City-Manager Plan. A few years' experience with this form of government naturally revealed its defects. Like the old

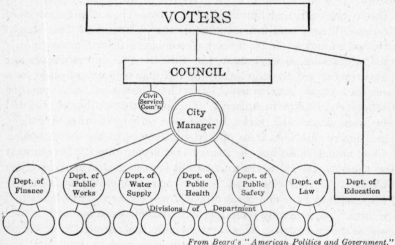

From Beard's "American Politics and Government."

CITY-MANAGER PLAN

Adapted from the National Municipal League's chart showing the city-manager plan, in which administrative responsibility is centralized.

type of officials, the commissioners often did not have the technical ability required to direct such matters as fire and police protection, public health, public works, and public utilities. Someone then proposed to carry over into city government an idea from the business world, where the stockholders of each corporation elect the directors, and the directors in turn choose a business manager to conduct the affairs of the company. It was suggested that the city commissioners, instead of attempting to supervise the details of the administration, should select a competent manager to take over this work. A scheme of this kind was put into effect in Sumter, South Carolina, in 1913. Like the commission plan, the city-manager plan became popular. Within eight years more than one hundred and fifty towns and cities had turned to it for relief. Among the larger municipalities were Dayton, Springfield (Ohio), Akron, and Phoenix. Later Cleveland and Cincinnati joined the list.

MEASURES OF ECONOMIC REFORM

The Goal of American Reform. Honest elections, direct government, and expert civil service were not the sole answers made by reformers to the critics of American institutions. Nor were they the most important. In fact they were regarded not as ends in themselves, but as means to serve a larger purpose — the promotion of "general welfare." The concrete objects covered by that broad term were many and varied; but they included prevention of unfair charges by railway and other corporations, protection of public health, the extension of education, improvement of living conditions in the cities, elimination of undeserved poverty, removal of gross inequalities in wealth, and more equality of opportunity.

All these things involved the use of the powers of government. Although a few citizens clung to the earlier doctrine that the government should not interfere with private business at all, the American people rejected that conservative theory as impatiently as they rejected the radical doctrines of an extreme socialism which would give all business to the state. It was the middle view that generally prevailed. "We must abandon definitely," insisted Roosevelt, "the laissez-faire theory of political economy and fearlessly champion a system of increased governmental control, paying no attention to the cries of worthy people who denounce this as socialistic." This conviction was affirmed by Taft when he said: "Undoubtedly the government can wisely do much more . . . to relieve the oppressed, to create greater equality of opportunity, to make reasonable terms for labor in employment, and to furnish vocational education." But he was quicker to add a word of caution that "there is a line beyond which the government cannot go with any good practical results in seeking to make men and society better."

The Regulation of Railways. The first attempts to use the government in a large way to control private enterprise in the public interest were made by the Northwestern states between 1870 and 1880. Charges were circulated by the farmers, particularly those belonging to Granges, to the effect that the railways extorted the highest possible rates for freight and passengers, that they gave low rates and other favors to large shippers, that fraudulent stocks and bonds were sold to the public. It was claimed that railways were not on the same footing as other enterprises, but were "quasi-public" concerns, like roads and ferries, and thus matters for government control. In response to such arguments laws were enacted subjecting railroads to state supervision. In some cases state legislatures fixed the maximum rates to be charged by common carriers, and in other cases commissions were created with the power to establish such rates after an investigation. Conservatives in the East frowned upon this legislation, and said that it amounted to a "confiscation" of the railways in the interest of the farmers. And some of the companies tried to induce the Supreme Court of the United States to declare it unconstitutional. The outcome was a kind of compromise. The Court said that the states could regulate rates but must allow railway companies to earn a "fair" return on the capital invested.

In a few years the Granger spirit reached Congress. An investigation revealed a long list of abuses committed by the railways against shippers and travelers. The result was the act of 1887 which created the interstate commerce commission, forbade discriminations in rates, and prohibited other profiteering practices on the part of railways. For various reasons, this measure was not strictly enforced, so that the evils at which it was aimed continued almost unabated. Hence a demand for more effective control grew louder and louder until Congress was forced to heed. In 1903 it enacted the Elkins law, which forbade railways to charge rates other than those published, and provided punishments for officers and agents of companies who granted secret favors to shippers, and for shippers who accepted them. A still more drastic step was taken in 1906 by the passage of the Hepburn Act which authorized the interstate commerce commission to receive complaints and, after a public hearing, to determine whether just and reasonable rates had been charged by any company. In short, the right to fix freight and passenger rates was thus taken from the owners of the railways engaged in interstate commerce and vested in a commission appointed by the President with the consent of the Senate. In effect property worth $20,000,000,000 or more was declared to be a matter of public concern and subject to government regulation.

Municipal Utilities. Similar issues were presented by the street railways, electric light plants, and other public utilities. In the beginning the right to construct such undertakings was freely, and often corruptly, granted to private companies by city councils. Many such concessions or "franchises" were made perpetual, or perhaps for a term of 999 years. Generally also the rates charged and services rendered to the people were left to the will of the companies themselves. Mergers or unions of companies were common; and stocks and bonds of doubtful value were "unloaded" on the public; bankruptcies were frequent. Furthermore the relations between the utility companies and the politicians were, to say the east, not always in the public interest.

Three lines of progress leading, it was said, to better service and more reasonable rates were marked out by the reformers. One group proposed to bring all utilities under municipal or state regulation, and to require government approval for the formation of new utility companies and all issues of stocks and bonds. In some cases state, and in other cases municipal, commissions were created to exercise this great power over "quasi-public corporations." Wisconsin, by legislation enacted in 1907, placed all heat, light, water works, telephone, and street railway companies under the supervision of a single commission. Other states followed this example rapidly. By 1920 the principle of public control over municipal utilities was accepted in nearly every section of the nation.

A second line of reform appeared in the "model franchise" for utility corporations, illustrated by the Chicago street railway settlement of 1906. The total capital of the company was fixed at a definite sum, its earnings were agreed upon, and the city was given the right to buy and operate the system if it desired to do so. In many states, as a part of the general program, it was provided that no franchises to utility companies could run more than twenty-five years, subject to renewal on precise terms.

A third group of reformers were satisfied with nothing short of public ownership. They insisted that regulation failed to bring about fair rates and that utility companies were still corrupting politics, press, and schools. They proposed to drive private companies entirely out of the field and vest the ownership and management of plants in the city, the state, or the federal government according to the nature of the utility. This plan was extensively applied to municipal electric-light and water-works plants, and to street railways in a few cities, including San Francisco and Seattle. In New York the subways are owned by the city but leased for operation. Congress provided in 1920 that water-power sites on the federal domain and navigable rivers should not be sold but should remain in the hands of the government even if the right to use them was sometimes leased to private companies.

Tenement-House Control. Among the most pressing problems of the cities was overcrowding in houses unfit for habitation. An inquiry in New York City, made under the authority of the state in 1902, revealed poverty, misery, slums, dirt, and disease, unsuspected by well-to-do citizens. A tenement-house law was then enacted, prescribing in great detail the size of rooms, air space, light and sanitary arrangements for all new buildings at least. An immense improvement followed and the idea was quickly taken up in other states having large industrial centers. In 1920 New York put a bridle on greedy landlords by assuring to the public "reasonable rents" for flats and apartments of certain grades.

Workmen's Compensation. No small part of the poverty in cities was due to the injury of wage-earners while working at their trades. Every year the number of men and women killed or wounded in industry mounted higher. Under customary law, the workman or his family had to bear all the burden, unless the employer had been guilty of some extraordinary negligence, and even in that case an expensive lawsuit was usually necessary to recover "damages." In short, although employers insured their buildings and machinery against necessary risks from fire and

Photograph by Ewing Galloway, New York

CROWDED CONDITIONS IN NEW YORK CITY

storm, they allowed their employees to assume the heavy losses due to accidents to their bodies. It was generally believed up to this time that labor should endure all the brunt of mishaps. It was said to be unfair to make the employer pay for injuries for which he was not personally responsible; but the argument was overborne.

About 1910 there set in a decided movement in the direction of lifting the burden of accidents from the unfortunate victims. Laws were enacted requiring employers to pay damages in fixed amounts according to the nature of the case, no matter how the accident occurred, as long as the injured person was not guilty of willful negligence. By 1914 more than one-half the states had such laws and, to avoid losses, owners of dangerous machinery now began to surround them with better safeguards. The next advance along this line took the form of industrial insurance providing for automatic grants by state commissions to persons injured in industries — these grants to be made from funds furnished by employers or the state or by both. By 1917 thirty-six states had legislation of this type.

Minimum Wages and Mothers' Pensions. Another prime source of poverty was of course the low wages paid for labor in many cases. Report after report furnished the facts to prove it. While some of the labor unions were able to maintain high wage-scales by organized efforts, women and children were more defenseless in the labor market; often the so-called "women" were merely young girls. In 1912 Massachusetts took a significant step in the direction of declaring the minimum wages which ought to be paid to women and children. Oregon, the following year, went further by creating a commission with power to fix minimum wages in certain industries, based on the cost of living, and to enforce the rates. Within a short time one-third of the states had legislation of this character, but its development was blocked in 1925 by a decision of the Supreme Court of the United States declaring void an Arizona minimum-wage law. To cut away some of the other evils of poverty by enabling poor widows to bring up their children in their own homes, "mothers' pensions" next became a popular measure of reform. At the opening of 1913 two states, Colorado and Illinois, had laws authorizing the payment from public funds of definite sums to widows with small children. Within four years, thirty-five states had similar legislation. From this it was but a step to pensions for all old persons unable to support themselves. By 1929 five states, Montana, Nevada, Wisconsin, Kentucky, and Illinois, had provided such pensions and the movement in favor of the principle was gaining rapid headway.

Taxation and Great Fortunes. As a part of the campaign waged against poverty the demand for taxes upon great fortunes grew stronger, particularly for taxes upon large inheritances. Roosevelt was an ardent champion of this type of taxation and dwelt upon it at length in his message to Congress in 1907. "Such a tax," he said, "would help to preserve a measurable equality of opportunity for the people of the generations growing to manhood. . . . Our aim is to recognize what Lincoln pointed out: the fact that there are some respects in which men are obviously not equal; but also to insist that there should be equality of self-respect and of mutual respect, an equality of rights before the law, and at least an approximate equality in the conditions under which each man obtains the chance to show the stuff that is in him when compared with his fellows."

The spirit of the new politics was, therefore, one of reform, not of revolution. It called for no utopian experiments, but for the steady and progressive enactment of measures aimed at admitted abuses and designed to accomplish tangible results in the name of the general welfare.

General References

E. S. Bradford, *Commission Government in American Cities*.
R. C. Brooks, *Corruption in American Life*.
J. Bryce, *The American Commonwealth*.
P. L. Haworth, *America in Ferment*.
W. Z. Ripley, *Railroads: Rates and Regulation*.
E. A. Ross, *Changing America*.
H. R. Seager, *A Program of Social Reform*.
E. R. A. Seligman, *The Income Tax*.
W. E. Walling, *Progressivism and After*.
C. Zueblin, *American Municipal Progress*.
The American Year Book (an annual publication which contains reviews of reform legislation).

Research Topics

"The Muckrakers." Paxson, *The New Nation* (Riverside Series), pp. 309–323.

Civil Service Reform. Beard, *American Government and Politics* (5th ed.), pp. 301–322; Ogg, *National Progress* (American Nation Series), pp. 135–142.

Direct Government. Beard, *American Government,* pp. 503–524; Ogg, pp. 160–166.

Popular Election of Senators. Beard, *American Government,* pp. 229–332; Ogg, pp. 149–150.

Party Methods. Beard, *American Government,* pp. 525–535.

Ballot Reform. Beard, *American Government,* pp. 535–557.

Social and Economic Legislation. Beard, *American Government,* pp. 672–699.

Questions

1. Who were some of the critics of American political practices?

2. What particular criticisms were advanced?

3. How did Elihu Root define "invisible government"?

4. Discuss the use of criticism as an aid to progress in a democracy.

5. Explain what is meant by the "merit system" in the civil service. Review the rise of the spoils system.

6. Why is the public service of increasing importance?   Give some of its new problems.

7. Describe the Australian ballot and the abuses against which it is directed.

8. What are the elements of direct government?   Sketch their progress in the United States.

9. Trace the history of popular election of Senators.

10. Explain the direct primary.   Commission government.   The city manager plan.

11. How does modern reform involve government action?   On what theory is it justified?

12. Enumerate five lines of recent economic reform.

Questions for Debate

1. The direct primary has been beneficial.

2. The initiative and referendum have been justified in their results.

Historical Fiction

Mary Dillon, *The Leader.*
Walter Hurt, *The Scarlet Shadow.*

CHAPTER XXV

THE NEW POLITICAL DEMOCRACY

Women in Public Life. The story of American politics and the spirit of reform is not the history of men's activities alone. On the contrary much of the new legislation just described was directly promoted by organizations made up exclusively of women. In other cases it was inspired by agencies for social improvement in which they were zealous participants. No cause escaped women's attention; no year passed without expanding the range of their labors. They served on committees that studied the problems of the day; they appeared before legislative assemblies and congressional bodies to advocate remedies for evils they discovered. By 1912 they were a force to be reckoned with in national politics, as actual voters in a few states and as a "moral" influence in others.

Nevertheless this advanced position had been attained only by slow stages from an almost rightless condition in the colonial era. Under the English common law generally applied in America at that time, unless there was a pre-wedding settlement arranging otherwise, a married woman's personal property — jewels, money, furniture, and the like — became her husband's property and her landed estate also passed to his control. Even the wages a woman or girl earned, when she worked outside the home, belonged to her husband or father respectively. In keeping with the law, custom of course dictated that women should not take part in political meetings or enter into public discussions on religion or anything else of consequence. So it is indeed a far cry from the banishment of Anne Hutchinson from Massachusetts in 1637 for daring to dispute with the church fathers and local magistrates to the national political conventions of 1920 in which women sat as delegates, made nominating speeches, and served on committees. In the contrast between these two events may be measured the evolution in the privileges and position of women since the hour when the first Englishmen settled the New World.

The account of this progress is a narrative of individual leadership by "rebellious" women who, after the style of masculine agitators, "condemned, assailed, and attacked" the opposition which in their case tried to bind them to one kind of life forever.

CONFERENCE OF MEN AND WOMEN DELEGATES AT A NATIONAL CONVENTION IN 1920

It is also a narrative of organized campaigns of education by disciples of such pioneers and of aid from men in sympathy with efforts to remove civil and political disabilities from all Americans. To a large extent this progress is due to irresistible economic forces which swept women into industry, created a leisure class, gave them property rights, and brought more economic independence. What agitation demanded, industry helped to achieve.

THE RISE OF THE WOMAN MOVEMENT

Protests of Colonial Women. Few significant reforms spring up full-armed in a single night. Even this republic did not arise that way. Independence was a product of gradual nurture by fireside discussions and debates in public forums, by reactions to episodes and English legislation. In similar fashion independence for women was matured. That colonial women shared in the domestic sifting of political principles and programs we know both from their own letters and from the correspondence of men. As for the making of public opinion, the force of their patriotism is indicated in the collections we have of their revolutionary writings for the newspapers, including songs, dramas, satirical "skits" on English rule, and special articles. Naturally therefore when everyone was arguing about the true basis of government and poring over Thomas Paine's *Common Sense*, some of the colonial women were led to apply the notion of government by consent of the governed to themselves and to insist on self-government all around. Thus did Abigail Adams, when her husband, John Adams, was in the Continental Congress at Philadelphia debating the future of America, for she wrote to him objecting "to all arbitrary power whether of state or males" and urging a "voice or representation" for women in the new state. Hannah Lee Corbin, sister of "Lighthorse" Harry Lee, likewise protested to her influential brother against taxation of either men or women without representation.

The Stir among European Women. Such "feminism" in America was quickened by events in Europe. English women were especially aggrieved because men were entering their industries and in protest they held a conference in London at which they coupled with their economic complaints demands for better education and the right to vote. In 1792 this budding revolt against custom was voiced by Mary Wollstonecraft in her *Vindication of the Rights of Women* — a book that was destined to serve women as the books of Locke and Paine had served men. Meanwhile French women were giving such energetic support to the great Revolution that "citizenness" ranked with "citizen" as a symbol of reform. This phase of French radicalism, like all its other phases, had a wide curve of influence which took in both hemispheres.

Leadership in the United States. In assuming the task of securing civil and political rights, American women had to study and write books useful to their cause. To be sure a library of sermons already existed to emphasize the domestic duties of women but there was very little material available on their economic condition, their rôle in the great civilizations of the past, or the public aspects of the family they were asked to guard and serve. So books were now prepared to meet this need. For example, Mrs. Elizabeth Ellet wrote a history of the American Revolution which brought out the part women had played in the war for independence. Lydia Maria Child and Margaret Fuller published works dealing with women of other times and places and bringing the record up-to-date. Margaret Fuller called her study *The Great Lawsuit: or Man* vs. *Woman; Woman* vs. *Man.* Mary Wollstonecraft was also read and discussed in this country as in England.

The Struggle for Education. With criticism was carried on a struggle for better educational facilities, since women had been from the beginning excluded from every college in America. In this field Emma Willard and Mary Lyon were conspicuous pioneers; the former founded a girls' seminary at Troy, New York, which ventured to make higher mathematics a part of the regular course of study; the latter started in Massachusetts a school which later became Mount Holyoke College. Sarah J. Hale, a prominent editor, waged a long and powerful campaign for equal educational opportunities, that went far toward paving the way for the founding of Vassar College, when the sectional war was over. Oberlin College in Ohio, established in 1833, astonished the nation by admitting girl students and then contributed Lucy Stone, Antoinette Brown, and other capable leaders to help engineer the movement for the extension of women's rights. An education association was formed in 1852 to promote equal opportunities and some of its speakers went up and down, east and west across the country agitating for a recognition of that educational right. This was preceded in 1848 by the founding of the American Female Medical Education Society.

The Desire to Effect Reforms. As soon as they knew more of their peculiar history and their part in previous civilizations, women grew more confident of their right to express themselves freely in public about the controversies of their own age. When the "Daughters of Temperance" were organized in 1846, they were so bold as to ask that habitual drunkenness be made a ground for divorce and they denounced the churches for indifference to excessive drinking. The slavery issue also called women into public life. The Grimké sisters of South Carolina emancipated their bondmen, and one of these sisters, socially exiled from Charleston for her "Appeal to the Christian Women of the South," went North to work against the slave system. In 1837 the National Women's Anti-Slavery Convention met in New York with seventy-one women delegates in attendance representing eight states. Three years later eight American women, five in Quaker costume, went as American representatives to the World Anti-Slavery Convention in London — much to the horror of the majority of male delegates, who promptly excluded them from the sessions on the ground that it was not proper for women to take part in such assemblies.

But this action only stiffened the backs of the women. Nothing human did they consider alien to them. They worked against cruel criminal laws and indecent prisons. They organized poor relief and led in private philanthropy. Dorothea Dix directed the movement that induced the New York legislature to establish in 1845 a separate asylum for the criminal insane. In the same year Sarah G. Bagley organized the Lowell Female Reform Association for the purpose of reducing the long hours of labor for women, safeguarding "the constitutions of future generations." Mrs. Eliza Woodson Farnham, matron in Sing Sing penitentiary, was known throughout the nation for her social work, especially prison reform. Wherever there were misery and suffering, women appeared with programs for relief.

Freedom of Speech for Women. To advance their causes women of course had to make public appeals and take part in open meetings. Though contrary to the general custom which forbade "ladies" to leave "the sheltered seclusion of the home," women insisted on making their voices heard in the fermenting intellectual life of the age. Frances Wright, who came to the United States from Great Britain in 1820, lectured all over the country for many years on labor, feminism, and politics. A Polish orator, Ernestine Rose, fleeing from oppression, spoke to crowded houses in all the large cities on "the science of government." Besides wielding her pen skillfully, Margaret Fuller gave "parlor conversations" on art, science, religion, politics, literature, philosophy, and society, exhibiting a range of interests much like Emerson's.

While some of these "new women" were cordially received, others were persecuted and mobbed. Antoinette Brown, although she had credentials as a delegate, was driven off the platform of a temperance convention in New York City. Nor did the forum of the press always remain hospitable as the women grew more independent and assertive. James Russell Lowell, editor of the *Atlantic Monthly*, declined a poem from Julia Ward Howe on the theory that no woman could write a poem; but he added on second thought that he might consider an article in prose. Nathaniel Hawthorne, another editor, even objected to something in prose because to him "all ink-stained women were equally detestable."

To the natural resentment against their intrusion into fields dominated by men was joined a dislike for women's ideas and persistence. As temperance reformers, they were apt to be merciless toward those who would not accept their opinions. As opponents of slavery, they seemed neither to sleep nor to rest. One of their conventions, held at Philadelphia in 1833, passed a resolution calling on all women to leave those churches that would not condemn every form of human bondage. This brought down upon them the enmity of many preachers who were accustomed to women's sitting silent in the churches and who were scarcely more inclined to treat a revolt leniently than were the Puritan clergy of Anne Hutchinson's day. Women next decided that they would preach themselves — out of the pulpit first and finally in it.

Women in Industry. The period of this mental upheaval was also the age of the industrial revolution and the growth of mill towns in America. Women's work was now in extraordinary measure transferred from homes to factories. And if the slavery system raised social questions, so did the factory system. Among these were hours of labor, sanitary conditions, the competition of foreign immigrants with native labor, comparative wages of men and women, and the right of women to their earnings. Moreover these problems were complicated by the constant shifting of men into women's hereditary occupations, such as the needle trades, and by women's invasion of men's industries — boot and shoe making, for instance. To deal with the new conditions women in some of the trades formed unions of their own and strikes occasionally occurred. The mill girls of Lowell, Massachusetts, who were at first mainly the daughters of New England farmers, published a magazine, *The Lowell Offering*, which contained such excellent poems and articles that the French statesman, Thiers, is said to have carried a copy of it into the Chamber of Deputies to show what working women could achieve in a republic. Winning their way in the world outside the home and the old type of family care, women began to talk of their "economic independence."

Another European Revolution Awakens Echoes in America.
Such was the quickening of women's minds in 1848 when the world was startled once more by a revolution in France which spread to Germany, Poland, Austria, Hungary, and Italy. Again the people of the Western nations began to examine the principles of democracy and to argue human rights. In these European agitations and uprisings women were active as usual. From their prison in France two, who had been jailed for their disturbances over women's rights, exchanged greetings with American women who were raising the same issue here.

The Women's Rights Convention of 1848. A few months after the outbreak of this new European revolution moral and intellectual forces crystallized in the first Women's Rights Convention in the history of America. It met at Seneca Falls, New York, in 1848, on the call of Lucretia Mott, Jane Hunt, Martha Wright, Elizabeth Cady Stanton, and Mary Ann M'Clintock, three of whom were Quakers. Accustomed to equality with men in their religious meetings, the Quakers suggested that men be invited to attend the convention. Indeed a man presided, for the other advocates of rights for women still felt that "chairing" was too exalted a performance to try as yet.

From this Seneca Falls convention was sent forth a Declaration of Rights modeled after the Declaration of Independence. The preamble began: "When in the course of human events it becomes necessary for one portion of the family of man to assume among the people of the earth a position different from that which they have hitherto occupied. . . ." So also it closed: "Such has been the patient suffering of women under this government and such is now the necessity which constrains them to demand the equal station to which they are entitled." Included in the text was a list of grievances, the exact number which had been handed to George III in 1776. Especially did these women scoff at the disabilities imposed upon them by the English common law imported into America — the law which denied married women their property, their wages, and their own legal existence. All these grievances they recited to "a candid world." Then they set down in detail their remedies: equal rights in the colleges, trades, and professions; equal suffrage; the right to share in all political offices, honors, and emoluments; the right to complete equality in marriage, including equal guardianship of children; and for married women the right to own property, to keep their wages, to make contracts, to transact business, and to testify in the courts of justice. In short, they declared women to be legal "persons" as men are persons and entitled to all the rights and privileges of human beings. Such was the clarion call for justice in 1848 — to an amused and contemptuous country, it must be admitted — but to a country fated to heed and obey.

The First Gains in Civil Liberty. The women's rights convention did not make the suffrage its leading demand. It looked first to the winning of civil rights, and the New York Legislature of that very year, as a result of a twelve years' agitation, passed the Married Woman's Property Act giving them many of the "rights of man." California and Wisconsin followed in 1850; Massachusetts in 1854; and Kansas in 1859. Other states soon fell into line. Women's earnings and inheritances were at last theirs, in some parts of America at least. In a little while laws

were passed granting women rights as equal guardians of their
children and permitting them to divorce their husbands on grounds
of cruelty and drunkenness.

By degrees more steps were taken. The Women's Medical
College of Pennsylvania was founded in 1850, and the Philadelphia
School of Design for Women in 1853. Other colleges soon emulated
the example of Oberlin in co-education: the University of Utah in
1850; Hillsdale College in Michigan in 1855; Baker University in
Kansas in 1858; and the University of Iowa in 1860. New trades
and professions were opened to women and traditional prejudices
against their activities and demands slowly gave way to concepts
more befitting the modern era.

THE NATIONAL STRUGGLE FOR WOMAN SUFFRAGE

The Beginnings of Organization. As women surmounted one
obstacle after another in the path of civil equality, the agitation
for equal suffrage came to the front. If any year is to be fixed as
the date for emphasis, it may very well be 1850, when the suffragists of Ohio urged the state constitutional convention to confer
the vote upon them, when state suffrage conferences were held in
Indiana, Pennsylvania, and Massachusetts, and when the leaders
of these meetings began to coöperate. The same year the first
national suffrage convention was held in Worcester, Massachusetts,
on the call of eighty-nine prominent men and women representing
six states. Accounts of the convention were widely circulated in the
United States and in Europe. English women — for instance,
Harriet Martineau — sent words of appreciation for the work thus
inaugurated. It inspired a leading article in the *Westminster
Review* which caught the attention of the distinguished economist,
John Stuart Mill, who married the author of the article. Soon
he became the champion of woman suffrage in the British Parliament and wrote an eloquent appeal, *The Subjection of Women*,
which was read throughout Western civilization. Thus do world
movements grow — French, English, Polish, American, and
English currents swinging to and fro.

The national suffrage convention was followed by an extraordinary outburst of propaganda. Pamphlets rolled from the press.

Petitions poured in upon legislative bodies.   Addresses were delivered by favorite orators, such as Garrison, Phillips, and Curtis; lectures were given by the great philosopher, Emerson; and poems were contributed by Longfellow and Whittier.   In 1853 a suffrage paper was founded by Anna W. Spencer, the wife of a member of Congress from Rhode Island.   By this time practically the last barrier to white manhood suffrage had been swept away and the woman movement was running a close second.

Woman Suffrage Checked by the Civil War.   Advocates of woman suffrage believed themselves on the high road to success when the Civil War came to claim the energies and labors of the whole people.   Northern women realized that the prime necessity was to preserve the Union so they held no suffrage conventions for five years.   Instead, they transformed their associations into Loyalty Leagues, aiding Lincoln and trying to induce him to make the terrible ordeal result in the emancipation of slaves.   To this end they rolled up monster petitions in favor of a war for Union and liberty.   They banded together to buy only domestic goods when foreign imports threatened to destroy American markets. In hospitals, in military prisons, in agriculture, and in industry they bore their full share of responsibility.   Even when the New York legislature took advantage of their unguarded moments to repeal the law giving the mother equal rights with the father in the guardianship of children, they refused to lay aside war work for agitation.   As in all wars, their devotion was unstinted and their sacrifices equal to the necessities of the hour.

The Federal Suffrage Amendment.   Plans and activities when the war closed were partly shaped by events beyond women's control.   The emancipation of the slaves and the proposition to give the ballot to freedmen made the question of suffrage a national issue for the first time.   Friends of the colored man insisted that the civil liberties just conferred would not be safe unless he was also granted the right to vote for officers to enforce them.   Suffragists very pertinently asked why the principle did not apply to women. But their query was ignored.   The fourteenth amendment to the federal Constitution, adopted in 1868, definitely put women aside by limiting the scope of its suffrage clause to male citizens.

This was the signal for the advocates of woman suffrage to carry their case to Washington. In March, 1869 their proposed amendment to the Constitution was introduced in Congress by George W. Julian of Indiana. It provided that no citizen should be deprived of the vote on account of sex, following the language of the fifteenth amendment which forbade disfranchisement on account of race. Support for the amendment, coming from many directions, led the suffragists to believe that it would soon be adopted. For example, in their platform of 1872, the Republicans praised the women for their loyal devotion to the Union, welcomed them to spheres of wider usefulness, and declared that the demand of any class of citizens for additional rights deserved "respectful consideration."

Experience quickly demonstrated, however, that praise was not the ballot. Indeed, the suffragists already had realized that a tedious contest lay before them. They had revived in 1866 their regular

Susan B. Anthony
Sculpture by Adelaide Johnson in the National Capitol.

annual convention. Elizabeth Cady Stanton and Susan B. Anthony gave the name of *The Revolution* to a paper they founded as a suffrage organ. A national suffrage association was organized and annual pilgrimages were made to Congress to present a claim to the vote. Such activities bore some results. Many eminent Congressmen were converted to their cause and presented it ably to their colleagues of both chambers. Still the subject was ridiculed by most newspapers and looked upon as freakish.

The State Campaigns. Discouraged by the outcome of the national campaign, suffragists turned to the voters of the individual states and sought the ballot at their hands. Even gains by this process were painfully slow. Wyoming, it is true, while still a territory, granted suffrage to women in 1869 and retained it on becoming a state twenty years later, in spite of strong protests in Congress. In 1893 Colorado established complete political equality. In Utah, the third suffrage state, the cause suffered its ups and downs: women were enfranchised by the territorial legislature; they were deprived of the ballot by Congress in 1887; in 1896 on the admission of Utah to the Union they recovered their former rights. During the same year, 1896, Idaho conferred equal suffrage upon the women. But this was the last victory for several years.

The Suffrage Cause in Congress. In the midst of such meager gains among the states there were occasional flurries of hope for quicker action by a federal amendment. Between 1878 and 1896 a Senate committee reported the suffrage resolution by a favorable majority on five different occasions and once the subject reached the point of a general debate. However, there were nine unfavorable reports and at no time could anything like the requisite two-thirds vote be obtained for its passage.

The Changing Status of Women. Meanwhile, strength to the suffrage movement was steadily coming through the activities of women in other directions. College after college — Vassar, Bryn Mawr, Smith, Wellesley, to mention a few — was founded to provide higher education. Other institutions, especially the state universities of the West, opened their doors to women, and they were received into the professions of law, medicine, and the ministry. By the rapid growth of public high schools, in which girls enjoyed the same rights as boys, education was extended still more broadly. The number of women teachers multiplied rapidly from coast to coast.

Women were also entering nearly every branch of industry and business. How many worked at gainful occupations before 1870 we do not know; but from that year forward we have the record of the census. Between 1870 and 1900 the proportion of women in the professions rose from less than two per cent to more than ten per cent; in trade and transportation from 24.8 per cent to 43.2

per cent; and in manufacturing from 13 to 19 per cent. In 1910, there were over 8,000,000 women gainfully employed as compared with 30,000,000 men and *What Eight Million Women Want* was quickly chosen as the title of a book written by Rheta Childe Dorr. When, during the World War, the United States government established the principle of equal pay for equal work and gave official recognition to the value of their services in industry, it was discovered how far women had actually traveled along the road forecast by the leaders of 1848. Facts were catching up with theories and ideals.

The Club Movement among Women. Over all the country women's societies and clubs were started to advance this or that reform or to study literature, art, and science. In time organizations of various kinds were federated into city, state, and national associations and drawn into debates on public questions. Under

Copyright by Harris and Ewing

MRS. NELLIE TAYLOE ROSS, GOVERNOR OF WYOMING (1925–27); DIRECTOR OF THE MINT (1933–   )

the leadership of Frances Willard some made temperance reform a vital issue. Others worked for laws pertaining to prisons, pure food, labor, public health, and municipal government, to list a few items. At their conferences, local, state, and national, civic problems were discussed, until finally, it seems, everything led to the quest for the franchise. By solemn resolution in 1914, the National Federation of Women's Clubs, representing nearly two million club women, formally indorsed the suffrage demand. In the same year the National Education Association, speaking for the public school teachers of the land, added its seal of approval.

State and National Action. The suffrage movement now swung along faster in the states. Washington in 1910, California in 1911, Oregon, Kansas, and Arizona in 1912, Nevada and Montana in 1914 by popular vote enfranchised their women. Illinois in 1913 conferred upon them the right to vote for President of the United States. To hasten victory all along the line, a number of younger suffragists next attempted political tactics such as men were wont to employ. They urged the women who already had the ballot to declare to both political parties that they would vote only for candidates who favored the federal amendment. This plan brought pressure upon Congress from every direction: from the older suffragists who now concentrated on Washington with appeals for justice; and from the "militants" who besought the women of the West to turn against candidates for President who would not approve the federal amendment. In 1916, for the first time, a leading presidential candidate, Charles Evans Hughes, representing the Republicans, and a distinguished ex-President, Theodore Roosevelt, indorsed the amendment.

National Enfranchisement. Events moved rapidly at last. The great state of New York adopted equal suffrage in 1917. Oklahoma, South Dakota, and Michigan took the same stand the following year; and several other states, by legislative action, gave women the right to vote for President. Appeals and petitions deluged Congress and the President, and "suffragettes" held daily demonstrations in Washington. Finally on September 30, 1918, President Wilson who, but two years before, had opposed federal action and indorsed suffrage by state adoption only, personally urged Congress to pass the suffrage amendment to the Constitution. The requisite two-thirds vote was secured in June, 1919, and the amendment was transmitted to the states for review. When on August 28, 1920, Tennessee ratified, the majority of three-fourths required by the Constitution was completed. Thus woman suffrage became the law of the land. With this direct weapon of reform in their possession, women soon set to work to remove various inequalities in state laws such as those affecting their property.

General References

Edith Abbott, *Women in Industry*.
Rheta Childe Dorr, *Susan B. Anthony*.
Charlotte P. Gilman, *Woman and Economics*.
Ida H. Harper, *Life and Work of Susan B. Anthony*.
E. R. Hecker, *Short History of Woman's Rights*.
S. B. Anthony and I. H. Harper, *History of Woman Suffrage* (4 vols.).
Anna H. Shaw, *The Story of a Pioneer*.

Research Topics

The Rise of the Woman Suffrage Movement. McMaster, *History of the People of the United States*, Vol. VIII, pp. 116–121; K. Porter, *History of Suffrage in the United States*, pp. 135–145.

The Development of the Suffrage Movement. Porter, pp. 228–254; Ogg, *National Progress* (American Nation Series), pp. 151–156 and p. 382.

Women's Labor in the Colonial Period. E. Abbott, *Women in Industry*, pp. 10–34.

Women and the Factory System. Abbott, pp. 35–62.

Early Occupations for Women. Abbott, pp. 63–85.

Women's Wages. Abbott, pp. 262–316.

Questions

1. Why does the history of reform involve women?
2. What was the nature of their activity in this field?
3. State the position of women under the old common law.
4. What part did women play in the American Revolution?
5. Explain the rise of the discussion of women's rights.
6. What were some of the early writings about women?
7. Why was there a struggle for educational opportunities?
8. How did reform movements draw women into public affairs and what were the chief results?
9. Show how the rise of the factory affected the life and labor of women.
10. Why is the year 1848 an important year in the woman movement? Discuss the work of the Seneca Falls convention.
11. Enumerate some of the early gains in civil liberty for women.
12. Trace the rise of the suffrage movement.
13. Review the history of the federal suffrage amendment.
14. Summarize the history of the suffrage in the states.

Question for Debate

Women now have equal opportunities with men.

CHAPTER XXVI

INDUSTRIAL DEMOCRACY

The New Economic Age. At the opening of the twentieth century the nation had passed from the era of agriculture to that of great machine industry. The number of city dwellers employed for wages as contrasted with the farmers tilling their own soil was continually mounting. Free land, once the refuge of restless workingmen of the East and immigrants from Europe, was but a memory. Labor had to choose other means for raising its standards of living. Realizing this full well, President Roosevelt said: "A few generations ago, the American workman could have saved money, gone West, and taken up a homestead. Now the free lands were gone. . In earlier days, a man who began with a pick and shovel might come to own a mine. That outlet was now closed as regards the immense majority. . . . The majority of men who earned wages in the coal industry, if they wished to progress at all, were compelled to progress not by ceasing to be wage-earners but by improving the conditions under which all the wage-earners of the country lived and worked."

With the disappearance of free land, Roosevelt continued, had come "a crass inequality in the bargaining relation of the employer and the individual employee standing alone. The great coal-mining and coal-carrying companies which employed their tens of thousands could easily dispense with the services of any particular miner. The miner, on the other hand, however expert, could not dispense with the companies. He needed a job; his wife and children would starve if he did not get one. . . . Individually the miners were impotent when they sought to enter a wage contract with the great companies; they could make fair terms only by uniting into trade unions to bargain collectively." It was for this reason that President Taft advocated reforms in law "to put employees of little power and means on a level with their employers in adjusting and agreeing upon their mutual obligations."

John D. Rockefeller, Jr., one of the great captains of industry, recognized the same facts when he said: "In the early days of the development of industry, the employer and capital investor were frequently one. Daily contact was had between him and his employees, who were his friends and neighbors.... Because of the proportions which modern industry has attained, employers and employees are too often strangers to each other. . . . . Personal relations can be revived only through adequate representation of the employees. Representation is a principle which is fundamentally just and vital to the successful conduct of industry. . . . It is not consistent for us as Americans to demand democracy in government and practice autocracy in industry. . . . With the developments what they are in industry to-day, there is sure to come a progressive evolution from aristocratic single control, whether by capital, labor, or the state, to a democratic, coöperative control by all three."

Coöperation between Employers and Employees

Company Unions. This changed economic life was similarly acknowledged by several great business concerns. Throughout the country decided efforts were made to bridge the gulf which industry and the corporation had created between employees and employers. Among the plans adopted to accomplish this purpose was the "company union." In a western lumber mill, for instance, all the employees were invited to join a company organization; they held monthly meetings to discuss matters of common concern; they elected a "shop committee" to confer with the representatives of the company; and periodically the agents of the employers attended the conferences of the men to talk over matters of mutual interest. It was the function of the shop committee to consider wages, hours, safety rules, sanitation, recreation, and other problems of this kind.

Whenever an employee had a grievance, he took it up with the foreman and, if it was not settled to his satisfaction, he brought it before the shop committee. If the members of the shop committee decided in favor of the man with a grievance, they attempted to settle the matter with the company's agents. All these things failing, the dispute was transferred to a common council including all the employees and the employers' representatives. A deadlock, if it ensued from such a conference, was broken by calling in impartial arbitrators selected by both sides from among citizens outside the mill. Thus the employees were given a voice in decisions affecting their work and welfare; and the rights and grievances of each were treated as matters of mutual interest rather than individual concern. Representatives of the regular trade unions, however, were rigidly excluded from all such negotiations between employers and the employees. As industrial workers became more efficient in organizing their own unions to enforce demands, corporations made still greater efforts to form unions on the company plan, with extraordinary success.

Profit-Sharing. To give workers an interest in the corporations that employed them, other projects were tried. Occasionally lump sums were paid as "bonuses" to employees who remained in a company's service for a definite period of years. In some places they were given a percentage of the annual profits. In other instances, employees were allowed to buy stock on easy terms and thus become part owners of the concerns for which they worked. This last plan was carried so far by a large soap manufacturing company that the employees, besides becoming stockholders, secured the right to elect representatives to serve on the board of directors which controlled the entire business.

Labor Managers and Welfare Work. Still another effort of employers to meet the problems of the machine age appeared in the appointment of specialists, known as employment managers, whose task it was to study the relations between masters and workers and discover practical methods for dealing with each grievance as it arose. By 1918, hundreds of big companies had recognized this modern "profession" and universities were giving courses of instruction in "personnel management." In that year a national conference of employment managers was held at Rochester, New York. The discussion revealed the wide range of duties assigned to managers: questions of wages, hours, sanitation, rest rooms, recreational facilities, and welfare work of every kind designed to make the conditions in mills and factories safer and more humane. Hundreds of employers had evidently abandoned the idea that their industrial obligations ended the moment hungry workers accepted whatever wage they were willing to pay. In short, they were seeking to develop a spirit of coöperation — to increase production by promoting the efficiency and happiness of the producers. Besides this, they were coming to see that high wages, by expanding the buying power of the people, enlarged the home market for American goods. This was a new phase in capitalist economy and was the next experiment which Europeans came to study.

The Rise and Growth of Organized Labor

The American Federation of Labor. Meanwhile a powerful association of workers representing all the leading trades and crafts, organized into unions of their own, had been built up entirely by labor's own initiative. This was the American Federation of Labor, a nation-wide union of unions, founded in 1886 on the basis of groundwork laid five years before. At the time of its establishment it had approximately 150,000 members. Its growth up to the end of the century was slow, for the total enrollment in 1900 was only 300,000. Then it had a boom. The membership reached 1,650,000 in 1904 and more than 3,000,000 in 1919. Also to be counted in the ranks of organized labor were several national unions, friendly to the Federation, though not affiliated with it. Such, for example, were the Railway Brotherhoods with more than half a million members. By the opening of 1920 the total strength of organized labor of the independent type was put at about 4,000,000 members, meaning, if we include their families, that nearly one-fifth of the people of the United States were in some positive way dependent upon the operation of trade unions.

Historical Background. This was the culmination of a long and significant labor history. In the age when the American republic was launched, certain skilled workmen — printers, shoemakers, tailors, and carpenters — had, as we have seen, formed local unions in the large cities. By the time the slavery issue drew the very existence of the Union into question, the number of local unions had increased by leaps and bounds in all the industrial towns.   Moreover, in every large manufacturing city a central labor body, composed of delegates from the unions of the separate trades, had been formed to advance general interests.   In the local union the printers or cordwainers, for instance, handled only their special trade problems.   But in the central labor union, printers, cordwainers, iron molders, and other craftsmen considered common labor problems and learned, by helping one another, to strengthen all.   A third step was the nation-wide federation of the unions in each skilled craft.   To illustrate, the printers of New York, Philadelphia, Boston, and other towns, drew together and formed a national trade union of printers built upon the local unions of that craft.   On the eve of the Civil War there were four or five powerful national unions of this character.   The expansion of the railway facilitated travel and correspondence and national conventions became possible for workmen of small means.   About 1834 an attempt was made to federate the unions of all crafts into a national organization; but they were not yet ready for that advanced stage.

The National Labor Union.   The plan which failed in 1834 was tried again in the sixties, at the close of the Civil War.   Industries and railways had expanded to meet Northern military requirements; prices had risen rapidly; the demand for labor had increased; and wages had climbed steadily.   Workers were forming unions in the cities for self-protection and eight or ten national unions had sprung into being.   The time was ripe, it seemed, for a continental consolidation of all organized labor to hold the war gains.

In 1866, therefore, the year after the surrender of General Lee at Appomattox, the "National Labor Union" was formed at Baltimore under the leadership of an experienced organizer, W. H. Sylvis of the iron molders.   The prime purpose of this union was not merely to secure labor's standard demands respecting hours, wages, and conditions of work or to maintain the gains already won.   It leaned rather toward political action based on radical theories.   Above all, it sought to eliminate the conflict between capital and labor by making workingmen themselves owners of shops through the formation of coöperative industries. For six years the National Labor Union continued to hold conferences and carry on its propaganda; but most of the coöperative enterprises failed, political differences arose within the organization, and by 1872 it had come to an end.

The Knights of Labor. While the National Labor Union was experimenting, a still more radical organization was formed, known as the "Noble Order of the Knights of Labor." It was founded in Philadelphia in 1869, first as a secret society with rituals, signs, and passwords; "so that no spy of the boss can find his way into the lodge room to betray his fellows," as the Knights said. It sought to bring all laborers, skilled and unskilled, men and women, white and colored, into a mighty body of local and national unions without distinction of trade or craft. By 1885, ten years after the national organization was established, it boasted a membership of over 700,000. Although they also believed that workers should coöperate in owning and managing factories and stores, the Knights of Labor went further in a socialist direction by advocating government ownership of railways and other public utilities.

By avowing such aims, the Knights awakened hostility among captains of industry and the people at large, especially when they added numerous and prolonged strikes to their record of propaganda. Weaknesses within, as well as foes without, pushed the Knights along the path to dissolution. They waged more strikes than they could carry on successfully; their coöperative experiments failed as those of other labor groups had failed before them; and the rank and file could not be kept in line. The majority of the members wanted immediate gains in wages or the reduction of hours. There was a limit to the time that hungry workers could remain unemployed merely for a principle and, when their hopes for better conditions faded, they drifted away from the Order. Its troubles were next aggravated by the appearance of the American Federation of Labor composed mainly of skilled workers who held the more strategic positions in industry. When the Knights of Labor failed to secure the support of the Federation in their efforts to organize the unskilled, employers closed in upon them. By 1890 they were a negligible factor and in a short time they passed into the limbo of dead experiments.

The Policies of the American Federation. Unlike the Knights of Labor, the American Federation of Labor sought, first of all, to be very practical in its objects and methods. It avoided every kind of socialistic theory and attended strictly to the business of organizing unions for the purpose of increasing wages, shortening hours, and improving working conditions for its members. It did not try to include everybody in one big union or indeed all the workers in separate unions. It brought together the more skilled groups of employees whose craft interests were clearly the same. To prepare for strikes and periods of unemployment, it raised large funds through heavy dues and created a benefit system to hold members loyally to the union. To permit action on a national scale, it gave the superior officers extensive powers over local unions.

While declaring that employers and employees had much in common, the Federation strongly opposed company unions. Employers, it argued, had united in the National Manufacturers' Association or in similar employers' organizations; every important industry was now national in scope, that is, it had plants all over the country; therefore, in view of competition in prices and output among countless shops from coast to coast, wages and hours could not be determined for a single plant alone without reference to standards in other plants. Even if conditions were excellent in one factory or mine where the company and its workers met on friendly terms, that did not solve the problem for all the employees in the same industry throughout the land, as the union undertook to do. For these reasons the Federation declared that company unions and local shop committees were unsatisfactory. It insisted that hours, wages, and other labor standards should be fixed by general trade agreements applicable to all the plants of a given industry, even if subject to local modifications.

On the basis of its strong organization, the Federation sought to avoid strikes and persuade employers that the relation between capital and labor might become one of peaceful bargaining. In taking this position it had the support of certain manufacturers, financiers, and professional men interested in public affairs, who founded the National Civic Federation in 1900 to promote better industrial relations. Though radical workers objected to this alliance, officers of the Federation frankly welcomed aid from the new ally, for they accepted the present economic system and had no intention of trying to overthrow it. Their ideal was to secure within this system definite terms and conditions for their members.

The Wider Relations of Labor

The Political Appeal. To strict trade unionists the labor problem seemed to involve nothing more than businesslike negotiations, man to man, with employers. But in fact it could not be kept in that simple form. The Federation was only six years old when a new organization, the Socialist Labor party, appealing directly to the industrial workers, nominated a candidate for President and demanded thoroughgoing changes in the capitalist system itself. Trade unionists were now told that mere bargaining with employers was not enough to bring about good working conditions and they were urged to go into politics for the purpose of accomplishing reforms by government action.

Modern Socialism. The theories of this political party were founded mainly on the teachings of a German scholar and agitator, Karl Marx. Unlike the "Utopians" of the early nineteenth century, Marx did not advocate the formation of "socialistic" labor colonies. On the contrary, he called upon workingmen of the whole world to unite against capitalists, take possession of the machinery of government, and introduce collective or public ownership of railways, lands, mines, mills, and other instruments of production. Marxian socialists were therefore political, as well as economic, in their aims. They sought to organize labor and to win elections.

Like the other parties they put forward candidates and platforms. The Socialist Labor party, for instance, in 1892, declared in favor of government ownership of utilities, free school books, woman suffrage, heavy income taxes, and the referendum. A similar position was taken by the Socialist party, founded in 1900, with Eugene V. Debs as its candidate; it too demanded public ownership of monopolies, mines, railways, and the chief means of production. Gradually the socialists became more revolutionary in tone. The Socialist party officially refused to support the United States in the war on Germany in 1917. Some individual

SAMUEL GOMPERS (FRONT ROW, SECOND FROM LEFT) AND OTHER LABOR LEADERS

socialists, influenced by the Russian revolution of that year, advocated the overthrow of the American industrial system by violence.

In their appeal for votes, the socialists of every type turned first to industrial workers. At the annual conventions of the American Federation of Labor they urged the delegates to indorse socialism.

But its president, Samuel Gompers, on each occasion, took the floor against them. He repudiated socialism and socialists, both on theoretical and practical grounds. He opposed too much public ownership, declaring that the government was as likely as any private employer to oppress labor. The approval of socialism, he believed, would split the Federation on the rock of politics, prejudice the public against it, and weaken it in its fight for higher wages and shorter hours. Throughout his long term as president, he was able to vanquish the socialists in the Federation, although he could not prevent it from favoring one of their planks in 1920 — public ownership of railways.

The Extreme Radicals. Defeated in their efforts to capture organized labor and to carry elections, some of the socialists broke away from both trade unionism and politics. One faction, the Industrial Workers of the World, founded in 1905, declared themselves opposed to all capitalists, the wages system, and craft unions. They asserted that the "working class and the employing class have nothing in common" and that trade unions only pit one set of workers against another set. They repudiated government ownership of industries, sought to unite all working people into one big union, and made plans to seize the railways, mines, and mills of the country in the name of revolutionary labor. This doctrine called down upon the heads of its advocates the condemnation of the American Federation of Labor and the general public also. At its convention in 1919, the Federation went on record as "opposed to Bolshevism, I. W. W.-ism, and the irresponsible leadership that encourages such a policy." It announced its "firm adherence to American ideals."

The Federation and Political Issues. The hostility of the Federation to socialists of every kind did not mean, however, that it was indifferent to political issues or political parties. On the contrary, from time to time, at its annual conventions, it indorsed specific reforms, such as the initiative, referendum, and recall, the abolition of child labor, the exclusion of Oriental labor, old-age pensions, and government ownership in certain lines. To forward its projects it adopted the policy of "rewarding friends and punishing enemies:" that is, it advised its members to vote for or against the candidates of political parties according to their stand on the specific demands of organized labor.

This policy the Federation pursued with especial zeal in dealing with the use of court injunctions in labor controversies. An injunction is a bill or writ issued by a judge ordering some person or corporation to do or not to do some specific thing. For example, a judge may order a trade union to refrain from interfering with non-union men or to continue at work handling goods made by non-union labor; and he may fine or imprison those who disobey his injunction, the penalty being inflicted for "contempt of court." This legal device came into prominence during nation-wide railway strikes in 1877. It was used effectively against Eugene V. Debs, director of the Pullman strike of 1894, and then applied with increasing frequency as a method for blocking labor tactics.

With strikes broken and leaders imprisoned under injunction orders, organized labor demanded that the power of judges to issue such writs in industrial disputes be limited by law. Representatives of the unions asked both the Republicans and the Democrats to approve their proposal and received from the latter a very definite and cordial indorsement. In 1896 the Democratic platform denounced "government by injunction as a new and highly dangerous form of oppression." While refusing to commit the Federation to the Democratic party as such, Gompers privately supported its candidate, William Jennings Bryan. In 1908 he came out openly for Bryan and boasted that eighty per cent of the votes of the Federation were cast for the Democratic candidate. Again in 1912 the same policy was pursued.

And the reward was the enactment in 1914 of a federal law exempting trade unions from prosecution as combinations in restraint of trade, limiting the use of the injunction in labor disputes, and prescribing trial by jury in case of contempt of court. This measure was hailed by Gompers as the "Magna Charta of Labor" and a vindication of his policy. As a matter of fact, however, it did not prevent the continued use of injunctions against trade unions. Even so, Gompers refused to sanction an independent labor party or radical economic plans. When the American Federation of Labor supported Senator La Follette for President in 1924, it did not join a third party; it merely gave him its official encouragement for the time being. After that experiment it continued its former "non-partisan" position.

Organized Labor and the Public. Besides its relations to employers, to radicals within its own ranks, and to various political questions, the Federation had to face obligations to a third factor in industry — the general purchasing public. With the passing of time these became heavy and serious. While industries were small and conflicts were local in character, a strike seldom affected anybody but the employer and the employees immediately involved. When, however, industries and trade unions became organized on a national scale, a strike could paralyze a basic enterprise like coal mining or railways, and thus put in jeopardy the vital interests of all citizens.

For the purpose of avoiding as far as possible such ruinous strikes, it was suggested by various reformers that employers and employees lay their disputes before commissions of arbitration for review and settlement. In a message of April 2, 1886, President Cleveland approved this idea and two years later Congress applied it in a law which made arrangements for the voluntary arbitration of labor controversies arising on interstate railways. The principle was later extended by Congress and fully incorporated in the Railway Labor Act of 1926, providing for a board of mediation to hear disputes respecting wages, hours, and rules of employment.

The initial success of this legislation led certain students of industrial questions to urge that unions and employers should be compelled, not merely permitted, to submit all their disputes to official tribunals and to accept their decision. Kansas actually passed such a "compulsory arbitration" law in 1920, but it was strongly opposed by both labor and capital. In the course of time the Supreme Court of the United States declared the Kansas statute unconstitutional and it seemed generally agreed that the scheme was not practical.

IMMIGRATION AND AMERICANIZATION

Labor and the Problem of Immigration. From its very beginning, the Federation of Labor had to meet numerous questions created by an ever-swelling stream of immigrant workers flowing into the United States. When it tried to unionize all the employees in a given trade, the Federation usually had to deal with many foreign language groups. Carrying on meetings in five or six tongues was not easy! Then after it had managed by hard labor to organize all the workers in a certain craft and raise their

Hine Photograph from Ewing Galloway, New York

MODERN SCENE AT ELLIS ISLAND — THE IMMIGRATION STATION AT THE
PORT OF NEW YORK

wages, it sometimes saw its efforts undone by a fresh influx of foreigners willing to accept lower rates. So labor leaders came to the conclusion that they could not form successful unions and uphold good standards of living as long as aliens poured into the country to underbid Americans and act as strike breakers.

Outside the labor movement, citizens at large also began to have some doubts about the wisdom of keeping the nation's doors wide open for the "alien invasion." These doubters saw whole sections of great cities occupied by people speaking foreign tongues, reading only foreign newspapers, and tied fast to the Old World by loyalty and custom. They witnessed an expanding army of total illiterates, men and women who could read and write no language at all; while among those aliens who could read, few there were who knew anything of American history, traditions, and ideals. Official reports revealed that over twenty per cent of the men of the draft army during the World War could not read a newspaper or write a letter home. Perhaps most alarming of all was the discovery that thousands of alien men were in the United States only on a temporary sojourn, solely to make money and go back to Europe or Asia with their savings. These men, willing to work for almost any wage and live in places unfit for human beings, had no stake in this country and did not care what became of it. They could not share in the progress of the labor movement or feel any interest in American citizenship.

The Restriction of Immigration. Yet in all this there was no cause for surprise. Since the foundation of the republic the policy of the government had been to encourage immigration. For nearly one hundred years no restraining act was passed by Congress, while two important laws actually promoted it; namely, the Homestead Act of 1862 and the contract immigration law of 1864. Not until American workingmen came into collision with Chinese labor on the Pacific Coast did the federal government pass its first measure of limitation.

With the discovery of gold and particularly after the opening of the railway construction era, a horde of laborers from China had descended upon California. Long used to starvation earnings and to poverty-stricken conditions of living, they threatened to cut American standards of wages to the lowest point of subsistence. In time the protest of American labor against this invasion was strong enough to compel both Republicans and Democrats to heed it. Accordingly in 1882 Congress by a law prohibited the admission of Chinese laborers to the United States for a term of ten years — a rule later changed into permanent exclusion. In a little while the demand arose for a bar against the Japanese, but in this case no exclusion law was passed. Instead, an understanding was reached with Japan, in 1907, known as the "Gentlemen's Agree-

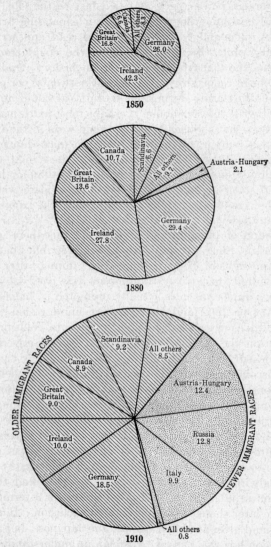

1850

1880

1910

GRAPH SHOWING PROPORTION OF FOREIGN-BORN OF DIFFERENT
NATIONALITIES IN THE UNITED STATES AT THREE PERIODS

ment." Under this arrangement Japan promised to stop issuing passports to laborers permitting them to sail for the United States and President Roosevelt made a pledge that the government would not adopt a Japanese exclusion act.

Having embarked upon the policy of restriction in 1882, Congress readily extended it. In that same year it forbade the admission of paupers, criminals, convicts, and the insane. Mainly owing to the pressure of the Knights of Labor, it forbade, in 1885, any person, company, or association to import aliens under contract to work for any specific employer. By an act of 1887, the contract-labor restriction was made even more severe. In 1903 anarchists were excluded and the bureau of immigration was transferred from the Treasury Department to the Department of Commerce and Labor, in order to provide for a more rigid execution of the law. In 1907 the classes of persons denied admission were extended to embrace those suffering from physical and mental defects and otherwise unfit for citizenship. When the Department of Labor was established in 1913 the enforcement of the law was placed in the hands of the Secretary of Labor — usually chosen by the President from among labor leaders or persons in sympathy with trade-union ideals.

Not yet appeased, organized labor demanded further protection against the competition of immigrants. In 1917 it won another advance in its thirty-year battle by the passage of a bill, over President Wilson's veto, excluding "all aliens over sixteen years of age, physically capable of reading, who cannot read the English language or some other language or dialect, including Hebrew or Yiddish."

By this time a lively opposition to the restriction of immigration was raised in many quarters. Naturally, certain races already in the United States objected to every barrier that shut out their own kinsmen; while some Americans of the old stock still held to the belief that the United States should continue to be an asylum for "the oppressed of the earth." And many employers, desiring an increase in the number of wage-earners, also protested against further restraints.

But Congress leaned toward more rather than less restriction.

Indeed in 1921 it adopted a principle which made a deep cut in immigration. It absolutely limited the number of aliens to be admitted from most countries to a certain percentage of their citizens already in the United States in 1910. In 1924 it made the rule more drastic, abolished the arrangement with Japan, known as the "Gentlemen's Agreement," and put the Japanese on the same basis as the Chinese (page 679).

Americanization. Intimately connected with the problem of immigration was a call for the "Americanization" of the aliens already within our gates. The revelation of illiteracy in the army helped to start this cry and the demand was intensified when it was found that many of the leaders among the extreme radicals were foreign in birth and citizenship. Innumerable programs for assimilating the alien to American life were drawn up, and in 1919 a national conference on the subject was held in Washington under the auspices of the Department of the Interior. All agreed that the foreigner should at least be taught to speak and write the English language and to understand the government of the United States — even if he continued to use his native tongue and read the newspapers of his race. Partly as a result of this movement, there was an enormous increase in the money spent for popular education. America, as Roosevelt had said, was to find out "whether it was a nation or a boarding-house."

General References

J. R. Commons and Associates, *History of Labor in the United States* (2 vols.).

Samuel Gompers, *Labor and the Common Welfare* and *Seventy Years of Life and Labor.*

W. E. Walling, *Socialism as It Is.*

W. E. Walling (and Others), *The Socialism of Today* and *American Labor and American Democracy.*

R. T. Ely, *The Labor Movement in America.*

T. S. Adams and H. Sumner, *Labor Problems.*

Alice Henry, *Women and the Labor Movement.*

J. G. Brooks, *American Syndicalism* and *Social Unrest.*

P. F. Hall, *Immigration and Its Effects on the United States.*

F. J. Warne, *The Immigrant Invasion.*

Research Topics

The Rise of Trade Unionism. Mary Beard, *Short History of the American Labor Movement*, pp. 10–18, 47–53, 62–79; Carlton, *Organized Labor in American History*, pp. 11–44.

Labor and Politics. Beard, *Short History*, pp. 33–46, 54–61, 103–112; Carlton, pp. 169–197; Ogg, *National Progress* (American Nation Series), pp. 76–85.

The Knights of Labor. Beard, *Short History*, pp. 116–126; Dewey, *National Problems* (American Nation Series), pp. 40–49.

The American Federation of Labor — Organization and Policies. Beard, *Short History*, pp. 86–112.

Organized Labor and the Socialists. Beard, *Short History*, pp. 126–149.

Labor and the Great War. Carlton, pp. 282–306; Beard, *Short History*, pp. 150–170.

Questions

1. What are the striking features of the new economic age?
2. Give Rockefeller's view of industrial democracy.
3. Outline the efforts made by employers to establish closer relations with their employees.
4. Sketch the rise and growth of the American Federation of Labor.
5. How far back in our history does the labor movement extend?
6. Describe the purposes and outcome of the National Labor Union and the Knights of Labor.
7. State the chief policies of the American Federation of Labor.
8. How does organized labor become involved with outside forces?
9. Outline the rise of the socialist movement. How did it come into contact with the American Federation?
10. What was the relation of the Federation to the extreme radicals? To national politics? To the public?
11. Explain the injunction.
12. Why are labor and immigration closely related?
13. Outline the history of restrictions on immigration.
14. What problems arise in connection with the assimilation of the alien to American life?

Questions for Debate

1. Compulsory arbitration in labor disputes should be established.
2. Immigration should be further restricted.

Historical Fiction

Ernest Poole, *The Harbor.*

CHAPTER XXVII

PRESIDENT WILSON AND THE WORLD WAR

"The welfare, the happiness, the energy, and the spirit of the men and women who do the daily work in our mines and factories, on our railroads, in our offices and ports of trade, on our farms, and on the sea are the underlying necessity of all prosperity." Thus spoke Woodrow Wilson during his campaign for election. In this spirit, as President, he summoned Congress in a special session on April 7, 1913. He invited the coöperation of all "forward-looking men" and indicated that he would assume the rôle of leadership. As proof of his resolve, he appeared before Congress in person to read his first message, reviving the old custom of Washington and Adams. Then he let it be known that he would not give his party any rest until it fulfilled its pledges to the country. When Democratic Senators balked at tariff reductions, they were informed that the party had plighted its word and that no excuses or delays would be tolerated.

Domestic Legislation

Financial Measures. Under his vigorous leadership, Congress enacted a program of somewhat sensational legislation. First on the list was the Underwood tariff act of 1913 which still recognized the protective principle but admitted some foreign competition by fixing the rates on the average about twenty-six per cent lower than the figure of 1907. Now that the sixteenth amendment to the Constitution made it lawful, Congress, as a part of the revenue act, included a tax on incomes — to the horror of conservatives.

Having disposed of the tariff, Congress took up the currency question which had vexed the country since colonial times and offered a new solution in the form of the federal reserve law of December, 1913. This measure, one of the most interesting in the history of federal finance, had four leading features. In the first place, it continued the bar against the issue of notes by state banks and provided for a national currency. In the second place, it put the new banking system under the control of a federal reserve board composed entirely of government officials. To prevent the growth of a "central money power," it provided, in the third place, for the creation of twelve federal reserve banks, one in each of twelve great districts into which the country was divided. All local national banks were required and certain other banks permitted to become members of the new system and share in its management. Finally, with a view to expanding the currency, a step which the Democrats had long urged upon the country, the issuance of paper money through federal reserve banks, under strict safeguards, was authorized.

Mindful of the agricultural interest, ever dear to the heart of Jeffersonians, the Democrats supplemented the reserve law by the Farm Loan Act of 1916, creating federal agencies to lend money on farm mortgages at moderate rates of interest. Within a year $20,000,000 had been lent to farmers, principally in Western and Southern states, with Texas in the lead.

Anti-trust Legislation. When it took up the trust question, the Wilson administration rejected the Progressive doctrine of regulation. Wilson himself declared that it was the purpose of the Democrats "to destroy monopoly and maintain competition as the only effective instrument of business liberty." The first step in this direction, the Clayton Anti-trust Act of 1914, carried into great detail the Sherman law of 1890 forbidding and penalizing combinations in restraint of interstate and foreign trade. In every line it revealed a fixed design to tear apart the great trusts and to put all business on a competitive basis. Its terms were reinforced in the same year by a law creating a Federal Trade Commission and giving it the power to inquire into the methods of corporations and lodge complaints against concerns "using any unfair method of competition." In only one respect was the severity of the Democratic policy relaxed. An act of 1918 provided that the Sherman law should not apply to companies engaged in export trade, the purpose being to encourage large corporations to enter foreign commerce.

Just what effect this anti-trust legislation had is difficult to say.

At all events very few combinations were dissolved as a result of it. Startling investigations were made into alleged abuses on the part of trusts; but it could hardly be said that huge business concerns had lost their leadership in American industry.

Labor Legislation. By no mere accident, the Clayton anti-trust law of 1914 made many concessions to organized labor. It declared that "the labor of a human being is not a commodity or an article of commerce," and it exempted unions from prosecution as "combinations in restraint of trade." It likewise defined and limited the uses which the federal courts might make of injunctions in labor disputes and guaranteed trial by jury to those guilty of disobedience (page 604).

The Clayton law was followed the next year by the Seamen's Act giving American sailors more rights in dealing with their employers and requiring an improvement of living conditions on shipboard. Indeed the law was so strict that shipowners declared themselves unable to meet foreign competition under its terms, owing to the low labor standards of other countries.

Still more extraordinary than the Seamen's Act was the Adamson law of 1916 fixing a standard eight-hour workday for trainmen on railroads — a measure wrung from Congress under a threat of a great strike by the four Railway Brotherhoods. This Act, hailed by union leaders as a triumph, called forth from some capitalists a bitter denunciation of "trade union tyranny," but it was easier to criticize than to find another solution of the problem.

Three other laws enacted during President Wilson's administration were popular in the labor world. One provided compensation for federal employees injured in the discharge of their duties. Another prohibited the labor of children under a certain age in the industries of the nation — later declared void by the Supreme Court. A third prescribed for coal miners in Alaska an eight-hour day and modern safeguards for life and health. These were positive proofs that trade unions had obtained a large share of power in the councils of the country.

Federal and State Relations. If the interference of the government with business and labor was a departure from the old idea of "the less government the better," what can be said of a large body of laws affecting the rights of states? The prohibition of child labor everywhere was one indication of the new tendency. Wilson had once declared such legislation unconstitutional; the Supreme Court declared it void; Congress, undaunted, tried to carry it into effect under the guise of a tax on goods made by children below the age limit, and only gave up the battle when this second law was also annulled by the Court. There were other signs of the drift. Large sums of money were appropriated by Congress in 1916 to assist the states in building and maintaining highways. The same year the Farm Loan Act thrust the federal government into the sphere of local money lending. In 1917 millions of dollars were granted to states in aid of vocational education, incidentally imposing uniform standards throughout the country. Evidently the government was no longer limited to the duties of the policeman.

The Prohibition Amendment. A still more significant form of intervention in state affairs was the passage, in December, 1917, of an amendment to the federal Constitution establishing national prohibition of the manufacture and sale of intoxicating liquor as a beverage. This was the climax of a historical movement extending over half a century. In 1872, a National Prohibition party, launched three years before, nominated its first presidential candidate and inaugurated a campaign of agitation. Though its vote was never large, the cause for which it stood found increasing favor among the people. State after state by popular referendum abolished the liquor traffic within its borders. By 1917 at least thirty-two of the forty-eight were "dry." When the federal amendment was submitted for approval, the ratification was swift. In a little more than a year, namely, on January 16, 1919, it was proclaimed. Twelve months later this eighteenth amendment went into effect, coupled with the Volstead Act which defined "intoxicating liquor" as a beverage containing more than one half of one per cent alcohol and created machinery for enforcing prohibition.

COLONIAL AND FOREIGN POLICIES

The Philippines and Porto Rico. Independence for the Philippines and larger self-government for Porto Rico had been among the policies of the Democratic party since the campaign of 1900. President Wilson in his annual messages urged upon Congress more autonomy for the Filipinos and a definite promise of final independence. The result was the Jones Organic Act for the Philippines passed in 1916. This measure provided that the upper as well as the lower house of the Philippine legislature should be elected by popular vote, and declared it to be the intention of the United States to grant independence "as soon as a stable government can be established." On signing the bill, the President said: "This is a very satisfactory advance in our policy of extending to them self-government and control of their own affairs." Yielding to Wilson's advice, Congress passed in 1917 a new organic act for Porto Rico, making both houses of the legislature elective and conferring American citizenship upon the inhabitants of the island.

American Power in the Caribbean. While giving more self-government to its dominions, the United States enlarged its sphere of influence in the Caribbean. The supervision of finances in Santo Domingo, inaugurated in Roosevelt's administration (page 539), was changed into a "protectorate" under Wilson. In 1914 dissensions in the republic led to the landing of American marines to "supervise" the elections. Two years later, an officer of the American navy, with authority from Washington, placed the entire republic "in a state of military occupation." He suspended the government and laws of the country, exiled the president, suppressed the congress, and substituted American military authority. In 1924 a new constitution was written under American scrutiny and a government installed. American marines were then withdrawn — on the tacit understanding that they would be sent back again in case of trouble.

In the neighboring republic of Haiti, a revolution broke out during the summer of 1915 — one of a long series beginning in 1804 — and American marines were landed to restore order. Peace was established at a heavy cost in the lives of natives — more than 1800 in a single year. Elections were held under the supervision of American officers, and a treaty was drawn up placing the management of Haitian finances and police under American

THE CARIBBEAN REGION

authority.   In taking this action, our Secretary of State was careful to announce: "The United States government has no purpose of aggression and is entirely disinterested in promoting this protectorate."   Still it must be said that many natives and American citizens did not view the conduct of our agents in the island in just that light.

In line with American policy in the West Indian waters was the purchase in 1917 of the Danish Islands just off the coast of Porto Rico.   The strategic position of the islands, especially in relation to Haiti and Porto Rico, made them an object of American concern as early as 1867, when a treaty of purchase was negotiated with Denmark, only to be rejected by the Senate of the United States.   In 1902 a second arrangement was made but this time it was defeated by the upper house of the Danish parliament. The third treaty brought an end to fifty years of bargaining and the Stars and Stripes were raised over St. Croix, St. Thomas, St. John, and numerous minor islands scattered about in the neighborhood.   "It would be suicidal," commented a New York newspaper, "for America, on the threshold of a great commercial expansion in South America, to suffer a Heligoland, or a Gibraltar, or an Aden to be erected by her rivals at the mouth of the Panama Canal."   On the mainland American power was strengthened by the creation of a protectorate over Nicaragua in 1916 (below, page 657).

Mexican Relations.   The spread of American enterprise southward into Latin America, illustrated by the operations in the Caribbean regions, naturally carried Americans into Mexico to develop the natural resources of that country.   Under the iron rule of General Porfirio Diaz, established in 1876 and maintained with only a short break until 1911, Mexico had become increasingly attractive to our business men.   On the invitation of President Diaz, they had invested huge sums in Mexican lands, oil fields, and mines, and had made the beginnings of an industrial system. The severe methods of government practised by Diaz, however, stirred popular discontent.   Mexican peons, or serfs, demanded the break-up of the great estates, some of which had come down from the days of Cortes.   Their clamor for "the restoration of the land to the people" could not be silenced. And in 1911 Diaz was forced to resign and leave the country.

Revolution in Mexico. Mexico now slid down the path to disorder. Revolutions and civil commotions followed in swift succession. A liberal president, Madero, installed as the successor to Diaz, was deposed in 1913 and brutally murdered. Huerta, a military adventurer, hailed for a time as another "strong man," then came to the top as dictator. Although Great Britain and nearly all the powers of Europe accepted the Huerta government as lawful, the United States withheld recognition. In the meantime Mexico was torn by local revolts under the leadership of Carranza, a friend of Madero, Villa, a bandit also called a reformer, and Zapata, a radical leader of the peons. Without the support of the United States, Huerta was doomed.

In the summer of 1914, the dictator resigned and fled from the capital, leaving the field to Carranza who was soon officially recognized by the United States. For six years the new president held a precarious position which he strove to strengthen against various revolutionary movements. But in 1920, he too was deposed and murdered, and another military chieftain, Obregon, installed in power.

The Mexican Policy of the United States. These events right at our door could not fail to involve the government of the United States. In the disorders many American citizens lost their lives, American property was destroyed, and land owned by Americans was confiscated. A new Mexican constitution, in effect nationalizing the natural resources of the country, struck at the rights of foreign investors in mines and oil wells. Moreover the Mexican border was in constant turmoil. Even in the last days of his administration, President Taft felt compelled to issue a warning to the Mexican government against the violation of American life and property.

President Wilson, shortly after his inauguration, sent a commissioner to Mexico to inquire into the situation. While he adhered to a general policy of "watchful waiting," on two occasions the system broke down. In 1914 some American sailors at Tampico were arrested by a Mexican officer; the Mexican government, although it immediately released the men, refused to make the required apology for the incident. As a result the President ordered the landing of American forces at Vera Cruz and the seizure of the city. A clash of arms followed in which several Americans and many more Mexicans were killed. War seemed at hand, but at this juncture the governments of Argentina, Brazil, and Chile tendered their good offices as mediators. After a few weeks of negotiation, during which Huerta was forced out of power, American forces were withdrawn from Vera Cruz and the incident closed.

In 1916 a second break occurred. In the spring of that year a band of Villa's men raided the town of Columbus, New Mexico, killing several citizens and committing robberies. At once President Wilson sent an expedition under the command of General Pershing to capture the offenders; and against the protests of President Carranza, American forces advanced far into Mexico — without effecting the object of their undertaking. They were engaged in this operation until January, 1917, when the growing difficulties with Germany led to their withdrawal. Friendly relations were resumed with the Mexican government and the policy of "watchful waiting" was renewed.

THE UNITED STATES AND THE EUROPEAN WAR

The Outbreak of the War. In the opening days of August, 1914, the age-long jealousies of European nations broke out in a general conflict such as had shaken the world in the time of Napoleon. On June 28, the heir to the Austro-Hungarian throne was assassinated at Serajevo, the capital of Bosnia, an Austrian province occupied mainly by Serbs and Croats. Believing that Serbia had been lending aid to conspirators, Austria-Hungary laid the blame for the incident on the government of that country and made humiliating demands on it. Germany at once insisted that the issue should be regarded as "an affair which should be settled solely between Austria-Hungary and Serbia." Russia refused to take this view. Great Britain proposed a settlement by mediation. Germany at first backed up Austria to the limit. To use the language of the German authorities: "We were perfectly aware that a possible warlike attitude of Austria-Hungary against Serbia might bring Russia upon the field and that it might therefore involve us in a war, in accordance with our duties as allies. We could not, however, in these vital interests of Austria-Hungary which were at stake, advise our ally to take a yielding attitude not compatible with his dignity nor deny him our assistance." Later, however, Germany did urge moderation but Austria-Hungary, refusing to accept Serbia's counter-offer, declared war on her in July, 1914. Almost immediately Russia mobilized for general war.

Every day of the fateful August, 1914, was crowded with momentous events. On the first, after the Czar refused to stop mobilizing his troops, Germany declared war on Russia. On the second, the Germans invaded the little duchy of Luxembourg and notified the King of Belgium that they were preparing to violate the neutrality of his realm by marching through it on their way to Paris. On the same day, Great Britain, anxiously besought by the French government, promised the aid of the British navy if the German warships opened hostilities in the Channel. The following day, Great Britain asked Germany to respect Belgian neutrality and, failing to receive a guarantee, broke off official relations. On the fifth, the British Prime Minister announced that war had begun between England and Germany. The storm now raged in pitiless fury. All the countries involved had long been armed to the teeth, getting ready for it. Now their "day" had come.

The State of American Opinion. Emulating the example of Washington in 1793, Wilson proclaimed the neutrality of the United States. But as in that far-off time, the public was divided and neutrality was even more difficult to maintain for many reasons. Germany and England were now on opposite sides and the German population in this country had increased enormously. Of course it was natural for the Americans of English descent or sympathies to look upon the German imperial government, with its autocratic power in military hands, as a menace and to view the Kaiser, William II, and the Crown Prince as the symbols of arrogance. Especially when the Germans invaded Belgium and occupied almost the entire country did resentment flame high. On the other hand, many Americans of German descent found it almost impossible to cast off inherited preferences for the Central Powers; and others of Irish ancestry, mindful of the tedious and bitter struggle for home rule, wished for the defeat of Great Britain as a redress of grievances in Ireland.

Once more Europeans sought to overcome American neutrality and the warring nations commenced to "drench" the United States with propaganda. Germany sent over Dr. Bernhard Dernburg, the former colonial secretary, as a special agent; and for months the newspapers, magazines, and periodicals were filled with interviews, articles, and notes on the justice of the Teutonic cause. A magazine, *The Fatherland*, was founded to secure "fair play for Germany and Austria." The German language press and many German societies came to the support of the Central Powers. On the other hand English and Canadians in the United States and special British agents were at least equally active with schemes for turning American opinion in favor of the Entente Allies — Great Britain, France, and Russia.

Before two weeks had elapsed, American feelings about the war had become so intense that President Wilson (August 18, 1914) was moved to caution his countrymen. "Every man," he said, "who really loves America will act and speak in the true spirit of neutrality which is the spirit of impartiality and fairness and friendliness to all concerned. . . . We must be impartial in thought as well as in action, must put a curb upon our sentiments as well as upon every transaction that might be construed as a preference of one party to the struggle before another."

The Clash over Trade. But commercial relations as in the time of the Napoleonic wars (page 230) complicated issues for the United States. Vital questions respecting rights of Americans trading with countries at peace as well as those at war were raised. On this point there existed on August 1, 1914, a fairly definite set of rules by which nations were bound. Among them the following were of special importance. In the first place, neutral ships carrying goods not useful for war purposes were free to sail where they would. In the second place, military supplies, or "contraband of war," found on a neutral ship was lawful prize; any ship suspected of carrying it was liable to search and if caught with such forbidden goods was subject to seizure. In the third place, international law declared that a peaceful merchant ship, whether belonging to an enemy or to a neutral country, should not be destroyed or sunk without providing for the safety of crew and passengers. In the fourth place, it was understood that a belligerent had the right, if it could, to blockade the ports of an enemy and prevent the ingress and egress of all ships; but such a blockade, to be lawful, had to be effective.

British Interference with American Commerce. These general principles left two important questions unanswered: "What is an effective blockade?" and "What is contraband of war?" But Great Britain, as mistress of the seas, soon furnished the replies. Although the German submarines made it impossible for her battleships to maintain a regular patrol of the waters in front of blockaded ports, she declared the blockade to be none the less "effective" because her navy was supreme. As to contraband of war, Great Britain put a broad interpretation upon the term which included nearly every important article of commerce. Early in 1915 she declared even cargoes of grain and flour to be contraband, defending the action on the ground that the German government had recently taken possession of all domestic stocks of corn, wheat, and flour. Thus American trade with Europe was seriously limited.

Furthermore, a novel problem arose in connection with American commerce with the neutral countries surrounding Germany. Great Britain early began to intercept ships carrying oil, gasoline, and copper — all war materials of prime importance — on the theory that they were either destined ultimately to Germany or, if sent to Holland or Norway, for example, would release goods for sale to Germans. On November 2, 1914, the English government alleged that the Germans were sowing mines in open waters and therefore declared the whole of the North Sea a military zone. Ships bound for Denmark, Norway, and Sweden were ordered to come by the English Channel for inspection and sailing directions. In effect, Americans were now licensed by Great Britain to trade in certain commodities and in certain amounts with neutral countries.

Against these extraordinary measures, the State Department at Washington lodged pointed objections, saying: "This government is reluctantly forced to the conclusion that the present policy of His Majesty's government toward neutral ships and cargoes exceeds the manifest necessity of a belligerent and constitutes restrictions upon the rights of American citizens on the high seas, which are not justified by the rules of international law or required under the principle of self-preservation."

Germany Begins the Submarine Campaign. In retaliation against British rules Germany now announced that, on and after February 18, 1915, the whole of the English Channel and the waters around Great Britain would be deemed a war zone and every enemy ship found therein would be destroyed. The German decree added that, since the British admiralty had ordered the use of neutral flags by English ships in time of distress, neutral vessels would be in danger of destruction if found in the forbidden area. It was clear that Germany intended to employ submarines to destroy shipping. A new factor was thus introduced into naval warfare, one not provided for in the accepted laws of war. A regular warship when overhauling and sinking a merchant vessel could easily take its crew and passengers on board for safe keeping as prescribed by international law; but a submarine ordinarily could do nothing of the sort. Of necessity the lives and the ships of neutrals, as well as of belligerents, were put in mortal peril. This conduct Germany defended on the ground that it was made imperative by British violations of international law ruinous to German trade in the necessities of life.

The response of the United States to the ominous German order was swift and direct. On February 10, 1915, Wilson warned Germany that if her commanders destroyed American lives and ships as threatened by that decree, the action would "be very hard indeed to reconcile with the friendly relations happily subsisting between the two governments." The American note added that the German imperial government would be held to "strict accountability" and all necessary steps would be taken to safeguard American lives and American rights. This was firm and clear language, but the only response received from Germany was a suggestion that, if Great Britain would allow food supplies to pass through the blockade, the submarine campaign would end.

Violations of American Rights. Meanwhile Germany continued to ravage shipping on the high seas. On January 28, a German raider sank the American ship, *William P. Frye*, in the South Atlantic; on March 28, a British ship, the *Falaba*, was sunk by a submarine and many on board, including an American citizen, were killed; and on April 28, a German airplane dropped bombs on the American steamer *Cushing*. On the morning of May 1, 1915, Americans were astounded to see in the newspapers an advertisement, signed by the German Imperial Embassy, warning travelers of the dangers in the war zone and notifying them that anyone who ventured on British ships into that area did so at his own risk. That day, the *Lusitania*, a British steamer, sailed from New York for Liverpool. On May 7, without warning, the ship was struck by two torpedoes and in a few minutes went down by the bow, carrying to death 1153 persons including 114 American men, women, and children. A cry of horror ran through the country. German papers in the United States and a few American people argued that the passengers on the ill-fated steamer had been duly apprised of the danger and had deliberately taken their lives into their own hands; but the terrible deed shocked the general public.

The *Lusitania* Notes. On May 14, the Department of State at Washington made public a note to Germany on the *Lusitania* case. It said bluntly to the German government: "No warning that an unlawful and inhumane act will be committed can possibly be accepted as an excuse or palliation for that act or as an abatement of the responsibility for its commission." It called upon that government to disavow the act, make reparation as far as possible, and take steps to prevent "the recurrence of anything so obviously subversive of the principles of warfare." The note closed with a caution to Germany that the government of the United States would not "omit any word or any act necessary to the performance of its sacred duty of maintaining the rights of the United States and its citizens and of safeguarding their free exercise and enjoyment." The die was cast; but Germany in reply merely temporized.

In a second note, made public on June 11, the position of the United States was again affirmed. William Jennings Bryan, the Secretary of State, had resigned because the drift of President Wilson's policy was not toward mediation but the strict mainte nance of American rights, if need be by force of arms. The German reply was still evasive and German naval commanders continued to sink merchant ships. In a third and final note of July 21, 1915, Wilson made it clear to Germany that he meant what he said when he wrote that he would maintain the rights of American citizens. Finally after much discussion and shifting about, the German ambassador on September 1, 1915, sent a brief note to the Secretary of State: "Liners will not be sunk by our submarines without warning and without safety of the lives of non-combatants, provided the liners do not try to escape or offer resistance." Editorially, the New York *Times* declared: "It is a triumph no-only of diplomacy but of reason, of humanity, of justice, and of truth."

The Presidential Election of 1916. In the midst of the crisis raised by the European war came the presidential campaign. On the Republican side everything seemed to depend upon the action of the Progressives. If the breach created in 1912 could be closed, victory was possible; if not, defeat was certain. A promise of unity lay in the fact that the conventions of the Republicans and Progressives were held at the same time in Chicago. Admirers of Roosevelt hoped that both parties would select him as their candidate; but this hope was not realized. The Republicans chose, and the Progressives accepted, Charles Evans Hughes, an associate justice of the federal Supreme Court who, as governor of New York, had won a national reputation by attacking "machine politicians."

Confronted by demands that they take sides in the European quarrel the Republicans steered a middle course, declaring that they would uphold all American rights "at home and abroad, by land and by sea." This sentiment Hughes echoed in his acceptance speech. By some it was thought to mean a firmer policy in opposing British interference with American commerce; by others, a more vigorous handling of the German submarine menace. The Democrats, on their side, renominated Wilson by acclamation, reviewed with pride the new laws passed by Congress under their direction, and commended "the splendid diplomatic victories of our great President who has preserved the vital interests of our government and its citizens and kept us out of war."

In the election which ensued Wilson's popular vote exceeded that cast for Hughes by more than half a million, while his electoral vote stood 277 to 254. The result was regarded, and not without warrant, as a great personal triumph for Wilson. He had received the largest vote yet cast for a presidential candidate. The Progressive Party practically disappeared and the Socialists suffered a severe setback, falling far behind the vote of 1912.

President Wilson Urges Peace. Believing that his pacific policies had been approved by his countrymen, President Wilson, soon after the election, addressed "peace notes" to the European belligerents. On December 18, he asked them to avow "the terms upon which war might be concluded." To these notes the Central powers replied that they were ready to meet their antagonists in a peace conference; but Allied powers, in answering, made certain demands in advance, which put a stop to the negotiations. Not discouraged by this, Wilson, in an address before the Senate on January 22, 1917, declared it to be a duty of the United States to take part in bringing about a stable peace on the basis of certain principles: "peace without victory"; the right of nationalities to freedom and self-government; independence of Poland; freedom of the seas; reduction of armaments; and abolition of entangling alliances. The whole world was discussing the President's message when the newspapers announced, on January 31, that the German ambassador at Washington had given notice of the intention of his government to renew the submarine warfare.

The United States at War

Steps toward War. Three days later, Wilson broke off relations with the German empire and sent the German ambassador home.

Still he explained to Congress that he desired no conflict with Germany and would await an "overt act" before taking further steps to preserve American rights. "God grant," he concluded, "that we may not be challenged to defend them by acts of willful injustice on the part of the government of Germany." Yet the challenge came. Between February 26 and April 2, six American merchant vessels were torpedoed, in most cases without warning and without regard to the loss of lives. The President therefore called upon Congress to meet this crisis, and it answered on April 6 by passing, with only a few dissenting votes, a resolution which declared that war existed with Germany. Austria-Hungary at once severed official relations with the United States; but it was not until December 7 that Congress, acting on the President's advice, also declared war on that country.

American War Aims. In many addresses delivered during the war, Wilson stated the purposes for which our government had taken up arms. First he emphasized the fact that it was a war of self-defense. "The military masters of Germany," he exclaimed, "denied us the right to be neutral." Proof of that, he said, lay on every hand. Agents of the German imperial government had destroyed American lives and American property on the high seas. They had planted bombs in ships and munition works. They had fomented discord among American citizens.

But Wilson insisted that the resort to arms meant no desire for material rewards. "The world must be made safe for democracy. Its peace must be planted upon the tested foundations of political liberty. We have no selfish ends to serve. We desire no conquest, no dominion. We seek no indemnities for ourselves."

In a very remarkable message read to Congress on January 8, 1918, Wilson laid down his famous "fourteen points" stating in brief form the ideals for which we were fighting. They included open treaties of peace, openly arrived at; absolute freedom of navigation upon the seas; the removal, as far as possible, of trade barriers among nations; reduction of armaments; adjustment of colonial claims in the interest of the populations concerned; fair and friendly treatment of Russia; the restoration of Belgium; righting the wrong done to France in 1871 in the matter of Alsace-

Lorraine; adjustment of Italian frontiers along the lines of nationality; more liberty for the peoples of Austria-Hungary; restoration of Serbia and Rumania; the readjustment of the Turkish Empire; an independent Poland; and an association of nations to afford mutual guarantees to all states great and small. On a later occasion Wilson dwelt more fully on the fourteenth point, namely, the formation of a league of nations to guarantee peace and establish justice among the powers. Democracy, the right of nations to decide their own fate, a pledge of enduring peace — these were the ideals for which the American people were to pour out their blood and treasure.

The Selective Draft. Whatever its purposes, the World War was a war of nations. The powers against which the United States was arrayed had every able-bodied man in service and all their resources, human and material, thrown into the scale. For this reason, Wilson called upon his whole country to make every necessary sacrifice. Congress decreed that the national army should be chosen from all male citizens and males not enemy aliens who had declared their intention of becoming citizens. By an act of May 18, 1917, it fixed the age limits at twenty-one to thirty-one inclusive. Later, in August, 1918, it extended them to eighteen and forty-five. From the men of the first group so enrolled were chosen by lot the soldiers for the World War who, with the regular army and the national guard, formed the American Expeditionary Force upholding the American cause on the battlefields of Europe. "The whole nation," said the President, "must be a team in which each man shall play the part for which he is best fitted."

Liberty Loans and Taxes. In order that the military and naval forces should be stinted in no respect, the nation was asked to place its financial resources at the service of the government. Some urged the "conscription of wealth as well as men," meaning the support of the war out of taxes upon the fortunes of the rich; but more conservative counsels prevailed. The major portion of the cost was met by the sale of bonds. Four great Liberty Loans were floated, all the agencies of modern publicity being used to enlist popular interest. The first loan had four and a half million subscribers; the fourth more than twenty million. But combined with loans were heavy taxes. A progressive tax was laid upon the incomes of private persons, beginning with four per cent on incomes in the lower ranges and rising to sixty-three per cent of that part of any income above $2,000,000. A progressive tax was levied upon inheritances. An excess profits tax was imposed on all corporations and partnerships, rising in amount

THE LAUNCHING OF A SHIP AT THE GREAT NAVAL YARDS, NEWARK, N. J.

to sixty per cent of the net income in excess of thirty-three per cent on the invested capital. "This," said a distinguished economist, "is the high-water mark in the history of taxation. Never before in the annals of civilization has an attempt been made to take as much as two-thirds of a man's income by taxation."

Mobilizing Material Resources. No stone was left unturned to provide the arms, munitions, supplies, and transportation required for the gigantic undertaking. Between the declaration of war and the armistice, Congress enacted law after law relative to food supplies, raw materials, railways, mines, ships, forests, and industrial enterprises. No power over the lives and property of citizens deemed essential to winning the war was withheld from the government. The farmer's wheat, the housewife's sugar, coal at the mines, labor in the factories, ships at the wharves, trade with friendly countries, railways, banks, stores, private fortunes — all were mobilized and placed at the service of the government.

For example, a law of August 10, 1917, gave the President power to fix the prices of wheat and coal and to take almost any steps necessary to prevent monopoly and excessive prices. By a series of measures, enlarging the principles of the Shipping Act of 1916, ships and shipyards were brought under public control and the government was empowered to embark upon a great shipbuilding program. In December, 1917, the government took over the operation of railways under a presidential order which was elaborated in March, 1918, by act of Congress. In the summer of 1918 the express, telephone, and telegraph business of the entire country passed under government control. By war-risk insurance acts, allowances were made for the families of enlisted men, compensation for injuries was provided, death benefits were assured, and a system of national insurance was established in the interest of the soldiers and sailors. Never before in the history of the country had the government taken such a generous view of its obligations to those who served on the field of battle or on the seas.

The Espionage and Sedition Acts. By the espionage law of June 15, 1917, and the amending law, known as the Sedition Act, passed in May of the following year, the government was given a drastic control over public opinion. The first measure penalized those who gave information to a foreign country to be used to the injury of the United States; those who made false statements designed to interfere with the military or naval forces of the United States; those who tried to stir up disobedience or disloyalty in the army and navy; and those who willfully sought to obstruct the enlistment of soldiers. The Sedition Act was still more severe and sweeping in its terms. It imposed heavy penalties of fine and imprisonment upon any person who used "abusive language about the government or institutions of the country." It authorized the dismissal of any officer of the government who committed "disloyal acts" or uttered "disloyal language" and permitted the Postmaster General to close the mails to persons violating the law. This measure, prepared by the Department of Justice, was strenuously opposed in the Senate where twenty-four Republicans and two Democrats voted against it. Senator Johnson of California condemned it as a law "to suppress the freedom of the press in the United States and to prevent any man, no matter who he is, from expressing legitimate criticism concerning the present government." But he could not prevent the passage of the bill. The Sedition Act was upheld by the Supreme Court and stringently enforced.

Labor and the War. In view of the unrest among the working classes of Europe and especially the proletarian revolution in Russia in November, 1917, there was some anxiety in America as to the stand which organized labor might take in regard to the war. Yet it was soon dispelled. Samuel Gompers, speaking for the American Federation of Labor, declared that "this is labor's war" and pledged the united support of all the unions. There was, it is true, some dissent. The Socialist party denounced the war as "a capitalist quarrel"; but all the protests combined were too slight to have much effect. American labor leaders were sent to Europe to encourage the wavering ranks of trade unionists in war-worn England, France, and Italy. Labor was allowed to have delegates on the important government boards and on commissions dealing with industrial questions. Trade-union standards respecting hours and wages were adopted by the government and generally applied to industry. In a public address to the American Federation of Labor, Wilson assured trade unionists that labor conditions would not be made unduly onerous by the war and received in return a pledge of complete loyalty from the organization. At the close of the conflict the services of labor were rewarded by a special section in the treaty of peace, which provided for a permanent international labor office to promote world-wide improvement in the lot of toiling mankind. "The league of nations has for its object the establishment of universal peace," runs the preamble to this section, "and such a peace can be established only if it is based upon social justice. . . . The failure of

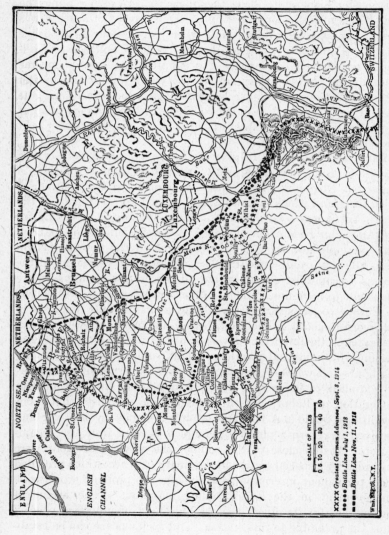

WESTERN BATTLE LINES OF THE VARIOUS YEARS OF THE WORLD WAR

SCALE OF MILES
0 5 10 20 30 40 50

XXXX Greatest German Advance, Sept. 8, 1914
•••• Battle Line July 1, 1918
━━━ Battle Line Nov. 11, 1918

Wm. Emry do., N.Y.

any nation to adopt humane conditions of labor is an obstacle in the way of other nations which desire to improve the conditions in their own countries."

The American Navy in the War. As soon as Congress declared war the fleet was mobilized, American ports were thrown open to the warships of the Allies, provision was made for increasing the number of men and ships, and a contingent of war vessels was sent to coöperate with the British and French in their life-and-death contest with submarines. Special effort was made to stimulate the production of "submarine chasers" and "scout cruisers" to be dispatched to the danger zone. Convoys were provided for the transports conveying soldiers to France. Before the end of the war more than 300 American vessels and 75,000 officers and men were operating in European waters. Though the German fleet did not come out and challenge the sea power of the Allies, the battleships of the United States were always ready to do their full part in such an event. As it happened, the work of the American navy was limited mainly to helping in the patrol that wore down the submarine menace to shipping.

The War in France. Owing to the peculiar nature of the warfare in France, it required a longer time for American military forces to get into action. But soon after the declaration of war, steps were taken to give military assistance to the Allies as quickly as possible. The regular army was enlarged and the national guard was brought into national service. On June 13, General John J. Pershing, chosen head of the American Expeditionary Forces, reached Paris and made preparations for the arrival of the troops. In June, the vanguard of the army was in France. A slow but steady stream followed and as soon as the men enrolled under the draft were ready, it became a flood. During the period of the war the army was expanded from about 190,000 men to 3,665,000, of whom more than 2,000,000 were in France when the armistice was signed.

Although American troops did not operate on a large scale until the last phase of the war in 1918, several battalions of infantry were in the trenches by October, 1917, and had their first severe encounter with the Germans early in November. In January,

1918, they took over a part of the front line as an American sector. In March, General Pershing placed our forces at the disposal of General Foch, commander-in-chief of the Allied armies. The first division, which entered the Montdidier salient in April, soon was engaged with the enemy, "taking with splendid dash the town of Cantigny and all other objectives, which were organized and held steadfastly against vicious counter attacks and galling artillery fire."

When the Germans launched their grand drives toward the Marne and Paris, in June and July, 1918, every available man

TROOPS RETURNING FROM FRANCE

was placed at General Foch's command. At Belleau Wood, at Château-Thierry, and other points along the deep salient made by the Germans into the French lines, American soldiers distinguished themselves by heroic action. They also played an important rôle in the counter-attack that "smashed" the salient and drove the Germans back.

In September, American troops, with French aid, "wiped out" the German angle at St. Mihiel. By this time General Pershing was ready to drive northeast into the Argonne forest, while he also coöperated with the British in the assault on the Hindenburg line. In the Meuse-Argonne battle, our soldiers ran into some of the most severe fighting of the war and pressed forward steadily against the most stubborn resistance from the enemy. On the 6th of November, reported General Pershing, "a division of the first corps reached a point on the Meuse opposite Sedan, twenty-five miles from our line of departure. The strategical goal which was our highest hope was gained. We had cut the enemy's main line of communications and nothing but a surrender or an armistice could save his army from complete disaster." In five days the end came. On the morning of November 11, the order to cease firing went into effect. The German army was in rapid retreat, demoralization had begun, and the Kaiser had abdicated and fled into Holland. The World War, involving nearly every civilized nation on the globe, was brought to a close. More than 75,000 American soldiers and sailors had given their lives. More than 250,000 had been wounded or were missing or were in German prison camps.

The Settlement at Paris

The Peace Conference. On January 18, 1919, a conference of the Allied and Associated powers assembled to draw up the terms of peace with Germany, Austria-Hungary, Bulgaria, and Turkey. It was a moving spectacle, with seventy-two delegates from thirty-two nations. The United States, Great Britain, France, Italy, and Japan had five delegates each; the others, from one to three each. President Wilson spoke in person for the United States. England, France, and Italy were represented by their premiers: David Lloyd George, Georges Clemenceau, and Vittorio Orlando.

The Supreme Council. The real work of the settlement was first given to a Supreme Council of ten, representing the United States, Great Britain, France, Italy, and Japan. This was later reduced to five members. Then Japan dropped out and finally Italy, leaving only Wilson and the Premiers, Lloyd George and Clemenceau — the "Big Three" — to make most of the great

decisions.   Their task was finished on May 6, and in a secret
session of the full conference the whole treaty of peace was approved, though a few of the powers made reservations or objections.   The next day the treaty was presented to the Germans
who, after many protests, signed on the last day of grace, June 28.

PREMIERS LLOYD GEORGE, ORLANDO, AND CLEMENCEAU AND PRESIDENT
WILSON AT PARIS

This German treaty was followed by treaties with Austria and
Hungary — and finally, their allies, Bulgaria and Turkey, with
which the United States had not been at war.

Terms of the Settlement.   Together the treaties make a huge
volume.   The German treaty alone embraces about 80,000 words.
Collectively they cover an immense range of subjects which may
be summarized under five heads: (1) the territorial settlement
in Europe; (2) the destruction of German military power; (3) reparations for damages done by Germany and her allies; (4) the

EUROPE ACCORDING TO THE

(1) Saar Basin under League of Nations until 1935, then plebiscite; coal mines to France. (2) Eupen iscites here favored Germany. (5) Upper Silesia, rich mining district divided between Germany and annexed to Italy in 1924. (8) Zara, ceded to Italy. (9) Memel, district given by Allies to Lithuania, under international commission; boundaries changed in 1923. (12) Occupied by Greece under treaty was recognized as republic by treaty, 1920, but western part was conquered by Turkey and eastern

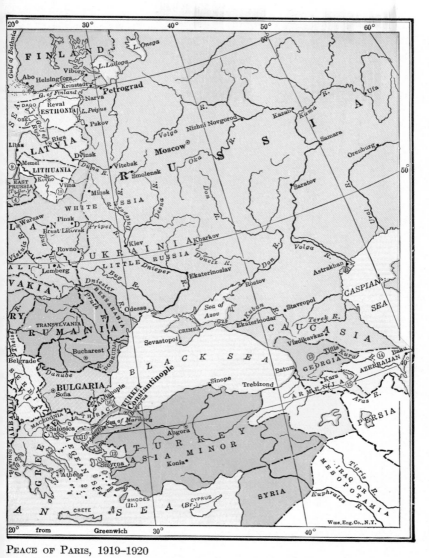

PEACE OF PARIS, 1919–1920

and Malmédy to Belgium. (3) Northern Schleswig annexed by Denmark after plebiscite. (4) Pleb-
Poland. (6) Klagenfurt, voted to remain in Austria. (7) Free State of Fiume, established 1920, but
1923. (10) Vilna was part of Lithuania but was annexed by Poland, 1922. (11) Zone of the Straits
of 1920, regained by Turkey in 1922. (13) and (14) Republics federated with Russia. (15) Armenia
part federated with Russia, 1921. (16) Ceded to Greece, 1920; regained by Turkey, 1923.

disposition of German colonies and protectorates; and (5) the League of Nations.

Germany was reduced by the cession of Alsace-Lorraine to France and the loss of several other provinces. Austria-Hungary was dissolved and dismembered. Russia, which was not permitted to share in the Peace conference, was cut down in size by the creation of new states on the west. Bulgaria was stripped of her gains in the recent Balkan wars. Turkey was broken up. Six new independent states were created: Poland, Finland, Lithuania, Latvia, Esthonia, and Czechoslovakia. Italy, Greece, Rumania, and Serbia were enlarged by cessions of territory and the Kingdom of the Serbs, Croats, and Slovenes was organized by the union of various regions inhabited largely by South Slavs.

The destruction of German military power was thorough. The entire navy, with minor exceptions, was turned over to the Entente allies; Germany's total equipment for the future was limited to six battleships and six light cruisers with certain small vessels but no submarines. The number of enlisted men and officers for the army was fixed at not more than 100,000; the General Staff was dissolved; and the manufacture of munitions was restricted.

Besides yielding to this restraint on her war powers, Germany was compelled to accept responsibility for heavy damages caused by the World War, to pay five billion dollars in cash and goods, and to make certain other payments as ordered from time to time by an interallied reparations commission. Until these debts were paid, parts of Germany were to be occupied by troops of the victorious nations.

The disposition of the German colonies presented knotty problems but it was finally agreed that they should be placed under the tutelage of certain of the Allied governments acting as "mandatories," holding them in a "sacred trust of civilization." An exception to the mandatory principle arose in the case of German rights in Shantung, all of which were transferred temporarily to Japan. It was owing to this action that the Chinese delegates at Paris refused to sign the treaty.

The League of Nations. High among the specific reasons for entering the war, President Wilson placed the desire to establish permanent peace. All through the United States people spoke of the "war to end war." No slogan met a deeper response from the public. The President himself repeatedly declared that a society of nations must be formed to guard the peace and protect all countries against the ambitions of the few. "As I see it," he said, "the constitution of the League of Nations and the clear definition of its objects must be a part, in a sense the most essential part, of the peace settlement itself."

It was mainly for the purpose of carrying out this pledge that Wilson went to Paris in person. At all events it was largely owing to his efforts that the peace conference wrote into the treaty with Germany a section providing for the League of Nations. And with good reason that action is said to mark a new epoch in the history of humanity. With the idea of banishing war hatreds, Wilson insisted that all nations should finally be included in the League — the former enemy countries by a two-thirds vote of the League Assembly.

The agencies of the League of Nations were to be three in number: (1) a permanent secretariat, located at Geneva; (2) an Assembly consisting of one delegate from each country, dominion, or self-governing colony (including Canada, Australia, South Africa, New Zealand, and India); (3) and a Council consisting of representatives of the United States, Great Britain, France, Italy, and Japan, and four other delegates selected by the Assembly from time to time.

Numerous duties were imposed on the League, and its members had to make important pledges in the interest of peace. The League Council was instructed to draw up a plan for reducing armaments and a plan for a permanent Court of International Justice. The nations belonging to the League bound themselves in Article X to respect the territory and political independence of each associated nation. They furthermore agreed that, when they could not settle any dispute by diplomatic negotiation, they would submit it to the Council for review and on no account would go to war over it until three months after the Council made its report on the quarrel. In case the decision was unanimous the members affected by it were to abide by its terms. If, however, any member refused to stand by its pledges, then its conduct was to be regarded as an act of war against the League and to be dealt with accordingly — by cutting off its trade and taking other measures of compulsion.

Such, in general, was the settlement at Paris and such was the association of nations formed to promote the peace of the world. They were quickly approved by most of the powers, and the first Assembly of the League of Nations — "a Parliament of Mankind" — met at Geneva late in 1920.

The Treaty in the United States. When however the treaty was presented to the United States Senate for approval, it was greeted by a decided opposition. In that body the Republicans had a slight majority and a two-thirds vote was necessary for ratification. Sentiment for and against the treaty ran mainly along party lines; but the Republicans were themselves divided. A large group, known as "reservationists," favored ratification with certain conditions respecting American rights; while a small though active minority, calling themselves "irreconcilables," absolutely refused to give their support to the League of Nations on any conditions.

The grounds of this Republican opposition lay partly in the terms of peace imposed on Germany and partly in the Covenant of the League of Nations, but the burden of criticism was directed against the League itself. Article X guaranteeing the independence and territorial integrity of the members of the League was subjected to a specially heavy fire; while the treatment accorded to China and the sections laying on the United States the duty to take part in European disputes were attacked as "unwise and dangerous." As an outcome of their deliberations, the Republicans drafted a long list of reservations which touched upon many of the vital parts of the treaty. These Wilson refused to accept on the theory that in effect they "nullified" the whole program for permanent peace. No compromise could be reached. In the end the Senate rejected the treaty of Versailles and the United States therefore failed to enter the League of Nations. In vain did the President make a tour of the West, appealing to the people to force a ratification of his program.

General Reference

L. B. Shippee, *Recent American History.*
W. E. Dodd, *Woodrow Wilson and His Work.*
Woodrow Wilson, *The New Freedom.*
C. L. Jones, *The Caribbean Interests of the United States.*
H. P. Willis, *The Federal Reserve.*
J. F. Rippy, *The United States and Mexico.*
E. E. Robinson and V. J. West, *The Foreign Policy of Woodrow Wilson.*
S. B. Fay, *Origins of the World War.* Best work on the subject.
Carlton J. H. Hayes, *A Brief History of the Great War.*
J. B. McMaster, *The United States in the World War.*

Research Topics

President Wilson's First Term. Elson, *History of the United States,* pp. 907–925.
The Underwood Tariff Act. Ogg, *National Progress* (The American Nation Series), pp. 209–226.
The Federal Reserve System. Ogg, pp. 228–232.
Trust and Labor Legislation. Ogg, pp. 232–236.
Legislation Respecting the Territories. Ogg, pp. 236–245.
American Interests in the Caribbean. Ogg, pp. 246–265.
American Interests in the Pacific. Ogg, pp. 304–324.
Mexican Affairs. Haworth, *The United States in Our Own Times,* pp. 388–395; Ogg, pp. 284–304.
The First Phases of the European War. Haworth, pp. 395–412; Ogg, pp. 325–343.
The Campaign of 1916. Haworth, pp. 412–418; Ogg, pp. 364–383.
America Enters the War. Haworth, pp. 422–440; pp. 454–475; Ogg, pp. 384–399; Elson, pp. 926–945.
Mobilizing the Nation. Haworth, pp. 441–453.
The Peace Settlement. Haworth, pp. 475–497; Elson, pp. 945–951.

Questions

1. Enumerate the chief financial measures of the Wilson administration. Review the history of banks and currency and give the details of the Federal Reserve Act.
2. What was the Wilson policy toward trusts? Toward labor?
3. Review again the theory of states' rights. How has it fared in recent years?
4. What steps were taken in colonial policies? In the Caribbean?
5. Outline American-Mexican relations under Wilson.

6. How did the World War break out in Europe?

7. Account for the divided state of opinion in America.

8. Compare the events leading up to the War of 1812 with the events from 1914 to 1917.

9. State the leading principles of international law involved and show how they were violated.

10. What American rights were assailed in the submarine campaign?

11. Give Wilson's position on the *Lusitania* affair.

12. How did the World War affect the presidential campaign of 1916?

13. How did Germany finally involve the United States in the war?

14. State the American war aims given by the President.

15. Enumerate the measures taken by the government to win the war.

16. What part did the navy play in the war? The army?

17. How were the terms of peace formulated?

18. Give the principal results of the war.

19. Describe the League of Nations.

Historical Fiction

H. G. Wells, *Mr. Britling Sees It Through.*
Stallings and Anderson, *What Price Glory.*

CHAPTER XXVIII

BUSINESS ENTERPRISE AND DEPRESSION

The times seemed ripe in 1920 for a return to "peace and prosperity." By creating a huge demand for military supplies, including iron and steel, the World War hastened the changes which had long been transforming the United States into a manufacturing nation. When the war came to a close, the country had more industries, more people living in cities where the industries were located, and more millionaires with money to invest in new manufacturing plants. Once American bankers had borrowed money abroad for American railways and industries. Now they were lending money to foreign governments and business men. Once English and Germans had bought American bonds by the billion. Now American citizens were investing in foreign loans which promised a high rate of interest, often seven or eight per cent. Commerce with Europe, Asia, and South America had increased. In short the United States came out of the war, to all appearances, the industrial and financial victor.

Business men were therefore confident that their prospects would be bright if they could just get rid of "government interference" with their affairs and recover the liberties they had enjoyed when McKinley was President. This was called by Senator Warren Gamaliel Harding returning to "normalcy." Income taxes were high but these they hoped to reduce and perhaps abolish entirely. Their hearts were set on going back to "the good old days when everybody had a chance to make money." Having made big profits out of war, they hoped to make more profits out of peace. This prosperity labor expected to share in the form of the high wages received in war time. Farmers had sold their produce at high prices during the war, and they too looked forward to sharing the good things.

REPUBLICANS VICTORIOUS IN THREE CAMPAIGNS

Republicans Return to Power. If business enterprise was to have "a free hand," it needed a change in the federal government. Woodrow Wilson had attacked "big business" in 1912 and declared that "our government has been for the past few years under the control of heads of great allied corporations with special interests." He had pushed through Congress bills to aid farmers and trade unions. During the war the Government had taken over railways, express companies, telegraph lines, and other concerns. At the close of the war, Wilson's Secretary of the Treasury had urged that the government continue to operate the railways. It was said that business leaders were treated coldly by Wilson and that farmers and trade unionists were specially favored by him. Moreover, the Democrats had lowered the protective tariff. This state of things Republican leaders proposed to change and, with the aid of business leaders, they carried three presidential elections, one after the other. For twelve years, from 1921 to 1933, Republican presidents occupied the White House.

The Campaign of 1920. When they began their battle to recover power, Republican leaders found several allies besides business men eager to throw off government interference with their affairs. Many German-Americans were angry because the United States had helped to defeat the German Empire. Many Irish-Americans were equally angry because we had aided Great Britain in the war. Other citizens were dissatisfied with the treaty of peace, which they thought was "too hard" on Germany. As things stood, a popular view was summed up by Senator Boise Penrose of Pennsylvania, when he said: "Any good Republican can beat any Democrat." And when the ballots were counted in November, 1920, the Republican candidate, Senator Harding of Ohio, came out victorious. He was at least a "good Republican." He had said that he loved "the good old times when the Republican protective tariff filled the Treasury and at the same time gave protection to American industry." He was described by newspaper men as a "Hail fellow, well met," and "a good average citizen." Besides a popular plurality of seven millions over the Democrats, Harding received 404 out of 531 electoral votes. The

Democratic candidate, James M. Cox, also of Ohio, did not carry a single northern state; even Tennessee went Republican.

The Victory of Coolidge in 1924. For a time everything seemed to favor the Republicans; but President Harding died in the summer of 1923 and shortly afterward several "scandals" broke out in Washington. A Senate investigating committee charged Albert B. Fall, former Secretary of the Interior under Harding, with accepting bribes from certain oil companies in return for leasing to them some government oil lands reserved for the Navy. Charges were also made against other members of the Harding cabinet. These allegations, President Calvin Coolidge, who as Vice President had succeeded Harding, greeted calmly. He said that the guilty would be punished. One thing followed another. Although not accused of wrongdoing, the Secretary of the Navy, Edwin Denby, resigned, for he had approved the oil leases. In the face of popular criticism, President Coolidge asked Harry M. Daugherty, the Attorney-General, to hand in his resignation. Later the Supreme Court of the United States decided that there had been fraud in the oil leases and ordered the lands returned to the government. Then another court found Albert B. Fall guilty of bribery, while the alleged briber was allowed to go scot-free.

Convinced that President Coolidge had cleared up the scandals, the Republicans nominated him for the presidency in 1924, with Charles G. Dawes for Vice President. Naturally the Democrats made much of the scandals. They chose John W. Davis of West Virginia as their candidate for President and, for the office of Vice President, they presented Charles W. Bryan of Nebraska, brother of the great Democratic leader, William Jennings Bryan. Discontented with both parties, a group of farmers, trade unionists, former Progressives, and Socialists formed a third party. It selected as its candidates Senator Robert M. LaFollette, Sr., of Wisconsin and Senator Burton K. Wheeler of Montana. It condemned the policies of President Coolidge. It favored government ownership of railways, popular election of federal judges, the abolition of the injunction in labor disputes (page 604), and giving citizens a chance to vote for or against any resolution of Congress declaring war in the future. But in spite of this political revolt, the Republicans were once more victorious in a "landslide." Their vote exceeded the combined votes of the Democrats and the new Progressives. With this general indorsement, President Coolidge became President in his own right by a direct election.

The Third Republican Triumph. As his term drew to a close, President Coolidge was urged to run again, but he replied laconically, "I do not choose to run." Meanwhile his Secretary of Commerce, Herbert C. Hoover, was making his way into public favor as presidential "timber." He had won fame during the World War as head of American relief work in Belgium and for other war services. Since 1921 he had been building up the Department of Commerce by doing all he could to find more foreign markets for American industries. After the withdrawal of President Coolidge, Hoover was easily victorious in the Republican convention. Associated with him, as candidate for Vice President, was Senator Charles Curtis of Kansas, who boasted of Indian ancestry.

At this moment the most popular man in the Democratic party was Alfred E. Smith. Four times he had been elected governor of the great state of New York. He had taken leadership in reforming the state government. He had favored humane labor laws. He had urged public ownership of water-power sites. He had opposed the Lusk bills designed to suppress free speech in New York, and had released from prison men accused of making "radical" speeches. Besides, Governor Smith had been an outspoken opponent of prohibition. For these things he was hailed as a "liberal" and "progressive." So the Democrats nominated Governor Smith for President and added to their ticket Senator Joseph Robinson of Arkansas for Vice President. Minor parties also offered candidates to the public. Among them were the Prohibitionists, the Socialists, and the Communists, who placed the "workers party" in the field.

Judging by their platforms, no very sharp issues divided the Democrats and the Republicans. This time the former omitted from their program the usual attack on the protective tariff. Neither side was clear-cut about prohibition. Hoover opposed the repeal of the Prohibition Amendment (page 615). Smith said that it was a failure, but promised to enforce it while it remained as law. Unfortunately the religious question was raised in the campaign. Governor Smith was a Catholic and was criticized on that ground by many citizens. As a Quaker, Hoover opposed injecting the religious issue; but some voters were intolerant by nature and others really feared that Catholic influence might become too strong if Smith were elected. Doubtless many votes were cast for and against him on religious grounds, but they did not account for the outcome. In the election Governor Smith received nearly twice as many ballots as were cast for the Democratic candidate four years before. Yet Hoover swept the country by a majority of more than six million votes and carried the electoral vote in forty states. So for the third time in succession the Republicans were to control the government.

Taking Down the War Machine

Dismantling the War Machine. As soon as the armistice with Germany was signed on November 11, 1918, plans were made for bringing the American forces home and reducing the army to a peace footing. There was some demand for universal military service on the old German model, but under the Army Reorganization Act of 1920, the regular army was held down to about 125,000 men. While Congress voted large sums for national defense, it refused to adopt projects for making the United States "the biggest military power on earth."

The Struggle over the Bonus. In fact the country was more interested in rewarding generously the soldiers of the World War. Within three years, a majority of the states had granted to each of their service men either a lump sum of money or an amount based upon the length of his service, or had made provision for assisting him in completing his education. Congress likewise voted large appropriations to aid sick and injured soldiers. Meanwhile the veterans of the World War, organized in the American Legion, made a demand for a national bonus "as an act of justice." Twice bills providing such "adjusted compensation" were passed by Congress, only to be vetoed by the President. Finally, in 1924, the law was enacted over his head by the requisite two-thirds vote. Thus an extra allowance in the nature of insurance was granted to the veterans. In 1931 Congress passed a law which permitted veterans to obtain large advances on their certificates.

Railways and Shipping. Since the federal government, as a part of its war program, had taken over the management of the railways, the return of peace brought the railway issue into politics in a new form. There was some demand for continuing the experiment of government operation, but it was not strong and Congress declined to adopt any such scheme. On the contrary, by the Transportation Act of 1920, the railways were returned to their former owners. This Act allowed the companies to raise their rates and to work out plans for uniting various short lines. It enlarged the powers of the federal interstate commerce commission (page 572) over railway rates, finances, and operation.

The principle of private ownership was also applied to the vessels in possession of the government. Once American ships carried nine-tenths of the American trade on the high seas, but at the opening of the World War the proportion had fallen to about one-tenth. For years Congress had been urged in vain to vote subsidies to American shipowners to enable them to compete with foreigners. At last, however, in 1916, when the war had made ships very scarce, Congress created the United States Shipping Board, giving it the power to buy, build, and operate merchant vessels. After America entered the war, efforts at shipbuilding were redoubled, and at its close the government found itself the owner of a great merchant fleet. What was then to be done with the ships?

By the Merchant Marine Act of 1920, Congress ordered the Shipping Board to continue to operate, many of them even at a loss, and to sell others gradually to private concerns. But it was said that American shipowners could not compete with foreigners without a subsidy from the federal treasury. Harding and Coolidge both urged Congress to grant such a bonus, but they could not have their way. Instead, in 1928, by the Jones-White Act, Congress reached a kind of compromise. On pioneer lines that were not paying, the Shipping Board was to continue to operate ships. Other lines were to be turned over to private concerns and government ships were to be sold to them on favorable terms. To assist American companies in meeting foreign competition, the government agreed to lend large sums of money at a low rate of interest to be used in building new vessels and it also gave to successful bidders the right to carry mails at high rates of pay.

HANDLING FOREIGN AFFAIRS

The League of Nations Issue. It was fairly easy to bring home American soldiers, to disband the draft army, and return the railways to their former owners. It was more difficult to decide about the foreign affairs of the United States. In the forefront, naturally, stood the question: Shall the United States join the League of Nations? President Wilson insisted that the refusal of the Senate to ratify the treaty of Versailles did not mean a final refusal to enter the League. So he declared that his party should appeal to the country on the issue in the campaign of 1920.

Somewhat doubtful about the opinion of the people, the Republicans did not come out squarely against Wilson's project. At their convention in Chicago they vaguely indorsed the idea of an international association to preserve peace, without expressly approving the League; and they chose as their candidates two men supposed to be in sympathy with it. At least, while in the Senate, Harding had favored the League with reservations and during the campaign he expressed a hope that the nations of the earth would form a society of some kind for maintaining peace. Moreover, a number of eminent Republicans issued a manifesto declaring that the election of Harding actually meant the entrance of the United States into the League of Nations, if changes could be made in the interest of American independence. But other Republicans repudiated it root and branch. So the Republicans were not united in throwing over the League altogether. Acceding to the wishes of Wilson, the Democrats urged the ratification of the peace treaty without any alterations that would "impair its essential integrity." Their candidate for President, James M. Cox, while willing to accept minor changes in the treaty, declared that our country ought "to go into the League." Taking little stock in the peace professions of the old parties, the Socialists offered Eugene V. Debs, who had been imprisoned for opposing the last war, and renewed their criticisms of the "capitalist system as the source of war and poverty."

Separate Peace Treaties. The significance of the Republican victory was revealed after the election of 1920. It then became evident that a two-thirds majority could not be mustered in the Senate in favor of ratifying the Versailles treaty. Wilson, now weakened by long illness and fated to die within four short years, was no longer able to direct his party and the issue of the League gradually faded away. As the country was still nominally at war with the Central Empires, Congress finally decided to put an end to that strange state of affairs by passing a joint resolution, signed July 2, 1921, declaring the armed conflict officially closed. A short time afterward, separate treaties of peace were made with Germany and Austria, securing to American citizens all the rights asserted in the Versailles treaty without assuming any of the obligations of that agreement. Ambassadors were then exchanged and trade and travel opened as before the war.

American Attitude toward European Conferences. Nevertheless the country seemed resolved to maintain a "splendid isolation." When the Assembly of the League of Nations met at Geneva in the autumn of 1920, no delegate from the United States was present. Although he sometimes sent "unofficial observers" to watch the proceedings, President Harding refused to take any part in the conferences held by the Allied powers to discuss questions growing out of the treaty of Versailles. In his eagerness to get out of European entanglements, he withdrew the last of the American troops from the Rhine region in July, 1922. Our government was then on good terms with all the nations of Europe, except Russia. Harding refused to recognize the government of that country as long as it adhered to communist principles, and his successors, Coolidge and Hoover, took the same stand.

In the course of time, opposition to the League of Nations softened a little. At first the Secretary of State ignored the letters sent to him by officials of the League but later he decided to reply courteously. As the League began to hold special conferences on matters affecting the welfare of America, such as public health and commercial relations among countries, our government adopted a policy of sending delegates. At first these delegates were merely "unofficial observers." After a few years, however, the President sent official agents to take part openly in certain conferences held under the auspices of the League. In 1931, an American delegate sat unofficially in the council of the League when it was considering the form of protest to be made against the conduct of Japan in seizing Manchuria, a part of the territory of China (page 659). In 1934, President Franklin D. Roosevelt made the United States a member of the International Labor Office — a branch of the League.

The Washington Conference (1921–22). In declining to have anything to do with the League of Nations, President Harding was

Photograph from Wide World Photos

ARMS CONFERENCE IN SESSION AT WASHINGTON, D. C. IN 1921

not wholly indifferent to foreign affairs. The truth was, as he said, "with Europe prostrate and penitent, none feared the likelihood of an early conflict there. But the Pacific had its menaces and they deeply concerned us." He found many points of trouble in the Orient; and with anxiety he watched England, Japan, and the United States building battleships at breakneck speed. So, to remove grievances and relieve taxpayers, he invited Belgium, China, England, France, Italy, Japan, the Netherlands, and Portugal to send delegates to a conference at Washington beginning on November 12, 1921. They all accepted with apparent pleasure, and on the appointed day the assembly was opened with an address by the President, and another by the Secretary of State, Charles E. Hughes.

As a result of its work the Washington conference reached four fundamental conclusions: (1) England, France, Japan, and the United States made a "four-power" treaty in which they agreed to respect one another's island possessions in the Pacific Ocean and to confer with one another if any dispute arose over them. As a part of this understanding, England and Japan dissolved their alliance which the United States had long regarded as a possible menace to its interests. (2) England, France, Italy, Japan, and the United States entered into a compact to stop building capital battleships, to destroy certain ships already afloat or in construction, and to keep their battleship tonnage at a fixed figure. England and the United States were to be equal, while Japan was to have three-fifths of the tonnage assigned to each of them. (3) England, Japan, and the United States pledged themselves not to fortify certain islands in the Pacific, the Philippines included. (4) A number of understandings were reached with regard to China. All the powers once more consented to respect the "open door" policy (above, page 527). Japan promised to return to China the province of Shantung which she had taken from Germany during the World War and in 1922 she carried out the promise. All in all, the compacts drawn up at the Washington conference relaxed the tension in the Pacific and made for good-will. With a slight reservation, the Senate ratified the treaties to which the United States was a party.

The World Court. While still decided in his opposition to the League of Nations, President Harding declared that the United States should join other powers in submitting their disputes to the "Permanent Court of International Justice" established at The Hague by the League of Nations. He was warmly urging this proposal, when he died suddenly in San Francisco in August, 1923. His successor, President Coolidge, indorsed the idea very soon after taking office, and in 1926 the Senate voted in favor of entering the Court with several "reservations touching American rights." But many nations associated with the League objected to the terms laid down by the Senate and so the project was allowed to drop temporarily. At length in 1929 the Secretary of State, Frank B. Kellogg, revived it again. He asked the governments already in the Court to reconsider their decision, and President Coolidge sent Elihu Root abroad to smooth the way for America's admission. With much difficulty, Mr. Root induced the leading countries to agree to a treaty admitting the United States to the Court with a number of reservations touching American rights. Coolidge's successor, President Hoover, submitted this treaty to the Senate for ratification but action was delayed until 1935 when the Senate rejected it, in spite of President Roosevelt's approval of it.

Reparations and Interallied Debts. Whether in or out of the World Court, the United States was still tangled up in European affairs. Our former associates in the World War, especially England, France, and Italy, owed the federal government large sums of money borrowed mainly for war purposes — in all about ten billion dollars. How were they to pay and when? That issue was tied into another: How and when were the Allies to collect from Germany? Speaking of these questions, the United States government said that it would have nothing to do with attempts to make Germany meet her bills and it insisted that the Allies should pay their debts as obligations, no matter what Germany did.

However, in spite of such statements, the government agreed, very unofficially, to allow American citizens, among them General Charles G. Dawes and Owen D. Young, to serve on an Allied commission to work out a scheme for dealing with Germany's indebtedness. In 1924 the commission's project, known as the Dawes Plan, was put into effect. To help start the program, a huge issue of German bonds was floated, partly in the United

States, and thus American citizens furnished many million dollars to aid Germany in discharging her war bills.

But the Dawes Plan did not work well. So, in 1929, President Coolidge permitted American experts to take part in a conference held in Paris under the chairmanship of Owen D. Young for the purpose of drawing up another plan for adjusting Germany's "reparations." After the adoption of this new plan a huge issue of German bonds was sold to private investors in different countries. In this way a large amount of cash was raised to start Germany off again, but the respite was only temporary (page 654).

In the meantime, the federal government was gently pressing the Allies to arrange for the settlement of their debts, provoking in the process a lively debate among American citizens. On the one side it was said that the Allies were our brothers in a common war and that in view of their great sacrifices we should cancel the billions they had borrowed. On the other side it was argued that the Allies were at least equally guilty with the Central Empires in starting the war, that their debts were honestly incurred, and that anyway they were not so poor, because they were spending billions a year in preparing for the next war. While this wordy contest was on, the federal government continued to insist that the debts must be paid in some fashion at least and made easier terms with the debtors. It allowed them to pay over a long period of time and in fact blotted off the books a large part of their obligations. Figuring interest at the rate of $4\frac{1}{4}$ per cent, the British debt was scaled 17 per cent, that of France 52 per cent and that of Italy 75 per cent, amounting in reality to a considerable repudiation. In time all the important countries, except Russia, agreed to pay their debts to the United States on the installment plan.

This arrangement had scarcely been completed when the business panic (page 664) made it evident that some new settlement would have to be drafted. Germany could not pay reparations unless she could sell large quantities of goods abroad and hard times all over the world now made this out of the question. In the summer of 1931 Germany was on the verge of bankruptcy and could not pay the huge sums charged up against her as war damages. Her position was made the more difficult because the German government, German cities, and German business concerns had borrowed immense sums of money abroad, especially in the United States, and found difficulty in paying the interest as it fell due. So the German government said in effect to the world: "We cannot both pay reparations and meet the charges on these private debts."

At this critical moment, President Hoover managed to secure a temporary settlement. The United States postponed for a year all payments on debts owed to it by its former associates in the World War and they in turn promised to wait a year for payment from Germany. Thus a moratorium gave all the countries a short "breathing spell."

When the moratorium expired in 1932, the troublesome debts and reparations came up again. Convinced that Germany could not pay the reparations fixed by the Young plan, the former Allies, led by England and France, canceled them, except for a small sum, on the theory that the United States would cancel their debts. President Hoover and Congress then refused to extend the moratorium. In December, 1932, France and certain other debtors failed to pay. England and Italy paid, but under protest. The next year several of the debtors made small payments on account, "token" payments they were called. Then all except Finland quit paying entirely, despite the efforts of the new President, Franklin D. Roosevelt, to make some kind of arrangement with them. In 1934 the whole business of the debts was in a deadlock.

Peace, Arbitration, and the Kellogg Pact. While trying to settle each European question as it arose, the United States continued to favor methods for establishing permanent peace. By various treaties, it was already pledged to the principle of arbitrating its disputes with other governments. Indeed a series of compacts with twenty-five different countries, negotiated by Elihu Root, as Secretary of State, in 1908, bound the United States to arbitrate all disputes of a legal nature, not involving "national honor" or "vital interests." Carrying this idea a step forward, William Jennings Bryan, Secretary of State under

President Wilson, made "cooling off" treaties with twenty-two nations. By these compacts the United States agreed to submit all disputes "of every nature whatsoever" which could not be settled by friendly discussions, to a commission for inquiry and

PRESIDENT COOLIDGE SIGNS KELLOGG PEACE TREATY, 1929

report, and then bound itself not "to declare war or begin hostilities" during such inquiry, allowing at least one year for that operation.

In connection with the renewal of the Root treaties in 1928, the whole question of international peace came up for discussion. The subject could not be avoided, because it was being debated among all classes. At its convention three years before, the American Legion urged that Armistice Day be "used as an occasion for reckoning the progress made by America in the promotion of world peace as the great objective of the World War." In this spirit, Frank B. Kellogg, Secretary of State, replying to a proposal from France, suggested a general treaty positively pledging all nations to peace. In all parts of the earth the project was received with approval, and in the summer of 1928 a treaty incorporating the idea was signed in Paris by representatives of France, Germany, Great Britain, Italy, Japan, the United States, and other powers. On January 15, 1929, it was ratified by the Senate of the United States.

By this action the signers of the document, to use the words of the treaty, "condemn recourse to war for the solution of international controversies and renounce it as an instrument of national policy in their relations with one another." They also agree that the settlement of such disputes, "of whatever nature or whatever origin," shall "never be sought except by pacific means." Complete certainty was marred, however, by the fact that several of the signatory powers made reservations which impaired the strict pledges of the treaty. Yet the principle was established that aggressive war was to be condemned and peaceful methods were to be used in settling all disputes. By general consent this was a milestone in the history of efforts to "outlaw" war, especially as it was supplemented about the same time by new treaties of arbitration and conciliation with European and Latin-American governments.

Naval Rivalry with Great Britain. Nevertheless at that very moment the powers of the world, except Germany and her former allies, now forcibly disarmed, were spending more money than ever preparing for war. At the Washington conference, as we have pointed out, Great Britain and the United States agreed on equality in battleships, but not in cruisers, destroyers, and submarines. And so each country began building vessels in the second, or unrestricted, class. Seeing no end to such rivalry but war, many American citizens urged their government to promote a new limitation of armaments for the purpose of avoiding an inevitable conflict, to say nothing of the immense expenditure of money involved.

The London Conference of 1930. People in Great Britain were also disturbed by this state of affairs. The premier, Ramsay Macdonald, bent on doing something if possible, visited the United States and had long talks with President Hoover about another conference to limit naval armaments. This was in 1929. In principle they agreed and the next year delegates from Great Britain, France, Italy, Japan, and the United States assembled in London to draft a plan. Unfortunately for the smooth working of the assembly, France and Italy could not come to terms. But Great Britain, Japan, and the United States agreed on the amount of tonnage each was to have in cruisers of different types, destroyers, and submarines. At a special session of the Senate in 1930 the London conference treaty was duly ratified.

Mexico and the Caribbean. In dealing with international affairs in the New World, the government of the United States also made many efforts to adjust disputes by peaceful negotiation. Although a committee of the Senate, headed by Albert B. Fall, urged war on Mexico if American claims were not paid (page 617), President Harding chose the way of peace. He was encouraged in this course by the fact that order had been established in that country by President Obregon, who rose to power after the murder of Carranza. To reach a settlement of contested points, Harding sent a commission to Mexico City and it was at work on the task when he died. This peaceful policy Coolidge continued and as soon as the commission arrived at a general understanding official relations were renewed between the two nations. By choosing Dwight W. Morrow as ambassador, he sent to the Mexican capital "an envoy of good will" who relieved the strain by introducing to the Mexicans such delightful guests as the aviator, Colonel Charles Lindbergh, and the humorist, Will Rogers. When another revolution broke out in Mexico in 1929, President Hoover took a position friendly to the Mexican government during its effort to suppress the uprising.

With some other Latin-American countries, however, relations were not so happy. During his campaign for election, Harding attacked President Wilson for seizing territory in the Caribbean, especially Haiti and Santo Domingo, and for using American marines to interfere there (page 616); but after his election he decided not to make a sudden break in the policy of his predecessor. Nor did Coolidge depart from it. Marines were not withdrawn from Santo Domingo until 1924; they were extensively used in Nicaragua "to maintain order," but finally brought home in 1933; they were kept in Haiti until 1934. Indeed it was said that the Caribbean had become "an American lake."

Incensed by this development, many Latin-American leaders thundered against "Yankee imperialism," as they styled it. They declared that the Monroe Doctrine was merely used by the United States as a shield to keep off Europe while it extended its own power throughout the western hemisphere. In reply Coolidge protested that this nation wanted no more territory and would gladly withdraw its troops from all Latin-American countries if order were established and business put on a safe basis. In any case the gravity of the controversies called for coöperation with Latin-American governments in an effort to work out a scheme for the peaceful settlement of disputes. And on January 20, 1929, the Senate ratified a general treaty of conciliation with Pan-American nations, binding all parties to resort to pacific negotiations "when there is a prospect of disturbance of peaceful relations."

Copyright by Harris and Ewing

HERBERT HOOVER

To this conciliatory policy President Hoover gave his cordial support. Before his inauguration he made a good-will tour to

South America. The next year, 1930, he sent a commission to Haiti to study conditions there (page 616). At the opening of 1933 he withdrew the American marines from Nicaragua.

The Manchurian Question. In 1931, the Japanese government, which held railway rights in Manchuria, began a kind of war on Chinese in that neighborhood. It claimed that Chinese bandits were keeping the region in turmoil. On this ground it sent troops to Manchuria, against the protests of the Chinese government at Nanking, and occupied southern Manchuria.

Against this action by Japan the League of Nations and the government of the United States made strong objections. Japan was reminded that she had agreed to the "open door" policy (page 527), that she had joined other countries in the "nine-power pact" drawn up at the Washington conference (page 651) which confirmed that policy anew, and that she had signed the Kellogg Pact (page 656) binding herself to adjust her disputes with other countries by peaceful means. These objections, however, had no effect. Japan pursued her course of conquest, occupied Manchuria, set up there a puppet government called Manchukuo, withdrew from the League of Nations, and ignored the refusal of the United States to recognize the new government of Manchukuo.

The Rise and Fall of Business Prosperity

Higher Tariffs on Imports. While taking down the war machine and seeking to maintain friendly relations with other countries, the Republicans once more came to the aid of industry by giving it more protection against foreign competitors. They repealed the low tariff law enacted under President Wilson, enacted an emergency bill, and then passed in 1921 the Fordney-McCumber Act making duties more protective. By these measures they raised the rates on imports higher than they had ever been in the history of American industry. Since the new tariff brought increased revenues into the treasury, attempts were made to induce Congress to cut down the income taxes, especially the high taxes levied on people of great wealth. And, in 1924, Congress consented to a general reduction, with radical cuts in the surtaxes laid on large incomes. Still the taxes left on wealth were heavy — far beyond any weight dreamed of by the Democrats when they passed the income tax law of 1894, which made a furor in its day.

Not yet content with the tariff rates of 1921, the Republicans made the subject an issue in the campaign of 1928. The victory of Herbert Hoover over the Democratic candidate, Alfred E. Smith, encouraged them to believe that the country favored another increase in customs duties on foreign imports. Accordingly in 1929 Congress, at a special session, set to work on a tariff revision. After a long and heated debate it passed the Hawley-Smoot bill of 1930 which raised the rates still higher on the average. However, to provide for changes in the future, it created a tariff commission (appointed by the President and Senate) and empowered the Commission on motion of the President or either house of Congress to investigate the rates on any commodities. On its recommendation the President could raise or lower duties, within fixed limits. The idea of this plan was to establish a "flexible" tariff — one that could be easily changed as the costs of production at home and abroad varied.

An Era of Business Prosperity. The first of the permanent tariff bills passed by the Republicans in Congress in 1921 was followed shortly by a great upswing in business. Under President Coolidge, prosperity became a great boom. Wages and prices were high. The stocks of great industrial concerns rose to figures which seemed fantastic in many cases. Thousands of people put their savings in the stock market, hoping to get rich easily and quickly. From month to month business men and statesmen prophesied still bigger profits. Economists declared that America had entered upon a new age of permanent and increasing prosperity. A few bankers and captains of industry urged caution, reminding the people of the great disasters that followed booms in 1837, 1873, and 1893, but their warnings fell on dull ears. A general frenzy seized the people in the towns and the slogan "Two cars for every garage" became a symbol of the age.

The Crisis in Agriculture. While industries enjoyed this rosy prosperity, farmers remained in a sad plight. On the return of peace, the demand for agricultural produce dropped rapidly, for the European governments stopped their purchases and the impoverished people of the Old World could not buy as lavishly as in former times. In the two years between 1920 and 1922, wheat fell from $2.14 a bushel to 93 cents, while other commodities also sagged in price. All over the country farm mortgages were foreclosed, farmers went into bankruptcy and moved to town in search of work, and the value of land sank lower and lower. Immediately this state of affairs was reported in Congress by the election of a few Farmer-Labor members and by the formation of a "farm bloc" composed mainly of Republicans and Democrats pledged to vote together on bills of agricultural relief. By a number of acts Congress made it easier for farmers to form coöperative marketing societies, arranged for them to borrow money at Farm Loan Banks on produce as well as on land, regulated the stock-yards, and tried to prevent certain kinds of speculation in grain.

But such legislation did not meet the real crisis in agriculture. So a new measure was drafted, known as the McNary-Haugen bill, which was intended to help farmers by raising the prices of their produce. When this bill was passed by Congress in 1927, President Coolidge vetoed it with a critical message.

President Hoover's Agricultural Marketing Act (1929). Inevitably agricultural distress became an issue in the campaign of 1928. Both candidates, Hoover and Smith, promised to do something about it if elected. In accordance with his pledge, President Hoover called a special session of Congress, gave it his views in general terms, and left it to work out a relief plan. The result was the Agricultural Marketing Act of 1929, containing a number of special features. It created the farm board, appointed by the President and the Senate, and placed $500,000,000 in the hands of the board. On its part, the board was to encourage the formation of coöperative marketing associations among farmers, lend money to them, buy farm produce through special corporations, and generally seek to stabilize prices on a fair level. The board, however, had no power to curtail production or to bring pressure to bear upon farmers to keep them from growing too much. In spite of its efforts, the prices of agricultural produce continued to fall.

Labor and Immigration. If, as the farmers said, trade unionists fared better by controlling wages, the fact remained that many industrial workers felt that their wages had not kept pace with the rising cost of living. Indeed during the war and the years that followed, there was an epidemic of labor disputes. In 1922 a great coal strike called out over half a million miners and almost at the same moment thousands of shopmen employed by the railways struck for higher wages. In both cases attempts at arbitration failed and courts issued injunctions against strikers, raising that issue again for political discussion. While this question was uppermost in labor circles, the Supreme Court declared unconstitutional the second child labor law (page 614). Congress then passed an amendment to the Constitution authorizing the abolition of child labor, but ratification by three-fourths of the states could not be secured. In an effort to curtail the use of the injunction by courts, Congress passed another anti-injunction act, in 1932.

Contending that the American labor market was overcrowded, trade unions urged a reduction in immigration. In their demands they were supported by other citizens who held that more immigrants were coming into the country than could be assimilated, that is, merged easily with the older population. In response to such arguments Congress passed in 1924 the most drastic immigration law ever enacted. The rule of exclusion long applied to China and other Oriental countries was now extended to Japan. The Act provided that at a later date (1929) the total number of immigrants allowed from countries permitted to send immigrants at all should not exceed 150,000. To each of these countries it assigned a quota or fixed share of the total. This quota depended upon the number of people from the country in question already in the United States in 1920. For example, if one-sixth of the people in the United States in 1920 were of German origin, then Germany's quota under the new law would be one-sixth of 150,000. In effect the Act materially reduced immigration from southern and eastern Europe; but it was not applied to Canada, Mexico, and some other countries in this hemisphere.

Water Power and Utilities. Among the issues of the period none was more important than control over the development of electric power. On the one side was involved the use of the water-power sites on the national domain and along navigable rivers under the direction of the federal government. With respect to such sites Congress adopted a definite policy in 1920. Henceforward they were not to be given away or sold, but to be kept in the hands of the government and leased for development to private concerns at a fixed rental or leased to cities and states free of charge. Other questions were raised by the rapid combination of local power companies under the ownership of a few giant corporations, operating within states and across state boundaries. Should the regulation of their rates be left to state commissions or should the federal government assume that function?

Special circumstances emphasized the power question. During the World War the federal government had built a great hydroelectric plant at Muscle Shoals for the purpose of manufacturing chemicals useful in warfare. At the conclusion of the conflict it became necessary to make some disposition of this establishment. One group in Congress demanded that the government operate the plant and sell the electric power to individuals and companies in the neighborhood. Another group insisted that the government should get out of the business and sell or lease the plant to a private concern on a rental basis. After years of debate the first plan was adopted in a bill passed by Congress in 1931, but it was vetoed by President Hoover. Meanwhile the Muscle Shoals plant remained undeveloped — indeed largely idle until 1933 (page 675).

A second undertaking also reinforced the power issue. For the purpose of making use of the power and water along the Colorado River, the federal government, with the consent of the states involved, decided to build a great dam at a strategic site. How was the power to be distributed and sold? Here again the issue of public ownership and operation came into review. Finally it was decided to lease the falling water to a private company, but most of the electric power was to be sold to states and municipalities in the region. Only a small part of it was allotted to private companies.

THE DECLINE IN PROSPERITY

The Business Crash. On top of the depression in agriculture, which had continued almost steadily after the World War (page 661), came, in 1929, the signals of a depression in the business world.

In the autumn of that year there was a crash on the New York stock market which brought down the prices of stocks from the high figures of the boom days. After a lull, stocks continued to fall. Business dropped off. Factories were shut for want of orders. The prices of farm produce fell still lower. By 1932 millions were out of employment and thousands were in distress, calling for relief.

Old scenes were enacted again. During each of the great war periods of American history — 1812–1815, 1861–1865, and 1914–1918 — the industries and agriculture of the United States enjoyed abnormal prosperity. In each period, large quantities of paper money were issued and the prices of commodities produced by farmers, miners, and manufacturers rose to unusual heights, as compared with gold. Wages soared in the cities. With the rise of prices and wages, people came to believe that a new era had arrived — an era of increasing prosperity. Farmers bought more land, manufacturers built new plants to take care of growing business, and new houses and office buildings were erected everywhere. To embark on such enterprises, people borrowed money and mortgaged their farms, industries, and homes as security. Thousands engaged in speculation in farm land, city lots, and railroad and industrial stocks. In other words, "they lost their heads" on the theory that boom times would last forever.

Had they studied the history of such abnormal times, they would have known that, with the amount of gold fixed at a given number of grains per dollar, the prices of commodities would drop in due time to something like the old normal level on a parity with gold. But they were not so prepared during the years following the World War and were caught unawares by the calamity which began in the autumn of 1929.

An example will illustrate. During the World War, when wheat was $2.00 a bushel, a farmer bought 160 acres of excellent wheat land at the boom price of $250 an acre and put a mortgage of $20,000 on the farm. If wheat had remained at $2.00 a bushel, his crop of approximately 3200 bushels would have brought him $6400 a year and he could have paid off the mortgage in the course of four or five years. But when wheat dropped to fifty cents a bushel, his crop brought him only $1600 a year. After he had paid his living expenses and taxes, he was unable to meet the annual interest of $1200 on his loan.

Since the price of wheat had fallen, the value of the farm dropped to $100 an acre and could not be sold for enough to cover the mortgage. So the bank which had made him the loan foreclosed and took the farm away from him. Having a large number of farms of the same kind on its hands and being unable to sell them for the amount which it had lent on them, the bank could not raise money to pay its depositors on call. So the bank closed its doors and its depositors lost a part of their money — large or small according to circumstances.

Incidents such as this happened all over the United States in the years of distress which followed the crash of 1929. In the cities people whose homes were heavily mortgaged lost their property when their wages were cut or their employment stopped. Businessmen lost their stores and manufacturers their plants. Speculators who had once been rich were reduced to poverty. And suffering spread throughout all sections of the population.

Plans for Avoiding Economic Disasters. In the midst of this distressing condition, leaders in public affairs began discussing ways and means of averting such calamities or at least mitigating their evils. All agreed apparently that, as a committee of the United States Chamber of Commerce suggested, it was "painful" and "stupid" for people to be hungry in the presence of a surplus of food, cold when clothing and coal were available, and idle when machinery waited on workers. That much was scarcely debatable, but agreement on remedies was not easily reached.

Great industrialists, such as Gerard Swope and Owen D. Young, said that a way out of the trouble could be found if the members of each main branch of industry, electrical manufacturers, for example, would organize an association, take steps to equalize supply and demand, and insure their employees against idleness. A committee of the United States Chamber of Commerce advocated a similar project. Senator LaFollette, Jr. of Wisconsin introduced a bill providing for the creation of an economic council to study and devise plans for stabilizing business.

A few economists advocated "nation planning" on a large scale, including all branches of industry and agriculture in a common scheme to steady production, prices, and employment — sometimes with projects for insurance against unemployment. Other economists insisted that the chief trouble lay in the currency system. A demand was heard once more for the free coinage of silver (page 488) and there was a call for an increase in the amount of paper money issued by the Federal Reserve banks (page 613). A third currency program proposed that, while retaining the gold standard (page 501), the government should reduce the number of grains of gold in the gold dollar, thus automatically raising the prices of commodities in terms of the new dollar. Advocates of this project cited in support of their reform the example of France. That country did not attempt a drastic deflation of prices after the World War but stabilized its money — the franc — at about four cents as against its old price of approximately twenty cents.

President Hoover, however, did not favor any extensive programs of planning or radical changes in the currency system. In fact, he said that the idea of planning had been adopted from the Russian "five-year plan" which had alarmed so many economists and political leaders. On his part, therefore, President Hoover proposed only measures of temporary relief. He laid before Congress, late in 1931, a series of recommendations. One, as already noted, was the moratorium on European debts (page 654). A second, which he had also previously advanced, was an increase in the expenditures of the federal government for public improvements — waterways, buildings, roads, and similar works — to give employment to the idle. To assist railways, banks, real estate concerns, and other enterprises that were in trouble, President Hoover proposed the creation of a Federal Finance Corporation.

In response to a widespread demand for action Congress passed a number of important laws in the winter of 1931–1932, including most of President Hoover's suggestions, often with changes. It created the Finance Corporation advocated by the President. It placed huge sums of money in the hands of the Corporation and other federal agencies to be lent to railways, banks, industrial concerns, farmers, and others in financial difficulty. A large grant was made to states and municipalities for use in building public works to give employment and in affording other relief to the unemployed. Provision was also made for allowing the Federal Reserve system to issue additional currency. In spite of differences of opinion respecting these measures, it was clear that the best leadership of the nation was bent on finding ways and means for meeting the evils of the panic and for preventing the recurrence of such economic disasters.

The Republicans Beaten in the Election of 1932. While the country was in the throes of the depression the campaign of 1932 arrived. Claiming that President Hoover had done his best, the Republicans re-nominated him and Vice President Curtis. This time the Democrats chose as their candidate Governor Franklin D. Roosevelt of New York and associated with him John N. Garner of Texas as candidate for Vice President. The election was a Democratic "landslide." Roosevelt carried forty-two states, leaving only six for President Hoover. The popular vote stood as follows: Roosevelt, 22,800,000; Hoover, 15,700,000; Norman Thomas, the Socialist, 880,000; W. Z. Foster, the Communist, 102,000; with scattering votes for other minor party candidates. Besides winning the presidency, the Democrats secured a majority in both houses of Congress. Thus the Republican era of twelve years was brought to a close.

References

W. A. White, *Politics: The Citizen's Business* (for platforms of 1924).
World Almanac (platforms of 1928 and election returns).
R. L. Buell, *The Washington Conference.*
J. T. Shotwell, *War as an Instrument of National Policy.*
Parker T. Moon, *Imperialism and World Politics.*
Isaiah Bowman, *The New World* (4th ed. 1928).
C. A. Beard, *America Faces the Future* (1932) (the business depression and plans for avoiding panics).
For all questions of international relations see pamphlets of the Carnegie Endowment for International Peace, 405 West 117th St., New York City.
For domestic questions, *Current History* and *The American Year Book* are useful.

Questions

1. Did the election of 1920 decide the League of Nations issue?
2. How was the World War officially closed?
3. How were relations with Germany and Austria renewed?
4. What had been the official attitude toward Europe? Russia?
5. Why was the Washington conference called? What countries took part in it? What were the chief results?
6. What has been the official policy with regard to Mexico? The World Court? The Caribbean?
7. What was the Dawes Plan? The Young Plan?
8. How were Interallied debts involved in German reparations?
9. What was President Hoover's moratorium?
10. Give the chief steps in the development of peace plans. Describe the Kellogg Pact.
11. What were the principal results of the London arms reduction conference?
12. Review the recent federal laws respecting railways, tariff, shipping, agriculture, water power, and immigration.
13. What were the effects of the business depression?
14. Discuss some of the plans for meeting the depression.

CHAPTER XXIX

THE NEW DEAL

The Emergency. Seldom in the history of the country had a President taken office in such a trying time as on March 4, 1933, when Franklin D. Roosevelt began "The New Deal" which he had promised during the campaign. A grave emergency existed. Banks were either failing or closing their doors in many parts of the country, so that depositors could not draw out their money. Industries were either shut down or running part time. Millions of men and women were unemployed. Railways were finding it hard to pay their expenses. Farmers had great piles of produce which they could sell only at ruinous prices, if at all. The federal government owed an immense war

FRANKLIN D. ROOSEVELT

debt. States, cities, and counties were heavily in debt. Companies and citizens were in debt. Mortgages on farms and homes were being foreclosed and property taken away from owners. Millions did not know where to turn for food, clothing, and shelter and looked to government for relief in their distress. Clearly Congress and the President had to act quickly and boldly.

Yet no large plans for dealing with such an emergency were ready and agreed upon. So President Roosevelt attacked one problem after another.

Emergency Measures

Control over the Banks. His first step was to close all banks throughout the United States, until federal officers could find out which were "sound" and fit to be opened. This action Congress quickly approved and "sound" banks were opened. It also passed a new banking law which gave the President more power over banks in the federal reserve system (page 612). In states which allowed banks to have branches, Congress permitted federal reserve banks to open branches, thus putting the federal government behind more banks. Congress retained the Reconstruction Finance Corporation set up under President Hoover (page 666) and widened its powers. It permitted the Corporation to lend more money to banks. It also authorized the Corporation to lend money to industries, as well as banks and railways. Within a few months the federal government promised to insure against loss all deposits up to the amount of $5000 in banks willing to take out insurance. Another step was to set up a Stock Exchange Commission to keep watch and ward on Wall Street and prevent a return of various abuses by which investors had lost so much money during the boom.

Control over the Currency. Connected with banking was the currency—the money with which business is carried on and debts are paid, if paid at all. In 1900, after many political battles, it had been settled that the standard dollar in the United States should be the gold dollar, containing a fixed number of grains of gold (page 501). All other dollars, paper and silver, were made redeemable in gold; that is, anyone who had a paper dollar could get a gold dollar for it at the Treasury of the United States. Moreover most debts were made payable in gold dollars if demanded. But in fact there was not enough gold in the country to meet the demand if all creditors insisted on having gold. In addition public and private debts in the United States were huge, especially on account of the borrowing done during the boom. The prices of goods had fallen, and it was alleged that this was due to the lack of money.

In this emergency Congress and the President took four important steps. They declared that it was no longer necessary for public and private debts to be paid in gold coins or their equivalents. The President was empowered to reduce the weight of gold in the dollar by at least fifty per cent, and he did reduce it to about fifty-nine per cent of its former amount. This was followed by an order calling all gold in banks and private hands (with some exceptions) into the federal Treasury. Later, in 1934, under act of Congress also, he called in silver. For the gold and silver he paid a fixed price in paper money. Besides reducing the gold content of the dollar, he issued large quantities of silver "certificates" based on silver in the Treasury. By these means, it was hoped, the dollar would be made "cheaper" and the prices of commodities raised to about the level prevailing in 1926. Thus both agriculture and industry were to be "stimulated."

NIRA. From banking and currency, Congress and the President turned to direct efforts to improve industry and agriculture. At this point we come to the "alphabet" of the New Deal. So many acts were passed by Congress and so many boards were established, bearing long names, that the habit of referring to them by initials came into vogue. NIRA, for example, stands for the National Industrial Recovery Act, which was signed in June, 1933. Its purpose was to bring all great industries under federal supervision, to promote united action of management and labor, to maintain the fullest possible use of industrial plants, to increase buying power among the people, to improve working conditions, and to conserve natural resources.

Under the Act each of the leading industries, such as coal, steel, automobile, electrical appliances, and foundry equipment, was called upon to draw up a code for its own government. Representatives of the employers in each industry were to meet and agree upon a plan for fair practices in the industry. The code fixed minimum wages and maximum hours in the industry, provided for bargaining with employees, and laid down rules for "fair dealing." One part of the Act, Section 7a, stated that employees had the right to organize and to bargain collectively with their employers through unions of some kind. President Roosevelt knew that it would take months to draw thousands of employers and employees together in such a nation-wide scheme, although he started the work immediately by appointing General Hugh Johnson head of the National Recovery Administration (NRA). So he called upon employers all over the country to enter into agreements with him. In such an agreement the employer bound himself to employ more workers, stop hiring children under sixteen years of age, fix minimum wages, and hold the prices of goods down. Every employer signing an agreement received from the Government a placard, a Blue Eagle, bearing the words: "We do our part." By the end of a year hundreds of industries had drawn up their codes and these took the place of individual Blue Eagle agreements. This plan lasted until 1935 when the Supreme Court declared it unconstitutional (below, page 680).

Agricultural Adjustment Administration (AAA). While the NRA was being put to work, another agency was being established in the Department of Agriculture under the Agricultural Adjustment Act, of May, 1933 (amended in 1934 and again in 1935). This Act authorized Henry A. Wallace, the Secretary of Agriculture, to enter into agreements with farmers for the purpose of reducing the amount of cotton, corn, wheat, rice, tobacco, hogs, cattle, peanuts, and certain other products raised on the land. In return for cutting down acreage under cultivation each farmer entering an agreement received from the government a certain payment in money. To meet these heavy bills a tax was laid upon industries engaged in "processing" agricultural produce, that is, for example, grinding wheat, ginning cotton, and manufacturing cigars and cigarettes. In addition, the Government bought huge quantities of farm products and distributed them as relief to unemployed. Later cotton farmers were compelled by an act of Congress to reduce their acreage whether they liked it or not. In this way it was hoped to cut down the "surpluses" of farm products which could not be sold at all or at prices below cost of production.

Railways. Like agriculture and industry, railways were in distress as passenger and freight business fell off. Some were bankrupt and in the hands of receivers appointed by federal judges. Others were hard pressed to meet running expenses. In part their troubles were due to the wastes of competition, such as maintaining separate stations and running too many trains between the great cities. In part also their difficulties came from the sharp competition of trucks, buses, and airplanes. So the government came to their aid. Under an act of Congress, President Roosevelt appointed as "coördinator," Joseph B. Eastman, of the Interstate Commerce Commission (page 492). At once the Coördinator tried to get the railway companies to agree to a common use of tracks, stations, yards, and warehouses, and thus reduce wastes and costs. Under other acts of Congress the government lent money to railways.

Providing Employment through the Public Works Administration (PWA). While seeking to promote employment in industry and agriculture, the federal government tried to create employment directly by starting public works of various kinds. It pressed the construction of post offices and other federal buildings. It set up the Public Works Administration under NIRA. It allocated hundreds of millions to the Army and Navy. It urged states, cities, counties, and towns to start roads, school buildings, water works plants, and other public improvements. It gave them outright thirty per cent of the cost of each approved project and lent them money for the balance. To speed up such enterprises the Civil Works Administration (CWA) was organized temporarily in November, 1933, to provide public works jobs until the rest of the plan could get under way. In 1935 Congress approved a plan for putting 3,500,000 people at work on federal and state projects.

Relief Work. Although efforts were made to speed up industry and public works, millions of people still remained unemployed and faced hunger and privation. In his inaugural address the President declared that no one should starve in America and that if the state and local government could not prevent it, the federal government must step in and help. Its aid took many forms. The President enrolled about 300,000 young men in the Civilian Conservation Corps (CCC), set up camps for them under the general management of army officers, and employed them in forestry work, the prevention of soil erosion, and other improvements. The men enrolled were provided with food, clothing, and shelter and paid a small sum monthly, a part of which they had to send home to help their dependents. In 1935 the number of men was increased to 600,000. To take charge of other relief, the Federal Emergency Relief Administration (FERA) was established and granted a large fund by Congress. It made allotments of money to states, cities, and other local governments. It bought and distributed food and clothing. At one time in 1934, according to reports, at least fifteen million people were receiving relief in some form from governments, federal, state, and local. In an effort to help farmers and home owners who were in debt, the Federal Government arranged to lend them money on easy terms through land banks (page 615), the Home Owners' Loan Corporation (HOLC), and other agencies.

Housing Projects. With a view to stimulating the building industry, which was in a bad way, and improving housing conditions, the federal government gave some attention to this subject. Through the PWA it tried to induce cities to clear up some of their worst slum areas by tearing down tenements and erecting new houses. But this proved to be slow work, and little was done. Then the government set aside a small sum for the purpose of experimenting itself in the building of better homes. Finally, in 1934, it established the Federal Housing Administration (FHA) to supervise lending money to home owners who wished to paint, repair, and otherwise improve their property. Despite these undertakings, the Secretary of Commerce declared that there was a shortage of 5,000,000 habitable dwellings in the United States and that "thousands of others were unfit for human habitation." As a result of many studies, agreement was reached that millions of Americans are not properly housed and lack most of the conveniences that make homes comfortable for living.

Paying for the New Deal. All these activities cost money—a huge sum in addition to the ordinary expenses of the federal government. From month to month, expenses mounted. To meet this situation, the government borrowed billions of dollars, issuing its bonds in exchange. It increased the taxes on incomes, especially the incomes of "the very rich," and laid new taxes, including taxes on intoxicating liquors after the repeal of prohibition (page 676). Money flowed out so fast that it was hard to tell just how much the government owed at any moment, but by 1935 at least eight billion dollars had been added to the national debt as it stood in 1933.

OTHER DOMESTIC PROBLEMS

The Tennessee Valley Development (TVD). One of the questions which confronted President Roosevelt in 1933 was the disposal of the Muscle Shoals power plant which had long been debated (page 663). Under his direction, Congress settled it by providing for the federal ownership and operation of the plant. It did more. It created the Tennessee Valley Administration (TVA)—a board of three members. It empowered this board to finish the Muscle Shoals plant, build new dams and plants, construct lines to transmit electricity, and sell power directly to states, cities, towns, companies, and individuals. The board was also authorized to make plans for "developing" the surrounding region in the Tennessee Valley, reforesting waste lands, preventing soil erosion, building houses, laying out homesteads, and starting industries to give employment. This, said President Roosevelt, is to be the beginning of similar planning for other regions in the United States.

The "Lame Duck" Amendment. For many years critics had complained that too much time elapsed between elections in November and the day on which the President was inaugurated and members of the new Congress met. Under old practice, members of Congress chosen in November, 1930, let us say, took their seats in December, 1931, unless called in special session by the President. In any case old members of Congress kept their places for about four months after new members were elected. The hold-over members who had been defeated were called "lame ducks." After much agitation, this state of affairs was changed by an amendment to the federal Constitution—the Twentieth— adopted in 1933. Under the new plan, members of Congress elected in November of each even year take their seats on January 3 of the following year. A new President elected in November is inaugurated on the next January 20, instead of March 4. By the same Amendment provision is made for succession to the presidency in case of vacancy by death or for any other reason (Appendix, page xvi).

The Repeal of Prohibition. The long and bitter debate over national prohibition resulted in the repeal of the Eighteenth Amendment in 1933 (page 615). This was done by the adoption of the Twenty-first Amendment to the Constitution (Appendix, page xvi). By the new Amendment control over the manufacture and sale of intoxicating liquors was returned to the states. Individual states may forbid the liquor traffic entirely or regulate it as they see fit. But Section 2 of the Amendment prohibits the transportation or importation of liquor into any state in violation of its own laws dealing with the matter. In other words, if a state forbids the sale of liquor within its boundaries, no person or concern can carry liquor into the state and sell it.

Having won back control over the liquor business, the states chose various ways of handling it. A few continued prohibition. By September, 1935, there were only three "bone dry" states in the Union. Others provided for licensing the sellers of liquor. In Pennsylvania and a few other states the state government itself took over the management of liquor selling. Although it was hoped that "bootlegging" or the illegal sale of liquor would stop, it did not disappear entirely. Owing to the high taxes imposed on liquor by the federal, state, and local governments, it was found profitable to smuggle liquor into the United States and sell it quietly to customers at prices below the taxed goods. Nor was it easy, in the age of airplanes and automobiles, to stop the unlawful carriage of liquor from one state to another. So the liquor question still remained in politics.

The Federal Drive on Crime. In earlier days, the Federal Government dealt only with criminals who violated its laws— smugglers, counterfeiters, and post-office burglars, for example. Other crimes were left to the control of the states. But after the World War the crime problem became national. Certain crimes became more frequent. Among these crimes were kidnaping rich people and holding them for ransom, bootlegging, and "racketeering" or wringing money from people by threats and unlawful schemes of one kind or another. Robbing banks and stores on a large scale became a desperate game of desperate men and women. And by using airplanes and automobiles, criminals could easily flee from the scenes of their operations into other states and distant places. Local sheriffs, policemen, and state governments simply could not cope with crimes in such conditions. Hence Congress took up the question in 1934 and enacted six important laws bearing on crime. It allowed two or more states to coöperate in combating crime; and it gave federal officers more power to deal with kidnapers, robbers, and other "gangmen."

DEVELOPMENT OF THE ROOSEVELT PROGRAM (1934–1935)

Making Permanent Plans. Many of the laws mentioned above were "emergency" measures. They were designed to cope with immediate troubles in banking, industry, and agriculture. After they were adopted in 1933 President Roosevelt and Congress began to consider more permanent plans for dealing with "hard times," unemployment, distress, and other problems of American life. As a result Congress passed several important acts in 1934 and 1935 and the Federal Government undertook to do a number of things which were novel in American history. In the meantime the Agricultural Adjustment Administration was made permanent; that is, the plan for controlling the production of certain farm crops was changed, strengthened, and declared to be a regular system for upholding the prices of farm produce. Federal control over banks was increased and the reduction of the weight of gold in the standard dollar was continued in force. In 1935 the huge sum of $4,800,-000,000 was voted to furnish relief for the unemployed and to provide more employment on federal, state, and local projects, such as highways, school buildings, and housing.

The Social Security Act. By a law signed on August 14, 1935, Congress sought to reduce the amount of poverty among the aged and to provide insurance against unemployment in the future. It voted money to aid states in paying pensions to aged people.

If a state will pay a pension to each old man or woman who has no other means of support, the Federal Government will furnish half of the amount up to $15 a month. That is, the Federal Government will pay half of any state old-age pension providing it is not more than $30 a month. Already about two-thirds of the states have old-age pension plans. In the second place, Congress set up a scheme by which certain classes of workers will receive larger old-age benefits after the year 1942. Such benefits are to be based on the wages of each person and may amount to a pension of $85 a month after the age of sixty-five. By the Security Act money is also voted from the Federal Treasury to aid the states in caring for dependent children, promoting child welfare, and improving the health of the people. If any state sets up a fund to insure people against unemployment, by imposing a tax on employers and employees, then the Federal Government will reduce its taxes on employers and employees. Thus states are encouraged to raise funds out of which to pay weekly allowances to certain classes of unemployed persons for a certain period of time. This new law is being carried out by the Social Security Board appointed by the President and Senate.

Labor and Industry. After the Supreme Court declared most of the National Industrial Recovery Act unconstitutional (below, page 680), Congress passed a new law—the Wagner-Connery Act—to promote "collective bargaining" between employers and employees. It provided that the employees in any factory or plant can organize a union of their own and elect their own officers to bargain with employers over hours and wages. At the same time Congress forbade employers to form unions among their employees and to interfere with independent unions organized by their employees. By another law Congress sought to improve conditions in the soft coal industry. For many years employers had been losing money and coal miners had been suffering from low wages and unemployment. The Guffey-Snyder Act, passed by Congress in 1935, empowered employers and employees in this industry to organize, bargain over hours and wages, and fix the minimum prices for coal. To provide pensions for aged railway workers, Congress imposed a tax on railroad companies. At the same time it made an attempt to help the companies by empowering the Interstate Commerce Commission (page 673) to regulate the rates and services of interstate bus and truck concerns. Buses and trucks had cut down the earnings of railways.

National Youth Administration. Owing to the large number of young men and women unable to find work, Congress established in 1935 a National Youth Administration with branches in all the states. Three main duties were laid upon the administration. It is to aid youths between sixteen and twenty-five in finding employment, and to provide employment for them, if necessary, on work-relief projects. For youths in search of more education it must furnish guidance in the choice of vocations and in training for them. Needy students in colleges and high schools are to receive in some cases part-time employment and in others small cash payments so that they may carry on their education. In each state a director is to coöperate with schools, colleges, and other institutions in providing opportunities for young people unable to finish their education or find employment.

Rural Resettlement. While coming to the aid of industrial workers in cities, the Federal Government attacked problems of poverty in rural regions. It found that thousands of farm families were trying to make a living on poor land that could not possibly support them. So it set up the Resettlement Administration. The Administration was empowered to buy up a large amount of infertile or marginal land, to help families in backward regions to establish homes for themselves on better land, and to found communities for such "new homesteaders." The marginal land bought by the Government is to be used mainly for reforestation. Millions of trees are to be planted, and dams built to check floods and prevent the washing away of land (soil erosion). In a way rural resettlement is intended to "abolish slums in the country" just as the housing plans are designed to destroy some of the worst spots in great cities.

The Holding Company Act (1935). Among the many measures of "The New Deal," none stirred up more debate than a bill to regulate electrical industries. The business of producing and selling electricity had grown up rapidly. It had begun with the building of local plants in cities and towns. Each was at first independent and sold electricity in the neighborhood. Then the business expanded. Larger and larger plants were built and companies commenced to send current across state lines into distant communities. Thus they were engaged in interstate commerce. The next step was to combine many little companies under one large company. In this process the "holding company" was invented. A holding company, as a rule, does not produce any electricity itself; it merely owns a number of companies that are making and selling current. Sometimes a holding company would own a number of holding companies which in their turn owned local companies. Although there were numerous advantages in the uniting of many producing companies in one system, abuses often appeared. Some holding companies forced producing companies to charge high rates to consumers or sold to the public stocks and bonds that proved to be worthless, or nearly worthless.

By the Holding Company Act of 1935 Congress tried to do three things. It gave the Federal Power Commission the right to regulate the rates and services of concerns engaged in transmitting electricity across state boundaries, that is, in interstate commerce. It required companies to secure government approval before selling stocks and bonds to the public. Then it provided for breaking up all holding companies except those that own operating plants linked together in a single region. At the time this law was passed, critics said that it violated certain clauses of the Federal Constitution, and in fact a Federal District Court, in November, 1935, declared it null and void, as contrary to the Constitution.

The Supreme Court Declares NIRA Invalid. In the winter and spring of 1935, the Supreme Court at Washington declared unconstitutional a number of laws passed by Congress under President Roosevelt's leadership. The most important law set aside was the National Industrial Recovery Act (page 671). The Court said that Congress could not give the President and industries the power to draw up codes for controlling hours, wages, and other matters. That was giving them the power to make laws, whereas under the Constitution all legislative power belongs to Congress. The Court also said that hours and wages in local plants were local matters and did not belong to "interstate commerce." Since Congress can regulate only commerce among the states, it cannot regulate hours and wages within the states. Other parts of the New Deal program, including the processing tax for AAA (page 672), were declared void by lower federal courts, and President Roosevelt expressed the fear that his whole program might be set aside by the Supreme Court. This raised a vital question: Shall the Constitution be amended in such a way as to permit more federal control over agriculture, hours, wages, and living conditions? So things stood as the year 1935 drew to a close.

FOREIGN AFFAIRS

The London Economic Conferences. One of the difficulties in domestic affairs was the problem of finding outlets abroad for goods that could not be sold at home. It was hoped that foreign trade could be helped by some kind of international agreement at a general conference held in London in 1933. To this conference President Roosevelt sent delegates, headed by Cordell Hull, Secretary of State. Two leading issues were raised: (1) the reëstablishment of the gold standard throughout the world and (2) the lowering of tariffs on goods. Some delegates wanted to raise also the matter of the debts owed to the United States by former associates in the World War on which they had stopped payments (page 654). But nothing came of the conference. President Roosevelt would not permit a discussion of the debts; neither was he ready to put the country back on a gold basis or reduce the American tariff by a single stroke. Representatives of other countries were not able to reach any common agreements either.

The Geneva Disarmament Conference. When President Roosevelt took office, American delegates had already been appointed to a conference at Geneva on the reduction of armaments. A pledge in favor of such action had been made in the Versailles treaty (page 638) when Germany had been disarmed; and Germany insisted on having the pledge fulfilled. Long discussions were held at the conference; but the delegates could not agree on any plan to reduce their expenditures for death-dealing weapons.

The Recognition of Russia. A few months after he was inaugurated, President Roosevelt took up the question of recognizing Russia. Under Republican administrations, the United States Government had repeatedly refused to have any official relations with that country on account of the policies pursued by its communist rulers. But President Roosevelt decided to change this strange state of affairs in which two great nations stood on unfriendly terms. On invitation from him the Russian government sent an agent, Maxim Litvinov, to the United States. Litvinov and the President talked over the situation and reached an agreement. Then an American ambassador was sent to Moscow, and a Russian ambassador came to Washington. The matter of the debts owed by the old Tsarist government to the United States was left to later settlement, but regular relations between the two countries were thus restored.

Relations with the Far East. Meanwhile relations with Japan, although officially friendly, were not very cordial. The United States continued firm in its refusal to recognize the new state, Manchukuo, which Japan had set up in Manchuria, at the expense of China (page 659). The exclusion of Japanese immigrants from the United States (page 610) remained a sore point with the Japanese people, and the action of Congress in voting large sums to build new vessels for the American navy caused excitement in Japan.

Philippine Independence. However, the risks of war in the Far East were reduced, perhaps, by an act of Congress in 1934 providing for the ultimate independence of the Philippine Islands. This act authorized Filipinos to hold a convention and draw up a constitution for their own government. It then added that at the expiration of ten years after the Filipinos have accepted the act and established a constitution the United States will withdraw its troops, and allow them to have complete independence. By 1935 the Filipinos had adopted a constitution and inaugurated their first president. In offering independence to the Islands, the American government seemed to say to the world that it would not join in any new scramble for territory which the great powers might start in the Far East.

The Caribbean. Nearer home, in the Caribbean, important changes occurred. The government of Cuba was overthrown by a popular uprising, but the United States did not send troops to intervene under the Platt Amendment of 1901 (page 544). On the contrary, President Roosevelt made a treaty with Cuba abolishing that part of the Amendment which permitted the United States to interfere in the affairs of Cuba to maintain order there; and the treaty was duly ratified by the Senate in 1934. Another treaty with Latin-American countries pledged the United States to a peaceful settlement of disputes in the future. Somewhat later, American marines were withdrawn from Haiti (page 658). Thus the Government of the United States was no longer using troops to "keep order" in any Caribbean country.

The Reciprocal Tariff Act. In the hope of enlarging commerce with other countries, Congress passed a new tariff law in 1934. This act gave the President sole power for a term of three years to make tariff agreements with other nations. In any such agreement he can raise or lower (within limits) the duties on imports from a particular country already fixed by Congress in the regular tariff laws. The President was expected to make bargains—to say to other governments: "If you will make it easier for your people to buy American goods, we will reduce the tariff on certain of your goods imported into the United States." Within a short time a reciprocity tariff treaty had been made with Cuba and a few other governments.

The Armament Outlook. While President Roosevelt was coming to friendly terms with Russia, taking steps to free the Philippines, and improving relations with Latin-American countries, the armament question was pressed upon his attention. All the great powers of the world, including the United States, were spending more and more money on armies and navies. Just as on the eve of the World War, they were piling up weapons of death and destruction. And it was rightly feared that the end of this race would be another war. The Geneva disarmament conference (page 681) came to nothing. The treaties limiting navies were soon to expire and a new naval conference was due in 1935. Could the competition in war machines be stopped? The outlook was not favorable when President Roosevelt accepted an invitation to send delegates to a new naval conference in London in December, 1935.

The Neutrality Act. Nevertheless there was a strong sentiment in the United States against becoming involved in any foreign war. In August, 1935, Congress passed a law known as the Neutrality Act. According to this act whenever a war breaks out between foreign countries and the President proclaims the fact, it then becomes unlawful for Americans to export any "arms, ammunition, or implements of war" from the United States to the warring nations. American citizens who travel on the ships of warring countries travel at their own risk. As soon as war broke out between Italy and Ethiopia in the autumn of 1935, President Roosevelt proclaimed the new law in full force and forbade Americans to export munitions to either belligerent. He also hinted that he did not look with favor on selling any other goods to the warring powers.

In this way the Federal Government refused to protect American citizens in selling goods and lending money to belligerents. Such protection had helped to involve the United States in the World War in defense of the "American right" to carry on profitable commerce with warring nations (pages 621-625). It was hoped that the United States might the more readily keep out of foreign wars if American citizens were prevented from making money out of such conflicts. This hope was due in part to revelations of huge profits in munition-making unearthed in 1934-1935 by a Senate committee of investigation, headed by Gerald P. Nye. "Take the profits out of war" and "Keep out of war" became two very popular slogans in the United States as the threats of new wars loomed up in Europe and Asia.

References

B. Y. Landis, *Must the Nation Plan* (1934), with excellent list of current books.

E. K. Lindley, *The Roosevelt Revolution* (for personalities).

C. A. Beard and G. H. E. Smith, *The Future Comes* (1933), for first steps in establishing the New Deal.

W. Macdonald, *The Menace of Recovery* (critical).

W. H. Mallory, *Political Handbook of the World* (1934).

B. Lasker and W. L. Holland, *Problems of the Pacific* (1934).

For a monthly review of domestic and foreign affairs, see *Current History*, published by the New York *Times*, and for a weekly review, *The American Observer*, published in Washington, D. C.

Questions

1. What were the domestic troubles which made the emergency in 1933?

2. Give the steps taken to restore confidence in banks.

3. Why was the gold content of the dollar reduced?

4. List the things done to aid industry, agriculture, the railways, the unemployed.

5. What plans were adopted to pay for the New Deal?

6. How was the question of Muscle Shoals decided?

7. Give the provisions of the two new amendments to the Constitution.

8. Give the chief terms of the Social Security Act.

9. What efforts were made to favor collective bargaining in industry?

10. Explain the terms: Youth Administration, Rural Resettlement, and Holding Company.

11. Why was the armament question important for the United States?

12. What policies did President Roosevelt adopt in dealing with the Far East and the Caribbean region?

13. Explain the purpose of the Reciprocity Tariff Act.

14. Discuss the Neutrality Act.

CHAPTER XXX

AMERICAN CIVILIZATION IN THE ENGINEERING AGE

Through the moving years of war and politics, business enterprise and labor organization, agitations over women's rights, and debates over public questions, the cultural interests of the American people — religion, science, letters, and the arts — advanced amid changing scenes. By the multiplying production of wealth fabulous sums were available for churches, schools, colleges, museums, magazines, and intellectual pursuits of every kind. From decade to decade the number who could read and write widened until it included almost the entire population. Transcontinental railways, the telegraph, radios, automobiles, and improved roads bound the whole continent into a tight unity, brought town and country together, and linked section with section. More than that; foreign commerce, finance, debts, cables, radios, and travel caught America up into the web of world civilization. While this bewildering transformation was taking place strange problems of life, labor, conduct, and opinion furnished new themes for writers and artists, new tasks for religious workers, new opportunities for scientific endeavor. Through the deeper speculation ran the question: What profiteth riches to the human soul?

RELIGIOUS AND INTELLECTUAL INTERESTS

The Churches. The principle of religious toleration, fairly achieved by the middle of the nineteenth century, continued to be held up as the national ideal. Under that principle practically all denominations enlarged their membership and activities. Recruited extensively by immigrants from European countries, the Roman Catholic Church showed a rapid growth, especially in the Eastern cities; in Rhode Island and Connecticut that denomination had on its rolls in 1926 more than one half the total church population. With immigration new congregations appeared; Russian Orthodox churches rose beside Jewish synagogues. Among Protestants, the ferment of opinion produced new denominations; for example, the Christian Science Church. A religious census of the United States for 1926 showed more than one hundred and fifty different sects or organizations for religious worship — an increase of thirty-two in ten years. At that date about one-half the people of the United States were listed as church members. Never before had such huge sums of money been given for buildings, missions, young people's societies, church publications, religious education, and the maintenance of religious worship.

Development of Secular Learning. While the churches were growing in wealth, numbers, and power, intellectual activities once monopolized by the clergy continued to pass into the hands of laymen, particularly among the Protestants. The great mass of students in the colleges of the country were not preparing for the ministry but for law, medicine, science, teaching, business, art, music, literature, and other secular occupations. The number of books on worldly themes multiplied more swiftly than those on theology and religion, as political and economic questions were calling for increasing consideration. Scientific discussions filled monthly and weekly journals and flowed over into the daily newspapers. Less and less of the teaching in Protestant colleges was done by clergymen; even instruction in philosophy, psychology, and other themes closely akin to religion was gradually handed over to laymen. Clearly immense changes had been introduced into the religious and intellectual realm described in the chapter on colonial culture.

Advancement of Science. Appropriate to the industrial age, natural science flourished in every form — chemistry, physics, biology, geology, botany, astronomy, and all the other branches. Courses in these subjects were given in high schools and colleges, richly equipped laboratories were established to foster research in such fields, and journals were founded to awaken scientific interest and spread the results of investigation among the people.

New scientific theories filled the air, that of evolution attracting the most attention. This hypothesis was fully expounded by

Charles Darwin, an English scholar, in the *Origin of Species,* which he published in 1859. Darwin held that the various species of animals on the earth had reached their present stage slowly through thousands of years of change from earlier forms of life. Some Christians, usually known as Fundamentalists, strenuously opposed such theories on the ground that they were contrary to the Bible or were at best mere guesses that could not be proved. But other Christians, called Modernists, said that most of the scientific ideas could be squared "with a liberal interpretation of God's Word." Under Fundamentalist influences Tennessee and Arkansas passed laws against teaching the doctrine of evolution in the schools supported wholly or in part by public funds; and debates over the subject made "live news" for the papers.

In keeping with the tradition started by Franklin natural science in America remained largely practical in its nature — that is, devoted primarily to useful inventions. Scarcely a year passed between 1865 and our own time without some sensational invention or scientific application. We shall name just a few. In 1876 Alexander Graham Bell sent his first telephone message by wire. In 1877 Thomas Edison heard "Mary had a little lamb" on his phonograph. In 1893 Henry Ford tested his first automobile on the road. In 1894 C. F. Jenkins gave a motion-picture show with his new machine at Richmond, Indiana. In 1902 a wireless message was sent across the Atlantic. In 1908 the Wright brothers made the "first public flight" with their aircraft at Fort Myer near Washington. In 1915 the sound of the human voice sped from New York to San Francisco by telephone and in 1927 from New York to London by wireless. In 1927 Colonel Charles Lindbergh flew from New York to Paris in less than thirty-four hours, and in 1932 Mrs. Amelia Earhart Putnam flew from Harbor Grace to Ireland in less than fifteen hours. In 1932 Captain James G. Haizlip flew from Los Angeles to New York in a little more than ten hours — a thrilling comparison with the old sea voyage around Cape Horn or the wagon trip across mountain, plain, and desert. By the use of the scientific method in medicine and public health, life was lengthened and suffering reduced. In 1901 the average American citizen could expect to live forty-eight years; in 1925 his expectation of life was fifty-eight years — an increase due in no small measure to medicine and sanitation.

While invention and practical application played the chief rôle in American science, great encouragement was also given to what was known as "pure science" — inquiry into the ways of

Photograph from Wide World Photos

"We" — Colonel Lindbergh and the Plane in Which He Crossed the Atlantic

nature without interest in useful ends. This assistance took the form of university laboratories, often magnificently equipped for every kind of speculative research, the foundation of research fellowships, and the creation of special endowments for investigation. There was no longer ground for Franklin's lament that the New World lacked implements for experimenting. And that some Americans were capable of noteworthy achievement in this field was attested by the award of the Nobel Prize, established in 1896, to four men of science: to A. A. Michelson and R. A. Millikan in physics; T. W. Richards in chemistry; and Alexis Carrel in medicine. Nevertheless, in spite of its splendid facilities for work, the United States lagged behind the leading nations

Photograph from Wide World Photos

Dr. R. A. Millikan in the Norman Bridge Laboratory of Physics at the California Institute of Technology

of the Old World in the realm of pure science. Money and laboratories did not automatically produce profound thinking; Pierre and Marie Curie discovered radium although they had only a crude little workshop in Paris.

Social and Economic Thinking. While inventors and manufacturers were extending the range of things the public could buy, thoughtful people were puzzling over the character of the civilization that was now taking shape. A growing concern about human welfare was manifest in the vast output of books, articles, and courses of instruction on such matters as capital and labor, feminism, social reform, the improvement of government, international relations, the arts, war and peace, imperialism, history, sociology, and ethics. If Chicago and San Francisco seem far removed from colonial Jamestown and Plymouth, nothing shows it better than the types of books written for boys and girls in the twentieth century in comparison with such a lone "juvenile" of the colonial age as the Catechism. Throughout the nation, teachers, editors, and other specialists were prying and inquiring into all manner of political and social questions — describing the changes that had been taking place, propounding new theories of society and education, and suggesting improvements in American ways of working and living and thinking. For the ancient tradition of sticking fast to the ways of the past was substituted to an amazing degree the idea of continual progress in all lines. For the poet's old creed that "whatever is is right" was substituted the modern belief that "whatever is can be improved."

History and Social Studies. All this discussion of social and economic questions, illuminated by the spirit of science, made nothing short of a revolution in the writing of history. Once it consisted mainly in telling exciting stories about heroes, warriors and politicians and it was thought that anybody who was fairly literate was fitted to be a historian. Moreover it was believed that his sole function was to praise his native land and his political party, to show that they were always right, and then to paint his foes in dark hues. But with the spread of the scientific spirit into the study of human affairs and with the multiplication of university chairs for research, historians began to declare that their prime duty was to discover the truth — to see things if possible as they actually were in the past — to understand rather than blindly to glorify or condemn. With this ideal in mind, they went straight to the sources for information, that is, to the original letters, papers, and documents of the people whose age they were seeking to describe, and from these sources they tried to build up a correct account of how things came to pass and why. Naturally this kind of history made duller reading than dashing romances or sentimental yarns told without respect to facts.

The rôle of romance in history was also reduced by the growing interest in "social studies" — in the problems of modern democracy, business enterprise, labor conditions, economic issues, municipal government, agricultural difficulties, feminism, and kindred matters. In treating such subjects writers were not dealing with flashing heroes and handsome heroines but with the masses of people engaged in the daily quest for food, clothing, shelter, and a fuller life. An account of the government regulation of railway rates, for example, may not be as uproarious as a tale about the shooting up of an Indian camp but it is likely to be a great deal more important. And interest was clearly veering in that direction, turning popular attention to the majestic crossword puzzles which American democracy must try to solve. From this standpoint it is an intellectual adventure to consult the catalogue of any large public library under such heads as Commerce, Business, Agriculture, Woman, Municipal Government, Railways or Social Studies.

EDUCATION

Colleges and Universities. Economic and intellectual changes of such magnitude inevitably influenced every phase of education. With some of the enormous wealth accumulated in industry, rich men and women founded new colleges. Sometimes these institutions were organized on novel principles; for example, Johns Hopkins University, the gift of a business man of Baltimore, was dedicated especially to science. But as a rule wealthy benefactors bestowed their millions on the older colleges, like Harvard, Yale, Princeton, Columbia, and Chicago; and in the process boards of trustees were generally widened to include members of various religious denominations so that these institutions tended to lose their sectarian aims and to swing over to secular objects, including business education. A third development of this industrial age was the rapid multiplication of technical schools — a development aided by the Morrill Act passed by Congress in 1862, which set aside large areas of public land to aid in industrial,

"The Magic City"
The lower New York skyline

JOAN OF ARC

A statue by Anna Hyatt which stands on Riverside Drive, New York

mechanical, and agricultural education. Not to be outdone by the rich, legislatures steadily raised their grants to the state colleges, enabling them better to compete with the institutions founded and maintained by millionaires. A fourth feature of educational development was the multiplication of colleges for women, following the establishment of Vassar in 1867.

As this wealth flowed into higher learning, laboratories, theaters, museums, and libraries were added to the colleges. Not only were the institutions bigger and richer; they taught more subjects and gave the students a freer choice. When Charles W. Eliot became president of Harvard in 1869 he started a revolution in that college by broadening the curriculum, with its limited courses in Greek, Latin, mathematics, logic, and religion, to cover all the interests of society — law, engineering, economics, sociology, political science, domestic science, business, drama, music, and the fine arts. At the opening of the twentieth century a college catalogue looked very much like an index to an encyclopedia. Moreover university presidents, such as Dr. Eliot, and teachers, such as William James and John Dewey, had become leaders in intellectual and social movements.

Secondary Schools. Equally striking was the great development in secondary education. The principle had been established in the period of Jacksonian Democracy that all children should have free elementary education; and it was applied in every part of the country by the succeeding age, out of its greater riches. The loyal labors of teachers made possible by huge funds can be partly recorded in figures. In 1880 seventeen per cent of the people over ten years of age were illiterate, that is, could not read and write; but in forty years the number was brought down almost to six per cent. When the "intelligence tests," used in the army during the World War, disclosed a still appalling lack of education among the soldiers, a cry went up for a redoubled assault on illiteracy and within ten years the annual outlay for public schools multiplied almost three times — from $750,000,000 to $2,000,000,000. What a sweep this represented from the poor little log schools of colonial days built for the few to the great public schools now built for all!

With this expansion of elementary education ran a remarkable rise in public high schools to carry training above the grades. When Lincoln was inaugurated there were only about one hundred such schools in the country; by 1880 there were eight hundred; at the opening of the present century the figure had passed six thousand and was mounting. In 1927 the number of boys and girls in the high schools of the country reached the total of four millions. Besides preparing pupils for colleges, the high schools

An Up-to-date High School in Birmingham, Alabama

were offering courses in the practical arts for those who were going immediately into occupations. If Henry Barnard and Mary Lyon could have returned to earth they would have found that the seed sown in the Middle Period had sprung up a thousandfold.

Adult Education. *Why Stop Learning?* is the query of a book by Dorothy Canfield Fisher published in 1927. She answers her own question by showing that education is extended in many ways to people who have completed their formal "schooling." Though a large proportion of Americans had been made literate, it was realized that beyond the classroom was another long "stretch of road leading toward an educated citizenry." And this way was lined with correspondence schools, university extension schools, continuation classes, lecture lyceums, women's clubs, Chautauquas, summer courses, and other aids to continuous learning.

Self-education is assisted in modern times by museums and free libraries as never before. When P. T. Barnum exhibited the first hippopotamus to bewildered Americans he laid the basis of the present-day zoölogical garden and natural history museum which are such important supplements to textbook work in science. Private gifts and public grants made it possible for every large city in the United States with any pretension whatever to culture to erect a popular library and usually a museum too. With readers' guides, trained library assistants, and collections of books in every field freely available to the masses, America was leading in many forms of adult education. In museums with their maze of paintings, furniture, textiles, porcelains, glass, jewelry, and other specimens of the work from all ages and climes, even the casual visitor has his view of the universe enlarged, while students draw inspiration for creative work in their turn. Pictures of Lincoln, with a handful of books, reading in a log cabin by the firelight, flash through the mind as one watches groups of school children and adults receiving explanations of Egyptian, Greek, and Oriental civilizations in libraries and museums well stocked and free as air!

Journalism. The popularization of learning was carried by invention into the realm of publishing. Four specific changes in the printing industry worked for mass production of newspapers and periodicals while reducing their cost. As early as 1867 paper made from wood pulp was used on presses and, owing to improvements in manufacturing, its price fell from about seventeen cents a pound at that date to less than two cents at the end of the century. The slow setting of type by hand was doomed in 1886, while Grover Cleveland was President, when Ottmar Mergenthaler placed in the office of the New York *Tribune* his linotype machine. Until then printers had been compelled to pick out each letter from a little box and fix it in place by hand. Now an operator could set type by pressing keys. A third extraordinary invention was the film to be substituted for the plate in photography, making possible cheap and exact illustrations. Then came quick engraving processes, especially by chemical methods, which freed publishers from dependence on the slow hand labor and enabled them to transform photographs almost instantaneously into "cuts" for printing. In fifty years the advances of four centuries were outstripped. In addition, the growth of business enterprise provided so much advertising that publishers favored with sufficient patronage could sell their papers below the cost of manufacture.

More people were learning to read, paper was cheaper, and journalists now tried to reach the largest possible audience. One

MODEL OF THE FIRST TELEPHONE

result was the rise of the sensational press, known as "yellow journalism." It specialized in crime, scandal, and adventure and advertised itself by the use of big type, flaming headlines, and crude drawings to attract the eye. Technology and democracy also invaded the magazine world and the outcome was the rise of popular weeklies and monthlies. The older periodicals had been heavy and serious and sold at a price beyond the reach of the man in the street and the woman in the kitchen. Now new national weeklies — illustrated and full of lively stories — were put on the market to sell for a few cents, some bidding for a circulation on a national scale and winning millions of subscribers. In the search for buyers, if not readers, publishers made more extensive use of illustrations. In 1884 the New York *World* introduced the cartoon as a regular feature and before many years the portrayal of the passing show in pictures spread from one end of the country to the other. Another radical departure was made in 1918 when the first illustrated daily, or "tabloid," appeared on the streets of New York, appealing to people who liked poster headlines, cartoons, comic strips, and other forms of picture writing. At last there were newspapers and magazines for the millions. Yet while the popular press flourished, the number of special and technical journals appealing to the higher intellectual interests multiplied also; there was not a science, art, religious faith, or economic reform which did not have its periodicals.

LITERATURE AND THE ARTS

Fiction. For readers in the greatest hurry the short story — a kind of miniature word-painting — was perfected and it rose to a fine art in America in the rushing era of the machine. Novels too came from the presses as thick as autumn leaves. Every section of the country, every phase of life, and most of the problems of the age were discussed by writers of fiction. Mark Twain covered no small part of the American scene: the Far West of early days in his *Roughing It;* life on the Mississippi in many a tale; and political corruption of reconstruction days in *The Gilded Age.* Machine civilization was glorified in a socialistic novel by Edward Bellamy, called *Looking Backward.* New riches, the growth of divorce, and the ambitions of "social climbers" were treated by Edith Wharton. Puritan New England, creole circles in New Orleans, pioneer schools in Indiana, the struggles of the Southern aristocracy through the poverty after the Civil War, life on the Main Streets of small towns, the hustling business man, the idle wife, strife between capital and labor, scandals in politics and industry, and the problems of women were all woven into novels so fully and so vividly that one could almost write a history of the period from fiction alone. Illuminating criticism of American modes and manners is to be found in this "imaginative" literature.

Poetry. After Edgar Allan Poe, Walt Whitman, and the New England school passed away there was a marked decline in poetry — to which Sidney Lanier of Georgia offered one of the few exceptions. But at the opening of the twentieth century came an outburst of rhyming and singing that seemed the harbinger of a true age of poetry. Edgar Lee Masters of Kansas and Carl Sandburg and Vachel Lindsay of Illinois in bold free verse celebrated heroes of the common life and painted the ruthless march of business enterprise in lurid colors. The feminist, Edna St. Vincent Millay, began during her student days at Vassar to "laugh and laugh into the sky" but in her later lyrics and ballads dwelt upon the tragedies as well as the liberties of mankind. If James Whitcomb Riley of Indiana could write of the simple life in lines of great popular vogue, William Vaughn Moody, born in the same state, could bring a fine, brooding spirit of appraisal to bear on the struggles of the industrial age.

The Drama. A number of things conspired to make the drama less rich in imagination than the other branches of literature. The old-fashioned stock company, composed of actors and actresses who traveled about giving plays that suited their fancies and talents, was now generally driven to the wall by the big theatrical manager who supplied capital, bought "strings of theaters," chose his own "stars," and chose plays that promised the largest box-office receipts. Then the moving picture — with its demand for "snappy stuff," movement, spectacles, and action — left little or no room for ingenious dialogue, for the play of mind, which gave distinction to the finest dramas. Broadly speaking, the plays of the latest age were built on a few routine ideas that appealed to the widest possible audiences; as one experienced actor put it: on "(1) tears, (2) laughs, and (3) thrills." Moreover in the epoch of quick lunches, automobiles, and flying machines, Shakespeare and tragedy almost disappeared to make room for light sketches that amused without straining the mind. It is true that there were notable exceptions; but efforts to reproduce on the stage the more complex human and social problems discussed in novels were "few and far between."

Painting and Drawing. From the same wealth that supplied laboratories for science and endowments for colleges were provided schools for the study of art. At the opening of the twentieth century nearly every section of the country offered facilities for instruction in all its branches. And out of the thousands of aspiring boys and girls who tried their talents in this sphere, many won fame and honor. It is hardly fair to choose from the long list any names for special mention but undoubtedly John S. Sargent, J. A. M. Whistler and John La Farge stand high on the record. They won prizes, commissions, and recognition in two hemispheres — "all the honors that come to artists." And these three men represent three stages of the artistic movement. Sargent painted portraits in the grand style so long in favor; Whistler was an "impressionist" seeking to convey the mood of what he

THE AUTOMOBILE AGE — PARKING CARS DOWNTOWN IN CLEVELAND

saw; La Farge was a scientist experimenting in his own factory with glass and other materials and breaking light with his brush as he saw it broken in the spectrum. Nor must we overlook the etchings and drawings of Joseph Pennell who portrayed the skyscrapers, mills, and giant industries of business enterprise (opposite page 478). Finally a school devoted to the modern art, still borrowing heavily from Europe, sought to reproduce on canvas and in commercial designs the motion, science, colors, materials, forms, and machines of the new industrial civilization.

Sculpture. In speaking of the arts, we have not mentioned sculpture up to this point because it was late in reaching distinction. Although several satisfactory American artists could be discovered to paint George Washington, it was thought necessary to import a Frenchman, Houdon, to immortalize him in marble. It is true that in the Middle Period work showing competence was done in stone and metal, but opportunities for accomplishment were sadly limited. It was the World's Fair at Chicago in 1892 that first gave American sculptors great responsibilities in the form of commissions to decorate public buildings — a dream city in which they were permitted to express their noblest imaginings. After that experience American sculptors displayed finer skill and won wider acclaim, women showing a peculiar talent for the requirements of the art. Among the best-known men in this field were George Grey Barnard, Daniel Chester French, Lorado Taft, and Jo Davidson; among the women, Anna Hyatt, Janet Scudder, and Mrs. Harry Payne Whitney. At the opening of the new century, the continent was being adorned by figures of military heroes, statesmen, pioneer mothers, Indians, war memorials, symbolic compositions, and every sort of sculpture that human fancy could devise.

Architecture. It was in architecture that American artists wrought their most brilliant achievements. When sufficient wealth had been amassed to make a selection of grand designs possible, our architects imitated European styles, tried to hold down the height of buildings, and decorated them after the fashion of Venetian or Parisian palaces. But the rising value of land in the cities, the perfection of elevators, and advances in steel construction forced them to accept height and bulk. So in 1902 the strange Flatiron Building was erected in New York — forerunner of structures higher and higher, more venturesome and more fantastic, until in 1913 the mighty Woolworth Tower was lifted sixty stories above the sidewalks of that city. When lofty towers such as these sprang up thick and fast, the streets were in danger of becoming dark canyons, and in the interest of light and air, builders were required to "step back" their structures every few stories. As a result of this practice skyscraper centers became mazes of staggered monoliths and turrets. Even churches adopted the new mode in order that their spires might not be lost in the wilderness, and finally the buildings for the "Century of Progress" Exposition at Chicago in 1933 were designed in the sharp, angular style appropriate to the mechanical age.

City Planning. Nor was this artistic interest limited to buildings. There was a decided revival of enthusiasm for city planning, the art so sadly neglected after L'Enfant laid the groundwork for the city of Washington. For a hundred years most cities had just grown up haphazard without much reference to convenience or beauty or health. At the opening of the twentieth century there was no regular city-planning office in any American city but within twenty-five years more than two hundred cities had planning agencies and a number had begun reconstruction along better lines drawn by competent minds and hands. In that span of time the profession of city planning had won public recognition; a national society for its promotion had been formed; a journal had been established; and a small library of books had been written on the subject. Cities began to divide the land within their borders into "zones," to limit the height and nature of buildings, and to widen streets so that sunlight and air might enter dark corners. Engineers were talking about "regional planning," that is the systematic control of broad areas around cities on principles of public welfare. Even the word "nation planning" had been coined.

Beyond all doubt, Lincoln's high resolve that the government of the people should not perish from the earth was now supplemented by a resolve equally firm that the standard of life for the people should be raised, that the benefits of civilization should be more equitably distributed, that science should be brought with increasing directness to the service of humanity, and that the quest for beauty in life and work should be as zealous as the pursuit of liberty.

SUMMARY OF PROGRESSIVE DEMOCRACY AND FOREIGN RELATIONS

The industrial progress of the period following the Civil War bequeathed to the new generation many problems connected with the growth of trusts and railways, the accumulation of great fortunes, the increase of poverty in industrial cities, the exhaustion of the free land, and the acquisition of dominions in distant seas. As long as there was an abundance of land in the West any able-bodied man with initiative and industry could become an independent farmer. People from the cities and immigrants from Europe had always before them that gateway to property and prosperity. When the free arable land had disappeared, about 1890, the country faced an entirely novel situation.

Though the new economic questions had been vigorously debated in many circles before his day, it was Theodore Roosevelt who first discussed them continuously from the White House. The natural resources of the country were being exhausted; he advocated their conservation. Huge fortunes were being made in business creating inequalities in opportunity; he favored reducing them by income and inheritance taxes. Industries were disturbed by strikes; he pressed arbitration upon capital and labor. There was no more free land; he declared that labor was in a less favorable position to bargain with capital and therefore should organize in unions for collective bargaining. There had been wrongdoing on the part of certain great trusts; those responsible should be punished.

The spirit of reform was abroad in the land. The spoils system was attacked. It was alleged that the political parties were dominated by "rings and bosses." The United States Senate was called a "millionaires' club." Poverty and misery were observed in the cities. State legislatures and city governments were accused of corruption.

In answer to the charges, remedies were proposed and adopted. Civil-service reform was approved. The Australian ballot, popular election of Senators, the initiative, referendum, and recall, commission and city-manager plans for cities, public regulation of railways, compensation for those injured in industries, minimum wages for women and children, pensions for widows, the control of housing in the cities — these and a hundred other reforms were adopted and tried out. The national watchword became: "America, Improve Thyself."

The spirit of reform broke into both political parties. It

appeared in many statutes enacted by Congress under President Taft's leadership. It disrupted the Republicans temporarily in 1912 when the Progressive party entered the field. It led the Democratic candidate in that year, Governor Wilson, to make a "progressive appeal" to the voters. It inspired a considerable program of national legislation under President Wilson's two administrations.

In the age of change, four important amendments to the federal Constitution, the first in more than forty years, were adopted. The sixteenth empowered Congress to lay an income tax. The seventeenth assured popular election of Senators. The eighteenth made prohibition national. The nineteenth, following upon the adoption of woman suffrage in many states, enfranchised the women of the nation.

In the sphere of industry, equally great changes took place. The major portion of the nation's business passed into the hands of corporations. In many of the leading industries of the country labor was organized in trade unions and federated in a national organization. The power of organized capital and organized labor loomed upon the horizon. Their struggles, their rights, and their place in the economy of the nation raised problems of the first magnitude. Then company unions complicated the situation.

While the country was engaged in debating its domestic issues, the World War broke out in Europe in 1914. As a hundred years before, American rights upon the high seas became involved at once. They were invaded on both sides; but Germany, in addition to attacking American ships and property, ruthlessly destroyed American lives. Warnings from President Wilson were without avail. In January, 1917, the German government announced an unrestricted submarine campaign.

After long and patient negotiations, Wilson in April, 1917, called upon the nation to take up arms against an assailant that was in effect making war upon America. The answer was swift and firm. The national resources, human and material, were mobilized. The navy was enlarged, a draft army created, huge loans floated, heavy taxes laid, and the spirit of sacrifice called forth in the titanic struggle.

In the end, American financial, naval, and military assistance counted heavily in the scale. American sailors scoured the seas searching for the terrible submarines. American soldiers took part in the last great drives that broke the might of Germany's army. Such was the nation's response to the President's summons to arms in a war "for democracy" and "to end war."

When victory crowned the arms of the powers united against Germany, President Wilson in person took part in the peace council. He sought to redeem his pledge to end wars by forming a League of Nations to keep the peace. In the treaty drawn at the close of the war the first part was a covenant binding the nations in a permanent association for the settlement of international disputes. This treaty the President offered to the United States Senate for ratification and to his country for approval.

Once again, as in the days of the Napoleonic wars, the people seriously discussed the place of America among the powers of the earth. The Senate refused to ratify the treaty. World politics then became an issue in the campaign of 1920. Though some Americans talked as if the United States could close its doors and windows against all mankind, the victor in the election, Senator Harding, of Ohio, knew better. The election returns were scarcely announced before he began to ask the advice of his countrymen on the pressing theme that would not be downed: "What part shall the United States — first among the nations in wealth and material power — assume at the council table of the world?"

President Harding called a conference of nine important naval powers in 1921 to bring about a limitation of naval armaments. This Washington conference resulted in an agreement to limit the building of battleships for ten years, and in a "four-power treaty" regarding problems of the Pacific. Under his successor, President Coolidge, the promotion of peace resulted in the signature of the Kellogg Pact in 1929 renouncing war as an instrument of national policy and pledging the great powers of the world to the pacific settlement of international disputes. The next year, Great Britain, Japan, and the United States, at a conference in London, agreed to a limitation of cruisers, destroyers, and submarines.

Among other questions of the age were the adjustment of the debts due to the United States from the Allies, a further reduction of armaments, which were huge in size, in spite of previous efforts at limitation, and the establishment of more friendly relations with Latin America. Notwithstanding all efforts at the peaceful settlement of international disputes, Japan made war in China in 1931, claiming that she was protecting Japanese lives and property against Chinese bandits, and attempts to stop her action failed. When the government of the United States and the League of Nations protested and asserted that the action of Japan violated various treaties, the Japanese government withdrew from the League in 1933 and continued in her course.

In domestic affairs many problems arising from the war had to be met — the reduction of the army, a bonus for soldiers, taxation, the repeal of war legislation, and the relation of business to the changing order. The tariff was revised upward, twice, according to Republican principles. Railways were returned to their owners. Federal aid was granted to the merchant marine. The troublesome issue of farm relief, raised by the long continued depression in agriculture, came to the front, and an effort was made to deal with it by the Marketing Act of 1929. A business depression which set in during the autumn of that year slowed down industries, threw millions of men and women out of work, pushed the prices of agricultural produce down, and spread distress far and wide throughout the country. Meanwhile the subject of prohibition was continually discussed and at length in 1933 the Eighteenth Amendment was repealed.

As the months passed the depression grew worse. Immediately after his inauguration, President Franklin D. Roosevelt induced Congress to pass many laws designed to cope with its evils. Aid was given to farmers burdened with debts and suffering from poverty due to the low prices of their produce. The federal government took charge of banks and lent money to many. It sought to bring industries together and stimulate them into greater activity. It provided employment for thousands in reforesting waste lands and building public works. It granted millions of dollars to furnish food, clothing, and shelter for the impoverished.

Amid all the debates over politics and wars, religious, intellectual, and artistic interests were promoted in terms of the industrial age. Elementary education was extended by enlarged appropriations of money; high schools were founded; new colleges and universities were created. Adult education through libraries, journals, museums, and other agencies was advanced, reaching an ever-widening area of the people. Literature and the fine arts flowered. Speaking at the dedication of the Bok Singing Tower in Florida, in 1929, President Coolidge urged upon the nation "a deeper realization of the value and power of beauty." On all sides writers, philosophers, and artists were discussing civilization, culture, and the good life, when a new business depression raised fateful questions.

How can America remove the great blots on civilization: poverty, unemployment, misery, and uncertainty for millions of the people? How can the American ideal of government by the people and for popular welfare be more fully realized? What part must leaders in education, science, letters, and the arts play in the effort to abolish misery and bring "the abundant life," to millions in despair, as President Roosevelt has put the case? By such questions, the easy-going optimism of the old days was challenged after 1929, and the nation was once more called upon to face grave problems of government and economy.

References

Cambridge History of American Literature. Vols. III and IV.

E. P. Cubberley, *Public Education in the United States.*

H. E. Barnes (Editor), *History and Prospects of the Social Sciences* and the *New History and Social Studies.*

W. Kaempffert, *A Popular History of Invention.*

J. M. Lee, *History of American Journalism.*

S. Isham, *History of American Painting.*

Lorado Taft, *History of American Sculpture.*

T. F. Tallmadge, *Story of Architecture in America.*

E. Weitenkampf, *American Graphic Art.*

N. P. Lewis, *The Planning of the Modern City.*

APPENDIX

CONSTITUTION OF THE UNITED STATES

We the people of the United States, in order to form a more perfect union, establish justice, insure domestic tranquillity, provide for the common defence, promote the general welfare, and secure the blessings of liberty to ourselves and our posterity, do ordain and establish this Constitution for the United States of America.

ARTICLE I

SECTION 1. All legislative powers herein granted shall be vested in a Congress of the United States, which shall consist of a Senate and House of Representatives.

SECTION 2. 1. The House of Representatives shall be composed of members chosen every second year by the people of the several States, and the electors in each State shall have the qualifications requisite for electors of the most numerous branch of the State legislature.

2. No person shall be a representative who shall not have attained to the age of twenty-five years, and been seven years a citizen of the United States, and who shall not, when elected, be an inhabitant of that State in which he shall be chosen.

3. Representatives and direct taxes [1] shall be apportioned among the several States which may be included within this Union, according to their respective numbers, which shall be determined by adding to the whole number of free persons, including those bound to service for a term of years, and excluding Indians not taxed, three-fifths of all other persons.[1] The actual enumeration shall be made within three years after the first meeting of the Congress of the United States, and within every subsequent term of ten years, in such manner as they shall by law direct. The number of representatives shall not exceed one for every thirty thousand, but each State shall have at least one representative; and until such enumeration shall be made, the State of New Hampshire shall be entitled to choose three, Massachusetts eight, Rhode Island and Providence Plantations one, Connecticut five, New York six, New Jersey four, Pennsylvania eight, Delaware one, Maryland six, Virginia ten, North Carolina five, South Carolina five, and Georgia three.

[1] Partly superseded by the 14th Amendment, page xiii.

i

4. When vacancies happen in the representation from any State, the executive authority thereof shall issue writs of election to fill such vacancies.

5. The House of Representatives shall choose their speaker and other officers; and shall have the sole power of impeachment.

SECTION 3. 1. The Senate of the United States shall be composed of two senators from each State, chosen by the legislature thereof, for six years; and each senator shall have one vote.[1]

2. Immediately after they shall be assembled in consequence of the first election, they shall be divided as equally as may be into three classes. The seats of the senators of the first class shall be vacated at the expiration of the second year, of the second class at the expiration of the fourth year, and of the third class at the expiration of the sixth year, so that one-third may be chosen every second year; and if vacancies happen by resignation, or otherwise, during the recess of the legislature of any State, the executive thereof may make temporary appointments until the next meeting of the legislature, which shall then fill such vacancies.[2]

3. No person shall be a senator who shall not have attained to the age of thirty years, and been nine years a citizen of the United States, and who shall not, when elected, be an inhabitant of that State for which he shall be chosen.

4. The Vice-President of the United States shall be President of the Senate, but shall have no vote, unless they be equally divided.

5. The Senate shall choose their other officers, and also a President *pro tempore*, in the absence of the Vice-President, or when he shall exercise the office of President of the United States.

6. The Senate shall have the sole power to try all impeachments. When sitting for that purpose, they shall be on oath or affirmation. When the President of the United States is tried, the chief justice shall preside : And no person shall be convicted without the concurrence of two-thirds of the members present.

7. Judgment in cases of impeachment shall not extend further than to removal from office, and disqualification to hold and enjoy any office of honor, trust, or profit under the United States : but the party convicted shall nevertheless be liable and subject to indictment, trial, judgment, and punishment, according to law.

SECTION 4. 1. The times, places, and manner of holding elections for senators and representatives, shall be prescribed in each State by the legislature thereof; but the Congress may at any time by law make or alter such regulations, except as to the places of choosing senators.

2. The Congress shall assemble at least once in every year, and such meeting shall be on the first Monday in December, unless they shall by law appoint a different day.

[1] See the 17th Amendment, page xv.   [2] *Ibid.*, page xv.

SECTION 5. 1. Each House shall be the judge of the elections, returns and qualifications of its own members, and a majority of each shall constitute a quorum to do business; but a smaller number may adjourn from day to day, and may be authorized to compel the attendance of absent members, in such manner, and under such penalties as each House may provide.

2. Each House may determine the rules of its proceedings, punish its members for disorderly behaviour, and, with the concurrence of two-thirds, expel a member.

3. Each House shall keep a journal of its proceedings, and from time to time publish the same, excepting such parts as may in their judgment require secrecy; and the yeas and nays of the members of either House on any question shall, at the desire of one-fifth of those present, be entered on the journal.

4. Neither House, during the session of Congress, shall, without the consent of the other, adjourn for more than three days, nor to any other place than that in which the two Houses shall be sitting.

SECTION 6. 1. The senators and representatives shall receive a compensation for their services, to be ascertained by law, and paid out of the Treasury of the United States. They shall in all cases, except treason, felony, and breach of the peace, be privileged from arrest during their attendance at the sessions of their respective Houses, and in going to and returning from the same; and, for any speech or debate in either House, they shall not be questioned in any other place.

2. No senator or representative shall, during the time for which he was elected, be appointed to any civil office under the authority of the United States, which shall have been created, or the emoluments whereof shall have been increased during such time; and no person, holding any office under the United States, shall be a member of either House during his continuance in office.

SECTION 7. 1. All bills for raising revenue shall originate in the House of Representatives; but the Senate may propose or concur with amendments as on other bills.

2. Every bill, which shall have passed the House of Representatives and the Senate, shall, before it become a law, be presented to the President of the United States; if he approve he shall sign it, but if not he shall return it with his objections to that House, in which it shall have originated, who shall enter the objections at large on their journal, and proceed to reconsider it. If after such reconsideration two-thirds of that House shall agree to pass the bill, it shall be sent, together with the objections, to the other House, by which it shall likewise be reconsidered, and if approved by two-thirds of that House, it shall become a law. But in all such cases the votes of both Houses shall be determined by yeas and nays, and the names

of the persons voting for and against the bill shall be entered on the journal of each House respectively. If any bill shall not be returned by the President within ten days (Sundays excepted) after it shall have been presented to him, the same shall be a law, in like manner as if he had signed it, unless the Congress by their adjournment prevent its return, in which case it shall not be a law.

3. Every order, resolution, or vote to which the concurrence of the Senate and House of Representatives may be necessary (except on a question of adjournment) shall be presented to the President of the United States and before the same shall take effect, shall be approved by him, or being disapproved by him, shall be repassed by two-thirds of the Senate and House of Representatives, according to the rules and limitations prescribed in the case of a bill.

Section 8. The Congress shall have power: 1. To lay and collect taxes, duties, imposts, and excises, to pay the debts and provide for the common defence and general welfare of the United States; but all duties, imposts, and excises shall be uniform throughout the United States;

2. To borrow money on the credit of the United States;

3. To regulate commerce with foreign nations, and among the several States, and with the Indian tribes;

4. To establish an uniform rule of naturalization, and uniform laws on the subject of bankruptcies throughout the United States;

5. To coin money, regulate the value thereof, and of foreign coin, and fix the standard of weights and measures;

6. To provide for the punishment of counterfeiting the securities and current coin of the United States;

7. To establish post offices and post roads;

8. To promote the progress of science and useful arts by securing for limited times to authors and inventors the exclusive right to their respective writings and discoveries;

9. To constitute tribunals inferior to the Supreme Court;

10. To define and punish piracies and felonies committed on the high seas, and offences against the law of nations;

11. To declare war, grant letters of marque and reprisal, and make rules concerning captures on land and water;

12. To raise and support armies, but no appropriation of money to that use shall be for a longer term than two years;

13. To provide and maintain a navy;

14. To make rules for the government and regulation of the land and naval forces;

15. To provide for calling forth the militia to execute the laws of the Union, suppress insurrections, and repel invasions;

16. To provide for organizing, arming, and disciplining the militia,

and for governing such part of them as may be employed in the service of the United States, reserving to the States respectively the appointment of the officers, and the authority of training the militia according to the discipline prescribed by Congress.

17. To exercise exclusive legislation in all cases whatsoever, over such district (not exceeding ten miles square) as may, by cession of particular States and the acceptance of Congress, become the seat of the government of the United States, and to exercise like authority over all places purchased by the consent of the legislature of the State in which the same shall be, for the erection of forts, magazines, arsenals, dock-yards, and other needful buildings; — and

18. To make all laws which shall be necessary and proper for carrying into execution the foregoing powers, and all other powers vested by this Constitution in the government of the United States, or in any department or officer thereof.

SECTION 9. 1. The migration or importation of such persons as any of the States now existing shall think proper to admit, shall not be prohibited by the Congress prior to the year one thousand eight hundred and eight, but a tax or duty may be imposed on such importation, not exceeding ten dollars for each person.

2. The privilege of the writ of *habeas corpus* shall not be suspended, unless when in cases of rebellion or invasion the public safety may require it.

3. No bill of attainder or *ex post facto* law shall be passed.

4. No capitation, or other direct, tax shall be laid, unless in proportion to the census or enumeration hereinbefore directed to be taken.[1]

5. No tax or duty shall be laid on articles exported from any State.

6. No preference shall be given by any regulation of commerce or revenue to the ports of one State over those of another : nor shall vessels bound to, or from, one State, be obliged to enter, clear, or pay duties in another.

7. No money shall be drawn from the Treasury, but in consequence of appropriations made by law; and a regular statement and account of the receipts and expenditures of all public money shall be published from time to time.

8. No title of nobility shall be granted by the United States; and no person, holding any office of profit or trust under them, shall, without the consent of the Congress, accept of any present, emolument, office, or title, of any kind whatever, from any king, prince, or foreign State.

SECTION 10. 1. No State shall enter into any treaty, alliance, or confederation; grant letters of marque and reprisal; coin money; emit bills of credit, make anything but gold and silver coin a tender in payment

---

[1] See the 16th Amendment, page xiv.

of debts; pass any bill of attainder, *ex post facto* law, or law impairing the obligation of contracts, or grant any title of nobility.

2. No State shall, without the consent of the Congress, lay any imposts or duties on imports or exports, except what may be absolutely necessary for executing its inspection laws: and the net produce of all duties and imposts, laid by any State on imports or exports, shall be for the use of the Treasury of the United States; and all such laws shall be subject to the revision and control of the Congress.

3. No State shall, without the consent of Congress, lay any duty of tonnage, keep troops, or ships of war in time of peace, enter into any agreement or compact with another State, or with a foreign power, or engage in war unless actually invaded, or in such imminent danger as will not admit of delay.

ARTICLE II

SECTION 1. 1. The executive power shall be vested in a President of the United States of America. He shall hold his office during the term of four years, and, together with the Vice-President, chosen for the same term, be elected, as follows:

2. Each State shall appoint, in such manner as the legislature thereof may direct, a number of electors, equal to the whole number of senators and representatives to which the State may be entitled in the Congress; but no senator or representative, or person holding an office of trust or profit under the United States, shall be appointed an elector.[1] The electors shall meet in their respective States, and vote by ballot for two persons, of whom one at least shall not be an inhabitant of the same State with themselves. And they shall make a list of all the persons voted for, and of the number of votes for each; which list they shall sign and certify, and transmit sealed to the seat of the government of the United States, directed to the president of the Senate. The President of the Senate shall, in the presence of the Senate and House of Representatives, open all the certificates, and the votes shall then be counted. The person having the greatest number of votes shall be the President, if such number be a majority of the whole number of electors appointed; and if there be more than one who have such majority, and have an equal number of votes, then the House of Representatives shall immediately choose by ballot one of them for President; and if no person have a majority, then from the five highest on the list the said House shall in like manner choose the President. But in choosing the President, the votes shall be taken by States, the representation from each State having one vote; a quorum for this purpose shall consist of a member or members from two-thirds of the States and a majority of all the States shall be necessary to a choice. In every case, after the

[1] The following paragraph was in force only from 1788 to 1803.

choice of the President, the person having the greatest number of votes of the electors shall be the Vice-President. But if there should remain two or more who have equal votes, the Senate shall choose from them by ballot the Vice-President.[1]

3. The Congress may determine the time of choosing the electors, and the day on which they shall give their votes; which day shall be the same throughout the United States.

4. No person except a natural born citizen, or a citizen of the United States, at the time of the adoption of this Constitution, shall be eligible to the office of President; neither shall any person be eligible to that office who shall not have attained to the age of thirty-five years, and been fourteen years a resident within the United States.

5. In case of the removal of the President from office, or of his death, resignation, or inability to discharge the powers and duties of the said office, the same shall devolve on the Vice-President, and the Congress may by law provide for the case of removal, death, resignation, or inability, both of the President and Vice-President, declaring what officer shall then act as President, and such officer shall act accordingly, until the disability be removed, or a President shall be elected.

6. The President shall, at stated times, receive for his services a compensation, which shall neither be increased nor diminished during the period for which he shall have been elected, and he shall not receive within that period any other emolument from the United States, or any of them.

7. Before he enter on the execution of his office, he shall take the following oath or affirmation: — "I do solemnly swear (or affirm) that I will faithfully execute the office of President of the United States, and will to the best of my ability, preserve, protect, and defend the Constitution of the United States."

SECTION 2. 1. The President shall be commander-in-chief of the army and navy of the United States, and of the militia of the several States, when called into the actual service of the United States; he may require the opinion, in writing, of the principal officer in each of the executive departments, upon any subject relating to the duties of their respective offices, and he shall have power to grant reprieves and pardons for offences against the United States, except in cases of impeachment.

2. He shall have power, by and with the advice and consent of the Senate, to make treaties, provided two-thirds of the senators present concur; and he shall nominate, and by and with the advice and consent of the Senate, shall appoint ambassadors, other public ministers and consuls, judges of the Supreme Court, and all other officers of the United States, whose appointments are not herein otherwise provided for, and which shall

[1] Superseded by the 12th Amendment, page xii.

be established by law : but the Congress may by law vest the appointment of such inferior officers, as they think proper, in the President alone, in the courts of law, or in the heads of departments.

3. The President shall have power to fill all vacancies that may happen during the recess of the Senate, by granting commissions which shall expire at the end of their next session.

SECTION 3. He shall from time to time give to the Congress information on the state of the Union, and recommend to their consideration such measures as he shall judge necessary and expedient; he may, on extraordinary occasions, convene both Houses, or either of them, and in case of disagreement between them, with respect to the time of adjournment, he may adjourn them to such time as he shall think proper; he shall receive ambassadors and other public ministers; he shall take care that the laws be faithfully executed, and shall commission all the officers of the United States.

SECTION 4. The President, Vice-President, and all civil officers of the United States shall be removed from office on impeachment for, and conviction of, treason, bribery, or other high crimes and misdemeanors.

ARTICLE III

SECTION 1. The judicial power of the United States shall be vested in one Supreme Court, and in such inferior courts as the Congress may from time to time ordain and establish. The judges, both of the Supreme and inferior courts, shall hold their offices during good behaviour, and shall, at stated times, receive for their services a compensation, which shall not be diminished during their continuance in office.

SECTION 2. 1. The judicial power shall extend to all cases, in law and equity, arising under this Constitution, the laws of the United States, and treaties made, or which shall be made, under their authority; — to all cases affecting ambassadors, other public ministers and consuls; — to all cases of admiralty and maritime jurisdiction; — to controversies to which the United States shall be a party; — to controversies between two or more States; — between a State and citizens of another State; [1] — between citizens of different States; — between citizens of the same State claiming lands under grants of different States; — and between a State, or the citizens thereof, and foreign States, citizens, or subjects.

2. In all cases affecting ambassadors, other public ministers and consuls and those in which a State shall be a party, the Supreme Court shall have original jurisdiction. In all the other cases before mentioned, the Supreme Court shall have appellate jurisdiction, both as to law and fact, with such exceptions and under such regulations as the Congress shall make.

[1] See the 11th Amendment, page xii.

3. The trial of all crimes, except in cases of impeachment, shall be by jury; and such trial shall be held in the State where the said crimes shall have been committed; but when not committed within any State, the trial shall be at such place or places as the Congress may by law have directed.

SECTION 3. 1. Treason against the United States shall consist only in levying war against them, or in adhering to their enemies, giving them aid and comfort. No person shall be convicted of treason unless on the testimony of two witnesses to the same overt act, or on confession in open court.

2. The Congress shall have power to declare the punishment of treason, but no attainder of treason shall work corruption of blood or forfeiture except during the life of the person attainted.

ARTICLE IV

SECTION 1. Full faith and credit shall be given in each State to the public acts, records, and judicial proceedings of every other State. And the Congress may by general laws prescribe the manner in which such acts, records, and proceedings shall be proved, and the effect thereof.

SECTION 2. 1. The citizens of each State shall be entitled to all privileges and immunities of citizens in the several States.

2. A person charged in any State with treason, felony, or other crime, who shall flee from justice, and be found in another State, shall on demand of the executive authority of the State from which he fled, be delivered up, to be removed to the State having jurisdiction of the crime.

3. No person held to service or labor in one State, under the laws thereof, escaping into another, shall, in consequence of any law or regulation therein, be discharged from such service or labor, but shall be delivered up on claim of the party to whom such service or labor may be due.

SECTION 3. 1. New States may be admitted by the Congress into this Union; but no new State shall be formed or erected within the jurisdiction of any other State; nor any State be formed by the junction of two or more States, or parts of States, without the consent of the legislatures of the States concerned as well as of the Congress.

2. The Congress shall have power to dispose of and make all needful rules and regulations respecting the territory or other property belonging to the United States; and nothing in this Constitution shall be so construed as to prejudice any claims of the United States, or of any particular State.

SECTION 4. The United States shall guarantee to every State in this Union a republican form of government, and shall protect each of them against invasion; and on application of the legislature, or of the executive (when the legislature cannot be convened), against domestic violence.

ARTICLE V

The Congress, whenever two-thirds of both Houses shall deem it necessary, shall propose amendments to this Constitution, or, on the application of the legislatures of two-thirds of the several States, shall call a convention for proposing amendments, which, in either case, shall be valid to all intents and purposes as part of this Constitution, when ratified by the legislatures of three-fourths of the several States, or by conventions in three-fourths thereof, as the one or the other mode of ratification may be proposed by the Congress; provided that no amendment which may be made prior to the year one thousand eight hundred and eight shall in any manner affect the first and fourth clauses in the ninth Section of the first article; and that no State, without its consent, shall be deprived of its equal suffrage in the Senate.

ARTICLE VI

1. All debts contracted and engagements entered into, before the adoption of this Constitution, shall be as valid against the United States under this Constitution, as under the Confederation.

2. This Constitution and the laws of the United States which shall be made in pursuance thereof and all treaties made, or which shall be made, under the authority of the United States, shall be the supreme law of the land; and the judges in every State shall be bound thereby, anything in the Constitution or laws of any State to the contrary notwithstanding.

3. The senators and representatives before mentioned, and the members of the several State legislatures, and all executive and judicial officers, both of the United States and of the several States, shall be bound by oath or affirmation to support this Constitution; but no religious test shall ever be required as a qualification to any office or public trust under the United States.

ARTICLE VII

The ratification of the conventions of nine States shall be sufficient for the establishment of this Constitution between the States so ratifying the same.

Done in Convention by the unanimous consent of the States present the seventeenth day of September in the year of our Lord one thousand seven hundred and eighty-seven and of the independence of the United States of America the twelfth. In witness whereof we have hereunto subscribed our names,

Gᵒ. WASHINGTON—
Presidt. and Deputy from Virginia
[and thirty-eight members from all the States except Rhode Island.]

Articles in addition to, and amendment of, the Constitution of the United States of America, proposed by Congress, and ratified by the legislatures of the several States pursuant to the fifth article of the original Constitution.

ARTICLE I[1]

Congress shall make no law respecting an establishment of religion, or prohibiting the free exercise thereof; or abridging the freedom of speech, or of the press; or the right of the people peaceably to assemble, and to petition the government for a redress of grievances.

ARTICLE II

A well regulated militia, being necessary to the security of a free State, the right of the people to keep and bear arms shall not be infringed.

ARTICLE III

No soldier shall, in time of peace, be quartered in any house, without the consent of the owner, nor in time of war, but in a manner to be prescribed by law.

ARTICLE IV

The right of the people to be secure in their persons, houses, papers, and effects, against unreasonable searches and seizures, shall not be violated, and no warrants shall issue, but upon probable cause, supported by oath or affirmation, and particularly describing the place to be searched, and the persons or things to be seized.

ARTICLE V

No person shall be held to answer for a capital, or otherwise infamous crime, unless on a presentment or indictment of a grand jury, except in cases arising in the land or naval forces, or in the militia, when in actual service in time of war or public danger; nor shall any person be subject for the same offence to be twice put in jeopardy of life or limb; nor shall be compelled in any criminal case to be a witness against himself, nor be deprived of life, liberty, or property, without due process of law; nor shall private property be taken for public use, without just compensation.

ARTICLE VI

In all criminal prosecutions, the accused shall enjoy the right to a speedy and public trial, by an impartial jury of the State and district wherein the

[1] First ten amendments proposed by Congress, Sept. 25, 1789. Proclaimed to be in force Dec. 15, 1791.

crime shall have been committed, which district shall have been previously ascertained by law, and to be informed of the nature and cause of the accusation; to be confronted with the witnesses against him; to have compulsory process for obtaining witnesses in his favor, and to have the assistance of counsel for his defence.

ARTICLE VII

In suits at common law, where the value in controversy shall exceed twenty dollars, the right of trial by jury shall be preserved, and no fact tried by a jury shall be otherwise reëxamined in any court of the United States, than according to the rules of the common law.

ARTICLE VIII

Excessive bail shall not be required, nor excessive fines imposed, nor cruel and unusual punishments inflicted.

ARTICLE IX

The enumeration in the Constitution, of certain rights, shall not be construed to deny or disparage others retained by the people.

ARTICLE X

The powers not delegated to the United States by the Constitution, nor prohibited by it to the States, are reserved to the States respectively, or to the people.

ARTICLE XI [1]

The judicial power of the United States shall not be construed to extend to any suit in law or equity, commenced or prosecuted against one of the United States by citizens of another State, or by citizens or subjects of any foreign State.

ARTICLE XII [2]

The electors shall meet in their respective States, and vote by ballot for President and Vice-President, one of whom at least shall not be an inhabitant of the same State with themselves; they shall name in their ballots the person voted for as President, and in distinct ballots the person voted for as Vice-President, and they shall make distinct lists of all persons voted for as President, and of all persons voted for as Vice-President, and of the number of votes for each, which lists they shall sign and certify, and transmit sealed to the seat of the government of the United States, directed to

[1] Proposed Sept. 5, 1794. Declared in force January 8, 1798.
[2] Adopted in 1804.

the President of the Senate; — The President of the Senate shall, in presence of the Senate and House of Representatives, open all the certificates and the votes shall then be counted; — The person having the greatest number of votes for President, shall be the President, if such number be a majority of the whole number of electors appointed; and if no person have such majority, then from the persons having the highest numbers not exceeding three on the list of those voted for as President, the House of Representatives shall choose immediately, by ballot, the President. But in choosing the President, the votes shall be taken by States, the representation from each State having one vote; a quorum for this purpose shall consist of a member or members from two-thirds of the States, and a majority of all the States shall be necessary to a choice. And if the House of Representatives shall not choose a President whenever the right of choice shall devolve upon them, before the fourth day of March next following, then the Vice-President shall act as President, as in the case of the death or other constitutional disability of the President. The person having the greatest number of votes as Vice-President, shall be the Vice-President, if such number be a majority of the whole number of electors appointed, and if no person have a majority, then from the two highest members on the list, the Senate shall choose the Vice-President; a quorum for the purpose shall consist of two-thirds of the whole number of senators, and a majority of the whole number shall be necessary to a choice. But no person constitutionally ineligible to the office of President shall be eligible to that of Vice-President of the United States.

ARTICLE XIII [1]

SECTION 1. Neither slavery nor involuntary servitude, except as a punishment for crime whereof the party shall have been duly convicted, shall exist within the United States, or any place subject to their jurisdiction.

SECTION 2. Congress shall have power to enforce this article by appropriate legislation.

ARTICLE XIV [2]

SECTION 1. All persons born or naturalized in the United States, and subject to the jurisdiction thereof, are citizens of the United States and of the State wherein they reside. No State shall make or enforce any law which shall abridge the privileges or immunities of citizens of the United States; nor shall any State deprive any person of life, liberty, or property without due process of law; nor deny to any person within its jurisdiction the equal protection of the laws.

SECTION 2. Representatives shall be apportioned among the several States according to their respective numbers, counting the whole number

[1] Adopted in 1865.   [2] Adopted in 1868.

of persons in each State, excluding Indians not taxed. But when the right to vote at any election for the choice of electors for President and Vice-President of the United States, representatives in Congress, the executive and judicial officers of a State, or the members of the legislature thereof, is denied to any of the male inhabitants of such State, being twenty-one years of age, and citizens of the United States, or in any way abridged, except for participation in rebellion or other crime, the basis of representation therein shall be reduced in the proportion which the number of such male citizens shall bear to the whole number of male citizens twenty-one years of age in such State.

SECTION 3. No person shall be a senator or representative in Congress, or elector of President and Vice-President, or hold any office, civil or military, under the United States, or under any State, who, having previously taken an oath, as a member of Congress, or as an officer of the United States, or as a member of any State legislature, or as an executive or judicial officer of any State, to support the Constitution of the United States, shall have engaged in insurrection or rebellion against the same, or given aid or comfort to the enemies thereof. But Congress may by two-thirds vote of each House, remove such disability.

SECTION 4. The validity of the public debt of the United States, authorized by law, including debts incurred for payment of pensions and bounties for services in suppressing insurrection or rebellion, shall not be questioned. But neither the United States nor any State shall assume or pay any debt or obligation incurred in aid of insurrection or rebellion against the United States, or any claim for the loss or emancipation of any slave; but all such debts, obligations, and claims shall be held illegal and void.

SECTION 5. The Congress shall have power to enforce, by appropriate legislation, the provisions of this article.

ARTICLE XV [1]

SECTION 1. The right of citizens of the United States to vote shall not be denied or abridged by the United States or by any State on account of race, color, or previous condition of servitude.

SECTION 2. The Congress shall have power to enforce this article by appropriate legislation.

ARTICLE XVI [2]

The Congress shall have power to lay and collect taxes on incomes, from whatever source derived, without apportionment among the several States, and without regard to any census or enumeration.

[1] Proposed February 27, 1869. Declared in force March 30, 1870.
[2] Passed July, 1909; proclaimed February 25, 1913.

ARTICLE XVII [1]

The Senate of the United States shall be composed of two senators from each State, elected by the people thereof, for six years; and each senator shall have one vote. The electors in each State shall have the qualifications requisite for electors of the most numerous branch of the State legislature.

When vacancies happen in the representation of any State in the Senate, the executive authority of each State shall issue writs of election to fill such vacancies: *Provided* that the legislature of any State may empower the executive thereof to make temporary appointments until the people fill the vacancies by election as the legislature may direct.

This amendment shall not be so construed as to affect the election or term of any senator chosen before it becomes valid as part of the Constitution.

ARTICLE XVIII [2]

SECTION 1. After one year from the ratification of this article the manufacture, sale, or transportation of intoxicating liquors within, the importation thereof into, or the exportation thereof from the United States and all territory subject to the jurisdiction thereof for beverage purposes is hereby prohibited.

SECTION 2. The Congress and the several States shall have concurrent power to enforce this article by appropriate legislation.

SECTION 3. This article shall be inoperative unless it shall have been ratified as an amendment to the Constitution by the legislatures of the several States, as provided in the Constitution, within seven years from the date of the submission hereof to the States by the Congress.

ARTICLE XIX [3]

The right of citizens of the United States to vote shall not be denied or abridged by the United States or any State on account of sex.

The Congress shall have power to enforce this article by appropriate legislation.

---

[1] Passed May, 1912, in lieu of paragraph one, Section 3, Article I, of the Constitution and so much of paragraph two of the same Section as relates to the filling of vacancies; proclaimed May 31, 1913.

[2] Ratified January 16, 1919.

[3] Ratified August 26, 1920.

ARTICLE XX[1]

[*"Lame Duck" Amendment*]

SECTION 1.   The terms of the President and Vice President shall end at noon on the 20th day of January, and the terms of Senators and Representatives at noon on the 3d day of January, of the years in which such terms would have ended if this article had not been ratified; and the terms of their successors shall then begin.

SECTION 2.   The Congress shall assemble at least once in every year, and such meeting shall begin at noon on the 3d day of January, unless they shall by law appoint a different day.

SECTION 3.   If, at the time fixed for the beginning of the term of the President, the President elect shall have died, the Vice President elect shall become President.   If a President shall not have been chosen before the time fixed for the beginning of his term, or if the President elect shall have failed to qualify, then the Vice President elect shall act as President until a President shall have qualified; and the Congress may by law provide for the case wherein neither a President elect nor a Vice President elect shall have qualified, declaring who shall then act as President, or the manner in which one who is to act shall be selected, and such person shall act accordingly until a President or Vice President shall have qualified.

SECTION 4.   The Congress may by law provide for the case of the death of any of the persons from whom the House of Representatives may choose a President whenever the right of choice shall have devolved upon them, and for the case of the death of any of the persons from whom the Senate may choose a Vice President whenever the right of choice shall have devolved upon them.

SECTION 5.   Sections 1 and 2 shall take effect on the 15th day of October following the ratification of this article.

SECTION 6.   This article shall be inoperative unless it shall have been ratified as an amendment to the Constitution by the legislatures of three-fourths of the several States within seven years from the date of its submission.

ARTICLE XXI[2]

SECTION 1.   The eighteenth article of amendment to the Constitution of the United States is hereby repealed.

SECTION 2.   The transportation or importation into any State, Territory, or possession of the United States for delivery or use therein of intoxicating liquors, in violation of the laws thereof, is hereby prohibited.

SECTION 3.   This article shall be inoperative unless it shall have been ratified as an amendment to the Constitution by conventions in the several States, as provided in the Constitution, within seven years from the date of the submission hereof to the States by the Congress.

[1] Proclaimed January, 1933.

[2] Ratified December, 1933.

POPULATION OF THE UNITED STATES, BY STATES:
1930, 1920, 1910

STATES	POPULATION		
	1930	1920	1910
United States	122,775,046	105,710,620	91,972,266
Alabama	2,646,248	2,348,174	2,138,093
Arizona	435,573	334,162	204,354
Arkansas	1,854,482	1,752,204	1,574,449
California	5,677,251	3,426,861	2,377,549
Colorado	1,035,791	939,629	799,024
Connecticut	1,606,903	1,380,631	1,114,756
Delaware	238,380	223,003	202,322
District of Columbia . .	486,869	437,571	331,069
Florida	1,468,211	968,470	752,619
Georgia	2,908,506	2,895,832	2,609,121
Idaho	445,032	431,866	325,594
Illinois	7,630,654	6,485,280	5,638,591
Indiana	3,238,503	2,930,390	2,700,876
Iowa	2,470,939	2,404,021	2,224,771
Kansas	1,880,999	1,769,257	1,690,949
Kentucky	2,614,589	2,416,630	2,289,905
Louisiana	2,101,593	1,798,500	1,656,388
Maine	797,423	768,014	742,371
Maryland	1,631,526	1,449,661	1,295,346
Massachusetts . . .	4,249,614	3,852,356	3,366,416
Michigan	4,842,325	3,668,412	2,810,173
Minnesota	2,563,953	2,387,125	2,075,708
Mississippi	2,009,821	1,790,618	1,797,114
Missouri	3,629,367	3,404,055	3,293,335
Montana	537,606	548,889	376,053
Nebraska	1,377,963	1,296,372	1,192,214
Nevada	91,058	77,407	81,875
New Hampshire . . .	465,293	443,083	430,572
New Jersey	4,041,334	3,155,900	2,537,167
New Mexico	423,317	360,350	327,301
New York	12,588,066	10,385,227	9,113,614
North Carolina . . .	3,170,276	2,559,123	2,206,287
North Dakota . . .	680,845	646,872	577,056
Ohio	6,646,697	5,759,394	4,767,121
Oklahoma	2,396,040	2,028,283	1,657,155
Oregon	953,786	783,389	672,765
Pennsylvania	9,631,350	8,720,017	7,665,111
Rhode Island . . .	687,497	604,397	542,610
South Carolina . . .	1,738,765	1,683,724	1,515,400
South Dakota . . .	692,849	636,547	583,888
Tennessee	2,616,556	2,337,885	2,184,789
Texas	5,824,715	4,663,228	3,896,542
Utah	507,847	449,396	373,351
Vermont	359,611	352,428	355,956
Virginia	2,421,851	2,309,187	2,061,612
Washington	1,563,396	1,356,621	1,141,990
West Virginia . . .	1,729,205	1,463,701	1,221,119
Wisconsin	2,939,006	2,632,067	2,333,860
Wyoming	225,565	194,402	145,965

TABLE OF PRESIDENTS

	Name	State	Party	Years in Office	Vice President
1	George Washington .	Va.	Fed.	1789–1797	John Adams
2	John Adams	Mass.	Fed.	1797–1801	Thomas Jefferson
3	Thomas Jefferson . .	Va.	Rep.	1801–1809	Aaron Burr
					George Clinton
4	James Madison . . .	Va.	Rep.	1809–1817	George Clinton
					Elbridge Gerry
5	James Monroe . . .	Va.	Rep.	1817–1825	Daniel D. Tompkins
6	John Q. Adams . . .	Mass.	Rep.	1825–1829	John C. Calhoun
7	Andrew Jackson . .	Tenn.	Dem.	1829–1837	John C. Calhoun
					Martin Van Buren
8	Martin Van Buren . .	N. Y.	Dem.	1837–1841	Richard M. Johnson
9	Wm. H. Harrison . .	Ohio	Whig	1841–1841	John Tyler
10	John Tyler [1]	Va.	Whig	1841–1845	
11	James K. Polk . . .	Tenn.	Dem.	1845–1849	George M. Dallas
12	Zachary Taylor . . .	La.	Whig	1849–1850	Millard Fillmore
13	Millard Fillmore [1] .	N. Y.	Whig	1850–1853	
14	Franklin Pierce . . .	N. H.	Dem.	1853–1857	William R. King
15	James Buchanan . .	Pa.	Dem.	1857–1861	J. C. Breckinridge
16	Abraham Lincoln . .	Ill.	Rep.	1861–1865	Hannibal Hamlin
					Andrew Johnson
17	Andrew Johnson [1] . .	Tenn.	Rep.	1865–1869	
18	Ulysses S. Grant . .	Ill.	Rep.	1869–1877	Schuyler Colfax
					Henry Wilson
19	Rutherford B. Hayes .	Ohio	Rep.	1877–1881	Wm. A. Wheeler
20	James A. Garfield . .	Ohio	Rep.	1881–1881	Chester A. Arthur
21	Chester A. Arthur [1] .	N. Y.	Rep.	1881–1885	
22	Grover Cleveland . .	N. Y.	Dem.	1885–1889	Thomas A. Hendricks
23	Benjamin Harrison .	Ind.	Rep.	1889–1893	Levi P. Morton
24	Grover Cleveland . .	N. Y.	Dem.	1893–1897	Adlai E. Stevenson
25	William McKinley . .	Ohio	Rep.	1897–1901	Garrett A. Hobart
					Theodore Roosevelt
26	Theodore Roosevelt [1] .	N. Y.	Rep.	1901–1909	Chas. W. Fairbanks
27	William H. Taft . .	Ohio	Rep.	1909–1913	James S. Sherman
28	Woodrow Wilson . .	N. J.	Dem.	1913–1921	Thomas R. Marshall
29	Warren G. Harding .	Ohio	Rep.	1921–1923	Calvin Coolidge
30	Calvin Coolidge [1] . .	Mass.	Rep.	1923–1929	Charles G. Dawes
31	Herbert Hoover . .	Cal.	Rep.	1929–1933	Charles Curtis
32	Franklin D. Roosevelt	N. Y.	Dem.	1933–	John Nance Garner

[1] Promoted from the vice presidency on the death of the president.

POPULATION OF THE OUTLYING POSSESSIONS: 1930 AND 1920

AREA	1930	1920
United States with outlying possessions	137,008,435	117,823,165
Continental United States	122,775,046	105,710,620
Outlying Possessions	14,233,389	12,112,545
Alaska	59,278	55,036
American Samoa	10,055	8,056
Guam	18,509	13,275
Hawaii	368,336	255,912
Panama Canal Zone	39,467	22,858
Porto Rico	1,543,913	1,299,809
Military and naval, etc., service abroad	89,455	117,238
Philippine Islands	12,082,366 [1]	10,314,310 [2]
Virgin Islands of the United States .	22,012	26,051 [3]

[1] Estimated population July 1, 1929.   [2] Population in 1918.   [3] Population in 1917.

A TOPICAL SYLLABUS

As a result of a wholesome reaction against the purely chronological treatment of history, there is now a marked tendency in the direction of a purely topical handling of the subject. The topical method, however, may also be pushed too far. Each successive stage of any topic can be understood only in relation to the forces of the time. For that reason, the best results are reached when there is a combination of the chronological and the topical methods. It is therefore suggested that the teacher first follow the text closely and then review the subject with the aid of this syllabus. The references are to pages.

Immigration
   I. Colonial immigration
      1. Causes: economic (19–20), religious (20–21), political (21), and enforced (39–41)
      2. How the immigrants came: the trading company (22–23), the congregation (23–24), the proprietor (24), paying their own way (37–38), indentured (38–39)
      3. Nationalities: English, Germans, Scotch-Irish, Irish, Jewish, and other peoples (41–46)
      4. Assimilation to an American type through the character of land holdings (51–56)
  II. Immigration between 1789–1890
      1. Nationalities: Scotch-Irish, Irish, Germans, and Scandinavians (303, 331–332, 467), other people who came with the gold rush (316), or to build railways (462, 607), Orientals (607, 660), and Mexicans (660)
      2. Relation to Southern slavery (430)
      3. Government policy (406, 607–609)
      4. Cities and immigration (446–448)
      5. Labor and immigration (605, 659–660)
 III. Immigration questions after 1890
      1. Changes in nationalities (448)
      2. Changes in economic opportunities (478–479, 686)
      3. Problems connected with competition and Americanization (605–610, 659)
      4. Government restrictions (607–610, 659–660)

Expansion of the United States

The Westward Advance of the People

Political Parties and Political Issues

I. The Federalists versus the Anti-Federalists (Jeffersonian Republicans) from about 1790 to about 1816 (198–212, 223–240)
  1. Federalist leaders: Hamilton, John Adams, John Marshall, Robert Morris (*see* Index)
  2. Anti-Federalist leaders: Jefferson, Madison, Monroe (*see* Index)
  3. Issues: funding the debt, assumption of state debts by the federal government, first United States Bank, taxation, tariff, strong central government versus states' rights, and the Alien and Sedition acts (*see* Chapters IX and X)

II. Era of "Good Feeling" from about 1816 to about 1824, a period of no organized party opposition (238–244, 279–285)

III. The Democrats (former Jeffersonian Republicans) *versus* the Whigs (National Republicans) from about 1832 to 1856 (*see* Chapters XII and XV)
  1. Democratic leaders: Jackson, Van Buren, Calhoun, (*see* Index)
  2. Whig leaders: Webster and Clay (*see* Index)
  3. Issues: second United States Bank, tariff, nullification, Texas, internal improvements, and disposition of Western lands (279–298)

IV. The Democrats *versus* the Republicans from about 1856 to the present time
  1. Democratic leaders: Jefferson Davis, Tilden, Cleveland, Bryan, Wilson, and Franklin D. Roosevelt (*see* Index)
  2. Republican leaders: Lincoln, Blaine, McKinley, Theodore Roosevelt, Coolidge, and Hoover (*see* Index)
  3. Issues: Civil War and reconstruction, currency, tariff, taxation, trusts, railways, foreign policies, imperialism, labor questions, and policies with regard to land and conservation (*see* Index)

V. Minor political parties
  1. Before the Civil War: Free Soil (355) and Labor parties (334–335)
  2. Since the Civil War: Greenback (494), Populist (495) Liberal Republican (456), Prohibitionist (493), Socialistic (494, 601–603), and Progressive (557–558)

Economic Development of the United States

I. Land and natural resources
  1. The colonial land system: freehold, plantation, and manor (48–53)
  2. Development of the freehold in the West (258–259)

American Foreign Relations
 I. Colonial period
   1. With the Indians (92–94)
   2. With the French (94–96)
 II. Revolutionary period
   1. With Great Britain (99–167)
   2. With European powers (159–161)
   3. The French alliance of 1778 (162)
   4. Assistance of Holland and Spain (162)
 III. Relations with Great Britain since 1783
   1. Commercial settlement in Jay Treaty of 1794 (207)
   2. Questions arising out of European wars, 1793–1801 (201–207)
   3. Blockade and embargo problems (209)
   4. War of 1812 (230–238)
   5. Monroe Doctrine and Holy Alliance (242–244)
   6. Maine boundary — Webster-Ashburton Treaty (298)
   7. Oregon boundary (313–314)
   8. Attitude of Great Britain during Civil War (396–397)
   9. Arbitration of *Alabama* claims (508–509)
   10. The Samoan question (509–510)
   11. The Venezuelan question (510–511)
   12. British policy during Spanish-American War (524)
   13. Controversy over blockade, 1914–1917 (621–623)
   14. The World War (619–639)
 IV. Relations with France
   1. The colonial wars (94–96)
   2. The French alliance of 1778 (162)
   3. Controversies over the French Revolution (203–206)
   4. Commercial questions arising out of the European wars (206–209, 230–234)
   5. Attitude of Napoleon III toward the Civil War (306)
   6. The Mexican entanglement (506–507)
   7. The World War (619–635)
 V. Relations with Germany
   1. Negotiations with Frederick, king of Prussia (160)
   2. The Samoan controversy (509–510)
   3. Spanish-American War (524)
   4. The Venezuelan controversy (530–539)
   5. The World War (619–635, 643–644)
 VI. Relations with the Orient
   1. Early trading connections (314)
   2. The opening of China (481); opening of Japan (481)
   3. The Boxer rebellion and the "open door" policy (526–528)
   4. Controversy with Japan over Manchuria, 1931–1933 (654)

INDEX

Abolition, 345–346

Abolitionists, attacks on, 345

Adams, Abigail (Mrs. John Adams), 74, 147, 156; protests women's exclusion from political rights, 143, 581

Adams, Charles Francis, 397

Adams, Henry, 442, 524

Adams, John, 127, 132, 147; American minister to Holland, 160; defeated as presidential candidate (1800), 212; delegate to Continental congress, 134; elected president, 208; selected as presidential candidate by Federalists (1796), 208

Adams, John Quincy, 272, 346; elected president (1824), 282

Adams, Samuel, 125; creates Committee of Correspondence, 141; delegate to Continental congress, 134; demands withdrawal of troops from Boston, 126; urges independence, 140

Adamson Law (1916), 614

Agricultural Adjustment Act (1933), 672

Agricultural Marketing Act (1929), 661

Agriculture, crisis in, 660–661; decline of, in East, 479; diversity of Western, 467–468; evolution in the West, 465–469

Aguinaldo, Emilio, 525

Alabama, admitted to the Union, 264

Alabama, 397; claims arbitrated, 508–509

Alamance River, 127

Alamo, 307

Alaska, purchased by the United States, 508

Albany plan of union, 97

Alien and sedition laws, 209–211

Allegiance, tests of, 144–145

Altgeld, John P., 496

Amendments. *See* Constitution, Federal

America, discovery and exploration, 3–17; migration to, 18–46; world power (1865–1900), 506–531. *See also* United States

American colonies, architecture, 84–85; art, 83–85; assemblies dissolved, 125–126; assembly, 89; churches, 66–72; compulsory religion, 66; contests between legislatures and governors, 90–91; control by Crown, 100–101; culture, 66–85; experiments in common tillage, 48–50; feudal elements in, 50–51; financial burdens, 97–98; fishing, 59–60; foreign conflict, 92–96; founding of, 21–37; growth of towns, 63–64; handicrafts, 83; histories, 77–79; Indian affairs, 92–94; intercolonial commerce, 63; iron industry, 57–59; judicial control, 101; land tenure in, 48–65; leadership of clergy, 70; literature, 77–81; manufacturing and commercial development, 56–64; natural science, 81–82; newspapers, 74–77; oceanic commerce, 61–63; opposition to Stamp Act, 119–123; painting, 84; parliamentary control, 102; poetry, 79–80; population, distribution of, 55; proprietary, 24, 31–34; Puritanism, 70–71; relations with French in Canada, 94; religious congregation, 23–24; religious toleration, growth of, 69–70; royal provinces, 87–89; schools and colleges, 72–74; science, 81–82; self-education, 74; self-government, 87–92; shipbuilding, 59; taxation, 116–123; textile industry, 56–57; trade laws, 103; trading companies, 22–23; training in government, 96–98; types of, 22–24; woman movement, 581. *See also* names of individual colonies

American Expeditionary Force, 628, 633

CHAPTER XXXI

CONFLICT ON THE HOME FRONT

New Deal Laws Declared Unconstitutional. In the beginning of President Roosevelt's administration, members of all parties generally supported his policies. But as time passed a strong opposition arose. Many critics insisted that the chief laws included in the New Deal program were unconstitutional. In 1935 the Supreme Court had given some grounds for this belief by declaring invalid most of the National Industrial Recovery Act (p. 680) and also by setting aside a law providing pensions for railway workers (p. 678). More grounds for the belief were furnished the following year, when the Court declared unconstitutional two more outstanding laws: the Agricultural Adjustment Act (pp. 672, 681) and the Coal Conservation Act, known as the Guffey-Snyder law (p. 678). The first of these two Supreme Court decisions seemed to destroy all plans for carrying out the farm-relief policy, and the second upset plans of mine-owners and miners for reviving and stabilizing the coal industry.

That the Supreme Court regarded efforts to regulate wages as unconstitutional was likewise made clear; for in 1936 it declared void a law of the state of New York which authorized fixing minimum wages for women and children. As leaders in the New Deal were planning a minimum-wages-and-hours act for men, women, and children in many industries throughout the country, the decision of the Court appeared to block further social legislation of this kind.

Republicans Choose "Progressive" Candidates in the Campaign of 1936. Nevertheless, at their national convention held in Cleveland in June, 1936, the Republicans did not choose as their candidates conservative men known to be hostile to the whole New Deal program. They were well aware that there was great

1

popular approval for many New Deal measures, especially those which had given relief to millions of unemployed men and women, helped home owners in distress, granted aid to farmers, and provided jobs for thousands of industrial workers. The idea of renominating Mr. Hoover and adopting a mere opposition program they rejected as utterly out of the question. Instead, the Republicans nominated for President Alfred M. Landon, governor of Kansas, a business man of progressive leanings, though far from radical. With Mr. Landon they associated, as candidate for Vice President, Frank Knox, a newspaper publisher of Chicago, who had joined the Progressive movement under Theodore Roosevelt during the revolt against the Republicans in 1912 (pp. 557–558).

The Republican Platform. In their platform the Republicans criticized many features of the New Deal and set forth their own proposals for reform. They charged the Roosevelt administration with wasting public money and driving the Government deeper and deeper into debt, with flouting decisions of the Supreme Court, with appealing to class prejudice, with prolonging the depression by discouraging business enterprise, and with trampling on the liberties of the people. In the proposals of their platform they pledged themselves to cut down the spending of public money and balance the budget and to maintain "a sound and stable currency." To farmers they promised credit on easy terms and continued federal grants of money in return for crop reductions made in the interest of soil conservation. To organized labor they promised support for the right to organize and bargain collectively with employers. As for assistance to persons in distress, the Republican platform declared in favor of four main measures: public works to furnish employment, federal grants to states for relief purposes, old-age pensions, and encouragement to states in providing unemployment insurance.

The question of child labor and minimum hours and wages for women in industry was "hot" for the Republicans. Many Americans were clamoring for such "protective" legislation, but the Supreme Court had just declared unconstitutional the minimum-wage law of New York. What was to be done? The

Republicans put in their platform a plank favoring the adoption of state laws and interstate compacts abolishing child labor and fixing minimum wages and hours for women in industries. This, they said, could be done "within the Constitution as it now stands." Could it? Mr. Landon had doubts. So he telegraphed the convention that, in case it could not be done lawfully "within the Constitution," he would personally favor the adoption of an amendment to the Constitution distinctly authorizing such legislation respecting women and children in industry.

Touching the subject of foreign affairs, the Republicans bound themselves to maintain peace by "all honorable means." At the same time they declared that America would not become a member of the League of Nations or of the World Court nor enter into any entangling alliances.

In short, though highly critical of the New Deal and though vigorous in asserting their allegiance to the Constitution, freedom of speech and press, and the authority of the Supreme Court, the Republicans by no means sought to abolish the New Deal root and branch. On the contrary, they promised to modify it, improve upon it, and uphold the main principles of social welfare put forward by the Roosevelt administration.

President Roosevelt Renominated on a New Deal Platform. In the Democratic party there was practically no difference of opinion over the candidates or the platform. At its convention assembled at Philadelphia late in June joyful harmony reigned. President Roosevelt and Vice President Garner were renominated by acclamation, and the New Deal was endorsed without a word of criticism. The Democratic platform for the campaign declared the pride of the party in its administration and announced that the course which had been followed would be continued. It cited the long list of measures which it had sponsored, having to do with savings and investments, old-age pensions and other forms of social security, rural electrification, housing, agriculture, labor, the regulation of private business enterprise in the interest of the public good, unemployment, the protection of youth, finance, and foreign affairs. It proclaimed that concern with the common life must be a national responsibility.

The platform contended that Republicans were mistaken when they insisted that the states could take care of every need of the people. It called attention to the kinds of disasters which sometimes embrace several states in a single region, such as floods and droughts, and the interstate business practices which affect wages, hours, and other conditions of labor. It maintained that these disasters and business practices called for federal as well as state action. In short the Democratic platform dwelt upon the national character of numerous problems affecting the people of the United States. Confronted with the outlawry of New Deal measures by the Supreme Court as unconstitutional, the Democrats called for an amendment to the Constitution which would "clarify" the status of their legislative program and acts, if such an amendment should prove to be necessary.

Minor Parties and Their Programs. The presidential campaign of 1936 was enlivened by the appearance of a new party, the Union party, composed largely of men and women who had rallied around four "stormy petrels" during the worst years of the depression — Father Charles E. Coughlin of Detroit, Huey P. Long of Louisiana, Dr. Francis E. Townsend of California, and William Lemke of North Dakota. Each of these men had a large and enthusiastic following.

Father Coughlin had his own broadcasting station, a strong organization known as the National Union for Social Justice, and his own newspaper called *Social Justice*, which was sold widely in many parts of the country. Huey P. Long had been a virtual dictator in Louisiana politics and had brought about his own election to the United States Senate. On a platform of "share our wealth" he had promised to give relief to all the poor and to make "every man a king." Owing to his high-handed methods he had been assassinated in 1935, but one of his aides, Gerald Smith, also a flaming orator, had continued to battle for his ideas. The third member of the quartet, Dr. Townsend, had sprung into national fame by advocating a pension of two hundred dollars a month for everybody over sixty years of age and had organized Townsend clubs in every state in the Union. The fourth member, William Lemke, had long been a farmer-labor leader in the West and, as a member of the House of Representatives, had demanded laws far more radical than any proposed by President Roosevelt.

In itself the Union party was a strange aggregation of people. Lemke, its candidate for President, had a farmer-labor following. Father Coughlin and his organization endorsed Lemke but not the Union platform. The followers of the late Huey Long and of Dr. Townsend were divided as to the merits of the Union party's claims, but many of them went along with Lemke. In the election, despite all the furor, Lemke received only 882,000 votes. The other minor parties were even less popular in their appeals. The Socialists, with Norman Thomas as their candidate, polled only 187,000 votes; for the Communist ticket, headed by Earl Browder, only 80,000 votes were cast.

Victory for President Roosevelt. The verdict of the voters at the polls was an overwhelming triumph for the Democratic leader already in the White House, promoter and defender of the New Deal. With the exception of Maine and Vermont, he carried every state. He polled 523 electoral votes as against eight votes for the Republican candidate. Much of his popularity, it was generally said, was due to his personality. But whatever the source of his popular strength, he was granted a second term, and he looked upon his re-election as a command from the people to go on with his political and social program for the United States on the home front.

President Roosevelt's Second Term Opens. When the President was inaugurated for his second term, on January 20, 1937, he delivered an address in which he reviewed the work of his first administration, dwelt upon problems of poverty yet unsolved, and declared that the country meant to solve them. "In this nation," he said, "I see tens of millions of its citizens — a substantial part of the whole population — who at this very moment are denied the greater part of what the very lowest standards of today call the necessities of life." That was the tragedy in the situation. But the President pointed a moral, the need of raising that low standard of living, saying: "It is not in despair that I paint you that picture. I paint it for you in hope, because the nation, seeing and understanding the injustice in it, proposes

to paint it out. . . . In our personal ambitions, we are individual-
ists. But in our seeking for economic and political progress as a
nation, we all go up — or else we all go down — as one people."

A Plan for Changing the Supreme Court. Believing that the
Supreme Court held a narrow view of the Constitution and that
its recent decisions interfered with his program for the country,
President Roosevelt, on February 5, 1937, proposed a scheme for
changing the membership of the Court by appointing at least six
new justices. He asked Congress to grant him the power to
appoint, with the approval of the Senate, a new federal judge
whenever a judge reached the age of seventy and did not then
resign. At the time there were six men over that age in the
Supreme Court. If Congress had agreed to this proposal, the
President, with the consent of the Senate, could have added six
new justices, thus increasing the number from nine to fifteen.

But the President's plan, though urged in strong terms, was
rejected by Congress. The debate over it was long and turbulent.
The country joined in the dispute. Party lines were broken in
Congress and among the citizens aroused by the conflict. Many
Democrats defended the President's proposal and assailed the
conservatism of "old men" on the bench; other Democrats
criticized the plan as too dictatorial and as an assault on the
independence of the judiciary. Some Republicans gave it a mild
support; other Republicans condemned it harshly as a move to
"pack the Court" and fasten the New Deal on the country. On
a test vote the Senate defeated it by a thumping majority, and it
never came to a vote in the House. But all judges were made
aware that people at large were taking sides, with intense interest,
on the question of the wisdom of the Supreme Court in declaring
void so many acts of Congress.

The National Housing Act. Other measures proposed in 1937
by President Roosevelt were more favorably received in Congress.
Prominent among them was the National Housing Act, signed on
September 1. By this law Congress provided for a National
Housing Authority, the issue of housing bonds, and both loans
and grants to local communities for the purpose of building houses
to be rented to families in the low-income groups. Under this

Act federal and state agencies set to work clearing away slums in cities and building low-rental apartments and separate houses.

Agricultural Legislation. To accomplish the main purposes of the Agricultural Adjustment Act, which the Supreme Court had declared unconstitutional, Congress passed new laws framed in different language: the Marketing Act of 1937, the Soil Conservation Act of 1937, and the Agricultural Adjustment Act of 1938. Under these laws three plans were carried out: the production of certain great staples, such as cotton, wheat, corn, and tobacco, was reduced, an immense acreage was turned to other uses, and farmers were paid subsidies for complying with the regulations. But none of these measures touched the question of tenants — the large number of farm workers who had no land of their own. After a long study of this problem had been made, Congress passed in 1937 the Farm Tenant Act, which authorized federal loans to farm workers for the purpose of helping them to buy homesteads and become independent farmers.

Labor Legislation. During his campaign in 1936 President Roosevelt had promised to "reduce hours overlong, to increase wages that spell starvation, and end the labor of children, to wipe out sweatshops." In a special message the next year he asked Congress to fulfill the promise. After heated debates lasting many months Congress answered by passing the National Wages and Hours Act of 1938. The law applied to certain groups of industrial and business workers. It provided that, by gradual stages ending in seven years, the national wage must be at least forty cents an hour and the national working time not over forty hours a week. This measure was preceded, in 1937, by the enactment of a new bituminous-coal bill and a new railway employees pension bill in such forms as to avoid the objections of the Supreme Court to old laws of a similar kind previously declared unconstitutional.

Changes in the Supreme Court and New Decisions. Although President Roosevelt's plan for enlarging the Supreme Court was defeated, he soon had opportunities to appoint new justices owing to resignations and deaths among the old members. In fact within a few years only two of the justices in office in 1936 were left. The first vacancy, which occurred in 1937, President Roosevelt filled by appointing Senator Hugo Black of Alabama. In 1938 he appointed Stanley Reed of Kentucky; in 1939, Felix Frankfurter of Massachusetts and W. O. Douglas of Connecticut; in 1940, Frank Murphy of Michigan; in 1941, James F. Byrnes of South Carolina and Robert H. Jackson of New York, while elevating Harlan F. Stone to the post of Chief Justice, left vacant by the resignation of Charles E. Hughes; and in 1943, W. B. Rutledge of Iowa to take the place of Justice Byrnes, who resigned to enter administrative service. Before his second term expired, President Roosevelt's appointees formed a majority of the nine justices constituting the Supreme Court.

In the meantime the Supreme Court altered some of its views respecting social legislation such as the New Deal favored. In March, 1937, while President Roosevelt's court plan was still being debated in Congress, the Court upheld a minimum-wage law enacted in the state of Washington, thus reversing its decision of the previous year on a similar law of New York. This action was quickly followed by two other decisions: the first declared constitutional the Labor Relations Act, which provided for collective bargaining in industry; the second sustained the Social Security Act, which dealt with old-age pensions, unemployment and other forms of insurance, and grants of money to states for the care of the sick and dependent. Thus by judicial rulings three primary reforms favored by the New Deal were declared to be in harmony with the Constitution of the United States.

American Affairs Disturbed by Aggressors in Europe and Asia. While Americans were trying to grapple with the depression, unemployment, poverty, and other domestic problems, their minds were agitated by the wars and threats of wars in Europe and Asia. In 1931 the government of Japan, ruled by a brutal military clique, seized the great province of Manchukuo in China (p. 659). In 1933 Germany, under the iron rule of the dictator Adolf Hitler and his National Socialists, began to rearm for another war. In 1934 Japan gave notice that she would no longer abide by the limitations on naval forces provided by the Washington treaty (p. 651). In 1935 the Fascist dictator in Italy, Benito

Mussolini, conquered and annexed Ethiopia. By this time it was clear that the disarmament conference at Geneva (p. 681) was a failure. In 1936 Hitler defied France and sent troops into the Rhineland contrary to Germany's pledges in treaties. That same year General Francisco Franco started a Fascist rebellion against the government of the Spanish republic, aided by men, money, and munitions from Germany and Italy. In 1937 Japan began a wholesale war on China. In 1938 Hitler occupied Austria and tore Czechoslovakia to pieces. In 1939 he finished the destruction of Czechoslovakia, and Mussolini invaded Albania. In the autumn of 1939 general war began in Europe between France and Great Britain on one side and Germany on the other.

These tumultuous events and still worse threats from the dictators of Germany, Italy, and Japan, finally united by treaty as "the Axis Powers," naturally made disturbances for Americans. They broke in upon the peaceful course of American trade with Europe and Asia. They violated pledges which Germany, Italy, and Japan had given to pursue pacific methods according to the Kellogg Pact (pp. 655–656). Japan's actions in China openly flouted the agreement she had made to respect the Open Door policy in the Far East (p. 651). Thus Americans were called upon, amid their discussion of domestic problems, to consider what was to be done by the United States in view of the turmoil in Europe and Asia. Grave questions of foreign policy confronted them. Could the United States stay out of another world war? If so, what methods must be adopted to gain this end? Or should the United States take steps to prevent the spread of the war by joining other nations in resisting the three aggressors among the nations?

The Early Stages of President Roosevelt's Foreign Policy. During his first term President Roosevelt sought to maintain peace by announcing and following policies of peace for the United States. He established official relations with Russia (pp. 681–682). He approved giving independence to the Philippines (pp. 682, 683). He pursued the "good neighbor" policy by promoting friendly relations with all nations in the Western Hemisphere. He strove to encourage peaceful commerce under the Reciprocal Trade Act. During his campaign for re-election in 1936 he declared:

I hate war. . . . I can at least make certain that no act of the United States helps to produce or promote war. . . . The Congress of the United States has given me certain authority to provide safeguards of American neutrality in case of war. . . . We can keep out of war if those who watch and decide have a sufficiently detailed understanding of international affairs to make certain that the small decisions of each day do not lead toward war and if, at the same time, they possess the courage to say "no" to those who selfishly or unwisely would let us go to war.

Congress Seeks to Maintain American Neutrality. When the Neutrality Act of 1935 (p. 684) expired in 1937, Congress renewed and made it more strict by adding amendments. In signing the first Act the President had said that he had done so "because it was intended as an expression of the fixed desire of the Government and the people of the United States to avoid any action which might involve us in war." He thought that the second Act was too rigid and left him too little discretion in controlling the export of munitions to belligerents, but nevertheless he signed the bill two days after it passed both houses of Congress. The new law, even more than the first, expressed a "fixed desire of the Government and the people . . . to avoid any action which might involve us in war." Many critics of the law maintained that it was wrong in principle, that the United States should stop the sale of munitions to aggressors and sell munitions to countries attacked by them. But the Act, whatever its shortcomings, seemed to show a resolve on the part of the American people and their Government to avoid being drawn into war through the assertions of American rights to travel and to sell and buy goods freely around the world as in the First World War.

Continued Expressions of the Desire to Keep Out of War. Although President Roosevelt, in a speech delivered at Chicago in October, 1937, declared that the aggressors should be "quarantined" and that it was vain to expect that, when the war came in terrible form, "America will escape attack," he proposed to Congress no plans for giving effect to his idea of a "quarantine" on the aggressors. When war broke out in Europe in 1939, he called upon Congress to modify the Neutrality Act in such a way as in effect to permit the sale of munitions to Great Britain and France. But in so doing the President said that this action "is a positive program for giving safety. This means less likelihood of incidents and controversies which tend to draw us into conflict, as they unhappily did in the last World War. There lies the road to safety!" Again, when in 1940 President Roosevelt transferred to Great Britain fifty "over-age" destroyers from the United States Navy and received in return leases for naval bases on British territories in this hemisphere, he informed Congress that the exchange "is not inconsistent in any sense with our status of peace." In the same way the Selective Service Act of September, 1940, which provided for a large increase in the armed forces of the United States, was treated by its advocates, in Congress and outside, as a measure for the defense of the United States.

Domestic and Foreign Questions in the Campaign of 1940. On the date fixed by the Constitution, a presidential election had to be held during the increasing turmoil in Europe and Asia. Hitler had overrun Norway, Denmark, Belgium, and the Netherlands. France had fallen before his conquering armies. Italy had joined him in the war on France. The aggressions of Japan continued in the Far East. Great Britain stood alone fighting bravely for her very existence. In these circumstances the merits of New Deal domestic measures and the issues of peace and war had to be submitted to American voters. To these questions was added another: Would President Roosevelt break the tradition established by Washington and Jefferson and seek re-election for a third term?

Brushing aside the "regulars" in their party, such as Senator Taft of Ohio and Thomas Dewey of New York, the Republicans at their national convention in Philadelphia in June nominated for President Wendell Willkie, a former Democrat, who had previously taken little part in politics. In their platform they went on record as "firmly opposed to involving this nation in war," and, though criticizing several features of the New Deal, they approved its main principles, as they had done in 1936. In his campaign Mr. Willkie declared in favor of aid to farmers, collective bargaining for labor, and a program for social security.

Until the very eve of the Democratic convention assembled at Chicago in July, President Roosevelt refrained from speaking out on the third-term question. Even then he merely let it be known that he did not seek the nomination. But no other member of his party could overcome his leadership, and he was nominated in a storm of acclamation. On his suggestion the convention selected as candidate for Vice President Henry A. Wallace, his Secretary of Agriculture. As in 1936, the Democratic platform endorsed the New Deal heartily. As to the war issue it declared: "We will not participate in foreign wars, and we will not send our Army, Navy, and Air Force to fight in foreign lands outside of America, except in case of attack."

During their campaign tours President Roosevelt and Mr. Willkie took similar positions on the issue of peace and war. Both condemned the aggressors in Europe and Asia. Both expressed sympathy with Great Britain, France, China, and their allies in their struggle for independence and liberty against the Axis Powers. Both approved the measures taken to increase the armed forces of the United States. But, declared Mr. Willkie: "The American people do not want war. . . . They are determined to keep America at peace. In that determination I stand with them. I am for keeping out of war." In language just as strong President Roosevelt assured the fathers and mothers of America: "Your boys are not going to be sent into any foreign wars. . . . The purpose of our defense is defense."

The returns at the polls on Election Day were more nearly balanced than in 1936, but President Roosevelt was nevertheless victorious. He received in round numbers 27,000,000 votes against 22,000,000 cast for the Republican candidate. His electoral vote was 449 to 82 for his opponent. The third-term doctrine had been submitted to the voters, and they had given an emphatic answer: It is not binding on the people of the United States.

CHAPTER XXXII

THE UNITED STATES INVOLVED IN THE SECOND WORLD WAR

President Roosevelt Warns Congress of Coming Perils. In his annual message to Congress on January 8, 1941, shortly before he opened his third term, President Roosevelt laid down his program for the future. He devoted eight-tenths of his message to the war, one-tenth to the social reforms of the New Deal at home, and one-tenth to advocating the spread of freedoms throughout the world. As to the war, he emphasized his belief that the security and peace of the United States were in danger from attacks by aggressors and that the United States should furnish munitions and other supplies to the Allies waging war against the Axis Powers, "even if a dictator should unilaterally proclaim" this American assistance to be an "act of war." Then the President declared "social and economic problems" to be "the root cause of the social revolution which is the supreme factor in the world," and he urged Congress to extend the social reforms of the New Deal to many citizens not yet enjoying its full benefits. In the last tenth of his message he spoke eloquently of looking forward to victory over aggression and the establishment of a new world order founded upon "four essential freedoms" — freedom of speech and expression, religious freedom, freedom from want, and freedom from fear.

Aid Given to Nations at War with the Axis Powers by Lend-Lease Act. In line with the intentions announced in his message, President Roosevelt had prepared and laid before Congress a measure, known as the Lease-Lend Bill, which authorized him to sell, lease, lend, or otherwise grant to all the countries at war with the Axis Powers huge supplies of munitions and implements of war. This proposal at once became the theme of heated discussions in committees of Congress, on the floors of both houses, and throughout the United States.

13

It was entitled a bill "to promote the defense of the United States," and its sponsors in Congress argued that it was designed to keep this country out of war by assisting the Allies to defeat Germany, Italy, and Japan. In an official statement the Secretary of State, Cordell Hull, declared: "This bill will make it possible for us to allocate our resources in ways best calculated to provide for the security of this Nation and of this continent in the complex and many-sided conditions of danger with which we are likely to be confronted."

Critics of the bill declared that it would violate definite rules of international law, that it was in effect an act of war, and that it would be followed by a "shooting war." But after a long and full discussion Congress amended the original bill and passed the amended bill; it became a law on March 11, 1941. In its final form it authorized the President to sell, transfer, exchange, lend, lease, or otherwise dispose of ships, aircraft, implements of war, and other goods "to the government of any country whose defense the President deems vital to the defense of the United States." Soon afterward Congress appropriated seven billion dollars for this purpose.

American Troops Occupy Iceland. The passage of the Lend-Lease Act was followed by vigorous actions in the Atlantic Ocean on the part of President Roosevelt. On July 7, 1941, he informed Congress that the armed forces of the United States had joined British forces in the occupation of Iceland, and he ordered the Navy to protect sea communication between the United States and Iceland. Thus American war vessels took over the patrol of the sea lanes to a point within seven hundred miles of Scotland, thereby releasing British warships from that patrol to concentrate their energies in what were then more dangerous submarine zones.

Roosevelt Reaches an Agreement with Churchill on Foreign Affairs. In August, 1941, after Germany and Finland had begun war on Russia, the President of the United States met the British Prime Minister, Winston Churchill, on shipboard "somewhere in the Atlantic" for conferences on war plans and aims. According to a report given to Congress by the President, he and the Prime Minister considered the dangers arising from the dictatorship of Hitler and the other governments associated in the Axis with him, and "made clear the steps which their countries are respectively taking for safety in the face of these dangers." The two men drew up an agreement of certain common principles "in the policies of their respective countries on which they base their hopes for a better world." This statement became known as "The Atlantic Charter" (p. 25).

The "Shooting War" Begins. In his Navy Day address of October 27, 1941, President Roosevelt announced that Germany had opened war on the United States. "Hitler," he said, "has attacked shipping in areas close to the Americas. . . . Many American-owned ships have been sunk on the high seas. One American destroyer was attacked on September 4. Another destroyer was attacked and hit on October 17. Eleven brave and loyal men of our Navy were killed by the Nazis. We have wished to avoid shooting. But shooting has started. . . . America has been attacked."

Increased Tension between the United States and Japan. Meanwhile, as Japan continued her war on China and moved more troops down into Indo-China, the relations of the State Department and the government of Japan became more and more strained. Again and again the State Department remonstrated with the Japanese government against its multiplying acts of aggression in China and its threats to other regions in the Far East, but always in vain. Japan, it is true, occasionally offered to make some concessions, and it was reported that late in November, 1941, a kind of agreement had been patched up. But Japan demanded that the United States stop giving military aid to China and in effect permit her to have a free hand in dealing with China. To that demand the Government of the United States would not yield; and every American proposal to settle the disputes on the basis of fairness to China was rejected by Japan.

The United States Takes Positive Action. Finding that pleas to Japan were without avail, the Government of the United States brought economic pressure to bear on Japan. In 1939 it notified her that the existing commercial treaty between the two countries would be ended at the expiration of six months, as provided by the terms of the treaty. This prepared the way for the economic embargo on Japan. From month to month the United States added to the number of articles useful for war purposes which could not be sold by American citizens and transported to Japan. By the spring of 1941 embargoes had been placed on the shipment of arms, munitions, gasoline, oil, iron and iron products, copper, aluminum, and other "strategic war materials." Japan protested against such measures in the name of "international law," but Secretary Hull of the State Department replied that it was "unheard of for a country engaged in aggression and the seizure of another country, contrary to all law and treaty provisions," to charge the United States with committing unfriendly acts because it stopped selling implements of war to the aggressor.

Final Efforts Are Made to Settle the Dispute. In November, 1941, Secretary Hull held many conferences with the Japanese ambassador and a special agent sent to Washington from Tokyo to aid in the negotiations. Again the efforts to reach a peaceful conclusion failed. On November 25 and November 28 Secretary Hull informed high officials of the United States Government that no settlement with Japan was "practically possible," that safeguarding the country was in the hands of our armed forces, and that Japan might spring surprise attacks on various points at any moment.

Japan Starts War on the United States. On Sunday, December 7, 1941, Secretary Hull held another conference with the Japanese agents in Washington, at which they accused the United States of interfering with Japan's affairs in a gross manner and declared that no agreement between the two countries seemed possible. Secretary Hull branded the Japanese charges as "infamous falsehoods and distortions" and grimly bowed the agents out of his office.

Without warning of any kind, one hour before this final interview between the diplomatic agents of Japan and Secretary Hull, Japanese armed forces attacked the American outpost at Pearl Harbor, Hawaii (Honolulu time 7.50 A.M.). About the same time

Japanese armed forces also attacked the International Settlement at Shanghai, the British possessions at Hong Kong, Malaya, the Philippine Islands, Guam, and Wake Island.

Though Secretary Hull had previously declared that surprise attacks on American territory might be expected, American forces at Pearl Harbor were not on the alert and could not make an effective defense. Many American ships were sunk or badly damaged in Pearl Harbor. Numerous airplanes on the ground were destroyed. Nearly three thousand American officers and men were killed, about nine hundred were wounded, and many civilians were slain or wounded.

. **The War Spreads.** Horrified by the Japanese attack, deemed especially treacherous in view of the request for an interview at the State Department by Japanese agents at almost the moment of its occurrence, the American people were instantly resentful and inflamed against Japan. The following day, on a ringing appeal from President Roosevelt, Congress, with only one dissenting vote, passed a resolution declaring war on Japan. Also attacked by Japan, at Hong Kong, Great Britain added her declaration of war. Three days later, on December 11, Germany and Italy joined Japan's program by declaring war on the United States and signed a pact with Japan binding themselves not to make a separate peace with the United States or Great Britain. One after another several Latin-American states declared war on Japan or Germany and Italy or on all these Axis Powers. By the opening of the new year, 1942, the war in Europe and Asia had spread until it encompassed all the great nations of the globe and nearly all the smaller nations and peoples. In Asia, Japan and Russia remained nominally at peace. Russia was fully occupied with her war on Germany along her western front. Japan, through fear or for other reasons, did not include Russia in her assault upon her neighbors.

The United States Expands Its Armed Forces for War. As soon as the global war opened, the Government of the United States took steps to multiply the number of men in its armed forces for combat at the widely scattered fronts — on land, on sea, and in the air. Since the limitation of nine hundred thousand placed on the number of men that could be inducted under the Selective Service Act had been removed, the Government started to call up men for the services as rapidly as it could provide barracks, equipment, and supplies. Plans were made for a total force numbering from twelve to fifteen million men. On November 13, 1942, the President was authorized to call youths eighteen and nineteen years of age for military-service training. By another law all males between the ages of twenty and forty-five were made liable to military service.

The administration of the Act, under presidential orders, was vested in the Director of Selective Service and in local boards — one board in every community in the country — supervised in each state by the governor of the state. Able-bodied males liable to service in the armed forces were summoned for induction according to certain rules. Young unmarried men without dependents were usually inducted first. Married men with children or other dependents were generally deferred, and so were men with dependents if they were employed in activities essential to war production or other support of the war effort. Deferred men, however, were subject to call as the number in the armed forces expanded.

The Government Organizes for War. With the war raging in many parts of the world and demands for aid to associates of the United States in the war mounting daily, the Government confronted numerous perplexing problems. An immense amount of supplies for American armed forces and for other nations fighting the Axis had to be procured and transported to places near and far by truck, train, ships, and planes. Industries and great branches of agriculture engaged in producing guns, tanks, bombers, foods, and other supplies for armed forces at home and abroad had to be promoted and regulated in a manner to assure the largest possible production and the quickest possible transportation. In order that war industries might have ample raw materials of iron, steel, oil, and other commodities for swift and steady and heavy production, it was necessary to allocate to each industry just the things it needed and in the right amounts.

While this was going on, the question of wages and prices,

especially of civilian goods, became acute. With a growing number of workers employed at good wages the demand for civilian goods increased among the wage-earners, and prices rose. And as the prices of food, clothing, and other consumer commodities soared, workers asked for higher wages to meet the mounting cost of living. If this runaway struggle between wages and prices kept up, the value of the dollar would become less and less, until "inflation" spread ruin everywhere. How could prices and wages be stabilized, held in balance, and goods be so distributed as to prevent some people from having too much and others too little?

To deal with these problems several new offices, agencies, and boards were created to supplement the work of the regular Departments. To the War Production Board was given the task of obtaining war supplies and increasing the amount of supplies. The function of regulating the transport of goods by land and sea was divided between two principal agencies, the Office of Defense Transportation and the War Shipping Administration. The regulation of prices was put in charge of the Office of Price Administration, and when the rationing of goods among consumers was adopted, this function was also put in charge of that office. Power to adjust disputes between employers and employees over wages and working conditions was vested in the National War Labor Board. For the purpose of mobilizing the labor power of the country and assigning workers to the places where they were most needed the War Manpower Commission was established.

The question of wages, salaries, and prices, which were so closely tied together, became more and more alarming, and to cope with this issue President Roosevelt recommended and Congress passed, on October 2, 1942, the so-called Anti-inflation Act, giving him larger powers to deal with this matter. The Act authorized him to fix, or stabilize, prices, wages, and salaries affecting the cost of living, with minor exceptions to the "ceilings." The prices, wages, and salaries so controlled were to be based on the levels or figures existing on September 15, 1942, subject to some changes necessary to correct "gross inequalities."

To enforce the new Act the President at once appointed a Director of Economic Stabilization and created a board to assist the Director. He instructed the Director to suppress inflationary tendencies in prices, wages, and salaries, and to effect an immediate stabilization of wages, salaries, rents in cities, towns, and rural districts, and the prices of goods, including farm produce. Late in May, 1943, the President set up the Office of War Mobilization, headed by James F. Byrnes, and gave it high authority over civilian affairs pertaining to the war.

Ideas as well as labor and material goods were mobilized by the Government in its war effort. In the field of ideas two major operations were involved. The first was to disseminate information that would help in the conduct of the war. The second was to prevent the spread of information that would hinder war efforts or give aid to the enemy countries — Germany, Italy, and Japan.

The first of these functions was given to the Office of War Information, with which was merged the older Office of Facts and Figures. The Office of War Information was made the agency of communication between the Government and the people of the United States, and indeed the world at large, on war aims, American war efforts, and the progress of the war. It distributed news and other information gathered from the Departments and agencies of the Government. It issued news releases, pamphlets, and articles. It attempted to co-ordinate the speeches of government officials in order to harmonize them as to war aims and plans. To counter the propaganda of the Axis Powers it distributed information, pamphlets, and documents, and fostered radio programs directed to the nations associated with the United States in the war and to the people of the Axis nations.

The second function in respect of ideas, that of controlling the news so that no information injurious to the war efforts might be published, was especially hard to execute, for it involved interfering with liberty of the press, of speech, and of communication — civil liberties ardently cherished in the United States. To discharge this duty the Office of Censorship was established. The Director of the Office was instructed to control and censor all communications between the United States and other countries, by mail, cable, radio, or any other method. At the same time he was required to arrange for and supervise a "voluntary censorship" of the press and the radio in the United States in co-operation with newspaper publishers and managers of broadcasting stations. The principal rule to be followed was that no news likely to help the enemy or disrupt war efforts in the United States should be given to the public.

Public opinion was further mobilized for the war under Acts passed by Congress similar to the Espionage and Sedition laws of the First World War (p. 630), but more stringent in some respects and more lenient in others. The Department of Justice, working through its Federal Bureau of Investigation (FBI), tracked down persons who committed deeds of violence against the United States and persons who expressed opinions deemed to be "subversive" and hampering to the prosecution of the war. A number of them were tried and sentenced — a few to death and others to fines and imprisonment.

The Productive Energies of the Nation Are Marshaled for War. To provide the buildings, machinery, and equipment for manufacturing munitions, implements of war, and war supplies on a mammoth scale, American industry was transformed and enlarged with remarkable speed. Existing industrial plants were converted and enlarged. New plants were erected in various parts of the country, often by private companies with the aid of government loans and sometimes as government-owned factories. Automobile, electrical, locomotive, and other plants became plants for making guns, tanks, planes, and other products essential to carrying on the war. With all their zeal and skill for manufacturing enterprise, American leaders in business and industry turned from peacetime work to pressing forward with the construction, management, and operation of the most gigantic plants ever seen in the history of the nation.

At the end of 1941 about seven million persons were employed at war production, according to official figures. In November, 1942, approximately seventeen million were so employed; and in that month the Office of War Information announced that the Government expected to have, before the end of 1943, at least sixteen million men and four million women in war plants. This announcement also stated that an additional number of women — between three million and four million — would have to be recruited for other demands, to replace the men called for armed services and to aid in the expansion of war industries.

While manufacturing for war purposes went forward by dramatic leaps, revealing the machine production power of the nation, the production of foodstuffs and other raw materials lagged behind. This lag was due in part to the very nature of agriculture, though the fact had been seriously overlooked. It was easy for a manufacturer to build an addition to a factory in a short time and double or treble its output quickly, notably in the case of shoes. But invention of machinery had not enabled the farmer to double or treble the produce of the fields so suddenly. To be sure, farmers could increase their output but certainly not rapidly enough to meet the tremendous demand for foodstuffs for the armed forces of the United States and its associated peoples. Indeed, an acute shortage appeared in many basic foods. The sharpness of the pinch, it was finally realized, was related to the excessive drafting of farmers and their laborers into the armed services. Therefore, in the administration of the Selective Service Act a deferred status was given to workers on essential farms, and plans were made for recruiting boys and girls from towns and cities to help the farmers during the coming summer season.

Civilians Undertake Defense Measures. To meet the question, "What can I do?" which the people at large were asking, the newly created Office of Civilian Defense in the Government issued on August 30, 1942, the *Citizen's Handbook for War.* In this publication everyone was told what he or she could do for civilian defense — adults engaged in trades and industry, in business and the professions, and on the farms, and even boys and girls. It described ways in which "each of us can become a fighting unit on the biggest front of all — the home front."

The Government informed the people as a whole that they could render important aid in the following ways: by contributing the man power and the woman power for production in war industries; by guarding the health of families and communities; by taking active interest in democratic government and helping to keep it vital; by getting along with smaller consumption of goods and less waste so that ample provisions might be available for the armed forces and for lend-lease shipments. To housewives was assigned the duty of guiding their families through the hard times of war. To boys and girls was given the role of being helpful in every possible manner at home, in school, and in their towns and cities.

Throughout the country, communities organized civilian-defense work to include such activities as watching for airplanes and reporting passing planes to the proper authorities, fighting fires and aiding rescue squads, carrying messages, driving automobiles in emergencies, serving in auxiliary police forces, working with road-repair groups, and giving medical and nursing aid to the sick and injured. For the guidance of persons engaged in each kind of civilian-defense work special leaflets and pamphlets were printed and spread broadcast.

The drive for the sale of war bonds and war savings stamps was pushed by all the great national organizations as a volunteer civilian movement. Regular portions of wages and salaries were voluntarily set aside for buying the government securities so necessary to carrying on the war. Even children were made familiar with this phase of the war as they were encouraged to fill little books with war stamps.

To stimulate alertness to possible attacks by enemy airplanes, black-outs and dim-outs were instituted far and wide. Citizens were drilled in ways of safety for emergencies. Air-raid shelters were devised in schools, office and hotel buildings, libraries, and other institutions, and the people, old and young, were instructed in their use.

For work in civilian defense in its manifold forms women rallied in large numbers. They built up the Red Cross membership and took its first-aid courses, rolled bandages, and performed other labor which it directed. Women offered their services as nurses' aides in hospitals to substitute for trained nurses dispatched to the fighting fronts. They opened and administered day nurseries for the young children of mothers working in war plants, and urged upon national, state, and local government the value of this enterprise.

Women's Auxiliary Military Corps Are Established. For the purpose of releasing men to fight at the front, women were organized into military bodies associated with the Army and the Navy. The first of these orders to be established was the Women's Army Auxiliary Corps (WAAC). The law establishing the Corps provided for a maximum membership of one hundred fifty thousand women between twenty-one and forty-five years of age.

The second organization was the Women's Naval Reserve Corps (WAVES). Its training program was framed by an advisory council of eight nationally known women co-operating with Navy officials.

The Women's Reserve of the Coast Guard Reserve (SPAR) was the third women's auxiliary corps to be established. The Auxiliary Marine Corps was the fourth.

As the women of these four corps emerged from their field camps and college schools they were quickly assigned work in connection with the release of men for combat zones. They were pledged to work on this continent or anywhere else they might be sent.

War Aims Are Officially Formulated. While American energies and materials were being mobilized for the war against Japan, Germany, and Italy, public officials, members of Congress, and political leaders entered into discussions of war aims and the kind of settlement to be made at the end of the war. In these arguments two main questions were explored: What are the specific aims of the war? and by what principles is the making of the peace to be guided?

Although no single official document was immediately issued giving all war aims in the summary style of President Wilson's Fourteen Points of the First World War, two official statements laid down the broad principles of American policy and were widely used in discussions of war aims. The first was the statement made by President Roosevelt in his annual message of January, 1941, before the United States became involved in this global war:

In the future days, which we hope to make secure, we look forward to a world founded upon four essential human freedoms.

The first is freedom of speech and expression — everywhere in the world.

The second is freedom of every person to worship God in his own way — everywhere in the world.

The third is freedom from want — which, translated into world terms, means economic understandings which will secure to every nation a healthy peacetime life for its inhabitants — everywhere in the world.

The fourth is freedom from fear — which, translated into world terms, means a world-wide reduction of armaments to such a point and in such a thorough fashion that no nation will be in a position to commit an act of physical aggression against any neighbor — anywhere in the world.

The second official document respecting war aims was the Atlantic Charter drawn up by President Roosevelt and the British Prime Minister, Winston Churchill, during their conference at sea in August, 1941. The Charter may be divided into three parts: (1) territorial boundaries and the rights of nations; (2) international relations and lasting peace; (3) the rights of peoples.

Under the first head they declared that "their countries seek no aggrandizement, territorial or other"; "they desire to see no territorial changes that do not accord with the freely expressed wishes of the peoples concerned"; and "they respect the right of all peoples to choose the form of government under which they will live, and they wish to see sovereign rights and self-government restored to those who have been forcibly deprived of them." In these declarations were incorporated, it is clear, some of the principles that President Wilson had laid down in his Fourteen Points.

Touching the subject of international relations and lasting peace, President Roosevelt and Mr. Churchill promised that their countries "will endeavor, with due respect for their existing obligations, to further the enjoyment by all States, great or small, victor or vanquished, of access, on equal terms, to the trade and to the raw materials of the world which are needed for their economic prosperity." That declaration was likewise in accord with one of President Wilson's main" points." On the subject of peace the President and the Prime Minister now agreed that after the "destruction of the Nazi tyranny" their countries hope to see established a peace which will afford security to all nations against external aggression, which will permit "all men to traverse the high seas and oceans without hindrance," and which will cut down the burden of armaments and stop the use of force in settling controversies.

Although the Charter did not use the word "democracy," it did deal with the idea of democracy by dwelling on human rights. It recognized the right of the people of each country to choose their own form of government. It expressed a desire "to bring about the fullest collaboration between all nations in the economic field with the object of securing, for all, improved labor standards, economic advancement, and social security." It also expressed a hope for a final peace "which will afford assurance that all the men in all the lands may live out their lives in freedom from fear and want." In presenting the Charter to the Congress of the United States, President Roosevelt stated that the Charter includes of necessity "the world need for freedom of religion and freedom of information," and he represented the Charter as covering the four great freedoms proclaimed in his message on war aims of January, 1941.

Popular Discussions of War Aims and World Order Take Place. Freely and fully in the press, in meetings, and with one another, private citizens also discussed war aims and the coming relations between nations. They referred repeatedly to the Four Freedoms and the Atlantic Charter. They also raised many specific questions: Is the League of Nations to be altered, and is the United States to join it? Or is a new form of world association to be organized for the purpose of establishing and maintaining a new "world order"? Is a "world police force" to be set up to maintain peace everywhere? Or is an alliance to be formed between the United States, the British Empire, Soviet Russia, and China, with a view to ordering the world and keeping peace in it by combined armed forces? Or is the United States, at the end of the war, to refrain from active membership in any world association that may be set up and, as in 1919, leave other nations to operate, as they did before, in a League of Nations or by forming alliances or unions among themselves or by carrying on diplomatic negotiations only?

Naturally, as freedom of thought reigned in the United States, there were differences of opinion among the American people over these questions. On only one point was there general agreement: the Axis governments must be disarmed and suppressed and rendered unable to commit more acts of brutality and terror against their neighbors. There was also a strong, if not unanimous, opinion to the effect that great efforts should be made to hold the United States, Great Britain, Russia, and China together in some kind of friendly and co-operative relation at least for a long period after the end of the war.

The United Nations Formed. On January 2, 1942, agents of twenty-six nations signed at the city of Washington a declaration of war aims and purposes. Some of these nations were represented by governments in exile, their lands having been seized by Hitler. Whether the governments were still functioning at home or in exile, representatives of these nations pledged their countries to employ all their resources, military and economic, in the war on those Axis Powers with which they were actually at war, bound themselves to co-operate for the prosecution of the war, and promised to make no separate peace or armistice. Victory over their enemies, they agreed, "is essential to defend life, liberty, independence, and religious freedom, and to preserve human rights and justice in their own lands as well as in other lands."

The signers of the United Nations Declaration were the President of the United States, the Prime Minister of Great Britain, the Soviet Ambassador, the Chinese Foreign Minister, and officials from Australia, Belgium, Canada, Costa Rica, Cuba, Czechoslovakia, the Dominican Republic, El Salvador, Greece, Guatemala, Haiti, Honduras, India, Luxembourg, the Netherlands, New Zealand, Nicaragua, Norway, Panama, Poland, South Africa, and Yugoslavia. Although this was not an alliance binding the United States by treaty, President Roosevelt expressed the hope that the union so formed might co-operate not only during the war but afterward also in making the settlement at the end of the war.

Great Funds Become Necessary for the War Program. To pay for a war which, besides the expenses of the United States as a belligerent, included aid to other nations associated with it in the conflict and feeding multitudes in Europe, Africa, and Asia, billions of dollars were needed. By comparison the $26,300,000,-000 spent by the United States on account of the First World War, during the years from 1917 to 1921, was trivial. Before the first year of this global war came to a close, Congress had authorized expenditures amounting to $240,000,000,000, the national debt had passed the one-hundred-billion-dollar mark, and no end was in sight. Estimates of future outlays, running up to five hundred billion dollars and more, were mere guesses, but on any reckoning the outlays would be tremendous.

In providing funds for war bills Congress laid in 1942 the heaviest taxes ever imposed on the people in the history of this nation. The Revenue Act of that year, designed to yield about $8,500,000,-000 additional money, increased to a high point the excise taxes on liquor, tobacco, telegraph, cable and radio messages, travel tickets, and other objects and transactions. The rate of the surtax on the normal earnings of corporations was raised, and the rate on unusual, or "excess," profits was fixed at 90 per cent flat. Taxes on incomes were so arranged as to compel millions of persons who had never paid an income tax to make returns and pay according to the amount of their wages, salaries, and other income, with certain exemptions and certain deductions for the care of dependents. The tax laws of 1943 promised to be still heavier. To bring in money enough to pay the bills which could not be met by taxation, Congress authorized the Treasury Department to sell war bonds and stamps by the billions to banks, companies, private persons, and other investors.

The Course of Combat Action Induces Encouragement. In the early stages of the war the American armed forces had to play a defensive role in both theaters of the conflict — Asiatic and European. The serious damage done to American naval and air equipment at Pearl Harbor prevented an immediate dispatch of forces for the defense of the Philippines or a frontal attack on Japan, even if that had seemed good tactics. Ships, planes, and men were soon sent into the western Pacific, but by the time they arrived within striking distance of Japanese positions the Japanese sweep southward was well along its way. All that could be done then was to hinder and delay that advance toward the shores of Australia.

Week by week for several months after the attack on Pearl Harbor, Japanese naval, air, and land power drove to the south, southeast, and southwest, conquering as it went. Before the end of that month the Japanese had seized Guam, landed in the Philippines, and taken possession of the British colony at Hong Kong. In January, 1942, they took Manila and were fanning out in every direction. American and Philippine troops, in command of General Douglas MacArthur, withdrew to the northwest of Manila and made heroic stands in Bataan and on the island of Corregidor in Manila Bay. Not until April did they yield to the overwhelming strength of Japan in Bataan. Not until May was the fortress at Corregidor given up. By that time General Mac-Arthur had made a miraculous escape to Australia, where he had been ordered for the purpose of organizing American forces to join the Australians in resisting the Japanese, who were threatening to invade that country, and in preparing for the turning of the war tide.

To the east, west, and south of the Philippines the Japanese lightning blows fell hard and fast. The British port of Singapore was conquered in February. The Dutch, in their East India islands and surrounding waters, aided by British and American naval and air power, tried to stem the flood in vain. By midsummer in 1942 Japan had control of the Philippine Islands despite the continuance of local fighting in which valiant Filipinos sought to defend their homes and lives, the Netherlands East Indies, and the southern mainland of Asia to the borders of India. They were strongly intrenched in the Solomon Islands and in other islands near Australia, close to the "life line" at sea along which American men and supplies would have to pass to Australia.

A year after the fall of Bataan the zone of water and land in possession of Japan was enormous. The western boundary ran from her part of the island of Sakhalin in the north, southward off the coast of Siberia, down along the mainland of China, and then westward on the mainland to the western border of Burma. From that point it ran southward and then eastward to include Sumatra, Java, and other Netherlands East Indies islands, to the northern shore line of New Guinea, then eastward to include the Solomon Islands and the Gilbert Islands. From the Gilbert Islands it ran northward in the Pacific to embrace the Marshall Islands, Wake Island, and three islands at the tip of the Aleutians. Then it ran westward, as surveyors say, "to the point of beginning."

Nevertheless, despite the general retirement of American forces toward Australia, these forces had struck many heavy blows at the Japanese. In a notable battle in the Coral Sea near the Bismarck Archipelago, in May, 1942, they inflicted great losses on the Japanese, checking and turning back their naval drive in that direction. In the same month American airmen bombed Tokyo. In June another naval advance by the Japanese in the direction of Hawaii was blocked near the Midway Islands, and such havoc was wrought upon their warships and planes that they were compelled to flee from the scene with their surviving equipment and men. In the autumn of that year, 1942, American sea, land, and naval forces, alone and in co-operation with the Australians, had begun to recover lost ground piece by piece. They had begun to batter the Japanese in Guadalcanal, and they kept up their pressure, until early the next year they had full possession of that strategic post so close to the sea lanes leading from the United States to Australia. In March, 1943, Americans sighted and utterly destroyed a huge fleet of Japanese warships and troop ships attempting to reinforce the Japanese positions in the South Seas. About the same time they began a successful drive on the Japanese in the Aleutians.

In the European theater of conflict during the first months of the war there was little that Americans could do in the way of direct attacks on Germany and Italy. American soldiers and pilots were sent in large numbers to Great Britain and Northern

Ireland. American warships hunted enemy submarines in the Atlantic and adjoining waters, and furnished convoys for merchant vessels carrying supplies to Great Britain or to Russia by the northern route. American airmen, equipped with giant bombers and other planes, soon, however, joined the British in blasting German industrial centers, submarine bases, railway stations, and other places essential to the enemy's aggression. Americans also helped to wage war against the Germans and Italians in Lybia. Their aid was valuable, too, to the Russians locked in their desperate struggle on the western front.

At length a general demand went up for "a second front" in Europe — for an invasion of the Continent by the associates of Russia in the war. In the summer of 1942 the Russian armies, though still intact, were being driven back by the Germans, and on October 4 of that year Premier Stalin openly called for more help.

While the second front and the possibility of success, if attempted, were being debated, while Russian armies were again taking the offensive against the Germans, American forces, in co-operation with the British, landed, on November 7, at many points on the Mediterranean and Atlantic coasts of French North Africa and soon went into action. In that month Americans also occupied the port of Dakar on the African "shoulder" extending out into the Atlantic toward Brazil. Important French officers and administrators in Africa, defying the French government at Vichy, which was then dominated by the Germans, joined the Americans and British and placed French armed forces by their side in the common war on the common enemies. In November, as the British drove the Germans and Italians westward across Lybia, the Americans, British, and French pressed forward for the conquest of Tunisia, recently seized by German and Italian troops.

At first there were some setbacks in Africa. But by April, 1943, the British had broken into Tunisia from the east, and American, British, and French forces were pressing forward from the west in a joint effort to capture the Germans and Italians. On May 12 the Axis forces surrendered to the British and Ameri-

cans.   During this period, American airmen took part in bombing
Sicily and other Italian places, and all these actions seemed to
forecast an invasion of Europe from the south.   Whether the
second front was actually to be opened in Italy and southern
France or along the coast from Norway to Spain or in the Near
East was a question often raised in the newspapers.   At all events,
for defense against invasion the Nazis built as fast as they could,
largely by forced labor, great walls and fortifications along the
Atlantic coast as well as in southern Europe.

Seventeen months after the Japanese attack on Pearl Harbor
therefore, a turn had really come in the long road of withdrawal
and defensive warfare.   The ability of the Germans and Japanese
to lunge forward victoriously, whenever and wherever they pleased,
appeared to be definitely broken and the power of Italy to be
reduced to a shadow.   American combatants fought according to
the greatest heroic traditions of our country, and many of them
were decorated for valor and publicly acclaimed.   But the global
war was not yet won.   The Government of the United States,
like that of Britain, warned the people of the two nations against
thinking that the end would soon come in victory.   Even so, the
armed power of the United Nations designed to bring their enemies
to the ground in "unconditional surrender" was growing steadily,
despite the submarine menace, and the resolve of the Government
and people of the United States to carry the war to a successful
conclusion became firmer as the drive increased on all fronts.